DISCOVERING MAHLER

Donald Mitchell with the score of Mahler's Sixth Symphony
*Photo* Toby Glanville

# DISCOVERING MAHLER
## Writings on Mahler, 1955–2005

## DONALD MITCHELL

*Selected by*
GASTÓN FOURNIER–FACIO *and* RICHARD ALSTON

*Edited by*
GASTÓN FOURNIER–FACIO

*Co-ordinating Editor*
JILL BURROWS

THE BOYDELL PRESS

First published 2007
The Boydell Press, Woodbridge

ISBN 978-1-84383-345-1

The Boydell Press is an imprint of Boydell & Brewer Ltd
PO Box 9, Woodbridge, Suffolk IP12 3DF, UK
and of Boydell & Brewer Inc.
668 Mt Hope Avenue, Rochester, NY 14620, USA
website: www.boydellandbrewer.com

A CIP record for this book is available
from the British Library

This publication is printed on acid-free paper

Typeset by
Agnesi Text, Hadleigh
Printed in Great Britain by
Antony Rowe Ltd, Chippenham, Wiltshire

*To*
COLIN and BELINDA MATTHEWS
*and*
DAVID and JENNIFER MATTHEWS

# Contents

# List of Illustrations

The author and publishers are grateful to all the institutions and persons listed for permission to reproduce the materials in which they hold copyright. Every effort has been made to trace the copyright holders; apologies are offered for any omission, and the publishers will be pleased to add any necessary acknowledgement in subsequent editions.

# Preface

## *Donald Mitchell*

Titles are always a problem, though less so perhaps as one grows older, writes less and possibly thinks more. However that may be, *Discovering Mahler* came to me as I was sitting at my desk in Bangkok. A moment's reflection suggested that it was immediately and wholly appropriate. It not only represents the overall character of much of what is compiled here but also narrates the evolving recognition of Mahler's huge creative significance with which, world wide, we are familiar today. The years of publication of the individual items tell their own tale.

While what matters, indubitably, is the living, pervasive presence of a music, an oeuvre, we now have the fortune to possess in unimaginable quantity and variety, it is still relevant and historically important, I think, to continue in awareness of the long, long period that preceded its establishment, when admiration of Mahler was rare and, when it occurred, was received with disbelief and even contempt.

All of this negative assessment, I soon came to learn in my youth, was based on ignorance and the absence of sources which might have provided reliable information as well as enlightenment, though there were of course highly valuable exceptions to which I trust I have paid sufficient tribute.

But what will give me the greatest satisfaction is the thought that in the future no aspiring Mahler lover, whether a student or a scholar, a passive admirer or passionate performer, composer or conductor, will be obliged, as I was, virtually *to start from scratch*.

A good half of my life's work has been devoted to Mahler, and if in some measure, however slender it may seem when compared with today's massive Mahler literature, I shall prove to have made a contribution to the fundamental change in perception to which I have referred, I shall be very well satisfied. For me, whatever I write or have written about Mahler will always remain as expressions of profound gratitude, however inadequate, for the miracle of a composer, the discovering of whose miraculous music was thenceforth to transform my life.

Bangkok and Hua Hin
12 October 2006

# Mining the Archive: A Fourth Volume

## Richard Alston

*Gustav Mahler: The Early Years*, Donald Mitchell's pioneering account of Mahler's early life and works, almost the first serious Mahler study in English, was first published in 1958. *The Wunderhorn Years*, which relinquished biography in order to concentrate on the music of the early songs and the first four symphonies, followed in 1975, and ten years further on came *Songs and Symphonies of Life and Death*, an unprecedented examination of *Das Lied von der Erde*, with the *Rückert Lieder* and *Kindertotenlieder*, and a final section on the Eighth Symphony. The major part of Mahler's output not so far covered by this survey – the middle symphonies (the Fifth, Sixth and Seventh) together with the Ninth and Tenth – will be found in the present volume. Plugging this gap was the original germ of the conception of this book. In this context it was immediately apparent that the work had already been done elsewhere, distributed among other publications. To take only the most outstanding example, after 'Eternity or Nothingness? Mahler's Fifth Symphony', which must be one of the most detailed in-depth studies ever published on any single musical work, who could quickly find much more to say about the symphony, and what would be the point of merely rehashing the chapter, for a new book?

However, like all conceptions, this one 'growed', as well as in some ways changed direction. The overall project has changed character at least once before, from a 'life-and-works' first volume to a progressive exploration of the music; so why not again? Donald Mitchell noted in his 1975 Preface to *The Wunderhorn Years* that he was moving away from 'a more or less comprehensive account of each work I surveyed' (with 'analysis' which might 'lapse into the purely descriptive') in favour of integrating given works into 'the broader perspectives of Mahler's works as a whole' – so to speak weaving the commentary on individual pieces into the main text. Now, in

*Discovering Mahler*, the content returns to a study of the music acces-
sibly work by work, at the same time providing a survey of virtually
the entire oeuvre. Inevitably there are similarities of approach across
the chapters. The essays on individual works (in the *Scrutiny* section)
stand alone and do not need to be read consecutively, but can be
used as a compendium. On the other hand, there are positive
advantages in reading them in sequence. Points that a layman might
find erudite in an isolated essay are consistently highlighted, so
insights into Mahler's work can be properly absorbed. Unifying
themes emerge: the concepts of 'the narrative' and 'the frame',
Mahler's innovative diversity of 'musics' and 'orchestras', the complex interrelationships between song and symphony.

Another good reason for supplementing the examination of
individual works in the earlier volumes is that in some instances
Donald Mitchell naturally has a desire if not a need to update his
previous work. To take one example, his major piece on the complete *Das klagende Lied*, for the world premiere, in 1997, of the original 1880 version of the piece in three movements, was delivered
forty years on from his first thoughts in *The Early Years*, based –
unavoidably – on a reported description of the score of the first
part of the work, *Waldmärchen*, which was unavailable at the time.
Meanwhile perennial controversies like the order of movements in
the Sixth have rumbled on over that whole period, and you will
find here his considered contribution, as well as a current summary
of the arguments.*

Thus this fourth volume has taken on some of the characteristics of an everyman's guide to Mahler. It belatedly fulfils, in some
ways at least, Mitchell's old promise to the publishers John Murray
and Frank Upjohn, of a book which he said (in 1975) 'was to be
simple and short'. This raises the question of the audience for
whom the present volume is intended. We hope the readership will be
wide. The original jacket of *Songs and Symphonies of Life and Death*
(1985) listed as 'the readership it addresses' scholars, performers,
'general readers and Mahler lovers', and certainly we wish to reiter-
ate all of those here. Perhaps it will be close to all our hearts, not

---

\*    See Appendix 1: 'The "Correct" Order of the Middle Movements in Mahler's Sixth
     Symphony', pp. 631–45.

least Donald's own, if we imagine a young student, intelligent and well informed and not needing to be talked down to, but who, none the less, having absorbed the readily obtainable background knowledge would like to look further into the realm of the specialists, in a non-elitist context. In this context it is relevant to stress that although many of these essays have been previously published elsewhere, the majority of them have either been lectures, published only in conference proceedings, or special celebratory publications or articles in academic journals, in none of these cases reaching the readership potentially open to a mainstream book.

Mahler devotees of course may already own a significant proportion of the republished chapters. However, given the range of their sources, which include celebratory books published in the Netherlands and notes for various recordings, it is unlikely that any prospective reader will possess all of them, let alone in one convenient format. In addition Donald Mitchell has reconsidered and occasionally revised all the contents for the current publication, sometimes adding new commentary, so we have here his most recent thoughts.

Furthermore, some of the contributions to this book are here published for the first time; to take two examples, the beginning and the end (in Mitchell-speak, as applied to Mahler, 'the frame'). The first chapter is particularly fascinating as it is the original draft, subsequently much reworked for publication, of the entry on Mahler's music for *The New Grove Dictionary of Music and Musicians* (1980). In a sense this essay provides its own 'frame' for the whole book, which is why it has a section all to itself (*Vision*). The last chapter (also a section in itself, *Resonance*) is strictly speaking a second publication, as it has already been issued in Dutch, but it is here making its very first appearance in English (the same applies to 'A Mahlerian Odyssey'). Besides proposing a quite new point about Mahler's use of cowbells, 'Dearest Ted' forms a poignantly personal envoi to this collection and hence to the whole gigantic quartet (as it now is) of Mahler studies. All these latest statements are markedly more autobiographical, befitting an author embarking on his eighties.

It remains to draw attention to, as well as the range of sources, the consequent range of styles, from early journalism in the *Daily*

*Telegraph* to recent prestigious lectures in Colorado and Amsterdam (all to be found in *Reflections*). It is a tribute to Donald Mitchell's authorial skills that in virtually every case he unerringly adapts the style to the situation. The lecture format perhaps shows him at his best, thanks to the combination of the stimulus of the live occasion with the discipline of the time limit. For this reason we have chosen not to edit out spoken exclamations or rhetorical questions, which add to the flavour of a live event. He is still an inspirational teacher, which reflects what is also encapsulated in this volume, a combination of scholarship with enthusiasm which is very rare if not unique (among other writers on music Deryck Cooke, H. C. Robbins Landon and David Cairns all share it, but few others). The range of styles may actually enhance the readability of the book, as bravura lecture performances are interspersed with slighter articles, even quizzical in tone, such as 'Mahler's "Abschied": A Wrong Note Righted', which however has a significance of its own.

The point about 'A Wrong Note Righted' is that the supposed fuss over a single note makes much more difference to the music than might at first appear. The one changed note restores the heterophonic relations that give the 'Abschied', the final song of *Das Lied von der Erde*, its special character, and had been previously obscured by consistent mistranscription. By taking his cue from the musical meaning (he was one of the first scholars to scrutinize Mahler's manuscripts thoroughly) Donald Mitchell was able to spot the tiny copying mistake that had slipped past the composer himself and every subsequent editor. This opened up for the first time the discussion of Mahler's revolutionary use of heterophony, which was then expanded in *Songs and Symphonies*. A parallel identification of meaning with the actual notes resurfaces in 'Dearest Ted', where the 'randomness and unpredictability' of life, exemplified by the July 2005 London bombs, are mirrored in Mahler's aleatoric (yet precise) scoring for the cowbells, another of his innovations.

Another perspective afforded by this volume is witnessing Donald Mitchell's development as a Mahler authority over fifty years (a major period of discovery for him as well as for the listening world) from the time of the Mahler centenary in 1960. This historical perspective is crucial, so for example a talk from

1961 should be read with an eye to the cultural climate then prevailing, which it illuminates, rather than from an exclusively twenty-first-century viewpoint. By the same token, the earliest article included, 'Some Notes on Mahler's Tenth Symphony', is a remarkable document in its own right when it is remembered that it predates Deryck Cooke's work on the sketches, let alone his own extensive commentaries. We have tried to highlight the most critical changes of view or emphasis over the years, often in authorial or editorial notes, without too extensive cross-referencing. Certain episodes, the young Britten's celebrated letter about *Das Lied von der Erde* being the most obvious example, naturally recur in two or three different chapters, but it is to Mitchell's credit that the context is invariably subtly different (he is never guilty of repeating an identical lecture). Therefore apart from reducing repetitions of complete quotations we have seen no reason to edit out such recurrences.

Next a word about performers, without whom after all the music would not exist as a living entity. Mahler conductors appear in the course of this book, which contains notes for (and references to) recordings by Claudio Abbado and Riccardo Chailly, while the *Das klagende Lied* occasion was a collaboration with Kent Nagano. However, the most distinctive feature in this respect comprises two major dialogues, Mitchell with Chailly and with Bernard Haitink, about the Fifth and Seventh Symphonies respectively. These represent a rare meeting of minds between musicologist and conductor (again, this is the first publication in a generally accessible form for both these pieces). Indeed, Riccardo Chailly in particular is a presence throughout the book, which includes a note for the boxed set of his complete Mahler symphonies recordings ('Chailly, Mahler and the Italian Connection'). Their work together on the Fifth Symphony, covered here, has been unusually close, as Donald Mitchell has so to speak toured the piece with the Royal Concertgebouw Orchestra, making his spoken contributions along the road. Chailly in his turn has expressed indebtedness to Mitchell: he has reported remembering his comments in the act of conducting the First Symphony.

The reader will find in this volume several allusions to other

arts, notably literature, and to writers including Proust, T. S. Eliot
and Virginia Woolf. Mitchell's early book *The Language of Modern
Music* had as its central thesis parallels with painting and with architecture (principally with the work of Picasso and Le Corbusier).
His wider erudition – the learning of a self-taught man – has
prevented him from ever becoming an academic in the narrow
sense of the word. I still recall his saying to me many years ago now
that too many musicians know nothing about any of the other arts.
His awareness of contemporary intellectual cross-currents facilitates
his placing Mahler, not as an isolated phenomenon but as part of a
continuum. *The Language of Modern Music* was eloquent on Mahler's
relationship with Schoenberg and hence his position vis-à-vis
tradition and 'the new', and more perspectives on all this are on
offer here, especially in the lectures given in Colorado, Rome and
Amsterdam. (Another example of Mahler's own openness to new
experiences is how on a visit to Berlin in 1907 he chose to see, and
enjoyed, Wedekind's then shocking play *Spring Awakening*.)* Thus
we can see how Mahler's 'vision' was lit by its historical context.
The story of how the flame has been carried forward to our own
day, flickering from time to time but essentially undimmed, and now
burning brightly, I leave to the author himself and also to Gastón
Fournier-Facio, who in his survey of the development of Mahler
studies attempts to define more precisely Donald Mitchell's
honoured place in this second continuum.

Poole, Dorset
October 2006

---

*   Another major example is his exploration of Chinese music and poetry (see 'Das
  *Trink*lied von der Erde?' (pp. 456–76)). DM himself has long had a significant interest in
  Far Eastern music, more especially the classical music of Thailand. He was responsible for
  bringing groups of Thai musicians to the UK in 1981, 1983, 1991 and 1998 (including
  appearances at the Aldeburgh Festival and the BBC Proms). This interest is reflected in
  depth in his now extensive writings on Oriental music in the music of Britten and
  Mahler. See the Nimbus CD (1994) of *Thai Classical Music*, performed by the Prasit
  Thawon Ensemble, for which DM wrote an extensive liner note.

# An Overview from the Inside

## Gastón Fournier-Facio

> I am well aware that as a composer I will not find
> recognition in my lifetime. That can be expected only
> beyond my grave. That distance is necessary for an
> adequate assessment of a phenomenon like me, the
> *conditio sine qua non*. As long as I am the Mahler who
> wanders among you, 'a man among men', I as a
> creator must expect all-too-human treatment.
>
> I shall first have to shake off the dust of the earth
> before justice is done to me. I am, in Nietzsche's
> expression, a man not of his own time. This applies
> above all to my kind of works.
>
> Gustav Mahler<br>(interview with Bernard Scharlitt, 1906)

Since Mahler made this statement, many historically significant
writings have been published devoted to his music. From celebrated
monographs to monumental biographies, from collections of documents and historical sources to lectures and conference papers on
specific subjects (e.g. Mahler's life, his personality, his conducting
and theatre-management career, the surrounding culture, etc.), the
body of literature on the composer is extremely rich and varied,
and ever growing.

Many of these texts have a historical significance for the understanding of his music, and have had an important role in stimulat-
ing its subsequent reception. Serious appraisals of his music now
cover over a century of writings, from 1901 to 2007, a period
through which perspectives on the composer have been continually
evolving.

The long list of historically relevant works starts with the first
author who ever published a book on Mahler's music: Ludwig

Schiedermair's 1901 monograph, published at the time of the end
of Mahler's *Wunderhorn* period. The author was of course dealing
with only part of the composer's total output, since only about a
third of it had been written at the time. The sequence continues
with the dedicatory texts edited by Paul Stefan in 1910 on the
occasion of Mahler's fiftieth birthday (a few months before his
death).

Other early texts, written at the end of the composer's life or
immediately after his death, were by celebrated musicologists of his
time as well as personal friends of the composer (Paul Stefan himself, Richard Specht, Guido Adler and Paul Bekker), who were
convinced advocates of his music. They concentrated on giving
Mahler's work a relevant position in the history of music and they
established the first attempt at a division of his works into compositional periods, spelling out the originality of his music and
characterizing its peculiar technique and contents. Many of these
analyses are still reckoned as valid and authoritative in our own day.

There were then the 1920 papers read on the occasion of the
first Mahler Festival, held in Amsterdam, when his complete works
were first performed as a whole, under the baton of Willem
Mengelberg.

Of special importance for the new generation's perspective on
Mahler were two famous lectures: the 1912 Prague Festival lecture
by Arnold Schoenberg, given a year after Mahler's death; and the
1960 Vienna Centenary Address by Theodor W. Adorno, given on
the occasion of the centenary of Mahler's birth. The latter anticipated all the main theses of Adorno's fundamental book, published
in the same year, *Mahler: Eine musikalische Physiognomik*, which
would have a major impact on every single study on Mahler to
come, and was one of the key factors in launching the 1960s
Mahler 'renaissance', which was then helped on its way by Leonard
Bernstein's first-ever integral recording of Mahler's nine completed symphonies.

Between Schoenberg's and Adorno's lectures, two invaluable and
justly famous memoirs were published, written by people who had
known Mahler intimately: the indispensable Natalie Bauer-Lechner's
*Erinnerungen an Gustav Mahler* in 1923 (which mostly reports what

Mahler himself had to say about his own music – which is what makes this book so invaluable); and Alma Mahler's *Gustav Mahler: Erinnerungen und Briefe* in 1940, one of the first major documents to fill out major details of Mahler the man and the artist which, despite its many inaccuracies, as a truly epic tale eloquently told proved to be not only an unrivalled source of information about the composer's personality but also a precious instrument for our understanding of Mahler's methods of composing and the compositions themselves.

Among the succession of personal accounts from those who had known Mahler personally are most relevant observations by Alban Berg and Anton Webern, which focus on single works, particularly *Das Lied von der Erde* and the Ninth Symphony.

The year 1936 saw the publication of Bruno Walter's significant memoir, *Gustav Mahler. Ein Porträt*. As assistant conductor to the composer in both Hamburg and Vienna, Walter had been Mahler's most intimate confidant during the composition of his last two completed scores (*Das Lied von der Erde* and the Ninth Symphony) and, after Mahler's death, he was to conduct the premieres of both works. Walter had, therefore, an absolutely privileged position in the assessment of Mahler's works, and his monographic study, written just before the *Anschluss* (which had disastrous consequences vis-à-vis the diffusion of Mahler's music) showed a profound understanding of that music as well as the utmost devotion to it.

In his 1951 *Erinnerungen an Gustav Mahler*, Otto Klemperer published valuable testimony about Mahler's personality, and about Mahler the conductor.

In this century of writings on Mahler, the multiplicity of approaches and perspectives begins to fill bookshelves. Illustrious scholars and editors have assembled anthologies and collected essential material on our composer: source documents about his life (Kurt Blaukopf and Zoltan Roman, *Mahler: A Documentary Study*, 1976; Norman Lebrecht, *Mahler Remembered*, 1987); contemporary essays on individual works (*The Mahler Companion*, edited in 1999 by Donald Mitchell and Andrew Nicholson); symposia on a single work (James J. Zychowicz (ed.), *The Seventh Symphony of Gustav Mahler: A Symposium*, 1990) or on a single feature of Mahler's oeuvre (Henry-Louis de La Grange (ed.), *Gustav Mahler et l'ironie dans la culture viennoise au tournant du siècle*, 2001). Constantin Floros is one of the important writers to have devoted very useful analytical volumes to the discussion of the composer's whole output.

In their chronological progression, the appraisals of Mahler's works evolve in a fascinating way, from exalted polemics against Mahler's attackers (Arnold Schoenberg's 1912 Prague Festival lecture) to the most thought-provoking controversy (Pierre Boulez's 1979 *Mahler actuel?*) on the superficiality of Mahler fanatics, described as worshippers of music that they do not understand and often distort.

Amid this proliferation of analytical and celebratory writings, the work of the two most illustrious Mahler scholars of our times should be singled out: that of Henry-Louis de La Grange and Donald Mitchell. From rather different perspectives, their complementary work has constituted the most comprehensive and profound approach to Mahler's music in our time. And it is the happiest of coincidences that the two of them, now in their early eighties, have managed to finish their fourth volumes, completing a life's work, their vast and invaluable panoramas dedicated to the composer. In this sense Norman Lebrecht was right to dedicate to the two of them the first edition of his important anthology of first-hand accounts on the composer, *Mahler Remembered*, using as his inscription Mahler's celebrated quotation (in his letter of 17 February 1897 to Arthur Seidl) of a happy Schopenhauer phrase: 'two miners who dig a shaft from opposite sides and finally meet underground'.

La Grange's *Gustav Mahler*, the monumental three-volume study published in French between 1979 and 1984, is not only the definitive biography of the composer, but it also provides a comprehensive panorama of all his works. Every single significant event in the composer's life is thoroughly described in the light of a vast array of period documents which are often presented in full. Furthermore, every single work of Mahler is systematically discussed, with all his preliminary manuscripts and their present location enumerated and all publication and first-performance details listed. La Grange also discusses texts used by the composer, and goes through all pertinent details of orchestration, key, metre, tempo, titles, form and analysis of every single lied or symphony movement. He also reviews all the important writings on the work in question by the most prestigious and relevant writers on Mahler from his own time to the present. Since 1995 he has been in the process of rewriting the French edition of his work, revising, updating and enlarging it in English; and he is currently completing the fourth and final volume of his new version. It is every Mahler lover's dream encyclopaedia: completely comprehensive, very readable and clear, yet always thorough and profound.

Donald Mitchell's work – and this volume completes and culminates his life's work on the composer – is of a rather different nature. His main interest is in the understanding of Mahler's *musical identity*. He is on the trail of the composer's own language, in all its subtle complexities. It is not by chance that one of his closest friends was the late Edward R. Reilly, the doyen of American Mahler scholars, who undertook tireless studies of the manuscripts and sketches as a key to the understanding of the essential nature of the music. Mitchell has always been fascinated by Mahler's scores and their exact meanings. This explains why he can concentrate sometimes even on detailed descriptions of the elaborate notation used; it is because he sees it as essential to understanding the nature of the musical language itself.

In this sense, biography has never been an end in itself. It appears to concern Mitchell only when it proves to be functional to the understanding of compositional processes and facts. A case in point is his study of the beginning of the Seventh Symphony ('Mahler on the Move'), of Mahler's boat trip across the Wörthersee and more specifically the rhythm of the oars, which suggested the introduction to the first movement, starting his journey through a nocturnal landscape which characterizes the whole of the score. Another eloquent instance is Mitchell's study of Mahler's stay in Toblach, now Dobbiaco in the Italian Dolomites ('Mahler and Nature: Landscape into Music'), where he advances a possible relationship between it and the *freedom* of the recitatives in the 'Abschied' of *Das Lied von der Erde*. With all their innovatory, improvisatory unmeasuredness, they are seen as a musical documentation

of the stirrings and twittering of the birds, as the composer responds to the auditory stimuli of a mountain landscape. Sight is
transformed into sound. This asymmetrical musical freedom
Mitchell then reads as signifying the *transcendence* of death, the
reconciliation and identification with the perpetual renewal of the
earth's beauties.

Mitchell's most recent Mahler book (*The Mahler Companion*,
edited with Andrew Nicholson) presents a most comprehensive
overall view of Mahler's life's work. It devotes individual chapters
not only to every single one of his works (his 'Eternity or
Nothingness? Mahler's Fifth Symphony' could easily be seen as the
most detailed, thought-provoking and profound analysis of a
Mahler score ever written), but also to grand panoramic perspectives where key aspects of his compositions are discussed with reference to his work as a whole.

In the opening chapter of the current volume, 'Gustav Mahler',
originally written in 1976 for *The New Grove Dictionary of Music and
Musicians* (though here published in its full, unabridged version for
the first time), Mitchell offers an extremely important overview of
Mahler's compositional techniques and how they developed from
one work to the other. Every crucial aspect of his music is discussed, in chronological order, mapping in a valuable way the
ground for the subsequent chapters devoted to every single work.
Two major penultimate chapters provide the climax of the book
('The Twentieth Century's Debt to Mahler: Our Debt to him in
the Twenty-first' and 'A Mahlerian Odyssey: 1936–2003'), where
Mitchell, again, looks at Mahler's works as a whole, from the perspective of our own times, giving his book a solid, unifying frame.

The enormous range of essential Mahlerian traits analysed by
Mitchell in this new book, always illustrated with concrete and
very relevant examples from the scores, may seem rather daunting,
but his eloquent style carries the reader away on a wave of convincing enthusiasm. Here are just some of the aspects he covers:

Mahler once declared to Bauer-Lechner (NB-L *Recollections*) that
'In my writing, from the very beginning, you won't find any more
repetition . . . for music is governed by the law of *eternal evolution,*

*eternal development* [my italics] – just as the world, even in one and the same spot, is always changing, eternally fresh and new' (1899). And again: 'A work of art must evolve perpetually, like life' (1900).

This is one of Mitchell's major concerns when looking at Mahler's work as a whole, always seen as a totality in a state of *continuous evolution*, never repeating itself. Adorno (TWA *Mahler*) believed: 'That each of Mahler's works criticizes its predecessor makes him the developing composer *par excellence*; if anyone, it is in Mahler's far from copious oeuvre that one can speak of progress. What he improves always becomes something different . . . Even where he goes back to earlier work of his own, there is progress.' 'Like the storyteller, Mahler's music never says the same thing twice in the same way.'

Though one finds in Mahler an innovative use of interrelated material between one movement and another (just consider how the Fourth or the Fifth Symphonies are constructed), as well as fascinating interrelationships between different works (e.g. the close relationship between the Third and the Fourth Symphonies), what according to Mitchell still perhaps remains under-appreciated in Mahler's oeuvre is the other side of the coin – the singularity and individuality of each specific work. If there is a consistency to be discerned in his works then it is the quite extraordinary *compulsion* to explore and occupy a new concept of musical time and space in each succeeding symphony; and, yet more importantly, a new philosophy that also on occasions might involve an altogether new aesthetic. *Dis*continuity is for Mitchell a key feature of Mahler's oeuvre. In more than one chapter ('On the Road to the Eighth Symphony: Mahler's New Worlds', 'A Mahlerian Odyssey: 1936–2003') he insists on the sheer *unpredictability* of Mahler's creative journey from one work to the next, where each of them constitutes an independent world of sound, form and thought; a plethora of diverse philosophies, aesthetics, and above all *narratives*.

For Mitchell *the narrative idea* is a crucial one in the understanding of Mahler's music: i.e. when a formal process that is initiated by the first idea of a work is sustained over the length of it, and completed only when the last note has sounded. This creates the insistent presence throughout of an anticipated and thus awaited resolution. This idea of a musical representation of an unfolding 'drama' – something that Mitchell sees as a clear appropriation of the opera house's concept of the *dramatic denouement* – implies a destination wholly distinct from the point of departure. This notion is foreign to the idea of classical symmetry in symphonic music, based on the reprise ('we are back where we started'). This theme of Mahler's very personal story-telling principle is developed chronologically across Mahler's works, from the narration of an actual story (*Das klagende Lied*) through to the sophisticated type of immediate 'autobiography' of the later works, where the composer's perspective becomes 'the artist as hero'.

This narrative idea is further refined by the use of a *frame*. Mitchell observes, across the whole of Mahler's output, how first movements and finales of individual works stand in a special formal relationship, where some prime materials from the first movement are left to be developed to their maximum potential in the finale. Hence we encounter a novel division of formal responsibilities, i.e. the complementary, and to some degree, expository/developmental relationship between first movement and finale, which was to become a characteristic Mahlerian procedure.

A similar dramatic–symbolic perspective is then applied to Mahler's blurring of the distinction between *major* and *minor*; and to his occasional revival of the ancient *modes*.

But above all it is manifest in his particular use of *progressive tonality* (beginning the piece in one key and finishing in another). It is an evolutionary tonal scheme which 'travels' along with the changing fortunes of the often travelling 'heroes', since these progressive key schemes clearly have their roots and their logic in their association with dramatic or narrative ideas. In this sense, abrupt switches of keys, and the juxtaposition of sharply contrasted keys without any attempt to effect a modulating transition from one to the other, are basically theatrical gestures in Mahler's music.

From this dramatic perspective Mitchell branches into the analysis of Mahler's coalition of genres: symphony, symphonic poem, song. He analyses the influence of the smallest of musical genres, the lied, in the *Wunderhorn* symphonies. And later on Mitchell looks at *Das Lied von der Erde* as the overt summation of the techniques associated with the hybrid medium of *the orchestral song-cycle*. He looks at the dialectics between the dramatic 'symphonic poem' versus the pure symphonic tradition, discussing the functionality of *programmes* (albeit later eliminated by Mahler) in the definition of the final shape of most of his early works. Despite the composer's ambivalence about them, they proved to have an essential role, often enabling him to conclude the interrupted composition of a work (cf. the notorious case of the Second Symphony). In this context Mitchell highlights the mutually enriching relationship between the first symphonies and the *Wunderhorn* songs; or, for that matter, the use of Klopstock's and Nietzsche's *texts*, respectively, in the Second and the Third, where Mahler makes verbal, and thus explicit, crucial aspects of the drama the particular symphony is enacting.

The exploitation of combined *onstage, offstage orchestras* and the particular acoustic relationship involved in this device: the delicate spatial and dynamic organization of different instrumental groups, with which Mahler was a pioneer in the exploration of *acoustic space* and even of *directional sound*, devices that, in his later works, were explored *within* the orchestra itself, rather than through the contrast of physically, spatially separated groups.

The mix of *high tragedy* and the '*mundane*': the 'vulgarity' of introducing *vernacular* languages into the sophisticated highbrow symphonic language, breaking down traditional cultural barriers. The bringing together, within one dramatic frame, of many different kinds of *musics* – a plural that in Mitchell is always deliberate.

The use of popular or naive musical materials for a particular aesthetic purpose: irony, parody, grotesque satire, the *locus classicus* being the 'symphonic' treatment of the 'vulgar', rowdy brass bands, with their swinging march tunes, military signals, fanfares and vigorous march rhythms.

(Mitchell has fascinating things to say about Mahler's use of Lisztian *thematic transformation*, often travelling backwards and forwards between the vulgar and the sublime).

Indeed, Mahler's music traverses the spectrum of the diverse musics – from the street, concert hall, theatre, parade ground, dance hall and ballroom – that serviced the society of which he was part. Mitchell believes that this huge *inclusiveness* must surely be one of the reasons for the breadth of appeal his works have proved to make to a global audience.

His prominent kind of *vocal melody*, 'folklike', influenced by Bohemian folksong, was different from the approach of the nationalistic schools, because there is a sharp discrepancy between the 'primitive' folksong materials used and Mahler's super-elaborate, often intensely ironic, treatment of them.

Finally, with the *chinoiserie* of *Das Lied von der Erde*, Mahler approached another non-classical music culture, being one of the major pioneers in the great interest of the West in all the arts, crafts and thought of the East at the turn of the century.

Mahler's deluge of *dynamic markings* often adumbrates a complex layering of dynamics between simultaneously combined parts. These markings form an independent compositional parameter, fundamentally affecting the sonorities and even the overall form.

Mahler's radically new way of handling *the orchestra* is one of Mitchell's most passionate fields of research. The crude and common-place denigration of his music, accusing it of being monumental, megalomaniac or grandiloquent, is, alas, only too familiar. Mitchell reminds us that Mahler's exuberantly large orchestra was used mainly as an assembly of *chamber groups* which were exploited as such. One finds a constellation of sectional orchestras that on and off achieve independence from their colleagues, with crossovers and cross-fertilization between sections grouping themselves into unique combinations of instruments. There are of course passages of overwhelming mass sonorities, of sheer weight of volume. But Mahler very swiftly progressed from the lavish deployment of resources in his early cantata (*Das klagende Lied*) to the famous clarity, refinement and *soloistic scoring* of, say, the Fourth Symphony, where he develops a sort of *concertante* style. He needed in the main a very large orchestra from which the wealth of constituent ensembles, which is a feature of his orchestration, might be drawn.

Paradoxically, although the sound grows more transparent, more slender, more *'economical'* – the more Mahler succeeds in achieving the *clarity* or the sharp pungency that was his goal – the orchestral forces at the same time increase in number, to allow for the largest number of possibilities in varying textures that are always functional to the articulation of the various elements that form the musical structure. In 'Mahler's "Kammermusikton"', Mitchell analyses in a most original way the exceptional *variety* of Mahler's *chamber-like orchestration*, specially in his lieder; where Mahler devised an independent chamber-orchestral sound of matchless clarity for each song. He lets us understand how Mahler developed his highly personal orchestral sound, for example through his decisive move away from *strings* as the basis of his orchestral sonority, to *wind*. This meant a growing emphasis on selectivity: the use of the precise resources to meet the precise needs of the moment. And there are significant passages where he even achieved the *liberation* of the *percussion*.

All this was connected to Mahler's complex *contrapuntal devices*. It is, in fact, impossible to divorce a consideration of his orchestration from his actual methods of composing. Mitchell believes that how it sounds *is* the idea. Through his *motivic polyphony*, Mahler analyses the structure of the melody in terms of its motives by distributing them in sequences of changing instrumentation; which, in its turn, develops into *motivic orchestration*. No wonder Mahler deeply admired the music of Bach who, during his last years, became for him an exemplar.

Certainly Mahler had a profound familiarity with and awareness of *the past*, seeing it as a creative influence in his own work. But his perspective was dialectic, and he also critically upset the musical conventions of his own time. He was very free in his handling of *sonata form*'s traditional principles. Mitchell often points out fascinating details about Mahler's idiosyncratic approach to it, in his use of both *tonality* and *recapitulation*. See, for instance, his study of the 'telescoping' technique: the sophisticated treatment of the moment of recapitulation of the first movement of the Fourth Symphony, where the expected sequence of formal events is chronologically displaced in a highly original way (cf. '"Swallowing the Programme": Mahler's Fourth Symphony'). Many experimental approaches to the idea of *the symphony* are pointed out in great detail in Mitchell's chapters on specific works such the Fifth, *Das Lied von der Erde*, the Ninth and the Tenth.

In the unmeasured, asymmetrical 'prose' style of the recitatives and free melodies of 'Der Abschied', Mitchell reads Mahler's abandonment of regular phrase length and metric period, matched by a no less significant modification of all rhythmic organization. In the Tenth Symphony, especially the melodic contours of the opening adagio, with its huge leaps and skips that exemplify the extremities of Mahler's expressiveness, he takes us to the borderline with *Expressionism*. And through his asymmetrical distribution of accents, the free arches of melody and the finale's closing pages in *Das Lied von der Erde* Mahler achieves the *ecstasy of dissolution*, opening the way to a crucial aspect of the twentieth century's aesthetics.

In two extended autobiographical passages ('A Mahlerian Odyssey: 1936–2003' and 'The Twentieth Century's Debt to Mahler'), Mitchell tells us how it was that Mahler became such a leading musical passion of his life. Through some of his personal musical experiences, Mitchell gives us a most valuable first-hand survey of the *history of the reception* of Mahler's music in the twentieth century, and its struggle for recognition.

One aspect of Mitchell's research is particularly marked: an intimate rapport between *musicology* and *performance*. His dialogue with Riccardo Chailly on the Fifth Symphony ('New Sounds, New Century') is an illuminating example. Mitchell's concern goes well beyond musicology. He is interested in the living future of Mahler's music. In many of our present-day performances, he perceives a growing danger. Some of today's renderings offer a cosmetic blandness, a softening, a smoothing over, in short a blunting of the sharp edges, thereby making too easily acceptable a corpus of music with which the composer more often than not wanted to arouse discomfort, anxiety, disbelief, pain or ambivalence. Mitchell wants to secure *authenticity of interpretation* in all Mahler performances. And for him that often should mean preserving the original *shock* tactics present in the music. Mahler was far ahead of his time, and the intent, the capacity to shock, was to become another of those leading features of the twentieth century that he had substantially anticipated. With his capacity to upset or surprise (for example by a highly original manipulation of the seemingly trivial in a context in which audience expectations would have led them to expect something quite other) Mahler was out to challenge those assumptions. Therefore Mitchell is convinced that one of our prime responsibilities to the composer is to oppose his music's 'beautification', and the smoothing out or reduction of the shocks he originally intended (cf. 'The Twentieth Century's Debt to Mahler: Our Debt to him in the Twenty-first').

I strongly believe that Mahler would have been extremely happy with Mitchell's new book. Regarding the composer's 1906 fears (which I quoted as my opening epigraph), it is probably true that real justice has been done to 'a phenomenon like him' only after he had 'shaken off the dust of the earth'. But, with Donald Mitchell, Mahler 'as a creator' and his new 'kind of works' receive here the recognition they deserved from the start. Mitchell has 'done justice' to Mahler, demonstrating that Mahler was after all 'a man of his own time'. He absorbed the whole musical culture around him, although he was creatively critical of and often shocked the traditional status quo, while his works opened up a path for the music of the future.

Rome
July 2006

# A Note on Editorial Method and Acknowledgements

The texts gathered together in this volume have been very lightly edited in order to establish a uniformity of style. Occasional minor changes have been made to clarify meaning or to provide a more accurate reference. Footnotes attached to the original texts appear with a numbered indicator. Additional footnotes supplied by the current editors are placed below a short line and are indicated in the text by *, §, etc. When an original footnote extends beyond one page, the run-on text is set below a short dotted line (⋯⋯).

Translations of foreign phrases and titles are supplied in the text only when they are considered necessary for clarity. All Mahler's own titles – of works, songs, movements, etc. – are included in the Chronological List of Works (pp. XXXV–XLVI).

For a modest number of books that are referred to frequently throughout the texts, abbreviations are used; a list is provided on pp. XLVII–XLVIII. Full bibliographical details are supplied in the Bibliography (pp. 650–56).

Details of the initial publication of the texts are given at the foot of the first page of each essay. Where applicable, copyright credits for illustrations are included in the List of Illustrations (pp. IX–XII).

Unless otherwise indicated, translations of texts set by Mahler are by Deryck Cooke and are taken from his *Gustav Mahler: An Introduction to his Music* (London: Faber Music in association with Faber and Faber, 1980).

The music examples have been set by Lloyd Moore, with the exception of those for '"Swallowing the Symphony": Mahler's Fourth Symphony'; 'Mahler's "Kammermusikton"', and 'Eternity or Nothingness: Mahler's Fifth Symphony' (pp. 155–352 inclusive), where the music examples from *The Mahler Companion* (Oxford University Press, 1999) have been retained. When referring to rehearsal figures in scores, some essays use the fig. $x^{-/+N}$ convention, to indicate N bars before or after fig. x.

# Chronological List of Works

## Piano Quartet in A minor
Incomplete
*Date of composition* 1876/77
*First performance* ?1876–78; 12 February 1964, New York
*First publication* Sikorski, Hamburg, 1973; edited by P. Ruzicka
First movement (*Nicht zu schnell. Entschlossen* – 'Not too fast. Resolute' – and fragment (24 bars) of scherzo only

## Rübezahl
Fairy-tale opera; libretto by GM
*Date of composition* ?1879–83
Music lost

## 3 Lieder
Songs for tenor and piano; text by GM; dedicated to Josephine Poisl
*First performance* 30 September 1934, Radio Brno
*First publication* Schott, Mainz, 1990, as *Verschiedene Lieder für eine Singstimme mit Klavier*; edited by Zoltan Roman
From projected set of 5 songs

1 Im Lenz
'In Spring'; in F–A flat
*Date of composition* 19 February 1880

2 Winterlied
'Winter Song'; in A–F
*Date of composition* 27 February 1880

3 Maitanz im Grünen
'Springtime Dance in the Countryside'; in D
*Date of composition* 5 March 1880
Early version of 'Hans und Grethe'

## Das klagende Lied
'The Song of Lament'
Cantata for soprano, alto, tenor, baritone, bass, mixed choir and orchestra;
poem by GM
*Dates of composition* 1878–80; revised 1893–94; 1898–99 without Part 1,
for soprano, alto, tenor and orchestra
Originally in three parts: *Waldmärchen* ('Forest Legend'); *Der Spielmann*
('The Minstrel'); *Hochzeitsstück* ('Wedding Piece')
*First performances* revised version with only Parts 2 and 3: 17 February
1901, Vienna; original version, including *Waldmärchen*: 28 November
1934, Radio Brno; *Waldmärchen* only: 2 December 1934; original
version, complete: 8 April 1935, Vienna Radio; original 1880 complete
version, in 3 parts: 7 October 1997, Manchester
*First publications* revised 1898–99 version with only parts 2 and 3:
Weinberger, Leipzig and Vienna, 1902; *Waldmärchen*: New York, 1973;
original 1880 complete version in three parts: Universal Edition, Mainz,
1999; edited by Reinhold Kubik

## 5 Lieder
Songs for voice and piano

*Date of composition* 1880–83; 1887, entitled, in the only known manu-
script, 5 *Gedichte komponiert von Gustav Mahler*
*First publication* Schott, Mainz, 1892, forming volume 1 of the *Lieder und
Gesänge*, entitled after GM's death *Lieder aus der Jugendzeit*

1 Frühlingsmorgen
'Spring Morning', in F; text by Leander
*First performance* 20 April 1886, Prague

2 Erinnerung
'Remembering', in G minor–A minor; text by Leander
*First performance* 13 November 1889, Budapest

3 Hans und Grethe
'Hans and Grete', in D; text by GM
A reworking of 'Maitanz im Grünen'
*First performance* 20 April 1886, Prague

4  Serenade aus Don Juan
'Serenade from Don Juan', in D flat; text by Tirso de Molina and GM,
translated by Braunfels
*First performance*  ?1887, Leipzig

5  Phantasie aus Don Juan
'Fantasy from Don Juan'; in F sharp/B minor; ; text by Tirso de Molina
and GM, translated by Braunfels
*First performance*  ?1887, Leipzig

## Der Trompeter von Säkkingen

Incidental music for the play *The Trumpeter of Säkkingen* by von Scheffel,
for orchestra
*Date of composition*  1884
*First performance*  23 June 1884, Kassel
Manuscript lost; first number, 'Ein Ständchen am Rhein' ('A Serenade
on the Rhine'), used as andante (*Blumine*) in the original five-movement
version of Symphony No. 1

## Lieder eines fahrenden Gesellen

'Songs of a Wayfaring Lad'; texts by GM
Song-cycle for low voice and orchestra or piano
*Dates of composition*  ?December 1883–January 1885; revised ?1891–96
*First performance*  piano version: December 1884; orchestral version:
16 March 1896, Berlin
*First publication*  Weinberger, Leipzig and Vienna, 1897 (orchestral and
piano versions)

1  Wenn mein Schatz Hochzeit macht
'When my love becomes a bride', in D minor–G minor

2  Ging heut' morgen über's Feld
'I went this morning through the fields', in D–F sharp

3  Ich hab' ein glühend Messer
'I have a red-hot knife', in D minor–E flat minor

4  Die zwei blauen Augen
'The two blue eyes', in E minor–F minor

## Symphony No. 1

for orchestra, in D

*Dates of composition* (?1884–) March 1888; revised 1893–96
*First performance* 20 November 1889, Budapest
*First publication* 4-movement version: Weinberger, Vienna, 1898
Originally Symphonic Poem, later 'Titan'; originally in 5 movements –
andante (*Blumine*, 'A Chapter of Flowers'), placed second, discarded in
final revision

1 *Langsam. Schleppend – Immer sehr gemächlich*
(Slowly. Dragging – Always very leisurely)
2 *Kräftig bewegt, doch nicht zu schnell*
(Moving strongly, though not too fast)
3 *Feierlich und gemessen, ohne zu schleppen*
(Solemnly and measured, without dragging)
4 *Stürmisch bewegt* (Stormily agitated)

## 9 Wunderhorn Lieder

for voice and piano

Texts from von Arnim and Brentano, *Des Knaben Wunderhorn* ('The
Youth's Magic Horn')
*Date of composition* 1887–90
*First publication* Schott, Mainz, 1892, forming volumes II and III of the
*Lieder und Gesänge*, entitled after GM's death *Lieder aus der Jugendzeit*

1 Um schlimme Kinder artig zu machen
'To Teach Naughty Children to be Good', in E
*First performance* 1899–1900 season, Munich

2 Ich ging mit Lust durch einen grünen Wald
'Full of Joy I Walked through a Green Wood', in D
*First performance* 13 December 1907, Stuttgart (?also earlier)

3 Aus! Aus!
'Finished! Finished!', in D flat
*First performance* 29 April 1892, Hamburg

4 Starke Einbildungskraft
'Strong Imagination', in B flat
*First performance* 13 November 1907, Stuttgart (?also earlier)

5  Zu Strassburg auf der Schanz'
'On the Ramparts of Strassburg', in F sharp/F sharp minor–B/B minor
*First performance* November 1906, Helsinki (?also earlier)

6  Ablösung im Sommer
'The Changing of the Summer Guard', in D flat minor
*First performance* 1904–05 season, Berlin

7  Scheiden und Meiden
'Farewell and Forgo', in F
*First performance* 13 November 1889, Budapest

8  Nicht wiedersehen!
'Never to Meet Again', in C minor
*First performance* 29 April 1892, Hamburg

9  Selbstgefühl
'Self-Assurance', in F
*First performance* 15 February 1900, Vienna

## Symphony No. 2

for soprano, alto, mixed choir and orchestra, in C minor–E flat
*Dates of composition* 1888–94; revised 1903
*First performances* movements 1–3: 4 March 1895, Berlin; complete:
13 December 1895, Berlin
*First publication* Hofmeister & Weinberger, Leipzig, 1897; Universal
Edition, Vienna, 1906

1  *Allegro maestoso*
2  *Andante moderato*
3  *In ruhig fliessender Bewegung* (With quietly flowing movement)
4  *Urlicht. Sehr feierlich, aber schlicht* (Primeval Light. Very solemn, though
simple); text from von Arnim and Brentano, *Des Knaben Wunderhorn*
5  *Im Tempo des Scherzos* (In the tempo of a scherzo); text by Klopstock
and GM

## Des Knaben Wunderhorn

Songs for voice and piano or orchestra
Texts from von Arnim and Brentano, *Des Knaben Wunderhorn*
*First publications* Weinberger, Vienna, 1899, first five originally titled
*Humoresken*

1  Der Schildwache Nachtlied
'The Sentry's Night Song', in B flat
*Date of composition*  28 January 1892
*First performance*  12 December 1892, Berlin (with orchestra)

2  Verlor'ne Müh'
'Wasted Effort', in A
*Date of composition*  1 February 1892
*First performance*  12 December 1892, Berlin (with orchestra)

3  Trost im Unglück
'Consolation in Misfortune', in A
*Date of composition*  22 February 1892
*First performance*  27 October 1893, Hamburg (with orchestra)

4  Wer hat dies Liedlein erdacht?
'Who made up this little song?', in F
*Date of composition*  6 February 1892
*First performance*  27 October 1893, Hamburg (with orchestra)

5  Das irdische Leben
'Earthly Life', in B flat minor (Phrygian)
*Date of composition*  between April 1892 and summer 1893
*First performance*  14 January 1900, Vienna (with orchestra)

6  Des Antonius von Padua Fischpredigt
'Antony of Padua's Sermon to the Fish', in C minor
*Date of composition*  8 July 1893
*First performance*  29 January 1905, Berlin (with orchestra)

7  Rheinlegendchen
'Little Rhine Legend', in A
*Date of composition*  9 August 1893
*First performance*  27 October 1893, Hamburg (with orchestra)

8  Lied des Verfolgten im Turm
'Song of the Prisoner in the Tower', in D minor
*Date of composition*  July 1898
*First performance*  29 January 1905, Vienna (with orchestra)

9  Wo die schönen Trompeten blasen
'Where the Splendid Trumpets are Sounding', in D minor

*Date of composition* July 1898
*First performance* 29 January 1905, Vienna (with orchestra)

10  Lob des hohen Verstandes
'In Praise of Lofty Intellect', in D
*Date of composition* between 21 and 28 June 1896
*First performance* 18 January 1906, Vienna (with piano)

11  Es sungen drei Engel
'Three Angels were Singing', in F
*Date of composition* 11 August 1895, for Symphony No. 3
*First performance* 9 June 1902, Krefeld (in Symphony No. 3)

12  Urlicht
'Primeval Light', in D flat
*Date of composition* ?1892
*First performance* 13 December 1895, Berlin (in Symphony No. 2)

Das himmlische Leben
'Heavenly Life', in G–E
*Date of composition* 10 February 1892
*First performance* 27 October 1893, Hamburg (with orchestra)
Used in Symphony No. 4

## Symphony No. 3

for alto, women's choir, boys' choir and orchestra, in D minor–D
*Dates of composition* 1895–96; revised 1906
*First performances* movement 2: 9 November 1896, Berlin; movements 2,
3 and 6: 9 March 1897, Berlin; complete: 9 June 1902, Krefeld
*First publications* Weinberger, Vienna, 1899; revised version: Universal
Edition, Vienna, 1906

1  *Kräftig. Entschieden* (Strong. Decisive)
2  *Tempo di Menuetto. Sehr mässig* (Very moderate)
3  *Comodo. Scherzando. Ohne Hast* (Without haste)
4  *Sehr langsam* (Very slowly) – *Misterioso*; text from Nietzsche, *Also sprach
Zarathustra*
5  *Lustig im Tempo und keck im Ausdruck* (Happy in tempo and bold in
expression); text: 'Es sungen drei Engel' ('Three Angels were Singing'),
from *Des Knaben Wunderhorn*
6  *Langsam – Ruhevoll – Empfunden* (Slowly, tranquil, deeply felt)

## Symphony No. 4
for soprano solo and orchestra, in (B minor)/G–E
*Dates of composition* 1892; 1899–1900; revised 1901–10
*First performance* 25 November 1901, Munich
*First publications* Doblinger, Vienna, 1902; revised version: Universal
Edition, Vienna, 1906

1 *Bedächtig. Nicht eilen* (Moderately. Not rushed)
2 *In gemächlicher Bewegung. Ohne Hast* (Moving leisurely. Without haste)
3 *Ruhevoll* (Peacefully) *(Poco adagio)*
4 *Sehr behaglich* (Very comfortably); text: 'Das himmlische Leben'
('Heavenly Life') from *Des Knaben Wunderhorn*

## 7 Lieder
Songs for voice and orchestra or piano; entitled, after Mahler's death,
*Aus letzter Zeit*
*First performances* Nos. 1–6, with orchestra: 29 January 1905, Vienna
*First publication* Nos. 1–6, piano and orchestral versions: Kahnt, Leipzig,
1905

1 Revelge
'Reveille', in D minor or C minor
Text from *Des Knaben Wunderhorn*
*Date of composition* June/July 1899

2 Der Tamboursg'sell
'The Drummer-Boy', in D minor
Text from *Des Knaben Wunderhorn*
*Date of composition* 12 July 1901

3 Blicke mir nicht in die Lieder
'Do not peep into my songs', in F
Text by Rückert
*Date of composition* 14 June 1901

4 Ich atmet' einen Linden Duft
'I sensed a delicate fragrance', in D
Text by Rückert
*Date of composition* July or August 1901

5  Ich bin der Welt abhanden gekommen
'I am lost to the world', in F
Text by Rückert
*Date of composition*  summer 1901

6  Um Mitternacht
'At Midnight', in B minor
Text by Rückert
*Date of composition*  summer 1901

7  Liebst du um Schönheit
'If you love for beauty', in C
Text by Rückert
*Date of composition*  August 1902 (with piano accompaniment)
*First performance*  8 February 1907, Vienna (?also earlier)
*First publications*  piano version: Kahnt, Leipzig, 1905; orchestral version
(by Puttmann): Leipzig, ?1910

## Symphony No. 5
for orchestra, in C sharp minor–D
*Dates of composition*  1901–02; scoring repeatedly revised
*First performance*  18 October 1904, Cologne
*First publications*  Peters, Leipzig, 1904; revised version: 1905

1  *Trauermarsch. In gemessenem Schritt. Streng. Wie ein Kondukt*
(Funeral March. In a measured pace. Stern. Like a funeral procession)
2  *Stürmisch bewegt, mit grösster Vehemenz*
(Moving stormily, with the greatest vehemence)
3  *Scherzo. Kräftig, nicht zu schnell* (Powerful, not too fast)
4  *Adagietto. Sehr langsam* (Very slow)
5  *Rondo-Finale. Allegro*

## Kindertotenlieder
'Songs on the Death of Children'
Song-cycle, for voice and orchestra or piano
Texts by Rückert
*First performance*  29 January 1905, Vienna
*First publications*  full and vocal scores: Kahnt, Leipzig, 1905

1  Nun will die Sonn' so hell aufgeh'n
'Now will the sun as brightly rise', in D minor
*Date of composition*  summer 1901

2  Nun seh' ich wohl, warum so dunkle Flammen
'Now I see clearly why such ardent flames', in C minor
*Date of composition*  summer 1904

3  Wenn dein Mütterlein
'When your mother dear', in C minor
*Date of composition*  summer 1901

4  Oft denk' ich, sie sind nur ausgegangen
'How often I think they're just out walking', in E flat
*Date of composition*  summer 1901

5  In diesem Wetter
'In this grim weather', in D minor–D
*Date of composition*  summer 1904

## Symphony No. 6

for orchestra, in A minor
*Dates of composition*  1903–04; revised 1906; scoring repeatedly revised
*First performance*  27 May 1906, Essen
*First publications*  Kahnt, Leipzig, 1906; revised version: Kahnt, Leipzig, 1906

1  *Allegro energico, ma non troppo*
2  *Scherzo: Wuchtig* (Powerful)
3  *Andante moderato*
4  *Finale. Allegro moderato*
The performance order of movements 2 and 3 is a matter for debate, see Appendix 1, pp. 633–47.

## Symphony No. 7

for orchestra, in (B minor) E minor–C
*Dates of composition*  1904–05; scoring repeatedly revised
*First performance*  19 September 1908, Prague
*First publication*  Bote und Bock, Berlin, 1909

1  *Langsam* (Slowly); *Allegro con fuoco*
2  *Nachtmusik 1: Allegro moderato*

3 *Schattenhaft* (Shadowlike)
4 *Nachtmusik II: Andante amoroso*
5 *Rondo-Finale: Allegro ordinario*

## Symphony No. 8
for 3 sopranos, 2 altos, tenor, baritone, bass, mixed double choir, boys' choir, orchestra and organ, in E flat
*Dates of composition* summer 1906
*First performance* 12 September 1910, Munich
*First publications* vocal score: Universal Edition, Vienna, 1910; full score: Universal Edition, Vienna, 1911

Part I *Hymnus: Veni, creator spiritus* ('Come, Creator Spirit'); text by Hrabanus Maurus
Part II *Schlußszene aus 'Faust'* (Final Scene from *Faust*); text by Goethe

## Das Lied von der Erde
Symphony for tenor and alto (or baritone) and orchestra, in A minor–C
Texts after Hans Bethge's *Die chinesische Flöte* (*The Chinese Flute*)
*Dates of composition* summer 1908
*First performance* 20 November 1911, Munich
*First publications* vocal score: Universal Edition, Vienna, 1911; full score: Universal Edition, Vienna, 1912

1 Das Trinklied vom Jammer der Erde
'The Drinking Song of Earth's Sorrow' (tenor); text after Li-Tai-Po

2 Der Einsame im Herbst
'The Lonely One in Autumn' (alto); text after Chang-Tsi

3 Von der Jugend
'Youth' (tenor); text after Li-Tai-Po

4 Von der Schönheit
'Beauty' (alto); text after Li-Tai-Po

5 Der Trunkene im Frühling
'The Drunkard in Spring' (tenor); text after Li-Tai-Po

6 Der Abschied
'The Farewell' (alto); text after Mong-Kao-Jen and Wang-Sei, and by GM

## Symphony No. 9
for orchestra, in D–D flat
*Dates of composition* 1908–09
*First performance* 26 June 1912, Vienna
*First publications* Universal Edition, Vienna, 1912

1 *Andante comodo*
2 *Im Tempo eines gemächlichen Ländlers. Etwas täppisch und sehr derb*
(In the tempo of a leisurely ländler. Somewhat awkward and very coarse)
3 *Rondo-Burleske: Allegro assai. Sehr trotzig* (Very obstinate)
4 *Adagio.*

## Symphony No. 10
for orchestra, in F sharp minor/F sharp
Incomplete
*Date of composition* 1910; scoring repeatedly revised
*First performances* 12 October 1924, Vienna (movements 1 and 3);
13 August 1964, London (complete performing version by Deryck
Cooke in collaboration with Berthold Goldschmidt, Colin Matthews
and David Matthews); see also Appendix II, pp. 648–9
*First publications* movements 1 and 3: New York, 1951; performing
version by Deryck Cooke: London and New York, 1976

1 *Adagio* (275 bars drafted in orchestral and short score)
2 *Scherzo* (522 bars drafted in orchestral and short score)
3 *Purgatorio* (170 bars drafted in short score, the first 30 of which were
also drafted in orchestral score)
4 *[Scherzo]* (about 579 bars drafted in short score)
5 *Finale* (400 bars drafted in short score)

UNFINISHED WORK COMPLETED BY MAHLER

## Die drei Pintos
Opera in three acts
Sketches and original music by Carl Maria von Weber, 1821
Rescored and completed by GM, 1887–88
Libretto by Theodor Hell, revised by Capt. Karl von Weber and GM
*First performance* 20 January 1888, Leipzig Municipal Opera, conducted
by GM
*First publication* Kahnt, Leipzig, ?1888

# Bibliographical Abbreviations

AM *Memories* – Alma Mahler, *Gustav Mahler: Memories and Letters*, translated by Basil Creighton, edited by Donald Mitchell and Knud Martner, 4th edn (London: Sphere Books, 1990)

DCGM    Deryck Cooke, *Gustav Mahler: An Introduction to his Music* (London: Faber and Faber, 1980)

DMCN    Donald Mitchell, *Cradles of the New: Writings on Music, 1951–1991*, edited by Christopher Palmer and Mervyn Cooke (London: Faber, 1995); [MC] indicates an annotation by Mervyn Cooke

DMANMC  Donald Mitchell and Andrew Nicholson (eds.), *The Mahler Companion* (Oxford: Oxford University Press, 1999)

DMSSLD  Donald Mitchell, *Gustav Mahler: Songs and Symphonies of Life and Death* (London: Faber and Faber, 1985); rev. edn (Woodbridge: The Boydell Press, 2002)

DMWY    Donald Mitchell, *Gustav Mahler: The Wunderhorn Years* (London: Faber and Faber, 1975); rev. edn (Woodbridge: The Boydell Press, 2005)

GM *Selected Letters* – Gustav Mahler, *Selected Letters of Gustav Mahler*, translated by Eithne Wilkins, Ernst Kaiser and Bill Hopkins, edited by Knud Martner (London: Faber and Faber, 1979)

GMWL    Donald Mitchell (ed.), *Gustav Mahler: The World Listens* (Haarlem: TEMA Uitgevers, 1995)

HLG *Mahler* – Henry-Louis de La Grange, *Mahler*, 2 vols.: I (London: Gollancz, 1974); II *Vienna: The Years of Challenge (1897–1904)* (Oxford: Oxford University Press, 1995)

HLG *Mahler CV* – Henry-Louis de La Grange, *Mahler: Chronique d'une vie*, 3 vols. (Paris: Fayard, 1973–84)

NB-L *Recollections* – Natalie Bauer-Lechner, *Recollections of Gustav Mahler*, translated by Dika Newlin, edited by Peter Franklin (London: Faber and Faber, 1980)

*NSNC*    Donald Mitchell and Henriette Straub (eds.), *New Sounds, New Century: Mahler's Fifth Symphony and the Royal Concertgebouw Orchestra* (Bussum: THOTH/Amsterdam, Royal Concertgebouw Orchestra, 1997)

TWA *Mahler* – Theodor W. Adorno, *Mahler: A Musical Physiognomy*, translated by Edmund Jephcott (Chicago and London: University of Chicago Press, 1992)

# Abschied

## *Donald Mitchell*

There can be little doubt that this current volume of my writings on Mahler will also prove to be the last. It is unlikely that I shall find nothing else to say about Mahler in the immediate future; on the other hand I am aware that the future itself cannot be too long prolonged or postponed. In other words, a line has to be drawn, and it is precisely that line that this compilation represents.

I am aware of course of how much my preceding books on Mahler owe to the conspicuous encouragement and – often – collaboration I have been lucky to receive worldwide from fellow Mahlerians, friends and scholars, over the period of my own contributions to the Mahler literature of – principally – the last century. In my already published four Mahler volumes, *The Early Years* (1958; new edition, 2003), *The Wunderhorn Years* (1975; new edition, 2005), *Songs and Symphonies of Life and Death* (1985; revised edition, 2002), and *The Mahler Companion* (1999, with Andrew Nicholson), I hope that I have adequately recognized, identified and expressed gratitude to all those who (or whose work) so generously helped me in my own efforts to advance our knowledge of Mahler, and, above all, knowledge of the unique experience embodied in his music. It would seem needless to repeat all those expressions of gratitude here, while observing with no little sorrow that some of those to whom I remain indebted are no longer alive. Even as I write these words, I am conscious of the absence of Edward R. Reilly, to whom I address a posthumous letter at the end of this book. I still find it hard to believe that I cannot pick up the phone, hear his voice and tap his wisdom. Instead I offer this book to him as an *Abschied*. Memories of him, however, and of many other predecessors, remain very much alive in these pages along, I hope, with recognition of their pioneering discoveries.

What I must do now, however, is express my thanks to all those who, over a period of more than fifty years, in ways however diverse, encouraged me to pursue my Mahler studies. I remain indebted to them as a source of both information and inspiration: Claudio Abbado, Richard Alston, Chris Banks, Paul Banks; Richard Barber, Boydell Press; the late Robert Becqué, the late Eileen Bell, the late Kurt and Herta Blaukopf, Asa Briggs, the late Benjamin Britten, Jill Burrows, Riccardo Chailly; Peter Clifford, Boydell Press; Concertgebouworkest, Amsterdam; the late Deryck Cooke, Mervyn Cooke, Milein Cosman-Keller, the late Norman Del Mar, the late Peter du Sautoy, Matthew Evans, Peter Evans, the late Boris Ford, Gastón Fournier-Facio; Chris Grogan, Nicholas Clark, and the staff of the Britten–Pears Library, Aldeburgh; Bernard Haitink, the late Paul Hamburger, Stephen E. Hefling, Gilbert E. Kaplan, the late Hans Keller, Somsak Ketakaenchan, Reinhold Kubik, Henry-Louis de La Grange, the late Christa Landon, H. C. Robbins Landon, Norman Lebrecht, Stephen McClatchie, the late Anna Mahler, Marina Mahler, Knud Martner, Belinda Matthews, Colin Matthews, David Matthews, Kathleen Mitchell, Lloyd Moore, Kent Nagano, Eveline Nikkels; Caroline Palmer, Boydell Press; the late Christopher Palmer, the late Peter Pears, the late Hans F. Redlich, Philip Reed, the late Edward R. Reilly, Zoltan Roman, Eric Roseberry, the late Edward W. Said, Martijn Sanders, the late Robert Simpson, the late Kamtorn Snidvong, the late Erwin Stein, Henriette Straub, Marion Thorpe, the late Harold Truscott, the late Paul Wilson, Judy Young.

VISION

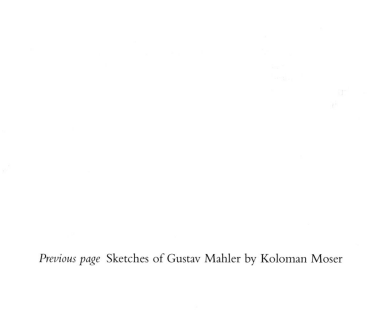

*Previous page* Sketches of Gustav Mahler by Koloman Moser

# Gustav Mahler

## ∻ 1976 ∻

Mahler himself considered *Das klagende Lied* to be the first work in which he found his own voice as a composer; and he was right. The precocious cantata of 1880 displays, for all its evident immaturities, an extraordinary number of mannerisms that we recognize at once as conspicuously Mahlerian. It is of particular interest, and hitherto hardly remarked, that his discovery of his musical identity was part of the chronological process of writing the cantata; hence the comparatively eclectic style, not to speak of the less cogently organized form, of the original first part of the cantata (if compared with the much more personal and shapely Parts II and III (which became the first and second parts of the revised and published version of 1899)). Since the rediscovery of the original first part, views have been expressed about the desirability of returning to the composer's original conception; but it seems to me that Mahler's revision showed his excellent critical judgement, and a precise assessment of

---

The text published here represents the original version of what I wrote in response to the invitation to contribute the entry on Mahler's music to *The New Grove Dictionary of Music and Musicians* (1980). What actually appeared was a text very heavily edited by Stanley Sadie and his colleagues. On renewing my acquaintance with it, while at the same time reading again my original text – I confess to having written at far greater length than I was asked for – it seemed to me that *The New Grove* ultimately conveyed very little of how I thought and felt about Mahler at the time I wrote it. A rather forbidding impersonality had been imposed that effectively drained from my words the excitement of the insights that were the main business of my first effort of length and (I hoped) substance to describe Mahler's creative evolution and its importance; we have to recall yet again that in the 1970s in England there was still relatively little general recognition of his genius, its character and its achievements. Perhaps I should add too that I was not *Grove's* first choice as author. This was to have been Deryck Cooke, who was also to have contributed the entry on Bruckner, which indeed he did. However, he found himself, so I was told, unable to take on the duo. The very coupling of Bruckner and Mahler, so often met with in the twentieth century, speaks volumes for itself. It was rare that each was afforded independent mention or evaluation; think for instance of the bonding of Bruckner and Mahler in 1955, when their names formed the joint title of a volume in Dent's famous 'Master Musicians' series. (Hans Redlich, its author, should have known better.) [DM]

where he began to speak his own language consistently, from *Der Spielmann* onwards. (As a result of the omission of Part I, the cantata's originally concentric tonal scheme, A minor → A minor, extending over the three parts, was lost; thus the 'progressive' scheme that remains, C minor → A minor, was not consciously planned but a consequence of the revision.)

The style of *Das klagende Lied*, even at its most personal, remains eclectic in the sense that, predictably, it shows its origins in the formative influences of the music to which Mahler was personally and enthusiastically responsive; to the music theatre of Weber and Wagner in particular in the case of the cantata, which feeds on a rich mixture of some of the principal sources of German Romanticism in the late nineteenth century: Magic, a revived Medievalism and murmuring Nature. But to all this the youthful composer gave a new twist by setting the catastrophe of the final scene of the work *against* the offstage contribution of a wind band, which pursues its festive music notwithstanding the calamitous dramatic context. This was a highly original climax – arguably it is the most original thing in the whole score – and in a single knot of sound we find tied together, as early as 1880, many of the threads that are thereafter continually to re-emerge in Mahler's music until his death, e.g. the exploitation of combined onstage, offstage orchestras and the particular acoustic relationship involved in this device; the mix of high tragedy and the 'mundane' (the offstage, emphatically *wind* band), the latter offering a simultaneously ironic commentary on the former; and the clear strike into the area of the opera house for the concept of the dramatic denouement. This complex of ideas Mahler was to plunder again and again and manipulate in various ways. Thus the early cantata presents at its peak moments a body of 'imagery', embedded in a quite specific handling of sound, which was to be of central importance for the future. Small wonder that when revising the work for publication, Mahler's attempt, in the interests of economy, to omit the stage band failed. The acoustic separation was essential to his purpose, as was its distinctive wind constitution.

There are four other aspects of the cantata which also demand specific mention. First, even in the original version, the handling of

Ex. 1    *Das klagende Lied, Der Spielmann*

the orchestra – an exuberantly large one at that stage – showed altogether unusual flair and imagination for a composer of his age. Second, there is a prominent kind of vocal melody, which in its directness and intensity, anticipates the comparable directness of utterance that marks the *Lieder eines fahrenden Gesellen*, the song-cycle on which Mahler was to embark in 1883–84. One is tempted to label this 'folk-like', and some commentators (e.g. Pamer and Newlin[1]) have indeed seen the influence of Bohemian folk song on the contours of these particular melodies. Such influence is in fact hard to estimate. What one can say, more precisely, is that the lyric vocal shapes embodied in Ex. 1 are quite distinct from anything that Mahler had written earlier for voice in the first volume of the *Lieder und Gesänge*, which offers songs relatively traditional in format (this not to overlook their very real merits and originalities, among them the first published appearance of Mahler's progressive tonality, in 'Erinnerung', which begins in G minor and ends in A minor). Even the folkiest of the songs, 'Hans und Grethe', which was to fund a whole movement in the first symphony, did not break new ground in quite the way that Ex. 1 does, which is remarkably free of the rounded, symmetrical period of the 'lied'; and which was perhaps assisted towards this freedom by the moment of drama that is being enacted. Indeed, rather than folk song, it seems to me that 'folk ballad', i.e., a form of dramatized story-telling, would give us a more appropriate description. Third, and in some ways most importantly, there is the complex, synthesizing form of the cantata itself, which brings together within one

1    Fritz Egon Pamer, 'Gustav Mahlers Lieder', and Dika Newlin, *Bruckner, Mahler, Schoenberg*.

dramatic frame, many different kinds of musics – the plural is deliberate – and exploits a wide variety of musical forms and resources.
Fourth, there is already a clearly defined dramatic/symbolic use of
tonality, e.g. F sharp minor, there is no doubt, is to be understood
throughout as the 'murder' key (the slaying of the younger brother
by the elder). The cantata proved to be a veritable seedbed of
inventive possibilities, but it was not until the Eighth Symphony,
years later, that Mahler attempted another composite work. In
between he pursued, more independently, those possibilities which
were practical and towards which the development of his personal
creativity clearly impelled him.

From the precedents revealed in *Das klagende Lied* it is obvious
that the potentialities of orchestral song, i.e. solo voice plus orchestra, was one of Mahler's preoccupations. It is not surprising, then,
that for his next work, the song-cycle *Lieder eines fahrenden Gesellen*,
which, because of the perfection of its formal design, should
properly be regarded as the masterpiece of his early years, he chose to
concentrate on a specific area in the voice/orchestra relationship.
There is little doubt that the cycle was envisaged at its earliest stage
with orchestral accompaniment, though first drafted (as indeed was
Mahler's custom with his later orchestral songs) for voice and
piano; the actual orchestration was done very much later (hence, of
course, the brilliant economy of it, as compared with the exuberant lavishness of the preceding cantata). The unique features of the
cycle may be summed up as follows: (1) the development, from the
cantata no doubt, of the narrative idea, an unfolding drama, but this
time applied to a sequence of four songs; (2) the musical representation of this 'dramatic' idea, which implies a destination wholly
distinct from the point of departure (a notion wholly foreign to the
idea of classical symmetry, based on the reprise ('we are back where
we started'), through an evolutionary tonal scheme which 'travels'
along with the changing fortunes of the travelling Hero (see Ex. 2);
(3) the clear perception by Mahler that within this exploration of
the orchestral song it was perfectly possible to attempt textures and
developments that were more 'symphonic' in their density and
elaboration than one would normally associate with the concept of
the lyric song (here Mahler was doubtless influenced by the large-

Ex. 2

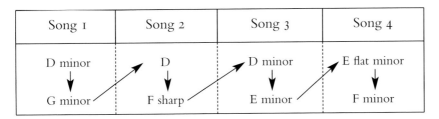

| Song 1 | Song 2 | Song 3 | Song 4 |
|---|---|---|---|
| D minor | D | D minor | E flat minor |
| G minor | F sharp | E minor | F minor |

scale thinking in Wagnerian music drama); and finally, (4) the unmistakable identification of the composer with his 'fahrende Gesell'. He is not, one feels, so much relating a history, as in *Das klagende Lied*, but appears as hero of his own work, i.e. the Artist as Hero. This was a role which we may think Mahler now continues to play to the very end of his creative life, though always in a phenomenal variety of guises (not disguises).

If the *Lieder eines fahrenden Gesellen* were not orchestrated after the songs had been drafted, it was probably because Mahler had started work (possibly as early as 1884, the year in which the cycle was brought to a conclusion) on his big new orchestral composition, which was to become the First Symphony but started life, and indeed was first performed, as a 'Symphonic Poem in Two Parts', and in five movements (the so-called *Blumine* movement – the original second movement (andante) – was later discarded). The shape and character of the 'Symphonic Poem' reveal many of the major features of the composer's music of this period, many of his major preoccupations, and also some of the problems with which he was faced.

These might be summed up as follows: first, the work, and particularly the work in its first version, shows that Mahler, like his aspiring contemporary, Richard Strauss, was dominated by the idea of programme music, by the concept of the dramatic symphonic poem. It was this new and innovatory form that magnetized him, though it was quite clear that at the same time he was acutely conscious of the 'symphonic' tradition, of the necessity to prove himself a symphonist. During this period of composition, say up to 1901, it was out of the friction between the two different concepts, symphony proper and symphonic poem, that some of Mahler's most interesting experiments emerged. The uncertainties and ambiguities which plagued him at this time proved creatively valuable. They led to the creation of (externally) very singular works of art. While it was true that Mahler was behaving like any ambitious young composer of his day in following the new trend – and the symphonic poem was certainly the dominant new form of the time – he brought to his own use of it certain highly personal angles of approach. For example, in the First Symphony, and also in the Second and even the Fourth – perhaps only the Third is the exception to the rule – Mahler maintained and further developed the narrative, chronological, story-telling principle (this is putting it crudely) which was the *raison d'être* of *Das klagende Lied* and the *Lieder eines fahrenden Gesellen*; and the change from the narrating a history (as in the cantata) to the immediate 'autobiography' of the *Gesellen* songs, this too was never to be modified. Indeed, it is plain that in the early cycle we encounter the personality whose fortunes Mahler was to document in one large-scale work after another over the ensuing decades. Furthermore, it was not only the story-telling principle that Mahler took over from the works of his early maturity, but also, and most importantly, actual musical materials, e.g. he made a substantial and dramatically apt quotation from the last song of the *Gesellen* cycle in the funeral-march slow movement of the First Symphony, made use of an early song in the scherzo, and built the work's ample first movement out of the cycle's second song, 'Ging heut' morgen . . .'. It is interesting to observe even in Mahler's early voice and piano sketch that this song is already the most complex and polyphonic in texture, thus offering the most possibilities for development in a more expansive formal area. This unique incorporation of the cycle into the symphony tells us a lot about Mahler's working methods; most interestingly, it underlines the need to consider the body of his work as a whole, as a totality in a state of continuous evolution. It would be exaggerated to suggest that there are no distinctions to be made between one category of work and another; but though compartments may indeed exist, they obstinately refuse to remain in isolation, and it is the interlinking, incorporating and mixture of categories which is a particular feature of the works up to the turn of the century (this was to diminish somewhat after 1901). (As Boulez remarks in his Preface to the Philharmonia miniature score of *Das klagende Lied*: 'This first Mahlerian epic makes us aware of future developments and implications. The great novel is sketched: we will read its chapters progressively in the works to come. Thus there are creators whose power, springing from a single source, is amplified according to certain constant data: this is how Mahler appears to me.') Most prominent and also most singular in this context are Mahler's *Wunderhorn* songs, settings of poems from the famous von Arnim and Brentano anthology of 1806–8. He was to use one of the earlier (and brilliant) voice and piano settings (of 1887–90), as the basis for the scherzo of the Third Symphony; but it was the later orchestral settings, from the 1890s, that were to prove of such creative significance. In pursuing yet further the voice–orchestra relationship and one must remember that at this time the *Gesellen* cycle still had not emerged in its final orchestral guise, the maturity of which reflects the experience he gained in drafting the *Wunderhorn* songs – Mahler was following up an old preoccupation. As in *Das klagende Lied*, for which he had written his own *Wunderhorn*-like text, Mahler gave a new twist to his *Wunderhorn* settings by lifting them out of the realm of fairy tale, of neo-medievalism, and reliving them in terms of an intense actuality of personal experience. Thus the archaic images of the poetry, embodied in intensely personal music, often came to be symbolic in Mahler's aesthetic of Man's (or the Artist's) experience of the world. For all that, i.e. the clear significance of the texts, it is the medium that remains the message, and when we speak of the vividness of Mahler's rendering of the poems, we mean the exceptional pungency of Mahler's orchestrations – for each song he devised an independent chamber orchestral sound of matchless clarity and the memorability and characterizing power of his vocal melodies. The orchestral songs met with a mixed reception at the time of their first performances. A minority readily appreciated their originality of content and craft. The majority was bothered by what (to them) seemed to be a sharp discrepancy between the 'primitive' folk-song materials and Mahler's super-elaborate, often ironic, often intense, treatment of them. But in fact this adverse criticism was based not on anything factual – i.e. Mahler's materials were anything but 'naive' – but on the contradiction of long-established conventions and predictions; folk-song settings should conform to certain comfortable orthodoxies, and Mahler's upsetting of the musical conventions – his declining to play the fairy-tale game led to constant misunderstandings.

The *Wunderhorn* songs are not only important in themselves as a valuable set of diverse orchestral songs, for which there were very few precedents outside the musical theatre – Berlioz, almost certainly, would have been one of Mahler's models: the great French innovator was without doubt a prime influence throughout this period of Mahler's life – but, most unusually, functioned as a storehouse of invention, symbol and image in parallel relation to the symphonies Mahler created during his *Wunderhorn* years; and sometimes as more than that, in the case of the Fourth Symphony indeed, generating powerhouse would be a more appropriate and accurate description of a song's relationship – e.g., that of 'Das himmlische Leben' – to a symphony – the Fourth (though not only to the Fourth, but also to the Third). The unique status of the orchestral songs of this period is in fact another and very striking example of the *totality* of Mahler's creativity, of the blurring of the conventional, clean-cut distinctions. He was engaged in symphony and song during these years, and where song could clarify an important moment in the dramatic structure of a symphony, e.g. 'Urlicht', in the Second, or 'Es sungen drei Engel' in the Third; or form the basis of a large-scale instrumental movement, e.g., the 'Fischpredigt' scherzo in the Second, the 'Kuckuck' scherzo in the Third; or function as the poetic and musical summit towards which an entire symphony might aspire, i.e. 'Das himmlische Leben' in the Fourth, Mahler without hesitation would turn to his available output of songs, or in certain cases write new ones, in order to complete, or make coherent, his dramatic schemes. At this period of his life indeed it is most useful, perhaps, to view Mahler's creative process as a kind of assembly line: music was composed (instrumental movements, songs, or song-cycle), and then blocks of invention, i.e. movements of various kinds, were chosen to fill out the dramatic outline, tried out in various sequences, added to or contracted, and finally shaped into the cogent overall structures with which we are familiar today. It was a uniquely evolutionary process this, which because of its very fluid and indeterminate nature, until the very final stage, sometimes meant that what was necessarily excluded from one work formed the basis of – or was included in – the next. The interrelationship of the Third and Fourth Symphonies provide a very clear instance of this practice. That part of the story that did not get told in the Third was meticulously and comprehensively explored in the Fourth, while the Second, and probably the First, too, if one knew more about the chronology of the first stages of its composition, provides a remarkable example of Mahler's assembly-line procedures. (In the First, apart from the exuberant utilization of the extant *Gesellen* cycle, Mahler cheerfully incorporated an instrumental interlude from the music he wrote in 1884 to accompany living tableaux based on Scheffel's *Der Trompeter van Säkkingen*. This was the so-called *Blumine* movement, later abandoned. I believe there is no doubt that this movement was a straight 'lift' from another source, planned to provide another episode in the symphony's narrative.)

It becomes clear then that while Mahler's *Wunderhorn* symphonies were programme symphonies, with their roots in Beethoven and Berlioz, they were also significantly influenced programmatically by the series of *Wunderhorn* songs, which introduced into the symphonies' various dramatic schemes a particular range of imagery very different from, say, the kind of scenarios that Strauss was pursuing. But though it is obvious that at this time Mahler needed a programme, whether uttered or kept to himself, in order to put his large-scale structures together, he simultaneously felt obliged to pay tribute to 'symphony' proper, for which reason, after completing his 'Symphonic Poem in Two Parts' (the First Symphony) he immediately embarked on completing the first movement of a symphony in C minor, on the grandest scale, which was plainly intended to establish his symphonic credentials. Thus the first movement of what we know now as the Second (so called 'Resurrection') Symphony is one of the most imposing of Mahler's sonata structures, unorthodox maybe in its tonal organization, but quite unambiguously, even 'classically', articulated as a thoroughgoing sonata shape. Hence, undoubtedly, the inscription 'symphony', although Mahler in fact got stuck after the first movement was done and was able to complete the work only after a long interval, when the devising of a programme enabled him to bring the work to a conclusion. While the sequence of the middle movements in the Second Symphony, and its gigantic finale, with its choral culmination, extend the idea of continuous narrative that was the thread on which the first movements of the original 'Symphonic Poem' (First Symphony) were hung, the great funeral march is a structure more explicitly and traditionally symphonic than anything that the very free and fantasy-like form of the immediately preceding work could have led anyone to expect. The trend, however, which in any case had not been sustained in the Second Symphony across the whole arch of the work, was not continued in the Third Symphony, the most idiosyncratic of Mahler's symphonies, the overall dramatic scheme of which only gradually evolved and crucial dramatic stages in which were only illuminated by recourse to orchestral song (Nietzsche) and choral song (*Wunderhorn* text) in the fourth and fifth movements. Moreover, to approach the huge first movement of the work with some pre-set idea of symphonic, i.e. sonata form, is to court analytic disaster and aesthetic disappointment. The first movement makes sense only in terms of the dramatic scenario which it enacts – the symbolic conquest of winter by summer – a scenario that was a good deal more minutely detailed in the original manuscript full score than is generally known. (It is fair to attribute, indeed, such formal failures as exist in the movement to precisely those moments, especially of reprise, where Mahler, surely mistakenly, felt obliged to go through the motions of sonata symmetry rather than follow through his dramatic conception.)

At a later stage, Mahler rid himself of any programmatic indications, not only in this work but also elsewhere. While this undoubtedly shows that he had ambiguous feelings about 'programmes', and often expressed himself as being powerfully opposed to the concept of the 'programme' and all the misunderstanding it entailed, this in no way diminishes in fact the importance of the programmatic idea for Mahler during the *Wunderhorn* years. In one case, the Second Symphony, he was unable to complete the work until he had formulated a programme, and in all the other works from the period, programmes, whether publicly acknowledged by Mahler or not, had an essential role to play. It was not until the Fourth Symphony that Mahler brilliantly returned to symphonic tradition, in a first movement of incomparable wit, subtlety and intelligence. This is certainly the finest and most complex of Mahler's symphonic structures from this period, not only a highly original approach to sonata form but also a fascinating commentary, in purely musical terms, *on* the sonata idea. Mahler emerges in the role of historian in this remarkable movement, quite deliberately (I submit) taking an historic formal model or concept and (literally) playing about with it. Witness the exquisitely sophisticated treatment of the moment of recapitulation which indeed recapitulates everything, but where the expected sequence of events is chronologically displaced (Ex. 3). Part of the unique character of this elaborate movement rests in the fact that we have here one of the earliest examples in the twentieth century of, to use Adorno's phrase, 'music about music' ('Musik über Musik'). Mahler's own analysis of the sonata principle – what it was, what might still be

Ex. 3    Symphony No. 4, first movement

Ex. 3(a)

achieved in the way of uncovering fresh possibilities in it – is built into the form of the movement, indeed is the form of the movement. It is a typical Mahlerian paradox that in the work, the Fourth Symphony, in which he wrote perhaps his most complex and meticulously organized sonata movement, one of his most perfect instrumental pieces, he also brought to perfection, and in its most sophisticated guise, the idea of the programme, in this case the poetic idea of the progress from experience (the first movement) to innocence (the *Wunderhorn* song-finale, 'Das himmlische Leben'), a progression symbolically represented in a sequence of forms and textures which gradually diminishes in complexity until the child-like vision of Paradise is attained in the 'heavenly' key of E major, a tonal destination already foreseen in the very opening B minor bars of the first movement, before the movement's – and the sym-

Ex. 3(b)

phony's – central tonality, G major, is unambiguously asserted. This
is the symphonic work that closes the *Wunderhorn* period, and in
which two of Mahler's preoccupations which were sometimes at
formal odds with one another – the obligations of the symphonic
tradition and the very different requirements of a developing
drama – were finally reconciled. The Fourth Symphony, furthermore, epitomizes in absolutely unambiguous fashion the significance of the *Wunderhorn* songs for the parallel symphonies from
these years. The Fourth was exclusively generated by one song, 'Das

himmlische Leben', and its long-term tonal organization, to mention only one factor, was strictly governed by the song's progressive
tonal scheme G → E.

This seems a convenient stage at which to sum up the major
features of Mahler's art as it had developed throughout this period.
One notes principally, in the realm of *form*, a coalition of symphony
and symphonic poem, with the latter a more substantial influence
than the former. (It was only after the Fourth Symphony that
Mahler settled for 'Symphony' as a designation without conflicts of
conscience.) One notes too his use of a dramatic, or poetic, narrative idea to underpin an evolving, sometimes suite-like sequence of
movements. To secure integration and induce coherence, Mahler
used interrelated material between one movement and another
(and across the whole span of a work) – i.e. the First, Third and
Fourth Symphonies – or cyclic procedures – e.g., the First
Symphony. On occasion, however, it was the narrative idea almost
alone which had to bear the weight of overall integration, e.g. the
Second Symphony.

There is then Mahler's striking use of *Wunderhorn* song, to make
verbal, and thus explicit, crucial aspects of the drama the particular
symphony was enacting (the same principle accounts for the use of
texts by Klopstock and Nietzsche in the Second and Third Symphonies, alongside the *Wunderhorn* poets) or to form the basis of
extended instrumental movements; and it was often with 'character' movements that Mahler filled out the frame provided by his
first movements and finales (in the First, Second and Third Symphonies, and again, later, in the Seventh). One observes already in
the First, how the first and last movements stand in a special formal
relationship, i.e. with some prime materials from the first movement
left to be developed to their maximum potentiality in the finale.
This novel division of formal responsibilities, i.e. the complementary, and to some degree, expository/developmental relationship
between first movement and finale, was to become a characteristic
Mahlerian procedure (e.g. the Sixth Symphony), and the principle
was sometimes extended to other pairs of movements (e.g. the first
and second as well as the fourth and fifth movements of the Fifth
Symphony).

To continue the tally: along with the stock of *Wunderhorn* song imagery, by which all the symphonies of this time were fertilized, we also find another very important consolidation of Mahler's creative personality, his 'voice' as a composer. We find it again in the First Symphony, in the use of popular or naive musical materials for a quite particular aesthetic purpose. In the early cantata, the offstage 'festive' band had commented ironically on high tragedy. In the First Symphony, the famous funeral march presented to a surprised and hostile audience at the first performance a parody funeral march based on a grotesque distortion of a familiar and friendly children's round ('Bruder Martin'/'Frère Jacques'); and the irony, with the exception of the middle part of the march based on the last song of the *Gesellen* songs (itself a vocal quasi-funeral march, a peculiarly Mahlerian invention which also crops up among the *Wunderhorn* songs), was sustained to the bitter end. Irony of course was not new to music; what was new about Mahler's use of the ironic mode was the comprehensiveness of it. In this instance, ironic method comprised virtually the total compositional act (not just part of it). It was just this radical comprehensiveness that early audiences found difficult to comprehend, i.e. the funeral march did not develop ironic features, but was ironic without any preliminaries and without any contrasting points or norms of reference. Parody, irony, satire: these were all elements that had their musical foundation in the works from Mahler's *Wunderhorn* years and became embedded permanently as part of his musical style. Moreover, these were components almost always inextricably mixed up with his singular use of popular musical materials, to which the ironic method and interest gave a new twist. A *locus classicus* is the 'vulgar', rowdy brass-band 'Resurrection' march from the Second Symphony, where the dramatic context – a march of the dead towards eternity – yet further charges with almost elemental power the seemingly mundane musical formulae that Mahler so energetically manipulates. He was certainly not above shock tactics, and this celebrated passage is an example of them. Through sheer compositional virtuosity – above all through a highly ingenious use of Lisztian thematic transformation – he almost succeeds in extinguishing the line between the Vulgar and the Sublime (he certainly

Ex. 4(a)  Symphony No. 2, finale

Ex. 4(b)  Symphony No. 2, finale

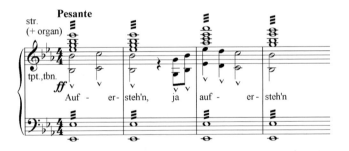

makes it a very thin one) (Ex. 4). But it would be a grave error to
assume that Mahler's ironic mode and his use of popular musical
materials always went hand in hand, though they often did. For
example, in the audacious first movement of the Third Symphony
he used all manner of popular invention – swinging march tunes,
military signals and fanfares, and vigorous march rhythms – to
embody his dramatic concept of summer marching in and sweeping winter away. No irony here; the popular materials are used
'straight', in an almost Ivesian fashion. The shock tactics here are
successfully employed – and again through orchestral mastery and
compositional virtuosity – to make these materials serve a sym-

phonic movement built on the grandest scale. The transforming power of Mahler's imagination was indeed prodigious, let alone his technical accomplishment.

Another important feature of these years was the development of the basis of his orchestration. (His reconstruction and pungent scoring of Weber's opera, *Die drei Pintos*, first performed in 1888, not only gave him further useful experience but also unmistakably reveals his own, rather than Weber's, orchestral personality.) From the very start of his creative life he showed quite unusual gifts in this sphere, but he very swiftly progressed from the lavish deployment of resources in the early cantata to the famous clarity, refinement and soloistic scoring of, say, the Fourth Symphony, a trend which was itself embodied in a decisive move away from strings as the basis of his orchestral sonority, to wind. The development of this highly personal orchestral sound meant a growing emphasis on selectivity, i.e. the use of the precise resources to meet the precise needs of the moment. It is certainly correct to refer to Mahler's orchestral practice as 'economical', and indeed his varying textures, wherever one may sample them, reveal an exact relation between the sought-after sonority and the instrumental constitution of it. On the other hand, so fine was Mahler's ear and so inventive in this area that he needed in the main very large orchestras from which the wealth of constituent ensembles, which is a feature of his orchestration, might be drawn. Paradoxically, then, although the sound grows more transparent, more slender, more 'economical' – the more that Mahler succeeds in achieving the clarity which was his goal – the orchestral forces at the same time increase in number, to allow for the largest number of economical possibilities in changing textures. It was often the case that the *refined* final version of a full score would in fact involve a larger orchestra than that used in a denser, thicker-textured first version. (One also ought to add that there were occasions where economy was not the aesthetic issue or intent, but sheer weight of volume, e.g. the culminating chorales of the Second and Eighth Symphonies, where Mahler did not hesitate to work in terms of an overwhelming mass sonority, using every resource available to him, rather than solo-inflected or highly individualized instrumental groups.)

The characteristic sound of Mahler's orchestra, despite many obvious and important exceptions to any rule one cares to propose – e.g. the languorous, seductive combination of strings and harp in the *Adagietto* of the Fifth Symphony – is its sharpness, its brightness and its pungency, all qualities, one might say, especially associated with the wind. Mahler showed a predilection for the sharp, cutting-edge potentialities of instruments like the E flat clarinet and the piccolo, which he used to articulate the elaborate motivic polyphony of his textures (a mode of composition particularly prominent in the *Wunderhorn* years), or, in his later period, the long stretches of counterpoint composed of extended independent parts, which became an increasingly prominent aspect of his music.

It is, in fact, impossible to divorce a consideration of his orchestration from his actual methods of composing. In few composers has the sound of the music been so intimately involved in the actual essence of the specific invention. For example, take Mahler's 'ironic mode', and the most celebrated early instance of it, the opening of the funeral march in the First Symphony. One cannot make any useful or real distinction between the musical 'idea' and the actual realization of it in terms of sound, in this case, a muted solo double-bass, playing at an unconventional and awkward high pitch, and projected over a drum ostinato. This is not 'idea' plus 'orchestration': how it sounds *is* the idea.

Another example of the hand-in-glove relationship between Mahler's orchestration and his musical thinking is embodied in his motivic polyphony. This has its *fons et origo* in the motivic construction of his melodies, e.g. the principal melody of the first movement of the first symphony, or the principal melody – on the orchestration of which Mahler spent no little labour – of the Fourth. My example shows how the seemingly impeded flow of the melodies is compounded of a chain, a row, of very small motives, the independent nature of which is demonstrated, very strikingly so, in the Fourth Symphony, by what one might describe as Mahler's 'motivic' orchestration, i.e. he analyses the structure of the melody in terms of its motives by distributing the motives in a sequence of changing instrumentation (Ex. 5). This principle applies not only to the horizontal statements of the melodies, but

Ex. 5 Symphony No. 4, first movement

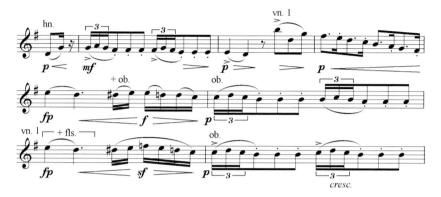

Ex. 6 Symphony No. 4, first movement

also to Mahler's motivic developmental practice, where he gives the constituent motives their independence, and without paying any attention to the chronological order in which the motives were originally unfolded as a melody, allows them life as a complex web of motivic polyphony, in which the motives continually appear in new vertical combinations, with the instrumentation again continuously clarifying and illuminating the motivic counterpoint. (Cf. Ex. 6, with Ex. 5 above.) This mode of minute motivic assembly of melodies (exposition) and their subsequent re-assembly in motivic polyphony (development) was a prominent feature of Mahler's composing in his *Wunderhorn* years, and was in fact to remain throughout his life a basic principle of his compositional method. Our comprehension of this principle also permits us to understand how the songs fertilized the symphonies, i.e. the motivic construction of the songs' melodies allows for just the kind of development that was to become habitual in the symphonies. Indeed, it is the type of development that one finds within the songs themselves (the second song of the *Gesellen* cycle is an obvious example), and one already foreshadowed in *Das klagende Lied*, especially in that work's orchestral interludes.

There is one final point to be made. Mahler often stated certain motives as prime building materials, without in fact formulating them as melodies. The slow introduction to the first movement of the First Symphony (in which work the unadorned motive of a fourth represents one dimension of his long-term integrating efforts), or the voluminous introduction to the finale of the Sixth Symphony, offer ample evidence of motives stated in isolation and not as part of an evolving, expository span of motivically assembled melody.

Not to be overlooked in the works of these years are other significant techniques which became permanent features of Mahler's technical vocabulary. There was, for instance, the exploration of the onstage/offstage acoustic already adumbrated in the closing stages of the cantata, which was then further exploited in later works, e.g. the delicate spatial and dynamic organization of different instrumental groups in the introduction to the First Symphony, or the combination (in different rhythms) of onstage/offstage orchestras in the Second Symphony's finale, and the audacious cadenza (the

'Last Trump' episode) in the same movement. In passages like this, Mahler showed himself to be a pioneer in the exploration of acoustic space and even of directional sound, and made a clear contribution to what has become a preoccupation of composers later in the century.

In his own later works, acoustic space was explored *within* the orchestra rather than through the contrast of physically, spatially separated groups; the Eighth Symphony revived the practice. The composer's extremely subtle dynamic markings and his actual mode of orchestration – moving between differently constituted bodies of sound within the orchestra as a whole (e.g. the chamber orchestra which suddenly emerges in the midst of the Ninth Symphony's first movement, cf. bars 376–91) – were themselves ways of exploring acoustic space, though without leaving the main arena of musical action.

While some aspects of these components may be attributed to the influence of a like-minded acoustic innovator like Berlioz, and also (especially in the Third Symphony) to Mahler's acoustic experience of open-air music as a boy and man (there is a link with Ives here), the principal generator of many of his acoustic experiments, most of which at this stage were of an explicitly dramatic character, was the musical theatre, the opera house, where he had already had years of experience and gained fame as a conductor of quite exceptional gifts. There can be little but speculation about the actual character of Mahler's conducting, though no doubt at all about the impact it made on his contemporaries.

However, of one thing we may be certain: that his performances of other men's music was re-creative rather than interpretative, i.e. he would have approached the works he conducted as if he had composed them himself and laboured to achieve the precision, the clarity and vivid characterization which we know he insisted on in performances of his own music, not from reports by orchestral players, but from the elaborate notation of his scores which attempts to find a sign for even the subtlest of nuances. If we accept this primarily re-creative spirit, much else becomes clear, in particular his activities as editor or arranger. His notorious retouching of Beethoven's orchestration, for example, or, a very different example,

his devising of a lengthy new recitative for Mozart's *Figaro*, should
not be regarded as meddling or evidence of his belief in the progressive march of history or in the technological or artistic superior-
ity of the nineteenth century, but rather as modifications made in
the image of his own compositional practice and convictions, in
which a passion for clarity – whether of sound or operatic plot –
was paramount. One may well think, rightly, that this was the wrong
kind of clarity for Beethoven, while recognizing none the less that
Mahler's 'editorial' motive had its roots deep in his own creativity.

The influence of theatrical music extends even to his 'dramatic'
use of tonality, e.g. progressive key schemes in the symphonies
which clearly have their roots and their logic in their association
with dramatic or narrative ideas. Clear examples of this are the
G→ E of the Fourth Symphony (Earthly Life → Paradise or
Experience→ Innocence, according to taste) or the more orthodox C minor→ E flat of the Second Symphony (Death→
Resurrection). Even in the symphonies which seem superficially to
be concentric in tonality, e.g. the First Symphony 'in D', we find
that the final affirmation of D has to be fought for: this is part of
the narrative of the work (the Hero wins through), while in the
case of the Third, again superficially concentric in tonality, the
ultimate D major represents the evolution of the work to a new
dramatic (and thus new tonal) plane altogether.

Although the first movement of the Third opens with a substantial slow introduction in D minor, the body of the movement
is in F (interestingly enough, Mahler for a long time designated the
work as 'in F'). The D major of the finale represents not only the
final conquering of the D minor or ice-bound winter, the dramatic
topic of the first movement's introduction, but also the decisive
shift from biological evolution (i.e. the animation of inert matter in
the first movement) to a final manifestation of Divine Love (the
adagio). (This is at least one of the many possible interpretations of
the Third's complex scenario.) At a different level of organization
altogether, Mahler's fondness for an abrupt switch of key, i.e. the
juxtaposition of sharply contrasted keys without any attempt to
effect a modulating transition from one to the other, was basically
a theatrical gesture, a technique that was particularly appropriate

Ex. 7   *Das klagende Lied*

Ex. 8   Symphony No. 7, finale

when Mahler was engaged on a dramatic work. There is an early example in *Das klagende Lied* (Ex. 7). In later works, the technique has become an established part of Mahler's style, and he used it freely without the need for the dramatic justification that had validated it in his early period. (This was the customary procedure by which new 'dramatic' techniques were incorporated into the general language of music. There came a stage when the overt dramatic associations could be dispensed with, and the technique, as it were, explains itself, as in the finale of the Seventh Symphony (Ex. 8).)

In this period of his work Mahler was unambiguously a tonal composer, though often using tonality in a very fresh way. There is certainly no feeling of tiredness or exhaustion about his language, in part, no doubt, because he was working in a style that was often unabashedly diatonic, with occasional forays into highly chromaticized harmonic textures. The First Symphony offers an admirable example of his uninhibited use of the available linguistic resources, which, in the 1880s, and after – and this was undoubtedly Mahler's historical good fortune – might still include clear-cut diatonic melody and the richness of chromatic, i.e. Romantic, harmony. As it had been for Wagner, so it was still for Mahler a valid juxtaposition, a possible combination, and it was not until later that his tonality diminished in stability, in definition, and one has to speak of a much more all-pervasive chromaticization of his harmonic style. This trend, though, is already apparent in the Fourth Symphony, which for all the emphatically diatonic character of some of its materials – which is part too of the aesthetic game the work plays – sometimes moves into an elaborately chromatic motivic polyphony where, though tonality may not be abandoned, it certainly becomes exiguous: cf., for example, the sturdy diatonic tune which is the first movement's second subject (Ex. 9), and the contorted chromaticism of a passage like Ex. 10, from the development, where one feels that any very strong sense of tonality has been temporarily suspended.

This free play of the tonal with the less tonal, the diatonic with the chromatic – to which one also ought to add Mahler's habitual blurring of the distinction between major and minor, and his occasional revival of the old modes – was particularly appropriate to his music up to the turn of the century, the diverse, explicitly dramatic build of which demanded just such a versatile, or, if one likes, inconsistent, style. It was part of Mahler's particular genius that he could be as eclectic as he was without putting at risk the independence or integrity of his own voice.

I have suggested that there was a significant friction or tension in these years between the opposed claims of symphonic poem and symphony, a formal dichotomy which certainly had significance for the kind of tonal style or styles that Mahler had available to him and called upon. The wealth of resources of which he made use was a particularly valuable factor, since the forms in which he worked –

Ex. 9    Symphony No. 4, second subject of the first movement

Ex. 10    Symphony No. 4, first movement development

hybrid forms, poised between the symphony and the symphonic poem – demanded an 'open' rather than a closed language. It is interesting that even when he was most self-consciously a symphonist, e.g. in the first movement of the Second Symphony, he none the less did not feel compelled to match up his 'classical' sonata form model with a comparably 'classical' tonal model, i.e. the second subject of the C minor movement moves to the remote key of E major for good 'dramatic' or 'narrative' reasons. To have done the 'correct' tonal thing at this point would have been to falsify the real drama of the movement which required a move not to the relative major but to another tonal 'world' altogether, which would represent an escape from or alleviation of the preoccupation with death. It was these dramatic considerations that shaped Mahler's tonal strategy, even when outwardly he was at his most formal. (On the other hand in this same movement he builds up a massive dominant preparation for the return of the tonic at the reprise which brings gigantic life and dynamic renewal to this traditional formula.)

This freedom of interpretation of a formal model, however traditionally based, Mahler applied in various and sometimes very innovative ways. He saw no obligation, for example, when embarking on an orthodox affirmation of the tonic at the reprise to recapitulate, as one would expect, the first subject – if he felt inclined to do otherwise. In the First Symphony's first movement, for example, D major makes its expected formal reappearance, but the theme which it affirms is not the first subject (which comes later) but an idea from the beginning of the development. The possibility of this divorce of tonal restatement from melodic restatement is an altogether characteristic example of Mahler's re-imagining in fresh ways time-honoured formulae and finding in them new potentialities.

I have mentioned some of the influences in and sources of Mahler's music. There are at least two literary sources which must be spelled out, apart from *Des Knaben Wunderhorn* (the military imagery of which, by the way, must have encouraged what was to be Mahler's life-long predilection for the march, military bands and military signals of every description). These are Nietzsche (for the Third Symphony) and the novelist Jean Paul Richter (1763–1825), whose writings were much admired by Mahler. One can understand why their style, a most curious amalgam of intense identification with Nature, despair, ecstasy, comedy, tragedy and the macabre, into which irony is interpolated from time to time, must have appealed to Mahler, and indeed influenced his aesthetic, as I am convinced they did. There is no need to look for a detailed programmatic relationship between Richter's novel, *Titan* (1800–1803) and Mahler's First Symphony, which came to be known by the same title. The symphony in many interesting ways reflects the novel – that is to say, the aesthetic of the novel – perhaps especially in the impetuous, arbitrary, juxtaposition of wildly contrasted moods and images, which is so fundamental to the novel's construction and manipulation of its language. It is the spirit of Richter that broods over the symphony, not a scenario based on his most famous novel.

Mahler drew musical inspiration and stimulus from a very wide range of other composers' music, from predecessors – Beethoven, Mendelssohn, Schubert, Schumann, Wagner, Weber, and increasingly as he grew older, J. S. Bach; and also from at least one contemporary, Richard Strauss. Given the dual nature of Mahler's creative life – his activities as conductor and composer, though these really have to be seen (despite Mahler's protestation to the contrary) as *one* creative life, not a duality – and the insatiable curiosity and appetite of his ear, it is not surprising that the 'literature' he conducted – or perhaps one should say the repertory, and above all the repertories of the many opera houses in which he conducted from his young manhood onwards – was creatively digested and assimilated; or that, on occasion, the model, whatever the transformation, is transparently obvious. I have pointed out elsewhere (in *Gustav Mahler: The Wunderhorn Years*, pp. 295–6) that we can identify the model for the funeral march in the First Symphony. It is none other than the parody march from Mendelssohn's *A Midsummer Night's Dream* music with which Mahler was familiar as a conductor in 1886. My two examples show the relationship. (Exx. 11 and 12).

But outside the concert-hall/opera-house repertory there is a whole body of music which Mahler knew as a *pianist* – he was an admirable pianist all his life, and in his early youth it was the piano that was his first study and as a prodigy that he commanded attention. There are many works for piano by Chopin, Schubert, Schumann and Liszt, which Mahler clearly knew intimately as a performer, and which left a marked impress on the make-up of his own music. I shall give only one example, the quite remarkable interconnection between Schubert's Piano Sonata in D, D. 850, and the Fourth Symphony, which can be tabulated as shown in Exx. 13 and 14. I think it will be admitted that this single example shows what a rich and rewarding field of investigation the piano-playing repertory of Mahler's offers the enquiring student. It has received very little attention and yet probably forms one of the most formative influences on the development of his art.

In his Fourth Symphony Mahler wrote himself out of his *Wunderhorn* period, although he retained and plundered for the rest of his life the dazzling array of techniques that he had assembled. The next period, from 1901/2 onwards, saw a disciplining of those techniques – it was no accident that the first movement of the Fourth was one of the most tightly organized and highly crafted

Ex. 11    Mendelssohn: *A Midsummer Night's Dream, Marcia funebre*

Ex. 12    Mahler: Symphony No. 1, funeral march

symphonic movements that he ever wrote – and the application of
them to very large-scale instrumental forms, 'dramatic' still in
organization, but in a new way, and without recourse to song or
song-based movements to clarify dramatic meaning, or to programmatic indications. (Although Mahler habitually issued a pro-

Ex. 13(a)    Schubert: Piano Sonata in D (D. 850), *Rondo: Allegro moderato*

Ex. 13(b)    Mahler: Symphony No. 4, last movement

and

Ex. 13(c)    Mahler: Symphony No. 4, last movement

gramme in his *Wunderhorn* years, only to suppress it later, this always meant that sufficient 'clues' had been in circulation for long enough to establish the right programmatic keys to the work in question.) At the same time, it would be a mistake to imagine that the narrative dramatic idea, which was so powerful a constructional principle up

Ex. 14(a)    Schubert: Piano Sonata in D (D. 850), *Rondo: Allegro moderato*

Ex. 14(b)    Mahler: Symphony No. 4, first movement

to the turn of the century, was laid aside. In no way was this the case. The narrative principle was as strong as ever, but now it had become totally 'internalized', self-explanatory in purely musical terms, above all in the meaning to be deduced from the overall musical shapes in which Mahler worked, which had no need for the intervention of the 'Word' to illumine the substance of the dramatic issue. It was as if Mahler had now established and made familiar his dramatic method and could afford to dispense with the song (and choral) elements which had been hitherto his chief aid to comprehensibility. This is not to say that Mahler quitted the sphere of the orchestral song or song-cycle. On the contrary, just as the *Gesellen* cycle and *Wunderhorn* songs had a very direct relationship to the whole creative period that followed, so now the two last *Wunderhorn* settings, the *Kindertotenlieder* and the Rückert songs, bear a very significant relationship to the symphonies that surround them.

At this time, inevitably, there was a decrease in Mahler's dependence on models for his music other than those provided by his own, a natural enough consequence of his evolving maturity and of the building-up throughout his *Wunderhorn* years of a massive stock of resources and experience upon which he might rely. It is of particular interest in this context to consider the significance of, say, the Rückert songs, which not only epitomize a delicate personal lyricism that was undeniably a growing trend in Mahler's art at this time but may also be regarded technically, especially because of their contrapuntal character (with the voice functioning as one 'voice' among its instrumental counterpoints), as preliminary studies for *Das Lied von der Erde*.

One can compare, for instance, Ex. 15 (from 'Um Mitternacht') with Ex. 16 (from *Das Lied*). The relationship is plain. Indeed, whether we look to these songs, or to the *Kindertotenlieder*, which Mahler conceived for an authentic chamber orchestra, no doubt with Berlioz's *Nuits d'été* in mind as a precedent, or to the last two *Wunderhorn* settings ('Revelge' and 'Der Tamboursg'sell'), which are built on a scale that reflects the degree to which 'symphony' had now infiltrated and fertilized 'song', there are everywhere interconnections and interrelationships between the songs and the parallel symphonies, e.g., cf. the second song of the *Kindertotenlieder* with the *Adagietto* of the Fifth Symphony; the final song of the same cycle with the introduction to the finale of the Sixth; 'Ich bin der Welt', a Rückert song, again with the *Adagietto* of the Fifth; the massive march of 'Revelge' with the first movement of the Sixth, and so on. These are all manifestations of the principle that we have earlier observed at work in Mahler's art: the totality of his creativity

Ex. 15    'Um Mitternacht'

Ex. 16    *Das Lied von der Erde*, 'Der Einsame im Herbst'

which in the most unusual way hangs together as a whole over large stretches of time, whatever the independence of the units of the works that make up the total picture. It is arguable in Mahler's case that it is the total life's work that is the *one* work of art that he laboured unremittingly to create, adding cumulatively one unit after another but never – and this would be true even had he finished his Tenth – placing the final unit in position. Only his death, retrospectively, could do that.

After the long *Wunderhorn* period, where Mahler so freely and colourfully, and with a wonderful lack of inhibition, shuffled between the modes of symphonic poem and symphony, he shifted decisively in the direction of symphony, though by no stretch of the imagination could the ensuing trilogy of works, the Fifth, Sixth and Seventh Symphonies, be held to be in the slightest degree orthodox in conception (the only exception, and for very special reasons, is the Sixth). Moreover, as I have suggested, the narrative idea has not disappeared but, as it were, gone underground: it was now inextricably involved with the profoundest levels of Mahler's compositional process. Furthermore, although the Hero in the *Wunderhorn* years had been explicitly *there*, first, in the *Gesellen* cycle, and then in the First and Second Symphonies – to name an obvious narrative sequence across a series of works – he was to be no less there in the ensuing symphonies, though non-explicitly, so far as clarification through the 'Word' was concerned. The fact that the concept of Artist as Hero was no longer projected through programmes, through *Wunderhorn* (or other) texts, meant in any case the development of an even stronger sense of autobiography in the music Mahler wrote after 1901: he became, ever increasingly, the programme of his own symphonies. Hence undoubtedly the development of the intensely personal vein of lyricism, which I have already mentioned, of which the two masterly song-cycles, the *Kindertotenlieder* and *Das Lied*, for all their differences, are particularly rich examples. It will be observed that in both cycles, though they retain a dramatically or poetically unifying idea and in fact progress towards a very carefully planned dramatic resolution, or denouement, explore the artist's experience, speak through his 'voice', rather than 'tell a story' in the narrative, ballad style of the

*Lieder eines fahrenden Gesellen.* (When the *Kindertotenlieder* were written, their topic was not an actual autobiographical experience of Mahler's, which was tragically to come later. But death and innocence – these were old preoccupations of his, hence the attraction for him, no doubt, of Rückert's poems.)

Although I have used the word 'trilogy' in connection with Symphonies Five, Six and Seven, the works are not a trilogy in any sense except that they represent three very different approaches – in the case of two of them, the Fifth and Seventh, one might say experimental approaches – to the idea of the symphony. The Fifth is in three parts and five movements, the whole enclosed within a tonal scheme, C sharp minor → D, which concentratedly (leading note → tonic) symbolizes the built-in dramatic narrative quite as unambiguously as the G → E of the Fourth.

An odd feature of Mahler's putting together of his symphonies, at this stage even, when he was preoccupied with the concept of the integral, large-scale instrumental composition, was the disorder in which the movements were composed. It is understandable that the works from the *Wunderhorn* years evolved in the process of composition rather than fulfilled a predetermined pattern. But the late symphonies too, though certainly not assembled in so ad hoc a manner as certain of their predecessors, were by no means composed in the actual order of the four-, five- or six-movement sequences that were their ultimate shape, although clearly the forms were pre-determined to a far greater degree than had been the case before, i.e. the choice of options was more severely restricted.

As it happens, we know that it was the big central scherzo of the Fifth – in D – that was the first movement to materialize, and we also know that Mahler himself envisaged this movement as depicting his Hero at the height of his powers, rich in energy and enjoyment. This was Mahler's way of indicating in conversation with Natalie Bauer-Lechner the character of the movement.[2] It was not a defined programme. On the other hand, his words clarify the interior drama that is played out across the whole span of the sym-

2    See NB-L *Recollections*, p. 173.

phony, a clear line of narrative unfolded from the opening funeral march and maintained throughout the ensuing agitated allegro to the pivotal scherzo, in which the Hero emerges from Part I, if not precisely unscathed, then at least able in the scherzo (Part II) to show the vitality and confidence that makes the triumphant conclusion of Part III a logical and climactic denouement. Given the fact that the musical weight of this remarkable symphony rests as much in the mid-point of the work as in the finale, the formal dramatic problem that Mahler had to solve was to avoid anti-climax at the finale stage by allowing the scherzo to resolve too many of the drama's conflicts too soon.

This meant that the scherzo had to function as a genuine pivot, a hinge on which the drama could turn from the dark to the light. One may also note that on this occasion Mahler was altogether more prudent in his scaling of the opening funeral march than he had been in earlier days in the case of the Second Symphony. There the sheer weight and mass of the musical invention and the grandeur of the form had made it excessively difficult for him to continue the work until he was rescued by the programmatic idea of Resurrection. The much less complex form of the Fifth's first movement, while not lacking in weight – a march and two trios – makes a suitably dramatic opening for a Part I that is all *Sturm und Drang* but very skilfully, from a formal point of view, leaves open developmental possibilities which are indeed taken up by the immediately following allegro, which in turn leads us on to the scherzo. Mahler had learned a great deal about *dramatic continuity* since burning his fingers with the Second.

The fact that the central scherzo occupies this central position and at the same time in the dramatic scheme is obliged to function also as a pivot, a transition, meant that Mahler had to find the musical ideas which would reflect the complexity of the role the movement was required to play. At one stage in his thinking he had indicated the seminal character of the movement by a title, 'Die Welt ohne Schwere' ('The World without Care') but it was essential that the scherzo should not in fact be too Care-free if the finale were not to be deprived of *its* proper role. With singular brilliance and originality, Mahler maintains the dramatic *tension* that is so conspicuous an aspect of the scherzo by an ingenious mix of two dances, the ländler and the waltz, the 'rustic' ländler bearing the weight of exuberance and optimism, while the 'sophisticated' waltz, though starting out in an innocent enough way, is unexpectedly subjected to the impact of Experience, and more particularly to the disintegrating, distorting impact of Mahler's ironic mode (see figs. 15–17). (It is of no little interest that in Mahler's treatment of – commentary on – the waltz in the scherzo of the Fifth there is already adumbrated the technique that Ravel was to use in *La Valse* of 1920.)

Thus it is that a tension between Innocence and Experience (in Blakean terms) is secured, through the manipulation of contrasting musical ideas, and the exercise of irony. The great scherzo ends positively and conclusively enough, but because of the ambiguities and ironies which the materials unfold we feel that the final affirmation is yet to come. (Perhaps one should add that through the elaborate obbligato part for solo horn in the scherzo Mahler gives us his version of concerto. This is one of his most concerto-like movements, but there are many other examples in the symphonies of similar, concerto-minded textures.)

Although the centrepoint of the symphony has been reached and passed through, there has still been no real slow movement. It is true that the first movement is in a slow tempo, but the *character* of the music, dynamic and dramatic, which is what counts, is far removed from what we normally expect of a slow movement proper.

Mahler fills the gap in a wholly novel way by opening Part III of his symphony with an *Adagietto*, the famous movement for harp and strings (the intense expressivity of which is, one might think, in direct proportion to its comparative brevity), which proves however not to stand as an isolated stretch of slow music but to serve, quite unambiguously, as the slow introduction to the finale (a rondo), into which it leads without a break.

More than that, the materials of the *Adagietto* – the contours of whose melody (see Ex. 17(a)) are wholly representative of Mahler's new lyric vein – are incorporated as episodes into the finale and subjected to all manner of variations and distortion: Mahler was

Ex. 17(a)    Symphony No. 5, *Adagietto*

never slow to take up an ironic or sceptical attitude to his own 'sentiment'. It is indeed the interpolating of the *Adagietto* into the exuberantly contrapuntal finale which provides the inner tension and contrast which are at last resolved, and the triumphant denoue-ment put beyond doubt, by the clinching statement of the chorale (see figs. 32–4), which has made two symbolic and unsuccessful attempts to assert itself as early as the second movement (cf. figs. 18 and 27) of the symphony.

To sum up: the Fifth Symphony presents a remarkably fresh symphonic shape, each main part of which reveals an innovating, experimental approach to form. Part I splits up 'exposition' and 'development' and treats the two areas as two huge independent units; Part II, the scherzo, functions as the large-scale central pivot, on which the inner drama of the work turns; and Part III unexpect-edly and brilliantly revives and renews the classical concept of slow introduction and allegro. The whole tri-partite, five-movement structure is contained within the framing tonal scheme C sharp minor → D, which encapsulates the symphony's dramatic scenario.

I have chosen to dwell on the Fifth at some length because the work cogently illustrates the kind of formal answers Mahler found to the formal problems he undoubtedly faced as a creator when he turned away from the very free exercise of his fantasy which was possible in the *Wunderhorn* symphonies, where the 'Word' could always be conscripted in the interests of clarification, and confront-ed instead the different disciplines and challenges represented by purely instrumental symphony. What is so admirable and so char-acteristic of Mahler's impatience with calcified conventions of any kind, is that he came up with attempted solutions that were gen-uinely fresh in their formal thinking and more often than not, convincing. The Fifth also tells us how important the programmatic idea, and the idea of dramatic continuity, remained for the composer, even though the programme was now implied, not made explicit. With the Fifth, moreover, was initiated a new period in Mahler's orchestration. It was a period of struggle, paradoxically, when, the acknowledged orchestral master laboured unceasingly, and often for years, to achieve precisely the ideal instrumental sound after which his imagination sought.

The major modification of Mahler's orchestral style in the middle-period symphonies was bound up with the establishment of the new lyric vein that I have mentioned above in connection with the melody of the *Adagietto* of the Fifth. This was above all a wholly characteristic music *for strings* (see Ex. 17(a), and cf. also the second song of the *Kindertotenlieder*), and the importation of unmistakably string melody into the middle-period symphonies, and the sustaining and extension of it in the late works, meant that from the Fifth Symphony onwards a vivid string presence was now a more substantial part of Mahler's orchestral sound.

The strings, used on this scale and in this melodic sphere, distinctively colour his music from the Fifth Symphony onwards, and the previous emphasis on wind-based sonority, which had been such a marked feature of the *Wunderhorn* symphonies and had indeed represented a shift away from both the classical string-based orchestra and the preoccupation with string melody of Mahler's Romantic predecessors, was diminished, though certainly not abandoned.

I am far from suggesting that there had not been prominent and characteristic string writing in the earlier works. There clearly had; e.g. the finale of the First (cf. figs 15–21); the andante of the Second; or the slow movements of the Third and Fourth Symphonies, examples that offer ample evidence of authentic string melody. But the balance after the composition of the Fifth was significantly altered, and the strings given a more consistent and integral role than before.

The change of timbre and colour must naturally be seen in direct relation to the forms and types of invention with which Mahler was working, because it was by them that the fresh recourse

Ex. 17(b)    Symphony No. 6, second subject of first movement

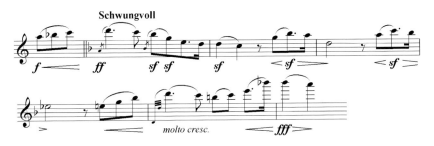

Ex. 17(c)    Symphony No. 7, second subject of first movement

to strings was generated. One cannot hope to cover every aspect of this complex topic in one composite music example, but Exx. 17(b) and (c) indicate the concept of lyrical string melody that emerged as part of Mahler's formal tactics when he was undertaking the big sonata first movements of the Sixth and Seventh Symphonies and when he turned, appropriately, to the strings to articulate an almost idealized type of the contrasting second subject beloved of analysts; and just because of the crucial role in the structure played by these melodies, their specifically string timbre accrues particular significance and weight in the context of each work as a whole. It is not a question of statistics, i.e. of counting the bars in which the strings are engaged, but of observing the crucial formal junctures at which Mahler introduces strings and the categories of theme which have their origin in string timbre.

If Exx. 17(b) and (c) are examples of timbre functioning in relation to form, Exx. 17(d) and (e) are examples of themes that are inseparable from – are shaped by – their instruments. Ex.17(f) is the last of Mahler's great adagio inventions, from the first movement of the Tenth, a theme with precedents behind it like the solidly string-based adagios of the immediately preceding symphony, the Ninth, and the Third, of 1895–96; while Ex. 17(d), from the finale of *Das Lied*, shows how the new asymmetrical development in Mahler's melody of his final phase, of which I write more in connection with *Das Lied* below, is again intimately involved with string techniques and timbre. Diverse though these examples are, they all display Mahler's uncommon instinct for exploring the potentialities of the strings and in so doing, creating that new vein of lyricism that was to become a major feature of his soundscape after the turn of the century.

To perceive afresh the continuing significance of the narrative principle for Mahler, one needs only to consider the immediately ensuing symphonies in the 'trilogy', the Sixth and Seventh. There is something to be said for looking at the Seventh first, where in fact we become aware that the lack of a defined scenario basically accounts for what strikes most students of the work, even the most sympathetic, as a conspicuous defect: it is hard to experience the work as a totality. All the customary ingredients are there, including a progressive tonal scheme that carries the work from the B minor/E minor → major of the first movement to the C major of the finale, but somewhere along the line, the sequence of the movements fails to convince; above all, the finale requires a major effort of faith on the part of the listener – this listener, at any rate – to hear it as the logical denouement of everything that has preceded it.

This is not to say that the Seventh is not full of magnificent things. The great first movement, a huge sonata structure which in many ways is a counterpart to the sonata first movement of the Sixth, though very different in atmosphere, is certainly not wanting in inspiration or originality, exploring as it does a sound-world which is quite its own and which offers a singular combination of Straussian luxuriance (a comparatively rare influence, this: cf. figs. 39–42) and Mahlerian austerity, an emphatically bony texture which methodically exploits chains of fourths, both vertically and horizontally (Ex. 18).

Although Mahler wrote the Seventh in his customary random

Ex. 17(d)    *Das Lied von der Erde*, 'Der Abschied'

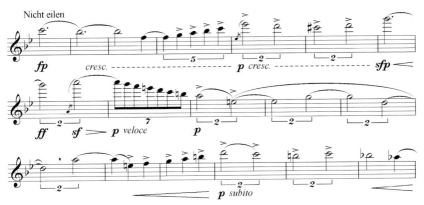

Ex. 17(e)    Symphony No. 9, opening of the adagio

Ex. 17(f)    Symphony No. 10, adagio

Ex. 18    Symphony No. 7, first movement

order, completing the first movement last, we must presume that he
had from the outset the concept of two large-scale outer movements framing a middle part; and for the middle part he devised
what in itself is a plausible triptych of contrasted nocturnes, the two
outer movements, both of them slow and each entitled *Nachtmusik*,
framing a shadowy, spectral scherzo, in which the disintegration of
the image of the waltz is carried to an even more extreme degree
than in the scherzo of the Fifth. (This is one of Mahler's nerviest
scherzos, and also rhythmically, one of his most sparse in texture:
the consequent exposure of the players, as soloists or in sections, is
uncomfortably thorough-going – there is no cover for which to
run if things go wrong in performance.)

   We have no 'dramatic' clues to the Seventh, but it is clear from
the organization (and the subtitles) of the middle part, and the
character of the various musics involved, that Mahler had in mind
a methodical exploration of nocturnal Nature; and indeed if we

read correctly the signs and images unfolded in the slow introduction to the first movement, which clearly harks back to the slow
introduction to the first movement of the Third Symphony (the
earth stirring from its winter sleep, etc.), then a good case can be
made out for the symphony as a whole having been consciously
built round the poetic idea of nocturnal Nature, progressing
through various shades of darkness – the blackest and bleakest pitch
is encountered in precise mid-point, in the scherzo – towards the
'light' of the finale.

In some respects, this kind of programme was typical of earlier
days, for which reason, no doubt, the slow march which is the first
of the two serenades, is 'fantastic' quite in the old *Wunderhorn*
manner, though carried through now with all the orchestral subtlety and sophistication of Mahler's maturity. In fact, what we have
here in the first serenade is a late *Wunderhorn* song, but for *orchestra alone*, a characteristic example of how at this period Mahler
was able to choose models from his own music and regenerate
them in often surprising ways.

However, it was perhaps as a tribute to another composer that
the second *Nachtmusik* may be apprehended. This is surely Mahler's
equivalent of a Schumann 'character' piece, i.e. a kind of extended
*Albumblatt*, not for Schumann's piano, however, but for a large and
idiosyncratic orchestra (mandolin and guitar are prominent).
Mahler marks the movement *Andante amoroso*, which gives us an
interpretative clue. The finale (a rondo), needless to say, is not all
loss. In some respects indeed, and especially in its ceaseless, restless,
rhythmic variation, the movement pursues paths (its stressedly
diatonic character is another singular feature) which are intriguing.
But the fact remains that, whatever its merits, the finale fails to convince us that it belongs irrevocably to the symphony which it
ostensibly completes. The sudden discontinuity – an arbitrarily
slapped-on C major – is disconcerting; and the final display of
cyclic conjuring tricks by the composer (see fig. 281ff.) does nothing to improve the situation.

Whether it be regarded overall as a success or failure, the Seventh
certainly sustains the innovating pattern of the Fifth, above all in
the organization of its middle movements, while at the same time

reflecting, in its first movement, the formal preoccupations of the
Sixth. The Sixth Symphony, indeed, is Mahler's most 'formal' symphony, and this despite the fact that it is at the same time one of his
most personal creations, one of the most highly charged with
intense emotion and one that yet again relies on a clear interior
dramatic organization to underpin its total structure. It is true that
this symphony, in the conventional four movements, conventionally
disposed (but see below), is one of the small number of Mahler's
symphonies that unambiguously assert a concentric tonality.

The work begins and ends in A minor; there is no progressing,
framing tonal scheme. But this concentration on and of A minor
(the scherzo, too, is in A minor) is as emblematic of the work's
drama as any of the progressive tonal schemes elsewhere, i.e. the
very fact that there is no escape (for the implied Hero) from the
fateful A minor that represents destiny and death constitutes the
drama that is played out across the work. Mahler at this time, like
Webster the Jacobean dramatist as described by T. S. Eliot, was a
man 'much possessed by death'[3] (cf. the *Kindertotenlieder*), even
though he himself had no reason yet to show concern about his
own health. It is well known that in the finale, one of the longest
and most massive of all Mahler's symphonic movements, the death
of the Hero is symbolically enacted, with the last of the movement's
famous climaxes finally extinguishing him. There were, originally,
three hammer blows, but at a later stage Mahler indicated that he
wanted a marked diminution in the power of the third climax, on
the grounds presumably that there should be a precise dynamic
relationship between the weakening Hero and the strength of the
blows required to finish him off, a dynamic scheme that had in any
case it seems been his initial intention, but based on three hammer
blows, not two.[4] So the third hammer stroke was deleted (and
omitted from the *Critical Edition* of the symphony). Mahler, however, was chronically uncertain in making just such judgements,
and there can be no certainty, in my view, that he might not have
had a change of mind and restored the third blow. For the same

3   See T. S. Eliot, *Poems 1920*, 'Whispers of Immortality'.
4   See AM *Memories*, p. 100.

reason, one cannot be sure that he would have adhered to his reversion to the original sequence of the inside movements, i.e. scherzo –
andante. He made the change because he feared too great a concentration of A minor after the first movement, but swapping the
middle movements round meant that what was the deliberately
planned relationship between the slow movement and the slow
introduction to the finale (E flat→ C minor) is thrown away.*
Once again, however, one cannot be dogmatic about Mahler's
second thoughts. A third or fourth thought might have followed.

It is a curious fact that Mahler's only 'tragic' symphony – i.e. in
which the Hero is defeated (elsewhere we encounter triumph or
resignation as a denouement, but not defeat) – should also be his
most formal in its outward organization. However, the formal con-
straint implied by the conventional, if hugely expanded, four-
movement shape was probably a reflection of his anxiety to keep
the dynamic energy and violent emotion released in this particular
work under strict formal control.

Many distinguished musicians, e.g., Berg and Webern, have
judged the Sixth to be among the greatest of the composer's works,
possibly just because of the remarkable equilibrium Mahler
achieved between form and drama. Certainly one feels here less
acutely than in some of the other symphonies the tension between
classical and narrative formal concepts, no doubt because the drama
in the Sixth does not so much develop or evolve, despite the fleeting turn to the major (A) at the end of the first movement or the
stretch of repose offered by the slow movement's E flat, as continually fall back to a resumption of the tragic situation and tragic
tonic minor out of which the work is born and which is established
at the outset of the enormous symphonic march which is the
Sixth's first movement. As a result, the emphatic recapitulatory procedures in the symphony – which are part of its 'classicism' – work
hand-in-glove with the leading dramatic idea: the recurring
inescapability of the Hero's tragic destiny. Thus does Mahler brilliantly reconcile classical formal gestures with programmatic
obligations!

---

* See also Appendix I, pp. 633–47.

The momentum of the march, and the associated array of military imagery, spills over and into the finale. The Sixth, indeed, offers the summation of Mahler's preoccupation with the march, serving, as it does here, as the embodiment of the poetic/dramatic idea (the Hero's battle against death) which is the symphony's nub. Once again we find Mahler using precedents from his own music as models, this time bringing to its symphonic apotheosis the military imagery that had been a permanent feature of his compositional landscape since his earliest days. (Ernst Krenek remarks: 'The fundamental feature of Mahler's music is the army march, running the whole gamut from the triumphal cortege to the muffled sounds of the funeral service . . . Mahler as an artist was impersonated energy, conscious of the dynamic character of his musical mission; and he was a fighter. No wonder that his propensity for striking symbols made him choose again and again the martial rhythm of bugle and drum.'[5]) But it is not only the exaltation of the march that is characteristic of all these three middle-period symphonies. There is also the striking development in Mahler's contrapuntal thinking. He had always been markedly polyphonic in his textures; from the very outset, for example in the First Symphony, he had established as a technique peculiarly his own a brilliant kind of motivic counterpoint, especially as a means of development (cf. also Ex. 6 above from the Fourth Symphony).

The motivic work is no less intricate in the post-*Wunderhorn*-period symphonies – the slow introduction to the finale of the Sixth is a perfect example of Mahler unfolding on an imposing scale the array of motives out of which the ensuing movement and its principal themes are to be built – and yet one is aware in these purely instrumental symphonies of the emphasis Mahler now gives in his textures to the elaborate polyphonic combination of extensive, independent melodies rather than the virtuoso juggling about with, or re-shuffling of, independent motives. To be sure, the melodies are still compounded of motives, but now one is more conscious than ever before of the profile, the contour, of each long independent voice as an entity.

5   Bruno Walter, *Gustav Mahler* (US edn), pp. 218–19.

Ex. 19    Symphony No. 6, finale

This new aspect of Mahler's technique emerges with altogether special force in the finale of the Sixth, which unfolds page after page of ecstatically sustained counterpoint, almost Palestrinian in its breadth, and showing that Mahler could bring as much skill to his contrapuntal treatment of the long theme as of the short motive (cf. Ex. 19, from the finale of the Sixth, with Ex. 6 above, from the Fourth Symphony). It was undoubtedly this modification of the character of Mahler's contrapuntal thinking that also contributed to the modification of his orchestration that I have already remarked upon; it is significant indeed that some (not all) of his most elaborate and long-breathed contrapuntal textures are now laid out for strings or are textures in which strings are prominent.

One should not leave the Sixth without remarking on one further unique feature, that it is the one symphony by Mahler in which – just because of the work's 'classical' shape – we encounter a slow movement that is to play its traditional role within a four-movement scheme. It is, in this sense, Mahler's only 'real' slow movement, because almost wherever elsewhere we look, either there is no real slow movement at all, e.g. as in the Seventh

Symphony, or the slow movement is obliged to function in some
other role as well: as a finale (the Third and Ninth); as the introduction to a finale (the Fifth); as a first movement (the Tenth); as a vocal
movement ('Urlicht', in the Second); or as a parody (the First). A
possible further candidate is the slow movement of the Fourth, but
even here one is properly kept aware of the explicitly dramatic role
the movement plays in relation to the *Wunderhorn* song-finale, e.g.,
the great dramatic outburst of E major which is the movement's
climax and which makes full sense only in the light of the finale's
switch to the 'heavenly' key. As for the *Poco adagio* of the Eighth, it
is undeniably the only stretch in the symphony to which the term
'slow movement' might appropriately be applied; and as such it has
been assumed to be by many, and without doubt was designed by
Mahler partly to be heard as such. But for all that, this adagio does
not – indeed, cannot, in view of its particular structural function –
achieve that degree of independence that a slow movement proper
normally displays. On the one (general) hand, the adagio in the
Eighth is too overtly part of the continuous form of the work as a
whole – an integral episode, but scarcely a self-sufficient movement –
and on the (specific) other, the unambiguously *introductory* role it
plays in relation to what follows in Part II, again, and necessarily,
diminishes the possibility of independent status. Even this brief
survey of the field shows that the anatomy of Mahler's slow movements is a subject in itself.

    After completing his remarkable and varied experiments in
purely instrumental symphony, Mahler wrote two works, the
Eighth and *Das Lied von der Erde*, both of which, in very different
ways, may be regarded as synoptic in character, i.e. each comprehensively sums up, and also develops on a very large scale, with very
large resources, musical ideas, forms, and media which had been
long-standing preoccupations of the composer. We cannot assume
that this was a conscious act on Mahler's part, an act of creative
retrospection which brought together in two major works a whole
range of 'themes' – I use the word in the broadest sense – which
had been thus far central to his life's work. But it cannot wholly be
chance that it was after the three imposing efforts – each one of
which attempted a different solution – to create a convincing sym-

phony, without recourse to the 'Word', that he returned again to vocal resources, and, in part, to vocal forms.

The often massively textured Eighth Symphony and the as often sparsely textured *Lied von der Erde* share a common influence, for all the contrasts of methods and media, an influence of the first importance for Mahler's later art, which had already been partly responsible for the increasing emphasis given to contrapuntal textures in his music from the turn of the century onwards: J. S. Bach.

Mahler's familiarity with and admiration of Bach were profoundly stimulated by his possession of the Bach Gesellschaft Edition; and it is not too much to claim that Bach became for him during his last years an exemplar. Hence, also, in 1909, the assembly of a suite of movements which Mahler selected from Bach's orchestral suites and edited, and for which he wrote a continuo part; he played this himself at a Steinway, the action of which had been modified by the manufacturers to make the instrument sound like a harpsichord. None the less, the Bach Suite is an important document, evidence not only of Mahler's personal enthusiasm for Bach but also, interestingly, of his feeling, faint perhaps, but still real, that 'authenticity' was something that could no longer altogether be ignored. Mahler in fact began to show signs of that historical conscience, which was to become a major preoccupation later in the century.

It is by holding Bach in view as a potent, active influence on the final years of Mahler's composing that much becomes clear. For example, the real key to understanding the first movement of the Eighth Symphony is not, I suggest, by references to 'choral symphony', whether it is precedents in Beethoven, Liszt or Mahler (the Second Symphony) that we have in mind, but by 'reading' the movement as Mahler's version of, or tribute to, one of Bach's great motets – probably 'Singet dem Herrn' – by the vocal polyphony of which Mahler confessed himself to be overwhelmed and which he surely attempted to emulate in his symphony.

As a gigantic motet for solo voices, chorus and orchestra – Bach, as it were, seen through the lenses of Mahler's creative spectacles (and one readily admits the element of distortion that accompanied the passionate admiration) – it is thus that an approach to 'Veni, creator spiritus' can be made that actually makes sense. For what we encounter, most unexpectedly, in the Eighth's first movement is an immensely vigorous celebration of the baroque as Mahler reimagined it – in 1906, a fascinating and historic musical event, the sheer mass and ambition of which may be interpreted as a typically late nineteenth-century conception but the actual execution of which, in terms of brilliantly articulated vocal and orchestral sound, was wholly characteristic of Mahler's late choral and orchestral manner.

There is of course something paradoxical, something of a duality, about Mahler's 'extravagant' version of baroque (not only double chorus, and a vast orchestra, etc., but also a complement of extra brass). On the one hand, it is based on what we in the later twentieth century feel to be a discredited conception; on the other, the very fact that the baroque provided Mahler with a model is irrevocably and significantly part of our century's rediscovery of the baroque. Mahler's commitment to his model, moreover, was a strikingly dynamic one, which resulted in music very different, for example, from the dreadful pallor of Mendelssohn's exercises in baroque revival, by which fortunately he seemed very little influenced, i.e. Mahler discovered Bach for himself, at least so far as his composing was concerned.

If Part I of the Eighth Symphony had its roots in Mahler's vivid experience of Bach, Part II was a vast synthesis of many of the forms and media that he had pursued since he first found his voice as a composer. Thus, the setting of Goethe's *Faust* represents an amalgam of dramatic cantata, sacred oratorio, song-cycle, choral symphony *à la* Liszt and instrumental symphony, the whole culminating in a final chorale (the famous 'Chorus Mysticus') which undoubtedly was modelled on the concluding chorale of the Second Symphony, though outshining its precedent in sheer volume and aspiration. Altogether, indeed, the Eighth is a consciously aspiring work of art, perhaps the most ambitious in this respect of Mahler's symphonies. Luckily, the aspiration and inspiration mostly coincide.

Although the Eighth occasionally unleashes monumental torrents of sound – which was undoubtedly part of the composer's aesthetic intent, i.e. to embody his great hymn to the redemptive power of Love in sonorities of appropriate dimensions – the vast resources are more often deployed, as was habitual with Mahler, to secure the most delicate of instrumental effects and subtlest of nuances. To name only two passages that illustrate the refinement that in fact is as characteristic of the sound of the Eighth as mass or volume: the *Poco adagio* for orchestra that opens Part II; and the quite extraordinary transition for a highly idiosyncratic chamber constellation of instruments (piccolo, flute, harmonium, celesta, piano and harps and isolated harmonics from a solo string quartet constitute the essence of the sound we hear at the juncture) which leads into the 'Chorus Mysticus', ***ppp***. An unexpected texture to find, delivered on the lowest dynamic level, in the midst of what has come to be misleadingly known as the 'Symphony of a Thousand'. (It would be helpful now if we could un-know what was no more than an advertising stunt that accompanied the premiere in 1910.)

If one accepts Part II of the Eighth as a collation, principally, of the vocal and choral forms that had long obsessed Mahler, and Part I as an attempted apotheosis of the baroque motet rather than a sonata movement (though the sonata model also lends another dimension to the movement); and if, furthermore, one recalls the flexibility with which he interpreted the concept of symphony during his *Wunderhorn* years, then one stands a reasonable chance of making a correct assessment of the position the Eighth Symphony occupies in his total output, i.e. not so much a new departure (though certainly tapping fresh sources of inspiration, Bach in particular) as a gathering together of a certain category of past formal pursuits and innovations, and as such, I think it may be fairly claimed that the Eighth genuinely and synoptically represents a crowning achievement.

The same may be claimed for the ensuing song-cycle, *Das Lied von der Erde*, and probably claimed without that element of controversy that is still aroused by the Eighth Symphony. Mahler described the new work – and from this point onwards, none of the works discussed was ever heard by the composer – as a 'symphony', but in this case we do not need to keep in mind the ambiguities and uncertainties that in earlier days surrounded his employment of this title in connection with hybrids like the First or Third Symphonies.

*Das Lied* brilliantly fulfils all the symphonic potentialities that he had always seen in the song and the song-cycle and consistently explored throughout the preceding years. (Some of the parallel techniques in Mahler's song-cycle and symphonies I have discussed in detail in *Gustav Mahler: The Wunderhorn Years*, pp. 27–44.) Thus, while some of the songs in *Das Lied* clearly dilate the developmental principles already adumbrated in the *Gesellen* songs and *Kindertotenlieder*, while at the same time using as models the contrapuntal textures that are the special feature of the independent Rückert songs, others – and 'Der Abschied' above all – demonstrate through a remarkable process of integration and juxtaposition the kind of fruitful symbiosis that Mahler achieved in this final stage of his creative life.

The central development section, for example, of 'Der Abschied' (cf. figs. 36–48) is not only a big 'song' for orchestra alone, from one point of view; from another, it is an example of a rigorous development of some of the principal motives out of which this great closing song is built: we shall find nothing more symphonic than this in Mahler's instrumental symphonies. (It is the motives that, in the customary Mahlerian manner, form themselves into the expanded melody that the orchestra, coming into its own as a soloist, sings.)

In the case of *Das Lied*, too, then, we are confronted by a work that seemingly makes an overt summation of the techniques associated with a medium – the orchestral song-cycle – that Mahler had made peculiarly his own and concerned himself with over a period of some twenty-five years, for half of his all too short lifetime.

If in this summing-up, synoptic respect *Das Lied* shares some common ground with the Eighth Symphony, in many others, the song-cycle is the symphony's direct opposite. Mass and volume of sound give way to a preoccupation with the most refined, the sparest, of orchestral textures, perhaps the most delicate instrumentation that we find anywhere in Mahler. It was a natural enough change in emphasis, because the relationship of solo voice to orchestra, the province of *Das Lied*, was quite other than the relationship of massive choral forces to orchestra in the Eighth; and while it might be fairly stated that the preceding symphony is the most public of Mahler's works – that it addresses itself to a hypothetically vast audience is surely a conditioning part of its aesthetic intent? – *Das Lied* is one of his most personal, literally so.

He had often, as I have already suggested, projected himself as the Hero of his own creations; but up to this critical stage in his life I do not think it would be at all correct to assume that Mahler expected his music to be understood as an attempt at total musical autobiography. In his middle-period symphonies, for example, he had been able to project himself into a given drama or narrative, and experience it *as if* it were indeed his own experience (the Sixth Symphony is a *locus classicus* of his method). But the '*as if*' is aesthetically crucial. It is guarantee of that degree of distance which distinguishes experience lived through the imagination from the direct, unimpeded transmission of the experience itself, albeit in whatever medium the artist happens to be working.

From the Eighth Symphony onwards I think it is undoubtedly the case that 'autobiography' took over from the narrative principle that, as we have seen, had been so important an organizing principle for Mahler, even in his middle-period symphonic projections of the Artist as Hero. The metamorphosis that had begun effectively with the composition of the Fifth Symphony (1901–2) was to be completed in the series of final works initiated by the Eighth in 1906.

Here, he attempted something he had not attempted before, a bold effort to unify a work through the committed expression of a highly personal philosophical idea, i.e. to relate the idea of human love – Eros and its redemptive power, which is the topic of Part II of the symphony, to both the creative spirit (which fires the artist) and the Creator – God – who endows the artist with creativity: this is the philosophical substance of Part I.

Mahler remains true to himself even in this changed context by availing himself, especially in Part I of as many 'dramatic' techniques as can be appropriately pressed to the service of a philosophical enterprise. Hence the preponderance of quasi-theatrical musical forms (cantata, oratorio, etc., not to speak of the occasional operatic gesture) in which he presents his philosophical ideas. In short, he

does his best to dramatize to the maximum the philosophic context of the work. (Nor was it accidental that he chose the last
scene of *Faust* for Part II of his symphony, a text that may not be
dramatic in the conventional sense of the word but none the less
uses some of the conventions of drama to get its ideas across, a
point that Mahler seized on and turned to musical account.) However, though we may concede that some aspects of the Eighth show
that the notion of continuing drama was still very much part of
Mahler's way of structural working, we also have to recognize that
we are far removed from the dynamically evolving dramatic structure that is manifest in, say, the Fifth Symphony.

This departure from the narrative principle is also apparent in the
concentric tonal scheme of the Eighth, which asserts an unshake-
able and enclosing E flat, with, of course, none of the traumatic
implications of the Sixth's all-embracing A minor, from which
there was a constant effort, dramatically and musically speaking, to
escape – to break out of the claustrophobic tonal cage.

From the Eighth onwards, Mahler's overall tonal schemes have to
be differently interpreted. We are confronted by late works each of
which, as John Bayley has said of three great European poems (by
Eliot, Akhmatova and Pushkin), seems 'to arrive out of the air, without their author's conscious volition, and which are seen to have
the quality of classic summation, the apprehension of a time and
place focused in the experience of the individual'.[6] It is significant
that in Mahler's final phase concentric or non-dramatic overall key
schemes prevail, i.e. the Tenth Symphony, focused on F sharp
major; *Das Lied*, whose A minor→ C frame is free of the evolutionary drama implied by the identical relationship which encloses
the Second Symphony (C minor→ E flat); and the Ninth, which
progresses (or does it regress?) from a D unstable in mode to the D flat
of the finale. The old *dynamic* concept of a co-ordinated, developing tonal scheme tied in with a clear narrative line has altogether
gone, and the new emphasis is on the primacy of personal experience. It is unfiltered personal experience that is now the 'topic' of
the work, that shapes its form and is guarantor of its integrity.

6   John Bayley, *The Times Literary Supplement*, 30 January 1976, p. 99.

Although it may be that it is the expression of personal experience, albeit in very various manifestations, that is the unifying feature of this last period, there are, over and above the sharp differences between individual works, common techniques; and once again, the influence of Mahler's study of Bach is often prominent.

He was not to repeat the busy, abundant polyphony of the Eighth's first movement, written for voices and genuinely vocal in character, but in both *Das Lied* and the Ninth Symphony, Bach's influence re-emerged in textures and forms that even someone equipped with gifts of prophecy could hardly have foreseen. Strange enough that the motet should act as springboard for the first movement of the Eighth. Stranger still that the statuesque recitatives of 'Der Abschied' in *Das Lied*, with their extraordinary woodwind obbligati, should have behind them Mahler's profound response to the recitatives of Bach's church cantatas and passions rather than his daily familiarity with recitative in the opera house.

In the Ninth Symphony, too, there are passages like the famously austere contrapuntal pages in the adagio finale (bars 88–107), many times remarked upon, which embody his new contrapuntal preoccupations; not to speak of an entire movement, the *Rondo-Burleske*, in which he consummated that brilliant motivic counterpoint that had long been a feature of his compositional method, a feat, at least part of the conspicuous virtuosity of which – a motivic polyphony comprising virtually the total activity of the movement – is attributable to his immersion in Bach. (I have suggested elsewhere that there are identifiable parallels between the *Rondo-Burleske* and the Fourth of the Brandenburg Concertos.[7]) But while this late manifestation of Bach as an influence is perhaps singular because of its intensity, and in any event of significance as an historical fact – Mahler's debt to Bach was a good deal deeper and far-reaching than that of most of the composers involved a little later in the 'back to Bach' movement – it is also prudent to recollect that as early as the scherzo of the Second Symphony (cf. fig. 38ff.), there were indications, above all in the concertante style of Mahler's orchestration, with its pronounced solo instrumental writing, of his

7   DMWY, pp. 360–61; and see pp. 345–62 for a wider discussion of Mahler's absorption of Bach.

attention to Bach, which was certainly already lively around the 1890s, if not as committed as it became after the turn of the century. Indeed it may not be an exaggeration to claim that Bach had a hand in shaping certain aspects of Mahler's orchestral techniques long before he became the formative musical influence of Mahler's last period.

*Das Lied von der Erde*, while undoubtedly standing as a culminating work in the line of the orchestral song-cycles, and at the same time executing that summation in terms of the techniques that were topical for Mahler at the time of its composition, also introduced some innovations which were to remain peculiar to the song-cycle, though one of them, the work's pentatonicism, was clearly bound up with the use of texts from the Chinese (in German adaptations); and the use of these particular texts was in turn intimately bound up with his life history, his failing health, above all.

One might think that this manifestation of exoticism – a breath of air from another continent – was characteristic of the culture of which Mahler was part. He was certainly not alone among European artists in seeking to refresh the language of his art from exotic sources. One thinks of many painters – of Van Gogh, of Monet – and in music, of Debussy, who was Mahler's exact contemporary, and whose music – even his very late music, e.g. the *Images* for orchestra, Mahler conducted (in New York, in 1910/11), though too late in his life for the music to influence him as a composer.

Indeed, it is of some historical interest that there are very few passages in Mahler to which one might meaningfully apply the term 'Impressionism'. Just occasionally, the creation or the building-up of an immobile, lingered-on harmonic texture, e.g. the final bars of the first movement of the Tenth Symphony, or the 'dissolve' – the unresolved dominant, left hanging in the air – which ends (or rather, does not end) the *Wunderhorn* song, 'Der Schildwache Nachtlied' – makes one think briefly of Mahler as Impressionist; but on the whole he was untouched I think by the Impressionist aesthetic, and where he does contrive a temporarily static harmonic texture in order to dwell on it, it is projected so powerfully that, like the notorious dissonant chord in the Tenth

Symphony (first movement and finale, see Ex. 20), there is more
sense in cataloguing the gesture as Expressionist rather than
Impressionist; and it is surely to some aspects of the Expressionist
aesthetic, and Expressionist techniques, that Mahler can be intelli-
gibly related. (So can Berlioz.)

It is probable, as I have already suggested, that Mahler arrived at
his pentatonicism in *Das Lied* through his texts, and that the choice
of these was at least partly conditioned by his personal need to
resign, or at least to reconcile himself, to his fate, which was to die
too young.

But the composer who for much of his life had made a compositional point of blurring the distinction between major and minor

Ex. 20    Symphony No. 10, first movement and finale

modes must in any case have been fascinated by the characteristic ambiguity of the pentatonic scale, even if its use in the first
place had been otherwise, i.e. poetically, motivated.

This blurring of the distinction between the modes is accompanied in *Das Lied* by an unmeasured, asymmetrical 'prose' style,
which may be most evident in the recitatives of 'Der Abschied' but
also significantly affects the shapes – often very free – of much of
the melody in this work; and, in turn, the abandonment of regular
phrase length and metric period is matched by a no less significant
modification of rhythmic organization. Once again it is 'Der
Abschied' (cf. Ex. 17(d) above) that can most profitably be consulted. We find there, substituted for Mahler's customary strong,
dynamic and regular pulse, an asymmetrical distribution of accents,
the location of which is determined by the points of climax within,
and the rise and fall of, the free arches of melody which are the
main substance of the finale's closing pages.

This accented and yet not *regularly* accented music undoubtedly contributes to the ecstasy of dissolution which is the poetic/dramatic idea on which the finale is based: at the same time, it is these specific techniques which themselves 'dissolve' the conventional symmetries with which Mahler's hypothetical audience would have been presumed to be familiar – a clear instance of the indivisibility in Mahler of the poetic/dramatic idea and its technical embodiment.

While not all the technical innovations of *Das Lied* were followed up in the ensuing symphonies – these might have been developed had Mahler lived beyond his Tenth, especially if he had returned again to song-cycle or orchestral song – the final works, the completed Ninth and the almost fully sketched but incomplete Tenth, show a clear resumption of his untiring efforts to create a convincing shape for the instrumental symphony, the individual form of which, in this last phase, was tailored to the personal narrative that (in my view) his art had become.

It is no distortion of perspective, then, to interpret the Ninth and Tenth Symphonies as a conscious return to the old formal concerns that had preoccupied him in the middle 'trilogy' of symphonies (Five to Seven), but with a fresh mobilization of all his imaginative and intellectual powers. There is no repetition of former patterns of overall organizations. The Ninth was the fourth of Mahler's experiments in four-movement shapes, but has virtually nothing in common in overall formal tactics with its predecessors (i.e. the First (in its final version), the Fourth and Sixth Symphonies). If it owes a formal debt at all, then it must be to *Das Lied* and to 'Der Abschied'; it was surely the case that the adagio of the Ninth was born out of the same mood of 'resignation' as the finale of the song-cycle, was an attempt indeed to realize a similar poetic/dramatic idea in terms of instrumental symphony.

But while from this one point of view the Ninth might be thought to continue the exploration of personal experience which *Das Lied* exemplifies, and thus to pursue some of its larger formal imagery – e.g. a slow last movement of departure – from almost every other point of view, and especially in the first movement (of which more below), the Ninth breaks new ground, maps out new formal excursions. In short, the composer was as vigorous as ever in restating the old problems and as fertile as ever in proposing new solutions. The Ninth even comes up with some fresh approaches to filling out the frame provided by the first movement and finale. The scherzo and *Rondo-Burleske*, considered from one angle, are genuine extensions of those 'character' movements that are an almost permanent feature of Mahler's symphonic landscapes, but to each example in the Ninth he brought fresh and formidable thinking.

The scherzo is the most emphatically ironized of all his ländler-based movements, i.e. the ländler is not used as an instrument *of* irony but as a subject *for* irony (and is indeed, finally, ironically dispatched (see fig. 27ff.); while the *Rondo-Burleske* introduces a new type of 'character' movement altogether, a big stretch of fiercely elaborate counterpoint, elaborately instrumented, which is as sophisticated and complex as the preceding scherzo is at times unequivocally primitive.

What unites these two movements in an otherwise seemingly arbitrary juxtaposition, is the satirical intention which is common to both. For the rondo is as satirical in and of its sophistication, as the scherzo is in and of its simplicities, and what these central movements present, in fact, are two faces, two possible physiognomies, of satire, delineated in materials and manipulated in techniques which have very little in common. Never was there a clearer instance of Mahler trying to extrapolate unity out of paradox.

The overall pattern of the Tenth shows Mahler launching out on yet another great symphonic enterprise, again a five-movement shape (cf. the Seventh Symphony, and also the Fifth), but organized this time as follows: (*Andante*) *Adagio*; Scherzo I (*Allegro*); 'Purgatorio' (*Allegretto moderato*); Scherzo II (*Allegro*); (slow Introduction) Finale (*Allegro moderato*). It is Deryck Cooke's brilliant and convincing reconstruction of a performing edition from Mahler's composition sketch that not only allows us to experience major examples of the composer's last inspirations in the context of his last work as a whole (even though we recognize, as does Cooke, that Mahler's final version of the symphony would inevitably have been very different, if more so in some movements than in others, from the performing edition) but also clearly indicates, as Cooke himself suggests, that Mahler had moved on, spiritually, from the resignation of *Das Lied* and the Ninth Symphony to the reconciliation which the Tenth, through a conscious choice on Mahler's part, makes perfectly explicit: he had at one stage considered bringing the work to a close in B flat but finally settled for a coda to the last movement that unequivocally affirms the tonic, F sharp, in the major mode.

But while acknowledging the significance of this assertion of concentric tonal organization in the Tenth, it is important also to remember that Mahler's dramatic key schemes were not confined to the overall organization of a work but were also a prominent aspect of the tonal organization within movements. The outwardly concentric Tenth itself reveals interesting instances of this inner dramatic organization, e.g., the fourth movement's progress from E minor to D minor and the fifth's from D minor to F sharp.

One might argue indeed that Mahler's final choice for the tonic to round off his finale was at least partly conditioned by the intense degree of tonal drama enacted within and across the movements and which required, if the sought-after reconciliation were to be made manifest, a concentric frame to contain and finally, to pacify it. While the Tenth offers an elaborate example of these internal dramatic key-schemes in action, the principle was by no means new to Mahler's art. It had already been adumbrated in the dramatically conceived key scheme, F minor → D major, of the finale of the First Symphony.

One should be suspicious of shorthand terms like 'resignation', which imply a crude identity of compositional method with mood. Mahler, in fact, in rather the same way that he juxtaposes two 'faces' of satire in the symphony, juxtaposes in *Das Lied* and the Ninth two contrasted conceptions of 'resignation', and finds for each the appropriate, but very different technical formulation. Compare, for example, the close of both works, the ecstatic dissolve into a void (oblivion?) of 'Der Abschied' and the exhausted sighs and whispers of the Ninth's adagio, in D flat, an ultimate decline in pitch (from the first movement's D major/minor) which powerfully reinforces the substitution in the symphony of an acquiescence in disintegration for the ecstatic plunge into dissolution of the song-cycle.

The overall tonal scheme of the Ninth, D major/D minor→ D flat, and the key sequence of the four movements, D major/ D minor→ C→ A minor→ D flat, reminds us of Mahler's avoidance of the conventional hierarchy of tonal relationships and his preference – in both the outward disposition and inner organization of his tonality – for third-related keys and stepwise or semitonal progressions, an organizing principle that emerged as early as the *Gesellen* cycle (cf. the diagram on p. 68 and especially the outlines of the last two songs).

Although all the works from Mahler's final phase, as I argue above, show an unmistakable inflection towards the autobiographical, it is still tried principles from the past, though newly formulated, that continue to form the basis of his methods of organization. But it is the fresh inflection that counts. The Tenth may share its concentric conception of tonality with the Sixth (or the Eighth), but now, one feels the achievement of a serene F sharp major is evidence of the triumph of an individual spirit, not the outcome of an externalized, objectified drama (which might be heard in terms of you or me or the 'hypothetical other' (to adopt Stravinsky's useful phrase[8]).

Again, the progressive key scheme, D major/minor→ D flat, of the Ninth Symphony may seem to be just another example of Mahler's habitual tonal symbolism, and so, from one point of view it is. But here the falling back by a semitone was not, one is convinced, conditioned by the pre-existence of a narrative scaffold – think of the Fifth, for example, which also happens precisely to present the reverse (i. e. C sharp minor→ D) of the Ninth's overall tonal scheme – but by Mahler's response to his own personal predicament.

To that same predicament he had already responded in *Das Lied*, once again a work conceived in terms of spiritual autobiography; and once again he made use of an overall tonal scheme that had its roots in past practice, i.e. a 'dramatic' shift (cf. the Second Symphony) from tonic minor to relative major, in *Das Lied*, A minor→ C. But now the drama, such as it is, is totally internalized,

8  When asked for whom he composed, Stravinsky is reported to have replied, 'The hypothetical other.'

and the key scheme not so much a dramatic emblem as a key to Mahler's spiritual life. One may also care to ponder on a superb Mahlerian paradox, that what had served in 1894 as a symbol of progress towards Resurrection emerged in 1908 as symbolic of an acceptance of oblivion.

'Autobiography' is a factor – or characteristic – hard to quantify, though none the less real for that; and if there are those who have doubts about the decisive shift to autobiography from the Eighth Symphony onwards, it is the Tenth that seems to me to provide at least one example of clinching significance, the catastrophic bass-drum strokes in the finale, a dramatic musical idea – unequivocal symbol of death – which has a crucial formal role to play and which we know to be based very precisely on an acoustic experience in Mahler's life.

It was from a New York hotel window, on Sunday afternoon, 16 February 1908, that he witnessed the funeral of a fireman.[9] The muffled drum of that funeral cortege, which so impressed him at the time, massively transformed, re-emerges as a unique feature of what was to be his last symphony, an unprecedented example of the close-knit texture of life and art in his final phase. One must concede that this is a particular instance, when the fact that we are able to locate the exact incident 'behind' the creation of a particular sonority brings us illuminating knowledge about Mahler's creative processes.

I am far from suggesting, however, that we have to identify the spiritual experience in order wholly to respond to its musical transformation. We should draw an almost total blank if we were foolish enough to approach Mahler's late works with such a crude principle of equation in mind. All that we can hope to know properly of his spiritual experience resides in his music and can only be known as music. The significance of the drum-stroke incident from 1908 lies in the exceptional indication it gives us of the autobiographical character of the experiences translated into music during these final years.

Even though it was only a partially completed stage to which the Tenth was brought, and which has been made accessible to us only through the skill of Deryck Cooke, it is possible to discern

9  AM *Memories*, p. 135.

many new stylistic and formal features which show Mahler as untiring as ever as a composer (though a sick man), proliferating fresh ideas about the creative matter in hand, i.e., the development of his concepts of 'symphony'.

There was certainly no slackening in intensity; and indeed this – yet another unquantifiable factor – might be thought to have led to some of the characteristics which lend the Tenth its singularity. It was, one suspects, the unleashed force of the expressive intent that in fact forces the great melodic shapes of the opening adagio to take the huge leaps and skips that exemplify the extremities of Mahler's expressiveness and are at the same time the means through which he achieves it.

But despite the intensity of feeling – and I have already pointed out above (see Ex. 20) that this same intensity, vertically formulat-ed, moves over the borderline that divides Expression from Expressionism – Mahler's constructive powers are no less evident. It is interesting, indeed, how rationally (from a technical point of view), he treats such highly emotive material as the great adagio theme itself, e.g. the inversion of the theme at bar 69 (see Ex. 21), a practice that makes one think of at least one aspect of the classi-cal manipulation of a note row; and given the intensely chromatic disposition of the theme, it is not surprising that Mahler should adopt this particular technique as a means of variation and devel-opment which at the same time preserves the 'order' represented by the basic melody. (It was no accident that inversion was to become such a pronounced feature of Schoenberg's attempt to re-introduce order into total chromaticism, and it is the adumbration of that

Ex. 21    Symphony No. 10, adagio

principle that we encounter in the first movement of Mahler's Tenth. I am not suggesting that inversion as such was an innovatory way of treating a melody, for which there is an immense volume of historical precedent. One naturally has to hear Mahler's use of the technique in its particular context.) The clearest evidence, however, of his undiminished creativity in his last symphonies lies in his continued exploration of large forms; and once again it is to his first movements and finales that he brings all his powers of renewal and innovation.

In so far as we can be confident in assessing the last movement of the tenth, it seems clear that it will have to be counted among the most remarkable of Mahler's finales. To the degree that it is cyclic, the movement is typical: there is only one exception – in the Ninth – to the rule that all Mahler's symphonic finales make use of cyclic procedures. (*Das Lied* provides one further exception.)

But it is just the degree of the recapitulatory procedures in the finale of the Tenth that makes the movement so atypical. Of all the finales it is the most extensive, the most comprehensive, in recapitulatory gestures, which, moreover, are not so much restatement or clinching, cyclical 'quotation', as development and the discovery of fresh potentialities in material from all the preceding movements. This new conception of the cyclic finale singles out the last movement of the tenth as a quite special achievement.

The first movement too shows Mahler breaking new ground, or rather consolidating the new formal ground that he had already opened up in the first movement of the Ninth Symphony, a movement that was justifiably hailed by Mahler's immediate successors in Vienna – Schoenberg, Berg, Webern – as one of the principal documents in the history of twentieth-century music; and more important, as one of the outstanding achievements in the first decades of the century. It was Berg who referred to the first movement of the Ninth 'as the most glorious [Mahler] ever wrote' and who, in the same letter, undated, but probably from the autumn of 1912, spontaneously and without calculation offered a clue to the correct analysis of this elaborate *Andante comodo*.[10]

10  Alban Berg, *Letters to his Wife*, p. 147.

Berg did not touch on such matters, significant though they are, and central though they are to the conception of the movement; likewise the juxtaposition of (D) major and minor, or the alternation of contrasted tempi, e.g. the andante of the first (major) section always quickening into the quasi-allegro of the (minor) second section. (The idea of a movement built round two tempi Mahler was to carry over into the first movement of the Tenth.)

Nor did Berg comment on the very interesting fact that in his Ninth and Tenth Symphonies, Mahler developed a new type of *slow first movement* that was something quite distinct from a slow movement placed as first movement, i.e., the andante of the Ninth, for all its basically slow pulse, develops the pace, the dramatic quality and complexity of organization that we have come to associate with – to expect from – a fully fledged symphonic first movement.

But Mahler achieves none of this through orthodox formal gestures, and although thousands of analytic words have been expended in the effort to relate the first movement of the Ninth to the traditional concepts of sonata or sonata-rondo, it was Berg in 1912 who stumbled on the key to the real form of the movement when he wrote: 'The whole movement is based on a premonition of death, which is constantly recurring . . . that is why the tenderest passages are followed by tremendous climaxes like new eruptions of a volcano.'[11]

It is not Berg's perception of the inner drama that need concern us here but his acute perception of the *dynamic* principle around which the whole vast movement is built, i.e. the bold idea of a recurring, expanding and exploding crescendo – Berg's volcanic eruptions – the last, longest and loudest of which gives rise to the ultimate disintegration of the movement's materials, the final reassembly of which offers a reconciliation of all the disparate components that have been involved.

So it is not to sonata or rondo (for rondo was the other influential classical formal model to which Mahler paid serious attention in his symphonies and which indeed sometimes modified his concept of sonata), that we must look as aids to comprehending the

11  Ibid.

Mahler: Symphony No. 9, *Andante comodo*

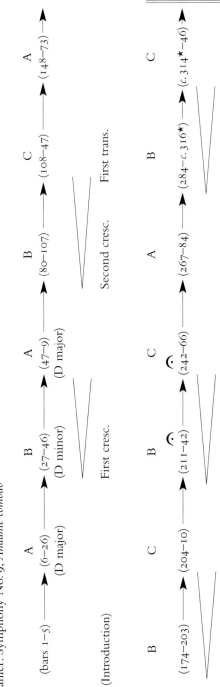

Key:  A = andante idea (D major); B = quasi-allegro + crescendo idea (D minor); C = transition idea
★ NB The fifth crescendo and fourth transition overlap.

organization of the Ninth's andante, but to the audacious and innovatory idea of a large and complicated instrumental movement having its basis (its very *raison d'être*) in a dimension of music – dynamics: specifically, the *crescendo* which had hitherto been an aspect of form, and often a major aspect, but never, I think, constituted the totality of a form, which is precisely the case in the andante of Mahler's Ninth and which the diagram opposite may help to elucidate.

If the first movement of the Ninth is, as Berg and many others have believed, one of the summits of Mahler's compositional feats, it is also one of his most original formal achievements, and one of the most original forms to be found in the history of the twentieth-century symphony, not only up to his death but beyond it.

It was entirely typical of his character as an artist, and of the character of his art, that in this, his penultimate work, he should have thrown out such substantial evidence of fresh symphonic thinking on so radical a scale; and the Tenth, too, as we have seen sustained the formal quest. Though Mahler did not live to complete his last symphony, perhaps it is not inappropriate to conscript at this point the words of Virginia Woolf's Lily Briscoe (in *To the Lighthouse*) and say for him, from the vantage point of the Tenth, and looking back over the extraordinary richness and boldness of his life's work: 'It was done; it was finished. Yes, she thought, laying down her brush in extreme fatigue, I have had my vision.' I do not think anyone could deny Mahler his vision or – like Lily Briscoe – his final victory.

Chiengmai-Bangkok-Kuala Lumpur-Barcombe Mills
1 January – 21 February 1976
Revised Bangkok, February 2007

SCRUTINY

*Previous page* Gustav Mahler in Rome in March or April 1907, studying scores
in the Library of the Orchestra dell'Accademia Santa Cecilia

# *Das klagende Lied*: Mahler's 'Opus 1'

## ᵔ 1997 ᵔ

The other week I was re-reading a remarkable article by my old and still much missed friend and colleague, Hans Keller. He wrote it in 1971, and it was entitled – characteristically – 'The Unpopularity of Mahler's Popularity' (*Listener*, 15 April). In the course of it, he observes that it was Mahler who was the first 'to invent the intra-musical style of irony, momentarily foreshadowed in one single work of the most universal composer ever – in *Così fan tutte.*' When Hans and I were talking about this in the late 1940s and early 1950s, it had not yet become part of everybody's critical vocabulary when writing about Mahler; after all he was still conspicuously 'unpopular' with – that is to say, unheard by – the critical establishment in those distant days. 'The function of irony in Mahler' was not likely to surface in the Arts columns of *The Times* as topic of one of those magisterial pronouncements by 'Our Music Critic' as he was known at the time.

One might think that there was in fact a certain irony bound up with the absence of immediate recognition of what we all know now is a leading feature – a very sharp edge – of Mahler's creative profile; it was not, however, to *become* a leading feature but was there from the very start, and nowhere more powerfully expressed than in the denouement that rounds off Part III of *Das klagende Lied* as it was composed by the youthful Mahler in 1878–80. At the height of the concluding marriage festivities, musically embodied in the exuberant presence of an independent wind and percussion orchestra, the guilty brother's awful secret is disclosed by the accusatory bone flute. The castle disintegrates, the lights are extinguished,

First published in the programme for the concert given by the Hallé Orchestra conducted by Kent Nagano in Manchester on 7 October 1997, and printed in the liner notes for the subsequent recording, issued in 1998, with the same forces, Erato 3984–21664–2.

the bride lies prostrate on the ground, the guests flee in terror, the drums are silent. The grand wedding party ends in darkness, dust and ashes: 'Leide' ('sorrow') is the last word we hear.

The innate theatricality of the scene is riveting enough; but what really drives home the horror and terror of it is the bold, unmitigated juxtaposition of the two musics and two orchestras involved, the celebrating, triumphal wind and percussion band on the one hand, on the other the tragic commentary of the main orchestra, soloists and chorus, each music functioning as an ironic comment on the other. Thus it was, and thus it is, that *Das klagende Lied* enables us to perceive that irony made its debut at a very early stage in the evolution of Mahler's creativity, and was to remain an established part of his creative strategy for the rest of his life.

It is fashionable these days to disparage Sigmund Freud, but his famous interview with Mahler in 1910 cannot be ignored, especially in the context of the denouement of the cantata. Freud reported that during his conversation with the composer, Mahler had recollected a 'specially painful scene' between his father and mother:

> It became quite unbearable to the boy, who rushed away from the house. At that moment, however, a hurdy-gurdy in the street was grinding out the popular Viennese air 'Ach, du lieber Augustin'. In Mahler's opinion the conjunction of high tragedy and light amusement was from then on inextricably fixed in his mind, and the one mood inevitably brought the other with it.

It seems probable to me still that the peculiarly Mahlerian conjunction of musics 'high' and 'low' may have had its roots in early experiences of childhood.

At this point I should like, if I may, to launch a Kellerism of my own: that it was in and with *Das klagende Lied* that Mahler *introduced himself to himself*. However, while it is obvious that the ironic confrontation of musics I have just described supports a reading of the cantata as a prime source of what, musically, the future had in store, it is by no means the only example of its kind, as I shall hope to show, and perhaps not even the most sophisticated or complex in its implications.

But before leaving the area of 'irony', let me, for a moment, dwell on a couple of other points that arise in that context. First, that the incursion of irony – how Mahler actually realizes it in terms of the impingement of one kind of music on another – inescapably involved him in the manipulation of acoustic space, of the relationship between sounds generated by different groups at different distances and at different dynamic levels; and sometimes too in a different rhythm and clashing tonalities. Indeed, one of the most extraordinary anticipatory 'events' in the cantata is the first emerging of the offstage orchestra in Part II, *Der Spielmann*, between bars 222 and 229, at this juncture a brief encounter, for sure, but Mahler makes certain we do not overlook it, i.e. fail to hear it, by setting off the brass (three trumpets!) and percussion (in 3/4) against the regular 4/4 of the rest of the orchestra. An extra-ordinarily extravagant – not to say, risky – idea for him to have introduced, given Mahler's youth and the fact that he would later submit his cantata to the (conservative!) committee of the presti-gious Beethoven Prize, a competition organized by Vienna's Gesell-schaft der Musikfreunde ('Society of the Friends of Music'). (What, one wonders, did the members of the committee make of what must be one of the earliest eruptions of uncompromising poly-tonality in the history of music – if not the earliest.) But already in this tiny but momentous seed there is a clear anticipation of that unique passage in the finale of the Second Symphony (between figs. 22 and 25) where an offstage orchestra (brass and percussion) is rhythmically independent of the main, on-stage orchestra. The rhythmic 'confusion' that results, two groups, two constellations of sound, quite distinct in character, combined in different acoustic perspectives, creates its own innovatory aesthetic – Mahler was certainly aware of the potentialities of random collisions of sound as he walked the streets – but again, the counter-rhythm, offstage, was a means of making certain that the 'collision' was effectively articulated, the same practical consideration that shaped the entry of the offstage band in the second part of the cantata, and in parti-cular the 'collision' between the offstage and onstage forces, each of which asserts its own independent tonal area(s). As Riccardo Chailly has observed, 'two different orchestras, talking two different languages simultaneously? This was absolutely unheard of in those days!'* A remarkable stroke of innovative imagination, and one that vividly foreshadows many similar combative juxtapositions in Berg's *Wozzeck*; but also an emphatic means of guaranteeing the audibility of the invasion from offstage.

One might think it sufficient that that handful of bars – a mere eight of them! – should disclose so much already about how Mahler's imagination would develop, and in what directions. But in fact there is more to observe, and in particular the grading of the dynamics, i.e. a crescendo (from $p$ in bar 222) for trumpets 1 and 2, culminating (bar 225) in a major third ([*mf*] and [*f*]) in which trumpet 3 participates, followed by a virtually identical repeat of the four bars but this time with the crescendo (again from $p$) culminating *ff* in a C major triad. (My square brackets are editorial but Mahler would surely have added a dynamic at the end of the first crescendo which would have represented an interim stage *en route* for the culminating *ff* at the end of the second crescendo.) By such nuancing of the dynamics, Mahler installs *within* an acoustic event that itself operates at one remove from the main body of sound an impression of sound 'on the move', i.e. the repeat of the crescendo should sound louder and thus 'nearer' (to us in the hall!), in relation both to the preceding crescendo and to the main orchestra.

This is a relatively simple example of a process, a technique, that Mahler was unceasingly to refine and define from *Das klagende Lied* onwards; it was to become, in his late symphonies, a concept of 'mobile' sound that remarkably anticipated one of this century's principal areas of exploration: acoustic space.

It is perhaps not surprising, then, that this early cantata crucially foreshadows the famous passage in the First Symphony – the long, slow introduction to the first movement – where Mahler, after a great deal of toil and sweat, finally succeeded in organizing to his satisfaction the potentialities of the acoustic space that that introduction represents: distances and dynamics were systematically laid out in their internal relationships, within the same group or between different groups of instruments, and in their relationship to the overall sound 'picture' of which they form part.

Moreover, it is in the overture (or prelude) to Part 1 of *Das*

---

*   See p. 359.

Alexander Rosé

Concertbureau

Wien, I. Kärntnerring 11.

**WIENER SINGAKADEMIE.**

(43. Vereinsjahr.)

Ausgezeichnet mit der goldenen Medaille für Wissenschaft und Kunst.

Grosser Musikvereins-Saal.

Sonntag den 17. Februar 1901, mittags halb 1 Uhr

**Ausserordentliches Concert**

der

**Wiener Singakademie.**

Zur ersten Aufführung gelangt:

# Das klagende Lied

für Soli, gemischten Chor und grosses Orchester von

## Gustav Mahler

unter persönlicher Leitung des Componisten.

**Mitwirkende:**

| | |
|---|---|
| Frau Elise Elizza | Frl. Edith Walker |
| k. k. Hofopernsängerin | k. k. Hofopernsängerin |
| Frl. Anna von Mildenburg | Herr Fritz Schrödter |
| k. k. Hofopernsängerin | k. u. k. Kammer- und Hofopernsänger |

das k. k. Hofopern-Orchester, verstärkt durch einen Bläserchor,

die Mitglieder der Wiener Singakademie u. des »Schubertbund«.

Vorher:

R. WAGNER: „Eine Faust-Ouverture".

Texte umstehend.

Programm: 20 Heller.

Programme for the premiere of *Das klagende Lied* in Vienna on 17 February 1901

*klagende Lied*, *Waldmärchen*, a slow, atmospheric and recurring introduction, that the foreshadowing of the First Symphony is most striking and fascinating. Much, of course, has been made in the past of the shared imagery between the cantata, the earliest orchestral song-cycle, *Lieder eines fahrenden Gesellen*, and the First Symphony, and it is undeniably true, and illuminating (up to a point), to recognize kindred features (horn calls, birdsong, fanfares, drum taps, and the rest). But for me what is fascinating is something a little beyond the imagery, the fascination of discovering how, even at this very early stage, the young composer begins to organize his sound, how the paths he will follow in the future are already revealed. Of course it is correct and perfectly appropriate to feel the associations between the magical horn calls of the First Symphony and those of *Waldmärchen*. But more exciting, I believe – hence the importance of the possibility we now have of hearing and assessing *Das klagende Lied* in its entirety – is to recognize that in the carefully graded dynamics of the horn calls and signals of *Waldmärchen* (not to speak of the similarly nuanced woodwind and other brass) a clear outline is being drawn – even while the composer was, so to speak, himself in the process of being born! – of the kind of mind that was bent on exploring the potentialities and *properties* of acoustic space and devising the techniques – and notation! – in which they might be embodied. (When the horn calls recur at the moment when the younger brother is discovered sleeping (bars 405 ff.), horns 1 and 2 (for the first time in the score) are actually marked 'wie aus der Ferne' ('as if from the distance'), a future Mahler hallmark.) These techniques were to stay with Mahler, in fact, long after he had abandoned the world of horn calls, fanfares and signals that were habitually the furnishings of fairy-tales in music.

Mahler himself was certainly aware of the evolutionary link between his first song-cycle and his First Symphony; indeed, in a famous concert in Berlin, on 16 March 1896, the occasion of the song-cycle's premiere, he went out of his way to spell out the connection by juxtaposing both works in the same programme.

It is again an important consequence of this revival of the cantata in its original version that it brings to our attention the precisely similar relationship between the cantata and the song-cycle. More important still, it makes us realize that these three early works, each cast in a distinctive form – cantata, song-cycle, symphony – also constitute, in part by means of cross-quotation and reference, a developing narrative that in fact was to be further sustained in the first movement of the Second Symphony. (Significantly, it was this movement, under the title of *Todtenfeier*, that Mahler also included among the trinity of works he performed in Berlin in 1896.)

The word I should like to emphasize here is 'narrative', the unfolding of a history, a drama, a story, a conflict, culminating (most often) in a denouement, a resolution, tragic and ironic in the case of the cantata, ambiguous in the case of the song-cycle (does the cycle's protagonist, who emerges here for the first time in Mahler's oeuvre, sleep and dream or die of a broken heart?), and, likewise, ambiguous in the case of the symphony. (Is the finale's triumph for real or to some degree illusory, as Mahler himself seems to have thought? Hence the 'funeral rites' of the first movement of the Second Symphony.)

What is unmistakable is the 'travelling' music common to all three works, an ostinato-like pattern of drum fourths (it was to become the basic interval uniting the disparate movements and materials of the symphony) that appears early on in the prelude to *Waldmärchen* and then is used consistently throughout the cantata as a whole, as emblem of a narrative continuity. This 'travelling' music, the very same idea that launches and accompanies Mahler's hypothetical hero on his travels in the *Lieder eines fahrenden Gesellen* and First Symphony, maintains the momentum, carrying us onwards to whatever denouement it is that lies ahead.

But once again I prefer to look a little beyond the identity of the 'travelling music' that binds together Mahler's first three major works, constituting a triptych almost. What grips my attention is Mahler's clear preoccupation with the *idea* of narrative, of 'travelling' from a given point of departure to a distant (yet-to-be disclosed) destination. If one puts aside the particular case of the travelling fourths in cantata, song-cycle and symphony, surely the more important observation is this: that Mahler was to continue as he began, a *traveller*, in his forms, for the rest of his creative life. For, virtually without exception, the later symphonies and song-cycles are all narratives, albeit that some are more explicitly so than others. But to the narrative principle, I would submit, each is faithful.

I think any thorough scrutiny of the score of *Das klagende Lied* must leave one astonished, in ever increasing measure, by the sheer comprehensiveness of the introduction it makes to the compositional techniques Mahler was to deploy and develop across his lifetime. To attempt a description of these in detail would consume altogether too much space, but for me one of the most arresting discoveries has been Mahler's systematic use – even in 1879–81! – of a motivic-based polyphony. Already, and perhaps especially in *Waldmärchen*, we find many pages of the score which consist exclusively of an elaborate combination of leading motives. This, after all, was to become one of the composer's principal contrapuntal techniques in his symphonies up to and including his problematic Fifth of 1901–2 – problematic, that is, in the composer's eyes (or ears, rather), who was of the opinion that the 'new style' the Fifth demanded was largely bound up with the articulation of its stressedly motivic polyphony. Whatever conclusions we may eventually reach about the 'problems' of the Fifth, there is no doubt to my mind that what is perhaps its leading feature, a ruthlessly motivic-based polyphony, is adumbrated at least, in the improbable fairy-tale context of the cantata. The technique was a thousand times refined and developed over the ensuing three decades, but what the symphonies were to demonstrate in this one regard at least was a fulfilment of a technique, a mode of contrapuntal thinking on Mahler's part, that unequivocally manifests itself in his early masterpiece. Small wonder that he was himself finally convinced that the cantata was his authentic Opus 1! In his own words (in a letter to Max Marschalk, [4] December 1896): 'The first work in which I really came into my own as "Mahler" was a *fairy tale* for choir, soloists and orchestra: *Das klagende Lied*. I number that work Opus 1.' He was yet more expansive when he had confided three years earlier to Natalie Bauer-Lechner on examining the score of his 'fairy tale', 'It's unbelievable, I find that the only advances I have made since then have been technical ones. But as regards the essentials, every aspect of the Mahler you all know was already there.'

There is another aspect of the motivic activity that is so pronounced a feature of *Das klagende Lied*, and that is the way in which the motives themselves perform. They are by no means passive, by which I mean to suggest that they do not simply function as identifying labels (of events, of landscape, of the principal dramatis personae) but behave rather like characters in a novel, changing, adapting, metamorphosing, according to the changed circumstances in which they find themselves. I have in mind here, the reader will not need reminding, Adorno's famous notion that the themes in Mahler's symphonies, as those works' narratives unfold, assume the status of 'characters' in the sense that we use the term in the context of the great literary narratives of the nineteenth century: 'characters' – i.e. themes, motives – that have a past, a present and – above all – an unpredictable future.

Of course the network of motivic associations is simple – naive, even – if one is making a comparison with the networking that goes on in a symphony like, say, the Fifth. But once again it is the point of principle that I am emphasizing, that here, in the youthful cantata, there is already present, albeit in embryonic form, a clear indication of the quasi-dramatic motivic system that was to be one of Mahler's most formidable technical resources henceforth, a resource, be it noted, irrevocably tied in with the concept of narrative, of travelling, of departure and arrival. After all, do we not embark on a journey, rich in people and incident, every single time we open one of the great European fictions of the nineteenth century and first decades of the twentieth?

For me one of the most remarkable of all the anticipations in the cantata of a technique that Mahler was to raise to unparalleled heights of ingenuity and originality is the use of one of the work's basic motives, a descending minor scale, spanning an octave, that we first hear early on in *Waldmärchen*, a punctuation – or 'cutoff' as I shall now describe it – immediately after the first chorale, 'O weh! Du wonnigliches Weib! . . .' (bars 145 ff.). This simple, economical and extremely telling gesture – the scale unwinds first in the cor anglais, then in the bass clarinet, then in the bassoons –

is the very epitome of the sorrow that is at the heart of the cantata.

What I find of particular significance, and perhaps especially in *Waldmärchen*, where this scale motive punctuates the narrative no fewer than six times, is its encapsulation, again in principle, of a gesture – my 'cut-off' – that will figure in ever increasing complexity as a leading feature of Mahler's style, of his expressive vocabulary, and indeed in one instance, the Fifth, plays a prominent role in the formal organization of one of the most innovative symphonic movements he was ever to compose, the second (allegro) movement, the 'Hauptsatz', of the symphony's Part 1. The 'cut-off' gestures imagined by Mahler at the height of his powers were almost invariably cries of sorrow and pain, though of a wildness and intensity that naturally enough the cantata does not match. But that, once more, is not the point at issue. There is, however embryonically in the case of *Das klagende Lied*, a shared gesture with a comparable formal function and of a similar expressive character. What in the Fifth is undeniably a surfacing of one of Mahler's most radical devices was launched, we must conclude, in his early cantata. Here again it is acquaintance with the original version *in toto* that proves so revealing.

If the passage in question is terminated by a gesture that opens a window on the future, it is preceded by one that (a) but for two repeats (plus a 'cut-off' in each case) is not to recur elsewhere in the cantata and (b) has the singular distinction of having no further role to play in the long-term assembly of Mahler's vocabulary. This is the pastiche chorale 'O weh! Du wonnigliches Weib!' (bar 139) that may at first strike one as an exercise in the manner of Bach but which I believe to have its roots, much more probably, in the oratorios of Mendelssohn. (In fact a vestigial reference to the chorale is to be found in *Der Spielmann* in bars 211–17. This was to be lost in the two-part revision of 1898, along with the epic first intervention of the offstage band.)

There is no specific narrative or dramatic reason that I can point to which would automatically justify or explain Mahler's choice of a style, a genre, that carried with it such a heavy burden of tradition and association (with Bach's Passions). The suffering we encounter in *Das klagende Lied* scarcely impinges on the sacred. On reflection, it seems probable to me that it was the role the chorus plays here, commenting on the drama, combined with the rhythm of the words and chorale-like concept of the text itself, that brought to the surface of Mahler's mind the expertise in chorale-writing that he must have acquired while so recently a student at the Vienna Conservatoire.

But in fact this deployment of pastiche – a rare event in Mahler – does not give us the whole story of the chorale idea and its involvement in the cantata. Something much more characteristic and redolent of things to come emerges in Part II, *Der Spielmann*, where what we immediately recognize as an authentically *Mahlerian* chorale in shape and sound emerges in bar 73 in a passage marked, uniquely, 'Religioso' (this must be the only known use by Mahler of this injunction: shades of Liszt and Berlioz?). Moreover the composer himself marks the passage 'Choral'. The impression of Mahler (as distinct from the pastiche chorale of *Waldmärchen*) having found his own voice is reinforced when the chorale – scored for two horns, two trumpets, three trombones and bass tuba – continues in bar 81. It would be difficult not to hear the chorales of the future lying ahead, more especially those of the Second Symphony; indeed, we may think this is particularly appropriate as *Der Spielmann* itself opens in C minor, 'Mit sehr geheimnisvoll Ausdruck', with a forceful *tremolando* (violas, *sff* $\Longrightarrow$ *pp*) and a leading motive, full of foreboding, assigned to the lower strings. We seem very close, and indeed are very close, to the sound-world and mood of *Todtenfeier*, as the first movement of the symphony was once entitled.

It is impossible to miss the prominent incorporation of a triplet into the rhythmic scheme outlined by cellos and double-basses:

Ex. I  *Der Spielmann*, bars 3–6

*pp*

The triplet as a rhythmic unit has a high profile throughout *Das klagende Lied*, but especially so in *Waldmärchen*, the omission of which when Mahler came to revise his cantata into two parts inevitably meant that some of the preparation of the importance of the triplet in Part I was lost. In fact the very opening of *Waldmärchen*, to take only the first forty bars or so, is rich in triplets. At the very start, the first motives we hear in the horns and clarinets reveal the triplet as a basic component, contributing to the vestigial 'pastoral' associations that the horn calls evoke. These prove to be short-lived, particularly when they find themselves in the context of a chilly F sharp minor, a piercing and sustained intervention by the flutes, oboes and cor anglais propelled by the cold wash of an F sharp minor arpeggio on the harp: we are warned, so to say, that this is unlikely to be a fairy-tale with a happy ending. It is triplets again that, in the immediately ensuing passage, whip the music up to its first big climax; and when that subsides, it is triplets again that service the feverish, agitated figuration exchanged between the bass clarinet and bassoon, a transition that returns us to the horn and woodwind calls of the outset, triplets again to the fore. Mahler's nervy agitation in the future was to assume on occasion just such a shape and sound.

Already at work here is Mahler's preoccupation with achieving coherence, vivid characterization and form-building through close motivic integration. However, it is the variety that obtains despite the consistency that is so remarkable; that is, the capacity of a single rhythmic unit – in this case the triplet, but there are others that might be mentioned – to metamorphose according to the changing needs of the narrative and its attendant situations. Thus (to stick to the triplet a moment longer) we find it servicing at opposite poles of the expressive scale, the threatening prelude to *Der Spielmann*, say, at one extreme, and, at the other, this time in *Waldmärchen*, where, in the marvellous rhapsody that responds to the song of the nightingale (bars 420 ff.), the triplets generate an embryonic exultant ecstasy that very clearly anticipates a feature of Mahler's later and late styles. Perhaps one might again draw a parallel here with the Fifth Symphony where the triplet is fundamental to the motivic network in which the work's narrative is embodied.

Think for instance of the role of the triplet in the opening fanfare with its intimations of mortality and high drama – it is this rhythmic unit that is the first thing we hear – and then of its transformation in the finale in a transcendental passage (figs. 21-3) which is an apotheosis of all that the triplet has come to represent over five movements during the course of seventy or so minutes. I exaggerate the parallel, of course; but what truth there is in it, is further proof of the main point I want to get across, that *Das klagende Lied*, above all in its original tri-partite state, allows us the unique opportunity to witness a composer's methodology and identifying battery of compositional techniques in the very process of their formation. And not only the evolution of his identity, but also the development – the sophistication and refinement – of those techniques across the three parts. For example, it is very evident to me that in Parts II and III of the cantata we are aware of a much more powerful, memorable and original *melodic* invention; and it is this sense of the composer growing along with the unfolding of his Opus I that makes the *Urfassung* an essential part of our knowledge and experience of Mahler. There is every reason, naturally, to continue to hear his two-part revision, which, now that we can get to grips with the *Urfassung*, represents a version of the cantata virtually independent of its predecessor. What has to be banished is the illegitimate, unlovely mix of both versions that to date has been the only form in which a three-part cantata could be heard.

Because my chief purpose has been to draw attention to some of the musical processes that must have led Mahler himself to accord his cantata the status of Opus I, I have deliberately overlooked the associations and links – one might describe them as 'inter-quotations' – between *Das klagende Lied* and certain of Mahler's earliest songs ('Im Lenz' especially), while another category of prominent ideas from the cantata was also to be carried forward and incorporated into the *Lieder eines fahrenden Gesellen* and the First Symphony. This whole area has been pretty extensively covered in the existing literature, though it is still not possible to establish beyond doubt the precise chronology of all the creative events involved. However, the 'quotations' made in the *Gesellen* cycle and – consequentially – in the First Symphony are readily identifiable, and I must confine myself here to drawing attention to the evidence these interpolations bring to the exceptional narrative continuity and overall integrity of the cantata, the first song-cycle, and Mahler's first attempt at symphony. However, the whole issue and complex practice of 'quotation' was to loom large in future years and works, perhaps reaching its apotheosis in the Fifth Symphony of 1901–2; thus once again *Das klagende Lied* anticipates – offers us a glimpse of – future events that would consume too much space if I were to enlarge on them here.

A few final points, matters of instrumentation first. In his *Urfassung* Mahler calls for an excessive number of harps, following no doubt the precedent of Wagner; in his revision he was to be more economic. On the other hand the conspicuous washes or splashes of harp colour, especially for example those chilling F sharp minor arpeggios that we hear at the very end of *Waldmärchen* – all six harps! – and comparable passages elsewhere (e.g. the A minor arpeggios (Mahler's 'tragic' key!) that precede (bars 361–4) the accusation of the flute in *Hochzeitsstück*), bring to the fore a gesture of Mahler's that was always to remain with him: think only of that glacial A flat minor harp (one harp!) arpeggio that precedes the terrifying dissonance that explodes in the opening adagio of the Tenth Symphony (bar 194).

The power with which even the youthful Mahler could charge these relatively 'simple' musical materials is also to be heard, vibrantly, in those isolated triads that sometimes disrupt or puncture the texture. There is an unforgettable instance in *Der Spielmann*, just before an intervention by the bone flute. The music has come to rest on a long-held F major. There follows (bar 336) a pungently scored E flat minor triad, sustained throughout on a pause bar, and succeeded by a wash of E flat minor arpeggios in the harps – after which the bone flute – the voice is marked by Mahler 'from the distance' – embarks on its tale of woe.

It is worth a moment's reflection on how Mahler achieves so uncommon an effect with a common chord. The four horns for a start are *hand*-stopped, a means much favoured by Mahler in later years to secure a suppressed sound, but one, unlike that produced by the conventional mute, with an uncomfortable edge to it. The horns' collective dynamic is >—— ***ppp***. The dynamics of the triad as simultaneously represented by the woodwind, on the other hand, are not the same. The pair of oboes is marked ***sff*** >——, but the cor anglais maintains ***ff*** for the entire duration of the bar, that is, without the initiating strong accents (***sff***) of the oboes. All the woodwind and horn parts, however, are given an overall wedge-shaped accent to emphasize the abrupt, dislocating entry of the chord.

This is a typical instance of the hyper-elaborate attention to dynamic detailing and consideration of timbre that we find throughout the original version of the cantata, and one could quote literally dozens of examples yet more complicated than this one instance that I have chosen for its relative simplicity. How extraordinary it is, that one of the leading features of the composer's preoccupation with notation – the attempt to indicate *precisely* the sound effect he was after – should have emerged, virtually fully fledged, at this unbelievably early age when, in fact, Mahler had had only the barest experience of conducting or working with an orchestra. So often in the past we have assumed the manic character of his notation to be a by-product of his professional life as a virtuoso conductor. Not at all, I submit. His notation, like everything else about him, was a creature of his imagination; and in *Das klagende Lied* we encounter the moment when that imagination was first ignited.

It is, I suppose, the comprehensiveness of that moment of ignition that is so surprising, embracing at one extreme something relatively esoteric – like Mahler's poeticization of the piccolo, an instrument he was to make his own in sonorous imagery sometimes the reverse of the shrill or piercing – or, at another, a direct evocation of a tiny motive – a sharply projected or falling semitone (most often entrusted to the woodwind: cf. bars 560–67 in *Waldmärchen*) – that throughout Mahler's oeuvre was time and time again to surface as an emblem of pain or lamentation. Or there are inklings of yet another field Mahler was to explore: the potentialities of tempo as organized form. There is rudimentary evidence of this in the very opening of the prelude to *Waldmärchen*, which takes the shape of a continuous *accelerando* without detriment to the diversity and contrasts of the materials out of which it is built. Or – and a last 'or' it must be, because one has to call a halt somewhere – there is the 'authenticity' of the intruding, destabilizing wind and percussion band at the conclusion of *Hochzeitsstück*. It is not the intrusion of irony that I want to return to but to remark instead on the formatting of the offstage band, in which strings have no role to play. This highlights not just Mahler's incorporation of the vernacular but unequivocally intimates what was to be a constant future preoccupation, the wind band itself, out of which developed his remarkable liberation of the brass and woodwind in his symphonies. Looking ahead, how piquant it is to find the mature symphonist, in the *Trauermarsch* of the Fifth, effortlessly able to convert his orchestra for a significant stretch into an 'authentic' windband off the streets (figs. 12–14). What was necessarily externalized in the cantata can now, where appropriate, be internalized, and function as part of the resources of Mahler's expressive language. But it was in *Das klagende Lied* that the process was initiated. Wherever the eye comes to rest in the score of the *Urfassung* one sees – hears – the composer that Mahler was to become, whether it is the unveiling of fundamental working methods that confront us or previews of the 'voice' that we recognize as uniquely Mahlerian.

'Song of Sorrow', 'Song of Woe', 'Song of Complaint (or Accusation?)', all of those verbal descriptions convey something of the cantata's dominant expressive character. In the event, it is Mahler himself who graphically identifies this for us by his use of a wholly typical motive – typical in rhythm, contour and intervallic build – at two critical and climactic junctures in *Hochzeitsstück* when the dire consequences of the guilty brother's murderous act take effect. My Ex. 2 below gives the motive as it is powerfully projected by the horns (with woodwind) at bar 388, while at the same time the soprano, on a falling octave, articulates 'klagen', the defining word itself. However, the association between defining word and specific motive has already been established earlier, in the (bone) flute's accusation (soprano), where again 'klagen' is articulated in tandem with the motive of sorrow, of woe (see Ex. 3); or, rather, 'klagen' *is* the motive (bars 269–71): word and pitches are inseparable.

Ex. 2  *Hochzeitsstück*, bars 388–91

Ex. 3  *Hochzeitsstück*, bars 269–71

A telling example, for sure, of Mahler's highly organized motivic practice, with its innumerable cross-references, anticipations and retrospections, and once again a clear intimation of what lies ahead, not so much practice this time as the disclosure of an idea, a sequence of pitches, a motive, a rhythm, that ever after were to comprise a permanent part of Mahler's working vocabulary.

I think my Exx. 4, 5 and 6 overleaf (in which Ex. 4 repeats Ex. 2) show the evolution of the motive of sorrow from *Das klagende Lied* into the motive of woe in the monumental Third Symphony. When we hear the eight horns pounding the motive out at the height of the symphony's great concluding adagio (see Ex. 5), behind it – audibly – is the model of the horn signal in *Hoch-zeitsstück*. I have shown in Ex. 3 above how Mahler in his cantata has identified the motive for us in advance by use of the defining word 'klagen'. Likewise in the Third Symphony, in the orchestral song that is the symphony's fourth movement (see Ex. 6), the horn signal there is identified for us in advance by the defining word, this time 'Weh!' ('woe'):

Ex. 4  *Hochzeitsstück*, bars 388–91

Ex. 5  Symphony No. 3, movement 6: *Langsam. Ruhevoll. Empfunden*, bars 180–83

Ex. 6  Symphony No. 3, movement 4: *O Mensch! Gib Acht!*, bars 100–101

As Mahler began, so – it seems – he was to continue!

# 'Hidden Treasure Within':
# The Early Songs for Voice and Piano
# and *Wunderhorn-Lieder*

### ∼ 1995 ∼

From the very start of his creative activity, when, so to say, the youthful Mahler was working out for himself what kind of a composer he was going to be, there was a relationship between a song (or songs) and a materialization of some part of a song in another location altogether, another format, another genre. The earliest complete songs known to us are the three songs for tenor and piano, 'Im Lenz', 'Winterlied' and 'Maitanz im Grünen', composed in 1880, in Mahler's nineteenth year; and two of them are of particular interest in the context of the comment I have just made. The third song, 'Maitanz im Grünen', he was later to include among the songs that made up the first volume of his *Lieder und Gesänge*, published in 1892. (It was Mahler's publishers, by the way, who later entitled the three-volume collection *Lieder und Gesänge aus der Jugendzeit*, which might have been an accurate description of vol. i but not of vols. ii and iii, made up of settings of *Wunderhorn* texts composed between 1887 and 1890, when Mahler was approaching thirty.) In its published form, 'Maitanz im Grünen' was re-entitled 'Hans und Grethe'; this 'Volkslied' was then to re-emerge as the basis of the ländler third movement in the original five-movement 'Symphonic Poem' shape in which what we know today as Mahler's First Symphony was launched in 1889. (Mahler's revision of 1896 entailed the omission of the *Blumine* andante, whereupon the 'Hans und Grethe' ländler moved into second place in the

First published in GMWL, pp. 2.58–65. Additional sections have been interpolated from the liner notes for two recordings of songs from *Des Knaben Wunderhorn*, Claudio Abbado's disc with the Berlin Philharmonic Orchestra, DG 459–646–2 and Riccardo Chailly's disc with the Royal Concertgebouw Orchestra, Decca 467–348–2, and from an additional note to 'Eternity or Nothingness? Mahler's Fifth Symphony' in the revised paperback edition of DMANMC.

Cover of the first edition of Mahler's *Lieder und Gesänge* (1892)

sequence of four movements.)* Moreover, it was not only this song from the trio of early songs that was to maintain its integrity as a solo song while also fulfilling an alternative and independent life elsewhere.

'Hans und Grethe' is a thoroughgoing example of what I have in mind. But the case of 'Im Lenz' is no less telling and equally symptomatic. This is not only a song very much in the style of the early cantata, *Das klagende Lied*, but also quotes a prominent theme from it. So here we have a process the reverse of that represented by 'Hans und Grethe', a large-scale dramatic cantata generating a song, as distinct from a song generating a symphonic movement.

There are other features of Mahler's early songs besides the inter-penetration of genres, which were also to prove of special signifi-cance for future developments in his music. For instance, take a song from the first volume of *Lieder und Gesänge*, 'Erinnerung'. Undoubtedly a fine, accomplished setting of Richard Leander's text, and one that reveals recognizably Mahlerian characteristics despite its debt to Schumann (a major influence on how Mahler devised his songs and song-cycles). I am not thinking of the inten-sity of its melancholy, which climaxes in an extended cry of grief – 'so kommen meine Lieder zu mir mit Liebesklagen!' ('so my songs return, lamenting love') – in the song's penultimate verse, but to what I would describe as its use of the narrative mode, one of the earliest examples of it in Mahler's music which indicates already, albeit on a miniature, lyrical scale, how integral to his thinking narrative was – departing from one point, arriving at another.

For while 'Erinnerung' sets out in G minor, it ends in A minor, Mahler's 'tragic' key, incidentally. But it is not this last point that I wish to emphasize, but rather that here, in 'Erinnerung', we encounter a narrative of lyrical feeling embodied in an unfolding tonal scheme which travels from G minor to A minor, thus articu-lating a principle that was henceforth to be of fundamental impor-tance to all Mahler's symphonies, let alone the songs and song-cycles that were to come. There could hardly be a clearer instance of the unique consistency of Mahler's thinking, irrespective of

---

* See also 'Gustav Mahler', p. 11.

genre or medium. A familiar example of the crossovers between genres, in this instance between song-cycle and symphony, we find in the conjunction of the *Lieder eines fahrenden Gesellen* (1884) and First Symphony ([1884]/1888). All I want to emphasize here is that in these two compositions, which together form a unit, the narrative implications of 'Erinnerung' come to major fruition; both the song-cycle and complementary symphony narrate poetic 'dramas', explicitly so in the texts of the *Gesellen* cycle and no less explicitly in the 'programme' that accompanied the symphony in its various early formats. By the 1880s, the narrative principle was well and truly on track.

There is perhaps one last point to be made about the earliest of Mahler's published songs, that in one of them, 'Frühlingsmorgen', again to a text by Leander, and again a Schumannesque inspiration, we find Mahler, as it were, tuned into Nature, to birdsong, to the acoustic imagery of spring, albeit in the largely decorative, imitative approach to Nature that one would expect of a young composer. The song itself, we might think, pre-shadows in some respects the spring-like mood and sounds of the second song of the *Gesellen* cycle, 'Ging heut' morgen über's Feld', though not that song's plaintive, poignant, conclusion; but there is an anticipation in 'Frühlingsmorgen' of that incorporation of Nature which was to become so striking a feature of songs and symphonies alike.

It was surely the rich imagery drawn from Nature that must have made a particularly powerful appeal to Mahler when seriously settling down to investigate the possibilities offered him by the famous anthology of 'old German songs', *Des Knaben Wunderhorn*, put together by von Arnim and Brentano and first published in three volumes in 1805 and 1808.

The *Wunderhorn* collection was, as Dika Newlin once put it, a 'typical product of the romantic *Zeitgeist*, with its stress on the simple, artless life of the "little people" and the glamour of bygone days'. One reason for the anthology's popularity was its appeal to the nineteenth century's nostalgic yearning after the lost innocence of a remote past. Mahler's approach was, however, stubbornly independent of this romantic indulgence. He eschewed all false

Title page of von Arnim's and Brentano's collection of songs,
*Des Knaben Wunderhorn* (first edition)

medievalism and self-conscious 'folkiness' (there are no folk-tune quotations, references or 'arrangements' in Mahler's *Wunderhorn* songs) and simply accepted the texts at their face value. He did not adopt a fairy-tale, 'once upon a time' approach to the texts, but relived them as if they were of the present moment. The reality – the immediacy and dramatic or lyrical truth – of his settings, their wellnigh anti-romantic character, is what lends them their singular flavour.

In his admirable study of the life and works of Theodor Fontane, Gordon A. Craig remarks on 'the great success Fontane had with his ballads', and continues:

> This method of telling a dramatic story in short stanzas with a striking or dramatic conclusion had, of course, been popular in Germany ever since the eighteenth century, encouraged in the first instance by Herder's interest in folk songs and attracting such poets as Goethe ('Der Erlkönig') and Bürger ('Lenore') in the Storm and Stress era and, in the Romantic period, Chamisso, Brentano, Eichendorff, and Uhland. In Fontane's day, both before and particularly after the 1848 Revolution, interest in the ballad revived because, in an apparently inert society with nothing in particular to look forward to, people took refuge in stories about the past triumphs or, failing that, about dramatic events in the remote history of Germanic peoples, the Danes and the Norwegians, the English and the Scots.

No less tellingly he observes:

> In [Fontane's] view, ballads had to be composed – that is, written according to a logical scheme – but must, at the same time, appear to be natural and free of any literary artifice. Success depended also on the skilful use of suggestion, omission, and abrupt transitions, on mastery of the art of repetition, refrains, and leitmotiv, on an ability to create effects with a minimal use of means, and, above all, on colour.[1]

---

[1]   *Theodor Fontane: Literature and History in the Bismarck Reich*, pp. 11–12.

Professor Craig's words – 'composed'! – might well serve as a remarkably precise description of the method and means that distinguish Mahler's many ballads, the generating source of which was, of course, *Des Knaben Wunderhorn*. Each of his settings is indeed a miniature drama; each has a distinctive colour; each combines extreme sophistication and simplicity; and each represents an encounter between the real world and historical fantasy. It should be no surprise, I suppose, that the genius of a composer so strongly driven by *narrative* should have seized on the potentialities of the *Wunderhorn* anthology, thereby raising to new heights the form's potentialities for the exploration of timeless and often bleak psychological truth while not forsaking the link with the Ballad's historical past.

The first fruits of Mahler's exploration of the *Wunderhorn* world were the voice and piano settings, published in 1892 as the second and third volumes of the *Lieder und Gesänge*.

To be sure, it is the later orchestral settings of *Wunderhorn* texts, published in their orchestral and voice-and-piano formats in 1899, under the title *Des Knaben Wunderhorn*, that have claimed most of the world's attention; and they are indeed marvellous songs. But this should not prevent us from enjoying – and paying attention to – Mahler's first excursions into the *Wunderhorn* field.

In saying that I am reminded, of course, that this is not quite true, for we know now that the text of the first song of the *Gesellen* cycle, 'Wenn mein Schatz Hochzeit macht', was itself modelled on a *Wunderhorn* poem; and while the remaining texts were Mahler's own, they are very much in the manner of the *Wunderhorn* anthology.

It is not surprising, then, that the *Gesellen* cycle itself often anticipates in character some of the ensuing *Wunderhorn* settings; for example, the cycle's concluding song, 'Die zwei blauen Augen', initiates a whole tradition of marching songs in Mahler's oeuvre, extending through 'Zu Strassburg auf der Schanz'' and – above all – 'Nicht wiedersehen!' among the *Wunderhorn* settings of volume III of the *Lieder und Gesänge,* to astounding vocal-march masterpieces like 'Revelge' and 'Der Tamboursg'sell', Mahler's last settings of *Wunderhorn* poems, composed respectively in 1899 and 1901 and published independently of the rest.

No less, we find vivid evocations of Nature, of birdsong, in these nine first settings of *Wunderhorn* texts, and – perhaps more importantly for the context in which I am writing – that same interpenetration of genres, of formats, on which I have commented before, e.g. 'Hans und Grethe' transformed into the ländler of the First Symphony while retaining its own identity and function as a solo song. Here, in volume III of the *Lieder und Gesänge*, we have 'Ablösung im Sommer', a song which, a few years after its composition, was to re-emerge, to form the basis of the Third Symphony's scherzo, the third movement, originally entitled 'What the animals in the forest tell me'. It was a movement about which Mahler himself had something to say:

> And this doesn't surprise me; for, while making the corrections at present, I myself find everything so strange that, to my amazement, I have to get used to it all over again. The scherzo in particular, the animal piece, is at once the most scurrilous and most tragic that ever was – in the way that music alone can mystically take us from one extreme to the other in the twinkling of an eye. In this piece it is as if Nature herself were pulling faces and putting out her tongue. There is such a gruesome, Panic humour in it that one is more likely to be overcome by horror than laughter.[2]

Mahler's comment on the symphonic movement is itself suggestive of the extension and transformation the song has undergone. The comparative proportions of song and symphony reinforce the point: 67 bars for the song and 590 for the scherzo and its trios, which incorporate the famous posthorn solos.

Some transformation! Moreover, mention of the scherzo by no means exhausts the relationships of the Third with Mahler's *Wunderhorn* songs, both the early and later series. But it is to the Second Symphony that I must turn back, because it was there that the kind of massive transformation and elaboration of a *Wunderhorn* song into a symphonic movement first occurred. I refer to the scherzo of the Second, born out of one of the most brilliant of Mahler's

2   NB-L, *Recollections*, p. 129.

later *Wunderhorn* settings, 'Des Antonius von Padua Fischpredigt'.

This amazing third movement of the Second – not an offshoot of the song but an alternative creation, independent and yet sharing its basic ideas with the song – constitutes a comprehensive critique of the platitudes and imbecilities of human existence; and Mahler had this to say about it to Bauer-Lechner:

> I asked Mahler how the 'Fischpredigt' came to grow into the mighty scherzo of the Second, without his having intended it or wanted it to. He replied, 'It's a strange process! Without knowing at first where it's leading, you find yourself pushed further and further beyond the bounds of the original form, whose potentialities lay hidden within it like the plant within the seed. In connection with this, it seems to me that only with difficulty could I conform to the limitations imposed by an opera libretto (unless I had written it myself), or even by composing an overture to somebody else's work.
>
> 'It is rather different with songs, but only because you can express so much more in the music than the words directly say. The text is actually a mere indication of the deeper significance to be extracted from it, of hidden treasure within. [. . .]
>
> 'In the "Fischpredigt", the prevailing mood – as in "Das himmlische Leben" – is one of rather bitter-sweet humour. St Anthony preaches to the fish; his words are immediately translated into their thoroughly tipsy-sounding language (in the clarinet), and they all come swimming up to him – a glittering shoal of them: eels and carp, and the pike with their pointed heads.
>
> 'I swear, while I was composing I really kept imagining that I saw them sticking their stiff immovable necks out from the water, and gazing up at St Anthony with their stupid faces – I had to laugh out loud! And look at the congregation swimming away as soon as the sermon's over: "Die Predigt hat g'fallen, Sie bleiben wie alle" ("They liked the sermon, but remain unchanged"). Not one of them is one iota the wiser for it, even though the Saint has performed for them! But only a few people will understand my satire on mankind.'

In connection with this, Mahler said: 'The Bohemian music of my childhood home has found its way into many of my compositions.

I've noticed it especially in the "Fischpredigt". The underlying national element there can be heard, in its most crude and basic form, in the tootling of the Bohemian pipers [aus dem Gedudel der böhmischen Musikanten].'[3]

'Hidden treasure within': could there be a better description of the unique creative excavation which generated the series of diverse 'alternates' to the songs themselves?

The 'Fischpredigt' is a *locus classicus* among Mahler's orchestral *Wunderhorn* songs, exploiting as it does that vein of sarcasm and caustic wit which he made peculiarly his own and for which he finds precisely matching instrumentation, e.g. the 'sarcastic' E flat clarinet. Each of these later *Wunderhorn* songs indeed is imagined for an orchestra tailormade to meet and match the imagery of the texts. There is no 'standard' orchestra here: each song inhabits its own sound world. It is no exaggeration to claim that for each song Mahler invents a unique orchestra.

In this connection it is worth remembering that among the early voice and piano settings, there are one or two of the songs, e.g. 'Zu Strassburg auf der Schanz' and 'Nicht wiedersehen!', in which Mahler inscribes instrumental indications in his piano parts as an aid to his accompanist, e.g. 'wie ein Schalmei' ('like a shawm'), 'wie fernes Glockenlauten' ('like the tolling of distant bells'), 'In allen diesen Trillern [in "Zu Strassburg"] ist mit Hilfe des Pedals der Klang gedämpfter Trommeln nachzuahmen' ('In all these trills, with the help of the pedals, imitate the sound of muffled drums'). In this respect, these early *Wunderhorn* songs make clear that one feature of the 'hidden treasure' Mahler was to uncover in his later settings was their rich instrumental possibilities.

He never himself returned to endow his early settings with an orchestral dress but, not surprisingly, composers of later generations have taken up the challenge, among them Luciano Berio and Colin and David Matthews.

The 'Fischpredigt', as song and symphony, stands pre-eminent as an example of independently invented, autonomous creations from

---

3   Ibid., pp. 32–3.

a common source, happily co-existing while at the same time inhabiting different locations and performing different functions. (The remorseless *perpetuum mobile* of the ostinato in the scherzo of the Second would surely continue to make its unnerving impression of dumb incomprehension even if we knew nothing at all of its origin in the song and its text.) But the Second was also to incorporate a further *Wunderhorn* text, this time 'Urlicht', which was to become the symphony's fourth movement, the work's only slow movement. 'Urlicht', in fact, was originally written as an independent *Wunderhorn* setting and then, at quite a late stage in the evolution of the symphony, pressed into symphonic service. Why? For a variety of reasons, no doubt, but principally, I suggest, because at this stage in the symphony's overall form Mahler needed a stretch of genuinely slow music and because, above all, the introduction of the Word at this juncture helped clarify the 'meaning' of the work, i.e. it articulated, intimated, the goal – Resurrection – in which the symphony will eventually culminate.

I almost used the word 'programme' instead of 'meaning' when writing that last sentence, but the whole question of the 'programme' in Mahler's music raises such complex issues that I hesitate to raise it here. In any case, I prefer the word 'narrative'; and in the context of that descriptive term propose the use of 'signpost' as a compact means of accounting for the interpolation of these *Wunderhorn* songs into the symphonies, of which 'Urlicht' was the first instance but was to be followed by others. 'Signpost' shows us where we have got to and/or indicates the direction in which our travels are taking us and where, we hope, we may arrive. Something that Mahler himself said to Bauer-Lechner, in the summer of 1895, about making himself 'intelligible' seems to bear out my interpretation:

> Coming thoroughly stirred up and excited from his work, Mahler told me as we walked, 'It was like balancing Columbus's Egg when I brought in the word and the human voice in the Second Symphony just at the point where I needed it to make myself intelligible. Too bad I didn't think of this in the First! But in the Third I feel no more hesitation about it. I'm basing the songs of the short

movements on two pieces from *Des Knaben Wunderhorn* and a glorious poem of Nietzsche's.'[4]

Thus it is that the Second lays out for us two distinct uses of *Wunderhorn* songs; song as signpost, and song as basis for a huge, purely orchestral paraphrase, extension and transformation. The Third Symphony, to which I now return, incorporates both these formats, one of which, the extended orchestral paraphrase, I have already mentioned: the scherzo generated by 'Ablösung im Sommer'. There follows a solo orchestral song, the precedent for which, undoubtedly, was 'Urlicht' and which likewise plays the role of clarifying signpost; but the text is Nietzsche's, 'O Mensch! Gib Acht!', and while the function of the song at this formal juncture in the symphony is strictly comparable with that of 'Urlicht', the musical character of its setting is entirely distinct from Mahler's *Wunderhorn* style. Indeed its long arches of string melody foreshadow the asymmetrical contours of his late melodic style, in *Das Lied* for example. This tells us something about an identifiable *Wunderhorn* manner, with which this same symphony, without more ado, and without any attempt at a bridge or transition, confronts us; the immediately ensuing number is not only a setting of a wholly characteristic *Wunderhorn* text, 'Es sungen drei Engel', but plunges us immediately into a typically *Wunderhorn* world of sound: boys' voices imitating bells, women's chorus, an orchestra in which wind instruments predominate, and only the *lower* strings are used, a perfect example in fact of the idiosyncratic orchestra that Mahler imagined and continually re-imagined for each of his *Wunderhorn* settings. 'Es sungen drei Engel' is also distinguished for another reason. It is the only *Wunderhorn* setting of Mahler's that *started* its life not as a song but as a choral symphonic movement, though a solo song version was in fact included among the twelve settings of *Wunderhorn* texts published in 1899.

The scrupulous reader will have noticed that while I have talked about *one* setting of a *Wunderhorn* text in the Third, and the setting of Nietzsche, Mahler, in the conversation I quote on p. 97, talked

3    Ibid., p. 40.

about two *Wunderhorn* movements in his new symphony. It was Mahler's original intention that his Third should culminate in 'Das himmlische Leben', the solo song to a *Wunderhorn* text that he had composed in February 1892. But as the symphony evolved, it became clear that the solo song could not function as an effective finale and, as we know now, the Third concludes with a great adagio; the architecture of the work as it progressed demanded a finale built on that scale. None the less, although 'Das himmlische Leben' was discarded, it remains a vivid presence in the Third, embedded thematically as it is in the enormous first movement and sharing significant musical ideas and instrumentation with 'Es sungen drei Engel'. We are kept aware throughout the Third indeed that 'Das himmlische Leben' was a goal that the composer had in mind until the adagio necessarily took its place, a movement that perhaps was another vision of 'heavenly life', albeit expressed in different terms and on a different scale from the song.

In a very real sense, then, we owe the creation of the Third to the existence of one *Wunderhorn* song, 'Das himmlische Leben'; and, as it happened, also the creation of the Fourth, whose goal the song had become. As the nineteenth century turned into the twentieth, Mahler composed his Fourth Symphony *into* its preexisting finale, the *Wunderhorn* song that was to have rounded off the Third. There is no comparable case elsewhere in the history of music, I believe, nor in the history of Mahler's own symphonies. Of all Mahler's *Wunderhorn* settings, it is 'Das himmlische Leben' that best exemplifies the fundamental significance of the relationship of song and symphony in Mahler's oeuvre; for here we have two great symphonic narratives guided towards the destinations by just one *Wunderhorn* song; indeed, in the case of the Fourth, the narrative tonal scheme of the symphony, completed in November 1901, was first adumbrated in the song in 1892, and Mahler remained faithful to every particular of it.

It is tempting to embark on a description of each individual *Wunderhorn* song, but rather than my words, let Mahler speak for himself. In his conversations with Bauer-Lechner, he had things to say, often on those occasions when he had been busy with setting

*Wunderhorn* texts, for example 'Rheinlegendchen'. Natalie had naively asked Mahler in the summer of 1893 'how music is composed', to which he responded,

> It happens in a hundred different ways. One minute it is the poem that is the inspiration, the next it is the melody. I often begin in the middle, often at the beginning, sometimes even at the end, and the rest of it gradually falls into place until it develops into a complete whole.
>
> Today, for instance, I had a theme in mind; I was leafing through a book, and soon came upon the lines of a charming song that would fit my rhythm. I call the piece 'Tanzreime' ['Dancing rhymes'] (he later called it 'Rheinlegendchen'); although I could christen it along with a group of other songs, or perhaps with 'Um schlimme Kinder artig zu machen' ['To make bad children good']. But this is quite different in type from the earlier songs that I wrote for Frau Weber's children. It is much more direct, but whimsically childlike [*kindlich-schalkhaft*] and tender in a way that you have never heard before. Even the orchestration is sweet and sunny – nothing but butterfly colours. But, in spite of all its simplicity and folklike quality, the whole thing is extremely original, especially in its harmonization, so that people will not know what to make of it, and will call it mannered. And yet it is the most natural thing in the world; it is simply what the melody demanded.[5]

Three years later, in the summer of 1896, Mahler composed 'Lob des hohen Verstandes':

> Although initially without his sketches, Mahler could not waste those first few days in his summer-house. So he set to music a song from *Des Knaben Wunderhorn*: 'Lob des hohen Verstandes' ['In praise

---

5   Ibid., pp. 33–4. 'Um schlimme Kinder artig zu machen' is one of the earlier voice and piano *Wunderhorn* songs (from vol. ii of the *Lieder und Gesänge*). At the time of composing these settings, Mahler was a close friend of the wife of Captain-Baron Karl von Weber, the grandchild of Carl Maria von Weber, hence his interesting comment that 'Um schlimme Kinder' was of a type of song written for 'Frau Weber's children'. Mahler surely continues that train of thought when he describes the orchestration of 'Rheinlegend-chen' as 'whimsically childlike', thus identifying one important feature of his *Wunderhorn* manner.

of great understanding'], a priceless piece of satire on criticism. 'Here,' he said to me, 'I merely had to be careful not to spoil the poem and to convey its meaning exactly, whereas with other poems one can often add a great deal, and can deepen and widen the meaning of the text through the music.'[6]

This 'priceless piece of satire' Mahler was to use against himself, by quoting from it ironically as a tiny prelude to the finale of his Fifth Symphony, in which he shows off, with maximum exuberance, every kind of 'learned' contrapuntal device.

I find it fascinating that in his words on 'Rheinlegendchen' Mahler singles out for special comment its orchestration (and we have evidence now to suggest that he thought of his *Wunderhorn* and Rückert songs as a kind of vocal chamber music, involving orchestral resources and an acoustic appropriate to that concept and its harmony – 'extremely original', as Mahler has it).*

The orchestral *Wunderhorn* settings are indeed replete with extraordinary harmonic inventions and inspirations, one of the most exceptional of which we hear in the very last bars of one of the most remarkable *Wunderhorn* songs of all, 'Der Schildwache Nachtlied', that ghostly ballad that at its very end fades with a ravishing poignancy into nothingness, much as the spectre of Hamlet's father fades with the coming of the dawn. Mahler accomplishes his stunning effect of fading into oblivion by leaving his song – and his performers and his audience – suspended on the unresolved dominant. It is a most extraordinary moment, and a bold technique to deploy in the early 1890s.

Ernst Decsey tried once, in a conversation with Mahler, to draw the composer out on this very passage: 'I made particular reference to one or two finer points of harmony and commented that at the end of "Der Schildwache Nachtlied" there was a remarkable evolution of the dominant chords that produced an ever-rising tension ...' But Mahler it seems 'refused to accept the point': 'Oh, go on! Just

6   Ibid., pp. 58–9.

---

*   See the quotation from Natalie Bauer-Lechner's 1893 report opposite.

accept things with the simplicity with which they're intended!'[7]

A wholly typical composer's response, intent, one might think, on protecting his 'hidden treasure' from the pedantic 'analysis' of critics. But we are free to recognize the innovative nature of Mahler's inspiration. 'Simple' it may be, in the effect it makes. But it is a simplicity that strikes deep, the kind of simplicity that only genius has at its command. And in any case, who had ever thought of doing anything like it before?[8]

'Der Schildwache Nachtlied', composed in Hamburg in 1892, is a dialogue between a lonely sentry on duty and his consoling girlfriend. For a start, the ambiguity of the song is a pronounced feature of it. Where does all the action happen – it constitutes in fact a miniature drama – and what is it that actually happens? Is the sentry recollecting in his imagination his lover's warmth and promises of reunion? Or does he overhear her song? There are two quite distinct types of music systematically involved, of a military character for the sentry, a seductive, slow ländler for the girl. Naturally enough, Mahler allots to each a quite differently assembled orchestra. After the second exchange between the two characters, in which there is reference specifically to the battlefield, the song embarks on a powerful military march proper, first heard at a distance and approaching ever nearer until the procession is commanded to halt, presumably by the sentry. We have reached the climax of the march, which then begins a diminuendo to which the band exits. We all know of Mahler's fascination with the acoustic events of the streets – music coming and going – and how altogether typical it is that even within the frame of a *Wunderhorn* song we experience the advance and retreat of a military band, created by Mahler's meticulous array of dynamics, the dynamics of departure.

But what is the sentry's fate? Has he been killed on duty, a victim of war? When the ländler returns, it is not the voice of his lover we hear but that of a third party, asking 'What song was here? Who sang just now?' And to those questions we receive no answer. The

---

7   See Norman Lebrecht, *Mahler Remembered*. Decsey's recollections were published in *Die Musik* in June and August 1911.

8   Perhaps only Smetana, in the famous lullaby from his opera, *Hubička*, which Mahler knew well and himself conducted. See 'Mahler and Smetana', pp. 537–49.

Programme of the concert on 29 January 1905

ländler loses its gentle momentum, the orchestra's textures thin out, the song is left unresolved, fading on the dominant. The rest is silence.

In a conversation with Anton Webern in 1905 Mahler said, 'After *Des Knaben Wunderhorn* I could not compose anything but Rückert – this is lyric poetry from the source, all else is lyric poetry of a derivative sort.'

By 1905 Mahler had completed his *Kindertotenlieder* and the orchestral *Rückert-Lieder*; and thenceforth, undeniably, if we are considering the interplay and interpenetration between song and symphony, it is the *Rückert-Lieder* that play the role that had formerly been played by the *Wunderhorn* songs, though the relationship now assumed new shapes, exercised new influence and – above all – opened up new formal vistas. But the completion of the Fourth Symphony, and the shift in the succeeding trinity of symphonies, Five, Six and Seven, exclusively to the orchestra (no orchestral paraphrases of songs, no vocal signposts), did not, in my view, mark the complete break with the *Wunderhorn* past that it has often been taken for. In any event there were, after the twelve orchestral *Wunderhorn* settings published in 1899, two last settings still to come, 'Revelge' and 'Der Tamboursg'sell' (1899 and 1901 respectively). About the latter song, Mahler spoke to the invaluable Bauer-Lechner – Mahler's Boswell! – in the summer of 1901:

He told me that ['Der Tamboursg'sell'] – almost as if according to a pre-established harmony between notes and words – came into being as follows. It occurred to him literally between one step and the next – that is, just as he was walking out of the dining room.

He sketched it immediately in the dark ante-room, and ran with it to the spring – his favourite place, which often gives him aural inspiration. Here, he had the music completed very quickly. But now he saw that it was no symphonic theme – such as he had been after – but a song! And he thought of 'Der Tamboursg'sell'. He tried to recall the words; they seemed made for the melody. When he in fact compared the tune and the text up in the summerhouse, not a word was missing, not a note was needed; they fitted perfectly!

He said that he felt sorry for himself that he should have to write

Friedrich Rückert (1788–1866); an etching from 1818

'Der Tamboursg'sell' and the *Kindertotenlieder*: and he felt sorry for the world that would have to hear them one day, so terribly sad was their content.[9]

These are indeed tragic, ironic, sometimes desperate songs, both of them – I use these words advisedly – towering masterpieces and each of them a march, in the case of 'Revelge' a vocal march of epic proportions. Again there is nothing quite like this elsewhere in music, nor in Mahler's vocal music. But precedents there are, of course, amply so, in the march movements of the *symphonies*; we come to realize in fact that these last two *Wunderhorn* settings reveal the reverse of the hitherto established relationship, i.e. in 'Revelge' and 'Der Tamboursg'sell' it is symphony that is now fertilizing song.

9  NB-L *Recollections*, p. 173.

The sheer scale of these songs speaks for itself, as does the high profile allotted the orchestra alone. Each song inhabits a unique sound-world, a consequence of the orchestra's transformation into something approximating to military wind bands. Percussion is prominent. The strings themselves in 'Revelge' are used as a percussive resource, while in 'Der Tamboursg'sell' only the lower strings – exclusively cellos and double-basses – are employed. The *intensity* of this music has few parallels, even elsewhere in Mahler. These final *Wunderhorn* settings remind us of one central truth about Mahler's approach to his texts. For him the poems were not artificial evocations or revivals of a lost age of chivalry and German Romanticism but, with the exception of a few genial, sunny inspirations, vivid enactments of *reality*, of sorrow, heartbreak, terror and pain. The *Wunderhorn* songs often tell an awful truth about the human condition.

There is a further refinement with which to close these thoughts on Mahler's 'hidden treasure'. While 'Revelge' and 'Der Tamboursg'sell' both crown and conclude the *Wunderhorn* settings, they also – perhaps not surprisingly, given the power of their invention – overlap with the succeeding works that are generally – and rightly – thought to relate to the Rückert lyrics: for example is the famous *Adagietto* of the Fifth not, in essence, a song without words for strings and harp in the style of the late *Rückert-Lieder*?

But the *first* movement of the Fifth, the *Trauermarsch*, is another matter altogether. We might perhaps regard it legitimately as another orchestral 'song without words', but this time it is not a Rückert lyric that is the relevant source but those last, momentous *Wunderhorn* march songs, 'Der Tamboursg'sell' especially. The symphony takes over the song's military wind band and there is a clear relation between the main melody of the second part of the song and the main tune of the symphony's opening funeral march.

The song ends with a repeated 'Gute Nacht!' from the singer. Perhaps it is not altogether fanciful to suggest that it is precisely in the first movement of the Fifth that the composer himself bade farewell to the *Wunderhorn* world he had explored over a long period with such energy and imagination and so productively. Now he was ready to explore a new world of lyric feeling and one which brought in train an entirely fresh phenomenon, the *new forms* developed in *Kindertotenlieder* which were profoundly to influence the formal build of *Das Lied von der Erde*, not to speak of the later instrumental symphonies.[10] Here was a new store of 'hidden treasure'. There was to be no end, it seems, to the fertilizing conjunction of song and symphony in Mahler's music. It was only his untimely death that imposed a last 'Gute Nacht' on his life's work, to which the *Wunderhorn* poems had made an unforgettable contribution.

10 In the 'Purgatorio' movement of the unfinished Tenth, however, some commentators have observed the influence of one of the *Wunderhorn* orchestral songs. e.g. Deryck Cooke, who suggests that we hear there 'the "treadmill" ostinato from . . . "Das irdische Leben"'. This was a song that was again the subject of a comment by Mahler: 'You can express so much more in the music than the words directly say . . . I feel that human life (in the poem to which I give the interpretative title "Das irdische Leben" ["Earthly life"] is symbolized by the child's crying for bread and the answer of the mother, consoling it with promises again and again. In life, everything that one most needs for the growth of spirit and body is withheld – as with the dead child – until it is too late. And I believe that this is characteristically and frighteningly expressed in the uncanny notes of the accompaniment, which bluster past as in a storm; in the child's anguished cry of fear, and the slow, monotonous responses of the mother – of Fate, which is in no particular hurry to satisfy our cries for bread.' NBL *Recollections*, p. 32.

# Lieder eines fahrenden Gesellen

## ～1995～

If one were looking for just *one* feature that united all three of Mahler's orchestral song-cycles, one would not go far wrong in coming up with the *narrative* idea, i.e. the concept of a cycle that is something more than a sequence, however carefully ordered that might be. In Mahler's hands the sequence became a narrative, beginning at one point, ending at quite another; and in between, a wide area of experience has been traversed by the supposed protagonist of all three cycles. It is of course the singer or, in the case of *Das Lied von der Erde*, singers who impersonate the various roles that Mahler entrusts to them, though by the time he was composing *Das Lied* he had left far behind him the narrative simplicity of the *Gesellen* songs: what we encounter in his last song-cycle is something much more complex than the relatively straightforward history of a single, simple hero and his frustrated passion (the *Gesellen* songs were inspired by Mahler's own highly charged feelings – they must have been! – for a singer at the opera at Kassel, Johanna Richter).

In *Das Lied,* we have a number of roles that the singers impersonate, while, in addition, the composer himself emerges – in the finale, 'Der Abschied', in particular – as protagonist-in-chief, summing up, transforming and finally transcending all the varied kinds of experience that the five previous songs (or movements, better) had explored; and it is *Das Lied*, by the way, that provides us with a classic example of ending up somewhere quite different from where we started out at the beginning.

More of that later. For the moment, let us stay with the *narrative* idea, which, as I think is incontrovertible, was fundamental not only to the song-cycles but also to the symphonies. Indeed, one of the most fascinating aspects of Mahler's oeuvre as a whole is the

---

First published in GMWL, pp. 2.120–23.

relationship between the song-cycles and the symphonies, or, as I prefer to describe it, the overlapping between a song-cycle and the surrounding (or in the case of the *Gesellen* cycle, ensuing) symphony. Of special importance in this regard is the influence the later song-cycles had on the form of the later symphonies; here, once again, *Das Lied* is a *locus classicus*, the song-cycle that is a symphony, or, if you prefer, the symphony that is a song-cycle. The use of either term requires no adjustment in one's thinking. Above all, as we shall see, what was, from the outset, a leading characteristic of the narrative idea – i.e. *not* ending up where one started – was developed by Mahler across his symphonies; from first to last, into the concept of the 'frame', where the finale not only lands us up somewhere else but also resolves, brings to a conclusion, what the first movement had, so to say, left unfinished in terms of narrative; and to the completion of the narrative Mahler added a further dimension, the resolution of a conflict, a drama, outlined in the first movement (or first song in the case of the song-cycles) while the denouement is kept for the last. The tension between these two poles provides the thread of continuity throughout the often varied intervening middle movements and songs.

It is clear already, that no sooner does one start thinking about the song-cycles than Mahler's symphonies become an integral part of the discussion; and there could hardly be a clearer case of this fundamental relationship than that between the first cycle, the *Gesellen* songs, and the First Symphony. Indeed, the first movement of the symphony is built out of the cycle's second song, 'Ging heut' morgen über's Feld', while the symphony's own parody funeral march, its third movement, quotes substantially from the cycle's fourth and last song, also a march, itself a funeral march of a kind – certainly the broken-hearted hero of the cycle buries his hopes beneath the linden tree, if not himself. It is of some significance that this particular passage derives from an earlier work, *Das klagende Lied*, where in that tale of fratricide, the younger knight sinks to rest beneath a willow tree, only to be slain by his elder and jealous brother. The equation sleep = oblivion = death is surely very telling when one hears the quotation in the last of the *Gesellen* songs and recalls its anticipation in the early cantata.

Inevitably, the *Gesellen* cycle does not at this early stage in Mahler's creative life display every feature that I have touched on in my preliminary remarks. But one basic feature is there: our hero starts from and finishes at tonal levels that are emphatically distinct. His point of departure at the beginning of Song 1 is D minor; he makes his exit in Song 4 in F minor.

In between, he 'travels', tonally, i.e. Song 1 concludes in G minor, which functions as an upbeat to the opening D of Song 2, which in turn closes on F sharp. Song 3 returns us to D minor and ends in E flat minor, thus initiating a semitonal ascent which, at the beginning of Song 4, establishes E minor, while it is in F minor that the song – the funeral march – comes to rest, as I have pointed out above. Thus our hero is in a state of perpetual mobility.

The four songs cover a wide range of preponderantly slow tempi: there is really only one genuinely fast song, the agitated third song – 'Ich hab' ein glühend Messer' (one remembers that it is with a sword that the younger brother is dispatched in *Das klagende Lied*) – which Mahler marks '*stürmisch, wild*', and only one extended stretch of a moderate tempo, i.e. the first three stanzas of the second song, 'Ging heut' morgens übers Feld'. The tempi indeed reflect the generally unhappy narrative that the *Gesellen* cycle unfolds, one of continually disappointed, frustrated love.

This results in fact in one of the cycle's singular features. Not one of the songs provides relief. There are glimpses of happiness vouchsafed by Nature, birdsong, especially in the brief E flat middle part of the first song, for example, or the vision of a beautiful, pastoral world in which the hero exults in the second song. But the first song returns to the compact motif of sorrow with which it opens – a motif that itself compulsively returns to the pitch with which it begins (an image of the lover trapped within his grief) – while the second, in a slow concluding section (F sharp) of the greatest poignancy, suggests that the preceding, ecstatic vision of Nature is all illusion:

> Nun fängt auch mein Glück wohl an?
> Nein! Nein! Das ich mein',
> mir nimmer, nimmer blühen kann!

> *Will my joy now flower too?*
> *No, no; well I know*
> *'twill never, never bloom again.*

– it is thus that the vision fades.

Likewise, the third song. There is a momentary respite from the reiterated cry of pain, a falling (sobbing) semitone, 'O weh! O weh!' ('Woe is me! Woe is me!'), in the middle part – 'Wenn ich in den Himmel seh'' ('When I look into the sky') (a vestigial C major, and distant, muted horn calls) – but after a few bars, the torrent of grief returns until it expires in a fragmented, scurrying *pianissimo* coda, the texture and instrumentation of which anticipate a desperate music that we encounter in the later symphonies, a case of late Mahler making an early appearance.

The stroke on the tam-tam that ends this song – virtually a scherzo for voice and orchestra – is still ringing in our ears as the fourth song opens, the march, the funeral march, as it must be. (The last bars of the preceding scherzo, by the way, are the only spot where Mahler uses the tam-tam; one cannot but look ahead to *Das Lied* and the strokes on the tam-tam that initiate 'Der Abschied'. The single resonating stroke here in the *Gesellen* cycle, as I suggest, provides a kind of sonorous symbolic upbeat to the song, 'Die zwei blauen Augen', that is also a kind of early 'Abschied', a farewell to life and love.)

A typical Mahlerian march of this period the song turns out to be, the first indeed of the whole procession of marches that marches its way through Mahler's works from beginning to end.

We hear the march song twice, first in E minor, then in an unstable C major/minor ('Ich bin ausgegangen in stiller Nacht' ('I went out at the dead of night')), then a modulation to F (harp prominent) and a visionary closing episode, 'Auf der Strasse stand ein Lindenbaum' ('By the wayside stands a linden tree'), in which the hero, we must suppose, finds final rest and ultimate peace beneath the linden tree. The march here – though its rhythm is never abandoned – is transformed into something altogether gentler and calmer, a change of character reflected in the instrumentation, which departs from the regimental windband model

that is close to the surface in the setting of the first two stanzas. And
yet, with that characteristic insistence that 'truth' rather than con-
solatory 'art' should have the last word, in the final three bars the
wind-band image returns and rounds off the F major transformation with a restatement of the basic march rhythm in an unequivocal F *minor*, thus discharging to the full Mahler's own direction
that the song should be interpreted '*ohne Sentimentalität*'.

Thus ends Mahler's first orchestral song-cycle, with a lyric
funeral march. One does not, of course, want to exaggerate the
point; and certainly there is something undeniably Wertheresque
about Mahler's hero, who wears his (broken) heart on his sleeve
without remission. None the less, it remains true that, the Sixth
Symphony apart, the *Gesellen* cycle is the most consistently pessimistic of Mahler's works, without one song that frees itself of
sorrow. It is salutary to remind ourselves how often in symphonies
and songs to come he was to celebrate joy and happiness. Furthermore, in his First Symphony he was able, so to speak, to give the
story of his hero a new slant. To be sure, the symphony has a funeral
march which incorporates a recollection of that ultimate peace our
hero finds beneath his linden tree in the *Gesellen* songs. But in the
ensuing finale of the symphony the hero is marvellously resurrected
and re-emerges, alive and kicking, and though still suffering the
pangs of frustrated love, rides to triumph in a blaze of D major as
the symphony ends. (Our hero was to be buried again in the first
movement of the Second and resurrected yet again, but this time
on a monumental scale, in the symphony's finale.)

As I have remarked, the *Gesellen* cycle reveals some of the basic
patterns and modes of thinking common to all Mahler's symphonies and song-cycles, while also revealing its own singularities.
But one important structural device it does not fully reveal: the
concept of the framing outer movements. The *Gesellen* songs of
course have their own unique shape, one determined however by
the unfolding of the poetic images and events rather than by formal
demands and obligations. The frame is there, very much so, in the
First Symphony; and thenceforth was to be virtually a permanent
feature of song-cycle and symphony alike. When Benjamin Britten,
still a student, heard the *Gesellen* songs in 1931 in London, he wrote

Gratis.

Concert-Direction
HERMANN WOLFF.

Montag, den 16. März 1896

Abends 7¹/₂ Uhr:

Im Saal der Philharmonie

# II. ORCHESTER-CONCERT

·von·

# Gustav Mahler

unter Mitwirkung des Herrn

## Anton Sistermans

sowie des Philharmonischen Orchesters.

## PROGRAMM

1. „Todtenfeier" (I. Satz aus der Symphonie in C-moll für grosses Orchester.)
2. Lieder eines fahrenden Gesellen, für eine tiefe Stimme mit Orchesterbegleitung, gesungen von Herrn *Anton Sistermans.*
3. Symphonie in D-dur für grosses Orchester.
   No. 1. Einleitung und Allegro commodo.
   No. 2. Scherzo.
   No. 3. Alla Marcia funebre; hierauf sogleich
   No. 4. Allegro furioso.

*Sämmtliche Compositionen sind vom Concertgeber.*

**Während der Vorträge bleiben die Saalthüren geschlossen**

Eintritts-Karten: Saal 3 und 2 Mk., Stehplatz 1 Mk., Loge 4 Mk.
sind in der Königlichen Hofmusikhandlung von ED. BOTE & G. BOCK, Leipziger Strasse 37.
und Abends an der Kasse zu haben.

**Gesangs-Texte umstehend.**

The poster for the concert on 16 March 1896, with the *Lieder eines fahrenden Gesellen* juxtaposed with the First Symphony and the *Todtenfeier*

in his diary, 'Lovely little pieces, exquisitely scored – a lesson to all the Strausses and Elgars in the world' (and a lesson Britten himself was quick to learn, one might add); and indeed the instrumentation of the cycle is of a clarity and refinement that anticipate the chamber-musical textures of *Kindertotenlieder* and *Das Lied*. The largest orchestra Mahler deploys in the *Gesellen* cycle is heard only in the tumultuous third song; the first song uses virtually a chamber orchestra, while the last excludes the brass entirely, but for the most sparing use of three of the four horns in sixteen bars only, four of those for horn solo!

There is no doubt that from the outset Mahler envisaged the *Gesellen* cycle as an orchestral song-cycle – so much is clear from the title-page of the earliest manuscript of the work known to us, for voice and piano. It seems probable, however, that Mahler did not get down to orchestrating the work until there was a possibility of a premiere for the cycle in its orchestral guise of some importance. Perhaps the cycle may have had a performance in its voice-and-piano version before 1896, but if there were one, we have no record of it; which leaves 1896 as the year in which the cycle made its first appearance in orchestral guise, when Mahler himself conducted the work in Berlin on 16 March 1896: the other work on the programme was his own First Symphony, a fascinating juxtaposition of two works so intimately related. It was for this occasion, I believe, that Mahler at last brought to fruition the orchestration of the *Gesellen* cycle which had always been his creative intention, helped, no doubt, by the experience he had now had of working on the orchestration of the symphony which itself had undergone many vicissitudes.

# Symphony No. 1:
## 'The most spontaneous and daringly composed of my works'

### ∿ 1996 ∿

In April 1896, when Mahler conducted performances of his First Symphony and the *Gesellen* song-cycle in the same programme in Berlin, he remarked to his confidante Natalie Bauer-Lechner: 'People have not yet accepted my language. They have no notion of what I am saying or what I mean, and so it all seems senseless and unintelligible to them. Even the musicians who play my works hardly know what I am driving at.'

What possible relationship could there be between the symphony and the song-cycle? The bewilderment of Mahler's listeners, of his players, can be understood. Not surprisingly they missed the whole point of the exercise, which, I believe, was Mahler's intention to elucidate – illuminate – his symphony *by means of the song-cycle.* In short, the song-cycle was to function as the explanatory note that was missing from the programme.

When Mahler launched his first big work for orchestra alone in Budapest in 1889, it was not described as a symphony at all, but as a 'Symphonic Poem', in two parts and five (not four) movements. Apart from the '*A la pompes funèbres*' inscription for the slow movement, which in any case only confused the audiences at the premiere by contradicting its expectations of a dignified funeral march, there was no programme. Discouraged no doubt by the hostile reaction of his listeners, Mahler then contrived a 'scenario' by way of elucidation.

For a later performance in 1893 at Hamburg, for example, he described the first movement as '*Frühling und kein Ende*' ('Spring

Liner note for the 1996 recording of Mahler's First Symphony by Riccardo Chailly and the Royal Concertgebouw Orchestra, Decca 448–813–2.

Moritz von Schwind, *The Hunter's Funeral Procession* (1850)

without end'), while the slow introduction was a representation of Nature awakening from its winter sleep. A clue to the slow movement was provided by referring to a parodistic picture, *The Hunter's Funeral Procession*, in which 'the beasts of the forest bring the huntsman's coffin to the grave. Hares carry a small banner, with a band of Bohemian musicians in front, accompanied by music-making cats, toads, crows', etc., which 'escort the procession in comic postures.' As for the finale, Mahler tried his hand at clarification by informing his audience: 'There follows *Dall'Inferno* (*Allegro furioso*) the sudden outburst of despair from a deeply wounded heart.'

It was that same wounded heart, of course, that had been on view in the *Lieder eines fahrenden Gesellen* cycle and was on view again at the aforementioned 1896 Berlin concert, but this time in immediate juxtaposition with the complementing symphony. This, indeed, was the very moment when the former 'Symphonic Poem' nomenclature was dropped, along with the original version's second movement, an andante, thus giving a four-movement shape to the work along with the title of 'Symphony'; and yet more significantly, all the attempted programmatic explanations were abandoned. All that was left was *Alla Marcia funebre* for the third movement, and even that inscription did not survive to reach the first published edition (1899) of the now four-movement Symphony No. 1 in D.

Hearing the first movement of the symphony after hearing the *Gesellen* cycle's second song, 'Ging heut' morgen über's Feld', might well have prompted the listener to some interesting and clarifying reflections. In both cases, we hear Mahler's hero setting off on his travels, striding across the fields in luminous spring sunlight. Same hero; same 'travelling' music. However, while the cycle's second song soon loses its exuberance and ends in poignant recollection of lost happiness (thus anticipating the consequences of unrequited love, of which the concluding song, itself a funeral march, is an unmistakable image), in the symphony the narrative goes differently. The first movement reaches quite another and optimistic conclusion, asserting the D major that will eventually prove to be the symphony's final tonal goal: the hero, so far at least, lives to fight another day.

It is entirely logical then that the quasi-funeral march that ends the song-cycle should resurface in the symphony's own *Todtenmarsch* (as Mahler described it at one stage). The implication of the haunting last song of the cycle, 'Die zwei blauen Augen von meinem Schatz', is, surely, that the hero has succumbed to his broken heart and lain down to rest beneath a lime tree. Mahler, we may feel, goes out of his way to emphasize this chilly, albeit romantic, denouement, by quoting the last stanza of the song and, most significantly, those dotted (march) rhythm chords in the woodwind, in an implacable, unyielding *minor* (G minor in the symphony, F minor in the song-cycle). It is as if in the new context of the symphony's slow movement, a Proustian reclamation of the past temporarily overwhelms our hero: he recalls the end of a consuming passion which must, at the time, have seemed like the end of life itself. Hence the delicate, fragile and nostalgic resurrection of the concluding song in the symphony's slow movement, of which it forms the contrasting middle part, a kind of trio, wearing very much its own orchestral guise – harp, strings, slow woodwind (as in the song-cycle) – quite distinct from the orchestra that surrounds it.

What surrounds it, in fact, is another funeral march, the famous (to some ears, infamous) parody funeral march, based, it must have seemed incomprehensibly so to its first audience, on the old nursery round 'Bruder Martin' ('Frère Jacques'), which Mahler converted into a dirge – he had always, he said, thought of it, even as a child, as 'profoundly tragic', not cheerful or humorous. In fact, what we encounter in this movement is not one funeral march but two, and the march that frames our hero's infinitely regretful look

Cover of the first edition of Mahler's Symphony No. 1 (1898)

back to the ashes of a disappointed love represents some of the most original, provocative, prophetic and calculatedly bizarre music Mahler was ever to unleash. Small wonder that his early audiences and players were disconcerted by it.

After the shock of the parody funeral march, a further and immediate shock was in store for audiences: a triple *forte* on the cymbal − struck with wooden drumsticks − and then a piercing dissonance − 'a horrifying scream', as Mahler described it, which initiates an outburst of stormy, agitated, despairing F minor music. The audience at the Budapest premiere was duly scandalized; it was reliably reported, indeed, that the cymbal crash caused one lady to add to the clatter by dropping her handbag.

The finale, however, for all the unconstrained violence of its rhetoric, is brilliantly organized, while at the same time making the impression of an exceptional freedom of form and feeling. What went unrecognized by the work's first audiences was the link with the first movement and its prophetic development section. It is precisely at the point when the development of the first movement anticipates the finale that the music significantly asserts F minor, the very tonality that is to emerge so powerfully in the finale, to be overcome, eventually, but only after prolonged struggle and conflict, by a D major that carries all before it. F minor it was in which Mahler, in three unforgettable bars, brings the funeral-march song − and the entire *Gesellen* cycle − to an end.

How the music has spoken to us determines how we 'read' that cold unmitigated F minor: does the hero dream − or die? What is certain, however, is that for Mahler it was a tonality symbolic of his hero's unhappy end, his tragic fate. Hence the re-emergence of F minor in the finale of the symphony and the important dramatic role allotted to it.

Yet more fascinating, what Mahler himself is recorded as having said about the finale confirms, I believe, the association of F minor and death, no less:

> A horrifying scream opens the final movement, in which we now see our hero altogether abandoned, with all the sorrows of this world, to the most terrible of battles. Again and again he gets

knocked on the head ... by Fate whenever he appears to pull himself out of it and become its master. Only in *death* [my italics] after he has overcome himself (and the wonderful reminiscence of his earliest youth [another Proust-like recovery of the past?] has brought back with it the themes of the first movement) does he achieve the victory (magnificent victory chorale!).

The 'victory chorale' materializes, along with the final, irresistible affirmation of D, as an exultant transformation of the very opening bars of the symphony, in which the slow sequence of falling fourths first appears in the woodwind. Thus the slow introduction to the first movement and the chorale in the last satisfyingly bind together the entire work in logical evolution, uniting the work's beginning and its end, a triumphant end, but in the light of Mahler's own words, not altogether free of ambiguity. Perhaps it is only in the ensuing Second Symphony, where the narrative of the preceding symphony is *resumed,* and specifically in the Resurrection celebrated in its choral finale, that Mahler's hero achieves the ultimate transcendence of death that may have eluded him in the First.

# Mahler's Hungarian Glissando

## ↝ 1991 ↝

When I was in Budapest at the end of last year I passed by the splendid Vigado, facing the Promenade along which residents and tourists stroll to enjoy a magnificent view of Buda, across the Danube.

The Vigado was built between 1859 and 1864 in what the guide-books tell us was a 'Hungarian Romantic style'; and it was there, in the concert hall (Redoutensaal) that Mahler's First Symphony was first performed on 20 November 1889, the composer conducting. At the time, Mahler was Director of the Royal Budapest Opera, a post to which he had been appointed a year earlier, in a country which, he exclaimed, 'will probably become my new homeland!'

Naturally enough, as I sauntered along, the symphony began to unroll in my mind like some accompanying soundtrack. More particularly, and perhaps stimulated by the overt attempt at something specifically Hungarian by the architect of the Vigado, Frigyes Feszl, a few bars from the slow movement insistently returned, demanding my attention.

The bars that haunted me were bars 58 and 59 of the slow movement, the famous funeral march – *A la pompes funèbres,* as it was first described in the 1889 programme. I reproduce the bars overleaf; it which it is easy to recognize the brief but arresting event they embody: in particular, a glissando for the strings which the composer clearly intended us not to miss.

The exaggerated dynamics, which accelerate from **pp** to **ff** and back to **p** again – the dynamic high point coinciding with the peak of the glissando – and the very intervention of the strings

Programme note written for a London performance of the First Symphony by the Vienna Philharmonic Orchestra under Claudio Abbado scheduled for 18 February 1991 but cancelled due to the First Gulf War; first published in DMCN, pp. 175–80. It appears here in a significantly revised form.

(reinforced by a pair of flutes) in a primarily wind-and-percussion-band texture indicate the emphatic articulation of these bars that Mahler wanted to secure:

I soon came to realize precisely why it was that it was this glissando that had invaded my inner ear as I dawdled along the Promenade. It was, of course, because – like all visitors to Budapest and at the receiving end of Hungarian hospitality – I had been serenaded by any number of gypsy ensembles, of varying degrees of authenticity, to be sure. But common to all of them when fiddlers were present was the ubiquitous – ascending or descending, but always swooning – glissando. Small wonder that it was Mahler's glissando that came to mind as I sauntered.

It further occurred to me that it was more than probable that this, as I was now beginning to hear it, specifically 'Hungarian' dimension of the funeral march was part of Mahler's compositional tactics. Here was a reference that the locals, so to say, might have expected to welcome as representing the familiar and entertaining; but it was a reference, an image, that proved to have such a sharp cutting edge that any pleasure of recognition must have given way to the pain of expectations incomprehensibly reversed. This was gypsy music with a vicious bite, an acid tongue.

This contradiction of expectations seems to me to be the *raison d'être* of the funeral march from its very outset. What, I wonder, had the audience expected of this movement at the Budapest premiere? Something along the lines of Beethoven, or Wagner, or Chopin in funereal mood? It was a shock for them, then, to encounter two bars of drum taps and then the strange, strangulated voice of a muted solo double-bass, singing as best it can an old nursery tune, 'Bruder Martin' (or 'Frère Jacques'), in the minor. What sort of funeral march was this? Moreover, this initial shock, the first section, was to be followed by another. As the march dies away, a pair of oboes introduces the popular tune that leads into the section that Mahler himself marks '*mit Parodie*' – an injunction to treat this passage in a parodistic manner. It is, I think, the first time this particular command found its way into one of Mahler's scores; and it is certainly the first time, on this sort of scale, that the caustic, sceptical, sarcastic and ironic Mahler emerges, as it were, in top gear.

The more I thought about it that sunny afternoon, the more intrigued I became by the thought that this first substantial manifestation of what we all know now to be a major feature of Mahler's capacity to disturb, to unsettle, his audiences we owe to the character of the musical culture that surrounded him. We cannot be absolutely sure of course that the gypsy glissando was not lodged in Mahler's inner ear pre-Budapest. After all, this was the time of the Austro-Hungarian Empire and the cultures of Vienna and Budapest were in some musical respects virtually interchangeable: there was nothing strange about gypsy music to the Viennese (think of Brahms). But Mahler, before Budapest, had been in Kassel, Prague and Leipzig; and it seems more than likely to me that the gypsy element in the First Symphony's funeral march was part of the furnishing of Mahler's musical mind that can be attributed more specifically to the influence of the musical culture amid which he himself evolved as a composer, where, I dare say, he had been a recipient of the compulsory gypsy experience that greets all visitors to the country, now as then; and in a typically ironic manner he used this music to criticize itself, placing it in a grotesque context – a funeral march – that was itself grotesquely conceived.

It is not surprising that it was precisely with this movement that the first audience in Budapest began to lose contact and perhaps its collective temper with the symphony. The first half of the symphony, which in 1889 was in five movements and entitled 'Symphonic Poem', had been moderately well received. The extraordinary slow introduction and ensuing first movement were certainly full of novel sounds; with hindsight we can hear just how many Mahlerian characteristics and formal features were adumbrated there, in profusion. Eyebrows may have been raised here and there but there was nothing to give actual offence or arouse hostility. There followed a sentimental andante, the so-called *Blumine* movement, later to be discarded (and properly so), and the scherzo (ländler), the most traditionally imagined movement in the whole work.

Everything changed, however, with the onset of the funeral march, as was Mahler's intention, I have no doubt. The opening 'Bruder Martin' idea was affront enough; but what followed was an insult: the parody of a domestic and 'national' music hit a target that was altogether too close to home. Mahler himself claimed that after the Budapest premiere, 'My friends avoided me in terror. Not a single one of them dared to speak to me about the work or its

Mahler's First Symphony caricatured in the magazine *Bolond Istók*, 24 November 1889: Hans Koessler, Professor at the Academy of Music, beats the drum of publicity; Ödön von Mihalovich tweaks a cat's tail, while Mahler himself, conducting, blows into a giant instrument, the 'Malheur Syphon' – a pun on 'Mahler Symphony'. (The Hungarian caption 'Hatás' means 'effect'.)

performance, and I wandered about like someone sick or outlawed.'[1]

In fact, Mahler had his friends and admirers in Budapest; rightly so, because he had, as Director of the Opera, identified himself with Hungarian national aspirations – 'my new homeland!' – to the serious and significant extent of his requiring that Wagner's operas should be sung no longer in German but in Hungarian. But respect for a nation's language was one thing. Respect for its café society and a café music masquerading as an exotic nationalism was altogether another; it is surely easy to understand why Mahler

---

1   HLG *Mahler*, vol. 1, p. 207. See also the authoritative French text, HLG *Mahler CV*, vol. 1.

chose to mock it in his funeral march. Was he not to turn his sceptical attention to the Viennese waltz in later symphonies?

The most – perhaps the only – intelligent review of the First Symphony's premiere was contributed to the *Pester Lloyd* on 21 November 1889 by August Beer, who did not fail to note the parodistic tone of the funeral march, both of its first section, the 'Bruder Martin' canon, and of its second, where the performers, he observed, kept to '*the Hungarian manner*' (my emphasis), with the parodistic intent of the composer revealed 'in the ironic accents of the violins'.[2]

Here, then, was one pair of ears that had received the full import and impact of Mahler's Hungarian glissando and survived the ordeal. The majority of the audience, one may surmise, was not so receptive. (There was even some booing when the finale was over.) Their views were probably summarized by another critic present at the first performance: 'The fourth movement . . . which includes a pitiful theme in canon in a very inadequate manner only to alternate it with one that is *offensively trivial* [my emphasis], is a complete disaster. The music is not humorous, only ridiculous.'[3] A different response to Beer's; but one that again vividly confirmed that Mahler's unsettling parody had achieved its object. It was a weapon, a strategy, that he was to refine and sharpen and use time and time again in the future. His Hungarian glissando was a warning of what was to come.

2    See DMWY, pp. 150–54, for the complete text of this review together with a facsimile of
     the original publication. [MC]
3    HLG *Mahler*, vol. 1, p. 205.

# Mahler's Second Symphony: His Epic Journey from Death to Afterlife

## ⌁ 2002 ⌁

It has become virtually a cliché to talk about Mahler's preoccupation with life and death, yet for all that, the observation remains true and illuminating of the music. Clearly these matters were fundamental to the sources of his creativity and inspiration.

What is odd, however, is something that has perhaps been less often remarked upon. His embarking, that is, upon the epic confrontation with mortality that is the Second Symphony at such an early stage in the chronology of his compositional life. When one thinks of the monumental scale of the symphony and the breathtaking range of its eschatological topics – no less than death, the afterlife and resurrection – and the likewise breath-taking range of its invention embracing a huge array of diverse forms, textures and kinds of music, some of which had certainly not been heard before in the traditional symphony, one is left wondering at the phenomenal boldness of Mahler's conception.

It is worth thinking for a moment about the works that preceded the Second Symphony: the cantata, *Das klagende Lied*; the *Lieder eines fahrenden Gesellen*; the highly influential *Wunderhorn* songs and, of course, the First Symphony. But without the hindsight we enjoy today – what the evolution of Mahler's own music has come to teach us about its origins, its development and innovations – it would, I suggest, even in the light of the First Symphony, have been impossible to predict what, finally, took shape as the Second. This head-on confrontation with mortality, the breadth of the vision, the sheer inclusiveness of the musical materials – all of this would have

First published as a liner note for the 2002 recording of Mahler's Symphony No. 2 performed by Melanie Diener (soprano), Petra Lang (alto), the Prague Philharmonic Choir and the Royal Concertgebouw Orchestra conducted by Riccardo Chailly, Decca 470–283–2.

been less astonishing if it had been attempted or achieved by a composer at a relatively late stage in his maturity. But not a bit of it. Mahler was still only in his late twenties when, in 1888, he set down his first thoughts for the great funeral march (for convenience this is how I refer to the movement) with which the symphony opens. Some years, however, were to pass before the eventual goal of the symphony was first clarified and then attained.

The story of the long period that ensued between the beginning of the symphony's composition and its end is too complex to spell out in detail here. I shall mention only those points that throw specific light on the work itself. For a start, it remains remarkable that Mahler began work on the first movement almost immediately after completing the First Symphony. Indeed, he might even have begun work before he was done with the First. Either way, there was scarcely a pause for breath. The funeral march, in fact, was none other than a continuation of the narrative unfolded in the First. Mahler made this perfectly clear in a letter he wrote to a friend, Max Marschalk, in 1896: 'It may interest you to know that it is the hero of my D major symphony that I bear to his grave, and whose life I reflect, from a higher vantage point, in a clear mirror.' In this same letter he also writes, 'I called the first movement *Todtenfeier* ["Rites of death"].' To the significance of this title I shall return. More important, I believe, was what he inscribed on the title page of his manuscript, which shows that what he had in mind was the composition of a 'Symphony in C minor', clear evidence of his intention and indeed ambition to write, as it were, a symphony proper.

It is vital for us to remember that at this time what we know today as the four-movement First Symphony was still in its original format of a five-movement 'Symphonic Poem in Two Parts'. I have no doubt that part of Mahler's initial ambition in conceiving the Second was to demonstrate that he had turned his back on 'programme music', a *genre* – and above all a mode of *thinking* about music – that was to arouse his vehement suspicion. Hence the grand, Brucknerian scale of the Second's first movement and yet more significantly its overtly 'classical' form, its allegiance to the great tradition of the symphony. If, in a sense, this movement looks back to the past, it also, even more compellingly, anticipates

Mahler's own future and in particular his preoccupation, often in his first movements, with sonata form. The regular scheme of that long-established form is clearly to be discerned in the funeral march. We have an exposition and an extensive development; and then after the high point of the development, an overpowering moment of recapitulation. There are, of course, endless subtle ways in which Mahler modifies his classical model; but a sonata movement it explicitly remains, and in so doing foreshadows the constant presence of sonata form in a high proportion of the first movements of the ensuing symphonies, in the Fourth, Sixth and Seventh, for instance.

The completion of the funeral march, however, was followed by what, in the story of Mahler's creative life, was a unique period of creative paralysis. He sketched out the first few bars of the *Andante moderato* that was to become the second movement, but the rest was a kind of restless silence sustained while Mahler, somewhat despairingly by some accounts, tried to work out how he might find a resolution. From 1888 to 1893, in fact, the incredible narrative thrust that had carried him through from the first note of the First Symphony to the last of the funeral march of the Second seems to have encountered a block. To this day, we still can only guess at possible or probable reasons. There were, as Edward R. Reilly has listed in his outstanding essay on the symphony,* family sorrows to be managed (the haunting presence of death close at hand), the development of his burgeoning career as conductor and opera-house administrator, his own health, the critical reception given his First Symphony in Budapest. Whatever the reasons, it was an unprecedented hiatus of *five years* – this was never to happen again in Mahler's life – before the great narrative of death and life was resumed.

At some stage in this strange and prolonged interim, the manuscript of the first movement had acquired a fresh title, *Todtenfeier*; and Mahler deleted the inscription 'Symphony in C minor'. Some have thought that this amendment was a kind of retrospective bestowal of independent symphonic poem status on the funeral march. But I doubt that. Was it perhaps the consequence of his not

---

* '*Todtenfeier* and the Second Symphony', DMANMC, pp. 84–125.

knowing for so long how to proceed and finding himself with a massive stretch of music on his hands? In any event, what is of much greater musical interest and significance was Mahler's use of the title when in Berlin in 1896 he opened a programme he conducted there with *Todtenfeier* and closed it with the First Symphony, thus demonstrating (at least to those in the know) the narrative link between the two works I have spelled out above. He was careful however to make clear that *Todtenfeier* was the first movement of the Symphony in C minor that had now been completed and performed in its entirety in Berlin the year before.

How was it then that the symphony came to be finished? Ironically enough it was, I believe, by Mahler's recourse to a mode of narrative – to a 'programme' – about which he was to be so scathing, so totally rejectionist, in attitude, in his final years. But in the end it was the 'programme' that saved the day. Even odder, it was Mahler himself who was to provide a highly detailed and colourful account of the symphony for a performance in Dresden in 1901 (and one observation from which I shall quote). But, one need hardly add, the 'programme' turned out to be a wholly unique Mahlerian narrative, unlike anything we find elsewhere in his oeuvre.

He rose at last to the challenge posed by the funeral march by completing his symphony, every succeeding note of it, as if seen – heard, that is – through the prism of death. The sequence of middle movements, for example, do not return us to the real world but to retrospective 'episodes from the life of the fallen hero'. They have to be imagined, I suggest – and this is of importance to the symphony's interpreters – as fleeting, fading recollections before death wipes the hero's slate of memory clean.

The andante, the second movement (Mahler had sketched out some thirty-eight bars in 1888), he described for Dresden as a 'happy moment' from the life of his hero, but one too that included 'a sad recollection of his youth and lost innocence'; Mahler was clearly referring here to the more agitated sections that alternate with the idyllic ländler. The third movement, the scherzo, introduces us to a fresh source of inspiration, Mahler's later settings of texts from *Des Knaben Wunderhorn*, which proved to be one of the principal means by which he made a breakthrough in his composing block. In July

1893 he had written 'Des Antonius von Padua Fischpredigt' which was almost immediately conscripted, less the voice, in an enormously expanded version, for service as the symphony's scherzo. Once again, Mahler's own words (this time remembered by Natalie Bauer-Lechner) are gripping in their imagery and immediacy:

> You must imagine that to one who has lost his identity and true happiness, the world looks like this – distorted and crazy, as if reflected in a concave mirror. The scherzo ends with the appalling shriek of this tortured soul.

And to these two 'episodes' was added yet another *Wunderhorn* setting, 'Urlicht', again composed in July – and once more Mahler found that he had unwittingly composed (for voice and what is virtually a *chamber* orchestra) a rapt, slow-moving song that functions as signpost to the symphony's eventual resolution.

Thus it was that Mahler's specific *Wunderhorn* activities in the summer of 1893 helped him build the bridge to the concluding stage of the narrative: the finale. There was to be no more retrospection of life as it had been lived but instead an unprecedented depiction of *after*life and in particular the moments of Judgement and Resurrection. There seems no reason why I should attempt a description of this fantastic finale, when Mahler himself, again in conversation with Bauer-Lechner, left us an account of the day of the Last Judgement that speaks to us with all the power of his musical imagination:

> The earth trembles. Just listen to the drum-roll, and your hair will stand on end! The Last Trump sounds; the graves spring open, and all creation comes writhing out of the bowels of the earth, with wailing and gnashing of teeth. Now they all come marching along in a mighty procession: beggars and rich men, common folk and kings, the Church Militant (*ecclesia militans*), the Popes. All give vent to the same terror, the same lamentations and paroxysms; for none is just in the sight of God. Breaking in again and again – as if from another world – the Last Trump sounds from the Beyond. At last, after everyone has shouted and screamed in indescribable con-

fusion, nothing is heard but the long drawn-out call of the Bird of
Death above the last grave – finally that, too, fades away. There now
follows nothing of what had been expected: no Last Judgement, no
souls saved and none damned; no just man, no evil-doer, no judge!
Everything has ceased to be. And softly and simply there begins:
'Aufersteh'n, ja aufersteh'n . . .' ['Rise again, yea, rise again . . .'] –
the words themselves are sufficient commentary.*

At the end, so Bauer-Lechner tells us, Mahler cried 'I absolutely
refuse to give another syllable of explanation!' There was no need,
indeed, though one explanation that he omitted was the story of
how the very last missing bit of the jigsaw – the ultimate 'Aufersteh'n' ('Resurrection') chorale – came to light.§ In 1894, Klopstock's ode (of which Mahler was to make his own version) had
been performed as part of the funeral service (death again!) for the
famous conductor Hans von Bülow. Mahler was among those
attending the ceremony. It is strangely appropriate that it was
another ceremony of death that vouchsafed Mahler his solution. By
the end of June the finale was done. How ironic that it was in fact
a 'despised' programme that was eventually to release Mahler from
his dilemma. But while the idea of the narrative stayed with him
for evermore, to a 'programme', of quite this kind, on this scale, he
never returned.

What is even more singular about the score is this: that despite
his misgivings and scepticism it was this very programme that
inspired him to a clutch of his most audacious, most innovative,
musical ideas, all of which were so profoundly to determine the
form, content and sound of his music in subsequent decades. Think
for example of the unique processional March of 'all creation' to its
final destination, in which Mahler for the first time raises the vernacular, the language as it were of the common people, to a new
height. Vulgarity – I use the word in its classical (*vulgus*) sense – had
never before been heard so unashamedly in the realm of the symphony. (All the more amazing when the march tune, we come to

---

\*   NB-L *Recollections*, p. 44.
§   Theodor Reik has written extensively on this subject in *The Haunting Melody:
    Psychoanalytic Experiences in Life and Music*, and see also DMSSLD, pp. 165–9.

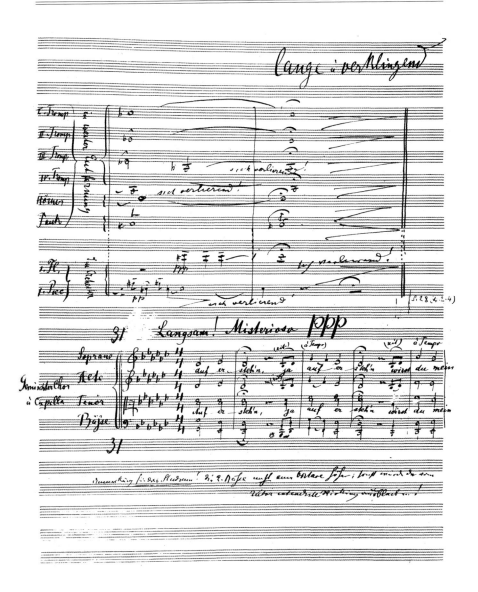

The opening of the 'Aufersteh'n, ja aufersteh'n' chorus from the final movement of the Second Symphony in Mahler's own hand

hear, has anticipated the contour of the sublime chorale that rounds off the movement.) Or there is the extraordinary passage which follows the end of the march, when a highly expressive theme, scored for its own orchestra (woodwind and strings) – we have heard it once before way back – returns and is developed this time in combination with an *offstage* ensemble of brass and percussion pursuing its own contrasting – and contrary – rhythms and fanfares.

Here Mahler is building on what he had unveiled already in principle in *Das klagende Lied*: the exploration of acoustic space. It is fitting indeed that this unique passage should eventually lead us into the extraordinary cadenza – which is what it is – for woodwind, brass and percussion, Mahler's depiction of the Last Trump; a symbolic moment certainly but also one in which the composer gathers together a variety of musics (my plural is deliberate) and launches them, onstage and offstage, in different dynamics and perspectives. Once again Mahler had brought the limitless potentialities of acoustic space into the concert hall.

Let me end more or less where I began and remark again on the feature of the Second Symphony that renders it, to my mind, without parallel. Mortality is not just what the symphony recognizes; it attempts to offer humankind an experience of it, in sound, not only death but beyond death. Death was merely Mahler's point of *departure*. This was a journey from post-cessation to and through the afterlife. How extraordinary that no sooner was the Second off his desk that Mahler started work on his Third, no less than an evolutionary history of the creation of the world. There was no stopping him, was there?

# Mahler's Third Symphony:
# His Encounter with Evolution

## ∻ 1997 ∻

When Mahler arrived on vacation at Steinbach am Attersee in the summer of 1895, he was accompanied by his faithful friend and confidante, Natalie Bauer-Lechner (1858–1921), herself a viola player and member of the Soldat-Röger (women's) string quartet; and in the years that followed – until the advent of Alma Schindler, and Mahler's subsequent marriage to her – Bauer-Lechner remained a frequent companion. More than that, she kept a diary in which she recorded her conversations with Mahler about the progress he was making on the symphonies on which he was currently engaged, and especially, as it so happens, the Third Symphony.

Mahler's Third is indeed a unique concept, but one that fulfilled precedents and parallels already adumbrated in the preceding First and Second Symphonies. However, one might argue that the Third did not itself reach its ultimate fulfilment until Mahler had incorporated 'Das himmlische Leben', at first intended to be used as the finale of the Third, into his Fourth Symphony. For this reason I provide overleaf a chronological table that will, I hope, enable those interested to see for themselves the crossovers and interrelationships that were a distinctive feature of Mahler's first four symphonies. In a very real but unusual sense, the Third was to evolve from the First and Second and then leave its mark on the Fourth. I think my table makes this clear.

One other detail. As far as possible I have included in my account of the symphony, Parts I and II, many of Mahler's own detailed comments made to Bauer-Lechner on a regular basis,

First published in the programme book for the performance of Mahler's Symphony No. 3 by the Associazione Orchestra Filarmonica della Scala, conducted by Riccardo Chailly, 12 May 1997.

CHRONOLOGY: SYMPHONIES NOS. 1–4

Symphony No. 1
in D major

[1884]/1888

For orchestra. Originally in five movements and entitled 'Symphonic Poem in two parts', and first performed as such in 1889. First performed as Symphony in D major in four movements in 1896.

Symphony No. 2
in C minor → E flat

1888–94

five movements, for soprano and contralto soloists, chorus and orchestra.

Symphony No. 3
in D minor / F → D major

1895–96

six movements, for contralto soloist, women's and children's chorus, and orchestra.

Symphony No. 4
in B minor / G major → E major

1899–1900

four movements, the last, 'Das himmlische Leben', with soprano soloist. It was Mahler's original intention to use this song as the finale of Symphony No. 3.

sometimes no doubt at the end of a day's work, sometimes while walking or bicycling together (Mahler was a keen cyclist).

Already in this summer of work on the symphony, Mahler had established the order – and titles – of the individual movements that came to comprise the symphony:

1  Der Sommer marschiert ein
   (*Summer marches in*)

2  Was mir die Blumen auf der Wiese erzählen
   (*What the flowers in the meadow tell me*)

3  Was mir die Tiere im Walde erzählen
   (*What the animals in the forest tell me*)

4  Was mir die Nacht erzählt (Der Mensch)
   (*What night tells me (Man)*)

5  Was mir die Morgenglocken erzählen (Die Engel)
   (*What the morning bells tell me (the Angels)*)

6  Was mir die Liebe erzählt
   (*What love tells me*)

Six movements in all; and indeed these are the six movements that we are familiar with. But at the time when Mahler was spelling out this list to Bauer-Lechner, there was in fact a seventh movement:

7  Was mir das Kind erzählt
   (*What the child tells me*)

And what Mahler had in mind here, it seems, at this early stage in his thinking about the overall shape of his new symphony, was the use of the already existing setting for voice and orchestra of a *Wunderhorn* poem, composed in 1892, 'Das himmlische Leben', the song in fact we all know today as the finale of the Fourth Symphony.

This intention did not only express itself as an addition to a list of the titles. On the contrary, early sketched material for the first

Mahler's handwritten list of proposed movements for the Third Symphony

movement clearly shows that it was precisely that song and its unforgettable melody that was to be the Third Symphony's long-term objective. But it was not to be. However, while the melodic anticipations in any extensive sense did not survive beyond the sketch stage, crucial motivic references to the song *do* remain in the first movement, as evidence of Mahler's original scheme, for example, the shrill repeated note motive of the clarinets, followed by a descending arpeggio, unmistakably outlines the 'himmlische Leben' melody, though it is a signpost to an event for which, as things turned out, we had to wait until the *next* symphony had been composed. However, the fifth movement, 'die Engel' ('the Angels'), as Mahler put it – see No. v in the list of titles above – was to share some of its materials with the movement that was finally diverted elsewhere.

Naturally enough, when it was a work built on such a massive scale, Mahler's concept of it changed as his composing of it progressed. It is strange but true that in fact Mahler first composed the sequence of five movements that make up Part II of his symphony *before* he composed the gigantic first movement that makes up Part I.

However, from the very start he had a pretty clear idea in his head about how the vast first movement should be planned, the character of it, and what it should contain. The idea that it should include contrast and conflict was already uppermost in his mind. This was how Mahler saw things in the summer of 1895, when he described the concept of 'Summer marching in', for which he said:

I need a regimental band to give the rough and crude effect of [Summer's] arrival. It will be just like the military band on parade. Such a mob is milling around, you never saw anything like it! Naturally, it doesn't come off without a struggle with the opponent, Winter; but he is easily dispatched, and Summer, in his strength and superior power, soon gains undisputed mastery.*

Certainly Mahler was to remain faithful to this scenario in outline, but as time and work themselves marched on, so too did his ideas develop. In particular the notion of 'Winter' evolved into something much closer in Mahler's imagination to a sound-picture of the world *before* it was animated by life. This is what he told Bauer-Lechner a year later, in the summer of 1896:

It has almost ceased to be music; it is hardly anything but sounds of Nature. It's eerie, the way life gradually breaks through, out of soulless, petrified matter. (I might equally well have called the movement 'Was mir das Felsgebirge erzählt' ['What the mountains – or mountain rocks – tell me'].) And, as this life rises from stage to stage, it takes on ever more highly developed forms: flowers, beasts, man, up to the sphere of the spirits, the 'angels'. Once again, an atmosphere of brooding summer midday heat hangs over the introduction to this movement; not a breath stirs, all life is suspended, and the sun-drenched air trembles and vibrates. At intervals there come the moans of the youth, of captive life struggling for release from the clutches of lifeless, rigid Nature. In the [march], which follows the introduction, *attacca*, he finally breaks through and triumphs.§

---

* NB-L *Recollections*, pp. 40–41.
§ Ibid., p. 59.

In fact, what we hear first, briefly but unforgettably, in this most remarkable soundscape is not 'soulless, petrified matter' but an epic unison statement (eight horns!) of the great marching song that will, eventually, carry the movement to triumph (and its conclusion in F major). But first there is the introduction proper, in D minor, music 'that has almost ceased to be music'. Mahler exaggerates; but it is certainly true that this is music without a human dimension, suggestive of the pre-history of Man.

In finding the music to match this unique vision of a world that has not yet been stirred into life, Mahler introduced all manner of innovations, above all the liberation of wind and brass, groups which play a much more important role than the strings, throughout. Indeed, it is not too much to claim that here, in this slow introduction, Mahler reverses the hitherto established balance between the wind instruments and the strings (the latter normally associated, by the way, with human preoccupations, passion, lyricism, exalted love, etc., etc.). Nothing as virtuosic for the brass, the trombones especially, had been heard in the symphony before this passage in Mahler's Third; perhaps the only exception might be Berlioz's *Symphonie fantastique*, which Mahler knew, often conducted, and enormously admired.

So much for the introduction. When the great march ensues, which forms the main body of the movement, we are once again back in touch with the vibrant marching song with which the eight horns opened the symphony. It is always a problem to find the right words or terms in which to describe music as idiosyncratic as this huge march for a very large orchestra, in which the strings now have a great deal to do. Perhaps if we respond to it as an expression of the 'Life Force' – Henri Bergson's 'élan vital', the creative urge at the heart of evolution which carries all before it – we come near to what Mahler, consciously or (more probably) unconsciously, had in mind.

But whatever conclusion we come to, what is beyond doubt – fact, not speculation – is the absolute novelty of the musical materials that Mahler incorporates, thereby expanding the very vocabulary and resources of music as a 'language'. I refer to Mahler's use of the vernacular, the 'pop' music of the day – marching songs, military signals and fanfares, the very sonorities and gestures of a regimental band on the street – in a context, the first movement of a symphony, no less, in which such 'vulgar' materials normally had no place. There had been a precedent for this in Mahler's preceding symphonies, above all in the finale of the Second where it is a regimental street band that accompanies the march of the resurrected dead, but nothing on the scale of this monumental march that completes Part 1 of the Third. If one had to single out one movement of Mahler's that changed the history of music, and more particularly the history of the symphony, the choice would have to be this first movement of the Third.

There are two last points I should like to make. First, that the triumphal march itself is by no means without interpolations of contrast and conflict. These disquieting dramatic interventions – interruptions, almost – of the momentum of the march, the last just before the movement's end, remind us that the path followed by evolution has not been without its setbacks. Second, another but very different example of Mahler's innovating techniques, this time at the end of the development section, when the march builds up to a tremendous climax. As it fades out in the tempo that has been established at the climax, a side-drum, 'placed in the distance', suddenly begins to play in the *original* tempo of the march and to continue 'without consideration' of the tempo maintained in the cellos and basses.

Thus it is that in a brief passage of not more than eleven bars, two different tempi are simultaneously combined while, at the same time, Mahler explores the acoustic phenomenon of sound that is both *close* to the auditor, the onstage lower strings, and *distant*, the intervention of the side-drummer. It is the latter who marches off, the sound fading, in the tempo in which Mahler begins his recapitulation, with – naturally enough – the eight horns thundering forth the marching song that opened the movement some 35 minutes earlier. Has a *tempo primo* ever been returned to and re-established by such an arresting and highly original means?

The first of the sequence of five movements that follows Part 1 is – most unusually – a minuet, almost, one might suggest, a minuet that deliberately looks back to a now vanished classical past. The movement provides the contrast and relaxation that are certainly

required after the exertion and monumentality of the march –
there is a parallel here, perhaps, with the ingratiating A flat ländler
that, in the Second Symphony, is juxtaposed with the enormous
opening first movement (another huge march) – not only in character of invention but in quality of sound. Mahler excelled himself
here in orchestration of an exceptional refinement. It makes all the
more impression after the exuberant din of the march.

However, there are also subtleties and sophistications, entirely
characteristic of the composer, that should not go unobserved. For
example, when the main tune returns after the contrasting and
faster alternative section, it makes its entry prematurely, in the lower
strings, while the *alternativo* is still winding – and slowing – down;
by the time the minuet proper is restored a significant segment of
the principal melody has already been recapitulated as it were
downstairs, while other things have been happening upstairs.

We have already had an example of simultaneity in the twin tempi
of the first movement; this overlapping of ends and beginnings in
the minuet is a variation of that same idea but applied to themes as
distinct from tempi. So even this charming, seemingly uncomplicated movement offers glimpses of Mahler's innovating techniques.
(By the way, the last time the minuet tune comes round, and just
to keep us on our toes, Mahler drops his overlapping method and
simply starts the tune off halfway through. You can't miss it, because
it is accompanied by an unexpected modulation to E major, which
then paves the way for the close in A major, the movement's tonic.)

Mahler himself had something to say about the minuet to
Natalie Bauer-Lechner, who wrote in her diary:

This is the movement that Mahler composed last summer [1895]
directly after his arrival at Steinbach. On the very first afternoon, as
he was gazing out of his summer-house that nestles amidst grass and
flowers in the meadow, the music came to him. He sketched it
quickly, completing the draft at one sitting.

'You can't imagine how it will sound!' [Mahler said.] 'It is the
most carefree thing that I have ever written – as carefree as only
flowers are. It all sways and waves in the air, as light and graceful as
can be, like the flowers bending on their stems in the wind. [. . .] As
you might imagine, the mood doesn't remain one of innocent,

flower-like serenity, but suddenly becomes serious and oppressive. A stormy wind blows across the meadow and shakes the leaves and blossoms, which groan and whimper on their stems, as if imploring release into a higher realm.'*

There is something of special significance, I believe, in Mahler's reference to a 'higher realm'. As we saw in his original list of movements, he entitled the minuet, 'What the flowers in the meadow tell me'; and the next movement, the third, 'What the animals in the forest tell me'; in short, it is as if we were *moving up the evolutionary ladder*, i.e. from inert matter (introduction) to Life-creating energy, to flowers, and now in the scherzo, to the life of the forest, the sounds of Nature, of birds and beasts. Here again is Mahler's own description, from the summer of 1899:

> The scherzo in particular, the animal piece, is at once the most scurrilous and most tragic that ever was – in the way that music alone can mystically take us from one extreme to the other in the twinkling of an eye. In this piece it is as if Nature herself were pulling faces and putting out her tongue. There is such a gruesome, Panic humour in it that one is more likely to be overcome by horror than laughter.§

There is a number of points that seem to me to add to our understanding and enjoyment of a movement that follows the precedent of the scherzo in the preceding Second Symphony, the 'sermon to the fish' of St Anthony of Padua. This had been a brilliant transcription and vast extension of what had originally been composed as an independent setting of a *Wunderhorn* text for voice and orchestra in 1893. In the case of the scherzo in the Third, Mahler turned to another and earlier *Wunderhorn* setting, but this time for voice and piano, composed between 1887 and 1890, 'Ablösung im Sommer'.

Like the 'fish' scherzo in the Second, this 'animal' scherzo in the Third represents a radical transformation of the song. To begin with, Mahler follows the relative simplicities of his voice and piano setting, but very soon the movement develops to incorporate all

---

\*    Ibid., p. 52.      §    Ibid. p. 129.

kinds of materials and dramatic and poetic incidents that are certainly not to be found in the original *Wunderhorn* poem that tells us
only that the song of the nightingale will remain to beguile us when
the cuckoo is silenced by death. The most important of all the new
imagery, not only for the movement itself but for the overall, evolutionary scheme of the symphony as a whole, is related to the introduction for the first time of a *human* dimension, by means of the
marvellous posthorn solo which forms the scherzo's trio, and is recollected once again before the end of the movement. This magical
sound of the postilion blowing his horn from the post-coach (shades
of the trio in the scherzo of the Fifth Symphony) comes not from
the world of animals but from the world of *human beings*.

Then, there is an extraordinary 'event' just after the reappearance of the posthorn solo, and not long before the end of the
movement, one of those threatening 'interruptions' that were a
feature of the first movement and even of the elegant minuet, when
the music, as Mahler remarked to Bauer-Lechner, 'suddenly
becomes serious and oppressive'. Exactly the same abrupt change
of mood overtakes the scherzo and once again Mahler's own
words, that I have already quoted, are particularly appropriate: 'One
is more likely to be overcome by horror than laughter.' And he
went on to elaborate this further in a description that must refer to
this very passage towards the end of the movement: there falls, he
said, once more 'the heavy shadow of lifeless Nature, of as yet
uncrystallized, inorganic matter. But here it represents a relapse into
the lower forms of animal creation before the mighty leap towards
consciousness in the highest earthly creature, Man.'

One may perhaps wonder too if that sudden eruption of terror
does not also represent the response of the animals to the invasion
of their forests by Man? However that may be, the posthorn solo
unequivocally – and unforgettably – defines the presence of Man,
and of Man as part of the natural soundscape and landscape of the
world, and, as it happens, without menace to animals.

It is with absolute logic, then, that in the fourth movement,
following the scherzo, Man himself is revealed, a slow movement, a
*meditation* for contralto soloist and orchestra, taking as its text
Nietzsche's 'Midnight Song' from *Also sprach Zarathustra*:

O Mensch! Gib Acht!
Was spricht die tiefe Mitternacht?
Ich schlief! Aus tiefem Traum bin ich erwacht!
Die Welt ist tief!
Und tiefer, als der Tag gedacht!

Tief ist ihr Weh!
Lust, tiefer noch als Herzeleid!
Weh spricht: Vergeh!
Doch alle Lust will Ewigkeit!
Will tiefe, tiefe Ewigkeit!

*O Man, take heed!*
*What does the deep midnight say?*
*I was asleep, from deep dreams I have awoken.*
*The world is deep,*
*And deeper than the day imagined.*

*Deep is its grief!*
*Joy, deeper still than heartache!*
*Grief says: Die!*
*But all joy seeks eternity,*
*Seeks deep, deep eternity.*

There is much that could be said about this marvellous expression of absolute stillness at the heart of the symphony. It is an extraordinary technical achievement to compose music that moves, as it must, and yet create the impression of immobility, until, that is, its final pages – 'Doch alle Lust will Ewigkeit!' – when the song magically flowers into a brief anticipation of the late lyrical style of *Das Lied von der Erde*. In fact, every parameter of the song (for which the precedent again is to be found in the Second Symphony, the setting there of a *Wunderhorn* text, 'Urlicht', another slow movement for voice and orchestra) is dedicated to realizing in sound a long-sustained contemplation of the universe as it slumbers, with questioning Man (Zarathustra) at its centre. 'Was spricht die tiefe Mitternacht?' asks the poem; and the answer is returned, 'Die Welt ist tief! [. . .] Tief ist ihr Weh!' As if to make sure we do not miss the prime significance of the words and the sequence of pitches to which they are set, Mahler repeats the motive: 'Tief ist ihr Weh! Tief ist ihr Weh!'

We may think that we have heard this phrase before, though in wordless form; and we should be quite right, for it has been twice thundered out by the horns in the first movement, on the first occasion at an early stage in the slow introduction, and on the second, as the climax of one of those dramatic 'interruptions' of the march that I have referred to earlier. Nor is this the last that we shall hear of this crucial motive; it will emerge again, and for the last time, during the course of the finale, the concluding adagio. It is certainly no accident that the verbal identification of the motive with the idea of grief and sorrow in this vocal movement that is itself placed at the centre of the symphony and is focused moreover on D, both minor and major, thus outlining the overall tonal progression of the symphony from D minor, with which it opens (the slow introduction), to D major, in which the great adagio ends. From many points of view, indeed, it is this slow movement for voice and orchestra that gives us the key to understanding what this remarkable work is all about.

The last bars of the 'Midnight Song' act as an upbeat to the fifth movement, the movement that fulfils the promise in the original list of titles that a song would be heard from the Angels, accompanied by the morning bells. The *Wunderhorn* text this movement sets is indispensable and follows below. What I would wish to emphasize is the breathtaking boldness of Mahler's conception: a four-minute (or so) childlike depiction of heaven in which truly penitent sinners are forgiven, to enjoy eternal bliss. To realize this extraordinary vision – and one could hardly imagine a stronger contrast after the solemnities of the 'Midnight Song' – Mahler summons up a whole range of fresh sounds and timbres that have not so far played any role in the symphony. To the bells of the orchestra Mahler adds a boys' chorus, colouring the strokes of orchestral bells with a repeated pair of onomatopoeic syllables, 'bimm bamm', while the poem itself is allotted to the alto soloist and women's chorus. Note, however, that at the very end of the movement, the boys' voices too participate in the final stanza, promising 'Die himmlische Freud', die kein Ende mehr hat!' It is undoubtedly significant that it was to children's voices, for Mahler the image of trenchant 'innocence', that he entrusted these crucial lines of text.

Es sungen drei Engel einen süssen Gesang;
Mit Freuden es selig in dem Himmel klang.
Sie jauchtzen fröhlich auch dabei,
Dass Petrus sei von Sünden frei.

Und als der Herr Jesus zu Tische sass,
Mit seinen zwölf Jüngern das Abendmahl ass,
Da sprach der Herr Jesus: Was stehst du denn hier?
Wenn ich dich anseh', so weinest du mir!

'Und sollt' ich nicht weinen, du gütiger Gott?
Ich hab übertreten die zehn Gebot.
Ich gehe und weine ja bitterlich.
Ach komm' und erbarme dich über mich!'

Hast du denn übertreten die zehn Gebot,
So fall auf die Knie und bete zu Gott!
Liebe nur Gott in alle Zeit!
So wirst du erlangen die himmlische Freud'.

Die himmlische Freud' ist eine selige Stadt,
Die himmlische Freud', die kein Ende mehr hat!
Die himmlische Freude war Petro bereit't,
Durch Jesum, und Allen zur Seligkeit.

*Three angels were singing a sweet song.*
*In blissful joy it rang through heaven.*
*They shouted too for joy,*
*That Peter was set free from sin.*

*And as the Lord Jesus sat at table,*
*And ate the supper with his disciples,*
*Lord Jesus said: Why do you stand here?*
*When I look at you, you weep at me.*

*'And should I not weep, thou bounteous God?*
*I have broken the ten commandments,*
*I wander weeping bitterly,*
*O come and have mercy on me!'*

*If you have broken the ten commandments,*
*Then fall on your knees and pray to God.*
*Love only God all the time!*
*Thus will you gain heavenly joy.*

*Heavenly joy is a blessed city,*
*Heavenly joy, that has no end!*
*Heavenly joy was granted to Peter,*
*Through Jesus, and to all men for eternal bliss.*

The overall very bright character of the sound of 'Es sungen drei Engel' is achieved by the format of the orchestra that Mahler uses to accompany the voices, predominantly wind, percussion and two harps; only the lower strings participate. It is yet another example of his ceaselessly inventive orchestral imagination. But orchestration is not only colour; it is also architecture; and it is with a supreme stroke of form-building logic that Mahler, having revealed the orchestra in multiple guises across the span of the preceding five movements, rebuilds the orchestra in its totality for the finale.

In particular, and I have no doubt consciously, having altered the traditional balance between wind and strings in the first movement, in the slow introduction in particular, he restores the full splendour of the strings in the great adagio that rounds off the symphony. Indeed, for the first fifty bars of the movement it is a string orchestra *alone* that we hear. Thereafter, the textures fill out and the dynamics gradually increase, until, in the movement's final pages, the whole very large orchestra is assembled in asserting D major. This indeed is sound functioning as form.

That overwhelming release of D major, embodied in the resplendent, brassy triumph of the chorale, brings us to the end of the epic journey we have travelled from the first movement to this great hymn to Love which is the finale, a journey that has encompassed the evolutionary process from the 'heavy shadow of lifeless Nature' to 'the mighty leap towards consciousness in the highest earthly creature, Man'. (It could only have been Mahler who would have attempted a symphonic enterprise on this cosmic scale.)

That 'heavy shadow' of which Mahler spoke recurs again before the adagio ends; and just before it, we are reminded once more, by all eight horns in unison, of the 'Tief ist ihr Weh!' motive, that we heard in the 'Midnight Song'.

Mahler had originally thought of calling his Third 'Die fröhliche Wissenschaft' ('The Happy Science'; after Nietzsche); another option was 'Das glückliche Leben' ('The Happy Life'). But as he came to compose the work in the summers of 1895 and 1896, the concept of 'suffering' became more prominent, as if it were an inescapable component in the evolution of Life on earth and, above all, inherent in the very act of creation that is the purpose of an artist's life. Mahler touched on this in a comment to Natalie Bauer-Lechner that I find very moving and certainly central to our understanding of this symphony:

> As sometimes a personal experience will illuminate and fully bring home to one the significance of something long known, so today it came to me in a flash: Christ on the Mount of Olives, compelled to drain the cup of sorrow to the dregs – and willing it to be so. No one for whom this cup is destined can or will refuse it, but at times a deathly fear must overcome him when he thinks of what is before him. I have the same feeling when I think of this [first] movement, in anticipation of what I shall have to suffer because of it, without even living to see it recognized and appreciated for what it is.[*]

Mahler had hoped that in his Third he might put behind him the tragedies, frustrations and suffering enacted in his First and Second Symphonies. But it was not to be. The Third, too, was to acquire elements of suffering and anguish as the composition of it progressed. However, it should certainly be remembered that the world premiere of the work in Krefeld on 9 June 1902 was one of Mahler's greatest successes as a composer.

As I wrote at the start of this note, the chronology of the symphony's composition is complex. We do know for sure, however,

---

[*]   Ibid., p. 62.

that it had been Mahler's intention to install 'Das himmlische Leben' as the finale of the Third. Indeed, the preceding fifth movement, 'Es sungen drei Engel', was conceived perhaps as a kind of upbeat to the sublime vision of Heaven and its music that the discarded finale attains in its final (E major) stanza.

Mahler himself, in a letter from 1896 remarked that the adagio represents the 'highest level of the structure', which is undeniably the case; and then goes on to add, 'God! Or if you like, The Superman', Nietzsche's *Übermensch*.

But not, we notice, Heaven, or at least not yet. That was an objective that still had to be grasped. For that he had to embark on was an entirely new symphonic journey – the Fourth – during which a state of innocence and grace was achieved that allowed 'Das himmlische Leben' to take up its rightful place at the top of the evolutionary ladder. It was only then, we may think, when Mahler completed his Fourth Symphony in 1900, that he also brought to completion his mighty Third. Heaven could at last be revealed and confirmed as Man's ultimate goal.

# 'Swallowing the Programme': Mahler's Fourth Symphony

*To Steuart Bedford*

## ∾ 1999 ∾

Man was made for Joy & Woe;
And when this we rightly know
Thro' the World we safely go,
Joy and Woe are woven fine,
A Clothing for the Soul divine;
Under every grief & pine
Runs a joy with silken twine.

William Blake, *Auguries of Innocence*

There is no contradiction between playfulness and pedantry; the one brings on the other.

. . . nothing tugs at the heartstrings so much as a quavering mechanical toy; think of the touching music boxes of bygone times.

Günther Grass, *Dog Years* (trans. Ralph Mannheim)

For the euphoria which we endeavour to reach . . . is nothing other than the mood of a period of life in which we were accustomed to deal with our physical work in general with a small expenditure of energy – the mood of our childhood; when we were ignorant of the comic, when we were incapable of jokes and when we had no need of humour to make us feel happy in our life.

Sigmund Freud,
*Jokes and their Relation to the Unconscious*
(trans. and ed. James Strachey, 1960)

First published in DMANMC, pp. 187–216.

I have just this minute received your letter and am
delighted by the entrancing analysis of my Fourth. I
hasten to reply at once, to tell you how touched I am
at being so well understood. In particular, I find your
approach to this work quite new and extraordinarily
convincing. You actually say what had never before
occurred to me whenever *I* had to say something
about it. It now seems child's play, so obvious! One
thing seems to me to be missing: did you overlook
the thematic relationships that are so extremely
important both in themselves and in relation to the
idea of the whole work? Each of the first three
movements is thematically most closely and most
significantly related to the last.

Mahler to Georg Göhler, New York, 8 February 1911
( GM, *Selected Letters*, pp. 371–2)

Any exploration of the Fourth Symphony of Mahler has to confront the issue of the 'programme', not only in relation to this
particular symphony but to its predecessors and successors. It is a
complicated matter, made the more complicated, as we shall see, by
Mahler's own complicated attitudes to it. But let me start with a
characteristically pungent and provocative observation by Adorno,
from his 1960 monograph on the composer, in which he writes:

Even the Fourth, with its overflowing intentions [Adorno has previously established the 'image-world' of childhood as the determining source of its materials], is not, however, programme music. It
differs from it not merely by using the so-called absolute forms
sonata, scherzo, variations, song; the three last, extensive symphonic
poems of Strauss also use these. Equally, even when he no longer
had any truck with programmes, Mahler cannot simply be subsumed under the practice of Bruckner or Brahms or even the aesthetic of Hanslick. *The composition has swallowed the programme* [my
italics]; the characters are its monuments.[1]

---

1    TWA *Mahler*, p. 58.

Adorno goes on to clarify what he means by his reference to 'characters' by making a comparison with the practice of Strauss. Mahler, he writes, 'does not subscribe to the programme because he [does not wish] to fix the meaning of the musical figures by decree', while in Strauss, 'Characterization founders . . . because he defines the meanings purely from the standpoint of the subject, autonomously.' 'Mahler's medium', Adorno continues, 'is that of objective characterization':

> Each theme, over and above its mere arrangement of notes, has its distinct being, almost beyond invention. If the motives of pro-gramme music await the labels of the textbooks and commentaries, Mahler's themes each bear their own names in themselves, without nomenclature. But such characterization has a prospect of validity only in so far as the musical imagination does not produce inten-tions at will, does not, therefore, think out motives that express this or that according to a plan, but works with a musical–linguistic material in which intentions are already objectively present. As pre-conceived entities [Adorno has earlier identified some of these, e.g. 'The sound of the great drum [*recte* bass drum: Adorno of course writes 'Grosse Trommel'] . . . is as drums once seemed before the age of seven', while in the first movement's development, 'The unison of the four flutes . . . does not just reinforce the sound. It creates an effect *sui generis*, that of a dream ocarina: such must have been children's instruments that no one ever heard'[2]] they are quoted, as it were, by the musical imagination and dedicated to the whole. The materials that achieve this are those called banal, in which meaning has generally sedimented, before the advent of the individual composer, and has been punished by forfeiting the spon-taneity of living execution. Such meanings stir anew under the staff of composition and feel their strength.[3]

For Adorno, of course, 'banal' bears a meaning entirely different from that of Mahler's early critics, who used it so often as a term of mindless abuse. I am not sure that 'banal', specifically in the

<hr>

2 Ibid., pp. 55 and 53.
3 Ibid., p. 58.

context of the Fourth, is the word that I would use, though I can certainly see what Adorno was getting at. 'Innocence' or, better still, 'a state of innocence' are what I would prefer, not only in relation to the symphony's musical ideas and images, the work's 'characters' as Adorno hears them, but to its eventually declared and explicit goal, its finale, the *Wunderhorn* song 'Das himmlische Leben', the conscription of which to serve as the symphony's last movement has to remain an event of unique significance and fascination. There is nothing like it elsewhere in Mahler's oeuvre and, as I shall hope to suggest, much more is bound up with it than the novelty of Mahler's composing a symphony *into* a pre-existing finale, especially when that finale itself was a model of the unorthodox, a song for solo voice and orchestra.

It is not my intention to rehearse here the long history of 'Das himmlische Leben' and its involvement in the creation of both the Third and Fourth Symphonies; the history is now both familiar and accessible.[4] Nor, for the same reason, shall I dwell, unless incidentally, on the evolution of the Fourth, for which an unusual number of preparatory programmatic, multi-movement schemes existed. It is sufficient for my purpose to remind readers that the song that was to be installed, virtually unamended, as the finale of the symphony had been composed in Hamburg in 1892.

It was there, on 26 April, that Mahler brought to completion his 'Fünf Humoresken/ "Wunderhorn-Lieder"', for voice and orchestra, among them 'Wir geniessen die himmlischen Freuden' (i.e. 'Das himmlische Leben'), which had been composed in its voice and piano version on 10 February and in its orchestral format on 12 March (see Ex. 1(a)).[5] The compositional substance of the song indeed remained unamended; on the other hand, Mahler was to

4   See e.g. DMWY, pp. 311ff.
5   The manuscript full score of the five 'Humoresken' is in the possession of the Gesell-schaft der Musikfreunde, Vienna. 'Das himmlische Leben' in its original version as an independent *Wunderhorn* song is included in the volume of the complete orchestral scores of Mahler's *Wunderhorn-Lieder*, published in 1998 by Universal Edition, Vienna, in collaboration with the International Gustav Mahler Society, edited with a full critical apparatus by Renate Hilmar-Voit and now forming vol. 14/2 of the Society's *Critical Edition* of Mahler's works. I am grateful to Dr Hilmar-Voit for bringing to my attention the instrumental differences between the early and later version of the song that I have briefly illustrated in Exx. 1(a) and 1(b) (cf. *Critical Edition*, 14/2, pp. 55–87).

'Das himmlische Leben': the first page of the voice and piano version,
dated 10 February 1892

make by no means insignificant instrumental retouchings and refinements, so that the version of the song we hear as the finale of the symphony varies in its orchestration from its original conception as an orchestral song (see Ex. 1(b)). A comparison of Ex. 1(a) with the corresponding passage in the symphony – the opening of the finale – makes clear the evolution of the orchestral sound that we are familiar with today when we hear the song in the context of the symphony.

In 1893, on 27 October, in Hamburg, Mahler included the song – its first performance in the programme of a 'popular concert', along with two others of the original five 'Humoresken' and three further orchestral settings of *Wunderhorn* texts. Finally, all these *Wunderhorn* orchestral settings were gathered together and published as *Des Knaben Wunderhorn*, less of course 'Das himmlische Leben', which, by the time of publication (1899), had already been incorporated into the symphony. The Fourth itself was composed across the turn of the century. The completion date for the symphony as distinct from the song was 5 August 1900, the date Mahler inscribed at the end of the slow movement (he got the date wrong, in fact, by one day, but his additional inscription of 'Sunday' tells us that it must have been the 5th on which he brought the first three instrumental movements of the symphony to their conclusion (the 6th – the date he inscribed – was in fact a Monday).

I wish to concentrate on what, finally, Mahler himself concentrated on: the four-movement symphony that we know today as Mahler's Fourth. And that, necessarily, returns us to that striking observation of Adorno's that has been my point of departure, that in the Fourth, absolutely unlike its predecessors, the composition has swallowed the programme.

Most penetrating observations have an element of exaggeration about them, and to that rule the quotation from Adorno is no exception. It is undeniably the case that in the Fourth the programme has been 'swallowed' by the composition – perhaps 'suppressed by' or 'submerged in', though less arresting, might be a shade more accurate? – swallowed, that is, until, by analogy with Adorno's own concept, the 'programme' is disgorged in the shape of the song-finale. It is, furthermore – and this, to my mind, is one of the most interesting things about it – a *retrospective* enlightenment as to what the

symphony, up to that point, has been all about; more than that, not
only a retrospective act of illumination, but also an enactment and
affirmation of the goal, we now come to realize, that all along has
been the symphony's objective, the goal to which the 'characters',
assembled in the first three movements, 'sonata, scherzo, variations'
and freed, as Adorno has it, from their 'thing-like rigidity'[6] – have
guided us, though to be sure what we arrive at is less a programmatic destination than the achievement of a state of mind, that idea
of 'Innocence' to which I have referred earlier.

This is a point to which I shall often return, but to emphasize
the singularity of the solo song's function in the Fourth, it may be
useful to remind ourselves how explicitly programmatic in outward
conception at least the first three symphonies were.[7] After all, the
First started life, without reservation, as a symphonic poem in two
parts and five movements (1888), and a significant period was to
elapse before the four-movement symphony we know today
emerged (1896). For the Second (1888–94), Mahler at one stage
provided a lengthy and elaborate programme; and indeed in an
early printed edition of the symphony, Hermann Helm's arrangement of the Second for two pianos, four hands, published by
Friedrich Hofmeister in Leipzig in 1896, we find installed there
unequivocal 'programmatic' indications. e.g. at fig. 74 in the finale,
'Der Rufer in der Wüste' ('The Caller in the Desert'), and at
fig. 96, a bold title – 'Der grosse Appell' ('The Last Trump') – forms
the heading at the top of the first page of the great cadenza that
precedes the chorus of Resurrection.

In later editions, of course, all such programmatic clues or clarifications were expunged and Mahler's own detailed scenario, written originally in connection with a performance of the symphony
in Berlin in 1901, categorically withdrawn. We must note, too, that
for a time at least, while Mahler was still bringing the work to
completion, he accorded quasi-independent symphonic-poem
status to the first movement, entitling it *Todtenfeier* and indeed
performing it himself as a work temporarily in its own right in a
concert in Berlin on 16 March 1896, though spelling out in the

6   TWA *Mahler*, p. 58.
7   See also Donald Mitchell, 'Symphony No. 1: "The most spontaneous and daringly com-
    posed of my works"', pp. 117–22.

Ex. 1(a) A transcription from the autograph of the first two pages of
'Das himmlische Leben' in its original guise as the fourth of the
five 'Humoresken' for voice and orchestra composed in 1892.

## IV.

Ex. 1(b) The first two pages of 'Das himmlische Leben' as orchestrated by Mahler for the finale of his Fourth Symphony

programme that this was the first movement from a symphony in C minor. But we should not, because of this, hasten to identify the movement as a 'Symphonic Poem', as the title-page of its first publication (as Supplement (vol. 1) in the *Critical Edition* of Mahler's symphonies published by the International Gustav Mahler Society, Vienna) imprudently had it. It is more than likely in my view that Mahler added this title as a *continuation* of the scenario that is narrated in the First Symphony, i.e. to indicate that the protagonist – the hero – in the First was presumed by Mahler to have *died*, his demise to be solemnly celebrated in the first movement of the 'new' symphony (the Second), hence the inscription *Todtenfeier* and of course the Resurrection that follows in the famous finale. This is something quite different from the conception of an independent 'symphonic poem', which I think *Todtenfeier* never was.

Finally, there is the Third (1895–96), which evolved in its six-movement form only after Mahler had committed to paper a whole batch of movement titles in a variety of sequences in which the actual number of contemplated movements was also subject to change.[8] The work represents from many points of view the most elaborate and sophisticated of any of the 'programmes' that, before Mahler ruthlessly banished them – or attempted to banish them – from public knowledge, had formed an indispensable part of his aesthetic strategy: and part, too, of the means by which he clarified his intentions to his audience; or, to put it another way, a means of disseminating 'information' about a work in the interests of comprehensibility (it is in this light, bearing in mind a parallel with the *Trauermarsch* inscription of the first movement of the Fifth, that we should consider the *Todtenfeier* title).

Mahler's later antagonism to his programmes stemmed from a number of sources, some relatively superficial, some, I suggest, profound. There can be no doubt that he became increasingly exasperated by responses to his music which were seemingly conditioned or predetermined by the 'programmes'; far from clarifying the music or promoting intelligent discussion of it, they obscured it.

8    See DMWY, pp. 187–94, *passim*; also Peter Franklin, *Mahler: Symphony No. 3*, ch. 3.

A danger of programmes is that the listener, in seeking to hear the descriptive account, even when it is the composer who has provided it, does not hear the music. Ultimately, Mahler's hostility to programmes was to extend to analysis of any kind; the idea of 'programme notes', it seems, became anathema to him. For example, when the Seventh was first done in Prague in 1908, the only information Mahler permitted to appear in the programme comprised the tempo (character) indications for the five movements, absolutely nothing else.)[9] Then there may have been a desire to distance himself, musically speaking, from his great contemporary, Richard Strauss, and to make the point, at least by the time his hostility to programmes had become explicit and he was retrospectively fighting a rearguard action to erase them, that while Strauss was undeniably the presiding genius of the symphonic poem, his – Mahler's – territory was the symphony.

There is a certain irony about this, to be sure. After all, Mahler himself, as I have just mentioned, began his life as a symphonist with one foot in the symphonic-poem camp. It is true, of course, and as subsequent events (i.e. successive revisions) were to prove, that all along there was a symphony awaiting its excavation, its release, from its symphonic-poem carapace; nor should it be overlooked that for an aspiring and ambitious young composer, still not out of his twenties, there was powerful motivation to hitch one's flag to the mast of the 'progressives' rather than enter a field – the symphony – that was already crowded and where the competition, to put it mildly, was intense.

However, while the stripping out of the symphony from the initiating symphonic poem speaks for itself, so too does the continuing

9   See, for example, the reproduction of the programmes for the Prague and Vienna premieres, reproduced in the facsimile edition of the Seventh published by Rosbeck Publishers (Amsterdam, 1995), pp. 41 and 67 of the volume of commentaries to which Edward R. Reilly and I contributed. The absence of a 'programme' was widely complained of by the work's early critics, e.g. Richard Batka, who wrote: 'Unfortunately, Mahler subscribes to the principle of the minimal programme . . . I understand that the all-too-often literal use made by the audience of more detailed programmes would arouse the opposition of a composer like Mahler. But his refusal to provide even very brief hints concerning the meaning of, and the connection between, the individual parts of his work serves only to take us from misunderstanding to incomprehension' (p. 45). See also below, 'Mahler's Seventh: A Dialogue with Bernard Haitink', pp. 414–15.

presence of the 'programme' in the ensuing symphonies, up to and including, though in a rather special way, the Fourth. It is not my purpose here to attempt a comprehensive exploration of the programmatic dimension of the first three of Mahler's symphonies. For one thing, the ground has been pretty well covered elsewhere; for another, it is self-evident that the idea of a programme, however varied its execution, was fundamental to the concept and creation of the early symphonies, that no amount of retrospective deprecation on Mahler's part could (or indeed, should) do anything to alter. If I omit at this stage specific reference to the Fourth, it is because I believe it represents a quite particular case, the natural but momentous consequence, if it may be stated thus, of what strikes me as the single most interesting and important feature of these so-called *Wunderhorn* years (1888–1901 is my estimate): the tension generated by Mahler trying to pursue two opposed ideologies simultaneously, one dedicated to the path of the symphonic poem, to the programmatic idea, the other to the path, the tradition, of 'symphony', unpolluted by programmatic affiliations or associations.

This creative tension was never entirely extirpated from Mahler's formal thinking, his formal conscience – much to posterity's benefit let it be immediately said, since the competing aesthetic strategies gave rise to some of his most innovative music. The tension was the spring that kept the pendulum swinging between the two poles.

There is no clearer instance of this than the first movement of the Second, the special formal profile of which – *pace* its *Todtenfeier* entitling – surely indicated a bid to *abandon* the 'symphonic-poem' territory occupied by its predecessor and undertake a big symphonic project: a 'Symphony in C minor', opening with a movement that was the first of Mahler's unequivocal affirmations of sonata form. Can we doubt that he revealed thereby his ambition to write a work in the Great Tradition? The monumentality of the gesture itself was an indication of the scale of the ambition. But what happened? The 'Symphony in C minor' – the work that Mahler's inscription (from 1888!) had originally implied – was never, perhaps, to materialize. What did, finally, emerge after a painfully long period of gestation, did so – ironically – only by courtesy of the 'programme', the dissemination of which

he came later to regret. But there is no denying that it was fundamental to the continuation and completion of the work that we
know today as 'Mahler's Second'. Years of creative frustration and
uncertainty interposed, while he was trying to find an answer to
the question, 'how to continue?'; and it was not until he found the
'programme' that he found the answer. No question here of the
composition 'swallowing the programme'. The 'programme', at
long last, was the indispensable means by which the composition
came to be completed.

Among the group of Mahler's first three symphonies, it is the
Second that unequivocally juxtaposes the concepts of symphony
(the first movement) and symphonic poem (the sequence of ensuing movements). To be sure, the tension shows up again in the
Third, in the first movement, where, as has so often been observed,
a sonata scheme is to be discerned behind the elaborate programmatic concept. It is revealing, indeed, that Mahler clung to the
skeletal sonata frame even when, as I have suggested elsewhere, it
would surely have been more rational and convincing in terms of
the given programme to have ditched it. But for Mahler, it seems,
this foothold, or in this case, toehold, in the past, was a kind of
certificate of immunity against total immersion in the aesthetic of
the symphonic poem.[10]

It is indubitably of significance as a piece of evidence when trying to assess Mahler's picture of himself. But does anyone, when
experiencing the first movement of the Third, really 'hear' it as a
sonata movement, as one certainly does the first movement of the
Second? One hears it, surely, as the huge initiating stage in an
evolving sequence of programmes which culminates in the crowning, elevated, and elevating adagio, representing, in Mahler's own
words, 'What Love tells me'. We have made a long ascent, onwards
and upwards, from the heaving introduction to the first movement,
about which Mahler said to Natalie Bauer-Lechner in June 1896,
'It has almost ceased to be music; it is hardly anything but sounds
of Nature. It's eerie, the way life gradually breaks through, out of

---

10 See DMWY, pp. 206–8, and DM, 'The Modernity of Gustav Mahler', in G. Weiss (ed.),
  *Neue Mahleriana: Essays in Honour of Henry-Louis de La Grange on his Seventieth Birthday*,
  pp. 175–90.

soulless, petrified matter. (I might equally well have called the movement . . . "What the mountains tell me")'; and he continued: '. . . as this life rises from stage to stage, it takes on ever more highly developed forms: flowers, beasts, man, up to the sphere of the spirits, the "angels" . . .'[11] And so on, and so on. There may have been an apparent surfacing of the symphony/symphonic-poem dichotomy in the compositional histories of the First and Second Symphonies, but confronted by the Third at the time of its earliest performances it would have been hard – impossible, I suggest – to have predicted not only Mahler's abandoning of the concept of the 'programme' but his hostility to its resurrection, even in those contexts where it had been fundamental to the creation of a specific work; the case of the Third is perhaps the most striking of all.

It would have been equally hard to predict that the ensuing Fourth would have taken the shape it did; for what it was to reveal, in absolute distinction from the preceding Third, was a marked preoccupation with the idea of 'symphony' from which, virtually, the 'programme' (at least in the sense that it is immediately identifiable as such in the Third) is excluded (or 'swallowed', as Adorno has it); until, that is, we reach the finale, the *Wunderhorn* song.

Up to that point – and of course the act of *retrospective* illumination is an incomparable stroke of genius – up to that point, we have three perfectly articulated and constructed instrumental movements in 'so-called absolute forms, sonata, scherzo, variations' which – if we did not know otherwise – might well have culminated in a 'conventional' finale, a brilliant and engaging rondo, say; given the 'right' instrumental finale, i.e. one that fulfilled the thematic, motivic, and tonal implications – tonal, above all – adumbrated in the sonata-form first movement, we should have had not the work heralding the close of the period when Mahler and the 'programme' symphony were inextricably bonded, but the work that, so to say, established his credentials as a symphonist proper, and was to initiate the sequence of purely instrumental symphonies, Five, Six, and Seven. No one in his right mind would want a

---

11  NB-L *Recollections*, p. 59. See also 'Mahler's Third Symphony: His Encounter with Evolution', pp. 137–52.

Fourth without 'Das himmlische Leben'; but that a Fourth might be so envisaged is a point worth making simply because it shows just how far at the turn of the century Mahler's *dependence* on the explicit programme had weakened; the new shape it was to take I shall want to discuss in relation to the Fifth. But the paradoxical truth about the Fourth is this: that it demonstrated how close Mahler was to the idea of 'symphony' in 1899–1900 – is it not the case in the Fourth, indeed, of the idea of 'symphony' swallowing the *composer*? – while at the same time revealing his subtlest, most original, and most perfectly executed 'programme'.

Part of that perfection that 'Das himmlische Leben' vouchsafes is embodied in the fact that the song – unthinkable as a finale until Mahler brought it off – performs all the functions that were expected of a finale as the nineteenth century was on the brink of expiring. The song clarifies and justifies all that has preceded it, rounds off everything, tidies everything up, explicates what hitherto has been a shade inexplicable (not much of that, in fact, but perhaps those seemingly eccentric opening three bars, chinking sleigh-bells, chirruping flutes, the 'wrong' key, etc., etc., fall into that category until illumination dawns with the onset and evolution of the song).

I have already sufficiently emphasized, I think, the unique act of fulfilment *plus* retrospection that 'Das himmlische Leben' represents, while not forgetting, naturally, that *Wunderhorn* orchestral songs (or in the case of the Third, a setting of Nietzsche (the fourth movement), in addition to that of a *Wunderhorn* text (the fifth)), had already been incorporated in two of the preceding symphonies.

But if we examine their function in the contexts of the symphonies that contain them, we find it differs fundamentally from the role of 'Das himmlische Leben'. If it is 'Urlicht', the fourth movement of the Second, that we have in mind, then its function – apart from providing an absolutely obligatory intervening moment of repose after the agitation of the scherzo and before the unleashing of the epic theatre of the finale – is akin to that of a signpost, pointing the direction in which the symphony must travel, and anticipating its final destination; in short, playing its role as part of an evolving programme, a stage, a station, on the way to the eventual denouement. The building of *Wunderhorn* songs into the symphonies was a novel way of installing compact sources of information for the hypothetical traveller seeking enlightenment about the route he was following, as it were in the steps of the composer. The orchestral songs in the Third function likewise. The Nietzsche setting, 'Was spricht die tiefe Mitternacht?', performs much along the same lines as 'Urlicht' in the Second, a moment for reflection, meditation, that also anticipates the symphony's denouement, not only the final triumph of D major but the conquest, by incorporation, of the motive of verbally identified suffering from the Nietzsche setting – 'Tief ist ihr Weh!' (the information process in action!) – into the great concluding adagio; a recapitulation (at fig. 20) that is surely meant to remind us of the suffering that necessarily precedes victory. But this event is not an example of the finale clarifying the song, but of the *reverse* process, the song acting as signpost to the finale, which will, as we shall hear for ourselves, come up with the answer to Nietzsche's question, 'What does deep midnight have to tell us?'

As for 'Es sungen drei Engel', the fifth movement of the symphony and a setting that shares the source and imagery of its text and much of its musical material with 'Das himmlische Leben' – which, it will be remembered, at one stage was envisaged as a potential finale for the Third – it does not so much clarify as represent a further stage in the evolving programme, evolving, that is, towards the sublime concluding adagio, 'Was mir die Liebe erzahlt'. It is a movement to my mind that can be understood, so marked is the contrast it offers to the movement to which it functions as a kind of prelude, only as a reminder that before we can enter into and perhaps be redeemed by the spirit of Love, man must first aspire to or achieve – or at least hold intact within him – a condition of childlike innocence. This is a point of some significance; as I shall come to suggest, in the case of the Fourth, it is precisely towards the establishing of that condition that the thrust, the drive, of the symphony is dedicated, and made explicit, in terms of its techniques, tone, and style.

Little or any of that was comprehended by the work's first audiences. The symphony was first performed in Munich on 25 November 1901, when Mahler conducted the Kaim Orchestra; we may savour the irony that it was this work above all that was to be the agent of changed attitudes to Mahler in the years after the Second World War. Its relatively modest resources, and relative brevity, were also an influential factor; none the less it was the 'approachability' and 'appeal' of the Fourth that won it admiring audiences.

This was not at all Mahler's experience in 1901. In general, it is safe to say, the symphony was received with blank incomprehension and hostility. There were a few, very few, voices dissenting from the overall adverse judgement, and the majority seemed to think that they were the victims of a scandalous joke, of a hoax, even. Those who may wish to scrutinize for themselves the sorry parade of prejudice and ignorance – the critic of the Munich *Allgemeine Zeitung* of 26 November complained that the first movement of the Fourth was reminiscent [*sic*] of the andante (the A flat ländler) of the Second, while a further weakness was the similarity [*sic*] of the scherzo to the first movement, 'too much like [the first]' in the critic's own immortal words – will consult the relevant and thorough documentation in Henry-Louis de La Grange's second volume.[12]

Of greater interest is what some early critics of the symphony, whether favourable or unfavourable, had to say about the issue that directly concerns us – the 'programme'. Mahler's, by this time, explicit opposition to 'programmes' (or at least to the dissemination of information about them) only added to the confusion. As the critic of the *Münchener Zeitung* remarked, 'only a programme could possibly have "made the work's images and points of departure comprehensible to the listener". As it was, the Fourth repeatedly touched on the dubious genre [i.e. programme music] which, as the saying went, was "the only one not permissible".'[13]

Likewise, the critic of the *Allgemeine Musik-Zeitung*, Karl Potgiesser, found it 'incomprehensible without a programme',[14] as did his colleague on the *Neue Musikalische Presse,* who wondered if Mahler 'was not simply making fun of his audience, since he even refused

12 See HLG *Mahler*, vol. II, pp. 392–416.
13 See ibid., p. 400.
14 Ibid., p. 401.

them the explanation and "programme" they so sorely needed'.[15] And so on, and so on. The critical reception of the work during the remainder of the tour was not one whit better. The strange, profoundly ironic truth was that not a single critic had observed the single most striking fact about the symphony, that it did indeed have a 'programme', but one that was not revealed until the song-finale spelled it all out, whereby the 'programme' that underpinned the symphony from its first note to its last was retrospectively made manifest.

A further layer of irony was provided by the success 'Das himmlische Leben' occasionally enjoyed in comparison with the preceding movements. Here, at any rate, there was a modestly positive response, though it was emphasized that this of course was not a legitimate, serious symphonic finale; notwithstanding, it was a song that might be enjoyed in its own right. Did Mahler ask himself, one wonders, after the disastrous sequence of performances, if he had not been altogether too successful in composing a symphony which 'swallowed the programme' so consummately that in 1901 the climactic moment of revelation went unheard, unremarked by virtually everyone?

There was, however, one exception, Max Graf, who heard the first Vienna performance of the Fourth on 12 January 1902 and wrote about it in the *Neues Wiener Journal*.[16] The reception of the work in Vienna was as hostile as it had been in Munich, and Graf was no less negative – indeed destructive – than his colleagues. There is something almost sublimely ironic, if not comic, about his launching a reproach that at the same time, though evidently unappreciated by its author (still in his twenties), precisely described the retrospective process which every other critic had apparently not noticed. 'This symphony', he declared, 'has to be read from back to front like a Hebrew Bible.' Given the tragi-comic history of the Fourth's reception, it seems entirely appropriate that one of the few genuine insights about the symphony should have been expressed (and intended) as an adverse comment.

Graf himself was a Jew, so it may have been that Mahler was not offended by what may have been intended or at least understood

15  Ibid., p. 402.    16  Ibid., p. 475.

as a good Jewish joke. In any event, wittingly or unwittingly, Graf's perception matched Mahler's own, who had remarked to Bauer-Lechner after a reading rehearsal of the Fourth in October 1901, 'In the last movement . . . the child – who, though in a chrysalis-state, nevertheless already belongs to this higher world – *explains what it all means*' [my italics],[17] (It is of no little interest in this context that in a letter to Weingartner from the autumn of 1901 he explained his opposition to a *vocal* work preceding his symphony because he wanted 'the appearance of the soprano to come as a complete surprise before the finale'.[18])

Adorno, as we have read above, places a good deal of emphasis on the roots of the Fourth, as he hears it, having their location in the events and experiences of our early years. 'Its image-world is that of childhood . . . No father figures are admitted to its precincts. The sound avoids all monumentality, which had attached itself to the symphonic idea since Beethoven's Ninth.' Later, he continues, 'The *entire* [my emphasis] Fourth Symphony shuffles non-existent children's songs together; to it the golden book of song is the book of life.'[19] And so on.

If, as I have suggested, we substitute a state or condition of innocence for Adorno's 'golden book of song', or any other of the many vivid metaphors he employs, we find ourselves not so far removed from Adorno's conceptualizing, providing, that is – and for me this is fundamental to our comprehension of what the Fourth is 'about' – that 'innocence' is acknowledged to be the symphony's goal, the *condition to which it aspires,* and which the finale, 'Das himmlische Leben', at the last moment, unveils.

The progression, or, rather, the possibility of the progression, is brilliantly contrived from the outset of the symphony, from the jingling sleighbells of the introduction and the beguilingly simple 'cut', i.e. character, of the ensuing first subject. But is the first

---

17 NB-L *Recollections*, p. 178. There is a further remark of Mahler's to Bruno Walter in 1902 recorded by Bauer-Lechner which should be read in the light of his comment from 1901: 'They [the public] don't really know *what* to do with this one: *which end* [my italics] should they start gobbling it up from?' (ibid., p. 185).
18 HLG *Mahler*, vol. II, p. 394.
19 TWA *Mahler*, pp. 53 and 55.

movement in fact quite as simple, i.e. childlike, as Adorno would have us believe? One wonders, indeed, if the simplicity that he equates with childhood were not also a remarkable anticipation of an aesthetic that in the history of music in the twentieth century was eventually to be known as neo-classicism – 'Der neue Klassizismus' that was the object of Schoenberg's derision in his identically entitled cantata of 1925 (Op. 28, No. 3).

But neo-classicism in fact did not have to await the advent of Stravinsky and Hindemith, or for that matter of Schoenberg himself, who had pursued his own form of neo-classicism, less immediately assimilable (audible) than, say, Stravinsky's, but no less part of his creative strategies in the 1920s and 1930s. We often discuss or think about neo-classicism as if it were wholly a matter of 'style', of explicit references to the manners of the past: and to be sure the 'past' must be integral to any attempt at defining the concept of neo-classicism. There is, however, another approach, another perspective, which perhaps transcends the issue of style or manner as the prime means of 'reviving' the past. It manifests itself, rather, as an awareness of the evolution of an established form to that critical point in time at which our hypothetical composer himself begins to work at extending the chosen form – the symphony, say – and, thereby, its pre-existing history. In short, the *history of the form itself* then becomes a subject of the composer's discourse.

I use the word 'critical' advisedly, because it was at just such a critical moment that Mahler (our composer unmasked!) was, so to say, suspended between two centuries and the two symphonies which it is my business to survey, the latter of which, the Fifth, was to mark a fresh departure, something for which the composer himself, perhaps to an unexpected degree, found himself unprepared. In the Fourth, on the other hand, where he had encountered none of the difficulties (in the sphere of instrumentation in particular) that were to haunt him as he undertook successive revisions of the Fifth, there is, interestingly enough, not a sense of a new start, no hint of an experimental initiative (the finale excepted), but more a conscious reference to past practice, past styles even; to form, above all, and to first-movement sonata form, emphatically so.

Indeed, it is surely a brilliant dimension of the symphony's first movement that in the wittiest and most sophisticated manner, Mahler seems to hold up for our inspection an 'innocent' age in the history of the symphony, though only to show that any kind of literal return to the past is no longer possible, that there has to be both renewal and innovation if the past is not to petrify. It is thus that I read the unique telescoping (or overlapping) technique that Mahler applies to a critical moment in the form of the movement, the recapitulation. This is what I wrote in 1975:[20]

> But it is in the first movement of the Fourth Symphony that Mahler offers us the most brilliant and sophisticated example of his telescoping technique; rightly so, because in this case the technique is pressed into service at a highly important formal moment: the recapitulation in an elaborate sonata movement (at fig. 18). Because of the 'formality' of the movement, Mahler's treatment of it is all the more riveting. This is a well-known passage in the symphony and one of which Mahler himself was clearly proud. He remarked about it to Bauer-Lechner that the audience would discover only later 'how artful [*kunstvoll*] it is'.[21] The artfulness rests in the ingenuity with which Mahler manipulates his telescoping principle. We recognize the principle involved just as soon as we hear the way in which Mahler recapitulates the principal theme [see Ex. 2]. We drop into the tonic, G major, but the theme itself is picked up in midflow. In characteristic Mahler fashion, what he recapitulates is not in any case the first statement of the principal theme from the exposition but the varied repeat of it (see three bars after fig. 1 *et seq.*), which, in the recapitulation, he surrounds with a whole nest of fresh motives (see, however, the lower strings, one bar after fig. 18, where the principal tune persists). It is with bar 3 of the principal theme, in fact, that the recapitulation opens; and . . . precisely as in the minuet [of the Third Symphony], the thematic recapitulation has started on the 'wrong' side of the double bar at fig. 18.[22] If one looks back to the point of climax of the development (at fig. 17) and then at the ensuing lead-back to the recapitulation, one finds

20  DMWY, pp. 322–4.
21  NB-L *Recollections*, p. 183.
22  See DMWY, pp. 318–22.

not only the 'missing' opening bars of the principal theme in an augmented version (bars 234–8) that carries one right up to the double bar and proves to dovetail precisely with the continuation of the melody (bar 3) with which the recapitulation so surprisingly opens, but also the introductory motives (cf. bars 1–3) which in the exposition precede the main tune.[23] At bar 225, flutes and sleigh-bells reintroduce the very opening idea of the symphony, and there-after, and before the double bar is reached, all the introductory motives are recapitulated in a mosaic-like pattern of motivic com-binations, as well as the principal tune's opening bars; and to all this Mahler adds a nice touch of symmetry by using the version of the introductory motives that actually opens the development (fig. $8^{+3}$) and now returns to close it (bars 233–8), while at the same time serving in a recapitulatory role.

This is altogether an amazingly elaborate passage, the more so when one remembers that this subtle recapitulatory process also has to work smoothly and effectively as part of a transitional process, in which the development winds down and in which we are finally led back through an ingenious modulatory scheme[24] to the tonic and the recapitulation proper. 'Kunstvoll' indeed, and certainly a more complicated compositional exercise than the minuet in the Third Symphony. None the less, it was in that 'simple' movement that the essential principle underpinning this complex construction in the Fourth Symphony was first outlined.

I notice that when I came to continue that text I did not fail at least to raise the issue of neo-classicism, while not pursuing it very far:

Undoubtedly the complexity of this passage was part of the aesthetic game that Mahler was playing in his Fourth Symphony: an out-wardly simple-minded, even backward-looking symphony (an early manifestation of neo-classicism?), that creates a peculiar world of its own by contradicting, in developments of a demanding complexity and sophistication, the anticipations of simplicity and guilelessness

23  See ibid., p. 366, n. 10.
24  See ibid. n. 11.

Ex. 2 Fourth Symphony, first movement: overlapping technique at recapitulation

that the very opening of the work seems to arouse (though only momentarily).

Now, however, I believe that greater weight and consideration should be given to it, as an early example, indeed, of what Adorno himself describes as 'Musik über Musik' ('music *about* [my emphasis] music').[25] For all its urbanity and playfulness, is this first movement not saying to us in fact that there can*not* be a return to the 'simplicities' of the past (they were never that, of course) at any level, formal, thematic or tonal, while at the same time saluting the certainties, the symmetries, the proportions – though none of these was invariably so – of classicism?

Typical of Mahler that his gesture to the past should simultaneously incorporate patent and elaborate innovations (cf. Ex. 2 above) that, so to speak, turn the past on its head, in order to make the very point that at this critical juncture in the history of the symphony, innovations were obligatory if the form – and its future – were to remain alive and kicking. In the first movement of the Fourth, then, Mahler was in a sense bidding farewell to the ideals of classicism, rather than reasserting them as models that might service the future of the form.

Thus the Fourth, to my mind, represents a manifestation of neoclassicism peculiar to Mahler himself, an awareness of and reflection on the role he himself and his work(s) in progress might play in the still evolving history of the idea of the symphony. The Fourth, or one significant dimension of it, spells out the impossibility of rolling history back or complacently attempting to continue in the line of – wake of, rather – the Great Tradition. We should remember too that the symphonies that preceded the Fourth, all three of them, exploited the still new and intriguing concept of the 'programme' symphony; and that it was in the Fourth that Mahler, so to say, turned his back on programme music (while at the same time, as I have already suggested, creating his most perfect example of the genre). Goodbye to an illusory golden past, goodbye to the illusions of the 'programme'. The Fourth quite remarkably proved

25  See Theodor W. Adorno, *Philosophy of Modern Music*, pp. 181–4.

to be the vehicle of change, the symphony in which the ground was cleared to make way for the new symphonic initiatives of the first decade, the Fifth and its successors; the symphony too in which some of the most conspicuous features of Mahler's later orchestral manner were anticipated.

All of this, however, does not argue against the basic concept of the 'innocent' and the 'childlike' which I believe to be the *fons et origo* of the symphony's inspiration, though I stress again that this must not be approached as a static concept but a mobile one, as a journey from Experience to Innocence.[26] In this sense, the first movement is all Experience. To be sure, Adorno has a point in his promoting the 'image-world . . . of childhood' as a defining influence on the character of Mahler's themes, the often bright colours of their instrumentation, the choice of percussion, etc., etc. There is indeed something of the celestial nursery to be discerned, obligatorily so in the light of what the finale is to vouchsafe. But there is nothing very childlike or naive about the organization of the first movement's recapitulation, while the intense and intensive polyphony that we encounter throughout the movement, and in its development section in particular, is hard to read as a manifestation of 'childhood' or the 'childlike'; or if so, then this is an exceptionally clever, knowing child, playing an exceptionally sophisticated game.

This last factor is of quite special importance, for in fact it is in the first movement of the Fourth that for the first time in a Mahler symphony we are confronted by a show of that hyperactive motivic counterpoint which, in the succeeding instrumental symphonies, was to be a hallmark of his 'new' polyphonic orchestral style. As we shall see, this technique was to land Mahler in no end of trouble, about which he himself was unusually forthcoming; for example, as late as February 1911 – almost a decade after the symphony's completion – he was writing to Georg Göhler from New York, 'I have finished [*sic*] my Fifth – it had to be almost completely

---

26 I capitalize Innocence and Experience henceforth to remind readers that my use of these concepts in relation to the Fourth derive from William Blake, i.e. his *Songs of Innocence and Songs of Experience: Shewing the Two Contrary States of the Human Soul,* published in 1794.

re-orchestrated. I simply can't understand why I still had to make such mistakes, like the merest beginner. (It is clear that all the experience I had gained in writing the first four symphonies completely let me down in this one – for a completely new style demanded a new technique.)'[27]

That 'new style', although Mahler himself did not amplify the statement nor point to any precedents, has always been assumed to be the onset of the polyphony that characterizes the symphonies (but not only the symphonies) from the Fifth onwards; and surely rightly so – after all, Mahler himself in 1904 in a letter to his publisher had remarked on the difficulty of getting every last detail right in 'such a very polyphonic' work as his Fifth.[28] But as Adorno remarks, it was in the first movement of the Fourth that 'he writes counterpoint for the first time in earnest, although polyphony did not dominate the imagination of the earlier pieces'.[29]

How odd, then, and, to some significant degree inexplicable, that the Fifth was plagued by such problems when the first copious manifestation of the new contrapuntal style, the new polyphonic thinking, had been executed with such remarkable clarity in the first movement of the Fourth, and with seeming ease; like the rest of Mahler's symphonies, the Fourth was also the subject of pretty continuous revision, but on nothing like the scale of the obsessive revisions of the Fifth. There is not a commentator on the Fifth who, parrot-like, does not echo the established opinion that 'new style' meant a new preoccupation with counterpoint, while remaining seemingly oblivious to the fact that the 'new style' was adumbrated, however improbably, in the first movement of the Fourth.

It is true that our apprehension of the movement's polyphonic profile does nothing to help explain why it was that Mahler found himself in such a predicament when coming to realize the polyphony of the Fifth. If anything, indeed, it heightens the enigma, about which I shall have more to say in my chapter on that

27  See GM *Selected Letters*, p. 372.
28  See HLG *Mahler*, vol. II, p. 801.
29  TWA *Mahler*, p. 54.

symphony.* But a failure to perceive that the new contrapuntal thinking was, so to say, launched in the Fourth, is to diminish the pivotal role the symphony plays in the evolution of his compositional resources and techniques. There can be no doubt that the overt contrapuntal features of the first movement were widely misunderstood as a means of jokey reference to the past; so much emerges from many of the notices of the work's first performances. We can reinterpret it in our own day as an early signal of a revived classicism yet to materialize, though the motivation for Mahler's salutation, as I have suggested, was probably somewhat distinct from that of his successors, the later proponents of neo-classicism proper. But much more seriously and illuminating, the Fourth's polyphony we now realize was an intimation of the new polyphonic style that was to service, virtually without exception, Mahler's music thenceforth.

But it was not only counterpoint that was a signpost to innovations to come. Scarcely less significant was another dimension of the work altogether, though one clearly related to the burgeoning contrapuntal component, which brought in its wake the obligation to achieve clarity of articulation: a marked reduction in the orchestral forces involved (no trombones or tuba). Adorno did not fail to take note of the new dispensation: 'The means are reduced, without heavy brass; horns and trumpets are more modest in number. No father figures are admitted to [the symphony's] precincts. The sound avoids all monumentality, which had attached itself to the symphonic idea since Beethoven's Ninth.' And he continues: 'The reduction of the orchestra caused the symphonic writing to approach chamber-music procedures, to which Mahler, after the alfresco quality of the first three symphonies, returned again and again, most markedly in the *Kindertotenlieder* . . .'[30]

30  Ibid., p. 53. Some comparative figures: whereas in the Fourth Mahler uses 4 horns and 3 trumpets, his First had required 7 horns, 5 trumpets (+ 3 trombones and bass tuba); his Second, 10 horns, 6–10 trumpets (+ 4 trombones and bass tuba); and his Third, 8 horns, 4 trumpets (ideally 6 + 4 trombones and bass tuba). Numbers, when Mahler is involved, cannot tell anything like the full story, and in each of the Fourth's predecessors one can locate passages and textures of a chamber-musical character. But the Fourth represents a defining stage in Mahler's progress towards the concept of a chamber orchestra.

*  See 'Eternity or Nothingness: Mahler's Fifth Symphony', pp. 225–351, *passim*.

It was *Kindertotenlieder,* one might claim, that finally gave birth to the idea of the *chamber orchestra,* an event of no little consequence for the future of twentieth-century music, and again a topic to which I shall return in the ensuing chapter.* But its foreshadowing here in the Fourth, in the symphony's very constitution, has to be spelled out in order to heighten the work's peculiar status and achievements, and to remind us of its singular history, greeted by scorn and mockery on its first airing and then, decades later, earning a reputation as the most accessible and approachable of the symphonies.

How wonderfully ironical that it was this symphony above all that fired the enthusiasm of many of those hearing a Mahler symphony for the first time, an enthusiasm made possible only by its relative accessibility – even amid the constraints of war in the 1940s – an accessibility itself facilitated of course by the deployment of (relatively) slender orchestral resources; while that, in turn, as I have suggested above, represents to us one of the symphony's most original and, in Mahler's terms, forward-looking gestures. Represents *now,* I should have written, in the light of everything we know about Mahler today. But it says something about the symphony that it could speak so directly, eloquently, and expressively in virtually the total absence in those far-off days of anything like the contextual information we have ready to hand, not to speak of the torrent of performances and flood of CDs.

There is no doubt in my mind that Adorno was correct in identifying the childlike as one of the most important stimuli, both symbolic and sonorous – that is, as image and sound – to Mahler's imagination. But exaggeration blunts the sharp point he is making. A symbolic representation of childhood, of the childlike, we may all agree, was obligatory at an early stage in the symphony if the narrative were to culminate, in the finale, in the unveiling of Innocence; and indeed Mahler wastes no time at all in making the point himself in the very first three bars of the first movement: the jingling bells and repetitive patterns in the woodwinds are akin in their bright, arresting simplicity to a musical box, a bit of nursery equipment, the machinery of which, however, is imperfectly synchronized.

---

*   See 'Mahler's "Kammermusikton"', pp. 200–224.

Was that perhaps what Mahler had in mind when organizing the slight but calculated rhythmic confusion that attends the winding down of the introduction, the flutes marked 'ohne rit.', the last beat of the clarinets marked 'poco rit.', while the upbeat in the violins to the first statement of the first subject and the establishment of G major is also marked 'Etwas zurückhaltend' (i.e. 'poco rit.')? Clearly, this is what he wanted to happen, this teasing dissynchronization; but in fact it is only in a very recent edition of the symphony, incorporating Mahler's very last corrections made, probably, between October 1910 and May 1911 – an invaluable note of which was kept by Erwin Stein – that his wish is made adequately explicit (cf. this introduction as it appears in the first publication of the work in 1902 with its parallel in the corrected edition of 1995, forming part (vol. IV) of the *Critical Edition* of the symphonies supervised by the International Gustav Mahler Society, Vienna).

The choice of ideas to initiate the symphony cannot have posed much of a problem for Mahler. These were ready to hand in the already existing finale, the song, 'Das himmlische Leben' (it is not only the symphony itself that has to be read backwards but also the chronology of its composition). What Mahler had to be mindful of was not to divulge *too much Innocence too soon*; hence, no doubt, the exceptional brevity of this introduction. (The only comparable example of extreme economy is the introduction to the first movement of the Ninth and even that runs for a bar or two beyond the three bars of the Fourth, the briefest of all the composer's introductions.)

It is exactly in this manipulation of balance and proportion, in keeping the symphony's goal in his sights, setting up the objective, but avoiding a premature denouement, that we encounter the very considerable and conscious art – artifice might be the better word here – Mahler brings to this first movement. In short, Innocence has to be signposted, but then held in check and subjected to the challenge of Experience. It is the conflict between those two prime areas of the human condition – and the resultant tension – that forms the principal business of the first movement, a tension that is skilfully sustained by Mahler across the whole span of the symphony until its final dispersal in the finale's closing stanza.

In this respect, we do well to note, the Fourth behaves virtually as does every other Mahler symphony, its predecessors and successors. For example, the overall concept of the Fifth was to be entirely different, as we shall see. But the narrative *process* is there, unmistakably, and in all important respects identical with that of the Fourth, i.e. the basic conflict articulated at an early stage and a significant indication vouchsafed of a possible (probable), albeit still distant, resolution of the drama. It is always the finale, without exception in Mahler's oeuvre, that clinches the narrative, unfolds the denouement; and the ultimate denouement of the Fourth, which will make final sense of the B minor musical-box introduction that I have described above, is of course the last stanza of 'Das himmlische Leben' – 'Kein Musik ist ja nicht auf Erden . . .' ('There's no music at all on the earth') – floated on a sublime E major (from fig. 12).

Already, I suggest, there is sufficient to encourage us not, as it were, to swallow Adorno whole (leaving on one side the question of the programme); as is often the case with the best of critics, perhaps necessarily and fruitfully so, the overestimation of one dimension of a work, important and illuminating though that may be, leads him or her to underestimate one that may be equally (or perhaps even more) important. Adorno zooms in on Innocence, thereby excluding Experience; all the odder, one may think, since he shows himself to be alert to many of the novel features of the Fourth that I believe run counter to the images (or practices) of childhood, and which I believe to belong incontrovertibly to the sphere of Experience.

A case in point is the explosion of counterpoint in the Fourth, something that Adorno was quick to observe while seeming not to have sufficiently recognized the specific role it plays in the contest between Innocence and Experience; how, so to say, it emerges at its most potent and challenging in the first movement in that crucial section, the development, where Mahler explores areas of feeling and expression the farthest *removed* from Innocence. The development, indeed, demands separate scrutiny in its own right and I shall turn to it in a moment. But in any event counterpoint alone does not exhaust a list of features that decisively contribute to the interplay between the opposed ideas out of which conciliation will eventually emerge. After all, what sort of resolution or denouement would it be, if challenge, contrast, and opposition had not preceded it?

So, in pursuit of our qualifications of Innocence, we have to add to our list such things as the elaborate, 'knowing' treatment of critical formal junctures in a sonata-form movement with a long musical history behind them, and which depend for their effect on a kind of tacit complicity between the educated, historically minded listener and the historically minded composer, e.g. the lead-back to the recapitulation in the first movement that my Ex. 2 above illustrates; the shift towards a chamber-orchestral style that Mahler was soon to establish in *Kindertotenlieder* and the late Rückert settings,[31] his 'Kammermusikton', as he was himself to describe it; the explicit references to a spirit of classicism by no means confined to the forms Mahler expounds, e.g. 'textbook' sonata form in the first movement, 'textbook' variations in the third, but extending also to the very configuration of themes, motives, textures and, not least, rhythm, e.g. in the first movement, figs. 2–3, figs. 19–20, and the movement's very last four allegro bars, remarkable anticipations, one might think, of the neo-classicism with which the first half of our century has made us familiar; these are like neo-classical windows opened up in the façade of the symphony. Nor should one overlook an often unblemished assertion of the diatonic, as if, say, *Tristan* had been temporarily erased from the historical record.

All of this, the sheer sophistication and technical virtuosity of it, seems to run significantly counter to Adorno's surely too exuberant and indiscriminate categorizing of the symphony, its ideas, its 'characters' and characterizing sonorities, as having their origin in the 'image-world . . . of childhood'. At the same time we should not fall into a similar trap ourselves, thereby underrating the importance of the role of childlike imagery in the symphony as a whole. But it would count for little if it were not for the context of

---

31  And not only in the Rückert song-cycle and songs I mention here, but also in at least some of the *Wunderhorn* settings. See the section on 'Mahler and the Chamber Orchestra' in 'Mahler's "Kammermusikton"' (pp. 213–19), where I examine some of the statistical – and other – implications of the historic 'Lieder-Abend mit Orchester' that Mahler conducted in Vienna on 29 January 1905. The first half of the programme was made up exclusively of *Wunderhorn* songs.

Experience, from which indeed Innocence has to be seen to be – heard to be – at last extrapolated.

If there is an agenda that appears not to have claimed Adorno's full attention, then it surfaces unmistakably and audaciously in the first movement's development section, from figs. 8 to 18, about which there is nothing very childlike in character or seraphic in mood. On the contrary, what we encounter here, after the relatively benign exposition, is what might be described as distinctly unsettled weather, accompanied by constant fluctuations of temperament and temperature. There is no other part of the symphony comparable to this abrupt destabilization of the prevailing mood; to respond adequately to this remarkable music, we have to fall back on words like 'doubt', 'anxiety', 'scepticism', 'irony', 'agitation' – again, a vocabulary remote from the texts of an imagined 'golden book of song'[32] belonging to childhood that Adorno suggests is the Fourth's generating source.

For the song Mahler sings in his development is a very different kind of song. His manipulation, distortion, and distending of his invention surface in ever new and intricate counterpoints, projected, more often than not, in startlingly unpredictable instrumental combinations; some of these – they form a continuous array between figs. 8 and 16 – unequivocally reverse the 'classical' relationship between winds and strings. There have been plenty of precedents for this calculated dis-balance in earlier symphonies, of course; perhaps one becomes particularly conscious of it here because of the no less calculated tribute he seems to pay to classicism in the Fourth in so many of its parameters, and perhaps more specifically because the exposition, relatively speaking – everything is relative in Mahler! – has been homogeneous in texture. But with the onset of the development at fig. 8, a radically different sound-world manifests itself.

The very first eight bars of the development initiate the shift away from anything recognizable as classical homogeneity of orchestral sound; we hear nothing but woodwind, bells, solo horn, and solo violin! We are borne back – which was of course Mahler's

32  TWA *Mahler*, p. 55.

intention – to the complex of motives and identifying instrumentation with which the symphony was launched in bar 1. But any
illusion we might have that we are to embark on a further exploration of the guileless naiveties of the introduction and the generally affirmative, shadowless character of the ensuing exposition – all
G major and D major but for a five-bar recall (bars 72–6) of B
minor along with the introduction (what follows is a seeming
'classical' repeat of the exposition which is then cut short (no second subject!)) – is shattered by the path the development pursues.

I have already mentioned the dazzlingly varied, eccentric textures, from which the strings are often absent or relegated to a sub-
ordinate role; woodwind and brass predominate. When the strings
do participate, on a highly intermittent and selective basis, their
function is to contribute yet another means of articulating and
colouring the web of motivic polyphony that is the development's
*raison d'être*. If one needs to isolate one single example in the development that embodies a sound-world as remote as one could get
from the 'noise-fields' of infancy that Adorno seems to have had
(too much) in mind, then we need look no further than, say, bars
160–67 and their restatement in bars 200–208: first time round
repeated high chords in the flutes, **p**, accompanied by muted trumpets and cymbal strokes (with the soft stick); second time round, the
high chords repeated, **pp**, distributed among flutes, oboes, and clarinets (clarinet 2 in E flat), while harp harmonics, **f**, punctuate and
articulate the soft vibrations of the cymbal.

On both occasions, the chords function as interpolations –
interruptions – in the midst of ceaseless motivic variation and fragmentation and no less ceaseless motivic counterpointing, though
naturally enough, because (second time round) we are approaching
the climax of the development – when E flat minor and F minor
are not so much replaced as ejected by a robust C major – the
motivic activity (vertical and horizontal) becomes ever more
intense and elaborate. To be sure, the music withdraws from this
encounter with foreboding and agitation, and unequivocally
reasserts its 'optimism'. But for a significant stretch of musical time
we have, so to say, been suspended over an abyss.

These specific passages in the development cannot be left without one further comment on the extraordinary ingenuity with which Mahler expounds his materials. For a start, why this emphasis *here* on the three repeated chords? That these repetitions derive, rhythmically and motivically, from the main theme of the 'himmlische Leben' melody (see, for example, the opening bars (clarinet) of the finale) must of course be part of any answer. But perhaps a little less obvious is, on reflection, their clear relationship to the first bar of the second subject (at fig. 3); whereupon it will be recalled that the expected restatement of the big D major tune in the (only seeming) repeat of the exposition was never to materialize. True to past practice, Mahler compensates for what is apparently 'missing' in one spot by resuscitating it, albeit in disguised form, in another. Hence the development's concentration on a derivative which continuously, once it has been remarked, is heard to evoke the omitted second subject. (The precedent for this may be found in the first movement of the Second Symphony.)[33]

I have referred above to the development's withdrawal from foreboding and its eventual reaffirmation of the symphony's 'optimism'; and it is precisely at the climax of the development, and in an exuberant C major, that the reversion is made. This is a critical passage (figs. 16–17) from many points of view, not least Adorno's, for whom this climax is 'an intentionally infantile, noisily cheerful [noise-]field . . . the forte growing increasingly uncomfortable until the retransition [the lead-back] with the fanfare.'[34] It seems to me, however, that he once again overstates one dimension at the expense of all else.

For example, it is here for the first time that the thematic source and eventual thematic goal of the symphony is spelled out – proclaimed *fff* – by the solo trumpet, simultaneously combined, however, with a whole nest of related motives (cf. figs. 2–3), not excluding the repeated-note (chord) motive which has attained such prominence in the development and now continues to enjoy a high profile, but one stripped of its former expression of anxiety.

Moreover, while it is perfectly true that this brilliant climax

33  See DM, 'Mahler's Longest Journey'.
34  TWA *Mahler*, p. 54.

serves as a kind of apotheosis of the calculated naivety which is an essential part of the symphony's aesthetic, we should not fail to remark the ingenuity of the counterpointing, a demonstration, surely, in this prime location that, in the Fourth, counterpoint does not necessarily belong to the torments and trials of Experience but can also wear the face of Innocence. The polyphony here represents the obverse of that which has held sway between figs. 11 and 16; thus it is that one compositional principle assumes two contrasting roles in the evolution of the narrative, and contributes to the interplay between the opposed poles of Innocence and Experience. If counterpoint is one of the 'characters' involved, then, it seems, 'characters' can from time to time change sides.

How, then, are we to read that C major climax and the trumpet tune? Has Mahler, so to say, given the game away, arrived prematurely at his denouement? I think not. For a start, the projection of the 'himmlische Leben' tune, forcible though it is, is but one motivic strand in a complex of motives; as we shall hear, when Mahler does finally release the melody in its entirety, it not only uncoils itself in a wholly relaxed way – there is no sense of it having to justify its existence – but comprises virtually the total experience the symphony has to offer at this (still distant) point, by when everything will have been stripped away, pared down and simplified.

It is an extensive melody that embodies the symphony's resolution, that tells us, retrospectively, all we need to know about what has preceded it; and its consummatory E major indicates that the C major of the development's peak, no matter its motivic/thematic importance, its triumphalism even, could not possibly be taken to represent to us that the 'conflict', the tension, was near to being solved; least of all did Mahler intend us to read that *C major* as his symphony's eventual tonal destination. In any case, while this critical passage is certainly not wanting in confidence, its staying power is limited; at fig. $17^{+4}$ there is an intervention – the famous fanfare, which is followed by the overlapping lead-back I have described above to the recapitulation by way of F sharp minor, B minor, and *E minor* (bar 229 *et seq.*).

I emphasize E minor because the sleighbells we hear at the

beginning of the development (fig. 8) indisputably function, as I have already mentioned above, as a recall of the movement's introduction, and, along with it, the introduction's own B minor (bar 102 *et seq.*). Eight bars later, 'classically' enough, it is in E minor that the development really gets under way; whereupon one becomes acutely conscious of what might be described as the movement's *double tonic*; there is not only G, as it were, to be accommodated, but also E, in both its minor and major mode.

This is a fundamental aspect of the first movement, and – eventually – an issue – i.e. G or E? – that is fundamental to our understanding of the work as a whole and its narrative. It is a feature of the Fourth about which the New Zealand Mahler scholar, Graeme Downes, has written exceptionally well in his 1991 doctoral thesis,[35] and especially so in relation to the character and organization of the first movement's development. He suggests that the 'tonal direction' of the development becomes 'crucial to the question of overall tonicity. G major could be confirmed if another strong structural dominant is reached, but on the other hand, the failure to provide such a dominant could place G's tonicity in jeopardy'. He continues:

> The first sign that the development section might take the latter course is the return of the sleighbell introduction. Not that this is disruptive in itself, but here it begins to assert its tonal independence and, in so doing, realizes a different tonal function that has remained latent up until this point. Specifically, B minor functions as the dominant of E: not as a modal colour subsidiary to the tonic G major. Here it is strengthened by a stronger modal implication thanks to the tonicizing leading note in the solo violin part, which therefore implies B minor more strongly than B Phrygian, thus avoiding the modal connection with G.
>
> Very quickly the development section establishes the key of E, which will ultimately be the work's tonal destination. But it is not merely a case of beginning the development in the relative minor

35  Graeme Alexander Downes, 'An Axial System of Tonality Applied to Progressive Tonality in the Works of Gustav Mahler and Nineteenth-Century Antecedents', Ph.D. thesis, pp. 143–59.

of G. The development section here is the most unusual Mahler has written so far in his career, inasmuch as it avoids any goal-oriented drive towards a preparatory dominant and subsequent resolution to the tonic. In other words the development ends up as a disconnected structural unit, one which begins and ends in E minor no less . . . In terms of the local tonal context, the return of G major [at the recapitulation] is entirely gratuitous. So the muted articulation of the structural outlines that Mahler achieves with his thematic dove-tailing [Ex. 2 above] actually points out a more serious situation – namely the growing crisis over the tonicity of G.

Such a claim may seem far-fetched at first sight, but it is never-theless a fact that the development fails to establish a goal-oriented structural dominant that seeks to tonicize G.[36]

Dr Downes has much more to say that is illuminating; those who wish to pursue his line of thinking should consult his thesis. What captured my attention – and indeed my imagination – was his clear recognition that this development section was not only the 'most unusual' that Mahler had yet written but 'a disconnected structural unit', an analytic insight that I think spells out in another way what I have already remarked upon as the development's unique detach-ment, its decoupling almost, from the movement's – the exposi-tion's – principal concerns.

Dr Downes adduces a tonal strategy that I believe supports what I have written about at length above: that the virtually self-con-tained development explores territories that the exposition has not led us to expect. Above all, its failure to confirm a 'goal-oriented structural dominant', combined with its own structural independ-ence, beginning and ending in E minor, makes one acutely con-scious of the competing claims of the symphony's 'alternative' tonic, E; not only of its eventual status – as Dr Downes observes, the 'latter stages of the work will effect [the] transition whereby E becomes the tonic'[37] – but of the role it plays in the overall narra-tive of the symphony, the 'character' allotted it by the composer.

If I can put a gloss of my own on what Dr Downes has to say

36 Ibid., pp. 147–8.
37 Ibid., p. 149.

about E, then it seems to me entirely appropriate that at this first-movement stage of the symphony it is E *minor* that, by association, comes to represent the impact of Experience on Innocence: in short, it is the disconcertingly restless, uneasy character of the development that defines for us what, in terms of tonal symbolism, E minor embodies.

That it may eloquently represent unmitigated lamentation is revealed in the third movement, the adagio, in which, after the first unfolding of the theme in a serene G major, there follows at fig. 2 a long lament initiated by the oboe in E minor, music that again anticipates significant features of Mahler's later style, of *Kindertoten-lieder* in particular, from which, in bars 80–81, Mahler *seems* to make a quotation (cf. the opening bars for the voice in the cycle's second song, 'Nun seh' ich wohl, warum so dunkle Flammen').

However, if – as important research[38] has suggested – 'Nun seh' ich wohl' post-dated the symphony, i.e. was composed in fact in 1904, then it must be that the song took as its point of departure the oboe lament from the slow movement of the symphony.[39] Whichever option may be thought to be correct, the result does not affect my argument: that the idea of mourning, of pain and suffering, are inextricably associated with the advent of E minor in the adagio of the Fourth, thus retrospectively clarifying the function of the E minor that frames the development section in the first movement (everything in this symphony has to be read backwards!).

This unmediated juxtaposition of G major and E minor that opens the adagio articulates in its clearest guise the conflict, the spiritual drama if you like, that as I have already suggested is the work's *raison d'être*. Or as Dr Downes puts it succinctly from his own perspective: it was clearly Mahler's aim in the slow movement 'to juxtapose the work's *main tonal combatants* [my emphasis]'[40] – I would only add, 'from the movement's very outset'.

---

38  See Christopher O. Lewis, 'On the Chronology of the *Kindertotenlieder*', *Revue Mahler*, 1 (1987), pp. 21–45.

39  Odd if this were, in fact, the case: all Mahler's markings in bars 80–81 of the *Adagio* of the symphony go out of their way to indicate a 'quote'. Should we perhaps rethink – investigate further – the chronology of *Kindertotenlieder*?

40  Downes, 'An Axial System', p. 154.

The overall form of this adagio has often been described as a double-variation form after the model of Beethoven's Ninth, but this is surely not the case? We have a theme, and then two chains of variations, *between* which is interpolated the lament, the first time round in E minor (and then extensively and agitatedly developed), the second time round in G (Phrygian) minor and again extensively and likewise developed.

It is in the second chain of variations (like the theme, both units of variations centre on G) that for the first time E *major* is energetically asserted, in the fast – *Allegro subito* – variation that precedes the even faster final variation in G. It is perhaps not without significance that this last and very short variation borrows its rapid figuration from its E major predecessor. E major, so to speak, is intensifying its infiltration, gaining the upper hand in its contest with its rival. But the moment of triumph is not yet; indeed, the closing section, based on the main theme, that follows the final variation must have led early audiences to believe that the adagio was to be rounded off in the blissful G major with which it had opened. However, the climax of the movement is still to come; a huge – *fff* – affirmation of an undiluted E major, from within which horns and trumpets triumphantly articulate that complex of motives, themes, and rhythms that we heard originally at – or, rather as – the climax of the first movement's development. But there it was in the 'wrong' key.

The eruption of E major at last fulfils almost all the implications of its role as an alternative tonic that have been a fundamental part of the composer's tonal strategy since the symphony's initial handful of bars. It massively dispatches the E minor of the lament – and though E minor, inevitably and necessarily, continues to be a vivid presence in the song-finale, it is an E minor purged of its associations with pain and anguish – and proclaims unequivocally the vision of 'heavenly life' that is but a step, a song away. The continuity of the narrative that is enacted across the adagio and ensuing song-finale is secured by the concluding D major chord of the slow movement functioning as dominant upbeat to the ensuing G of 'Das himmlische Leben'. The final attainment of Innocence, of freedom from the pains and tribulations of Experience, is still to come; and Mahler, with characteristic skill, reserves the very last moments of his symphony for his apotheosis of E.

There is another feature of the adagio that I should like to mention before we come to that final stanza in the fourth movement. I have referred before to the systematic reduction in complexity of virtually all parameters of the symphony, of textures and forms in particular. This is an important part of the process by which, gradually, perhaps without our being always conscious of it, Mahler effects his evolving transition from Experience to Innocence across all four movements. The adagio, I suggest, usefully illustrates the point. To be sure, Innocence and Experience are forcefully juxtaposed; but there is nothing like the elaborate and sophisticated 'mix' of contrasting moods that we have encountered in the first movement's unique development; nor any comparable display of the intricate polyphony that distinguishes the movement as a whole, though in the interpolated lament, in the G (Phrygian) minor version in particular (at fig. 6), we are suddenly made aware of the linear preoccupations that were to surface around the turn of the century, and distinguish the textures of *Kindertotenlieder, Das Lied von der Erde*, and the Ninth Symphony. In bars 179–86 of the Fourth's adagio, the long lines of the counterpoint, scored for solo woodwind and solo horn, open a window on a type of polyphony that was to become an identifying characteristic of Mahler's later and last style. (Cf., for example, *Das Lied*, 'Der Einsame im Herbst', figs. 15–17.)

Appropriate enough, one might think in the light of all I have said, that these manifestations of counterpoint belong to the slow movement's lament, to the sector of Experience, to the plaintive minor mode (E minor, G (Phrygian) minor). On the other hand, the 'innocent' sector, the G major theme and variations, carries a rapturous simplicity to an extreme we have not witnessed before. This is especially true of the second chain of variations, from fig. 9 onwards, which – but for a momentary passing shadow between bars 267 and 277 – are of an artlessness that indeed has its roots in childhood: this is a kind of music that ingeniously evokes those simple sets of variations that are part of the experience of every child musician – especially aspiring infant pianists – for which reason, perhaps, the very figuration that Mahler introduces evokes, uniquely for him, the keyboard and the agilities required of young fingers. No doubt, too, it is precisely because this second variation chain attains an unprecedented simplicity of spirit that we find there (at fig. 10), as I have already observed, the first accommodation, the first intimation, of the forthcoming avowal of E major, the symphony's terminus.

If I have chosen to concentrate on the adagio, it is because the movement so aptly illustrates and represents the diminishing complication that we experience as the sequence of movements progresses. That I have said nothing about the scherzo should not in any sense be interpreted as mute adverse comment. On the contrary it is a strikingly original and often very beautiful movement in its own right, one too from which one may well conclude that Experience, in the shape of the spectral solo fiddler, 'Freund Hein', has an important role to play, beckoning those who follow him 'to dance out of life into death'.[41] Mahler himself, it seems, in a conversation with Natalie Bauer-Lechner, referred to the 'screeching and rough-sounding' tone of the *scordatura* fiddle part, 'as if Death were fiddling away'.[42]

But what I wish to emphasize here is not so much the self-evident and perfectly explicit character of the scherzo as its relatively simple *form*, a sequence of dances, i.e. three statements of the main scherzo section (and its repeats, second time round), into

41 See my note on the Fourth in *GMWL*, 2.54–7, where I specifically mention (2.56) the covert references Mahler makes in the scherzo to the contour of the melody of 'Das himmlische Leben' (cf. for example the passage between fig. $9^{+10}$ and fig. $11^{+13}$).

42 NB-L *Recollections*, p. 162, who writes, 'He is altering the violin solo of the scherzo by having the instrument tuned a tone higher, and rewriting the part in D minor instead of E minor', which prompts Peter Franklin to ask in an editorial note, 'Is Natalie mistaken here, or did Mahler originally conceive the scherzo in E minor?' (ibid., p. 222). Professor Edward R. Reilly, to whom I was much indebted, confirmed that the earliest manuscript known to him, a sketch in short-score format for the opening of the movement, 'clearly shows the key to be C minor'. It seems most probable, wrote Professor Reilly, 'that a slip was made in transcribing Bauer-Lechner's text, with E accidentally written instead of C'. I was also grateful to him for pointing out that while the short-score sketch is inscribed by Mahler '2. Satz', a later fair copy in full score of virtually the same passage is inscribed '3. Satz (Scherzo)', another fascinating example of the habitual uncertainties that attended the ordering of the middle movements of Mahler's symphonies; and yet, once the final sequence has been determined, one realizes that it was, after all, and from the start, the only possibility.

which are interpolated two trios (the second repeated). There are of course a hundred subtleties in Mahler's treatment of his ideas; but the generally straightforward character of the overall form is matched by invention and textures that on the whole are similarly uncomplicated[43] and certainly free of the polyphonic hyperactivity that crowds in on our ears in the first movement. If Experience *is* a presence in the scherzo, then it must be attributed to the symbolic figure of Freund Hein, rasping away on his rustic fiddle (?*klezmer*).

And so to the finale, and to the finale's finale, the magical onset of E major that accompanies the setting of the last stanza of the *Wunderhorn* poem:

> Kein Musik ist ja nicht auf Erden,
> die unsrer verglichen kann werden.
> Elftausend Jungfrauen
> zu tanzen sich trauen!
> Sankt Ursula selbst dazu lacht!
> Cäcilia mit ihren Verwandten
> sind treffliche Hofmusikanten!
> Die englischen Stimmen
> ermuntern die Sinnen!
> Dass Alles für Freuden erwacht.

> *There's no music at all on earth*
> *Which can ever compare with ours.*
> *Eleven thousand virgins*
> *Are set dancing.*
> *Saint Ursula herself laughs to see it!*
> *Saint Cecilia with her companions*
> *Are splendid court musicians.*

---

43 There is another ambiguous comment by Natalie Bauer-Lechner in her memoirs in which she recalls Mahler revising 'the part-writing in the second movement', which had 'become too elaborate and overgrown – "like limbs with ganglia" (*Recollections*, p. 162). If this were indeed the scherzo that Mahler was talking about, then it would seem he was himself conscious of the progressive diminution in textural complication that to my ears is a highly innovative feature of the symphony and one, again, that brilliantly relates to the 'programme' from a different angle of approach.

*The angelic voices*
*Delight the senses,*
*For all things awake to joy.*[44]

It is an extraordinary experience without parallel elsewhere in Mahler, this retrospective 'explanation' by the pre-existing *Wunderhorn* song-finale of what the three preceding movements have been 'about', and why they took the shape they did; and in particular, as I believe Dr Downes to have very convincingly shown,[45] how, in the vocal last movement, E is finally established as the symphony's authentic tonic. Here again, the tonal organization of the finale retrospectively clarifies the emerging role of E, both minor and major, in the first movement and the adagio.

As for the long journey from Experience to Innocence, how, so to say, is it left as the movement ends — as it has to do, naturally — on those low, repeated Es on the harp punctuating a low E, ***ppp***, on the double-basses, gradually dying away? A stroke of genius that an unadorned E should be the very last sound we hear. But no less inspired, surely, is the long-breathed, seamless melody, occupying virtually the totality of the last stanza's available musical space, a quietly rapturous celebration of a music that awaits us when Experience has been purged. Not Paradise, perhaps, but Innocence Regained; and by reserving that sublime melody for his final act of simplification, by his concentration on melody alone to bear the weight of the ultimate transformation, Mahler seems to return us to an age of innocence in music when (if I may echo Freud) such things were still possible.

44  Translated by Deryck Cooke.
45  Downes, 'An Axial System', pp. 156–8.

# Mahler's 'Kammermusikton'

## ∽ 1999 ∽

### *Kindertotenlieder*

Mahler's second orchestral song-cycle, *Kindertotenlieder*, composed over an unusually long period, overlaps with the Fourth,[1] Fifth, and Sixth[2] Symphonies, and, scarcely less important, with the last two settings of *Wunderhorn* texts, 'Revelge' and 'Der Tamboursg'sell', and the four independent orchestral settings of lyrics by Rückert. There are many fascinating crossovers and revealing relationships between songs and symphonies from this period in Mahler's creative life; but it is probably in the area of *form* that we encounter the most important relationship between *Kindertotenlieder* and the surrounding and ensuing symphonies. It could be expressed, albeit crudely, like this: that as Mahler developed towards his last works there emerged a profound symbiotic relationship between his late songs and his symphonies, the songs evolving ever more symphonically – a striking case in point is that masterpiece of symphonic song, 'Der Tamboursg'sell' (see pp. 220–24 and 'Eternity or Nothingness: Mahler's Fifth Symphony', pp. 225ff.) – while his late symphonic thinking shows the influence of the innovative forms adumbrated in *Kindertotenlieder*.

Mahler himself, one has to conclude, demonstrated this integral relationship in the very last years of his life by writing *Das Lied van der Erde,* the symphony that is also a song-cycle (or the song-cycle that is also a symphony, which was Mahler's choice of nomenclature). This concept of the formal relationships between songs

---

1   On the assumption, that is, that the symphony, in its adagio, quotes from the song-cycle's second song. See, however, '"Swallowing the Programme": Mahler's Fourth Symphony' nn. 38 and 39, and pp. 192–4.
2   See DMWY, pp. 40–43 and 322–3.

---

First published in DMANMC, pp. 217–35.

and symphonies is embodied for me not only in the forms of individual songs and symphonic movements but also in the dominant idea of the 'frame', that is, the idea of a first movement outlining the start of a narrative or interior drama and a finale supplying the denouement, the resolution of what has intentionally been left incomplete; an elaborate example of this practice we have already encountered in the case of the Fourth Symphony. Mahler's first song-cycle, the *Lieder eines fahrenden Gesellen*, certainly had unfolded a narrative, but a 'frame' there was not; in *Kindertotenlieder*, however, 'frame' and narrative are virtually indissoluble, and were to remain so until the very end of Mahler's life, as indispensable, for example, to the form and total experience of the Tenth Symphony in *its* entirety as to the First (something we should never have known, by the way, if it had not been for Deryck Cooke's feat of creative scholarship in transcribing Mahler's composition sketches).

It is just this remarkable dimension, generated by the preceding symphonies, that constitutes a unique feature of *Kindertotenlieder*. Who could have predicted that an outwardly 'poetic' sequence of songs, narrow in focus – each song in its way a meditation on mortality, on the special poignancy of the loss of children – and seemingly devoid of the possibility of 'drama', of narrative progression, should in fact represent one of Mahler's subtlest and most sophisticated treatments of both 'frame' and narrative.[3] At this stage in the development of his phenomenal compositional techniques, *Kindertotenlieder* revealed the clearest indication of the coincidence of song-cycle and symphony, though in fact it is only in recent years that the unique characteristics of the work have been recognized.

---

3   Perhaps it might be useful here to be reminded of my definition of the 'narrative idea' in Mahler, i.e. the practice of 'not ending up where one had started' which was developed by the composer 'across his symphonies, from first to last, into the concept of the "frame", where the finale not only lands us up somewhere else [Heaven, as it happens, in the Fourth, an ecstatic Void in *Das Lied*, acceptance (of death?) in *Kindertotenlieder*) but also brings to a conclusion what the first movement (or song) had, so to say, left unfinished in terms of narrative; and to the completion of the narrative Mahler added a further dimension, the resolution of a conflict, a drama, outlined in the first movement (or first song in the case of the song-cycles). Thus the denouement, both musical and narrative, is kept for the very final stage. The tension between these two poles sustains the thread of continuity throughout the often varied intervening middle movements and songs.' See GMWL, to which I contributed an article on 'The Orchestral Song-Cycles' 2.120–39. It is from that text that these comments on *Kindertotenlieder* have been taken in a revised form. See also DMSSLD, pp. 74–108.

It is helpful, I believe, to consider the 'frame' first, comparing the first song, 'Nun will die Sonn' so hell aufgeh'n', and the fifth, 'In diesem Wetter, in diesem Braus'. In the first song, the image – message – of the poet is ultimately one of hope: that the sun will after all rise again and disperse the darkness and shadows of the night. Mahler brilliantly mirrors the poet's imagery by purely musical means. He sets out by striking a note of mourning, of grief (D minor), and then, in the second half of the first stanza, moves gradually towards D major – the promise that the sun *will* rise; it is out of this initial alternation of minor and major, the accents of grief giving way to hope (or if not hope, then at least consolation), through this basic minor/major contrast, that the eventual 'goal' of the work is established. Mahler is careful not to establish D major at the end of the first song, as careful as he had been not to release too early the competing tonic, E major, in the Fourth Symphony, and as careful, as he was to prove to be again in the Fifth, to avoid a premature affirmation of D. The outcome in the first song had to remain open; and indeed it is to be the chief function of the finale to resolve the D minor/D major conflict, as we shall see.

The first song not only initiates the evolution of the frame – by implication there has to be a finale to complete it – but also discloses in its own method of formal organization a novel relationship with symphonic form, specifically first-movement sonata form. For the characteristic duality of that historic formal scheme – in Mahler's own time and in many of his own symphonies this continued to survive in the shape of emphatically contrasting first and second subject groups, despite the tonic–dominant axis having been drained of its original form-building power – for that now disestablished complex of dualities, Mahler substitutes a fresh duality, the juxtaposition and alternation of D minor and D major,[4] while

---

4   Mahler had long been preoccupied with the expressive and symbolic potentialities of major and minor. From his earliest years he had made use of the device, examples too numerous and too familiar to spell out here. But I believe it was in *Kindertotenlieder* that, for the first time, he introduced the novel idea of the minor and major modes of the same key functioning, effectively, not only to characterize and occupy what previously might have been thought to be the contrasting territories which were the special preserve of first and second subject groups, but also in terms of longer-range tonal organization to replace the discarded functions of tonics and dominants. A case in point is the Ninth Symphony, its first and last movements in particular, in which this process is carried

each of the four stanzas in the song also plays the role created for it by a novel application of sonata form to strophic song. To be precise, Stanza 1 = Exposition; Stanza 2 = Repeat of Exposition; Stanza 3 = Development; and Stanza 4 = Recapitulation. I cannot stress too strongly the evolution of this unique formal scheme from the preceding symphonies and their preoccupation with sonata form and its potential. If one wants proof of that, then look back no further than to the first movement of the Fourth, to the critical moment of the leadback – a passage I have already dwelt on in detail in '"Swallowing the Programme": Mahler's Fourth Symphony'; see Ex. 1, pp. 162–5. The overlapping technique we hear again in *Kindertotenlieder*, at exactly the same structural juncture, at the end of the first song's third, developmental stanza: while the leadback is still continuing, the recapitulation begins (see Ex. 1, p. 204).

The consequences of these formal innovations were to be immense, and nowhere more so than in the planning and execution of Mahler's last song-cycle, *Das Lied von der Erde*, a work built on a vastly more elaborate and extended scale.[5] However, immediate confirmation of the direct influence of *Kindertotenlieder* in matters of form on *Das Lied* is brought to us by the very first song of Mahler's last song-cycle, the outline scheme of which follows precisely the pattern of the first song of *Kindertotenlieder*, i.e. Stanza 1 = Exposition; Stanza 2 = Repeat of Exposition; Stanza 3 = Development; Stanza 4 = Recapitulation. Small wonder that Mahler's elucidating subtitle for *Das Lied* was 'Eine Symphonie' for solo voices and orchestra.

Before I continue with the sequence of the songs contained within the 'frame' of *Kindertotenlieder*, i.e. Songs 2, 3, and 4, I think logic demands that we take first the finale, the fifth song, which completes the 'frame', and proves to function, I suggest, precisely as

---

to yet further and more elaborate lengths, i.e. the D major/D minor complex of the first movement, and its symmetrical reflection, a semitone lower, the D flat major/C sharp minor complex of the finale. All of this makes the more pointed Mahler's 'textbook' procedure in the first movement of the Fourth, in which the second subject is allotted its proper dominant in the exposition (fig. 3) and re-emerges in the tonic of the recapitulation (fig. 20$^{+1}$). This show of tonal rectitude is of course part of the work's aesthetic strategy, a deliberate 'pedantry' which can also, as Günter Grass suggests, wear the guise of 'playfulness' (see the epigraph to '"Swallowing the Programme": Mahler's Fourth Symphony').

5   See DMSSLD, pp. 173–205; and GMWL, 2.132–9.

Ex. 1   *Kindertotenlieder*, 'Nun will die Sonn' so hell aufgeh'n'

I have sketched out in my opening paragraphs. The first movement
having set up the conflict and the possible 'goal' which might
resolve it, the finale proceeds to do just that, with perfect formal
logic. The formal and narrative parallels with the Fourth are compelling.

What Mahler does in the song-cycle's finale, the fifth song,
'In diesem Wetter, in diesem Braus', is to dilate the initial contrast
with which we are confronted in the first song, the alternation of
D minor and D major, on a greatly expanded scale. Indeed, the
basic form of the finale is one huge, dichotomous strophe, the first
part in a stormy D minor, from 'In diesem Wetter, in diesem Braus',
the second part, from 'In diesem Wetter, in diesem Saus' (bar 99),
a mitigating lullaby from which D major only very gradually
emerges, finally to be established with and on the word 'ruh'n' (bar
119). The lost children have at last found peace, acceptance has been
achieved: what was left an open question at the end of the first song
has been answered. In a marvellous epilogue, the song of the solo
horn reaffirms the attainment of what has been the work's goal, an

unclouded D major. (The model for this postlude Mahler must have taken from Schumann, whose songs are sometimes distinguished by a similar feature, an extended consummatory coda for the piano.)

I hope these comments on the 'frame' may make clear that it is through the first and fifth songs that we come to understand the 'story', the narrative, that this extraordinary cycle tells; some may be surprised by a suggestion that there is a narrative involved in so outwardly a 'poetic' work. And yet the truth is, surely, that a story is told each time the sun sets – and rises again? It is a recurring image that tells us something about the human condition, about the sunrise and sunset that are part and parcel of every single human life. In the last of the song-cycles, *Das Lied*, Mahler was again to pursue his constant preoccupation with matters of life and death – indeed, he was to do so until the sun set on his own life in 1911, with the Tenth Symphony left incomplete.

This might be the place, by the way, to clear up any misconceptions about an autobiographical interpretation of *Kindertotenlieder*. It is true that Mahler was to suffer the tragic loss of his elder daughter in 1907, but this was after the song-cycle had been composed. Nor, as some commentators have implied, was there a morbid, unnatural preoccupation on Mahler's part with the death of children. On the contrary, he transforms what might have been a topic too painful to dwell upon into an experience that is ultimately ennobling and itself transcendent, even of our sorrow at the loss of innocence, of lives intolerably abbreviated by the unpredictable and the unforeseen; that is what Mahler's 'storm' in the finale is about: it is an image of turbulent emotion – as in Britten's opera *Peter Grimes* – not a climatic event. Even so great a tempest of sorrow can be withstood; the psychic destruction caused by the 'storm' can be healed and at length accepted. The profound conciliation that Mahler's D major affirms at the conclusion of his finale is a philosophy to which he was to turn again in the finale of *Das Lied*.

The three songs that are contained within the frame in *Kindertotenlieder* are strongly contrasted, but at the same time each of them explores an aspect of loss; each unfolds a memory and a vision of the lost one or ones. The second, 'Nun seh' ich wohl, warum so dunkle Flammen', reveals as its principal image eyes that now live on in the memory like stars burning in the night; in the third, 'Wenn dein Mütterlein', a father is constantly reminded of the void left by the loss of a daughter; the fourth, 'Oft denk' ich, sie sind nur ausgegangen!', is again a memory, this time of the children who departed on a journey from which they were never to return; in an exultant, even ecstatic, coda (in E flat), the singer has a vision of the lost ones climbing ever higher, iridescent in radiant sunlight: 'Der Tag ist schön auf jenen Höh'n!' But we have to live through the immediately ensuing storm of the first half of the fifth song before that vision is sublimely fulfilled.

Each of these interior songs, moreover, is strongly contrasted in orchestral treatment. The second, 'Nun seh' ich wohl', through-composed, with its passionately yearning appoggiaturas and prominent harp arpeggios, stands close in style and texture to the independent settings of Rückert texts but closest of all perhaps to the famous *Adagietto* (for strings and harp) from the Fifth Symphony, which, as I suggest in 'Eternity or Nothingness: Mahler's Fifth Symphony' (pp. 330–31), is itself a 'song without words' for orchestra in the manner of the Rückert settings. All three songs are independent and each creates its own distinct world; but what must fascinate all students of Mahler are the common features of style, embracing both songs and symphonies, that lend this particular period its stylistic unity, a unity of techniques that Mahler developed and had at his disposal during the first decade of the new century. There is certainly no more convenient way of scrutinizing them than by observing how they function in Mahler's settings of Rückert, in the independent settings or *Kindertotenlieder*.

To conclude our survey of the three songs that form the middle part of the cycle, 'Wenn dein Mütterlein' and 'Oft denk' ich, sie sind nur ausgegangen', though inimitably Mahlerian in tone, traverse widely disparate historical traditions and styles. While the warm and glowing sixths of the horns at the opening of 'Oft denk' ich' vouchsafe resonances of, say, Brahms, the austere character of 'Wenn dein Mütterlein', where a long cor anglais solo is projected over a *pizzicato* bass, calls to mind, irresistibly, an aria or arioso by J. S. Bach, with the cor anglais playing a traditional obbligato role.

Mahler was among the first to make overt gestures to the past, consciously to incorporate into his own work aspects of the history of music; on occasion taking distant predecessors, e.g. J. S. Bach, as models, using them as sources for his own creative innovations. Bach was a constant and profound stimulus to Mahler's imagination; but there were other composers too, representing a more immediate history, one of whom, Bedřich Smetana (1824–1884), was bound up with the history of Mahler's own life and experience as a performing artist – as a conductor, that is, and yet more specifically, as a conductor in the opera house.

Many years ago now I isolated in *Kindertotenlieder* a melodic contour in the second song, 'Nun seh' ich wohl', that quite clearly had its origins in a virtually identical vocal contour from the entombment of the doomed lovers in the final act of Verdi's *Aida*.[6] A crucial contour, one might say, because, as I point out above (see pp. 192–3), it is also to be found in the F minor lament of the adagio of the Fourth, either as a quotation from, or as an anticipation of, the song in question; and what unites all three manifestations of an identical contour is their common source in feelings (whether Mahler's or Verdi's) of pain, suffering, grief and awareness of mortality.

This conjunction of musical imagery fascinated me at the time because it showed, on however a miniature scale, how Mahler's imagination might be serviced by external sources; how an identical dramatic or poetic situation might give rise to identical music; how, in the first instance, the idea might owe its origins to the hand of another creator altogether. This is not to diminish the transformation the idea would undergo, whereby it would attain its own unique Mahlerian character. But it memorably vouchsafes a glimpse of how a composer's set of distinctive responses may initially be shaped by ideas, by invention, other than his own, above all by specific ideas situated in specific contexts, which, albeit

6   See DMWY, pp. 38–9. A further striking Verdi parallel has been brought to my attention by the kindness of O. W. Neighbour. See *La Traviata*, Act III, Violetta's aria, 'Addio, del passato' (A minor!), which clearly influenced the contour of the melody of the second trio (A minor!) of the *Trauermarsch* in the Fifth. And see 'Chailly, Mahler, and the Italian Connection' (pp. 550–55).

unconsciously, have made a quite specific impression on him. (They must also have exerted a quite special and profound *appeal*.) Opportunities thus to sink a tiny illuminating shaft into a composer's psyche are few and far between. This particular example enables us at least to understand why, yes, it had to be *that* idea that seized Mahler's imagination, and not another.

Smetana's operas were works that Mahler knew well and often had conducted himself. I have written elsewhere about possible meaningful influences of Smetana on Mahler, meaningful in the sense that I have just defined above, i.e. they extend well beyond the reach of explanation as casual or inadvertent reminiscence.[7] Thus a special savour was attached to uncovering the same influential contour that I had identified in *Aida*, in Smetana's opera *Dalibor*. Mahler conducted a celebrated production of the work at the Vienna Opera in 1897, but of course had known the opera – indeed conducted it – long before then.

Once again, it is not the replica of Smetana's idea (see Ex. 2, bars 286–9) that is of principal interest, though it demonstrates how familiar Mahler was with the music of his great Czech predecessor. (It is a replication by the way that also embraces timbre and instrumentation, primarily plaintive woodwind in both instances.) What is significant – as in the comparable case of *Aida* – is again the conjunction of imagery. In Smetana's *Dalibor*, my Ex. 2 is generated by the mourning of Milada for her brother, the murdered Burgrave of Ploškovice. The idea stayed with Mahler and then took vital shape in the third song of *Kindertotenlieder*, 'Wenn dein Mütterlein', as Ex. 3 shows (cf. bars 3–4, *et seq.*). It is singular indeed that two operas, one by Verdi, one by Smetana,[8] should have been influen-

---

7  See ibid., p. 209, and 'Mahler and Smetana: Significant Influences or Accidental Parallels', pp. 537–49.
8  Parallels between Smetana and Mahler offer an enterprising student of Mahler – of both composers, perhaps – a valuable research topic that has still not been thoroughly explored. What I have written about Ex. 2 from *Dalibor* by no means exhausts the interest of this passage, where in fact one finds juxtaposed with the contour that has particularly claimed my attention a type of appoggiatura-laden, surging chromaticism (strings prominent!) that is also typical of *Kindertotenlieder* (e.g. the cycle's second song), albeit Mahler's version of this style is more sophisticated and refined than Smetana's. (See Ex. 2, bar 290 *et seq.*)

Ex. 2  Smetana, *Dalibor*

tial in the making of Mahler's second song-cycle; singular, without doubt, but not surprising given the shared context of grief and sorrow. For in a very real sense, the choice of *musical* image had already been made for Mahler by his predecessors, before he began to compose his own sequence of threnodies.

Ex. 2 (contd)   Smetana, *Dalibor*

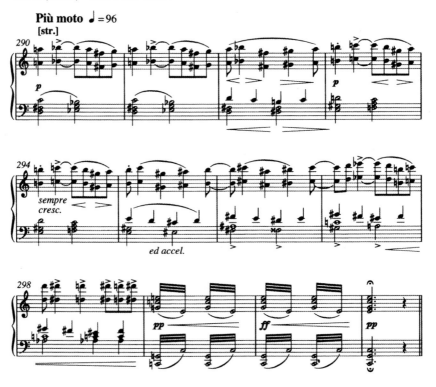

The anatomy of the compilation of Mahler's musical imagery, especially, it would seem, in the field of mourning, is undeniably an absorbing topic. But it must give way to something, I think, of greater significance. I have mentioned above how, in the Fourth Symphony, the concept of the 'chamber orchestra' is already a presence: it became, one might say, in Mahler's hands, a combination of slender resources and counterpoint, both of which innovations are foreshadowed in the symphony. The very first ten bars of the opening song of *Kindertotenlieder* establish the new world of sound; we hear (voice apart), only one oboe, one horn, and two bassoons (strings and harp enter only at the end of the tenth bar: see also 'Eternity or Nothingness? Mahler's Fifth Symphony', p. 345 n. 109). This was a revolutionary development, and it requires a note to itself.

Ex. 3 *Kindertotenlieder*, 'Wenn dein Mütterlein', bars 1–15

Allgemeiner Deutscher Musikverein.

Tonkünstlerfest in Graz.

Donnerstag, den 1. Juni, abends 6 Uhr

(Hauptprobe vormittags 10 Uhr)

Im Stephaniensaal

## Erstes Orchesterkonzert.

**Roderich v. Mojsisovics: Romantische Fantasie für die Orgel** (op. 9), III. (letzter) Satz.

Herr Otto Burkert.

**Guido Peters: Aus der Sinfonie No. 2, E-moll.**

I. Satz.  Frei rezitatorisch; mit Leidenschaft und großem Ausdruck; heroisch.

IV. (letzter) Satz.     Möglichst rasch; feurig; trotzig; bachantisch.

Pause.

**Gustav Mahler: Gesänge für eine Singstimme mit Orchester.**

I.

1. Der Schildwache Nachtlied.
2. Das irdische Leben.
3. Der Tamboursg'sell.
4. Ich bin der Welt abhanden gekommen.

Herr Friedrich Weidemann.

II.

1. Lied des Gefangenen im Turm.
2. Wo die schönen Trompeten blasen.
3. Des Antonius von Padua Fischpredigt.

Herr Anton Moser.

III.

1. Revelge.

Herr F. Schrödter.

2. Um Mitternacht.

Herr Erik Schmedes.

IV.

1. Nun will die Sonne so hell aufgeh'n.
2. Nun seh ich wohl.
3. Wenn dein Mütterlein.
4. Oft denk ich.
5. In diesem Wetter.

Herr Friedrich Weidemann.

Pause.

**Paul Ertel: „Der Mensch".**

Sinfonische Dichtung für großes Orchester und Orgel, nach dem gleichnamigen Triptychon von Lesser Ury, in Form eines Präludiums und einer Tripelfuge (op. 9).

Orgel: Herr Alois Kofler.

The programme for the 'Mahlersoirée' in the Stephaniensaal,
Graz Festival, 1 June 1905

## Mahler and the Chamber Orchestra

On 29 January 1905 a remarkable concert took place in Vienna (and was repeated on 3 February).[9] It was advertised as a 'Lieder-Abend mit Orchester' – an 'Evening of Songs with Orchestra' – and it was given in the Kleiner Musiksaal – the small hall (also known as the Brahmssaal) – of the Musikverein. Three singers participated – Anton Moser (baritone), Fritz Schrodter (tenor), and Friedrich Weidemann (baritone) – and the orchestra, made up of members of the Vienna Philharmonic, was conducted by Gustav Mahler.

The programme consisted exclusively of Mahler's songs with orchestra. It included a number of his *Wunderhorn* settings, among them two of the most recent that he had composed, 'Revelge' and 'Der Tamboursg'sell'. They were also to prove to be the last settings of *Wunderhorn* poems that Mahler was to compose (see below). Indeed, he had already turned to a new poetic world of imagery and feeling represented by the lyrical poems of Friedrich Rückert (1788–1866). Two of Mahler's Rückert settings, now among the most celebrated of his orchestral songs – 'Ich bin der Welt abhanden gekommen' and 'Um Mitternacht' – brought the programme to an end. But there was also another Rückert item on the programme, the first performance of *Kindertotenlieder*, composed between 1901 and 1904, in which Weidemann was the baritone soloist.

We can surmise from the programme announcement what Mahler was after. Something novel, to be sure: an evening of songs – a 'Lieder-Abend' – with a rather special kind of orchestra in place of the customary piano, performed in an acoustic and a hall appropriate to the intimacy implied by the tide of the programme. The substitution was seized on by one of the critics attending the later Graz performance and used – inevitably – to make an *adverse* point:

9   The programme was virtually identical with that of 29 January [see p. 107] but Marie Gutheil-Schoder (mezzo-soprano) joined the team of soloists and contributed a group of *Wunderhorn* songs that included the premiere of 'Lob des hohen Verstandes'.

In his *Kindertotenlieder* (to words by Rückert), Gustav Mahler has
treated a subject that is in part related to [Otto] Naumann's [*Der Tod
und die Mutter*, a large-scale choral work performed at the same
Festival]; but there is no doubt that in his choice of resources he
reveals himself the superior artist since, in order to stage this miniature domestic tragedy, he needs only a small orchestra and a single
vocal soloist. It should be added that the merits and inwardness of
Mahler's songs continue even today to provoke lively and heated
discussion. And not without good reason. Far from warming their
hearts, Mahler's new songs from *Des Knaben Wunderhorn* simply
seem to have left their audiences hot under the collar.

In terms of their craftsmanship, each of these songs is a phenomenon unto itself, and there is no other orchestra that sounds like
Mahler's chamber orchestra. Its characteristic qualities are its tear-
fully muted trumpets, its thrusting *sforzati*, its rattling side drums
and so on. As an example of humour in music, the 'Fischpredigt des
heiligen Antonius' is a collector's item with its leering thirds, its
strokes of the switch [*Rute*] and bubbling cymbal tremolo
[*Tschinellenwirbeln*]. These vocal character pieces reveal tremendous
artistry in their execution; but in those places where the profun-
dities of simple emotion are to be laid bare, not even the most
sophisticated musical staging can hide the fact that the musical
emotion often has little depth to it.

Among all Mahler's songs, there is not one in which a great and
impassioned idea pulsates from start to finish, as it does, for example,
in Wolf's Suleika setting, 'Hochbeglückt in deiner Liebe', which
positively burns with emotional fire. At the same time, there are
some songs by Mahler that it is impossible to remember but which,
at the same time, are impossible to forget. What an impression was
left by 'Der Tamboursg'sell'! And by the *Kindertotenlieder*! The mere
fact that Mahler has chosen such touchingly beautiful poems as the
poetic basis for his songs would speak volumes for him and for the
musician in him. But once again we have the same fussy instrumentation, which is no doubt a pleasure to listen to, but which seems so
'studied' and affected, often contradicting the naive and popular
melodies that Mahler uses. One is left wondering whether the
orchestra, however subtly it may be deployed, is really the best means

of expression for the lied? Or is it not, rather, the piano, an instrument which, in its artistic way, merely hints at what the orchestra
expresses more robustly? . . . Be that as it may: whatever objections
one may have to Mahler and however much he may repel or fascinate
his listeners, he has real personality and is one of the most complex
figures ever to have existed. Whether vocal music will develop further on the basis of his art is something that no one can tell today.[10]

Well, at least the critic in question recognized the unique sound
of Mahler's chamber-orchestral concept, something to which perhaps these days we pay too little attention, especially in the field of
performance practice.

Mahler's radical reduction of his orchestral forces in *Kindertotenlieder* is self-evident in the areas of woodwind, brass, and percussion; they are spelled out by the composer. But what about the
strings? We have no precise instructions from the composer, though
surely the physical circumstances of the premiere serve as an indicator of the string forces for which he conceived the work. The
choice of the Kleiner Musiksaal speaks for itself; and we know too
that not only was the same hall used on 3 February for the repeat
of the 29 January programme but that a similar chamber-music
venue in Graz (the Stephaniensaal) was also chosen for the programme on 1 June, when Mahler was again the conductor.

His consistent choice of a small hall, which permitted the
employment of only a much reduced string band, has been fascinatingly illuminated by some recent and telling research by Renate
Hilmar-Voit, who has enterprisingly investigated two Viennese
archives in search of the sets of orchestral parts that Mahler might
have used for his 'Lieder-Abend' in January 1905.[11] So far, it is only
the parts for the *Wunderhorn* settings that have come to light,
together with those for one Rückert setting, 'Blicke mir nicht in

10 This (unsigned) article appeared in the *Grazer Tagespost*, no. 161, of 11 June 1905. The
performance itself had been given on 1 June. Dr Renate Hilmar-Voit, whose seminal
study I mention above, has been unfailingly generous in providing me with much of the
information and illustrations on which this section of the chapter is based.
11 See 'Symphonic Sound or in the Style of Chamber Music? The Current Performing
Forces of the *Wunderhorn* Lieder and the Sources', *News about Mahler Research*, 28
(October 1992), pp. 8–12.

die Lieder', for the performance of which, it seems, Mahler could have employed a maximum orchestra of thirty-six players![12] Parts for *Kindertotenlieder* and the other Rückert songs have yet to be located, if they still exist. But it seems safe to assume that the string band would have remained numerically constant throughout, in *Kindertotenlieder*, at least, while perhaps allowing for departures elsewhere from the 'norm'. In any case, the size of the hall (the platform) would not have permitted significant expansion.

The scrutiny of the original string parts that had come to hand enabled Renate Hilmar-Voit to establish an average for the number of strings that Mahler might have used on the occasion of the first performance and subsequently: 8–10 players respectively for first and second violins; 6–8 violas; 4–6 cellos; 2–4 basses, a total that strongly contrasts with the size of the string body that we still too often hear in our concert halls in performances of the cycle. There are undoubtedly grey areas remaining, and further research needs to be done.[13] But we can be reasonably confident that Hilmar-Voit's speculations about the numbers of string players involved come close to what Mahler had in mind when composing *Kindertotenlieder*. Perhaps in future, when performing the cycle, we should attempt to implement what we now know of his intentions when he mounted his 'Lieder-Abend mit Orchester' in the Kleiner Musiksaal of the Musikverein in Vienna in January 1905, thereby introducing to the world his chamber-orchestral masterpiece. It seems, however, as if Benjamin Britten, without the benefit of statistics or research, had already, in the 1960s, perfectly apprehended Mahler's requirements. It was in 1966, at the Aldeburgh Festival, that I heard Britten conduct a remarkable interpretation of *Kindertotenlieder*, with the English Chamber Orchestra and, as baritone

12  The song is scored for a wind quintet – flute, oboe, clarinet, bassoon, and horn – harp, and strings (less double-basses), for which reason it is possible that an even smaller number of strings would have participated in this song than Hilmar-Voit's 'average'. *Kindertotenlieder* apart, did Mahler perhaps adjust the size of the string body according to the individual needs of each independent song? See also GMWL, 2.127 and 2.129, where the statistics in respect of 'Blicke mir nicht' should be corrected.

13  For example, there is an intriguing reference by Mahler in the context of his correspondence with Strauss (see below, n. 16) to '*twenty-four* Philharmonic players', but this could not possibly represent a total, i.e. the final song of *Kindertotenlieder* alone requires minimal forces well in excess of that number.

soloist, John Shirley-Quirk. Britten, in the 1930s, was among the earliest admirers of Mahler in England and possessed an ear famous for its refinement. At that time, there was no information available of the kind we owe to the initiative of Hilmar-Voit, and I thought it would be highly interesting to try to discover the precise string resources employed by Britten on the basis alone of his intuitive ear and his insights into Mahler's mind. After all, in the 1930s he was writing in his unpublished pocket diary, *Kindertotenlieder* 'restores my faith in life' (1935); 'cheered by Mahler's glorious *Kindertotenlieder*' (same year); 'Listen also for the 12th time to Mahler's peerless *Kindertotenlieder*' (same year); '. . . play Mahler's divine *Kindertotenlieder*. I feel it is worth having lived, if only for those little miracles' (1936); and finally, in the same year, 'Music that I think I love more than any other'.[14]

I cannot say that I was altogether surprised, given the discrimination of Britten's ear, by what I found: that the numbers of players he used almost exactly conformed to Hilmar-Voit's suggested averages. These were the figures for Britten in 1966: 9 first violins; 8 seconds; 4 violas; 5 cellos; 2(!) double-basses. I find them remarkable and convincing confirmation, arrived at through consideration of the score alone, of Hilmar-Voit's calculations extrapolated from the evidence available to her. Is it not high time that Mahler's performing practice in 1905, Britten's in 1966, and Mark Wigglesworth's in 1993,[15] should be widely adopted, with modification only when *Kindertotenlieder* is to be played in an acoustic larger than that envisaged by Mahler? With his own acute sensitivity to acoustic space he would surely himself have adapted his resources according to the needs of the particular occasion; but that does not mean that we should not ourselves be equally sensitive, whatever the

14  See also the section on 'Britten and Mahler' in DMANMC.
15  See the Aldeburgh Festival Programme Book for 1966, pp. 27–9 and 52, and the programme for the London Philharmonic Orchestra concert conducted by Mark Wigglesworth, at the Royal Festival Hall, London, 7 December 1993. On 26 May 1994 I contributed a lecture to the British Library's Stefan Zweig Series entitled 'Mahler's Chamber Music: His Late Orchestral Songs', an altogether wider investigation of his *Kammermusikton* than is possible here. In a slightly amended form I read this same paper at Oxford on 31 October 1995, as part of a series of seminars, 'Gustav Mahler and *fin de siècle* Vienna', convened by Daniele Reiber and James Ross.

occasion, to Mahler's explicit wishes, that is, continually to keep in mind the ideal acoustic space for which these songs were created.

The truth is that *Kindertotenlieder* represents what, for Mahler, was *his* form of chamber music – in his case, *vocal* chamber music, with a small, highly selective instrumental ensemble accompanying the voice. So much is confirmed by what Mahler himself wrote to Richard Strauss from Vienna in May 1905:

> Dear Friend
>
> I do not desire a 'special position' [i.e. the 'preferential treatment' Strauss mentions in the letter to which Mahler replies]! That would be a great misunderstanding on your part. Only a *small hall* for my songs that would be performed in the manner of *chamber music* [*Kammermusikton*]. – And just because I should not wish to take away an *evening*, I suggest a matinee. And in the interests of the *whole* it does not seem dignified to put on a few songs as the *conclusion* of a *Festival* . . . Moreover, you yourself know best that I am not forcing myself upon you, and that I really am not vain. – Here, for artistic reasons (despite all the pressure of 'commercial' considerations), I have put on these songs only in the *small* hall [i.e. in the Kleiner Musikvereinssaal, in January], and they were only appropriate there. To perform them in a large hall to round off a Festival is *decidedly lacking in taste* and really would expose us to those reproaches!

Mahler goes on to add in a postscript:

> . . . I suggested the songs, as they are less trouble to prepare, being a more modest gift. But as they *are* being performed, it must be done in appropriate style. So – only in the small hall!
>
> That I should cut a better figure at a large festival concert is self-evident. So it cannot be ostentation on my part to prefer a matinee in the small hall.

To round off the story, Strauss wrote to Mahler on 18 August, 'I have had enthusiastic reports of your songs in Graz from many friends . . .'[16]

16  Mahler had his way, and when the 'Lieder-Abend' was repeated at Graz on 1 June 1905,

In the context of this discussion of Mahler and the chamber orchestra, it is fascinating to find that of a performance of Mozart's G minor Symphony (K. 550) conducted by Mahler at Carnegie Hall on 29 November 1910, the same occasion on which he conducted Elgar's *'Enigma' Variations* (see DM, 'The Mahler Renaissance in England' in DMANMC, p. 554 n. 4), the critic of the *New York Times* wrote,

> Mr Mahler gave the audience a surprise. He had it played by a much reduced number of orchestral players, on the basis of eight first violins instead of the sixteen that make up the normal number of the orchestra. The other stringed instruments were reduced in proportion; some of the wind instruments were also lessened in number, but there were four flutes, though they did not always all play. The intention obviously was to give, as far as might be, the effect of such an orchestra as Mozart had in mind when he composed the symphony – an effect in which the wind instruments have a larger share than they have in performance of such works by the modern orchestra. But it may be doubted whether the results falling upon the ears of auditors in Carnegie Hall were such as were heard by listeners of Mozart's time; for they were those of a small orchestra in a large hall, instead of a small orchestra in a hall suited to its number. They were interesting results, however. The sonority was greater than was to be expected, and the quality of the orchestral colour, with the increased proportion of the wind instruments, was no doubt new to many to whom the symphony has been a life-long friend. It may be questioned whether this attempt was convincing to those who know the symphony as it is usually played in these days, or whether many will wish to hear Mozart's symphonic music hereafter in no other guise.'

(See Zoltan Roman, *Gustav Mahler's American Years: 1907–1911 – A Documentary History*, pp. 415–16.)

----

as part of the Tonkünstlerfest des Allgemeinen Deutschen Musikvereins, the concert was given in the Stephaniesaal. The programme, substantially, was the same as its Vienna counterpart, but Gutheil-Schoder (a later addition) did not participate and the original team of male singers was joined by Erik Schmedes (tenor). The exchange of letters between Mahler and Strauss is to be found in Herta Blaukopf (ed.), *Gustav Mahler–Richard Strauss: Correspondence 1888–1911*, pp. 77–82.

## *The Two Last* Wunderhorn *Songs:* 'Revelge' and 'Der Tamboursg'sell'

By 1905 Mahler had completed his *Kindertotenlieder* and independent settings of Rückert, and thenceforth, undeniably, when we are considering the interplay and interpenetration between song and symphony, it is the Rückert songs that play the role in the symphonies that had formerly been played by the *Wunderhorn* songs, though the relationship now assumed new shapes, new orchestral sounds, and – in *Kindertotenlieder* above all – opened up new formal vistas. But the completion of the Fourth Symphony, and the shift – unequivocally anticipated in that symphony – in the succeeding trinity of symphonies, Five, Six, and Seven, exclusively to the orchestra (no orchestral paraphrases of songs, no vocal signposts), did not, in my view, mark the complete break with the *Wunderhorn* past that it has so often been taken for; indeed, as I shall come to suggest in my discussion of the unique characteristics of the Fifth Symphony, the *Wunderhorn* world that Mahler had made his own up to the turn of the century was still, after it, a potent creative force; it had not been abandoned so much as assumed new guises. In this crucial cross-centuries evolution, it was the two final *Wunderhorn* settings, 'Revelge' (1899) and 'Der Tamboursg'sell' (1901), through which, in significant part, the transition to the 'new' symphonic manner was effected.

About the latter song, Mahler spoke at length to the invaluable Bauer-Lechner – Mahler's Boswell! – in the summer of 1901, adding the comment that 'he felt sorry for himself that he should have to write "Der Tamboursg'sell" and the *Kindertotenlieder,* and he felt sorry for the world that would have to hear them one day, so terribly sad was their content'.[17]

As Mahler himself recognized, these are indeed tragic, ironic, sometimes desperate songs, both of them – I use these words advisedly – towering masterpieces and each of them a march, in the case of 'Revelge' a vocal march of epic proportions. There is nothing

17  NB-L *Recollections,* p. 173.

quite like this elsewhere in music, nor in Mahler's vocal music. We come to realize, moreover, that these last two *Wunderhorn* settings reverse the hitherto established relationship of song to symphony: in 'Revelge' and 'Der Tamboursg'sell' it is symphony that is now fertilizing song. It is not at all fanciful to regard these extraordinary songs as the spiritual ancestors of the great opening march movements that distinguish the ensuing trinity of symphonies, Five, Six, and Seven.

The sheer scale of the songs speaks for itself, as does the high profile allotted the orchestra alone. Each song inhabits a unique sound-world,[18] a consequence of the orchestra's transformation into something approximating to military wind bands. Percussion is prominent. The strings themselves in 'Revelge' are used as a percussive resource, while in 'Der Tamboursg'sell' only the lower strings – exclusively cellos and double-basses – are employed. The *intensity* of this music has few parallels, even elsewhere in Mahler. These final *Wunderhorn* settings remind us of one central truth about his approach to his texts, that for him the poems were not artificial evocations or revivals of a lost age of chivalry and German Romanticism but, with the exception of a few genial, sunny inspirations, vivid enactments of *reality*, of sorrow, heartbreak, terror and pain. The *Wunderhorn* songs often tell a chilling truth about the human condition.

It is generally received opinion that the *Wunderhorn* songs contributed fundamentally to the character and period of Mahler's first four symphonies, while it was the Rückert settings, albeit in a different way, which made a contribution of scarcely less importance to the character and period of the symphonies from the Fifth onwards. That was a view to which I subscribed, perhaps helped formulate, myself; and it remains largely true. But there is no doubt in my mind now that it represents an over-simplification, and in particular overlooks the peculiar complexities of the overlapping(!) that occurred during this critical phase of evolution. This is fascinatingly represented by a passage from 'Der Tamboursg'sell', one of the crowning glories of the *Wunderhorn* world, which, on

18  See also DM, 'Mahler's "Lieder-Abend": Many Songs, Many Orchestras'.

examination, unequivocally has its roots in the 'new' style that Mahler was developing in *Kindertotenlieder* and independent Rückert settings: not only a unique slenderness of sound but – counterpoint! Moreover, in 'Der Tamboursg'sell' it takes the canonic shape that is often at the heart of the counterpoint in *Kindertoten-lieder* and the Rückert songs. In the remarkable passage I quote as Ex. 4 we have, so to say, stepped out of the *Wunderhorn* world and – in compositional techniques, I must emphasize, *not* character – into the world of the Rückert songs. The point is clearly made if we compare Ex. 5 from *Kindertotenlieder* (Song 1) with Ex. 4 from 'Der Tamboursg'sell'.

Everything – timbre, the slenderness of sound and refinement of instrumentation, the insistently canonic thinking – points to this singular coincidence of the *Wunderhorn* and 'Rückert' worlds in these last *Wunderhorn* settings. At the very time that he was, from one point of view, quitting that world, he was rethinking it in terms of the techniques that were to service the new world of song he was about to explore. As for the high profile allotted canonic for-mulations, it is not in *Kindertotenlieder* alone that we find striking examples. Some of the independent Rückert settings are rich in canonic activity, on a simple scale in 'Blicke mir nicht . . .' and on an elaborate, innovative scale in 'Ich bin der Welt . . .', the counter-point of which directly anticipates the unique heterophonic poly-phony of *Das Lied von der Erde* (see also 'Eternity of Nothingness? Mahler's Fifth Symphony', pp. 339 and 350–51 and n. 115). This is a huge subject in its own right. It must suffice for me to say here that in the evolution of the heterophony that was often to character-ize – indeed, to revolutionize – Mahler's late contrapuntal style, an altogether logical developmental stage was the priority given to canonic thinking. Here too, then, there is further evidence of the signposts to later and radical events in Mahler's music that study of the two final *Wunderhorn* songs, and of 'Der Tamboursg'sell' in particular, will reveal. It is entirely typical of Mahler that in the very songs that seemingly close the door on his *Wunderhorn* period, he was at the same time opening a window on works to come as seemingly remote in style and contrasted in character as *Das Lied* (which, heterophony apart, is also rich in canonic incident!). Thus

Ex. 4 'Der Tamboursg'sell'

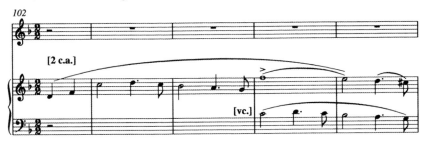

Ex. 5 *Kindertotenlieder*, 'Nun will die Sonn' so hell aufgeh'n'

my Ex. 4 not only palpably 'belongs' to the mind that – I have no doubt – was already preoccupied with *Kindertotenlieder* but also to that same mind that was, four years later, to create *Das Lied*.

All this should make us cautious, as I have already remarked, about establishing clear lines of demarcation in pursuit of a tidy chronology. There were certainly shifts in textual sources, narrative preoccupations, and compositional techniques; but as I hope our scrutiny of the works, symphonies, and songs is beginning to show, there was no specific moment in the history of Mahler's creativity which one could describe as a condition of stasis. His oeuvre was always in a state of evolution, one thing beginning as another was ending, irrespective of genre or 'period'. 'Overlapping' which, as we have seen, surfaces not only in the first movement of the Fourth Symphony but also in the first song of *Kindertotenlieder*, at identical formal junctures, might well serve as a motto for the whole of this chapter; and indeed as we move into the final phase of it, and embark on an exploration of the Fifth Symphony, overlapping yet again must rivet our attention; for it is 'Der Tamboursg'sell' that proves to be the vehicle of transition to the new symphony's first movement, itself an epic *Trauermarsch*. It is no more than the truth to claim, quite simply, that the last *Wunderhorn* song from 1901 provides us with an upbeat to the symphony on which Mahler had started work in the same year, an upbeat both in general and in particular because, as we shall see confirmed by Ex. 1 (p. 228) in 'Eternity or Nothingness? Mahler's Fifth Symphony', it is precisely an upbeat that is one of the features that distinguishes – and unites – the song that is a *Trauermarsch* and the *Trauermarsch* which is the movement with which the Fifth begins.

# Eternity or Nothingness? Mahler's Fifth Symphony

*To – and for – Riccardo Chailly*

~: 1999 :~

> He was afraid she would ask him to explain some-
> thing he had written, and he always winced at
> that – perhaps too timidly – for to his own ear the
> explanation of a work of art sounded fatuous.
>
> Henry James, *The Lesson of the Master* (1892)

## Part I
### (i) 'Trauermarsch'
### (ii) Stürmisch bewegt, mit grösster Vehemenz ['Hauptsatz']

*The 'Trauermarsch' and 'Der Tamboursg'sell'*

As I have already mentioned in the concluding sentence of
'Mahler's "Kammermusikton"', the characterizing upbeat that distinguishes the last *Wunderhorn* song, composed in July 1901, itself
forms the no less characterizing and ubiquitous upbeat that is the
distinguishing feature of the *Trauermarsch* of the symphony. The
song in fact comprises two funeral marches, the second appreciably
slower than the first; it is virtually an independent Part II, an independence further emphasized by its own independent tonality and
characterizing instrumentation: the first (vocal) march is accompanied by a military wind band, while the second emphatically introduces the strings. Here already is a manifestation of the dichotomy
fundamental to the concept of the symphony, both its instrumentation

---

First published in DMANMC, pp. 236–325.

and its narrative. In a typical gesture, Mahler, for Part II, forsakes the
E minor of Part I, and shifts a whole tone downwards, to D minor.
Thus the concluding march of the song is yet more sombre, yet
darker, than its predecessor. The penultimate statement of the dead
drummer-boy's last farewell, before night envelops him, his desperate 'Gute Nacht!', is launched, *fortissimo*, on the rhythm of the
upbeat itself, returning the song in fact to the motive that was its
genesis (bars 4 and 156).

In 'Mahler's "Kammermusikton"' I quoted Mahler's remark to
Bauer-Lechner in August 1901 that shows how conscious he was
of the burden of tragedy that both 'Der Tamboursg'sell' and *Kindertotenlieder* carried; an infinitely touching example, I find it, of the
artist's capacity (his need, perhaps?) to distance himself from his
creations, to grieve for himself – that he is compelled to act as a
vehicle of sorrow – and for the world that 'one day' would have to
listen to the products of his grieving; and yet there is no hint of an
option that might have relieved him of his burden to act, to create,
to communicate, as spokesman for the suffering inherent in the
human condition. Mahler's (I dare say) casual comment to Bauer-
Lechner reminds us of how it is that the world itself learns *how* to
suffer, from and through the work of artists, who suffer, without
complaint for the most part, on the world's behalf.

It was on this same occasion, it seems, that he recounted to
Bauer-Lechner how 'Der Tamboursg'sell' 'came into being':

> [The song] occurred to him literally between one step and the next –
> that is, just as he was walking out of the dining room. He sketched
> it immediately in the dark ante-room, and ran with it to the spring
> [adjacent to Mahler's land on the Wörthersee] – his favourite place,
> which often gives him aural inspiration. Here, he had the music
> completed very quickly. But now he saw that it was no symphonic
> theme – such as he had been after – but a song! And he thought of
> 'Der Tamboursg'sell'. He tried to recall the words; they seemed
> made for the melody. When he in fact compared the tune and the
> text up in the summerhouse, not a word was missing, not a note
> was needed; they fitted perfectly![1]

1   NB-L *Recollections*, p. 173. See also below, n. 10.

A page from Mahler's autograph full score of the Fifth Symphony. The passage comprises bars 351–8 of the second trio in the *Trauermarsch*.

Ex. 2   Fifth Symphony, first movement, march melody, bars 89–120

It is a recollection, if accurate, that seems to anticipate a similar creative incident that was to occur a few years later: the first intimation of the music for 'Veni, creator spiritus' in the Eighth, hurriedly written down in the absence of a full text which later proved to match up with the initiating musical genesis.[2]

But of more significance for our present purpose is the issue of chronology which the circumstances of the song's composition bring to the fore. It is already clear, I believe, from a comparison of

2   See also DMSSLD, pp. 523–6.

Ex. 4 (p. 223) in 'Mahler's "Kammermusikton"' with Ex. 2, that 'Der Tamboursg'sell' and the opening *Trauermarsch* of the symphony share the same world. My earlier quotation of a passage from the song's second march is sufficiently revealing; but if one juxtaposes the melody of the song's first march (Ex. 1) with the principal melody of the symphony's first movement (Ex. 2), from which I cite the march tune's second appearance (and expansion), the convergence is yet more striking. Moreover, while the first limb or contour of the march melody in either case adheres to the established pattern of a funeral march, each departs from that 'model' when embarking on its continuation or, as in the case of the song, a second (related) march is added by way of conclusion. In both cases, however, it is precisely during the process of extension or addition that each march, in the song as in the symphony, incorporates references to a further prime source, the first song of *Kindertotenlieder*: my Exx. 4 and 5 (p. 221) in 'Mahler's "Kammermusikton"' make this very point, the unique surfacing of the song-cycle's characterizing techniques in a *Wunderhorn* context, thereby constituting what I designate Part II of 'Der Tamboursg'sell', while the evolution of the symphonic march, second time round, after its repeat of its basic march profile, itself seems to assume the character of the song's second march and, at the same time, even more closely approximates to the contours of 'Nun will' die Sonn' ...'. Indeed, it is exactly this conscious or unconscious convergence that then logically permits the direct quotation from the song in which the final statement of the symphony's *Trauermarsch* culminates, just before the onset of the first trio of the march at fig. 15.

There are, then, three independent yet intimately related items for consideration,[3] each of which had a role to play in the critical period of transition following the completion of the Fourth Symphony: 'Der Tamboursg'sell', the first song of *Kindertotenlieder*, and

---

3   There might be four if, as I speculate in '"Swallowing the Programme": Mahler's Fourth
    Symphony', nn. 38 and 39, and 'Mahler's "Kammermusikton"', n. 1, further research on
    the chronology of the composition of *Kindertotenlieder* indicates a change in the relation-
    ship between the second song in the cycle and the slow movement of the Fourth Sym-
    phony, with its seeming 'quote' from, or reference to, 'Nun seh' ich wohl'.

the first movement, the *Trauermarsch*, of the Fifth, the movement which represented the first stage in a symphonic narrative in which, in my submission, the transition from the *Wunderhorn* world to a new world, of which the move to settings of Rückert was *emblematic*, was accomplished. (I emphasize 'emblematic' because of course the innovations in form alone, not to speak of style, of manner, of technique, far outweigh the significance of setting fresh texts. There is no denying that the imagery of Rückert is something very different from the characteristic imagery of the *Wunderhorn* anthology. But it would be simple-minded in the extreme to attribute Mahler's radical formal innovations, say, to his 'discovery' of Rückert. Other forces were at work; hence the critical importance of the Fourth, in which so much of the 'new' that was to come is anticipated. None the less, 'Rückert' remains a useful shorthand to indicate the changes that were afoot.)

Everything, naturally, could be clarified if we were able to introduce into the jigsaw-puzzle-like constellation of interrelationships a tidy chronological account of when the works, whether song, song-cycle, or symphony, were composed. First, some known dates and information of relevance. As my Table 1 shows, there are relatively few firm dates amid a quantity of information of probable chronological relevance. This is particularly true with regard to the detailed creative evolution of the symphony. What follows is inevitably largely conjectural; but it seems to offer, on the basis of our present knowledge, a reasonable account of when, and in what sequence, the Fifth came to be composed.

*Table 1   Chronology of the Fifth Symphony*

| | | |
|---|---|---|
| 1899 | June/July | 'Revelge', the first to be composed of the two last *Wunderhorn* settings (see also 1901). |
| 1900 | 5 August | Mahler completes the slow movement of his Fourth Symphony, thus bringing to a conclusion the symphony as a whole (the song-finale-to-be had been composed as an independent orchestral song (see Ex. 1, pp. 162–5) in 1892). (See also nn. 38 and 39 (p. 194) and n. 1 (p. 200).) |

| 1901 | June/August | Mahler composes four of his independent Rückert settings, among them 'Ich atmet . . .' and 'Ich bin der Welt . . .'. |
| | 12 July | 'Der Tamboursg'sell' composed in its voice and piano version. |
| | 25 July–10 August | 'During these past few days, Mahler talked to me [Bauer-Lechner] for the first time about the work he is now engaged on, his Fifth Symphony, in particular the third movement, which he is writing at present.' (NB-L *Recollections*, p. 172.) |
| | 10 August | Mahler plays through 'Der Tamboursg'sell' to Bauer-Lechner, according to her diary (NB-L *Recollections*, p. 173). |
| | Summer [A] | *Kindertotenlieder:* three songs composed, among them 'Nun will' die Sonn' so hell aufgeh'n', the first song of the cycle. |
| | | Fifth Symphony: works (probably) on first three movements, i.e. the scherzo (Part II) and the two movements of Part I (*Trauermarsch* and 'Stürmisch bewegt' (allegro)). |
| | end of year | Works on *Adagietto* (fourth movement)? (See below, pp. 336–9.) |
| | 27 December | Announcement of engagement to Alma Schindler. |
| 1902 | 9 March | Marriage of Mahler and Alma. |
| | Summer vacation (June–August) | 'He had the sketches for his Fifth Symphony with him, two [*sic*] movements completed and the rest in their earliest stages.' [AM *Memories*, p. 42.] |
| | | Fifth Symphony: Part III (movements four and five) completed. |
| | Autumn | 'He played me the completed Fifth Symphony.' [AM *Memories*, p. 47.] |
| 1903 | October | To initiate the publishing process, Mahler sends Alma's manuscript fair copy of the full score to Heinrich Hinrichsen, his publisher (Peters). His inscription to Alma ran as follows: 'Meinem lieben Almscherl, der treuen und |

---

A   No specific dates, but we know Mahler's vacation extended from early June until late August: these are generally assumed to have been his working months, compositionally speaking.

|      |                                                  |                                                                                                                                                                                                              |
|------|--------------------------------------------------|--------------------------------------------------------------------------------------------------------------------------------------------------------------------------------------------------------------|
|      |                                                  | tapferen Begleiterin auf allen meinen Wegen' Wien, Oktober 1903.' ('To my dear Almscherl, the faithful and brave companion on all my journeys.')                                                               |
| 1904 | Summer vacation (late June– August)              | *Kindertotenlieder:* two further songs composed, the last and No. 2, 'Nun seh' ich wohl, warum so dunkle Flammen'. (See, however, 1900 and n. 3, above, and 'Mahler's "Kammermusikton"', p. 207.)              |
|      | September (Leipzig)                               | Publication by Peters of study score, the first printed edition of the symphony.                                                                                                                               |
|      | 17 and 26 September (Vienna)                      | Two runs-through ('reading' sessions) with Vienna Philharmonic heighten Mahler's dissatisfaction with his scoring.                                                                                              |
|      |                                                  | There was to follow a seemingly endless series of revisions that was to continue until the end of his life, though in fact the process had begun even in advance of the 'reading' sessions.                     |
|      | 18 October (Cologne)                             | First performance of Fifth Symphony in Gürzenich concert hall (see illustrations on pp. 266 and 267).                                                                                                           |
|      | November                                         | First edition of full score published, incorporating some of Mahler's revisions of study score.                                                                                                                |
| 1905 | 13 March                                         | First Hamburg performance of Fifth under Mahler. 'Brecher . . . told us . . . [the Scherzo] came first in order of composition.' (Frau Dehmel's diary quoted in AM *Memories*, p. 92.)                           |
|      |                                                  | At the general rehearsal on 12 March, Hermann Behn, a close musical friend of Mahler's, had made a note of the timings of the individual movements. Part I: 1 = 12'; 2 = 15'. Part II: 15'. Part III: 1 = 9'; 2 = 15'. There was a pause of 2' between the *Trauermarsch* and ensuing allegro, a pause of 3' after the end of Part I and a pause of 3' after the scherzo.[B] |
| 1907 | 22 October (St Petersburg)                       | 'By day I revised my Fifth Symphony.' (AM *Memories*, p. 295.)                                                                                                                                                 |

B   See the 'Verbesseter Ausgabe' of the symphony, vol. v in the *Critical Edition* published by C. F. Peters and the International Gustav Mahler Society, Vienna, ed. Karl Heinz Füssl (1988), p. iv. In 2001 the International Gustav Mahler Society, Vienna, announced for publication a new edition of the symphony edited by Reinhold Kubik in association with Robert Threlfall.

|          |             |                                                                    |
| -------- | ----------- | ------------------------------------------------------------------ |
| 9 November |           | The Fifth performed in St Petersburg.                              |
| 1908     | (and after) | Constant revisions of orchestration of the Fifth (AM *Memories*, p. 143). |

★

First, we should bear in mind as a kind of backdrop to our consideration the singular fact that during the summer of 1901, more probably the early summer, Mahler was much preoccupied with the idea of death. Perhaps it was, as some have suggested, Mahler's near-mortal illness in February that made him peculiarly conscious of death as a neighbour.[4] On the other hand, the idea of death, above all as an imaginative source, had been part of his creative personality long before 1901; and again, can we really interpret *Kindertotenlieder* as a response to the sharp shock of being reminded of the possible and unpredictable immediacy of his own death? One must be cautious, in any event, to avoid the trap of confusing an artist's life and his art, while at the same time recognizing that, in this particular period, there was an altogether unusual *concentration* on the image of death in the works on which Mahler was currently engaged, varied though the genres were and widely differing in their modes of expression: *Kindertotenlieder*, 'Der Tamboursg'sell', the symphony's *Trauermarsch*.

## Questions of Chronology

Perhaps the best start on the chronology of the symphony can be made by focusing on the scherzo, because it seems likely that this movement, which was to become Part II of the symphony, was the first to be completed.[5] For one thing, it is certain that Mahler had had a movement of this character in mind well before embarking on the Fifth, i.e. a scherzo (in D major), entitled 'Die Welt ohne Schwere' ('The World without Gravity'), had formed part of a draft programme for the Fourth, where it was located as a possible

---

4   Notably La Grange; see HLG *Mahler*, II, pp. 367–9. See also Edward F. Kravitt, 'Mahler's Dirges for his Death', pp. 329–53.
5   See also n. 66 below.

penultimate movement, preceding the 'himmlische Leben' finale.[6] We know for a fact that Mahler was working on the scherzo between (early) June and 25 July because Bauer-Lechner documents a conversation with the composer in which he refers to it, describing it indeed in terms that almost precisely correspond to the title that formed part of the draft programme for the Fourth: 'Every note is charged with life, and the whole thing whirls around in a giddy dance . . . There is nothing romantic or mystical about it; it is simply the expression of incredible energy. *It is a human being in the full light of day, in the prime of his life* [my italics].' Furthermore, in this same conversation, Mahler, it seems, told Bauer-Lechner that his new symphony was to be 'a regularly constructed symphony in four movements [*sic*], each of which exists for itself and is self-contained, linked to the others solely by a related mood [*sic*]'.[7] If that report is authentic, then it lends credibility to the supposition that the scherzo was the first movement to be conceived, since it appears that even before the movement was completed Mahler still had no very clear idea of how the symphony as a whole was to be shaped (he could hardly have talked of a regular four-movement overall form if he had already had in mind, or in part worked on, two pairs of interdependent movements, i.e. Parts I and III of the symphony as we know it today).

There is one further bit of evidence that supports the view that the scherzo was the first movement to materialize. This is a reference to be found in an excerpt from the diary of Ida Dehmel, the widow of Richard Dehmel, the German poet (1863–1920); it was Dehmel's poem 'Verklärte Nacht' that inspired Schoenberg's work of the same title. The Dehmels, it seems, were with the Mahlers in Hamburg in 1905, where the Fifth Symphony was performed on 13 March. Frau Ida wrote of the occasion:

> This Fifth Symphony of his carried me through every world of feeling. I heard in it the relation of adult man to everything that lives, heard him cry to mankind out of his loneliness, cry to man,

6   See DMWY, pp. 138–9, and n. 67 below.
7   NB-L *Recollections*, p. 173.

to home, to God, saw him lying prostrate, heard him laugh his defiance and felt his calm triumph. For the first time in my life a work of art made me weep, a strange sense of contrition came over me which almost brought me to my knees. The *Adagietto* may for me have lacked something, and in the last movement I noticed some check to the logical development. Nevertheless, this symphony is a masterpiece of the first rank, and at a second hearing it was precisely the last movement which engaged my passionate attention: I positively drank in every note. Mahler had warned me in advance that the scherzo might seem obscure – no critic so far had known what to make of it. It was the scherzo that made the strongest impression on you, as by the way it did on Brecher too, who told us it came first in order of composition . . .[8]

The 'Brecher' mentioned by Frau Ida was Gustav Brecher (1879–1940), the conductor, who collaborated with Mahler in the preparation of a new performing edition of Weber's *Oberon*.[9] He was a distinguished musician who had the opportunity to be close to Mahler and thus a source to be taken seriously, especially as he confirms what seems to be the credible chronology that may be extrapolated from Bauer-Lechner's recollections.

I believe, then, that everything points to the scherzo as the first movement to be done, to be sketched out, perhaps while Mahler was still thinking of his new symphony as a four-movement shape. But to what next did Mahler turn his attention?

8   AM *Memories*, pp. 91–2.
9   Tragically, Brecher – a Jew – committed suicide with his wife in 1940, on board ship off the Belgian coast, while attempting to flee from the Nazi invaders. How ironic to reflect that Alma Mahler's stepfather, the Austrian painter Carl Moll (1861–1945), committed suicide for the opposite reason; he was known to be an anti-Semite and feared the liberation of Vienna by Russian troops as the Second World War came to an end, 'like a good many Viennese Nazis', as Alma herself remarks (Alma Mahler Werfel, *And the Bridge is Love*, p. 274). Important information about Moll's tragic last years and hours can be found in G. Tobias Natter and Gerbert Frodl, *Carl Moll*, the catalogue published to accompany the exhibition, 'Carl Moll: Maler und Organisator', at the Belvedere, September–November 1998.

### 'Der Tamboursg'sell' again

At this point we must return to Bauer-Lechner's recollections and more specifically her memory of the composition of 'Der Tamboursg'sell'. This relevant excerpt has already appeared above; I shall repeat here only comments of particular relevance. Mahler, it seems, was searching for a 'symphonic theme' when what came to him was the march melody that proved then to be a song, the carrier of the text of 'Der Tamboursg'sell'. We know the song was written by 12 July 1901 (see Table 1), which means that Mahler in the weeks preceding that date, and on the assumption that he had brought the scherzo to completion (in outline at least), may have been seeking for the 'theme' (the crucial idea, perhaps?) that would get him going on the movements that remained to be composed; not only composed, but conceived.

All of this I hasten to emphasize must be speculative, until such time as more precise chronological information emerges (if ever). Meanwhile, we must do what we can with what the music tells us, often the best and most revealing source of all. It has always puzzled me a little that, according to Bauer-Lechner, when Mahler ran off to the spring with his new idea in his head, 'he saw that it was no symphonic theme . . . but a song!' I began to wonder, in fact, if it were not the case that 'Der Tamboursg'sell' and the possible setting of it had been stored away in Mahler's mind for who knows how long, and came, albeit unconsciously, to influence the contours and rhythm of the melody that surfaced in the summer of 1901 when he was in search of a 'theme' for his new symphony. This would account for what otherwise seems inexplicable, that the words, after the melody had been imagined, 'seemed made for the melody'.[10] But even if that did prove to be the case, the truth is,

---

10  Long after I had written this passage I was astonished to discover the following comment of Britten's, made in a broadcast interview with the Earl of Harewood in 1960. What he says goes a very long way indeed to confirm for me my guess about the sequence of creative events with regard to 'Der Tamboursg'sell'. This, as I have always supposed, is exactly how composers' minds work, whether they be a Britten or a Mahler:

'Quite often I find that I am in the mood for writing a song about a certain kind of subject or in a certain kind of mood, and I have even had in my experience the suggestion

surely, that *it was the words that had given birth to the melody*, even if
Mahler had not recognized the connection as he wrote the melody
down.[11]

How the melody of 'Der Tamboursg'sell' came to take the shape
it did is undeniably fascinating. But what is surprising, if Bauer-
Lechner's recollection can be trusted, is Mahler's opinion − 'no
symphonic theme . . . but a song!'; perhaps not only surprising
but amusing even, when one observes what I guess was the next
creative step in the chronology of Mahler's summer activities, his
embarking on the *Trauermarsch* that was to form the first movement
of Part I of the new symphony. Amusing, because − as I think I have
already demonstrated by the juxtaposition of Exx. 1 and 2 − the
great march melody in the symphony is clearly a sibling of the
song. If Mahler did indeed commit himself to the view that this
type or character of theme was inherently alien to the concept of
symphony, then he would have soon had to change his mind (eat
his words would be the better metaphor, perhaps). For I have little
doubt that once 'Der Tamboursg'sell' was, so to say, fulfilled and off
the creative agenda, Mahler must have realized that the song, not
only musically (that is to say, melodically) but also image-wise, provided him with the point of departure for the narrative that the
new symphony was to unfold.[12] It is thus, I believe, that in this
overlapping of the last *Wunderhorn* setting with the *Trauermarsch* of
the symphony we can hear the *Wunderhorn* tradition and influence
sustained beyond the point where received opinion has it that the

of a tune which would like to have words attached to it. I then look through volumes
until I find such a thing, but nearly always, and I suppose this is where the subconscious
comes in, it is a poem I've known, and I suspect that that poem has been going on ringing in my subconscious, *and has produced the tune but I haven't been aware of it* [my italics]'.

11  For individual studies of 'Der Tamboursg'sell', see Susanne Vill, *Vermittlungsformen verbalisierter und musikalischer Inhalte in der Musik Gustav Mahlers*; Michael Johannes Oltmanns,
'"Ich bin der Welt abhanden gekommen" und "Der Tamboursg'sell" − Zwei Liedkonzeptionen Gustav Mahlers', and Elisabeth Schmierer, *Die Orchesterlieder Gustav Mahlers*, and
Schmierer, 'Between Lied and Symphony: On Mahler's "Tamboursg'sell"'.

12  Once again I must emphasize that any attempt to sort out the chronology of the Fifth's
composition must be speculative. However, that the song was a prime source for the
*Trauermarsch* seems to me to be highly probable. Even if it proved otherwise − and I am
not simply covering my tracks in the event of evidence surfacing that shows the reverse
chronology to have been the case − it would make no great difference to the point of
substance that I am trying to make, that is, it would leave unaffected the mutually influential and interdependent relationship between the two works.

*Wunderhorn* period ended, that is, with the Fourth Symphony. On the contrary, there seems to me to be good reason, as I suggested some years ago,[13] that the *Trauermarsch* (not the trios!) might be regarded as an example of a wordless song for orchestra in his (late) *Wunderhorn* manner. (In a work that is replete with singular symmetries and overlapping I shall have something to say later about the *Adagietto* in a similar context, though the movement owes its origins to Mahler's development of a quite different song style.)

## The 'Trauermarsch'

The 'song' then that the orchestra sings in the *Trauermarsch* is the same song – or a continuation and extension of it – that the doomed drummer sings in 'Der Tamboursg'sell'; and therein resides an overlapping with the long line of preceding *Wunderhorn* songs which are specifically military in their imagery.[14] It was perhaps only appropriate, if somewhat grimly so, that the tradition should expire – but for its extension in the *Trauermarsch* – in a song itself dedicated to the process of extinction. But having, I hope, established the relationship of 'Der Tamboursg'sell' to the new symphony, the next step must be to examine how this orchestral song functions as the initiator of the narrative that will unfold itself across the whole span of the symphony; above all to determine how Mahler sets up the basic conflict that the symphony must have resolved by the time it has ended, along with those indispensable indicators of the means, the mechanisms, by which that resolution will be achieved. As we shall see, the investigation of the narrative techniques involved mean that we have to take into account not only the *Trauermarsch* but the succeeding A minor allegro, 'Stürmisch bewegt. Mit grösster Vehemenz', the fast movement that constitutes the second part of the symphony's Part I.[15] It has often

---

13  In a paper I contributed to the Rondom Mahler II Congress and Workshop, Rotterdam, May 1990, 'Mahler's "Orchestral" Orchestral Songs'. See also below at n. 97.

14  For example, 'Zu Strassburg auf dem Schanz'', 'Der Schildwache Nachtlied', 'Lied des Verfolgten im Turm', 'Wo die schönen Trompeten blasen' and, of course 'Revelge', the first of the two last *Wunderhorn* songs.

15  Inscribed 'Hauptsatz' (main movement) by Mahler in his manuscript full score. However, this highly significant designation was not included in the first published edition of the symphony, nor thereafter.

been suggested in the past that the bipartite concept of Part I represents a divorce of the idea of exposition from the idea of development, each process, in the opening two movements of the Fifth, occupying its own autonomous area. In a very loose descriptive sense, there is an element of truth in the observation. But as we shall see, in order to appreciate the unique characteristics of the Fifth we must be prepared to look at those old terms, exposition and development, in a new light.

Self-evidently, the *Trauermarsch*, through its song of sorrow, 'exposes' the theme of grief, of mourning, which is the symphony's starting point. The slow march makes its (brief) first appearance at fig. 2, in the midst of the very grandly conceived ceremonial gestures which open the movement. At the start, of course, is the initiating fanfare for solo trumpet (see bars 1–20), with which almost every commentator draws a parallel with the fanfare that intervenes at the height of the development of the first movement of the Fourth Symphony (at fig. $17^{+4}$). It is in the nature of fanfares to share common features, or so it seems to me; and the contexts in which the two fanfares are used are so very different that the parallel of the most obvious kind, of which we have heard most in the past, has struck me up to now as a distraction. It is a personal observation of Colin Matthews's that has made me change my mind, i.e. that the opening fanfare of the Fifth is launched on the same pitch – C – as its counterpart in the Fourth, a fact that is highly suggestive of a possible *narrative* relationship. The fanfare in the Fourth emerges at the very end of the development of the first movement, during which all manner of complexities, tensions, and confrontations have been revealed. The movement then returns to its state of grace and innocence; and eventually the symphony ends with a vision of 'heavenly life' (we are even permitted to hear in the last stanza of the *Wunderhorn* song that is the symphony's finale the kind of music that awaits us if we are lucky: it will all be in E major). By recalling – or reviving – the fanfare from the Fourth – if that indeed were the case – was Mahler forcefully making the point that, albeit he had vouchsafed his audiences a glimpse of heaven at the end of the Fourth, the *larger* narrative that had underpinned his symphonic oeuvre from its outset – the

The first page of the autograph manuscript of the Fifth Symphony,
showing the trumpet fanfare

established conflicts and combats – had by no means run its course?

There will be no disagreement, however, about the significance of Mahler's use of the fanfare at the beginning of the Fifth as an agent of overlapping. The Fourth, we may recall (see '"Swallowing the Programme": Mahler's Fourth Symphony'; Ex. 1, pp. 162–5) is especially rich in examples of this compositional technique; and in this respect perhaps a further parallel can be drawn in the ways both fanfares perform in both symphonies: the fanfare in the Fourth not only signals the climax of the first movement's development but also the premature return of the recapitulation; indeed, while the ascending fanfare fades, the sleighbells make their unscheduled entry. Perhaps then, it is not altogether accidental that one of the most overtly dramatic and gripping examples of overlapping surfaces in this first movement of the Fifth, at a critical formal moment of transition at the end of both trios (of which more, much more, below): as each trio winds down, so too does the fanfare start up, puncturing the texture. The principle of simultaneity here – one event beginning even while another ends – is identical with the principle that we encounter in the Fourth (and before that in the Third); and it is this transitional technique, no less than the parallel in narrative imagery, that decisively unites the fanfares of the Fourth and Fifth.

The fanfare, it seems, has led us, quite naturally, into a consideration of the two trios. Quite naturally and also, as it happens, quite appropriately, since in fact the fanfare not only leads us, overlappingly, *out* of both trios, but also *into* each trio, though in this latter case there is no simultaneity involved: it is the unaccompanied and unadorned fanfare that functions as transition to the first trio (fig. 7⁻³) and also to the second (fig. 15⁻⁷), though here Mahler effects a surprising switch in instrumentation – the solo trumpet is eschewed and instead the rhythmic profile of the fanfare is transferred to the timpani, albeit a profile that conserves one of the intervals (a minor third) that is integral to the fanfare in its basic form. Mahler rarely introduces a surprise for the sake only of creating a surprising effect; and in this instance, as we shall see, the surprise of the timpani heralds an even greater surprise in instrumental colour. But we must give our attention first to the

character of both trios and the calculated implications these interpolations have for the overall narrative of the symphony, from its
beginning to its end.

Perhaps I may be allowed here to introduce an interpolation of
my own, an enlargement of what I have already remarked on
above, that this first movement of the Fifth has a successor in the
second movement, the first *Nachtmusik*, of the Seventh, which again
is basically a march with two trios, preceded by an initiating gesture comparable in its function, though distinct in character, to the
fanfare and its forceful continuation at the opening of the *Trauermarsch*.[16] But having said that, and having acknowledged that the
Seventh's patrolling nocturne is one thing and the Fifth's funeral
march quite another, what drives the radical contrasts between the
movements is Mahler's treatment in either case of the trios. In the
Seventh, the trios perform their traditional function, certainly
providing serenade-like contrast with the enfolding march but as
certainly never assuming responsibilities other than those that are
properly theirs. They are trios that have no status as commentary;
they are interludes, rather, relaxations of the steady pace of the
march.

### The Trios, their Function and Significance

The trios in the *Trauermarsch*, however, turn tradition on its head.
They come as a shock, and were no doubt designed to shock us
into an awareness of the symphony's principal issues and concerns,
both dramatic and musical. The precipitating role played by these
trios is to confront us with the symphony's main business, the
struggle to overcome, to conquer, the image or threat of implacable
mortality that the funeral march itself represents. This is an extraordinary *reversal* of the customary role that a trio plays. In place of
relaxation or relatively simple contrast we have two eruptions of
protest *against* the implications of the march, eruptions which at the

---

16 Something of Mahler's *Wunderhorn* manner may linger on in the second movement of
the Seventh doubtless because of its march character. But this is nocturnal music that is
not bathed in a ghastly or ironic light, as is so often the case in the most typical of the
*Wunderhorn* military songs.

same time constitute a music or musics in often desperate search for a resolution of, or solution to, the fateful conflict. If one had no more to suggest than this, it would already be apparent how profoundly Mahler has transformed the idea of the trio in this opening march. Never before, one begins to think, has it borne such a weight of feeling and narrative responsibility. For if these trios are a protesting commentary on the context in which they find themselves, they also perform developmental and expository roles. For example, the first (B flat minor) trio (figs. 7⁻¹¹)[17] not only develops materials from the preceding fanfare and march sections, but introduces during its middle part (fig. I:9) an ascending theme (at fig. I:9⁺⁹, G flat major) that is to recur in the second (A minor) trio (see fig. I:16, D minor) and, yet more importantly, in the ensuing (A minor) allegro (see, for example, figs. II:7, D flat minor, and 12⁺⁹, E flat minor). Thus the first trio combines expository and developmental roles, while the second both develops materials from the first trio while also functioning as a source of important themes and motives for the second *movement*. In short, if one is seeking processes which are identifiably 'symphonic' in character and execution, it is precisely in the trios of the *Trauermarsch* that one locates them; it is thus that Mahler endows the 'trio' with an entirely new formal status and capability.

There is a further arresting feature of the trios which must claim our attention, perhaps the most crucial of all. Each trio, each in its own unique way, rehearses the drama that, at the outset, is the *raison d'être* of the symphony's narrative: the attempt to counter and, finally, to dispel the sorrow, grief, and mourning that the *Trauermarsch* represents; each enactment of the basic conflict in each trio, however, ends in defeat, thus anticipating the defeat with which the second movement is to end. Necessarily so, of course, because if Part I of the Fifth were to end in consolation or triumph, we

---

17  Figs. I:7⁻¹¹ = *Trauermarsch*, the *first* movement of Part I, the passage between figs. 7 (reherasal numbers) and 11. Figs. II:7, D flat minor and 12⁺⁹, E flat minor = the *second* movement of Part I, the allegro, the passage beginning at fig. 7, and next, the passage that begins nine bars *after* fig. 12. Fig. II:29⁻¹ = the *second* movement of Part I, fig. 29 less one bar; and so on. It is the complex relationship of movements I and II sharing the same numerical sequences for bar numbers and rehearsal numbers that makes it essential to precede each reference with a roman numeral to identify the movement.

should have no need of the rest of the symphony. Likewise, there can be no possibility of either trio prematurely disclosing the means by which victory will eventually be achieved; this would put at risk the *coup de théâtre* – the chorale, which is the distinguishing feature forming the dramatic climax of the second movement, the stormy allegro. At the same time, if the trios were to amount to more than local eruptions of frustration, pain, and indignation at the inescapable reality of non-negotiable death, they must, with a longer perspective in view, indicate at least the possibility of a goal, a denouement, that will finally, in this symphony at least, reach an accommodation with the idea of mortality.

It was with characteristic ingenuity that Mahler solved the problem of premature disclosure in the trios. Each trio has somehow to suggest, as each does, the possibility of escape from the *douleurs* of the march, for there can be no – albeit obligatory – defeat if hope has not been created, thence to be suppressed. Thus the aspiring dimension of each trio is serviced by the aspiring theme that I have already mentioned in the context of discussing the first trio's expository role. But 'expose' as it may (fig. I:9$^{+9}$, G flat major), and anticipate though it may the aspiring function this same theme fulfils in the succeeding allegro (e.g. fig. II:12$^{+9}$), disclosure falls far short of revealing a goal that, if achieved, will mitigate the conflict and round off the narrative, when the torrents of protest captive in the trios will at last have run their course.

Mahler brilliantly manipulates his long-term strategy by divorcing, at this stage in the symphony, his thematic and tonal strategies. To be sure, the aspiring theme will continue to aspire; but there is no unequivocal disclosure of the ultimate *tonal* goal – D major – that the conclusion of the finale will eventually and confidently confirm. It is true that even the most modest analysis will show a key scheme – C sharp (leading note) for the *Trauermarsch* and A (dominant) for the ensuing allegro – which, if nothing else, shows how conscious Mahler was, at one level, of preparing the long-term evolution of an ultimate D major; he clearly needed to have the sense of a logical scaffolding in place. Having said that, it seems to me that, in the music he actually went on to create in Part I, in all its eruptive and disruptive ferocity, he tested his scaffolding to destruction. We may intellectually be aware of the 'logic' under-pinning the chaos, but I doubt if we hear it, or that Mahler wanted or expected us to hear it. Hence, in the *Trauermarsch*, neither trio affords us a glimpse of that destination, even when, as in the second trio, the critical moment of aspiration (fig. I:16ff.), followed by defeat (fig. I:18, '*Klagend*'), is enacted in a handling of sound that almost exactly parallels the comparable passage in the second move-ment, where D major is divulged and established (fig. II:29⁻¹), briefly held, and then – as if life itself were audibly drained out of the music – its texture and dynamics, the very density of the chords in the brass, thin out, fade into nothingness (fig. II:29⁺⁵): the final moment of extinction comes with the onset of D minor and the shrill intervention of the woodwind. one of the interruptive ges-tures ('cut-off', about which I shall have much more to say below) that are such a prominent – and dramatic – feature of the move-ment.[18]

The principle generating this procedure – which, as I have just described, is to give us, in the second movement, one of the most remarkable passages in all Mahler – is precisely adumbrated in the second trio at fig. I:18, this time in the shape of a sustained chro-matic slide conceived as a diminuendo.[19] The sound gradually fades and decays as step by step the slide descends and retreats from the initiating dissonance unleashed *fortissimo* in bar 369, the texture thins out, and we are so to say on the brink of silence (in the wake of collapse) until the intervention of the trumpet fanfare and resumption of C sharp minor remind us that while the trios may have revealed ample evidence of the search – of the need – for a solution to the spiritual crisis that the idea of mortality engenders in Everyman, they reveal no hint, musically speaking, of what that solution may prove to be.

---

18  See Table 2A–C below.
19  All too often underplayed these days by the composer's interpreters, as are so many com-parable passages elsewhere in the symphonies. If a passage like this – the climax of the second trio – is not very carefully considered in terms of its novel dynamics and above all without thought being given to its singular role in the drama of the symphony as a whole, and in particular as an anticipation of a critical event in the ensuing allegro, then its significance will pass unheeded. If the interpreter does not comprehend it, then audi-ences certainly won't.

As we have seen, we are to encounter the parallel collapse in the second movement, but this time with a vital difference: collapse the affirmation may, and fade to extinction, but not before the brief-lived, but unambiguous D major at fig. II:29⁻¹ (Mahler marks the bar with its up-rushing D major scale and D major triad, asserted *fff* in the brass, '*Hohepunkt*')[20] has indicated unequivocally that, though we are by no means at the end of the search, D major is potentially the goal towards which the symphony must strive. It is this dimension, the assertion of an unequivocal tonality as potential target, that is conspicuous by its absence from the anticipatory collapse at the end of the second trio. It is, so to say, *Hamlet* without the Prince, and the more chilling, the more 'negative' in its impact, for that very reason.

### A Collective of Orchestras: Instrumentation and Revisions

I may seem to have expended an excessive amount of attention on the two trios of the march; but in fact there has been relatively little comment in the past that has measured up to their importance; and that, if nothing else, I hope to have got across. How we hear those trios is fundamental to our apprehension of what Mahler was about in Part I of his Fifth. If I have concentrated on the 'collapse factor', it is because collapse is their point of consummation (if that is the right word). But by concentrating on this feature common to both trios I do not want to overlook the very significant and intriguing differences between them, especially those that distinguish the second trio from the first. Indeed, the very opening of the second trio introduces a sound-world that hitherto has not impinged on our ears. There is nothing surprising, one might think, in Mahler conjuring out of his hat one of those many independent instrumental constellations that go to make up the orchestra we think of as 'Mahler's orchestra'. (The plural – 'Mahler's orchestras' – might be the more appropriate description of the resources deployed in any-one of his symphonies, songs, or song-cycles.) The *Trauermarsch* provides us with an example of the diverse orchestras involved in

---

20 See below, n. 55.

the march itself: for example, between figs. 1:12 and 14, Mahler abandons the 'conventional' symphony orchestra and converts it, temporarily, into an authentic wind-and-percussion band, precisely the sonority that is associated with ceremonial funeral processions.[21] This vivid interpolation of wind-band instrumental colour is reserved for the final appearance of the principal march melody, preceding the second trio, the opening of which, after the obligatory dotted rhythm upbeat, introduces another and yet more radical change in instrumental constitution. What takes the stage is, basically, a string orchestra (it is unequivocally that, for the fifteen bars between figs. 1:15 and 16), plus – from fig. 1:16 onwards – solo horn (such (soft) brass chords as there are – bars 345–8 – simply fill out the harmony), and, from fig. 1:17, solo trombone(s), plus a pair of horns, effectively, for the two bars immediately preceding the collapse at fig. 1:18.

Furthermore, a scrutiny of the orchestral revisions that Mahler made to his Fifth – a huge subject in its own right[22] – shows him intent on stripping out from his first conception of the second trio all those instrumental redundancies and needless doublings, as a result of which it is a string-orchestral sonority, pure and simple, that magically materializes. This not only provides the maximum contrast to the heavyweight orchestral turbulence and rhetoric of the first trio (not to speak of the imposing funerary ceremony (the fanfare and the rest) with which the *Trauermarsch* opens). If one studies pp. 250–65, where I juxtapose the first conception Mahler had of the sound of his second trio with a version that is close to what we currently hear performed in our concert halls or on disc,

---

21 The addition of a viola line (first for solo, then tutti) at fig. 1:13 in no way materially modifies the wind-band character of this passage. In fact, it is only there to guarantee and sustain the seamlessness of the solo trumpet's melody. Typical of Mahler's fanatically precise ear that, of the violas' nine bars, the first five are for a solo viola, while the remaining four are marked *tutti* ('with mutes'). The solo viola bars, naturally, form part of a dynamic scheme that nowhere exceeds *p*, while the violas tutti are summoned to participate in a texture culminating in the climax (with horns and woodwind) of the trumpet melody. Even so, the mutes, along with Mahler's fastidious distribution of his dynamics among the instrumental groups, ensure that there is no assertion of an *independent* string timbre to dilute the authentic wind-band sonority of this section of the march.

22 See Sander Wilkens, *Gustav Mahlers Fünfte Symphonie: Quellen und Instrumentationsprozess*, and Colin Matthews, *Mahler at Work: Aspects of the Creative Process*. See also Irene Lawford-Hinrichsen, *Music Publishing and Patronage: C. F. Peters, 1800 to the Holocaust*.

the paring-away process – in effect the extrapolating of an orchestra of strings alone from the larger orchestra that is the basic resource – is clearly exposed. The relevant pages from the first published edition (the study score of 1904) are faced in the main by the comparable pages from a later published edition, probably the second edition of the full score, published in 1919 and incorporating many of the revisions he made, unceasingly, to the symphony up to the time of his death. This bringing to bear of a micro-lens, so to say, on the string body is characteristic of Mahler's revisionary practice; one must always – while acknowledging that an important minority of his orchestral revisions derived from the changing acoustic environment in which he found himself performing his music – seek the profounder creative motive behind the façade of seeming practicality.

Was then his prime creative motive to find a way of establishing a radical contrast? Up to a point, yes; but beyond that there is also what one might call the anticipatory function of the second trio, which is part of the special role the trio is designed to play, both musically and narrative-wise. For a start, with the benefit of hindsight (which of course the very first auditors of the symphony did not have), this remarkable opening of a window on the string band cannot but strike us as a prefiguration of a kindred sonority to come (string orchestra plus harp) that is exclusively to service the symphony's fourth movement, the famous *Adagietto*; and since the *Adagietto* has now surfaced in the context of our discussion of the first movement's second trio, perhaps I may emphasize how underrated is Mahler's pioneering of a movement for (primarily) string orchestra in the frame of a large-scale symphony – representing, in fact, its only slow movement. A most unusual step to take, given the evolution of the symphony in the nineteenth century. Is there a meaningful precedent? I have not been able to uncover one.[23]

23  No doubt someone will be able to produce a precedent from somewhere. But will it be relevant? For that reason I exclude the eighteenth century as a possible or probable source. This is something different from suggesting that models for the character of the *Adagietto* may not have been stored away in Mahler's imagination, e.g. the *Adagietto* from Bizet's *L'Arlésienne* Suite No. 1 (1872), while the exploration by other composers towards the end of the nineteenth century of the specific potentialities of the string orchestra, e.g. Grieg's brilliant *Holberg Suite* (first composed for piano solo (1884) but very soon

Fifth Symphony, first movement, second trio: (A) first edition (1904 study score):
bars 312–28. This version of the trio was recorded for the first time together
with Mahler's revised version of the trio by Riccardo Chailly and the Royal
Concertgebouw Orchestra in 1997 on the CD which accompanies *New Sounds,
New Century* (see n. 26 below).

(B) Revised edition (full score, second edition, 1919): bars 312–28.

1904 edition (contd): bars 329–43

1919 edition (contd): bars 329–40

1904 edition (contd): bars 344–50

1919 edition (contd): bars 341–52

1904 edition (contd): bars 351–57

1919 edition (contd): bars 353–65

1904 edition (contd): bars 358–65

I think we have to conclude that this novel isolation of the strings as an independent string band owes most to the development in Mahler's own music of his concept of the orchestra as a *collective of orchestras,* including, it must be added, from the turn of the century onwards, the idea of the chamber orchestra.[24] There are essential things of course still to be said about the clear relationship of the *Adagietto* to Mahler's late orchestral song style, manifest in the settings of Rückert; and just because of that it is worth recapitulating here that, for Mahler, those songs represented his 'Kammermusikton' (see 'Mahler's "Kammermusikton"'). I think in the context of the symphony, as it unfolds, the switch to the string orchestra (not to speak of the intimate, song-like character of the *Adagietto*, that Mahler seems to have recognized himself; see n. 97 below) created the atmosphere – perhaps illusion might be the better word – of a *chamber music conceived for the large concert hall*; and that in turn brings to mind Mahler's string orchestral arrangements of Schubert ('Death and the Maiden' String Quartet (D. 810), the slow (variation) movement of which Mahler performed in Hamburg in his 1894–95 season) and Beethoven (the F minor Quartet, Op. 95, performed in Vienna in 1899). These arrangements were greeted with incomprehension and hostility by their first audiences. To us, however, they are evidence of his preoccupation with string orchestral sound during those last years of the nineteenth century, a fascination that surely was to influence, at and after the turn of the century, his own forays in the medium.[25]

emerging in its string orchestral guise (1885)), may well have stimulated Mahler's own interest in the medium. It is worth noting that there are significant stretches in the Ninth Symphony, in its first movement, e.g. figs. 11–12$^{+13}$, where it is virtually a string orchestra that carries the weight of seething expression. Other instrumental sectors are intermittently involved but it is the timbre of the *strings,* virtuosically exploited, that is predominant.

24  I have pointed out in the previous note how the string orchestra, as an entity, surfaces in the Ninth. So too, even more decisively, does the concept of the chamber orchestra, again in the first movement. See bars 376–98.

25  Nor should we exclude the first twenty-four bars of the opening of the Fourth Symphony's adagio, though there is a distinction, I believe, to be made between string orchestral passages interpolated into a movement, as in the Fifth and Ninth Symphonies, and a third movement in a sequence of movements which opens with the string body and only after the obligatory break between movements. In the context of the Fourth and its adagio, and, more specifically, its string-orchestral character, it is perhaps worth

1904 edition (contd): bars 366–74

1919 edition (contd): bars 366–74

1904 edition (contd): bars 375–83

1919 edition (contd): bars 375–83

1904 edition (contd): bars 384–401

1919 edition (contd): bars 384–401

The cover of the programme for the premiere of the Fifth Symphony at
Cologne on 18 October 1904, the first Gürzenich Concert

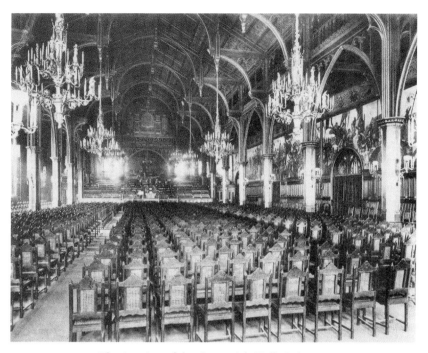

The interior of the Gürzenich Hall, Cologne

All of this, I suggest, speaks strongly for the impact the second trio makes in terms of contrast and anticipation; and, as we have already seen, both these considerations raise the issue of Mahler's notorious revisions. After all, it was he himself who was writing in a letter as late as 8 February 1911, to Georg Göhler, from New York, 'I have finished [*sic*] my Fifth – it had to be almost completely re-orchestrated. I simply can't understand why I still had to make

mentioning that already there are clear anticipations of the 'new' melodic style that was taking shape in Mahler's works around the turn of the century. For example, see in the Fourth's adagio fig. $2^{+8}$–fig. $2^{+10}$ and fig. $3^{+4}$–fig. $3^{+8}$, both of which passages (violins) directly foreshadow the manner – the '*Ton*'– of the *Adagietto*. It seems, then, that here too the Fourth shows itself to have been a vital stage in the evolution of the new style and new sound that were to be fully revealed in the Fifth and co-terminous settings of Rückert. So it was not only the polyphony of the Fourth that brought with it news of Mahler's future style, but also the profile (in the adagio) of its melody. This makes the question of the 'quote' of *Kindertotenlieder* in the adagio of the Fourth the more intriguing. See '"Swallowing the Programme": Mahler's Fourth Symphony', n. 39, and 'Mahler's "Kammermusikton"', n. 1.

such mistakes, like the merest beginner. (It is clear that all the experience I had gained in writing the first four symphonies completely let me down in this one – for a completely new style demanded a new technique.)'[26] (See also illustrations on pp. 269 and 270.)

The few pages that I have chosen to illustrate the fresh sound that accompanies the opening of the second trio also clarify the general principles underpinning Mahler's revisionary practice, principles that we encounter time and time again not only in the Fifth but in later and – up to a point – preceding works. It is the volume, character, and extent of the revisions in the Fifth that are singular.

The illustrations on pp. 250–64 (1904) perhaps show what it was that Mahler had in mind when referring to himself as the 'merest beginner' when contemplating the errors of judgement he made in his orchestration(s) of the Fifth, at least in its early stages. The extirpation of the entire woodwind section from fig. 1:16 to fig. 1:17⁻⁴, for example, and again from fig. 1:17 for eight bars, shows how ruthless he was in disencumbering himself of overweight textures – those dense, obscured, syncopated chords in clarinets and bassoons! – and doublings surplus to requirements; and if we scan the facing pages and note, as we proceed, his omissions and deletions, we can experience the very process by which he achieved the clarity and transparency of sound that was his objective.

But even as one writes about this comparatively simple example of how Mahler went about his revisions, *necessary* revisions to be sure, one also has to introduce an important qualification. Yes, of course Mahler was ridding himself here of a frank miscalculation, but at the same time the obligatory remedy, the radical surgery, was also motivated by a singular creative ambition, to upgrade the basic string-orchestra character of the trio almost up to the moment of collapse at fig. 1:18. This mix of the purely practical and an unprecedentedly inventive orchestral imagination seeking to make yet more explicit the materialization of a fresh body of sound is typical of his revising methods; one must always be on the lookout for

---

26 GM *Selected Letters,* Letter 443, p. 372. For Göhler's own note on the revisions he incorporated into the score of the Fifth for his performance in Leipzig on 9 January 1914 of a so-called 'new version' of the symphony, see NSNC.

**ALBERTHALLE ZU LEIPZIG**
MUSIKALISCHE GESELLSCHAFT

❑❑

Freitag, den 9. Januar 1914, 7½ Uhr
(Einlaß 7 Uhr, Ende 9½ Uhr)

# III. Abonnement-Konzert

Dirigent:
Dr. Georg Göhler.

Mitwirkende:
KÖNIGL. HOFOPERNSÄNGERIN GRETE MERREM
DAS BEDEUTEND VERSTÄRKTE
WINDERSTEIN-ORCHESTER

❑

Reihenfolge der Vorträge:
1) RICHARD WAGNER, Siegfried-Idyll
2) GUSTAV MAHLER, 4 Lieder mit Orchester

Pause von 10 Minuten.

3) GUSTAV MAHLER, Sinfonie Nr. 5
(Uraufführung
der neuen Fassung des Werkes)

❑

Text- und Programmbuch 25 Pfennige.

Kleine Partituren zu 1) und 3) bei den Saaldienern.

■ Nach dem dritten Klingelzeichen werden die Saal-Eingänge ■
■ geschlossen und der Zutritt ist ausnahmslos nicht gestattet. ■

The cover of the programme for the performance of the Fifth Symphony in Leipzig on 9 January 1914 conducted by Georg Göhler, who had incorporated into the score many of the revisions of the performing materials Mahler had continued to make up to the time of his death

Die Sinfonie kommt heute zum ersten Male in der neuen Fassung zur Aufführung, die Mahler vollständig fertig hinterlassen hat. Ich erzählte ihm bei seiner Anwesenheit in Leipzig zu den Proben, die er mit dem Riedel-Verein für die erste Aufführung seiner „Achten" abhielt, daß ich seine „Fünfte" einmal mit dem Karlsruher Hoforchester habe aufführen wollen, aber wegen nicht genügender Streicherbesetzung nach einer Probe vom Programm abgesetzt hätte. „Führen Sie die überhaupt jetzt nicht auf. Die habe ich völlig umgearbeitet, die ist schlecht instrumentiert." Er äußerte dann allerhand über die Mängel, die darin bestünden, daß ein so polyphones Werk gerade sehr durchsichtig instrumentiert werden müsse, damit alles Thematische klar zur Geltung komme.

Ich kam dann einige Male brieflich auf das Werk zurück und erhielt von ihm in einem Brief vom 8. Februar 1911 die Nachricht: „Die 5. habe ich fertig — sie mußte faktisch völlig uminstrumentiert werden. Es ist mir unfaßbar, wie ich damals wieder so völlig anfängerhaft irren konnte. Offenbar hatte mich die in den ersten vier Symphonien erworbene Routine hier völlig im Stich gelassen — da ein ganz neuer Stil eine neue Technik verlangte."

Man darf wohl diese Zeilen veröffentlichen, die beweisen, welches Maß von Bescheidenheit und Selbstkritik dem Komponisten eigen war, der gerade wegen seiner Instrumentationstechnik selbst von denen gefeiert wurde, die sonst nichts Gutes an ihm und seinen Werken ließen.

Durch die neue Fassung hat Mahler erreicht, daß das komplizierte polyphone Gewebe seiner Symphonie völlig klar zutage tritt. Denn er verstand unter Polyphonie nicht das möglichst krause Durcheinandergehen aller möglichen äußerlich aufgeklebten Kühnheiten, durch die die Harmlosigkeit und Dürftigkeit des eigentlichen Kerns verdeckt werden und „Modernität" erreicht werden sollte, sondern ernsthafte, durch die Idee des Werkes geforderte thematische Arbeit.

Der Verlag C. F. Peters würde sich den Dank aller Musikfreunde verdienen, wenn er sich zur Veröffentlichung der neuen Fassung des Werkes entschlösse, aber zu Studienzwecken auch die alte Partitur im Handel ließe. Denn es gibt wohl wenig so interessante Möglichkeiten, Instrumentation zu lernen, wie sie sich durch den Vergleich der beiden Partituren ergeben.

Aufführungen des Werkes nach der alten Fassung jedoch widersprechen nach den mündlichen wie schriftlichen Aeußerungen Mahlers seinem Willen und sollten künftig überhaupt nicht mehr stattfinden!

Mögen um so zahlreichere Aufführungen der neuen Fassung dazu helfen, immer mehr Klarheit über das Wesen der Mahlerschen Sinfonien zu verbreiten.

Dr. Georg Göhler.

The last page of the lengthy programme note Göhler wrote for the occasion

their purely creative dimension. In short, for Mahler, revising and composing (or recomposing) were locked together in an inextricable association.

We must note too how careful he was in his striving for clarity, which necessarily entailed much paring away, not to lose essential motives but, rather, to articulate them yet more clearly. For example, in the second trio, in its first orchestral format, the accompanimental motive in the divided violas, first emerging in bar 323 (fig. 1:15$^{+1}$) – this motive, rhythmically and intervallically,[27] has a fundamental role to play in the second movement, often as a means of energizing the long haul towards the summit of a climax (e.g. cf. figs. II:26$^{-7}$) – on its second appearance (cf. bars 1:345–51) was originally allotted (as p. 252 (1904) shows) to the bassoons. The bassoons, and the clarinets along with them, were to be excised, as I have already indicated; but the critical motive is transferred to the violas, thus sustaining the colour and character of their entry at fig. 1:15, while the clarinets' rhythmic punctuation, which would have done nothing to help expose the outline of the motive, is maintained by the second violins, **pp** and staccato, and functions, with perfect ease, as an accompanimental, undistracting, figure. Third time round (cf. bars 1:353–6), the winds have been restored and the motive heard in the penetrating oboes (as compared with the bassoons), along with (now for the first time) the clarinets' rhythmic punctuation. The motive in this passage, as p. 255 (1919) shows, has to compete with a cluster of other basic motives and themes

---

27 The motive itself, while almost always retaining its identifying outline, contracts or expands intervallically according to need. Perhaps its point of initiation is located, as Graeme Downes has suggested ('An Axial System of Tonality', 164–5), in the very first gesture of the first trio, i.e. the upbeat plus succeeding bar at I fig. 7, which already foresees the role it is to play in the second movement, again at an early initiating moment, II fig. 1$^{-8}$. It is a moment itself preceded by two bars (flutes, oboes, and clarinets) of the motive, the audibility of which Mahler, as I hope I will have shown, took so much trouble to secure at the opening of the second trio. The second movement confirms time and time again how essential it was in the cause of long-term comprehensibility for the significance of this motive to be unequivocally established. Once more, a critical interpretative point that conductors should take on board. There is one last observation I should like to make. Mahler *himself* virtually draws our attention to this fundamental motivic bond between the first trio and the second movement by accompanying its first appearance at the onset of the trio with an explicit injunction to the conductor: 'Geigen stets so vehement als möglich!' ('Violins as forceful as possible!'). It is precisely this form of words that he attaches to bar 8 at the opening of the second movement.

simultaneously combined; although by now its importance has been aurally established, Mahler takes care, notwithstanding, to secure again its clear articulation (triple oboes), relative to the surrounding motivic polyphony.

This same passage also offers an interesting and typical example of what one might describe as Mahler's motivic instrumentation, i.e. heightening the profile of the motives that go to make up a melody or theme by distribution of its constituent motives among a sequence of instruments. In the Fifth, unsurprisingly, it is the brass that is often involved. Consider, for example, the bars between figs. 1:16 and 18. The aspiring triplet theme (from fig. 1:16) is allotted in the first published edition (see p. 250 (1904)) to the horns (solo horn to begin with), and it is the horns that sustain the melody until fig. 1:17, when the trombones take over. Mahler's revision (see page 253 (1919)) maintains the horns until bar 352, but thereafter – at bar 353, a climactic quotation of the anguished opening of the first trio (see below, pp. 257–8) – it is the solo trumpet that provides the bridge (an early rhythmic anticipation, in fact, of the motive that generates the ensuing allegro, hence the spotlighting that the change of instrument secures) to the solo trombones, themselves conducting a motivic exchange; they also swap their directional thrusts (ascent and descent). This may be a simple example of the analytic instrumental thinking that was habitual for Mahler, but it also demonstrates how close was the association in his creative thought between motivic and instrumental texture. After all, in just two bars (bars 1:353–4), we have three levels of instrumentation – woodwind, brass, strings – and three levels of invention, each of which is distinguished by its own motivic profile, all of which are combined simultaneously, and all of which are directly related to some of the most prominent musical ideas of the forthcoming allegro. Indeed, it is precisely this motivic group that initiates the second movement, and rounds it off. (Once again, any interpretation that purports fidelity to Mahler's intention must take account of the complex anticipatory and retrospective motivic networking that is the *raison d'être* of his motivic polyphony.)[28]

---

28  In the *first* trio too there is evidence of Mahler's constant refinement of the dynamics and distribution of his instrumental parts. For example, how crude the concluding three

All of this, we may argue, is evidence of a composer intent on cleaning up, clearing out, what hitherto had been an overloaded texture. At the same time, as we can observe with fascination, the cleaning-up process also had the result of vastly extending the role of the string orchestra that, in Mahler's initial concept of his second trio, was confined to a first handful of bars. The orchestration of this particular passage would certainly have had to be amended; but that it came to be amended in the way that it did – therein lies the evidence of the hidden (creative) agenda that was ever the active collaborator in Mahler's revisionary practice.

A further remarkable feature of the Fifth, even allowing for the massive precedent that we find in, say, the slow introduction to the first movement of the Third Symphony, is the liberation of Mahler's writing for the wind, for the solo brass especially. The sheer *extent* of the materials entrusted there to the solo trumpet or solo trombone (not to speak of the virtuoso contributions from the horns, as a group) continues to astonish, however many times one hears the work. If there is a distinction to be made between his practice in this field in the Third and the development of his liberating instrumental techniques in the Fifth, it rests, I suggest, in this: that while the scale of the involvement of the wind in the introduction to the Third's first movement, and the potentialities of the individual instruments are innovatingly tested and exploited, the instruments are never, so to say, required to hijack the territory of another family of instruments altogether.

Something different happens in the Fifth.[29] For example, consider

---

bars of the horn melody look – fig. 1:10$^{-3}$ – if compared with the revision of 1919: it is not only the redistribution of the melody among all six horns that one notes but the introduction of a vastly more complex range of dynamics, a recurrent feature of Mahler's revisionary practice. The observant reader will note too in bar 1:210 the consequent excision of the doubling by the horns of the bassoons' descending figure. This was transferred to the trombones (as the 1919 score shows), but finally, it seems, Mahler indicated the excision of the transfer, committing instead the doubling of the bassoons to the cellos and basses, while an even later revision modified the lower strings' dynamics. (See the study score of the Fifth published as vol. v of the *Critical Edition*, fig. 1:10$^{-1}$, though for an example of a more radical modification of dynamics, cf. bars 1:361–3 in the *second* trio on p. 256 (1904), basses, with p. 255 (1919), where we find the dynamics have not just been modified but precisely reversed!)

29 Only the second trio of the *Trauermarsch* is shown on pp. 250–65. The attentive reader who cares to consult the first published edition (1904) of the score in full will notice that, while the solo for trumpet opens as a solo for the first six bars, the part is then allotted

to trumpets 1 and 2, and then resumed again as a solo until fig. 1:8. At fig. 10, however, it is a pair of trumpets that continues what from fig. 9 has been a solo flight. Clearly what Mahler had in mind here was the approaching climax at bar 221 and empowered his trumpet line, with characteristic precision, according to the changing dynamics and densities of the orchestral texture. If one follows the evolution of the music from fig. 10 to the peak of the climax at bar 221, it is obvious that he needed to keep a pair of trumpets at work to sustain the penetrative role of the trumpets in this crucial passage (bars 211–27). We can guess that Mahler wanted the peak pitch in the contour of the trumpet melody not only to ring out but ring *through* the texture, a high point also dynamically speaking. The pair of trumpets is of course retained in the 1919 revision, but we note there (see pp. 248–63) further refinements: a reduction, from bar 215 onwards, of the horns' doubling, from six horns to three; and, more significantly, for the first four bars after fig. 10 the two trumpets are reduced to a solo player (evidence of a calculated intent that I shall have more to say about below). It is in this guise that we hear the passage today.

But there are other refinements and nuances of colour that warrant attention. For example, as will be found if the first trio in the 1919 revision is consulted, the six horns on their collective entry in bar 159 are marked '*gestopft*', i.e. 'handstopped', whereas in the 1904 score no form of mute was indicated but the dynamic was *p*. In the 1919 score this is transformed into *ff*! Though the modification of the dynamics may appear to be dramatic, the effect of hand-stopping is to produce a horn sound which throws into contrast the high trumpet (which has embarked on its solo flight in bar 155) besides adding an uneasy colour to music that in any case is turbulent – '*Leidenschaftlich. Wild.*' – in character.

The sustained *p* euphony of the horns, as Mahler originally had them, would have padded out the middle part of the texture, conceivably masking or softening the sharp edge of the trumpets' articulation rather than providing in their own right a distinctive sonority. It is exactly this that hand-stopping the horns accomplishes – no cushioning, filling out or absorption but, in Norman Del Mar's vivid words, 'the savage bite of the best hand-stopped notes'. (Mahler prepares us for this radical switch in timbre, as the 1919 score shows, by doubling the existing oboe part with hand-stopped horn pitches while deleting the then redundant second violin and viola parts (see fig. 1:7$^{+5}$).)

It is clear that Mahler concluded that in the changed circumstances of the first trio's bars 155–64 the solo trumpet would not require further strengthening. I believe, however, that another factor may also have played an influential role. The Fifth, as I have suggested, is particularly rich in solo instrumental flights of many kinds: long, long arches of evolving melody, built out of motives, shuffled and reshuffled in ever new sequences. I believe that in entrusting these bold flights to a solo instrument and, above all, a solo*ist*, Mahler was not only enlarging and developing the scope of the instrument itself – what it could, technically, be pressed to deliver – but at the same time developing the technique of his players, not least perhaps testing their stamina, their nerves. There is a real difference in the spirit of a performance where the player, so to speak, is obliged to go it alone. The challenge creates its own characterizing tension which then forms an indispensable part of the musical idea itself, e.g. the opening trumpet melody of this first trio. It must remain speculation, inevitably, but I believe this sensitive and highly complex relationship between the performer and the composer, the latter bent on exploring his performers' capabilities to their limits, and beyond, was always part of Mahler's thinking, conscious or unconscious, when making his revisions. Thus when and wherever in the Fifth a solo role proved possible (perhaps only after Mahler had himself experienced the symphony in performance), he worked systematically, though always with high imagination, towards that end. This is not to say, however, that he failed to double up (or more) where the needs of his music made it obligatory. The passage I have already mentioned, figs. 1:10–11$^{-6}$, makes this very point. To sum up, what took a hand in the history of

the very opening of the first trio, where, in brilliant, vibrant counterpoint to the torrent of protest from the strings, the first trumpet
embarks on a huge, seamless, bounding solo that in other times
would surely not have been conceived for the trumpet. Indeed, it
is a passage that brings to mind a characteristic insight of Erwin
Stein's with regard to the orchestration of one of Britten's operas:
'The fiddles', he wrote, 'do not play first fiddle in *Billy Budd*.
Actually, the orchestral part of the first trumpet covers as many
pages as that of the first violins, and the parts of the first woodwind
players are still bulkier.'[30] Britten, in fact, was following in Mahler's
footsteps in pushing back the boundaries of what was thought to
be traditionally 'appropriate' to one instrument rather than another.
However, in my view, it was undoubtedly in the Fifth that Mahler
carried forward his liberation of the brass to a further critical stage,
not only in the passage I have just mentioned in the first trio, but
also in the second.

## The Second Trio

A feature of the second trio – a consequence of the process of
revisionary extrapolation that I have described above – offers us
further proof of Mahler's liberation of the brass. For hardly has he
established his string orchestra than we hear the first horn embark
on the long melodic flight (from fig. 1:16) that I have already mentioned in a different context. But here I want to emphasize the
concerto-like character that emerges along with the entry of the
horn. '*Concertante*' might be the more apt word; and that in turn
should remind us of the role of the *Corno obbligato* – designated thus
by Mahler himself – in the scherzo, the third movement, comprising Part II of the symphony.[31] I remarked many years ago that if

........................

Mahler's revising practice was the complex history of the capabilities of performers and
potentialities of instruments during his creative lifetime. Here is yet another example of
his both making *and* documenting the history that is embodied in his scores.

30  Erwin Stein, '*Billy Budd*', in Donald Mitchell and Hans Keller (eds.), *Benjamin Britten: A
Commentary on his Works*, p. 199.

31  I remember that at the first British public performance of the Fifth, at the old Stoll
Theatre in London on 21 October 1945, when the London Philharmonic Orchestra
was conducted by Heinz Unger, the orchestra's first horn, at the end of the second

one were looking for the horn concerto that Mahler never wrote, then it is to be found here, in the scherzo of the Fifth, the symphony which is particularly rich in *concertante* textures, in which the brass in particular predominate (not only the horn and trumpet, incidentally, but also the trombone). So it is, I suggest, that the horn entry in the second trio, sustained as a solo for twelve bars, anticipates the *obbligato, concertante* conception that we are later to encounter in the scherzo. A window is opened on a style that, in fully-fledged form, is yet to be revealed; likewise, the second trio's anticipation that I have already mentioned of the string orchestra that is (predominantly) to service the forthcoming *Adagietto*.[32] We note that in Mahler's earliest score (1904) the emphasis on the role of the horn was sustained from the end of the first horn's solo flight, when the third horn joins the first (bar 349), until fig. 17. Thus the horn colour in 1904 was dominant for a total of twenty-one bars (solo for twelve bars). But his revision of the preceding four bars (349–52) continues to assert the combination of horns and strings. Horns 1 and 2 unite in exclamatory extensions of the solo horn's unfolding of the 'ascent' theme (337 *et seq.*) from the first trio (203 *et seq.*), which theme is itself counterpointed (fig. 16) with the solo flight of the trumpet that opened the first trio but is now transferred to the violins, while at bar 345 it is the strings that accompany the horns with the 'ascent' theme! (Cf. pp. 252 (1904) and 253 (1919).)

The second trio, in short, is replete with anticipations of types and styles of music yet to come, in addition to the thematic and

---

movement, took up his place (his seat) at the front of the platform, alongside – or close to – the leader of the orchestra. Thus the concerto parallel was spelled out visually. I had no idea if the conductor were following his own instinct or responding to a performance tradition of which he was *himself* aware. But in Willem Mengelberg's conducting score the following note is to be found: 'Das Hornsolo immer hervortretend u. Horn beim 1. Konzertmeister zu placiren als Solist.' ('The first horn should always stand out and be placed as soloist at the front next to the leader of the orchestra.') It is possible, then, that this was a 'tradition' Mengelberg inherited from Mahler himself. See also Truus de Leur, 'Mahler's Fifth Symphony and the Royal Concertgebouw Orchestra', in *NSNC*, pp. 76–101.

32 I am aware, naturally, that the composition of the scherzo (probably) preceded the composition of the first movement and its second trio. But this does not affect my argument. It means merely that Mahler took account of the stylistic precedent the scherzo represented when composing (and, above all, revising) the trio.

motivic anticipations that I have already touched on. But there is one anticipation that I have not so far mentioned which is one of the most important of all: along with the marked contrast in character and sound that the opening of the second trio brings is the first intimation of the second movement's principal tonality, A minor. There has been little to prepare us for this onset of a new tonal area, though one recalls that the very fanfare that initiates the *Trauermarsch* culminates in an ascending A *major* triad (bar 1:11); and thereafter a grand orchestral tutti asserts, though only very briefly, A (bar 13).[33]

I shall return to the issue raised by Mahler's move to a fresh tonality below; or, rather, when Mahler himself returns us to it, in the second movement itself and, crucially, towards the end of that movement, where I believe the implication of the A major triad in the fanfare that opens the *Trauermarsch* audibly finds fulfilment, thus demonstrating its place in the narrative scheme and the long-term logic of Mahler's tonal symbolism.

However, this retrospective illumination still lies way ahead. I ventured to suggest at an earlier stage above that Mahler in Part 1 of his symphony divided his thematic and tonal strategies between the *Trauermarsch* and its two trios on the one hand, and the ensuing allegro on the other. One is struck, naturally, by the advent of A minor in conjunction with a radical change in texture and mood, but at this stage in the evolution of the symphony surely what commands our attention is the second trio's thematic profile? The opening melody for the violins could hardly offer a more vivid contrast to the turbulence of the first trio, or, one might think, a clearer contrast to the *Trauermarsch* itself. That we should listen, however, *beyond* (or *beneath*) the outward appearance of contrast is indicated by the ubiquitous upbeat at fig. 1:15 (bar 322; see pp. 250

33  Graeme Downes ('An Axial System of Tonality', p. 162) is one of those who comments on the significance of A emerging at this crucially early juncture. For him, the juxtaposition of C sharp minor and A major represents a further example of the 'axial relationships' that he believes to have been fundamental to Mahler's tonal strategy in his symphonies. I find his arguments entirely persuasive in the case of the Fourth, less so in the case of the Fifth. The strategy can be heard – experienced – by listeners to the Fourth, even if not accounted for in analytical terms. It is, so to say, *felt*. I wonder if the same can be said with quite the same conviction about the Fifth? None the less Dr Downes has good points to make which warrant our serious consideration.

(1904) and 251 (1919))[34] that has hitherto always introduced and
reintroduced the original march melody. In this context, it puts
us on notice that what follows in the ensuing trio will be *march*-
derived and thus *march*-oriented; and what in fact we hear from fig.
I:15 is a remodelled version of the *Trauermarsch*, in a new orchestral
guise – as remote as one could imagine from the regimental wind
band that we have encountered at an earlier stage in the movement –
a version, moreover, that accommodates, most intriguingly, the
triplets that up to now have represented musical and narrative ideas
opposed to the march, seeking escape from it, indeed. It is one of
the rare passages in Part I where there is some identifiable suggestion that a mitigation of the march of sorrow may eventually prevail. But here again, Mahler is careful not to overplay his hand.
Although the opening melody for violins, reflective, even gently
melancholic in character, may seem to distance itself from its generating source, the march is with us as an unmistakable rhythmic
presence from the start of the trio, from fig. I:15 to, say, fig. 16[+11],
which, with the advent of A minor, the interpolation of the string
orchestra, and the incorporation of the 'triplet factor' into the
remodelled march melody, seems to establish a rare, if fragile,
moment of calm. Here, certainly, A minor is not yet endowed with
the characteristics of Mahler's habitually 'tragic' (the Sixth) or tormented (*Das Lied*, first movement) key; nor even does it portend
the storm of nerves and agitation that A minor is to embody in the
succeeding allegro. (Once we have been engulfed by that storm at
the beginning of the movement, the trio's A minor, in retrospect,
inevitably takes on a new significance.) In any event, the march,
remodelled though it may have been, has not been subdued. It has
been submerged, rather. As Mahler's bass line asserts, the march
continues to prowl through the second trio downstairs, even while,
upstairs, in the violins' melody, it shows a new face. It is not, however, the bass alone that confirms that it is the march that we are
hearing, but also Mahler's insistence that the second trio, *unlike* the
first, should throughout, but especially at its outset, maintain 'always

34  See also Ex. 3 and related text on p. 282 below; also p. 207 n. 6 ('Mahler's "Kammer-
    musikton"') for a fascinating Verdi parallel.

the same tempo' – 'Immer dasselbe Tempo', he directs – as that of the immediately preceding principal march section. In other words, a conflation of tempo + rhythm + bass combines to remind us that the 'contrast' the second trio vouchsafes at its beginning is more apparent than real; and as we shall see, the remodelled march, bearing its load of particular symbolic significance, has an important role – a multiple role, indeed – to play in the allegro. The history of this one theme could be chosen to illustrate the highly complicated interrelationships, by means of exposition, development, and quotation, that exist not just between the two movements of Part I but between the two trios, and, in turn, their interrelationships with the march that frames them.

I have concentrated on the opening of the second trio, but what about the rest of the trio, which after all leads to the climax that I have already touched on above?[35] There is no doubt that the (relative) A minor calm of the trio at its start only heightens the awful intensity of the lament – a black hole, almost – into which (at fig. 1:18) the trio collapses.

## The Triplet Factor and Unveiling of the 'Quotation Principle'

The 'triplet factor' has an important part to play in this process. It is useful perhaps to remind ourselves, before the opening of the trio persuades us otherwise, that the triplets have their origin in the fanfare that opens the *Trauermarsch*. A triplet, indeed, is the first rhythmic unit we hear. Thereafter it becomes virtually a basic rhythmic leitmotiv, saturating much of the invention of the first two movements and the trios of the *Trauermarsch*. If the fanfare spawns triplets, so too does the immediate and agitated continuation of the violins' chromatic outburst at the very onset of the first trio (see fig. 1:7$^{+4}$ff.). It is not really until a later stage, at fig. 1:9$^{+9}$, that the triplets become irrevocably associated with the idea, of ascent, of 'aspiration', in a theme (in G flat, violins) that is to re-emerge in the second trio at fig. 1:16 (in D minor), but this time functioning not as a kind of contrasting 'second subject', the role it has played in the first trio, but as a triplet-related continuation of the second trio's opening A minor melody (the remodelled march). The thrust here of the 'triplet factor' seems to indicate an ascent that will climax on at least a glimpse of a resolution, however distant, which makes it all the more remarkable that the 'aspiring' triplets (cf. bar 352) are interrupted by a quotation, no less, of the cry of protest and anguish, *fortissimo*, that constitutes the opening bars of the first trio; as if to reinforce the authenticity of this interpolation, the violins' chromatic agitations are restated at their original pitch, a case of what is known these days as *pitch-specific*. The importance of this event can scarcely be overstated. It represents, in fact, the first unequivocal anticipation in the symphony of the 'quotation principle', the innovating technique that is to unite the pairs of movements in Parts I and III. That it should be first adumbrated by means of interaction and quotation between the trios of the *Trauermarsch* puts beyond doubt their unique formal and dramatic significance.

This unforeseen rupture-by-quotation raised to the status of a principle was something new in Mahler's art, an addition to his arsenal of musico-dramatic resources. At the same time it represents a radical development of a practice that he had long made his own, the reversal, reshuffling, and fresh combination of his themes and motives. As we have seen, the aspiring triplet theme in the first trio was in the first instance ejected by the turbulence of that trio's opening, to function as a mitigating contrast, almost, as I have suggested, like a 'second subject'. In the second trio, the chronology is reversed. What opened the first trio now interrupts – ruptures – the triplet invention that it had initially generated. The interruption, having made its dramatic appearance, now gives way, or so the casual listener might assume, to a resumption of triplet-inspired 'aspiration' (from fig. 1:17). But here again, and very typically, Mahler unfolds a nest of basic motives in a new combination. At the very beginning of the first trio, the violins' chromatic contours are simultaneously combined with the solo flight of the trumpet, itself generated by the symphony's opening fanfare. In the second trio, from fig. 1:16, the triplet theme, this time a flight of the solo horn, is simultaneously combined with a version of the trumpet's solo from the first trio, but transferred to the first violins. At fig.

1:17, when the triplet 'ascent' theme is resumed, this time by the solo *trombone*, the violins continue to counterpoint it with motives drawn from the trumpet solo (see figs. 1:7 and 16). The motivic web then exploits a fresh dimension, in the shape of a dialogue, an exchange, between trombones 1 and 2: the first having delivered its opening and ascending triplet limb (bar 357), it is answered by the second, in descending contra-motion, *its* limb based on motives from the solo trumpet (fanfare) flight. This exchange, which is also a development, is continued across twelve bars until at fig. 1:18, and, after a final upward triplet thrust from the first trombone (bars 367–8), the trio achieves its dynamic peak but only to collapse across the ensuing eight bars.

Thus it is that in the space of some fifty-five bars (the over-lapping transition to the coda begins in bar 376) we encounter both quotation and interruption; the unfolding of themes in a reverse chronology; the concept of ascent and collapse; development; and intensive, intricate motivic work, leading to ever new sequences, combinations, and exchanges of motives, a complex polymotivic texture throughout, in which the composer's instrumentation acts as a creative partner, articulating all the information that we need to have if we are to decode and thereby comprehend the signi-ficance of this second trio. For it is here, in miniature, that the narrative, the inner drama, of Part 1 of the symphony is rehearsed and played out to its bitter, protesting ('*Klagend*') end.

There is one final revision that I want to mention, that of the ubiquitous upbeat that almost in its own right accrues to itself the status of a leitmotiv throughout Part 1 of the symphony. It has a high profile, naturally, in the pool of motives on which the first trio draws for its thematic context (cf. e.g. fig. 1:7$^{+2}$, the first limb of the trumpet's solo) and functions likewise in the second trio, where it is all-pervasive from fig. 1:15 onwards. A presence, in fact, from the very first bar (fig. 1:15$^{-1}$), where, as I have already pointed out above, it introduces the remodelled version of the march, appropriately enough, since it is to the (original) march that the upbeat properly belongs. What I did not mention was the combining of the upbeat with the timpani's final triplet, the triplet that forms what one might describe as the very first thing we hear as the symphony begins; in fact, this simultaneity has already been anticipated at fig. 1:7⁻¹, but there the (crotchet) upbeat and its tumultuous continuation anticipates, rather, the motive that is to dominate the second *movement* (fig. II:1⁻⁸). Indeed, the trumpet's triplets (fig. 1:7⁻³) have the character of opening up a fresh vista – which they do – while the timpani's triplets, perhaps because they are stripped of the 'heroic' associations of the instrument to which they properly belong, convey much more the idea (muffled drums) of a winding down. In any event, the return to the upbeat in its original form at the beginning of the second trio provides us with another example, albeit on a tiny scale, of Mahler's overlapping technique, the more intriguing because it combines – within the space of one bar – an end, the last bar of the lead-back into the second trio, with a beginning, the upbeat which introduces the trio itself, while the 'end' derives, as I have said, from the very beginning of the symphony itself.

I have used above the words 'upbeat in its original form', and indeed this is true rhythmically, as a comparison of my pp. 250 (1904) and 251 (1919) shows. However, Mahler was to make a later revision of the upbeat which must have been overlooked, or had not yet been discovered, when the 1919 edition of the score was published. In the latest published edition of the symphony,³⁶ the upbeat appears as in Ex. 3, clearly articulating the A minor triad, in its second inversion. This is a revision, then, that yet more emphatically clarifies the onset of the 'new' tonality. A fine detail – cf. fig. 15 in the 1904 and 1919 editions of the symphony – but, in its context, one that tells.

Ex. 3  Fifth Symphony, first movement, bars 322–5

36  Vol. v in the *Critical Edition*, p. 39 (fig. 1:15).

*Problems of Instrumentation and Re-instrumentation and their Origin; the Paradox of Mahler's Loss of Nerve; his Revisionary Practice*

Before we quit altogether the topic of Mahler's revisions – only a fraction of which I have had the space to touch on – it is essential at least to raise the question that is always asked in the context of any discussion of this symphony: why was it that Mahler seemingly lost his nerve, orchestrally speaking, when embarking on the composition of the Fifth? How was it that he came to feel, in words that I have already quoted above, a 'merest beginner' in his first orchestral conception(s) of the Fifth?[37]

From the start, consideration of this complicated matter has been influenced by Alma Mahler's highly coloured account of an early reading rehearsal of the symphony in Vienna conducted by her husband. This is what she wrote:

> Early in the year [1904] there had been a reading-rehearsal with the Philharmonic, to which I listened unseen from the gallery. I had heard each theme in my head while copying the score, but now I could not hear them at all. Mahler had overscored the percussion instruments and side-drum so madly and persistently that little beyond the rhythm was recognizable. I hurried home sobbing aloud. He followed. For a long time I refused to speak. At last I said between my sobs, 'You've written it for percussion and nothing else.' He laughed, and then produced the score. He crossed out the side-drum in red chalk and half the percussion instruments too. He had felt the same thing himself, but my passionate protest turned the scale. The completely altered score is still in my possession.[38]

If we were to rely exclusively on an examination of the *extant* manuscript sources, there would be no option but to conclude that Alma got it wrong; it is an assumption that has been held by

37 Mahler's letter to Georg Göhler in 1911: see also above, n. 26. Göhler himself was interestingly to comment on Mahler's attitude, reporting that the composer told him '*the first version of the Fifth was never to be played again,* because it was badly orchestrated' (Göhler's emphasis). Mahler could not have put it more baldly. See GM *Selected Letters*, p. 448.
38 AM *Memories*, p. 73.

countless commentators, myself among them, that is, that what
emerges from any such scrutiny is the very reverse of what she
reports. Colin Matthews puts it succinctly in his 1977 thesis:

> However much truth there may be in this engaging story, the
> evidence of the manuscript and the printed scores does not, unfor-
> tunately, bear it out. In fact the first edition of the score actually has
> very slightly more percussion in the first movement (to which Alma
> is surely referring) than the manuscript; while the second edition
> merely omits a *mezzo-forte* cymbal and two *pianissimo* bass-drum
> strokes. The orchestral revisions are, however, all concerned with
> lightening and clarifying the texture – the first version was heavily
> scored, in places almost clumsily so, as if Mahler was unsure of how
> to deal with the middle-period change of style ushered in by this
> symphony.

But what had escaped my notice – and I am indebted to Edward
Reilly for bringing it to my attention – was a letter of Mahler's
written on 27 September 1904 to his publisher, Heinrich Hinrich-
sen, the day after the second run-through of the Fifth in Vienna, in
which he remarks: 'it was still necessary now and then to retouch a
little. *The percussion in particular was certainly overloaded* [my italics],
and would certainly have distorted the impression [made by the
work].' Alma's recollection of the (second?) run-through – confirmed by no less an authority than the composer himself –
reminds us that, though she may have had a penchant for exaggeration, her skills, memory and musical intelligence should not be
underrated. Is there a missing manuscript link – perhaps a percussion part – that was specific to the occasion of which Alma writes
and has since disappeared? It seems probable. The fact remains,
however, that while Mahler's revisions of the Fifth were voluminous and unceasing, it was not the percussion that consumed his
time and skill but, as Colin Matthews remarks, and as I hope to
have illustrated above, 'lightening and clarifying the texture': that
was his principal concern. And Mahler's textural clarifications, at
the heart of his revisory practice, not only addressed – as I think I
have amply demonstrated – the question of relative 'weight' but

were also intricately bound up with clarifying the symphony's narrative retrospections and anticipations, and the mosaic of its motivic content.[39]

## The Need to Revise: What Created It?

There is no disputing the *need* for the revisions in the light of what the study score of 1904 tells us. But what created the need? That is the major question that seems to me never to have been satisfactorily answered. After all, it was hardly the case that Mahler had had to struggle to establish a consummate orchestral style and the techniques to serve it. There were notable stretches of music at which he had had to work hard to achieve what his imagination demanded, for example, the slow introduction to the first movement of the First Symphony. But consider briefly the stage in the evolution of his mastering of the orchestra he had reached before starting work on the Fifth. He had behind him not only heavyweights like the Second and Third but also, and more relevantly, the Fourth, in which, as I have suggested, we not only encounter the shift to a pronouncedly polyphonic-cum-motivic style but also the shift to an emerging chamber-orchestral concept. Radical technical developments, both of these; and yet the novel Fourth was never subject to the uncertainties and consequent revisions that were to affect the Fifth. Even more extraordinary, as my chronological table clearly indicates, it was precisely at the time that the Fifth was on the drawing board that Mahler brought to fulfilment his 'Kammermusikton' in the two last *Wunderhorn* songs, *Kindertotenlieder*, and four independent Rückert settings. One simply has to emphasize the oddity of this – Mahler floundering badly as he drafted the Fifth, having just imagined the innovative but perfectly realized orchestral textures of the Rückert songs. There is no easy explanation of this seeming paradox. How was it that having accomplished

---

39  Matthews, *Mahler at Work*, p. 59. See also Eberhardt Klemm, 'Zur Geschichte der Fünften Sinfonie van Gustav Mahler: Der Briefwechsel zwischen Mahler und dem Verlag C. F. Peters und andere Dokumente'. For a clear exposition of the 'puzzle that nevertheless remains', see n. 14 to Edward R. Reilly's contribution to *Gustav Mahler: Adagietto: Facsimile, Documentation, Recording*, edited by Gilbert E. Kaplan, pp. 39–57.

*Kindertotenlieder*, say, on the one hand, he felt himself on the other –
as late as 1911! – to have undertaken the Fifth as 'the merest beginner'? The technical finesse of the one seems hard to reconcile with
the defects of the other. I have no simple answer. That it was primarily a question of 'style' – the advent of the 'new' polyphony as
is often suggested – I take leave to doubt. Even if one allows for the
evolution of a 'new' component, this was a feature that had distinguished virtually each new symphony that Mahler had composed;
and it had always proved the case that his compositional techniques
had kept pace with his innovating imagination.

### The Abandonment of 'Programmes'

I believe it was factors other than style (exclusively) that contributed to the undoubted crisis that Mahler experienced with
regard to the Fifth. First, though probably the less important of the
two factors I shall adduce, there was the swallowing of the programme in the preceding Fourth that I have already sufficiently
described in '"Swallowing the Programme": Mahler's Fourth
Symphony', a step that may well have left him with a feeling of
insecurity. To be sure, the rejection of the idea of the *overt* programme was a conscious decision, fiercely maintained in the years
(and symphonies) to come. No matter that, as we shall see, the 'programme', having been successfully swallowed in the Fourth, was to
resurface in the Fifth in a new guise – perhaps dis-guise might be
the better description? – but this time as an eventful but wordless
narrative generated solely by Mahler's manipulation of his musical
materials, themes, motives, tonalities, forms. As the work progresses,
its fundamental ideas acquire symbolic significance and evolving
identities, and thus come to play the roles allotted them in the
drama without their ever having been named.

This casting away of the props that the earlier 'programmes' had
constituted – we should not forget that they had been devised
initially to serve as instruments of elucidation – may well have left
Mahler feeling somewhat exposed. It is possibly significant that he
seemed himself peculiarly convinced (in his letters, for instance)
that his Fifth was a symphony no one was going to be able to

understand. Was this nervousness tied in, in some way, to his denying himself programmatic schemes, vocal movements, or movements composed 'after' songs? Now, so to say, Mahler's signposts
had become exclusively sound posts.

This dumping of an overt programmatic dimension was, we may
agree, part and parcel of Mahler's move away from synthesizing
symphonies like the Second and Third (though the Eighth was to
reinhabit the tradition) and his embarking, via the Fourth, on the
trinity of purely instrumental symphonies, initiated by the Fifth. It
has become virtually received opinion – perhaps even Mahler himself was influenced by it – that it was the critical distinction
between the 'synthesized', i.e. mixed, genres and the 'pure', i.e.
exclusively instrumental, concepts that was at the root of the crisis.
But as I have suggested, the purely instrumental symphony was
already significantly anticipated in the Fourth, without, it seems,
initiating doubts in the composer's mind about his competence.
Why the sudden loss of confidence? Of course in the Fourth there
was the concluding 'himmlische Leben' finale to 'explain', 'elucidate', the preceding three orchestral movements. Of course in the
Fifth, the 'programme' went underground, so to say. Was it, then, a
combination of all the considerations I have so far outlined above
that conspired to make Mahler stumble?

*Matters of Life and Death*

It would be senseless to deny the contribution these factors made
to the crisis of 'style' that Mahler was to experience while composing the Fifth; however, by 'style' I do not mean the issue of polyphonic clarity, which I take to have been already established in the
Fourth, but, rather, the inflexion of the voice that Mahler chose
specifically to serve the great issues of Life and Death – they
deserve their capitals – that the Fifth and its successor, the Sixth,
address.

It was particularly in Part 1 of the Fifth – the *Trauermarsch* and
allegro – that Mahler's revising of his orchestration was most
intensive; and it is precisely in Part 1 where the inner drama – the
contest, if you like, between Life and Death – is adumbrated. Once

we have comprehended what has been set in motion in Part I –
that the trios are locked into, held captive by, the funeral march;
struggle to achieve release in the ensuing allegro; encounter
implacable defeat; succeed eventually in their striving only through
the genial mediation and mitigation of the finale, which, in turn,
permits the materialization of the chorale – there is very little else
that requires 'explanation'. What does is the consistent overscoring
of that very part of the symphony where instrumental clarity (and
thereby formal and narrative clarity) was indispensable.

I believe that the factor that must be added to the others already
adduced was the question of 'voice' or 'tone' (perhaps the German,
'Ton', more economically conveys what we mean by 'tone of
voice'). How was the 'new' polyphonic style, already established in
the Fourth, but there serving a very different narrative and aesthetic,
effectively to function in the Fifth, a symphony that directly confronts the issue of mortality and man's battle with it?

There is no question that Mahler as an artist was no stranger to
the idea of mortality. It had haunted him since his earliest years,[40]
had been treated on an epic scale in the Second Symphony, and, as
we have seen, was a topic high on his creative agenda throughout
the period of the Fifth's composition.

Hitherto, moreover, each approach to the idea of mortality had
found its own sound-world, whether it was the unashamed theatricality and rhetoric of the Second or the unique intimacies of
Kindertotenlieder, the last Wunderhorn songs[41] and independent
Rückert settings. When it came to the Fifth, however, the first step
into the territory of the instrumental symphony with all the weight
of 'tradition' attached to it, one is almost obliged to conclude that
Mahler's nerve wobbled. But did it? One talks or thinks of 'tradition' but only if one forgets the breathtakingly original form that

40  In the text I wrote for Chailly's recording of the First ('Symphony No. 1: "the most
    spontaneous and daringly composed of my works"', pp. 119–24 above) I give specific
    consideration to Mahler's suggestion that his hero in fact has died in the finale, to be
    memorialized and then resurrected in the Second.

41  This is the place perhaps to remind ourselves of the unique orchestra Mahler assembled
    for 'Der Tamboursg'sell': 2 oboes, 2 clarinets, bass clarinet, 2 bassoons, 2 horns, tuba,
    percussion (timpani, side drum, bass drum, tam-tam), voice, cello, and double-bass (NB:
    lower strings only, throughout) and, in the second section of the song, 'Gute Nacht . . .',
    the unprecedented substitution of a *pair* of cors anglais for the oboes.

Mahler unfolds in the Fifth, innovative even by his own standards.[42] Amusingly enough, as I have already quoted (on p. 235), Mahler himself seems originally to have intended to conform to 'tradition', that is, to compose 'a regularly constructed symphony in four movements'. That ambition – and up to a point he had already done that in the Fourth, the 'regularly constructed' bit, quite consciously – was soon abandoned: the narrative drama that evolved as the Fifth progressed imposed its own overall form, as remote as one could imagine from classical precedents. Mahler, then, in the formal area, remained entirely true to himself, behaving exactly as one would have expected him to behave. When it came to the point, and whatever the pressures he may have felt himself under, and whatever the state of his nerves, there was no false obeisance to 'tradition'; which leaves us, still, with the paradox of the instrumentation, the strange miscalculations that, leaving on one side the category of refinements and motivic clarification that Mahler would have made anyway, even had there been no larger problem to circumvent, may be subsumed under the general heading of patent overscoring.

The explanation, surely, must reside in this first attempt to 'dramatize' in the 'new' context of the instrumental symphony the old preoccupations with Life and Death. For some reason, still not absolutely clear, Mahler's anxiety – *psychologically* rather than technically based? – led him blatantly to overscore, as if compelled to an excess of emphasis by his determination to match the challenge of the great issue cf mortality with a comparably 'weighty' body of orchestral sound. A momentary aberration, perhaps, though the impact of it was long-lasting, unnaturally so, which suggests to me that it was more than 'technique' that was at stake. In any event, Mahler finally succeeded in rescuing his symphony from a false aesthetic that he had pinned on it, releasing thereby a work, the sound-world of which and the techniques that created it were perfectly integrated. The comparative exercise on pages 250–65 clearly

---

42 See Colin Matthews, 'Mahler and Self-Renewal', pp. 85–8. There is not much to be gained from the pursuit of a 'classical' four-movement symphony in Mahler's oeuvre. The nearest approach that he made to that model was in the Sixth, the symphony that followed the Fifth, though the parallels cease to be of much significance as soon as the finale is reached.

articulates what was more a process of revelation than correction, the *release* of something that was already there, implicit, but which had been distorted, exaggerated, at the early stage of its evolution. Undoubtedly, Mahler came to see this, but that did not prevent him from indulging in a long-sustained bout of self-laceration (did it ever end, in fact?). All the more reason, I suggest, for supposing that the 'regression' that Mahler found so dismaying – his becoming again 'the merest beginner' – had touched on a sensitive area that had its roots in the depths of the composer's psyche rather than his technique; or to put it another way, it was the former that led in this instance to his problems with the latter.

### After the 'Trauermarsch'; the 'Hauptsatz'

Mahler himself, as I have noted, considered the second movement of Part I to be the main movement of the pair that make up Part I.[43] Rightly so; the movement has to be – and has been – assessed as one of the most original of all Mahler's symphonic movements. It is indeed a unique concept. However, while it is certainly the 'Hauptsatz' of Part I – of the symphony as a whole, I would argue – it is only so because of its extraordinary relationship to the preceding *Trauermarsch*, on which, indeed, it is entirely dependent and from which, unequivocally, its unique formal character derives. I have already indicated the complex exposition/development layout that underpins this formal scheme, while the significant role played by the trios in the *Trauermarsch* would almost alone single out the first movement as an altogether special achievement. But the truth is that the two movements of Part I are fundamentally interdependent, for which reason it makes no sense to approach them as separate entities, no more sense, in fact, than to consider a divorce of the finale from the preceding *Adagietto*; and in saying that, one has broached the topic of the larger symmetries that shape the Fifth, a topic that will arise naturally in the course of our further discussion.[44]

43  See above, n. 15.
44  Inconceivable, of course, even to think of the finale as an independent item, let alone perform it. This does not hold true of the *Adagietto* which, in the old days, represented

## Not Sonata Form but Discontinuity

Nor does it make any more sense to attempt, as so many commentators still do, alas, to try to account for the singular character of the second movement of Part I in terms of sonata form, for example, Floros,[45] who writes that Paul Bekker 'was right when he spoke of the [movement's] "ingeniously organized sonata form"'. Floros is not content even with that unequivocal statement, and goes on to add, 'The movement is indeed cast in normal [*sic*] sonata form. It contains everything considered typical: the division into three main parts and a coda, the contrasting themes, a clear disposition of tonalities, and finally the thematic treatment in the development' – and so on, and so on. This is not to mock Floros; but to observe, rather, the danger attendant upon a myopia which leads, it would seem, to treating the movement – hearing it even – as a 'normal' sonata form, whereas the whole point of it, its uniqueness, is inextricably bound up with the *Trauermarsch* and the role it plays in the ensuing allegro, to which it contributes an unprecedented series of interpolations and interruptions. It is precisely in these quite astonishing punctuations and ruptures (to gloss Adorno's word, *Durchbruch*) that the genius of the movement resides; and it is, in my view, a clear apprehension of their function which must provide the basis for any meaningful analysis of the allegro. To summon up a sonata scheme in this context is – grotesquely – to prevent us from hearing

---

all that we were actually able to hear of Mahler in public along with the occasional song. Furthermore, the movement achieved a kind of independent status in Mahler's own lifetime, a suspect 'tradition' that was maintained after his death. However, there is surely now little justification for performing the *Adagietto* out of context, and none at all for imposing on it a lugubrious valedictory character *à la* Bernstein. All the more reason for performers who want to programme the *Adagietto* as a separate item to bear in mind what we now know of its probable history and its integral relationship to the ensuing rondo: Part III of the symphony is as much an integral unit as Part I. (See also below, pp. 322 and n. 80 and 323ff.)

45  Constantin Floros, *Gustav Mahler: The Symphonies*, pp. 145–9. In this connection I commend to readers the thoughtful and refreshingly independent-minded account of the Fifth in Bernd Sponheuer's *Logik des Zerfalls: Untersuchungen zum Finalproblem in den Symphonien Gustav Mahlers*, pp. 219–79. Dr Sponheuer in his outline of the *Hauptsatz*, the unique formal significance of which he clearly recognizes, places alongside a column that describes the movement in conventional sonata-form terms a parallel column that is headed 'Peripetaler Verlauf' (peripatetic path), and articulates the movement's unpredictable and above all itinerant character. It offers an admirable corrective to Floros's narrow vision.

what Mahler was really up to.[46] Might it be argued that the composer himself suffered from the same misapprehension for which I chide Floros, since, in his autograph manuscript full score, he included repeat signs at the end of the section that Floros identifies as the 'exposition'? These appear in the manuscript (in the Pierpont Morgan Library, New York, Robert Owen Lehman deposit) at the *Hauptsatz*, bar 145, the double bar, five bars after fig. 9, and were included in the first published edition (study score) of the symphony. Mahler himself was soon to get rid of the repeat, if indeed, in terms of rehearsal or performance, he ever gave effect to it; how could he ever have envisaged that this would have been a possibility in a movement the very *raison d'être* of which is embodied in the calculated discontinuity of the music, barely a bar of which, let alone a substantial section, is repeated? Once again, I believe the explanation for what is otherwise inexplicable rests in a curious recess of Mahler's creative personality. It would seem as if he needed to reassure himself by making this gesture that he had not, after all, altogether abandoned 'tradition'. It was a kind of guarantee of propriety, a means of self-assurance and insurance. The more innovative the formal thinking, the more the need for a comforting sign of conformity, of orthodoxy. It is significant that exactly the same phenomenon was to recur in the case of the first movement of the Ninth, again one of the boldest of Mahler's formal schemes. The repeat signs are to be found in the Ninth's composition sketch but were again – as they had to be – deleted.

46 This whole aspect of Mahler's sometimes uneasy consciousness of the obligations to be paid to the past I have tried to clarify in 'The Modernity of Gustav Mahler', pp. 175–90. I must add here – because it has only just come to my notice as I prepare the final draft of this text – an exceptionally interesting article by Peter Gülke, 'The Orchestra as Medium of Realization: Thoughts on the Finale of Brahms's First Symphony, on the Different Versions of Bruckner's Sixth Symphony, and on "Part One" of Mahler's Fifth'. The few pages (pp. 273–5) the author devotes to the Fifth strike me as making the most enlightening (and enlightened) approach to the analysis of Part 1 of the symphony that I have yet come across.

*Interruptions, Quotations, Ascent/Collapse, and Cut-Off*

It is my purpose in what follows to try to articulate the *means* by which Mahler achieves the brilliant, continuous *discontinuity* to which I have referred above. For that reason, it seems to me redundant to plod through the movement, listing every single instance when there surfaces a reference to, or development from, the *Trauermarsch* and its trios. For one thing, this would be an endless task, given that the allegro is virtually dedicated to a total development of the first movement (of its trios, in particular); and for another, it is those crucial gestures that act consistently as agents of interruption and collapse that should have first claim on our attention.

I believe these may be broken down into four principal categories, one of which is itself subdivided: Interruptions (which may also take on the character of a 'rupture', or 'breakthrough' as Adorno has it: see Table 2A, column 5); Quotations, split between the march in its original form, which on one famous occasion functions also as Interruption (see column 2), its remodelled version (see column 4), and the theme and complex of associated motives I identify as Ascent (see column 3); and – my column 1 – a persistent and consistently descending scalic gesture, the best description for which I can devise is Cut-off (an association with the process of guillotining is perhaps by no means inapposite). My three Tables A, B, and C attempt to represent the second movement in tabular form, from different angles of approach.

If there is one further 'quotation' by means of which Mahler himself makes the point that I have been making time and time again myself, it is, surely, the unique resurfacing in F, between bars 392 and 399, of the opening bars of trio 1 of the *Trauermarsch*, though now in E minor, and not, as originally, in B flat minor (the unrelatedness of these two keys only further emphasizes the unprecedented character of this intervention).[47] It is as if Mahler

---

47 See also pp. 277–8 above, 'The Triplet Factor and Unveiling of the "Quotation Principle"', where I discuss the significance of the 'quotation' of this identical gesture in the *Trauermarsch*, trio 2.

## Table 2A

| 1 Cut-off | 2 Quotations of *Trauermarsch* [I¹] | 3 Quotations ('Ascent') from Trio 1 of *Trauermarsch* |
|---|---|---|
| (1) I² [i.e. the *Hauptsatz*], from fig. 5$^{-8}$ to fig. 5 (bars 66–73) Ww.ᴬ | (1) I², from fig. 15 to fig. 16 (bars 266–84) *March* + original tempo as in I¹ | (1) I², fig. 7, *Ascent* theme from I¹, trio I, (fig. 9$^{+9}$ to bar 221). NB Throughout the trio the pervasive intimations of simultaneous contrary motion, i.e. ascent and descent combined! |
| (2) I², from fig. 9 to double barline (bars 141–6) Ww. and str. | | (2) I², bars 222–33. *Ascent* theme combined with second quotation of (remodelled) *March* (see (6) in Table 2B) |
| (3) I², from fig. 11$^{-1}$ to fig. 11$^{+10}$ (bars 176–86) Ww. | | (3) I², bars 364–71. *Ascent* theme (see also (12) in Table 2B) |
| (4) I², from fig. 18 to fig. 18$^{+11}$ (bars 322–6) Ww. and str. | | (4) I², bars 392–9, first quotation of opening bars of trio 1 of I¹; the continuation at I², fig. 23 (bars 400–419) introduces the *Ascent* theme from trio 1 in combination with accompanimental motives first introduced in trio 2 |
| (5) I², from fig. 30$^{+1}$ to fig. 31$^{-3}$ (bars 521–6) Ww. and str. | | |

ᴬ The cut-off is itself accompanied by a further punctuation in the shape of a diminished seventh chord delivered by the brass. (See horns and trumpets, bars 66–7.( Note in particular the dynamics and colour of the horns: what begins *p*, crescendos into a hand-stopped *f* at bar 66, thereby transforming the chord into a (vertical) snarl that presages the first cut-off, a (horizontal) slash. This same punctuating chord recurs at all the

| 4 Quotations from Trio 2 of *Trauermarsch* | 5 Interruptions ('Collapse') |
|---|---|
| (1) I², from fig. 5 to fig. 7 (bars 74–116) *March*: theme (remodelled) + original tempo as in I¹ [NB cf. I¹, trio 2 from fig. 15 to fig. 16, bars 323–36] | (1) I² from double barline after fig. 16 (bar 288) A flat section leading to |
| (2) I², from fig. 11⁺¹³ *Recit.* (slow), from which *March* (remodelled) emerges (fig. 12, bar 213), tempo as in I¹ | (2) double barline (bar 316), attempt to establish A major and Chorale I |
| (3) I², from fig. 20⁺⁴ to fig. 21 *March* (remodelled) somewhat slower than tempo 1 of I² (i.e. see fig. 18). For the source of its continuation (bars 362–fig. 21), see I², fig. 2⁺⁷ *et seq.*, yet another example of Mahler's discontinuous continuity | (3) from fig. 27 to double barline at fig. 30 (bars 463–520), attempt to establish D major and Chorale II |

succeeding cut-off points, with the exception of bar 176, i.e. at bars 141, 322, and 520. Bars 66–73 provide a model example of Mahler's exploitation in a highly compressed space of open and hand-stopped pitches by the horns, not only in sequence and juxta-position (e.g. bars 69 and 70) but in simultaneous combination (bar 66).

## Table 2B

Cut-offs; Quotations; Interruptions: classified by type and in order of chronological appearance

(1)  First cut-off (I², bars 66–73)

(2)  First quotation of (remodelled) *March* (I², bars 74–116). Cf. I¹, trio 2, fig. 15 *et seq.*

(3)  First quotation (I², fig. 7) of *Ascent* theme from trio 1 (origins – 'triplet factor' – in I¹, bars 165–72, by which bars 203–10 are generated.

(4)  Second cut-off (I², bars 141–6)

(5)  Third cut-off (I², bars 176–86)

(6)  Second quotation (I², from fig. 12) of (remodelled) *March*, from bar 222 incorporating second quotation of *Ascent* theme (see (7) below)

(7)  Second quotation (bars 222–33) of *Ascent* theme from trios 1 and 2 of I¹, combined with continuation of *March* (see (6) above)

(8)  First quotation of *March* in its original form (I², fig. 15, bars 266–84)

(9)  First interruption (I², bars 288–316)

(10)  Second interruption: Chorale 1 (I², bars 316–22)

(11)  Fourth cut-off (I², bars 322–6)

(12)  Third quotation of (remodelled) *March* (I², bars 355–71), combined (bar 364 *et seq.*) with Third quotation of *Ascent* theme from trios 1 and 2 of I¹ (see also (7) above)

(13)  First quotation (I², bars 392–9) of opening bars of trio 1 of I¹ (cf. bars 155 *et seq.*)

(14)  Fourth quotation (I², bars 400–419) of *Ascent* theme from trios 1 and 2 of I¹ (cf. (12), (7) and (3) above)

(15)  Third interruption: chorale II (I², bars 463–520)

(16)  Fifth cut-off (I², bars 251–6)

(17)  Coda (I², fig. 33 to end)

## Table 2C

### Chronological Order

First cut-off

      First quotation of (remodelled) *March*

        First quotation of *Ascent* theme

Second cut-off

Third cut-off

      Second quotation of (remodelled) *March* incorporating —

        Second quotation of *Ascent* theme combined with continuation of (remodelled) *March*

      First quotation of *March* in original form

          First interruption

          Second interruption (Chorale I)

Fourth cut-off

      Third quotation of (remodelled) *March* combined with —
        Third quotation of *Ascent* theme

          First quotation of opening bars of trio I

        Fourth quotation of *Ascent* theme

          Third Interruption (Chorale II)

Fifth cut-off

goes out of his way to bring home to us, by the stitching in of this remarkable interpolation, the overwhelming importance of the *trios* of the march for the evolution of the second movement and, above all, for our comprehension of the drama of ascent and collapse that is enacted first in the trios of the march and then re-created in the ensuing allegro. If this anticipatory dramatic role played by the trios is kept in mind as a constant *backdrop* to the events of the allegro that I index variously in my tables, the patient reader – with score to hand! – may arrive, I believe, at a clearer picture of the unique formal and musical processes that generate the allegro, one more faithful to the movement and more relevant than the improbable sonata schemes foisted on it by too many commentators.

The tables, I hope, and their implications, speak for themselves. It is not my intention to comment on them, beyond here and there isolating one or two special features. The most straightforward category, and certainly one of the most important and arresting in concept, is that which I have named cut-off (Table A, column 1). The gesture itself – a shrill cry of pain or despair – requires no further elucidation. However, it does require forceful projection by the woodwind, and a conductor who understands its unchanging function; it should freeze our blood each time it occurs, like a scream in the dark. Its contour may change a little, it may be contracted or extended – its longest version runs to eleven bars (the *Hauptsatz*, fig. $11^{-1}$), its shortest to four (fig. 18) – but, after its first release at fig. $5^{-8}$, it is immediately recognizable, summing up, as it does, the scalic figuration in hectic descent that has been a feature of the trios of the *Trauermarsch*.

It is not my intention to pursue the retrospection principle even more thoroughly than the composer does himself in his symphony, and in the second movement of Part I in particular. But I cannot, in the context of our discussion of the evolution of the cut-off gesture, avoid making one last observation. I have just mentioned above the interpolation of the opening bars of trio 1 of the *Trauermarsch*, sited, as Table A shows (column 3, no. 4), well towards the end of the movement, approaching, in fact, the third and crucial interruption, Chorale II (column 5, no. 3; see also the chronological Tables B and C) which finally achieves D major, but only to lose it: it is the last cut-off (column 1, no. 5) that delivers the *coup de grâce*.

This sequence of events, one among many of the same type, variously put together but always leading to the same denouement – collapse – encapsulates the *fons et origo* of Part 1, both musically and dramatically. But overwhelming though this chain of quotation, interruption, and cut-off may be, we must not overlook, in the *Trauermarsch*, the first movement, the earlier quotation of the first trio's opening bars, to which I have already drawn attention on pp. 277–8 above. Almost as striking as the quotation itself (bars 1:353–4) is the sequence of 'events' that follows it. First, a cut-off (woodwind prominent, bars 355–6), a nascent version, surely, of what is to be established later and elaborated as the dominating cut-off that punctuates the allegro; next, the 'ascent' theme, as *Hauptmelodie* in a polyphonic web of motivic allusions (bars 357–68), a dialogue, no less, for two trombones, exchanging characteristic ideas that pull in opposite directions; and finally, the extraordinary climax at the *Trauermarsch*, fig. 18 – '*Klagend*' (an explosion of sorrow),[48] woodwind and (handstopped) brass with their bells up, so Mahler orders – that provides the model, as I have suggested, for all the collapses into the abyss that follow.

This further instance (Mahler's doing, not mine) of the high importance of the opening bars of trio 1 and their dramatic development in trio 2 – which affords an almost total glimpse of what is to come, of unflagging contrast between ascent and descent, triumph and collapse – together with the comparable sequence of events in the allegro that I have already touched on – confirms, if nothing else, what I have been arguing so strenuously: the prime generative function of the trios of the *Trauermarsch*. Who can doubt indeed, as Graeme Downes has pointed out,[49] that it is from the turbulent chromaticism of the opening of trio 1 that the principal theme of the *Hauptsatz*, the allegro (see bar 9 – fig. 2), evolves? Or that, ultimately, we may similarly ascribe the origins of the cut-off

48 It is important to remember that '*Klagend*' is not only an indication of sorrow but also an unleashing of protest, of complaint (e.g. '*Die klagende Partei*' = the plaintiff), a fist shaken at fate.
49 Downes, 'An Axial System of Tonality', pp. 160–61.

gesture to the seething (but needle-sharp) chromaticism of the 'wild', insistently descending violins of the first trio in the *Trauermarsch*? (It is no accident, Dr Downes makes clear, that in each case, the opening theme of the trio and principal theme of the allegro are initiated by an upbeat spanning an eleventh in the trio and a minor ninth in the allegro, the latter to assume virtually the status of an intervallic leading motive as the movement unfolds.)

So much for the cut-off column, its impact on, and some of its relationships to, the parallel columns. The march columns (2 and 4), again, are pretty straightforward in their disposition. Readers may use them as a guide and draw their own conclusions as to the validity or otherwise of what each column implies, i.e. the constant resurfacing of the *Trauermarsch*, in one guise or another (straight quotation or remodelled), so that its presence is never wholly dispersed or absorbed: our consciousness of mortality, it seems, is always at hand. As column 4 shows, the march most often emerges in its remodelled form (after the precedent established in the *Trauermarsch*, trio 1 (see above, pp. 277–9)), but there is once more a unique moment that calls for our special attention; its uniqueness, indeed, is represented by its having a column (2) to itself. The musical incident this, in every respect, singular entry embodies is the surfacing of the *Trauermarsch* in its original form (and tempo) in a context that has not led us to expect its intrusion. On the contrary, at the double barline (the *Hauptsatz*, bar 265) the ascending intervallic upbeat, which has gradually expanded from bar 261 onwards, would seem to prepare us for a return to, say, figuration directly related to the agitated principal theme of the allegro. But instead, the leap from E sharp (bar 265) to G sharp and thence to F sharp (a variant of the *Ur*-intervallic motive), together with the onset of B major, is audaciously *interrupted* in bar 266. Mahler makes the interruption graphically visible by interpolating *mid-bar* dotted vertical cut-off[50] lines from top to bottom of his score, at which point the *Trauermarsch* suddenly materializes, contradicting our thematic

---

50  Cf. a similar dotted line in bar 322, to mark the release of cut-off no. 4. Mahler undoubtedly added this graphic form of interruption to emphasize the significance of this particular cut-off, that it aborts the first attempt to establish the chorale (in A, bar 316).

expectations. It is as if a door had shut on one orchestra, and opened on another, in another room where the *Trauermarsch* is still in progress. An unmistakably Ives-like event this,[51] though perhaps more subtly conceived than if the American master had had a hand in it. In contriving this extraordinary interruption-that-is-also-a-quotation, Mahler, albeit unknowingly, was contributing a new page to the history of twentieth-century music.

Few interpreters, alas, as we move into the twenty-first century, show themselves to be alert to the significance of the passage: the general run of conductors play *through* it, paying little attention to Mahler's dynamics and least of all, most times, to the *triple forte* that Mahler demands for the proper articulation of the apex of the upbeat, without which there is no arousal of expectation and thus no contradiction of it either. Nor, apparently, do the composer's dotted lines impinge. Smoothness and unblemished continuity carry the day and erase all possibility of Mahler's brilliant innovation making its full effect. I shall be returning to this passage once more when I come to the final column, Interruptions (column 5), to which it might well be argued that this intervention by the *Trauermarsch* also – and quite properly – belongs.

I shall spend very few words indeed on the second of my Quotations columns (3) which lays out in sequence the genesis and evolution of the 'Ascent' theme (I can think of no better shorthand description than this). If the reader cares to take the list in one hand and a score in the other and follow the history of the theme from beginning to end, he will find himself in possession of everything he needs to know as the composer himself tells it, the best of all possible guides. The only caution I would enter is to avoid theme-

---

51 It continues to surprise me that the Ives–Mahler conjunction has received relatively little serious attention, though it is clear to me that the two composers often made a similar response to the sound-worlds by which they were surrounded, very different though those sound-worlds were. None the less, it was surely the case that both Ives and Mahler took a pioneering interest in multi-directional sound and the incorporation of the vernacular into their music – the deployment of the one often brought with it the use of the other – and I find the silence on the subject – which I aired as long ago as 1975 in DMWY, pp. 169–71, 280, and 373 – baffling. The more welcome, then, are two recent studies: Leon Botstein's 'Innovation and Nostalgia: Ives, Mahler and the Origins of Modernism', and Robert P. Morgan's 'Ives and Mahler: Mutual Responses at the End of an Era'.

spotting or theme-counting (the danger inherent in numerical lists) and always take into account, in this movement above all, context and location; a reasonably informed scrutiny of *where* a quotation occurs, with an eye (and ear) trained on what has happened before and after it, may help one to come up with an answer to the question, *why*?: that is, why *here*? I hope that in this specific respect the layout of Table c may be helpful. It represents an attempt to show how the particular events with which I have concerned myself are located and interrelated within the 'space' of the movement as a whole (something different, I think, from the laundry lists which make up Table a, say).

As for 'Ascent', my description, like the theme itself, speaks for itself. We need only add, at least in the context of this movement, that what ascends must also descend, or be cut off or otherwise terminated; and it is certainly obligatory to keep those consequences and implications in mind when categorizing the theme: it soars, as it were, only to fall. Here again Mahler goes out of his way to spell out the dichotomy – ascent and its obverse – simultaneously. I have already mentioned one example of this – the solo trombones' duet-dialogue in the *Trauermarsch*, trio 2, bars 357–68, which presents the 'Ascent' theme along with its directional opposite.[52] In fact, the contrary impulse in relation to the 'Ascent' theme has already been adumbrated at an even earlier stage, in trio 1, bars 165–72, and at the earliest stage in the evolution of the theme itself (cf. the version of the theme that establishes itself later in the same trio at fig. $9^{+9}$). All of which goes to illustrate the symbiotic relationship between ascent and descent with which the theme is identified from the start, and reconfirms yet again the almost manically anticipatory, indeed prophetic, role that the trios discharge.

What remains is the final column (5), dedicated to Interruptions (and their collapse), a short list, inevitably so, since the events both incorporate and effect their own termination and indeed bring Part 1 of the symphony to its close. The list, some may think, should be shorter; and I confess to some doubt about the justification for including the A flat section (beginning at the double bar, the

---

52  See above, pp. 280 and 299.

*Hauptsatz*, fig. 16⁺⁴) as an interruption proper, on the same scale, say, as the preceding intervention of the march.[53] On the other hand, this oddly swaggering, quasi-march episode undeniably strikes a new note even while – and perhaps because – the triplets that go to make up its profile recall, by association, the 'promise' of the 'Ascent' theme. It is, at the very least, a significant *remission:* is light, then, about to dawn, the promise of 'Ascent' to be fulfilled?

I noted earlier that the interpolation of the march was launched by the ascending leap of a ninth, thus contradicting our expectations of a resumption of the characteristic agitation of the allegro's principal theme; and it is again that same preparatory gesture that initiates the A flat mini-march, thus furnishing a further contradiction of our expectation that this time round the allegro will resume its pursuit of the conflict. But instead, there is this quirky switch to a more positive mood. It is of relatively short duration (some twenty bars), after which there follows a transition, based, in its last four bars, on the ubiquitous upbeat, which finally takes shape at the double bar (bar 316) as a leap from E natural to F *sharp* (317, and sustained for a semibreve), falling to E natural (again a semibreve). As we proceed, this sounds less like a forthcoming contradiction and more and more like a breakthrough; which, in fact, is exactly what happens: a triumphant A major is affirmed by strings, woodwind, brass, and timpani – even the triangle is conscripted to take part with a celebratory (*sempre fortissimo*) trill. For a moment it seems as if the battle (or whatever) is over, mortality banished, and the tonic *major* of the allegro unveiled as the goal after which Part 1 has been remorselessly seeking. But there is hardly time to be convinced, or indeed unconvinced by the breakthrough. For after two bars of assertion, the penultimate cut-off intervenes (column 1, no. 4) – at which critical point Mahler introduces another vertical dotted line mid-bar (322), an interruption in fact of an interruption (the aborted A major)[54] – and this time (same bar) the cut-off

---

53  Graeme Downes ('An Axial System of Tonality', pp. 170–71) locates a source for this passage in the *Trauermarsch*, bars 243–5, oboes. A typical instance, this, of a seemingly random counterpoint acquiring later a special motivic or thematic significance. The first movement of the Fourth is littered with like examples. See also my discussion of the apotheosis of the 'triplet phenomenon' in the finale on pp. 349–50 below.

54  See also above. n. 50.

is reinforced by – uncoils over – a diminished seventh chord (on A), brutally projected by the six horns, hand-stopped, bells up, for five bars, after which, at last, the *furor* of the allegro is resumed. Typically, however, it is not the principal theme that returns but the ascending upbeat, which, after frantically repeating itself (from bar 325), finally succeeds in reuniting itself (333) with the principal theme from which it had become detached. And so on and so on. There is no more remarkable passage in the whole movement than this complex sequence of discontinuities, executed, notwithstanding, with ferocious logic. One comes to realize, retrospectively, that the postponed reunion of the upbeat with its rightful continuation has all along been part of Mahler's long-term tactical thinking. If the seemingly unpremeditated is to make its effect, it must, paradoxically, be minutely, even manically, organized.

### A Chorale Collapses

Table B sets out the sequence of the events I believe to be of cardinal importance in the music that succeeds the penultimate cut-off (a double-strength cut-off, as I have just suggested); and I have already touched on the special significance of at least one of those events, the spectacular quotation (at bar 392) of the opening bars of trio 1, of an importance comparable, in its different way, to the resurfacing of the march in its original form and tempo in the *Hauptsatz* at fig. 15. In the light of what I have already had to say about the status acquired by the ascending upbeat as the allegro evolves and in particular its role as an agent, a creator, of expectation, there is perhaps nothing very surprising about its reappearance at fig. 26, once again screwing up the tension and preparing us – for what, exactly? After all, we have been through all of this before and landed up with the *Trauermarsch* at fig. 15; and again at fig. 16, when the A flat mini-march was interposed; and again at fig. 17$^{+8}$, when we were catapulted into the short-lived A major, almost immediately dispatched at fig. 18 by the fourth cut-off. What is afoot this time round? We are soon to know. Exiguous though the A major interruption was, it made its impact, a chorale, cut off – cut down – almost before it had announced itself; and when we hear the onset

of D major at fig. 27, jubilant string figuration, the noisy presence
of the timpani, and above all a lot of ascending triplets that finally
participate (from fig. 28) in the adumbration of an unmistakable
brass chorale, we may be forgiven for thinking that we are in the
midst of a replay of Chorale I but this time with the probability of a
final, positive outcome. This indeed is vouchsafed at bar 500, where
D major is unequivocally affirmed – Mahler takes care to mark the
bar 'Hohepunkt'.[55] But then something, to my ears, quite astonishing
happens over the ensuing twenty bars. A sustained, graduated diminuendo sets in; the dynamics fade; D major loses its brightness; the
mass of sound thins out; the orchestra itself, so to speak, packs its
bags and steals away, so that by bar 512 all the strings have departed but for the cellos and double-basses, all of the woodwind but for
the bassoon and double-bassoon, and all of the brass but for the
horns who keep alive – just – a spectral version of the chorale until
it expires altogether on a D played by the first horn only, *pianissimo*. What seemed to promise an unequivocal blaze of triumph has
been reduced to a whisper, if not a whimper.[56] And with awesome
logic, the fifth cut-off (*Hauptsatz*, bars 521–6) again provides the
*coup de grâce*, to confirm, if confirmation were needed, that Chorale
II, like its predecessor, has had its lifeblood drained out of it.[57] An
analogy with the photographic process might be drawn here, but in

55  It is not surprising perhaps that when Mahler came to compose the first movement of
his Ninth, like the second movement of the Fifth, a form built systematically around the
idea of ascent and collapse, he wrote above bar 308, after the tempo designation 'Pesante',
the words '*Hochste Kraft*' (maximum force). But he might just as well have followed the
precedent, '*Hohepunkt*', that we find in the Fifth (*Hauptsatz*, bar 500): the two bars in
question both represent the climactic peak of a final ascent followed by a final collapse.
I am much indebted to Henry-Louis de La Grange for drawing my attention to a remark
of Mahler's, made to William Ritter, probably in Munich in 1910, with reference to the
Ninth. 'Now', Mahler said, 'I am embarking on an entirely new path' (*Revue française de
musique*, 10/7 (15 July 1912); in French, Ritter's recollection of what Mahler said to him
runs like this: 'Maintenant je suis entre dans une voie toute nouvelle!').
56  'This is the way the world ends / Not with a bang but a whimper.' T. S. Eliot, *The Hollow
Men* (1925).
57  Incidentally, this passage provides for good measure a marvellous example of Mahler's
overlapping technique. For as the cut-off unfolds, its 'accompaniment' is made up of a
diminished-seventh chord (cf. bars 322 ff., but this time *piano*: it too, at first, has been drained
of its former power); the ascending upbeat (properly attached to its correct continuation), and the movement's opening, basic motive (see *Hauptsatz*, bars 1–5 ff.). A typical
instance of Mahler's passion for the simultaneous combination of ends and beginnings.

reverse: we start with a full-colour print but are left with a negative.[58]

Another extraordinary moment in the symphony, this expiring
of the chorale; and, I want to suggest, if we are listening correctly,
it should also represent an extraordinary moment of *déjà vu*, quite
in the manner of Proust. For what we hear – the recovery of a
moment of lost time – is a recovery, replay, a re-enactment, not so
much of the just aborted Chorale I, but of the similarly aborted
climax of the second trio of the *Trauermarsch*. Indeed, if one harks
back – to time past! – to that passage in the *Trauermarsch*, bars
368–76, it is immediately apparent that it is there that the model for
the ultimate collapse of the allegro has been set up. It is final proof
of the long shadow thrown over the allegro by the trios of the
funeral march; and the recovery of our memory of it in its very first
materialization must be an essential part of our experience of its
later manifestation.

There are of course differences. The volume of sound, for example,
is diminished overall, from **fff** to **p** *morendo,* by means of dynamics
alone, not by the reduction of instrumental resources that is the
radical procedure adopted in Chorale II. But the chief difference
resides in the substitution of the nascent chorale for the trio's
extensive chromatic slide. Mahler had no option but to find an
idea, a concept, that could act as both agent and symbol, of affirmation, a gesture that might, eventually, reverse the slide dramatically articulated as the failing climax of the second trio.

It was not just a matter of confirming the D major that had been
momentarily established and then withdrawn in the passage I
describe as Chorale II. The concept also, from the start, had to
incorporate a potentiality for ascent, the direction that would run
contrary to the predominant directional thrust downward of the
two trios of the *Trauermarsch* and much of the allegro. It was also
obligatory to light upon an idea that could effectively affirm and

58  The listener, however, will have to make all of this out for himself if the interpretation
     of the symphony does not do it for him, as it should. Conductors need to pay particu-
     lar attention to the preview of the allegro's final collapse that is disclosed in trio 2. An
     absolute commitment to Mahler's dynamics here, and in Chorale II, as it fades, would
     make a good start.

then unaccountably fade, while leaving behind an impression, at least, that a possible means to secure and then enact the obverse of collapse had been disclosed.

Hence, surely, Mahler's choice of 'chorale' as the concept that would meet his needs. Too many words, it seems to me, have been expended in a variety of attempts to elucidate its significance for the composer and thereby, naturally, the significance it should have for us. For example, was Mahler (improbable thought) evoking the shade of his great predecessor, Anton Bruckner? (This, it seems, was Alma Mahler's opinion, which she apparently expressed to her husband; in any case she thought it a mistake.[59]) Was Mahler's intent religious, mystical even? Or was it, as some have suggested, a suspect strategy, to achieve too easily a crowning moment of triumph, triumphalism rather than a genuine expression of joy?[60] On the whole, this last was Adorno's line of approach, who was a resolute *unbeliever* in the 'happy end' of the symphony, for reasons perhaps more to do with his own psychology (and psycho-politics?) than the facts of the music.[61]

It would be naive to imagine that Mahler was unaware of the weighty baggage of tradition, of various kinds, that the chorale, as an idea, carried; we must assume the contrary, that he was prepared to take advantage of its traditional affiliations and associations. But it is far more interesting and illuminating, I believe, to try to analyse those musical, even utilitarian, reasons why the chorale must have seemed to him to fit the bill precisely. In short, it was not the influence (or seductiveness) of tradition alone that made the choice of chorale as agent of resolution imperative.

Some of those reasons I have already touched on above, for example, directional thrust and the chorale's capability both to affirm and fade (and yet preserve its identity); but any scrutiny of the chorale's inherent properties must include two further items. First, what one might describe in the context of the music of Part I

---

59  See AM *Memories*, pp. 47–8.
60  Shades of the finale of another famous Fifth, Shostakovich's!
61  There is an admirable summary of many of the varied responses to Mahler's deployment of the chorale in the finale of the Fifth in HLG *Mahler*, II, pp. 822–85. The major statement of Adorno's scepticism with regard to the Fifth will be found in TWA *Mahler*, pp. 136–8.

as a whole, the 'alien' character of the chorale, an intrusion – interruption, in truth – from another aesthetic, another world of musical ideas, another *vocabulary* altogether, which Mahler must have realized to be exactly what he was seeking for: it is in its 'otherness' that the strength of the chorale resides. In this respect, indeed, it seems to me to be more like an *objet trouvé* than a symbol of traditional values. (This may develop later, as a matter of natural course, in the finale, but is not manifest here.) Second, and yet more importantly, while the chorale here, on its first materialization, offers, *because* of its drastic abridgement, a potentiality for future expansion, that very same *truncation,* in the unique context of the drama that Part I of this extraordinary symphony rehearses, consummately *completes* the cycle of ascent–collapse that is Part I's *raison d'être* – *not* by breaking it but by representing it in its ultimate guise! After which, one may well feel (along with the composer), that there is no more to be said, no absolute imperative that further music (movements, even) should transpire.

## The Coda of the 'Hauptsatz'

This is a major issue, to which I shall return in *my* coda below. Meanwhile, there follows one further brief burst of energy after the fifth cut-off (*Hauptsatz*, fig. 30) that very swiftly subsides into Mahler's coda (fig. 33), itself an exceptional feat of orchestral refinement. The orchestra is much reduced; the brass muted (a mixture of mutes (trumpets) and handstopping (horns)); the dynamics, but for a solitary *sforzando,* never rise above *p*, while bleached, spectral fragments of some of the movement's principal motives are recalled as if overheard in a dream. The only constant rhythmic feature is the unvaried triplet figuration of the divided first violins, a conflation of fourths, for which Mahler indicates artificial harmonics, and an overall dynamic of *pp*. This thin, ethereal string sound forms a backdrop against which the motivic shards are articulated. The very last sequence of motives we hear (see Ex. 4) unites the ubiquitous ascending upbeat and its consequent falling away, a graphic reduction at this last moment of the movement's life to the basic contour of its overriding obsession: ascent and

Ex. 4

Fifth Symphony: the last page of the coda in the 1919 score. A revision by
Mahler of this page in which he further refined and clarified the *glissandi* in the
concluding bars forms part of vol. v of the *Critical Edition* of Mahler's works
(Vienna, 1989), p. 115. A comparison provides a model example of his revisory
practice: the goal was always maximum transparency.

collapse.[62] A final touch of drained colour is provided by the over-lapping entries in the movement's closing bars of the ubiquitous ascending upbeat, detached from any immediate continuation,[63] allotted to solo strings – viola, then cello, then double-bass – the upwards leap now transformed into a glissando, *p*. We hear it three times, like sighs, or exhalations of a last breath.


## Reflections in the Shape of a Coda

It is just because of the perfect, albeit 'negative', conclusion that is achieved at the end of Part I, that a question remains uppermost in the mind during the interval that ensues – Mahler, as we can see, asks for a long pause, and conductors should observe this – before embarking on Part II: what is there left to say? Such is the extra-ordinary totality of the musico-dramatic experience that Part I unfolds, that one can feel (temporarily, in performance at least) that anything that follows has to be redundant.

No doubt this is an exaggeration; and I am not (I think) sug-gesting, at least not seriously, that Parts II and III are expendable. On the other hand, the very fact that this is an impression – more than that, a conviction – that is left with me in the wake of a con-vincing performance of the symphony, or immersion in the score, says something about the peculiar self-sufficiency of Part I, its unique form deriving from the interdependence of the two open-ing movements and the inspired obsessiveness and attention to detail with which the drama is worked out; one might, indeed,

---

62  It was Hans Keller who was the first to point out that one of the leading themes in Britten's *Peter Grimes* – 'What harbour shelters peace?' (Act I, scene 2) – had its source in this theme of Mahler's. Britten had first heard the Fifth, a broadcast from the Nether-lands, in 1934. It was this symphony of Mahler's above all that was a major influence on Britten's opera of 1945, e.g. cf. his 'Storm' interlude with Mahler's allegro in Part I. The contribution of the Fifth to *Grimes* is amply documented in Paul Banks (ed.), *The Making of 'Peter Grimes'*, vol. 2, Notes and Commentaries, and in particular, by Donald Mitchell, '*Peter Grimes*: Fifty Years On', pp. 125–51.

63  True to form – by which I mean Mahler, contrary to carefully calculated appearances (as here), always ensures that nothing integral is ever omitted – the upbeat is reunited in the last three bars with its rightful continuation, dispersed among the tuba (*morendo*!), harp, pizzicato cellos and basses, and a final stroke on the timpani, an A that Mahler marks *p* with an accent and an indication that this ultimate, isolated pitch must be perfectly tuned and clearly articulated ('*gut stimmen!!*').

quite properly describe Part I as a kind of *monodrama* in two acts.

It did not, in fact, surprise me when I had the rare opportunity to hear Part I of the Fifth as an independent item in the course of an orchestral programme,[64] to have confirmed the unique, detached integrity of the *Trauermarsch* and allegro, making perfect sense as a musico-dramatic unit: in other words, one did not, as Berg (his *Wozzeck* interludes) hove into view, really miss the unheard rest of Mahler's symphony. At the same time — because *of course* one cannot abandon Parts II and III — the very independence of Part I casts an illuminating light on our comprehension of the symphony as a whole.

I find here a parallel with the Sixth, interestingly enough to be the next symphony and the one that was to end in defeat, not triumph; and yet, as I have argued elsewhere, Mahler shows us, in the Sixth, by his rounding off the first movement in a brilliant A major, how the symphony might have concluded had, in fact, the tonic *major* proved to be its ultimate destination: 'this first movement . . . incorporates an alternative Sixth that was never composed'.[65]

---

64  This was at the Aldeburgh Festival of 1995, for which I devised a concert made up of music that had actively influenced Britten in the composition of his opera *Peter Grimes,* the fiftieth anniversary of the first performance of which the Festival was celebrating. Among the composers represented were Berg, Shostakovich, and Mahler, the last by a performance of Part I of the Fifth, when the City of London Sinfonia was conducted by Steuart Bedford. See also the Programme Book for the 1995 Festival, to which I contributed a note, 'Contexts of Violence: The Sources of *Peter Grimes*', pp. 91–6, and n. 62 above.

65  See my note on the Sixth in GMWL, pp. 2.71–7 and 74 in particular. The passage I have in mind is that from fig. 42 to the end of the movement, where the onset of A major plus jubilating timpani, not to speak of the upward thrust of the second subject, the leading motive of which is recalled at this point, cannot but call to mind the aborted A major Interruption towards the end of the second movement of Part I of the Fifth (in the Sixth, the second subject playing the role of the chorale (Chorale I)) that in fact does not fully materialize in the parallel passage of the Fifth's allegro until the later interruption that momentarily establishes D (*Hauptsatz*, bars 488 ff.). As the conclusion of the Sixth's first movement proceeds, it increasingly takes on the character of a displaced cyclic recapitulation of first-movement materials (cf. for example, the recapitulatory C major gesture that crowns the finale of the Seventh Symphony (fig. 293 ff.), for which the conclusion of the first movement of the Sixth was clearly a model) that in other circumstances might have brought the finale of the alternative Sixth, that I have referred to above, to a triumphant A major end. It is thus that Mahler's 'tragic' Sixth also informs us how an optimistic, conquering Sixth might have gone. (Colin Matthews believes that it is in fact the Seventh Symphony itself that represents Mahler's alternative to his Sixth.)

The parallel of course is not exact. For one thing, the 'alternative' that Part I of the Fifth proposes is much more elaborately fulfilled and at far, far greater length. What indeed we have in the Fifth is virtually an independent 'symphony' contained within the overall form of the symphony itself a uniquely self-sufficient and self-generating stretch of symphonic music in two movements, of an originality without parallel (almost) elsewhere in Mahler's oeuvre, that consummately enacts and brings to *tragic* resolution the 'tragic' drama that the symphony *as a whole* is designed to deny. That affirmative denial, we have to believe, awaits us in the finale, and indeed has been prepared. None the less, what the Fifth offers is not, as the Sixth does, a relatively brief glimpse 'of how the inner drama might have gone otherwise', but, rather, two independent 'readings', each complete in itself, each vouchsafing a reverse denouement of the basic conflict, that is, ascent or collapse, but one of which, Part I, can either work in association with Parts II and III combined or be decoupled and function in isolation.

There is, then, I believe, a case to be made for the very occasional occasion when Part I of the Fifth might be heard as a separate entity with its own identity, strictly for the reasons that I have outlined above; I am not, absolutely not, suggesting some kind of eccentric dismemberment of the symphony. But while I think Part I of the Fifth is an entirely special case, and before I am accused of vandalism or worse, it is surely of some relevance to consider a possible precedent like the first movement of the Second (an earlier *Trauermarsch*) and supreme inventions still to come, like the finale, 'Der Abschied', of *Das Lied* – in effect Part II of that symphony – or the first movement of the Ninth, again huge stretches of symphonic music that in some sense, and despite their incorporation into individual symphonies, can leave a marked impression of downright self-sufficiency. The first movement of the Ninth for me is comparable, for the impression of an integral completeness it makes, to Part I of the Fifth; it is again virtually a one-movement symphony, and I would not object here either to an occasional performance of that movement in isolation. It is certainly not my ambition to start a new performing tradition; but if nothing else, this discussion may provoke us to speculate a little about how Mahler's music might have developed had he been spared to live, say, for another decade. The arbitrariness of his death is too often lost sight of, with the consequence that we 'read' the last works as if they were the logical consequences of a pre-ordained fate. If there had been an 'alternative' *biography*, for example, had Mahler lived on to 1921 instead of dying in 1911, it is my guess, on the basis of those quite extraordinary independent movements that I have singled out (interestingly enough all of them first movements or parts and, in one case, a finale), that his innovatory, formal thinking might have led him to the creation of new concepts of what might constitute a symphony; Part 1 of the Fifth, the finale of *Das Lied,* the first movement of the Ninth, contain the seeds – the intimations – of an evolution that, alas, was never to be completed, the results of which might have had a profound influence on the development of the idea of 'symphony' in our century.

## Part II
### (iii) Scherzo. Stürmisch bewegt. Mit grösster Vehemenz

*Chronology and Sketches*

The very recent discovery of two further manuscript sources, one incomplete, though substantial, one more complete, for the composition of the scherzo, is an event of extraordinary interest – where, all these years, have these manuscripts been? – and of exceptional significance for detailed study of Mahler's working methods.[66] What they do not give us, it seems, is any helpful information about chronology; there are no dates, while the paper is of a type in general use by Mahler over a stretch of years that included the composition of the Fifth. We must assume, I think, until fresh evidence suggests otherwise, that these manuscripts – surfacing for

---

66  These are an addition to the magnificent Robert Owen Lehman deposit at the Pierpont Morgan Library, New York. I am much indebted to Edward R. Reilly for an early indication of the manuscripts' existence and whereabouts, though their provenance, it seems, has not yet been made known. See also Dr Reilly's 'The Manuscripts of Mahler's Fifth Symphony', in *NSNC*, pp. 58–63, where he discusses the new-found sketches in some detail.

the first time in 1996 – represent the sketches that Mahler would have had to hand, or under his hands, at the beginning of the summer of 1901, when he began seriously to work on the new symphony: I make the distinction because, taking into account the complex character of the new sources, it seems scarcely credible that the scherzo plus the two movements of Part 1 could all have been completed in this first summer of work on the symphony; for instance, does the first (partial) set of newly discovered composition sketches belong to an earlier chronological stage? Were these sketches that he might have brought with him to Maiernigg, to work up and flesh out, as was his habit, during his summer vacation? I often wonder if the division of creative labour between summer and the rest of the year was quite as absolute as established opinion has it. If not, perhaps it was a first set of sketches for the scherzo that accompanied Mahler to Maiernigg, at the beginning of his summer vacation in 1901.

In any event, we may safely assume that the scherzo had been round and about in Mahler's thinking for a (relatively) considerable stretch of time, as is indicated by the inclusion of it – as a title – in a projected scheme for the Fourth Symphony, in six movements, the fifth of which,[67] ran as follows: 'Die Welt ohne Schwere, D-dur [D major] (Scherzo)'. In 1975 (DMWY, p. 139) I translated Mahler's title as 'The World without Care', a version that I think now conveyed no sense of the weight, the heaviness, that 'Schwere' implies (along with seriousness and severity); in any case, my own inadequate terminology might have been better spelled out as 'The World without Cares' which would at least have had the merit of not flatly contradicting Mahler's own description of the movement to Natalie Bauer-Lechner in the summer of 1901: 'There is

67  Mahler's tentative numbering of the narrative scheme for a possible Fourth gives us *two* fifth movements, i.e. the movement that succeeds the scherzo, 'Das himmlische Leben, G-dur [G major]', is also marked as No. 5 in the sequence of titles, though placed sixth and last. The outline scheme was first published in Paul Bekker, *Gustav Mahlers Sinfonien*, p. 145. See also DMWY, p. 139, where I refer to the draft programme showing 'the dense intertwining of song and symphony characteristic of these *Wunderhorn* years' and further, on pp. 258–9 (n. 30), suggest that it 'must belong to the time when Mahler was engaged on the Third Symphony and still uncertain as to the exact disposition of the wealth of invention and creative ideas available to him. Already, it seems, even before the final shape of one symphony was determined, the shape of another was materializing . . .'

nothing romantic or mystical about it; it is simply the expression of incredible energy [*unerhörte Kraft*]. It is a human being in the full light of day, in the prime of his life . . .'[68] For Mahler, one might think already (with some disbelief), a remarkably shadowless, shadow-free, concept, a question to which we shall return. Meanwhile, still intent on decoding the title, we note Floros's – or his translator's, Vernon Wicker's – clever translation, 'The World without Gravity',[69] which accommodates the idea of a weightlessness of spirit and at the same time, of material things, 'Gravity' in its scientific sense; and – who knows? – given Mahler's interest in the physical sciences, it might well have been this meaning of 'Schwere' that attracted him to incorporate this word, and not some other, into his title.

*The Character of the Scherzo*

But more important than the title, which I guess Mahler would have formulated before he had a very detailed picture in his mind of how the music might eventually go, is the character of the music itself. Perhaps the first thing to observe, however, is the scherzo's principal tonality, D major. There was surely an element of risk here, of a premature affirmation of a D major that from the outset of the symphony Mahler had envisaged to be its goal. We have seen how, at the end of Part I, we are left in no doubt that there is much ground still to be travelled before there can be any chance of a secure D major establishing itself. Does, then, the exuberant D major in which the opening ländler of the scherzo declares itself, constitute a misjudgement, or perhaps a puzzling paradox? In other words, is this, at this stage, where we ought to be?[70]

68  NB-L *Recollections*, p. 173.
69  *Gustav Mahler: The Symphonies*, p. 111. Likewise, HLG *Mahler*, II, p. 800. I have gratefully adopted 'Gravity' and use it throughout this chapter.
70  Deryck Cooke, in *Gustav Mahler: An Introduction to his Music*, pp. 82–3, takes the view that it certainly is: the scherzo 'completely contradicts the nihilistic mood and minor tonality of practically everything that has gone before, by switching to the brilliant key of D major, and to an exploration of the joyfully affirmative view of life, both of which are to occupy the rest of the symphony. Thus the dark world of Part I is not gradually dispelled by a process of spiritual development: it is abruptly rejected [*sic*] in favour of a completely different attitude', etc., etc. As will emerge below, this is a view I do not share,

In attempting to answer that question we have to look back for a moment to Mahler's own concept of 'a human being in the full light of day, in the prime of his life', and remark that the movement he created, brimming over with energy though it may be, is in fact (and unsurprisingly) replete with extraordinary moments of darkness and frenzy which effectively undermine any conclusion we might reach that the scherzo's D major represents the D that is (still) Mahler's – his symphony's – ultimate goal.

For a start, even the most cursory scan of the movement reveals a notable accumulation of minor keys, among them F minor, D minor, A minor, E minor, which, if one takes into account the nervous, shadowy, sceptical, even desperate music associated with these tonal excursions, makes one realize how impossible it is to reconcile the image of Cooke's 'joyfully affirmative view of life' or indeed of Mahler's, of 'a human being in the full light of day', with what some of the most significant music of the scherzo is actually telling us.

Adorno, with his customary, if elliptical, economy, points to the scherzo's novelty, that is, to Mahler's concept of it as a 'development-scherzo',[71] thus isolating what is so striking about it, what Adorno himself goes on to describe as the composer's labouring 'at the possibility of a symphonic unity arising from dances arranged serially as in a suite', a *trouvaille* 'without which, incidentally, Strauss's *Rosenkavalier* [1911] would hardly be thinkable'.[72] And not only *Rosenkavalier*, but also perhaps, and much more relevantly, Ravel's *La Valse* (1919–20)? It was surely Mahler who, in the scherzo of this Fifth Symphony, was the first to deploy the waltz as an ironic icon, subjecting it to all manner of distortion and consistent reversal or contradiction of its traditional meanings? This, after

---

one moreover that seriously underestimates the compositional skills Mahler demonstrates in avoiding just such a crude contradiction that would have fatally weakened the overall evolution of the narrative. To be sure (and fair), Cooke concedes moments of 'nostalgia' and 'haunting music full of sadness and loneliness'. But these he suggests 'have nothing emotionally in common with the despairing laments of the first part of the work . . . The scherzo is really a dance of life, evoking all the bustle of a vital existence, as opposed to the concentration on the inevitability of death in the funeral marches and ferocious protests of Part I.'

71  TWA *Mahler*, p. 102.
72  Ibid. p. 103.

all, is what happens in the waltz section (F minor) that develops, after the very brief beguilement of its opening bars (bars 429ff.: the double bar marks the end of the movement's central trio section), into a veritable dance of death, especially when, in bars 472–5 and again in 482–5, the *Holzklapper* (whip), *fortissimo*, takes over its rhythm (forcefully doubled by the trumpets) – the horrible rattle of bones – from the glockenspiel (cf. bar 462). It is precisely here, in the scherzo of Mahler's Fifth, that the Viennese waltz, perhaps never an entirely virginal concept, finally lost its innocence.

### Mahler, Goethe, and Schubert

We owe to Constantin Floros the restitution of a bit of fascinating information that was originally included in Richard Specht's early monograph on Mahler first published in 1905,[73] who drew his readers' attention to a close parallel between a poem by Goethe, 'An Schwager Kronos' ('To Brother Time'), and the character of those parts of the scherzo that have particularly interested me. In so doing, Specht specifically mentions Bruno Walter's perception that Mahler's scherzo grew out of Goethe's poem; and given Walter's intimate association with the composer it must be highly probable that this was something that he had from Mahler himself.

What Specht does not mention (nor, oddly, does Floros) is the famous setting of the poem by Schubert (D. 369), similarly entitled 'An Schwager Kronos'. This would also certainly have been well known to Mahler; and I have no doubt that the conjunction of Goethe's text and Schubert's music offers us a source, a 'model', of some significance for the scherzo of the Fifth. The song gallops along in 6/8 from beginning to end in an unmodified moderate tempo ('Nicht zu schnell') and in an energetic D minor. Before the double bar is reached, however, Schubert registers the impact of the poet's vision of faltering old age and advancing death in a turbulent chromatic interpolation, climaxing on Goethe's image of

---

73 Floros, *Gustav Mahler: The Symphonies*, pp. 153–4, and Specht, *Gustav Mahler*, pp. 44–5. But Specht also refers to Goethe's poem – in fact he quotes a line from it – in his second, large-scale monograph published in 1913, pp. 290–91. The English translation I use is by Norma Deane and Celia Larner, in John Reed, *The Schubert Song Companion*, p. 47.

the 'dark gate of hell'. The 'gate', however, opens not on hell but on the postilion's cheerful horn signals that take over and round off the song in a brilliant, unqualified D major. The character of the narrative itself, which includes not only an unnerving vision of a 'dance of death' (Mahler's *Holzklapper!*) but also, we may think, a glimpse of 'a human being in the full light of day, in the prime of his life' (Mahler's words), plus the incorporation of the post-horn, plus – and perhaps most importantly – the song's tonality, seem to me good reason for including Schubert's song among the influential sources that contributed to the making of Mahler's scherzo.

| 'An Schwager Kronos' | 'To Brother Time' |
|---|---|
| Spude dich, Kronos! | *Hurry on, Time, on at a rattling* |
| Fort den raßelnden Trab! | *trot! The road runs downhill, your* |
| Bergab gleitet der Weg; | *dawdling makes things swim* |
| Ekles Schwindeln zögert | *before my eyes. On at a brisk pace,* |
| Mir vor die Stirne dein Zaudern. | *over stick and stone, stumbling* |
| Frisch, holpert es gleich, | *headlong into life!* |
| Über Stock und Steine den Trott | |
| Rasch ins Leben hinein! | |
| | |
| Nun schon wieder | *Now once more toiling uphill, out* |
| Den eratmenden Schritt | *of breath – up then, no slacking,* |
| Mühsam Berghinauf, | *upward striving and hoping.* |
| Auf denn, nicht träge denn, | |
| Strebend und hoffend hinan! | |
| | |
| Weit, hoch, herrlich | *High, wide, and glorious the* |
| Rings den Blick ins Leben hinein, | *prospect of life rings us round.* |
| Vom Gebirg zum Gebirg | *The eternal spirit soars from peak* |
| Schwebet der ewige Geist, | *to peak, full of intimations of* |
| Ewigen Lebens ahndevoll. | *eternal life.* |

| | |
|---|---|
| Seitwärts des Überdachs Schatten | *A shadowy doorway beckons* |
| Zieht dich an | *you aside across the threshold* |
| Und ein Frischung verheißender Blick | *of the girl's house, and her* |
| Auf der Schwelle des Mädchens da. | *eyes promise refreshment.* |
| Labe dich! – Mir auch, Mädchen, | *Take comfort! For me too,* |
| Diesen schäumenden Trank, | *lass, that sparkling draught,* |
| Diesen frischen Gesundheitsblick! | *that fresh and healthy look.* |
| | |
| Ah denn, rascher hinab! | *Down then, faster down!* |
| Sieh, die Sonne sinkt! | *See, the sun sinks. Before it* |
| Eh sie sinkt, eh mich Greisen | *sets, before the marsh-mist* |
| Ergreift im Moore Nebelduft, | *envelops me in my old age,* |
| Entzahnte Kiefer schnattern | *with toothless gnashing jaws* |
| Und das schlotternde Gebein. | *and tottering limbs;* |
| | |
| Trunkenen vom letzten Strahl reiß mich, | *snatch me, drunk with the* |
| ein Feuermeer | *sun's last ray, a sea of fire* |
| Mir im schäumenden Aug, | *boiling up before my eyes,* |
| Mich geblendeten Taumelnden | *blind and reeling through* |
| In der Hölle nächtliches Tor. | *the dark gate of hell.* |
| | |
| Töne, Schwager, ins Horn, | *Blow your horn, brother,* |
| Raßle den schallenden Trab, | *clatter on at a noisy trot. Let* |
| Daß der Orkus vernehme: wir kommen, | *Orcus know we are coming, so* |
| Daß gleich an der Tür | *that mine host will be there* |
| Der Wirt uns freundlich empfange. | *at the door to welcome us.* |

(Translation by Norma Deane and Celia Larner)

*The Character of the Scherzo Resumed: Retrospections and Innovating Anticipations*

The reference to the postilion's horn in Goethe's final stanza inevitably summons up the trio of Mahler's scherzo, which in turn looks back to the post-horn trio in the scherzo of the Third Symphony; this is the only feature of the scherzo in the Fifth that is unequivocally retrospective. For the rest, this 'development-scherzo' – Adorno's serial suite of dances – very clearly anticipates, in form and treatment, Mahler's late scherzos, that is, those of the Ninth and Tenth Symphonies, while those of the Sixth and Seventh pursue a different function and in quite a different manner. They are indeed brilliant inventions, pungently atmospheric – spooky – and profoundly idiosyncratic in character, as remote from the traditionally energetic and energizing role of the 'classical' (dance-) scherzo as it is possible to imagine. But the scherzo of the Fifth is something quite else, for which reason I believe Paul Bekker, in his magisterial study of 1921,[74] refers to it (p. 179) as 'Mahler's first traditional [*artgerechts*] scherzo' and, a few pages on (p. 188), as 'Mahler's first scherzo in the classical spirit of a dance-piece [*Tanzstück*]'.[75]

There is a further observation of Adorno's (pp. 102–3) that relates to wider issues: 'The structure of the movement', he writes, 'is itself governed by counterpoint' (likewise, he might have added, the second movement of Part I and the second movement of Part III). In isolating this fundamental feature that helps create the 'symphonic unity' of the scherzo, he also reminds us how much the unity of the work as a whole owes to its ceaseless counterpointing, despite the many different types of polyphony involved on a movement-by-movement basis. And that, in turn, reminds me of a relationship with the Fourth that has gone largely unremarked. There may appear at first sight to be an unbridgeable gulf between the scherzo of the Fifth and the sophisticated sonata-form first movement of the Fourth, about which I have already said so much. But I want to suggest that in fact, setting aside 'the obvious differences in the two movements' forms and the character of the musical materials involved, the treatment of them in the Fifth's scherzo derives from the composer's practice in the first movement of the

74 *Gustav Mahlers Sinfonien.* Why has this influential study never appeared in English translation?
75 Bekker goes on to state that in Mahler's later symphonies this 'type' of scherzo was not to return. But he oddly overlooked the scherzo of the Ninth, another 'dance-piece', surely? And the type in fact was to emerge again in the Tenth, notably in the second of the work's two scherzos, though of course in the 1920s Bekker would have had no way of knowing this.

Fourth. I am not just thinking of the counterpoint, though clearly much of the polyphony of the Fifth, as I have argued, can be heard as a logical evolution from the polyphony of the Fourth. Yet more striking, however, is the parallel in developmental and narrative strategy between the development section of the Fourth's first movement and the development(s) of Mahler's 'development-scherzo'. In short, we are unnerved by those developments in the scherzo of the Fifth in precisely the same way and by precisely the same means – thematic distortion, unforeseen motivic combinations, excursions into unsettled or unsettling tonal areas (often minor keys), shrill or hollow (e.g. the whip in the Fifth) instrumentation – that we encounter in the development of the Fourth's first movement. Indeed, taking into account that it is, for the most part, the most innocent-seeming of the scherzo's materials, the waltz, that is subjected to the most intensive and sceptical 'development', is it all that far-fetched to ask ourselves if we do not have here another example of the confrontation between Innocence – of which the waltz, at its first appearance in B flat at fig. 6, is the very picture – and Experience, that is so marked a feature of the first movement of the Fourth? It is, I submit, a technique and aesthetic strategy repeated here in the scherzo of the Fifth for exactly the same reasons, that is, to ensure that the D major that the scherzo 'affirms' is heavily qualified, just as the seemingly blithe and uncomplicated G major associations of the Fourth's first movement are subjected to critical developmental scrutiny. In both cases we are left, as the composer intends, with the conviction that there are still narrative and musical issues to be resolved before either symphony may be reckoned to have run its course.

I have briefly mentioned the trio's central episode and its retrospection: the obbligato horn here naturally recalls the post-horn solo in the scherzo of the Third. But in one respect at least the trio vouchsafes a glimpse of Mahler's innovating imagination, the extraordinary passage for a quartet of horns (fig. 10, bars 270–78). There is good reason for this. The timbre of the horn is fundamental to the character of the scherzo, and here we have a huge release of horn-sound, out of which, with perfect logic, emerges the obbligato horn, blowing the melody of the trio – 'Blow your horn,

Ex. 5    Fifth Symphony, Part II, scherzo, bars 271–7

brother . . .', as Goethe has it – and conducting an echo-like dialogue with differently constituted instrumental groups. Given the
*concertante* role that the horn has to play in the movement in its
entirety, this great tumult of horns that signals the onset of the trio
could not be more apt. But what could never have been foreseen,
and continues to astonish – another testing passage for the conductor – is the composer's articulation of his tremendous horn signal
(see Ex. 5). He lays this out for his four horns as if it were a highly
compressed canon or round (favourite contrapuntal forms for
Mahler),[76] made up of overlapping *fortissimo* entries, each horn in
numerical turn, all of them with their bells up, on a single pitch, F:
in short a sustained unison, across seven bars (fig. 10$^{+1}$ff.) that is also
a canon. One must not overlook the systematic detailing of the
dynamics which permits each successive horn entry to be heard

76  It is not just 'Bruder Martin' in the First Symphony that I am thinking of but the set-
    ting of 'Die du grossen Sünde rinnen' at fig. 136 in Part II of the Eighth. See also DMSSLD,
    pp. 587–8 and nn. 51 and 54, p. 612.

and then add to the crescendo, which the obbligato horn joins first by stealth, i.e. *pp*, so there can be no mistaking its participation as a fresh 'entry', and then, by matching the dynamics (in bar 278) with the *fortissimo* of horn 4, takes over in solo flight at the exact dynamic level at which horn 4 relinquishes its entry. This is an exceptional passage by any standards, and one which caught the ear of Mahler's successors, especially Berg[77] and Webern. After all, is there not bound up in the intricacies of how Mahler lays out his unison, the idea of the rhythmic canon, not to speak of the systematic sequential ordering of dynamics as a prime parameter of the musical idea as a whole? This horn signal, then, succeeds in launching a retrospection by compositional means which clearly presage the future, a characteristic Mahler paradox one may think.[78]

The scherzo brings to fulfilment one of the most striking aspects of the opening of the second trio in the first movement of Part I, where we first hear adumbrated the role of the horn as obbligato soloist,[79] the same trio that at its opening, as has been amply emphasized, introduces the concept of the string orchestra into the symphony as a sonority in its own right. This pregnant anticipation is now fully opened out, with the addition of harp, in the *Adagietto* which forms the prelude to the finale, and with it constitutes Part III. Thus the seminal second trio has an influential hand in both parts of the symphony that succeed Part I.

77  One only needs to look at the crescendo on a unison B in Berg's *Wozzeck*, Act III, fig. 110, to realize how deeply indebted was Berg's famous Expressionist gesture to Mahler's precedent in his Fifth. See also 'What is Expressionism?' in DMCN, pp. 219ff.

78  There may also have been a different kind of retrospection involved in this passage. On the one occasion that I heard Smetana's opera *Hubička* in the opera house (in Prague), a work Mahler first heard in the 1880s and later was to conduct himself at Hamburg in 1895, the interlude for orchestra alone between scenes 1 and 2 of Act II, representing night giving way to dawn in the shape of a continuous C major crescendo, very strongly evoked for me the horn unison in Mahler's Fifth. I think it not at all improbable that Mahler's signal had its distant origins in Smetana's interlude. As time passes I believe we shall uncover more and more instances of Mahler's debt to Smetana. See also 'Mahler and Smetana' (pp. 537–49), and above, 'Mahler's "Kammermusikton"', pp. 207–10.

79  A precedent for the obbligato horn in the scherzo of the Fifth is to be found, however, in the scherzo of the Fourth. Cf. e.g. fig. 5+4, where Mahler marks the first horn part *'sehr hervortretend'* ('very prominent'). Many of the ensuing solo flights for horn in this movement directly anticipate the role of the obbligato horn in the Fifth.

## Part III

### (iv) Adagietto Sehr langsam   (v) Rondo-Finale Allegro

#### Larger Symmetries

These days it is scarcely a revelatory observation to point to the
integral unit that the *Adagietto* and finale of the Fifth comprise;
worth making again however, because it emphasizes one of the
larger symmetries of the total form of the symphony that often
goes unnoticed but in fact is one of the work's distinguishing
features, especially in the context of Mahler's oeuvre as a whole: it
is his only symphony in which the two pairs of movements
(slow/fast) which form Parts I and III are conjoined by systematic
inter-quotation, that is, in each case the second movement extensively quotes from the materials surfacing first in the first movement. A novel process, and one peculiar to the Fifth, for which
reason it seems not at all inapposite to think of or refer to the work
as Mahler's 'quotation' symphony. (The only other writer whom I
know to have made this same point is Adorno, not in his monograph but in his Centenary Address, Vienna, 1960 (the hundredth
anniversary of Mahler's birth).)[80]

---

80  This – plus a new section, 'Afterthoughts' – was included in an English translation in
    Adorno's *Quasi una Fantasia: Essays on Modern Music.* Adorno writes: 'Because of their
    vast scope Mahler was induced to construct entire symphonies on the principle of cor-
    respondence. In the Fifth, for example, the funeral march is elaborated in the second
    movement parallel to a theme of the *Adagietto* in the finale, and between these two anal-
    ogously structured parts [Parts I and III] the great scherzo acts as a caesura' (p. 105).
    Edward Reilly (in conversation) has made an interesting further suggestion about the
    symmetries in the Fifth to which Adorno refers. If indeed it were the case that the first
    movement to be composed was the scherzo (Part II), then the brilliance of Mahler's sub-
    sequent articulation of his tripartite total structure shows up in his concept of Part I as
    exclusively 'tragic' or 'negative' in character while Part III concentrates on the life-
    enhancing and positive. In short, Part I makes a proposition (thesis), which Part III coun-
    ters with its opposite (antithesis), while the scherzo mediates the transition from one to
    the other. One might think the thesis/antithesis pattern can be discerned not only in the
    'analogously structured' Parts I and III, but in almost every parameter of the symphony's
    organization, e.g. *Wunderhorn* imagery (Part I, *Trauermarsch*) is replaced by 'Rückert'
    imagery in Part III; and since it is specific sonorities we are talking about (there are no
    verbal clues!), the thesis/antithesis conjunction (or *disjunction*, better) unequivocally

*The Adagietto in and out of Context: Its Peculiar Reception and Performance Histories*

It could well be that the famous *Adagietto*, the fourth movement of the symphony, the first movement of Part III, a prelude to the finale that at the same time is the symphony's only slow movement, might come out ahead in any attempt to identify the movement of Mahler's about which most has been written or which has stimulated most contention. It is not just that my description of it as the work's 'only slow movement' must immediately prompt the response, 'Yes; but *how* slow?', and thus raise an issue of interpretation that has engaged the attention of not a few students (and performers) of Mahler in recent years but – a yet more fundamental issue – how good is it, how faithful to – characteristic of – the creative personality whom we think we know, and whose 'truth' (his capacity to be true to himself) we think we can recognize from our experience of his music. In short, could – as some have thought – the *Adagietto* represent some sort of 'betrayal' by the composer of his own values and ideals?

Among the keenest sceptics is Adorno, who dismisses the *Adagietto* as 'shallow sentimentality',[81] a movement that 'borders on genre prettiness through its ingratiating sound'. At the same time he recognizes the importance of its conception 'as an individual piece within the whole',[82] a point to which I shall return. An earlier adverse opinion Mahler was to receive by post from Richard Strauss, who wrote, after attending a performance of the Fifth in Berlin conducted by Nikisch in February 1905 – 'Your . . . symphony again gave me great pleasure in the full rehearsal, a pleasure only slightly dimmed by the little *Adagietto*. But as this was what

---

manifests itself in the wind-band orientation of the *Trauermarsch* and the strings plus harp orientation of Part III[1]. One might discern the same 'pairing' at work even in the organization of the work's dynamics, e.g. compare the D major '*Hohepunkt*' that Mahler locates towards the end of the *Hauptsatz* (bar 500) – a climax that *fails* with a similarly calculated '*Hohepunkt*' (though not inscribed as such by Mahler) in Part III[2], a D major climax (bar 731) that this time *prevails*.

81  TWA *Mahler*, p. 51. Adorno's German, however, is more powerfully dismissive: '*kulinarische Sentimentalität*' (German edn., p. 74), for which 'cooked-up' or 'dished-up sentimentality' might serve as an English equivalent.

82  Ibid., p. 136.

pleased the audience most, you are getting what you deserve.'[83] Mahler certainly got what, by now, he must surely have *expected* in the way of a critical reception of his new symphony, a chiefly negative response, but – *pace* Strauss – for the *Adagietto*, which won almost uniform public approbation.

Irony, one might think, attended Mahler in his life, it was not only a component of his music; and virtually a compound of ironies has been a feature of the *Adagietto*'s history since it was first heard in 1904. For a start, how ironic that a movement that was conceived as prelude or slow introduction to a succeeding finale, as the first part of an integral two-part unit (the two parts in a differently executed but similar organic association as the two parts of Part I), was soon to be detached from its natural continuation and fulfilment, to lead a kind of amputated afterlife as an independent item in the concert hall or broadcasting studio, or on a ten-inch shellac disc.[84] This strange performance history reflects the strange history of the reception of Mahler's symphonies, shaped as that was not just by the familiar difficulties that narrative forms and innovative language habitually encounter before the breakthrough into public comprehension, but also by political events and swings in cultural fashion. Mahler's music had to contend not only with the cataclysm of the First World War but the appalling political ideologies that held sway in Germany from the early 1930s until the end of the Second World War in 1945. This meant that there were large areas of the world in which Mahler's music was suppressed;[85]

---

83  Herta Blaukopf (ed.), *Gustav Mahler-Richard Strauss: Correspondence*, p. 75.
84  The first recording of the *Adagietto* was made in May 1926 by the Concertgebouw Orchestra conducted by Mengelberg and issued on the Odeon label, o 8591. Interestingly, the title on the label runs as follows: '*Adagietto* a. d. [aus der] V. Symphonie/II. Teil (Mahler)'. Bruno Walter's recording of the *Adagietto* with the Vienna Philharmonic Orchestra was made in 1938, on 15 January. In GMWL, p. 1.15, Truus de Leur, 'Gustav Mahler in the Netherlands', writes: 'The *Adagietto* [as a separate item] was to become one of Mengelberg's showpieces – witness the performances and recordings he made of it in later years.' Small wonder that in our very own time – the 1990s – the *Adagietto* has found a home in more than one 'compilation disc', along with other severed limbs and parts.
85  An incident during a concert given in the Concertgebouw, Amsterdam, on 5 October 1939 is a painful reminder of the ideology that was shortly to oppress Europe (we should recall that just a month earlier, on 3 September, a state of war had been declared between Germany and the United Kingdom). Carl Schuricht was the conductor of the Concertgebouw Orchestra in a performance of *Das Lied*, with Kerstin Thorborg and Martin

and where it was not suppressed, there were pitifully few perform-ances because – to take Britain as an example – the dominant musical culture of the day, also in its way ideological rather than rational,[86] set its face against Mahler or, rather, closed its ears to him. The confidence of the adverse views expressed was equalled only by the ignorance of the music itself.

This is not the place to rehearse the generally sorry history of the reception of Mahler's symphonies between the two World Wars; there were of course brilliant exceptions, pairs of ears in England (Henry Boys's and Benjamin Britten's, for instance), in Russia (Ivan Sollertinsky's and Dmitri Shostakovich's), and in the States (Aaron Copland's), that 'heard' Mahler quite otherwise. If I use quotes, it is because knowledge of his scores had to be obtained from reading them; performances, opportunities actually to *hear* the music, were few and far between. For which reason early recordings took on a quite special significance, among them, inevitably, those of the *Adagietto*, which was also, because of its rela-tive brevity and slender resources, one of the few bits of Mahler that surmounted the culture barrier and was occasionally admitted into the concert hall.

Oehman as soloists. During a pause in the 'Abschied' a supporter of Germany and the Nazis shouted, 'Deutschland über Alles, Herr Schuricht!', an intervention greeted with whistles and boos from the scandalized audience. Seven months later the Netherlands were invaded and performances of Mahler's works banned, as they had been in Germany since 1933. I am indebted to Pierre Geelen, of Aerdenhout in the Netherlands, who drew my attention to this incident. The intervention can clearly be heard on a CD that was issued in 1993 of Schuricht's performance (Archiphon, ARCH–3.1). The recording was originally discovered in the archives of Dutch Radio (NAA).

86  For example, Vaughan Williams's famous dismissal of Mahler: 'Intimate acquaintance with the executive side of music in orchestra, chorus, and opera made even [*sic*] Mahler into a very tolerable imitation of a composer' (Ralph Vaughan Williams, *National Music and Other Essays*, p. 187). Or there was Julius Harrison's judgement, enshrined in a popular guide, *The Musical Companion*, edited by A. L. Bacharach, published in 1934 and many times reprinted. Having concluded that Bruckner's nine symphonies 'are in no wise worthy to rank with those of the great masters', he went on to add: 'Much the same can be said of the nine composed by Mahler; works of enormous size; interesting at times but laboriously put together and lacking that vital spark of inspiration that made Beethoven's nine the only nine springing direct from the nine Muses' (p. 237). I cannot forbear a mention of Dyneley Hussey's memorable prediction, in the same compilation, p. 456, that 'It is not improbable that, of Mahler's music, posterity will cling to the songs and let the rest go.' Posterity, it seems, has taken its revenge on Harrison and Hussey rather than the composer. But their views, like Vaughan Williams's, were thoroughly representative of entrenched conservative opinion in the 1920s and 1930s.

The highly unusual history of this one movement from a Mahler symphony – which, remember, had been heard much more often in isolation than as an integral part of the symphony from which it had become unnaturally detached – has contributed, I believe, to the ambiguities and contradictions that seem still to surround its interpretation, even though, as our century comes to an end, that performance history has been reversed: it is now relatively infrequent to encounter the *Adagietto* without the symphony to which it belongs.

It is to the divorce of the *Adagietto* from the finale that I attribute the extremes in variation of tempo that have in recent years been the subject of so much critical attention. I do seriously wonder, for example, if the funereal tempo of Bernstein,[87] who on one celebrated occasion – the funeral of Robert [Bobby] Kennedy in 1968 – performed the *Adagietto* in the spirit of a solemn valediction,[88] would ever have happened but for its promotion as an authentic slow movement by Mahler (the genuine article, of course, was often, and properly, very slow) that could stand alone; the hijacking of the movement – of the supposed emotion it represented, at least – surely reached its apogee when Visconti used the *Adagietto* in his film of Mann's *Death in Venice* (1971) as sonorous symbol of Aschenbach's nostalgia, frustrated passion, and hopeless longing: one might think, ironically, that the singular performance history of the *Adagietto* up to this point had been nothing but

87  More than 11 minutes in one instance. Slow enough, one might think, but this pales into insignificance when compared with such eccentricities as Scherchen's 13 minutes plus, or Haitink's 14 minutes with the Berlin Philharmonic Orchestra. I choose these examples more or less at random. The field of contrasting tempi is exhaustively documented in Gilbert E. Kaplan's facsimile edition. (See also Table 1, p. 231 above, for the details of Mahler's Hamburg performance in 1905.)

88  See Humphrey Burton, *Leonard Bernstein*, pp. 373–4: 'Jacqueline Kennedy [the former President's widow] called Bernstein . . . to ask him to supervise the music for the funeral at St Patrick's Cathedral in New York . . . He persuaded the appropriate Monsignor at the cathedral to agree to the inclusion of the *Adagietto* movement for strings and harp from Mahler's Fifth Symphony . . . It was, Bernstein recalled, a beautiful service. "The Mahler part of it was made more beautiful by the Kennedy children's procession up to the Altar carrying the Communion articles." There was an earlier occasion too when Bernstein had used the *Adagietto* to commemorate his old teacher and patron, Serge Koussevitzky, who died in 1951. Burton tells us further (p. 532) that 'a baton and the score of Mahler's Fifth Symphony were placed in the coffin alongside [Bernstein's] body'.

preparation for the iconic, cult status with which Mahler's prelude to the finale of his Fifth Symphony found itself lumbered as a result of the film.[89]

It is true that Mahler himself once, and once only, gave a performance of the *Adagietto* as an independent item in a concert that he conducted in Rome in 1907, in the Augusteo on 1 April, with the Orchestra of the Accademia di Santa Cecilia; but it would be an error to think that this constituted a precedent that thereafter legitimized the dissolution of the *Adagietto*'s marriage to the finale. Quite the contrary. Mahler's original intention when planning his programmes had been to perform the fourth and fifth movements – Part III – of his symphony as an integral unit. (I wonder what he might have made of my suggestion that we might, likewise, on occasion hear Part I as a self-sufficient item? See my 'Reflections in the Shape of a Coda', above, pp. 310–13.) What seems to have prevented this plan coming to fruition was the misrouting of the Mahlers' baggage when they were on their way to Rome – Alma spells this out in her memoirs – baggage that included Mahler's conducting scores and, presumably, orchestral material (of the Fifth, at least).[90] The scores and parts were recovered in sufficient time for Mahler to introduce the *Adagietto* into his second concert, along with Weber's overture to *Der Freischütz,* Tchaikovsky's *Romeo and Juliet,* and Beethoven's Seventh. Perhaps too these circumstances may have encouraged him to be cautious; the mediocre standards of the orchestra at that time might not have enabled it to rise to the challenge of the finale.[91] Incidentally, at an early stage in planning

---

89  See also Philip Reed, 'Aschenbach becomes Mahler: Thomas Mann as Film'. A memorable exchange on Classic FM between the Rt Hon. David Mellor and Vinnie Jones, reported in the *Guardian,* 9 January 1998, was a disquieting reminder of the continuing currency of the association. In one of his comments to Vinnie Jones, football's 'hard man' as the paper put it, Mellor remarks, 'I want to tell you about a piece of music that I came across in a film called *Death in Venice,* about the love of a middle-aged man for the beauty of a young boy. They played the *Adagietto,* the slow movement of a Mahler symphony. At the beginning of this film there is this gondola going across the lagoon into Venice. Every time I listen to this music I think about this film. And I am deeply moved by it [plays *Adagietto*] . . .'

90  See AM *Memories,* pp. 117–19.

91  See also HLG *Mahler CV,* III, pp. 20–26. An important fresh source of information regarding Mahler's Italian visit is *Mahler a Romo.*

this sequence of two concerts for Rome, Mahler had considered including the andante and scherzo from the Second Symphony. He was not celebrated as a composer in Italy. Did he have it in mind when turning over his ideas for the programmes that he would be addressing audiences not only unfamiliar with his music but inhabiting quite another musical culture?

It has not been my intention here to go over all the ground that has been exhaustively documented in the facsimile edition, and explored above all in Paul Banks's pioneering article,[92] but, rather, to make a note of the extra-musical factors, socio-political, historical, and cultural, that have conditioned, I suggest, our reception of the *Adagietto*, the way we hear it; and then there is performance practice, past and present, which in turn conditions *what* we hear.

I prefer to concentrate on what seems to me to be important aspects of the *Adagietto* that have not been sufficiently recognized. First, the altogether exceptional incorporation into the symphony – '*für grosses Orchester*' as the title-page has it – of a movement for string orchestra and harp. This certainly represented a radical departure from tradition. Indeed, can one think of a precedent in the orchestral tradition, i.e. post-Beethoven, which is surely the only relevant tradition here? To be sure, the character of Mahler's *Adagietto* may have been influenced by Bizet's *Adagietto* from the first *L'Arlésienne* suite;[93] but by far the most significant precedents are to be found in the evolution of Mahler's own orchestral thinking, e.g. in the gradual deconstruction across his oeuvre of 'the orchestra' into an assembly of diverse orchestras and instrumental groups, the string orchestra among them.[94]

## A 'Song Without Words' for Strings and Harp

But the principal source for the sonority of strings and harp must be looked for in Mahler's own settings of Rückert, not only the four independent settings for voice and orchestra, but also *Kinder-*

92 'Aspects of Mahler's Fifth Symphony: Performance Practice and Interpretation'.
93 See also above, n. 23; and what about the 'Meditation' (intermezzo) from Massenet's *Thaïs* (Act II)?
94 See also above, nn. 23 and 24.

*totenlieder,* where strings and harp often combine to colour – more than that, *incise* – the instrumental profile of a song. Think for example of 'Ich bin der Welt abhanden gekommen' or the second of the five *Kindertotenlieder,* 'Nun seh' ich wohl', where strings plus harp are at the very heart of the sound-world these songs inhabit. No matter, either, that while 'Ich bin der Welt . . .' belongs precisely to one of the summers when Mahler was working on his Fifth, the second of the *Kindertotenlieder,* 'Nun seh' ich wohl' might have postdated completion of the symphony. On the contrary, it is a chronology that helps make more emphatic the point that I want to make: that the late Rückert settings signify not only their marvellous individual selves but the onset of a late musical style[95] (new melodic contours as well as new sonorities) that spilled over into the symphonies, not only taking shape as the *Adagietto* of the Fifth but also generating (strings plus harp again) the remarkable lyrical effusions that constitute the second subjects of the first movements of both the Sixth and Seventh Symphonies, not to speak of 'Die liebe Erde . . .' in the 'Abschied' of *Das Lied* (the very apotheosis, one might think, of strings plus harp). This was a point I made as long ago as 1980 in *The New Grove,* vol. 11, pp. 520–21.

The near relationship of the *Adagietto* to 'Ich bin der Welt . . .' has often been claimed. I take a different view, as I argue below, and believe that the mistaken claim has itself been a source of interpretative confusion. To the evidence in support of a reconsideration of the supposed 'parallels' between the songs I shall turn later (see p. 339), evidence that is of some relevance, too, to our speculation about the probable chronology of the symphony's composition. But for the present let me take the short step that will bring us to perhaps the most important of the issues to which the *Adagietto* gives rise: its status, that is, a 'song without words', a wordless Rückert song for orchestra alone, or, rather, for string orchestra and harp.[96]

95  I use this term as Adorno uses it when describing *Das Lied* as 'one of the greatest achievements of a late musical style since the last quartets [of Beethoven]'. See Adorno, 'Mahler: Centenary Address, Vienna 1960', in *Quasi una Fantasia,* p. 92.

96  See also TWA *Mahler,* p. 22: 'The *Adagietto,* actually a song without words, is linked to "Ich bin der Welt abhanden gekommen" . . .', and below, n. 97.

## The 'Right' Tempo

Once that step has been taken, which involves rejection of the image of the movement as principally elegiac and valedictory, other matters usefully fall into place, in particular the question of the 'right' tempo. I would prefer not to attempt to impose a duration deduced from past documentation and recordings – it should never be forgotten that there are occasions when the 'wrong' tempo in the right hands can convince, whereas the obverse does not – but instead to repeat what I said in a paper contributed to a conference in Rotterdam in May 1990.[97] After referring to Banks's *Musical Times* article, I continued:

[97] 'Mahler's "Orchestral" Orchestral Songs', Rondom Mahler II Congress and Workshop, Rotterdam, 1990. I am again much indebted to Henry-Louis de La Grange for acquainting me with an unpublished, unedited article on Mahler's songs by William Ritter, written in 1914. Ritter had attended a performance of the Fifth Symphony in Munich in 1910, when the orchestra of the Konzertverein, Vienna, was conducted by Ferdinand Löwe. Mahler, it seems, was present and was addressed (reprimanded?) by Löwe after the *Adagietto* had been heard in rehearsal, Löwe holding that there could be no other explanation of it but that it was 'a parody'. Mahler, it seems, stopped, looked at Ritter, and shook his head in a gesture of denial that Ritter interpreted thus (I quote from his French text): 'Cela prouve à quel point on est incapable aujourd'hui d'un chant simple. On ne sait plus que la sincerité peut encore exister!' ('That shows how everyone today has lost the art of a simple song. It is no longer thought possible that sincerity can exist!') While Ritter makes clear that this was his interpretation of Mahler's gesture, not Mahler's own words, we should not necessarily discount it as evidence of his thinking about the *Adagietto*. Mahler and Ritter were in the midst of a long conversation – an 'interview', according to Ritter – and it is certainly not impossible that the *Adagietto* had been a topic already touched on in some way, which allowed Ritter thus to 'translate' Mahler's sign of dissent into words.

In this same context, an entry in the diary of Elisabeth Diepenbrock, the wife of the composer, Alphons, dated 23 March 1906, is of special relevance and interest, in particular Diepenbrock's reception of the *Adagietto* as 'a love song'. Diepenbrock was a member of the circle of very close friends surrounding Mahler on his visits to Amsterdam.

23 March [1906] – Yesterday and the day before again Mahler's Symphony (the 5th). This time such an overwhelming and wonderful impression. Sitting downstairs, where the sound is so bad, ruined everything the first time. Fons thinks it is so beautiful, so magnificent and regards Mahler as 'the only poet' of our time. At first he thought of the 5th as a step backwards after the 4th – but not any longer! The *Trauermarsch* is magnificent and yesterday we were also deeply moved by the *Adagietto*. Fons thinks it is almost too tender, especially at first, he understands it as a love song; to me it seems more like a solace, a caress from above after the scherzo's harsh reality [*sic*]. Lien [Jas] experienced it likewise; she thought of her mother. (Eduard Reeser (ed.), *Alphons Diepenbrock. Brieven en documenten*, vol. 5, p. 115.)

Lien [Eveline] Jas (1866–1951) was a close friend of the Diepenbrock family. I am most grateful to Henriette Straub (Amsterdam) for bringing this information to my notice.

He has a good deal to say about performance practice and refers especially to the widely differing tempi adopted for the *Adagietto* by various conductors, some very slow indeed – Hermann Scherchen takes 13' 07" over it – while others are relatively much more flowing – Mengelberg and Walter outstandingly are among those who linger the least, with durations respectively of 7' 04" and 7' 57". That sounds to me as if both Mengelberg and Walter had firmly in mind the song concept of the movement.[98] Because, if one accepts that, then the successful interpretation will be that which sustains the long melody as if it were written for the voice. No singer could possibly sustain Scherchen's tempo. Walter's and Mengelberg's tempi, on the contrary, are paced by that hypothetical singer. It's a point conductors might bear in mind, although I don't expect they will.

Or only, I would add in 1997, the most enlightened.

## Mahler's 'Spätstil'

The status of the *Adagietto* as a 'song without words' for strings and harp is one thing; another and perhaps more important feature is its character, that is, that it belongs to the same act of creative imagination that in the summer of 1901 gave us four of the independent Rückert settings and three (possibly) of the *Kindertotenlieder* cycle. One can have no quarrel at all with Adorno's invocation of the term 'Spätstil' in relation to *Das Lied*; but in fact the first genuine intimations and anticipations of that epoch-making 'late style' unequivocally surface in the Rückert settings *c.* 1901–4, while Adorno's own mention of Beethoven's late quartets in this context brings to mind (though evidently not to Adorno's) Mahler's own claim (see 'Mahler's "Kammermusikton"'), that his late songs

---

98 On the timings, see also above, nn. 87 and 92. In this same article, Dr Banks mentions a performance of the Fifth under Mahler in St Petersburg in November 1907, on the occasion of which one of the orchestral players noted a timing of 7' for the *Adagietto*. If this were accurate, or near accurate, then clearly Mengelberg and Walter, 'immediate disciples' of Mahler's as Banks remarks, were opting for tempi close or closer to Mahler's own than has been the case in many modern performances. A recording conducted by Boulez with the Vienna Philharmonic for Deutsche Grammophon (DG 453 416–2) challengingly and perhaps rather surprisingly offers a duration of 10' 59".

represented his 'Kammermusikton', his 'chamber-music manner' or 'tone of voice'. Thus, in one respect at least, the Fifth shares in the innovatory sound-world that was to be a distinguishing feature of his final decade.[99]

It was a future implicit in the late Rückert songs, of which, I continue to emphasize, the *Adagietto* was one, albeit minus a text by the poet himself, though as we shall see below, there is real probability that there *was* a (silent) sub-text linked to Mahler's courting of Alma Schindler, whom he was to marry on 9 March 1902; the engagement was announced on 27 December 1901.

*Symmetries again*

But before dwelling for a moment on the possible consequences for the chronology of the symphony's evolution if the association of the *Adagietto* with Mahler's courtship were shown to be likely, there is a point I wish first to make: that, irrespective of any identifiably autobiographical content or image, the very fact that we have here in essence a Rückert song for orchestra alone, asserts yet another of the remarkable symmetries that characterize, define, the Fifth as in no other symphony by Mahler. In short, whereas in Part I, a wordless *Wunderhorn* song for orchestra alone, the funeral march, serves as prelude to the ensuing movement and as source of that movement's 'quotations' ('Interruptions') in Part III, it is again an orchestral song, the *Adagietto*, that serves as prelude, as source of the *Rondo-Finale*'s contrasting episodes, thus demonstrating an even larger symmetry across the span of the symphony as a whole. These two orchestral 'songs' represent two sharply opposed styles, a brilliant consummation of the *Wunderhorn* manner ('Ton') in the shape

99  See also pp. 248–68 above, where I suggest that we can owe part of the development of Mahler's fascination with the potentialities of the string orchestra to his 'arrangements' of Schubert and Beethoven string quartets for string orchestra. It is significant, too, that one of the Beethoven quartets was a late masterpiece, Op. 95, in F minor; while it was certainly Mahler's intention to attempt a like arrangement of Op. 131, in C sharp minor, the last but one of Beethoven's quartets.

Critical editions of these arrangements by Mahler, by David Matthews and Donald Mitchell, were published in 1984 (Schubert) and 1990 (Beethoven) by Josef Weinberger, London.

of the funeral march that opens Part I, and an unmistakable intimation – evocation – of the late style that was increasingly to manifest itself in the later and last symphonies, in the shape of the *Adagietto*. Typical of Mahler, one might think, that the very symmetries in which is embodied the logic of the symphony's formal thinking, which provide the rational basis for the symphony's otherwise unique form, should at the same time represent an effortless transition from one creative phase to another, phases which in themselves represent two contrasting poles, two extremes, of the composer's creative imagination. If one thinks of 'Der Tamboursg'sell' as representing one extreme and, say, 'Ich atmet' . . .', 'Ich bin der Welt . . .', or 'Nun seh' ich wohl ..' (from *Kindertotenlieder*)[100] the other, it would be hard to conceive a starker contrast; and yet it is the case that both these seemingly contradictory worlds of sound and images cohabit in the Fifth, indeed are fundamental to the symphony's narrative. Without the *Trauermarsch* there could have been no beginning; without the *Adagietto*, no 'end', or at least not the finale that the *Adagietto* in fact enabled Mahler to compose and thus complete his narrative; and it is not the thematic bonding between the *Adagietto* and the finale that I have principally in mind.

## The Fifth, a Pivotal Symphony

Meanwhile, we can ponder on the curiosity of received opinion in the past (including my own) that insisted on Mahler's having abandoned the incorporation of 'song' into his symphonies after the Fourth, while in fact it is precisely in the idea of 'song', albeit wordless orchestral song, that the *genre* innovatively lives on in the Fifth, and in the instance of the *Adagietto*, which we should hear – and perform – *in context*, that is to say with the co-terminous Rückert settings in mind, opens a window on the late style of Mahler's last years. In all of these ways, then, that I have touched on

---

100  It matters, in my view, not at all if 'Nun seh' ich wohl . . .' were composed before or
    after the *Adagietto*. The song clearly belongs to the same mindset that generated the
    movement for strings and harp.

in this chapter, but in particular those relating to the character and function of the wordless orchestral songs, the Fifth has to be acknowledged as the symphony which acts as pivot between the period of the so-called *Wunderhorn* symphonies and the period(s) that ensued; and one may savour the strange irony that it is the two songs for orchestra that are emblematic of the evolution that is conducted within the confines of the symphony itself, 'song', the very *genre*, the supposed disappearance of which was taken to represent Mahler's radical ditching of a convention he had established and made peculiarly his own.

As we shall see, this very process of style-transition, which one might think to be principally bound up with the evolution of new techniques, Mahler deploys as part of the evolution of his *narrative*; the continuity of it is a consequence of the introduction of the *Adagietto* as agent of a change in style. Style, in short, has become a tool of narrative. But before I come to that, there is the subtext to the movement, the 'Alma dimension' one might name it, that calls for scrutiny.

### The Adagietto's 'Alma dimension'

It was in the full score used by Mengelberg for his performances of the Fifth that the link of the *Adagietto* to Mahler's courting of Alma was first plainly stated. This is what he wrote:

> This *Adagietto* was Gustav Mahler's declaration of love to *Alma!* *Instead of a letter* he confided it in this manuscript without a word of explanation. She understood and replied: *He should come!!!* (I have this from both of them!)[101]

This inscription has been the subject of commentary elsewhere, by Floros, for example, and Henry-Louis de La Grange,[102] Floros positive in his account, La Grange more sceptical.

It is true that the fact that nowhere in Alma's diary does she

---

101  See also DMSSLD, p. 31. The first page of the *Adagietto*, marked up by Mengelberg as described above, is reproduced in GMWL p. 1.25, and NSNC.

102  See Floros, *Gustav Mahler*, pp. 154–5; HLG *Mahler*, II, pp. 816–17; and Kaplan, facsimile edn, pp. 21–3 and 35–7.

mention this incident, that is, her receiving the manuscript (what might that have been? a composition sketch? a preliminary draft of the score?) and her decoding of it (skilled musician that she was, Mahler's 'letter' would not have presented her with any problems), undoubtedly suspends a question mark. As La Grange remarks:

> To my mind, however, some doubt remains about Mengelberg's story. It seems to me improbable that Mahler could have written two pieces so related in every way [i.e. the *Adagietto* and 'Ich bin der Welt . . .'] with such different meanings. I also find it highly improbable, if Mengelberg's story is true, that Alma should have failed to mention the true meaning of the *Adagietto* at some time during the half-century in which she survived Mahler. She was always very careful to record and preserve each one of her *Trophäen* ['Trophies'] and kept the autograph of 'Liebst du um Schönheit' [the song for voice and piano Mahler composed specifically for her in 1902] on her living-room wall in New York.[103]

On the other hand, I find it difficult to believe that Mengelberg made the whole thing up, and in particular am convinced by the authentic ring of his parenthetic, 'I have this from both of them!'

If I refrain from quoting the 'poem' that Mengelberg also wrote into his score – a text he envisaged accompanying the melody of the *Adagietto* – it is because I have no wish to lend further currency to a horrible, mawkish fabrication that can only shake one's confidence in his taste and judgement; but this is something different, I suggest, from his reliability when recollecting and recording what he claims to have been told by the composer and his wife.[104]

---

103 HLG *Mahler*, II, p. 817. But might it not have been the case that *she* at least told the story to Mengelberg *after* her husband's death? Much depends on the *date* on which Mengelberg wrote the ink inscriptions into his conducting score. A clear reproduction of the first page of the *Adagietto* may be found in GMWL, p. I.25.

104 However, this must have been on an occasion other than the premiere of the Fifth in Amsterdam on 8 March 1906, when Mahler himself conducted the Concertgebouw Orchestra. Interestingly, the second half of the programme was devoted to the Dutch premiere of *Kindertotenlieder* and, finally, as coda, a performance of 'Ich bin der Welt . . .', yet another example of Mahler's 'thematic' planning of his programmes. As his wife had not accompanied him, the story must have been related to Mengelberg later, by the Mahlers jointly or separately ('I have this from both of them' would seem to imply the latter?). The inscription itself, in ink, along with the 'poem', is quite distinct in character and execution from the red and blue pencil marks of Mengelberg's that were plainly

The case must inevitably remain open. But if what Mengelberg relates was basically accurate then there are at least two or three consequences of importance.

The first clearly raises the question of chronology: if the *Adagietto* were indeed a declaration of Mahler's love for Alma, then it must have preceded their official engagement, announced at the very end of December 1901. If that were so, then the *Adagietto*, in some shape or form – as a sketch of some kind? – must have been in existence at some stage between the summer and Christmas. The autumn and winter months were not, as we have so often been told, periods when Mahler sat down to compose. I have already expressed a lurking doubt about our accepting this as a *total* prohibition, especially in the absence of so much sketched material that must have existed but has mysteriously disappeared and, on occasion, as mysteriously resurfaces (the newly recovered sketches for the scherzo are a case in point). In any event, there can always be exceptions to any rule. Was, then, the *Adagietto* sketched during, say, the last six months of 1901? Was it a spin-off from the bout of song-writing that had occupied Mahler, along with work on his new symphony, in that year's summer months? Was it – even – an idea for a song that had not yet found its text, that Alma then proved to be? Speculation this, undoubtedly, but by no means wholly impossible. Mengelberg almost wrecks any confidence one might have in his veracity as chronicler by his perpetrating that abominable 'poem'. However, even if one discounts the whole Alma scenario, and with it the implied chronology, the important fact remains, that in the context of the symphony as a whole the *Adagietto* plays the role of a 'song without words', a 'song' in the

----

made in connection with his own first performances of the Fifth in the Netherlands, also in March 1906, but after Mahler's departure. The ink inscriptions suggest memories written into the score at a later date or dates, together with a related note written at the bottom of the page (it must have been at the same time). This reads: 'If Music is a language, then this is proof of it He tells her *everything* in *"notes"* [*Tonen*] and *"sounds"* [*Klangen*] in: Music.'

Floros (*Gustav Mahler*, p. 155) makes much of the 'Gaze' *Leitmotiv* from *Tristan* that he discerns, much more clearly than I do, as a significant presence in the contours of the *Adagietto*'s melody (in the movement's middle section, in particular). A conscious, knowing – if covert – 'quote' from *Tristan*? I don't hear it. Nor, it seems, did Mengelberg, who would surely have remarked on it, if he had.

manner of the *Rückert-Lieder* that had preceded it. From this point of view, Alma is immaterial. The fundamental source of the song was Mahler's own Rückert manner, the new style that broke surface in 1901. (We may note too that later manifestations of the style, e.g. the second subject of the first movement of the Sixth, were also Alma-oriented.)

## The Adagietto, another 'Ich bin der Welt . . .'?

Almost every commentator on the Rückert settings draws a parallel between the *Adagietto* and 'Ich bin der Welt . . .', Adorno, for example, and La Grange; indeed it is part of the latter's argument, consistent in its own terms, that just because the *Adagietto* and 'Ich bin der Welt . . .' inhabit the same spiritual world (of renunciation, of resignation) one must doubt the credibility of Mengelberg's suggestion that it was an avowal of human love, not a retreat from it.[105] The strict parallel between the songs, I believe, is based partly on reality, that is, that their respective codas ('closures' or 'liquidations' as current jargon would have it) are indeed very close in conception and execution, and partly on illusion, that is, too much has been read into the parallel between the closing sections, which, in turn, has been read *back* into performance practice, thus leading to those exaggeratedly slow, leave-taking misinterpretations of the *Adagietto*, in the manner of 'Ich bin der Welt . . .'. But the truth is, surely, that these are two highly individual songs (I am counting the *Adagietto* as one of them), distinct in their invention – where, for example, in the *Adagietto* is the pronounced pentatonicism of 'Ich bin der Welt . . .', or a sign of the latter's patent heterophonic thinking which unequivocally anticipates techniques Mahler was to deploy in *Das Lied*? – and thereby demanding distinctive tempi and interpretation. What they do share, undeniably, are the characteristic features of Mahler's emergent 'Spätstil', not only among themselves but with manifestations of that style yet to be composed, for example, as I have said before, the ardent second-subject groups in the first movements of the Sixth and Seventh Symphonies. It is by

105 See HLG *Mahler*, II, p. 818.

looking forward and then back that one can help oneself decouple
the *Adagietto* from its distorting association with 'Ich bin der Welt
...' and receive it instead in its own individual right as a typical
example of the type of inspirations, invention, and sound-worlds
with which Mahler was busy just after the turn of the century. It is
hardly surprising that among the songs there should be parallels
and cross-references; but if one insists on parallels there is much
more to be got out of a comparison with 'Nun seh' ich wohl ...',
the second song of *Kindertotenlieder*, in its own way another avowal
of love, though made (by the poet) in very different circumstances.)[106]


### A New Sonority Facilitating a Denouement

No doubt the *Adagietto* will continue to generate discussion and
disagreement. But on one feature of the movement, there must be
wide agreement: that in the context of the symphony its novel
sonority struck an entirely new note, to which I would add,
emphatically, that it was also precisely *this* that was required if the
symphony's narrative were to continue and reach a denouement.

I do not need to recall the drama(s) enacted so comprehensively
in the two movements of Part I, nor the uncompromisingly bleak
conclusion that is asserted at the end of the allegro. Likewise, I hope
to have sufficiently indicated the problem (of his own making) that
faced Mahler in the guise of his great central scherzo in D and the
dexterity with which he solved it, by his avoiding giving premature
birth to an unclouded D that had to be kept in reserve for the
finale and, when produced, prove to have retained sufficient vigour
convincingly to bring the narrative to an end.

The scherzo, with its emphatic inner tensions and contradictions, continued the drama of Part I, though on a much reduced
scale. With the onset of the *Adagietto*, a new sound and new character are introduced – remember that in the grand overall design,
the *Adagietto* replicates the functions, formal and thematic, of the
opening march, the other 'song', in Part I, but in a style that could

106 See also above, n. 100.

hardly be more powerfully contrasted to that of the *Trauermarsch*: a new sound and character, signifying that, after all, a resolution is possible, or if not a resolution, then at least a mitigation. We should feel, as the *Adagietto* slowly (but not sluggishly) unfolds, something akin to the poem by Stefan George set by Schoenberg as the finale of his Second String Quartet (Op. 10, 1907–8): 'Ich fühle Luft aus anderen Planeten' ('I feel an air from other planets'). In the context of Mahler's Fifth, the 'air' that his *Adagietto* exhales is comparable to the sense of an approaching new creative phase that is part of our response to Schoenberg's quartet. So it was that a new direction in his creativity provided Mahler with the means to embark on Part III and complete his symphony.

The enabling resource proved to be Rückert's poetry, and it must have come to Mahler as a heaven-sent intimation that rescue was at hand; for not only did he now have a wordless orchestral song (*à la* Rückert) to complement the wordless orchestral song (*à la Wunderhorn*) of Part I and thereby service the ensuing rondo, but, perhaps most importantly of all, the intermediary that would effect the substitution of human passion (whether or not Alma was the generating *raison d'être*) for the initiating rite of death, the march, in Part I, and thus open the door to what I can only describe as the humane preoccupations of the finale itself. In short, there was to be no more of the metaphysics of catastrophe but instead an affirmation of how, against the odds (Part I), however overwhelming, the individual spirit of man may after all survive (Part III): the interpolation of the *Adagietto* was the marker not only for the new style but also, in the context of the Fifth, for a radical switch in philosophy. It was that now newly defined goal that lent fresh impetus to the continuation of the narrative.

While the *Adagietto* may indeed strike a new 'tone', it also, almost literally so, strikes a new note, in so far as it explores a tonality, F major, that till now has not played an extensive role in any of the preceding movements: it is F *minor* that has made the majority of previous appearances. However, while the movement breaks new ground, at the same time it shows itself aware, in typical Mahler fashion, that there is still unfinished tonal business to be completed: between bars 63 and 72 there is an unequivocal, though undemonstrative, implication of a D yet to be conclusively affirmed, after which F resumes and brings this unique song to rest. The final goal, it seems, is now in sight and within reach.

## The Rondo-Finale

Inevitably, debate will continue about the third and last part of the symphony, above all about the status of the rondo. Adorno's notorious adverse judgement has already achieved wide currency: 'The finale, fresh in many details and with novel formal ideas like that of the musical quick-motion picture [wie der das kompositorischen Zeitraffers], is undoubtedly too lightweight in relation to the first three movements ... Mahler was a poor yea-sayer. His voice cracks, like Nietzsche's, when he proclaims values, speaks from mere conviction, when he himself puts into practice the abhorrent notion of overcoming on which the thematic analyses capitalize, and makes music as if joy were already in the world. His vainly jubilant movements unmask jubilation', and so on, and so on.[107] An ideological rather than a musical judgement, one might think, though, alas, one that has undeniably influenced some celebrated interpreters of Mahler and their performances, of the Fifth's finale in particular.

The assumption that Mahler was incapable of affirming a humane belief in humanity, that he was unequal to the task or uninterested in it, for me has the ring of ideological intolerance – an ideologically rooted pessimism – about it. If nothing else, I hope my suggestion that Mahler did not abandon an intelligible strategy when undertaking the completion of his symphony, even while recognizing that it was his own genius that, in Part I, had created some of the problems he had to face in Part III, may at least aid our understanding of how it was he went about his attempt to solve them.

Humour, I think even his most fervent admirers might concede, was not Adorno's strongest suit. Mahler, however, was a big enough and broad enough artist to know that humour, good humour that is, not just black humour (in which field he operated with a special

107 See TWA Mahler, pp. 136–7.

expertise; indeed he may be said to have invented a special language for it), was part of the human condition and proper to a finale in which geniality and energy are to have a high profile, and much else besides, as I hope to show.

## A Wunderhorn *Song Recollected*

It is not inappropriate then that the rondo's opening flourish (bars 3–4 inclusive) is a literal quote from Mahler's *Wunderhorn* song, 'Lob des hohen Verstandes' ('In praise of lofty intellect'), composed in the summer of 1896, a song (a competition between a nightingale and a cuckoo, of which a donkey is the judge and chooses – naturally – the cuckoo) that takes a knock at the critics; an alternative title for the song at one stage was 'Lob der Kritik'. Perhaps too, as I observed some years ago, the 'quote' may have had a special significance in relation to the movement that follows, a finale that was avowedly and artfully contrapuntal ('learned') in character. The quote, for sure, was aimed at the critics, 'daring the donkeys to fault his [Mahler's] contrapuntal art – and half expecting them to do just that, at the same time'.[108]

It is in the context of the satirical shaft aimed at his critics in the preludial quotation from the *Wunderhorn* song that I interpret the final manifestation of 'learned' counterpoint in the rondo's coda (from fig. 34), where Mahler (tongue in cheek, perhaps, or at least smiling) puts the song quotation through its contrapuntal paces. I find it hard to hear this as a covert comment on the chorale, that its triumph (like the chorale in Shostakovich's Fifth) is not 'meant', is not to be taken seriously. On the contrary, this was Mahler trouncing his critics with a final flourish of contrapuntal ingenuity, genially capping a movement that is, indeed, all about counterpoint (of more than one species). In all of this one has to note that a further internal symmetry is introduced. While the *Wunderhorn* and 'Rückert' styles are crucial to Parts I and III, in Part III itself, III[1] (the

---

108 See DMWY, pp. 261 n. 36 and 374–5 n. 30, where I refer to Mahler's irrational sensitivity about the adequacy of his contrapuntal technique. This might have been another motive for the quotation from the *Wunderhorn* song, a kind of joke against himself, though his critics would have been unlikely to know of the history that gave rise to it.

Rückert-like orchestral song without words) is complemented by III², which makes retrospective reference to an earlier *Wunderhorn* song. Thus the juxtaposition of movements in Part III itself juxtaposes the 'song' parallels that hitherto have traversed the *Trauermarsch* and Part III¹. Part III¹⁺² unites in sequence *both* song sources.

## *Mahler and Haydn*

The variety of energetic counterpointing in fact raises an interesting issue in itself. Closely linked though it is by quotation to the preludial 'song', the finale can hardly be said to belong to the 'new phase' in Mahler's composing represented by the *Adagietto*. The counterpoint itself is quite distinct from the innovatory motivic polyphony of the allegro, say, or that of the scherzo. I have suggested way back that the new (polyphonic) style of the Fifth, to which Mahler himself referred, had already been significantly anticipated in the Fourth Symphony's first movement, in its development especially. But there was in the Fourth, besides this intimation of an innovatory counterpoint, an intimation of another style that was to become of huge significance in the twentieth century and was not to leave Mahler untouched, well beyond the confines of the Fourth and its chronological place in his oeuvre. It is in fact, if one may put it a shade paradoxically, to the anticipations of neoclassicism in the Fourth to which Mahler returns in the finale of his Fifth. There *is* something arrestingly 'classical' about the rondo's principal sections and their industrious counterpointing, in which context Paul Banks, in conversation, made an observation of particular relevance to the topic of Mahler's classicizing. He drew my attention to the Haydnesque character of Mahler's invention in his finale, of the rondo's principal sections, that is, and the contrapuntal activity they ceaselessly generate. Haydn is not a composer that one often thinks of in association with Mahler; nor did he have much opportunity to conduct Haydn's music. The more remarkable, then, as Dr Banks went on to point out, that Mahler had conducted two performances of Haydn's 'Drum-roll' Symphony (No. 103 in E flat) – the only occasions on which he conducted this symphony – in Vienna on 18 March 1900 and in St Petersburg on

29 March 1902, dates spanning a period in which the Fifth was put together. I think even a cursory juxtaposition of Mahler's and Haydn's finales bears out Dr Banks's insight, who did not allow to go unremarked the fact that both finales open with prominent contributions from the horns.[109]

*The Quotation Principle again at work*

One of the novel features that Adorno presumably had in mind when writing of 'quick-motion movie music' (which would be my translation of his '*kompositorischen Zeitraffers*') is the speeded-up version of the *Adagietto* that serves as the contrasting episodes of the

---

[109] It is a strange but illuminating coincidence that during this very same period Mahler also conducted Tchaikovsky's 'Manfred' Symphony, Op. 58, in Vienna on 13 January 1901 and in St Petersburg on 23 March 1902. These were the years during which not only the Fifth was composed but also the first group of *Kindertotenlieder*. As my music examples (overleaf) show, it was not only Haydn who may have been an influential model for Mahler in his new symphony, but Tchaikovsky, in the shaping of the new song-cycle. It is clear that one of the most memorable contours developed by the melody of the cycle's first song, 'Nun will die Sonn' . . .', owes its identity to the first movement of Tchaikovsky's symphony and his tormented hero. Moreover, Tchaikovsky's movement opens with woodwind alone (bass clarinet and bassoons: cf. Mahler's oboes, bassoons, and horn).

With regard to Haydn, it is of some interest that Georg Göhler, with whom Mahler, as we have seen, corresponded about his Fifth, mentions Haydn when writing about the finale in the exhaustive programme note he prepared for the performance of the symphony he conducted in Leipzig on 9 January 1914. This was announced as the first performance of the so-called 'new version of the work [*Uraufführung der neuen Fassung des Werkes*]', for which Göhler had collated, in association with the publishers, C. F. Peters, very many (though, as it turned out, not all) of the revisions that Mahler had made ceaselessly up to the time of his death. These, however, had never been systematically incorporated into the published performing materials for the symphony. Hence the importance of Göhler's pioneering effort. The complete text of Göhler's note has appeared in *Muziek & Wetenschap/Dutch Journal for Musicology*, 7 (1999), pp. 65–74. His response to the *Adagietto* is perhaps of particular interest in the context of our discussion of this movement. Göhler first of all remarks that at the end of the scherzo, the third movement, in the evolution of the narrative we are hardly further along the road than at the end of the second; he continues: 'Once again one must imagine a longer break before the third part of the symphony (fourth and fifth movements). The noisy delights of the world were of no help. Peace, calm, consoling love alone ensure that the miracle happens. The fourth movement tells of this peace, this calm, of consoling, helping, kindly love, love that heals all wounds and restores to life the man who seemed to be dead to happiness and life, granting him the plenitude of the sunniest happiness.'

Finally, I am grateful to H. C. Robbins Landon for his reminder that it was Mahler who was responsible for one of the very earliest – if not the earliest – revivals in modern times of an opera by Haydn, *Lo speziale*, which he conducted in Hamburg (1895) and again in Vienna in 1899.

(a) Tchaikovsky's 'Manfred' Symphony, opening

(b) 'Manfred' Symphony, bars 14–19

(c) Mahler's *Kindertotenlieder*, 'Nun will die Sonn' . . .', bars 48–51

rondo.[110] A brilliant idea this, maintaining the formality of the quotation principle while at the same time throwing fresh light on the
*Adagietto*. This is an elegant, witty, compositional performance; and
if there is any satirical or parodistic intention involved, it is of the
gentlest, one might say, even, playful, kind, for example the subvert-
ing woodwind trills (flutes, oboes, clarinets) from fig. 29 ff., and, in
the bars immediately preceding this passage, the dynamic extremes
Mahler calls for from *ff* to *pp* in the space of four bars. However,
there is little hint of Mahler's habitual caustic tone of voice when
demonstrating that something that one has assumed to be the case
is abruptly stood on its head. This approach to the *Adagietto* returns
us for a moment to a further reflection on the parallel that is so
often drawn between the movement and 'Ich bin der Welt abhanden gekommen'. If it really were the case that both inhabit the
same spiritual world (with all that that implies for tempo or expressive character), is it likely, possible, even, that Mahler would have
risked seeming to trivialize what in those circumstances must have
been conceived as another solemn revelation of his profoundest
feelings about his life and his art? I take leave to doubt it.

There is much to admire as the finale proceeds in an atmosphere
that is remarkably shadowless and free of the volcanic tensions of
Part I. (One notices that the interpolations of the *Adagietto* in the
rondo never take on the character of interruptions; they are integrated variations, rather, of what we have heard before.) Does this
mean, then, that ingenuity and geniality reign supreme? Does
Mahler thereby risk blandness?

## A Narrative Parallel with the Fourth?

To arrive at that conclusion would entail overlooking a parallel
that, to my knowledge, has scarcely been remarked upon, with the
narrative strategy that governs the evolution of the Fourth from its
beginning to its end: the progressive reduction in complexity – of

---

110 It was surely this acceleration that Adorno had in mind, not as Floros would have it
(Floros, *Gustav Mahler*, pp. 157–8), the relatively orthodox variation by diminution of
the chorale.

texture, of invention, of tonal excursions – in which refining process the inner drama of the work – the passage traversed from Experience to Innocence (see '"Swallowing the Programme": Mahler's Fourth Symphony' above, pp. 186–8) – is embodied.

At least something of that same long-term strategy underpins the evolution of the Fifth, from the highly complex chromaticism, dissonance, and fractured textures of Part I (of the allegro, in particular) to the (almost) unblemished diatonicism and euphony of Part III, a sustained assertion of D major. The final extrapolation of a resounding D is comparable in its own way to the affirmation of E major at the end of the Fourth. The acute difference lies in the fact that it is an *entire movement*, the finale itself, that is required in the Fifth to lend sufficient weight and authority to the final attainment of D. (Small wonder, in the light of the hard time D major has been given in the allegro.)

Quite apart from this significant parallel in narrative strategies, it is intriguing to find a movement in the Fifth that overtly sustains the (neo)classicizing pursuits of the Fourth. Paul Banks's provocative suggestion that Haydn might have been an influential model opens up a highly interesting line of inquiry. In general, indeed, much more work needs to be done on the direct relationships between the music that Mahler was busy conducting and the music he was busy creating. There was a singular 'feeding' process in operation here that now warrants serious, systematic investigation.

It was Schoenberg who said there was still plenty of good music to be written in C major;[111] perhaps it might be claimed that Mahler was making that same point about D major already in the finale of the Fifth. The exceptional energy of the movement, which is one of its leading features, inevitably leads to that final act of reparation, no less, when the chorale that has twice been undermined by collapse in the allegro of Part I, returns to crown – to anoint – the denouement of the finale. There is never any serious doubt that this time round the chorale will survive and make its joyful statement, a perfectly legitimate joy (or so it seems to me,

111 See Dika Newlin, 'Secret Tonality in Schoenberg's Piano Concerto', pp. 137–9. (My thanks to O. W. Neighbour.)

*pace* Adorno); triumphant, yes, but free of triumphalism. Impossible in any event to put words to work when it is Mahler's untranslatable pitches that alone can provide the key to the 'parade sauvage' in which we ourselves, the world, Mahler, and his music, are all participants.[112] I find it moving in the Fifth that Mahler dumps transcendental solutions and instead offers as contra-assertions to collapse and catastrophe the consolations of human passion and mankind's unique capacity not only to find joy in a generally hostile world but to create it.

There is no question that in one major respect at least Mahler's finale departs from precedents established in the preceding symphonies: with the exception of the chorale there is no cyclic recall of materials from the two movements comprising Part 1, which normally would bring with them a vivid reminder of the tensions, the fundamental conflicts, that have led to the creation of the work.

This is not to say that there are no moments of retrospection, of music that suddenly puts us back in touch with notable events that have occurred at earlier stages in the symphony. A telling but minor example breaks surface at fig. 16 where for fourteen bars, and in the context of a reappearance of the *Adagietto*, the layout of the passage, for solo horn and the *Adagietto*'s very own string orchestra, spirits us back to the opening of the second trio in the *Trauermarsch* (fig. 15) and the opening of the scherzo, from fig. 1⁻¹, where the obbligato horn (for twelve bars) first embarks on its virtuoso, concerto-like solo flight, and again accompanied by strings alone (plus two solitary strokes on the triangle).

### The 'Triplet Factor' Apotheosized

A major recall, however, is to follow in the finale between figs. 21 and 23, where Mahler is limbering up for the materialization of the chorale. Once again we have a powerful affirmation of D and a further release of superabundant energy in a brilliant variation of the rondo's principal theme. But it is the detailed features of the

---

112 'J'ai seul la clef de cette parade sauvage', Arthur Rimbaud, *Les Illuminations*, no. IV, 'Parade', final line ('I alone possess the key to this barbarous sideshow').

variation that are wholly remarkable and that seem to have gone
unacknowledged but for the briefest of mentions by Paul
Bekker.[113] What is so riveting here is Mahler's reintroduction of the
*triplet* as a prime feature of his melodic invention at this point. We
have not in fact heard triplets – the *triplet phenomenon* – on this
torrential scale since Part I, where this rhythmic unit carried an
ever-increasing load of imagery, becoming one of the immediately
recognizable signifiers of Aspiration.[114] Its resurrection at this critical juncture in the finale, and the role it plays in the creation of an
almost incandescent web of polyphony, means that we have here a
mini-celebration of all the aspiring music that heretofore has met
with defeat. It is a unique apotheosis, in which Mahler lets loose
any ties with 'classicism' and liberates a type of ecstatic counterpoint that presages his late contrapuntal style. So the finale of the
Fifth too has its moment of disclosure of 'Spätstil'; and a tremendous moment it is.[115] A good case could be made for identifying it
as the real climax of the finale and, no less, the moment when the
symphony's initiating conflict is at last resolved.

## The Chorale Recovered

After which there remains the recovery of the chorale, which proceeds, if one may put it thus, without a hitch from fig. 32. On the
other hand, is there one among us, on reaching fig. 33 and its continuation at bar 730, who does not feel a tremor at the final statement of the chorale, especially at bars 740ff.? One knows, of
course, that this time round the chorale will not fade, will not have
its lifeblood drained from it, as was the case in the parallel passage

---

113  *Gustav Mahlers Sinfonien*, p. 200.
114  For parallel passages in Part I, Part I[1+2], see e.g. I[1], fig. 9+9ff., and in I[2], figs. 12–13, or bars
     356 (double bar) ff., or fig. 23, from double bar to double bar at bar 428. The downward
     thrust of the triplets in the finale at fig. 21 is of course bound up with the built-in direc-
     tion of the rondo's principal theme. But on this occasion the descending triplets are as
     elevating as their ascending precedents were signifiers of aspiration. Now at fig. 21, the
     triplets are freed of aspiration and can celebrate having arrived at their goal without
     directional restraint; and in fact Mahler disseminates his joyous triplets in both descend-
     ing and ascending forms.
115  Moments of high emotion in late Mahler (there are many examples in *Das Lied* and the
     Ninth Symphony) bring in their train an identifiable type of 'ecstatic' counterpoint.

in the *Hauptsatz*, fig. 29⁻² – fig. 30; and yet, even after the ultimate unison D has sounded (bar 791), one has to concede that one's memory of the chorale's fate in the *Hauptsatz* has not been entirely erased; nor could it be, nor perhaps should it be. Mahler might well have been of one mind with François Mauriac: 'Why are we always taught to dread annihilation? ...The really awful thing is to believe, against all evidence, in life eternal! To live eternally would be to lose the refuge of nothingness.'[116] Perhaps the truth is that the Fifth draws its strength from its juxtaposition of those options: Eternity (after a secular fashion) or Nothingness.

---

116 François Mauriac, *Le Mystère Frontenac* (1933); *The Frontenac Mystery,* translated by Gerard Hopkins (Harmondsworth: Penguin Books, 1986), p. 172.

Riccardo Chailly and Donald Mitchell discuss Mahler's Fifth Symphony

# New Sounds, New Century:
# A Dialogue with Riccardo Chailly

## ⌁ 1997 ⌁

### Part 1
### 1 *Trauermarsch*   2 *Stürmisch bewegt*

RICCARDO CHAILLY   Donald, I should like to start our dialogue in Heaven, with the very last bars of the Fourth Symphony, where Mahler has reached the 'himmlische Leben'. At the end of the symphony, the music describes *Verklärung* [Transfiguration], but *Verklärung* in a spiritual and positive sense. How could Mahler possibly start a new symphony when he had already reached Heaven and his soul was filled with spiritual pleasures? The earth-bound, physical *Trauermarsch* that opens the Fifth, in its idiosyncratic, even neurotic key of C sharp minor, must be a slap in the face to whomever expects the continuation of a similar mood after the last bar of the Fourth is over. You think you are still in Heaven, but the switch between *that* mood and this unbearable *ta-ta-ta-tam* [sings opening fanfare of the Fifth] of the trumpet at the beginning of the *Kondukt* [Procession] is quite unbelievable.

DONALD MITCHELL   This serenity, calmness and sublimity having been achieved in the Fourth, I think it is perfectly understandable how it might have been felt that everything now would go wonderfully well in the future. But I think the truth of the matter is, that while the 'himmlische Leben' does indeed round off the whole of the first period of Symphonies Nos. 1–4 with a glimpse of Heaven, in the first movement of the Fifth he had to start all over again, from zero, to confront all the same problems.

---

This discussion of Mahler's Fifth Symphony was recorded on 5 May 1997 in Milan and first published in **NSNC.** The publication included a CD of historic performances of passages from various versions of Mahler's Fifth Symphony and related songs.

People always go on about the trumpet fanfare, that supposedly 'links' the Fourth and Fifth Symphonies. The fanfare,
picking up from the height of the climax of the development
in the first movement of the Fourth, interrupts and then
returns to the recapitulation in the first movement. But all
fanfares have to have something in common, and up to now I
have not heard the opening of the Fifth principally as a continuation of something that had originated in the Fourth. On
the other hand, Colin Matthews, that very good friend of ours,
a fine composer and Mahler scholar, said to me, 'Well, that may
be, but just remember that in fact the trumpet fanfare in the
Fifth starts on the very same pitch with which the fanfare
makes its entrance in the first movement of the Fourth.' This,
I must admit, had not struck me; and perhaps there was a real
point in Mahler picking up from that earlier fanfare. Whereas
in the Fourth he, so to say, circumvented the implications of
the fanfare and was able to end up in the 'himmlische Leben',
in the Fifth he embarks on the whole drama all over again. It
is the C sharp in the Fifth that makes the connection.

RC  Mahler himself has said that he had to start from scratch, that
he had to forget the experience of his first four symphonies,
because he had found a new world, especially in his way of
orchestrating. He had continued revising the Fifth until the
end of his life. But I have a feeling that, even though he felt
that this was a new beginning, *la gemma portante ideologica* – the
ideological starting point – was already launched in the previous symphony by that same pitch (first movement, bars
226–8, second and third trumpet).

DM  This is a very interesting point, and should make us think
about very many aspects of the Fifth. You have just remarked
upon the constant revisions. It is a strange thing that Mahler, in a
letter from 1911 to Georg Göhler, wrote, 'I simply can't understand why I still had to make such mistakes, like the merest
beginner.'[1] This I find bewildering, especially when one thinks
of the perfection of the Fourth or *Kindertotenlieder.*

1  GM *Selected Letters*, p. 372.

RC  In your text on the Fifth you quote Ida Dehmel, who attended a performance of the Fifth, conducted by Mahler himself, in Hamburg in 1905.[2] It is clear from this that in spite of the difficulty of Mahler's language in the Fifth – the sudden change of gear, of tempi, of moods, of dynamics sounded almost neurotic, especially in the first movement – it did not put all listeners off, by any means. The symphony made a strong, immediate impact on some listeners and despite everything, won a lot of appreciation, including Richard Strauss's, except for the *Adagietto*.

DM  Well, I am sure that it was part of Mahler's genius that, however elaborate and innovative the music was – allowing us glimpses of an extraordinary future, of an extraordinary modernity that I think is absolutely basic to the Fifth – none the less his music succeeded in speaking to humankind.

RC  You refer to the extraordinary modernity of the Fifth Symphony. Here, I disagree with those who argue that the modernity of Mahler's music starts only from the Seventh.[3] The modernity of Mahler, in my view, starts with his Opus 1, *Das klagende Lied*, not with the Seventh Symphony! In particular, Nos. 5, 6 and 7 – the *trittico centrale* [the central trilogy] – embody the very heart of the modernity of Mahler's music. Those three central symphonies, especially, are clear anticipations of the Second Viennese School.

DM  In that case, I think, we are in agreement – and I feel very passionate about this – that Part 1 of the Fifth and in particular the relationship between the *Trauermarsch* and the allegro, the second movement, represents one of the most arresting and original concepts in twentieth-century music. It is indeed unique! These two movements share the same material, material that has been introduced in the *Trauermarsch* is quoted and developed in the second movement, the *Stürmisch bewegt* allegro. Memory plays an incredibly important role in this relationship. The compositional processes, and especially the functions of quotation and memory in the relationship of those

2  See 'Eternity or Nothingness? Mahler's Fifth Symphony', pp. 255–6.
3  Jean Matter, *Connaissance de Mahler. Documents, analyses et synthèses*, p. 231.

movements, I think, are not just part of our century, but of many centuries still to come. It remains an incomparable formal achievement.

RC In the second movement, as you say, Mahler constantly repeats material he has already introduced in the first movement. However, he never repeats it in a banal, let us say stereotypical 'neoclassical' way, but the repetitions always add something new, and there is always a reason for them. Repeating the same music is, for Mahler, a natural process of development. As he said himself, when he was actually working on the Fifth, 'There should be no repetition, but only evolution.'[4]

DM Or sometimes – as in the Fifth – interruption!

RC Yes; for which reason I'd like to talk about the recitative of the cellos at bar 191 in the second movement: a *notturno*-like, sorrowful (*'klagend'* says Mahler) *meditazione*. Before the recitative begins, the orchestra has been pressing forward – *Drängend* – generating a high intensity; and then – all of a sudden – silence . . . and after that a gradual *accelerando,* a roll on the timpani, and nothing else. What a modern idea, to interrupt the engine in this way!

DM And once more, this astonishing 'cut-off' is none other than one of the many transformations of the second trio of the *Trauermarsch.*

RC To me, this passage is so undogmatic, so free; an 'intrusion', perhaps, but not inconsistent or out of place. On the contrary, it is a bridge to the long development that starts when the cellos (bar 214) expand on the *meditazione* and soon lead us back to the prevailing mood of the movement, one of electrifying tension.

    I think it is crucial to focus on the function of the two trios in the first movement of this Fifth, as you do in your analysis.

DM Yes, it does seem immensely important to me. I don't think

4   NB-L *Recollections*, p. 172.

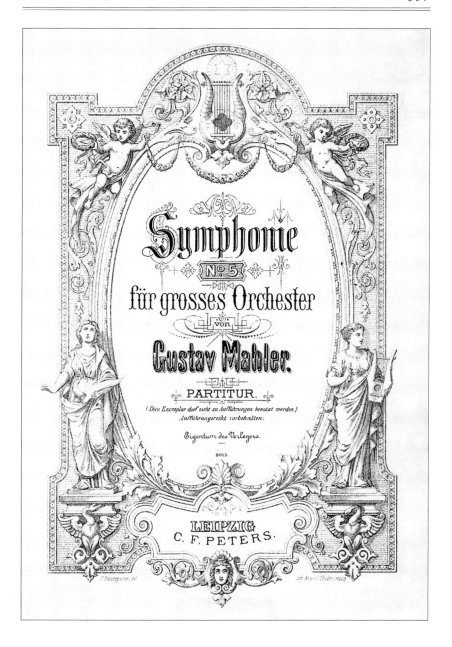

The title page of the 1904 edition of the study score of the Fifth Symphony

anybody really has quite understood the function of the trios, that each of them builds up to a huge climax and then each collapses, in the most terrifying way – I mean, one really seems to plunge into the abyss.

RC  The last climax at the end of the *Trauermarsch* is delirium-like, with this triple *fortissimo*, which collapses as you say very abruptly into a kind of oblivion, *la fanfara muore*.

DM  Absolutely. The second trio fades out into inaudibility in just that way, and I would be interested to know your view of that, Riccardo, because in the second movement, the chorale in D major similarly expires. Thus, the function of memory is all-important. We have to rely entirely on the interpreter to remind us, when we reach that fading of the chorale at the end of the second movement, of the second trio from the *Trauer-marsch* – it is almost Proustian this, the significance of memory in the Fifth. We must remember that we have lived through that once before and still await a resolution of the collapse.

RC  It is. I think, the so-called *memoria atavica* that is vital in Mahler's music. *Atavica* means the memory which descends from remote ancestors, or which human beings possess from the very beginning of their lives. Mahler's symphonies, more than any other compositions, rely on the *memoria atavica*. I have just come from Philadelphia, where I performed the First Symphony. I had studied the piece afresh, and went through a new experience of performing it. I was struck by how many features of the Fifth are related to the First, in particular to its huge finale. There are very strong links between these two pieces, and not only between these two works, but between all Mahler's compositions: from the First to the (complete) Tenth. It is up to the performer to make these internal affinities audible.

DM  If I may pick you up there, Riccardo, I think that is very important, what you have just said. There seem to me to be at least three categories of ways in which the memory, in the Fifth, is stimulated into action. There are affinities; there are, of course, variations: and then there are those extraordinary –

because literal – quotations. No composer, surely, in the nineteenth, or indeed early twentieth century, had ever used quotations in music like this before. In Mahler's second movement,
for example, there is that direct quotation of the *Trauermarsch*,
which simply re-appears, re-emerges. It is as if there is one
orchestra in one room playing the allegro, and somebody
opens a door and, good heavens, there is another orchestra in
the next room which is still playing the *Trauermarsch*. And this
is such a fantastic concept. People go on about Charles Ives or
whomever – but it was Mahler who was defining modernity
already at the turn of the century.

RC   And even before that, with *Das klagende Lied*. In the 'Urfassung' [original version], there is a multiple rhythm in the *Fern-
orchester* [offstage orchestra] three in a bar, against the main
orchestra's four in a bar (second movement, bars 222–9).[5] How
you could synchronize that in those days, I don't know. To me,
Mahler is the Charles Ives of Austria. How could an eighteen-
year-old have thought of something so completely modern?
His contemporaries must have thought the young composer
was off his head! Two different orchestras, talking two different
languages simultaneously? This was absolutely unheard of in
those days!

DM   Just to make one other point, I believe it is very important for
interpreters and audiences to realize that when all these quotations, variations and affinities emerge in the second movement,
the source of many of the most important of these memories
are the two trios from the *Trauermarsch*. Of course, there are
those major, literal quotations of the big march tune itself, but
those apart, one is constantly reminded elsewhere in the second
movement of the conflict first articulated by the two trios of
the *Trauermarsch*. That in itself is very extraordinary.

RC   I want to add an anecdote from Alma's autobiography: one
evening, Schoenberg tried to talk to Mahler about the concept

5   Gustav Mahler, *Das klagende Lied*: 'Erstfassung', edited by Reinhold Kubik.

of *Klangfarbenmelodie*, to which Mahler, it seems, reacted sceptically. I wonder why that was? Or did Alma get it wrong,
perhaps? Because for me, albeit unconsciously, Mahler had
already anticipated the concept. Think of the codas of the
*Nachtmusiken* of the Seventh . . . there we are already in what
we might call the antechamber to the principle of *Klangfarbenmelodie*.

DM  Indeed, but we are there also in the Fifth. If one compares the
early 1904 version and the revised version of the *Trauermarsch*,
and especially of the second trio, as we can now hear for the
first time on our CD, this whole *Klangfarbenmelodie* principle
was already in process. Whereas to begin with, Mahler, say, has
a continuous line in one colour, deploying one timbre, as the
revisionary process starts he breaks it down and distributes the
one timbre among a whole group of instruments. In this
respect, I have always thought that it was one of Schoenberg's
own pupils, Anton Webern, who, in developing the idea of
*Klangfarbenmelodie*, was possibly more influenced by Mahler than
by Schoenberg! Think, for instance, of Webern's wonderful
instrumentation of Bach's *Ricercar*, which has always impressed
me as a very clear example of Webern systematically following
in Mahler's footsteps.

RC  This is a meaningful comparison. I think. It is a matter of fact
that we live in the twentieth century, move towards the millennium and 'digest' contemporary music, some of which was
clearly composed by *discepoli di Mahler* [Mahler disciples],
Webern among them. We can now permit ourselves, with great
respect, to analyse, to look back, and 'intrude' so to speak, into
these matters discussed by Mahler and Schoenberg, and
Schoenberg's pupils. For them, this was simply not possible in
the same way. I find it fascinating to attempt to reach our own
conclusions by analysing their discussions of a new *ideologia di
composizione* [compositional ideology].

DM  There is one more point I should like to make, before we move
on to the scherzo. It is really not helpful to whomever is listen-

ing to, or studying, Mahler's Fifth, to think of the second movement in terms of 'sonata form'. I think this really is a big mistake. It is much more important to think of this movement in terms of interruptions, quotations, variations, and so on, and to avoid imposing a straitjacket on a radically innovative form.

RC    I never considered Mahler a *sinfonista* [symphonist] in the traditional meaning of the word. Mahler was a destroyer — he destroyed the classical symphony and built something completely new out of the debris. He wanted to expand the symphony into a new formula, which was going to be the bridge to the next century, for contemporary composers like Luciano Berio, for example. How could Mahler, who destroyed the symphony in its traditional form, have been *tradizionalista*, linked to sonata form? This is absolutely impossible, and that is why he is, today, still regarded as the *innovatore* of the twentieth century. That is the point.

DM    Well, then, you and I, Riccardo, are one hundred per cent in agreement that there was no greater total act of *creative* 'destruction' than Part I of this symphony!

RC    Exactly! What, Donald, I think, we should focus on, is the unique excess of different moods in the Fifth. In none of the other symphonies is it as extreme as in the Fifth, where he starts in such a tragic, sad, depressive, neurotic way and ends in the finale with the triumph of optimism. To me the happiness at the end of the First Symphony is illusory; it is a prelude to the real tragedy, with which the first bars of the Second Symphony confront us. But in the Fifth, he really means this D major. It is present throughout the finale, in which he hardly ever touches upon a minor key. He wants to finish in a positive mood, simply because he was happy at the time. For the one and only moment of his life, after he met Alma, he knew happiness — unfortunately it proved to be an illusion. The extreme contrast between the mood of the opening bars of the symphony and the opposite mood you find yourself in after sixty-five minutes, is in fact rather *anti-mahleriano, anti-tragico.*

DM  I agree. Part I really does end in total negation. There is not a
    tiny glimpse of hope for the future when you get to the end
    of Part I, which of course makes it all the more amazing when
    there follows the great scherzo and with it, a proclamation of
    D major. This was a big risk, don't you agree?

RC  Indeed: and that is why Mahler prescribes a long silence – '*folgt
    lange Pause*' – which prepares for the start of the new move-
    ment. It is a must that has to be respected. What he meant
    exactly by '*lange Pause*', I don't know; every conductor should
    take it into account, but I think you need at least two minutes.[6]
    It is not only our having reached the end of Part I that imposes
    a spiritually necessary moment of silence. In addition, the new
    mood and tonality of the scherzo, each so unexpected, should
    not be an irritation, a provocation. The switch, after the end of
    Part I, to the ensuing scherzo is enormous, and only time and
    silence can compensate for the abrupt start of such a powerful
    contrast.

## *Part II*
## *3 Scherzo*

DM  So, after at least two minutes' rest, the scherzo, which was
    almost certainly the first movement that Mahler composed.

RC  Mahler wrote to Alma that he feared that nobody would
    understand it, and that maestros would probably play it too fast
    for the next fifty years.[7] The prediction was wrong, and I feel
    that this movement is fully understood by my colleagues, by
    the public and by Mahler scholars. The reason why it might
    seem incomprehensible is not only the dramatic switch in
    mood between Part I of the symphony and the key, the tonal-
    ity, but – above all – the distorted *Wiener Walzer* of the scherzo.
    Mahler's *Wiener Walzer* is a parody, and an intended provoca-

6  See '1905 Hamburg' in *NSNC*, p. 31.
7  Henry-Louis de La Grange and Günther Weiss (eds.), *Ein Glück ohne Ruh'. Die Briefe
   Gustav Mahlers an Alma*, p. 221.

Riccardo Chailly rehearsing the Royal Concertgebouw Orchestra

tion of the listener. Do you think this was one of the reasons why the listeners might have laughed, and not taken the movement seriously?

DM I think it is perfectly possible, that the movement was misunderstood to be more exuberant and relaxed in mood than it actually is.

RC Exactly, look at the fourth bar of Fig. 2, the way the clarinet plays against the rhythm of the *Walzer* [RC sings the clarinet part], '*Schalltrichter in die Hohe*' [Bells up]! This is by no means the beautiful, elegant melody of a *Wiener Walzer,* this is a theatrical reaction to it – and much more serious in character than people might think. It is the waltz provoking a neurotic response, part of a movement that is itself quite specially characteristic of its composer's creative personality. It is a huge movement, by far the longest movement of the symphony.

DM And as the movement continues, it gets to be more and more a dance of death, doesn't it? Is the scherzo not telling us – among other things – that it is no longer possible to live in a beautiful world of Viennese waltzes? That that culture is now gone, is over, completely over . . . And the further the movement progresses, the more sceptical and critical it becomes, especially in its closing part, from fig. 15 onwards. After all, Mahler explores many minor tonalities before feeling able to release the final affirmation of D major at the end of the movement, while the use of the *Holzklapper* [whip] at fig. 16 evokes the rattle of bones. It really does become a wild dance of the dead here. And finally, is the scherzo not essentially a *pivotal* movement, a stage on the journey that will be completed only when we reach that ultimate triumph of D at the end of the finale? It was part of Mahler's problem that he had to avoid having a kind of conclusive D major celebration in the middle of his symphony, because that would have been premature. He still had to keep uncertainty and expectation alive throughout the scherzo which he did in the ways we've just been talking about.

RC    In this symphony, there are so many incredibly modern moments, and I think it is important to focus for a moment on 'Mahler the Modernist', 'Mahler the Innovator'.

DM    Absolutely; for instance, at fig. 10 of the scherzo, we come to one extraordinary passage: a kind of rhythmic canon for four horns on one pitch, a canon in unison![8] Unfortunately, very few conductors make this canon audible: hardly anyone takes notice of Mahler's detailed dynamics. When they do, Mahler, suddenly, is *in* our time, so modern is this passage in form and technique.

RC    This is pre-Penderecki – unbelievable. A composer of today, like Penderecki, who wrote in such a horizontal way in the 1970s, could have written something like that. The way Mahler had the instruments cut off independently, drop their notes one after the other . . .

DM    And if you don't have a conductor and orchestral players who actually play what Mahler wrote, and take the trouble to do that . . .

RC    You won't hear it . . .

DM    It will just sound like a unison.

RC    Exactly; I never thought of this before, Donald, but this passage also very much reminds me of another composer whose music I am studying at the moment: Edgard Varèse.

DM    Oh, Varèse! Yes.

RC    The way he treats the brass is typical Varèse. These five bars, from the second bar after fig. 10, might well been written by him. It is hard to believe, but absolutely true.

DM    Well, we are of a single mind here, because I too think that's one of the pages in the Fifth that was a hundred years ahead of its time.

8   See p. 322.

RC   And then, at fig. 11, there are the famous *pizzicato* spots, which Adorno nicknamed 'shadows'.[9] Mahler did not want *tutti gli archi pizzicati,* but *pizzicati soli.* He wants solo instruments, which sounds again very modern. It is almost as if after the *fermata* at fig. 11, after the silence, you find yourself all of a sudden in Op. 21 of Webern [Symphony (1928)]. We should also mention a spot of almost pure comedy further on, eight bars before the double bar. The oboe announces itself so very *timido* – 'schüchtern' [bashful]. It is a kind of 'May I, may I intrude?' Theatre again!

DM   [*whispering*] 'Can I say something? Can I? Can I? Is it all right for me to speak?'

RC   'The bassoon got it wrong twelve bars back, but perhaps I may interrupt?'

DM   Yes, I agree, it has to be like a fantastic dialogue between actors.

RC   Absolutely so. The scherzo is full of such delightful spots. Again, in the ninth bar after fig. 13: one single note makes the point. Into a very beautiful and elegant waltz-like melody, three clarinets burst in with one note, *fortissimo* – it should sound crazy! And if I do not succeed in getting a crazy sound, there is something wrong with my way of interpreting it. As for the modernity of Mahler's way of orchestrating . . .

There is one last spot in the scherzo I should like to draw your attention to: at the double bar after fig. 30, the feeling of a dance of death is given by the rhythm of the *gran cassa* [bass drum]. It is so dark, so sinister . . . Mahler chose the right colour for it.

DM   After that it is taken up with wooden sticks on the timps; and it is that basic rhythm there – we have had it before on the *Holzklapper* after fig. 16 – that is the heartbeat, the irregular heartbeat of death itself.

RC   And then, after eight bars, all of a sudden: *Più mosso.* Few con-

---

9   TWA *Mahler,* p. 103.

ductors are daring enough to do this sudden change of gear, perhaps also because it is technically rather difficult; almost all conductors play the *Più mosso* in the same tempo. They characterize it *Sehr wild,* but not *Più mosso.* The sudden acceleration in fact adds still more to the anxiety at the end of the movement. If you keep it in the same tempo, and fail to press forward, the modern character is lost. To have sixty players, the whole strings plus timpani and trumpet move on (bar 772) in a new tempo, without preparation or tempo modification, is like two overlapping tapes.

DM   And that pressure, that anxiety, really colours the scherzo, so that when we have got to the end of it, although it has been truly exhilarating, just because of the sheer energy of the movement and the whole extraordinary conception of it, none the less one has still *not* arrived at the final *terminus.* I mean the overall narrative is not concluded by the scherzo, even though it finally affirms D. I think it is particularly brilliant how Mahler leaves us feeling – knowing – by the means we have discussed, that we still have a journey to complete . . .

RC   Another important aspect of the Fifth is, I believe, Mahler's 'mania' for Bach which was so very much alive and present in those years. In none of his other symphonies does Bach play such an important role. The contrapuntal *bravura,* especially in the second movement, the scherzo and the finale, is obviously a constant *reminiscenza Bachiana.* Because of this contrapuntal, post-Bach, modern way of symphonic writing, he needed the *Adagietto.* The *Adagietto* is a moment of complete *arresto,* of relaxation; in its peaceful, horizontal way, it is reminiscent of Schubert and Schumann. It is a 'song without words'. Musically, I feel, the need for a relaxation at this point is also dictated by the mathematical and intellectual way in which, under the influence of Bach, Mahler constructed the second and third movements.

DM   Of course. It was vital that, after Parts I and II, he had to introduce an entirely new colour and new texture to achieve a total relaxation. It captivates our entire attention when the string orchestra with harp is introduced at this particular moment. What an extraordinary switch!! It is like opening a window to a breath of air from another planet, as Schoenberg might have said; but in this case it's not another planet, but another *orchestra*.

This was already anticipated in the second trio of the *Trauermarsch*.[10] It is there that the idea of a string orchestra begins to be defined; and conductors, I think, should make us sense the onset of something new at the beginning of that second trio. Then, when we hear the *Adagietto* itself, we are reminded of that anticipation of a string orchestra in the trio and realize that it has now, magically, materialized.

## Part III
### 4 Adagietto 5 Rondo-finale

RC  So now we embark on this delicate topic of the *Adagietto*. The Italian word 'Adagietto' leads me to a very important point: the suffix '-etto' indicates a *diminutivo*. 'Adagietto' thus means a *piccolo adagio* - a little adagio, purely in its shape, not in quality or intensity. It describes a miniature movement that we desperately need at this point in the symphony, a little calmness after the storm. Only strings and harp, no percussion, no brass, no wind. You consider the *Adagietto* to be a *canto senza parole* [song without words], don't you?

DM  Indeed, I do . . .

RC  But you don't want the words Mengelberg has written in his score![11]

DM  *No,* I certainly don't want those words! I am thinking more along the line of Mendelssohn's 'songs without words'. The character of the *Adagietto* is, to me, a wordless Rückert song.

RC  Perhaps we can think of it like this – that there is a secret text concealed in the melody of the first violins.

---

10 See *NSNC*, p. 35.    11 See facing page.

Mengelberg's conducting score: the opening of the *Adagietto*

At the third bar, Mahler writes '*seelenvoll*' [full of sentiment].
I think this word is often misinterpreted by conductors, who
seem to think it means 'sentimental'. But something that is full
of sentiment and something that is sentimental – these are two
entirely different things. Certainly the Visconti movie, *Death in
Venice*, which is a wonderful, brilliant movie, has contributed,
I think, greatly to the distortion of the piece into something
very sentimental. You named Mendelssohn, who brought his
own purity and noble simplicity to the concept of the *canto
senza parole*. If you indulge yourself in the *Adagietto*, also
tempo-wise, there is always a danger that you end up with sentimentality, instead of *seelenvoll,* which is a pity, don't you think?
To me this simple word, *seelenvoll,* is the key to the *Adagietto*.

DM  I could not agree more. I think you have made a very meaningful distinction between sentiment, the presence of sentiment – that is the presence of feeling – and the sentimental,
which is an *excess* of feeling out of proportion to the character
of the movement as a whole. This leads us to the question of
the tempo, on which I don't want to dwell too long. The
tempo should also reflect the designation of a *piccolo adagio,* but
I don't believe for a moment that there is some cast–iron
metronome tempo that must be the only 'right' tempo for the
movement.

RC  No, I believe still in the heartbeat of the conductor.

DM  Indeed, but it is worth remembering that we do have some
evidence concerning the tempo from the early days of the life
of the *Adagietto*. Performances under Mahler himself, along
with some of Mengelberg's performances, were between seven
and nine minutes, which seems to suggest that that was how
the *Adagietto* was heard at the start of its history. What seems to
have happened in later decades, right up to our own time, is a
tendency for the tempo somehow to get slower and slower,
and yet slower. The character of the music itself has been
changed by this, to my ears, 'alien' performing tradition. However, I don't think conductors today should be influenced by

Willem Mengelberg conducting

the wrong tempi established over a long period of time by some of their predecessors, however distinguished.

RC   Mengelberg noted a time of nine and a half minutes at the end of the *Adagietto* in his score. When he recorded it in 1926, and this recording is also on our CD, he needed only seven minutes and a few seconds. I do not believe this was purely for phonographic reasons! In the orchestral parts, which he used not only in Amsterdam but also on his tour of the United States, timings of about eight minutes are noted. I think he probably felt that the correct tempo should result in that sort of duration.

Donald, you may not care for Mengelberg's 'poem', but what about the story he tells with regard to Mahler's courting of Alma?

DM   Well, I think Mengelberg was probably right in suggesting that the movement was conceived initially as a declaration of love for Alma. It would be rather strange if Mengelberg had made this story up. Moreover, he wrote it in ink on the first page of the *Adagietto* in his full score, which means that he probably made it at a later date than when he was marking it up for performance; and he is also rather careful to say he had it 'from both of them'. This sounds to me very much like a genuine statement, and I myself see no reason at the moment to disbelieve it. I think it may be even a little helpful to regard it as a love letter, because I believe that it is of the first importance for interpreters to bear in mind when they are performing the *Adagietto* that it wasn't a message of condolence, but a signal of tender passion, with matrimony in view!

RC   I would like to add something to this. With all my respect and love for Mengelberg's tradition, in the specific case of the *Adagietto* I have certain doubts about his markings in the score. Mengelberg adds an extra *crescendo–diminuendo* – a double *forcella* – to almost every crotchet. He thus emphasizes every single note, not only of the melody, but also of the *Nebenstimmen* [subsidiary parts]. The effect this creates, is a sort of constant pumping, in and out. To me, it seems that his little poem 'Wie ich dich liebe', etc., which he wrote in the margin of the score, was the reason why he added those extra expression marks. It feels rather excessive to me, and I think he was probably carried away by his idea of adding a text to the melody. Because he could not in reality have this text, he automatically compensated for its absence by adding extra dynamics and agogics. The melody, however, does not ask for this, it should be pure, simple and *seelenvoll*, like Mendelssohn's melodies, as you mentioned before. What should be respected are the commas – there are no fewer then thirty-two of them! – with which Mahler divides the melody into small segments. They are very often forgotten.

I hasten to say that Mengelberg's recording of the *Adagietto* is tremendous. It sounds much more simple and more to the point than one might expect from reading his score with all the extra expression marks.

DM   All that is required of interpreters is to observe Mahler's own expression marks, but the commas especially. You were quite right to count them up! As you yourself noticed, these commas punctuate the continuity of the long arch of melody into a chain of phrases – communications to a loved one, if you like. (There is certainly no need to try to match the phrases with words!) Yet more importantly, these commas – and the unprecedented number of them – suggest a long line of vocal melody in which Mahler allows for the hypothetical singer to take breath. As you know, Riccardo, for many years now I have argued that the key to interpreting the *Adagietto*, and for that matter to finding the 'right' tempo for it, is to regard the movement as a song. It should move no more slowly than a solo voice might comfortably manage, the singer taking advantage of the 'breaths' that Mahler's thirty-two commas undoubtedly represent; and I stress that these commas are 'breaths' not pauses – a misunderstanding of them as the latter will result only in the unacceptably drawn-out tempo that we want to avoid. The overall continuity of the melody must be sustained. The key word here is punctuation, not pauses. If the commas

are correctly observed, then I believe most of the expressive
work is done for us and we don't need to add Mengelberg's
extra marks, a case of what, in English, we often describe as
'over-egging the pudding'.

RC   Of course, this is Mengelberg's very personal view of the
     *Adagietto*, but obviously he knew that '-etto' means *diminutivo*.
         I would like to add two things about the end of the
     *Adagietto*: from bar 96 Mahler noted '*Drängend*' [*stringendo*],
     which almost everybody translates into its opposite: *rallentando,*
     instead of moving forward. And this is typical of Mahler – an
     anti-conclusion to a *Lied*. It results in a feeling of anxiety, of
     not having reached any conclusion. However, the more you
     indulge in making a *rallentando,* the more you create the feel-
     ing of a conclusion. There *is* no conclusion, I think; and that is
     why Mahler wants the *Rondo-Finale* to follow without a break,
     *attacca*. In short, he merges the two movements: the *Adagietto* –
     which is not concluded – into the *Rondo*.

DM   I should also like, if I may, to add a comment to the very
     significant interpretative point you have just made, Riccardo.
     Just because that *rallentando* has become a kind of performing
     tradition, it has had the unwelcome effect of reinforcing what,
     in my view, is the misleading parallel so often drawn between
     the *Adagietto* and 'Ich bin der Welt abhanden gekommen'. The
     latter song does indeed reach a real conclusion in a sustained
     and very slow coda for orchestra alone, marked by Mahler
     '*verklärt*' [transfigured]. In addition, the whole final section of
     the song is marked '*ohne Steigerung*' [without increase of inten-
     sity], while the tempo marking for the song as a whole is
     '*Äußerst langsam und zurückhaltend*' [Extremely slow and held
     back]. With all these indications in mind, a very slow conclu-
     sion to 'Ich bin der Welt abhanden gekommen' happens as a
     matter of natural course. Compare that with the *Drängend* that
     Mahler demands for the parallel passage in the *Adagietto*, and
     the *contrast* between the worlds these two songs inhabit, for all
     their common stylistic features, is dramatically clarified.

RC  When I conducted the Fifth for the very first time in 1988 in
    Milan, and then, a year later on my farewell concert tour with
    the Radio Symphony Orchestra in Berlin, I remember I was
    tempted to slow down – because the music is so phenomenal
    and intense – instead of moving forward. This tendency to do
    the opposite of what Mahler wanted is too easy and self-
    indulgent.

      And while we are on the subject of fidelity – or otherwise –
    to the text, I am reminded of something else that occurred in
    Berlin, again in 1988. Before the final rehearsal of the Fifth, I
    asked the technician at the Philharmonie to play Mahler's his-
    toric Welte-Mignon piano-roll 'recording' of the *Trauermarsch* –
    we have included it on the CD that accompanies this book –
    to the members of the orchestra. I announced that something
    very special would be 'on air' and asked the players to pay
    special attention to the floating freedom of the pianist's tempo.
    It was to their great surprise, and embarrassment, almost, when
    I told them that the pianist was Gustav Mahler! The degree of
    elasticity he brings to the first movement is truly phenomenal.
    From that historic Welte-Mignon recording, and later too from
    Mengelberg's conducting score, I came to understand more
    about the freedom, tempo-wise, with which Mahler treated his
    text. It is quite different from modern practice. Today we are
    more cautious, too cautious, almost; we approach the text with
    a certain austerity. I feel it is very important to respect the text
    but not to exclude one's own personality when interpreting it.
    Imagination is something different from violation!

      The other point I want to make again involves performance
    practice, though not, this time, tempo; and it returns us to the
    end of the fourth movement, the *Adagietto*. There is a long-
    established German double-bass tradition, to play bars 95–8,
    from the low C of the double-basses where Mahler calls for
    '*viel Ton!*' [much tone!], an octave lower than was actually
    written. This makes the passage darker and gives it a funereal
    timbre. Mengelberg, who had ordered eight Otto double-basses
    (with a fifth string) for the Concertgebouw Orchestra, did not

use the fifth string in this spot in the symphony. Although Mengelberg had these instruments available, in fact he used them only if a composer required them. There is no indication in his score that he played those last four bars an octave lower. The custom of the modern orchestra, to play the C an octave lower, just to make it more dramatic, is a distortion.

DM This again, surely, adds to what we both agree, that these are practices based on a misunderstanding of the character of the song. It makes it too heavy, while the tendency to hold the tempo back at the end of the song instead of pressing forward, even further distorts the *Adagietto*'s character.

RC And now we attack the *Rondo-Finale*. I do not recall another symphonic movement in which you can read the word '*allegro*' four times on one page, more remarkable still, on the first page! I would like to know what you think of this, Donald.

DM Well, Riccardo, you may or may not agree, but by now we have been thoroughly prepared for a complete change of character in the finale of the symphony. The change – the possibility of change – has been effected by means of the *Adagietto*, a radical change of mood and also of orchestral colour, just strings and harp. Mahler has now really prepared us for the final stage in our long journey, for the ultimate affirmation of D major that will round off the whole of this great narrative. The continual repetitions of '*allegro*' – perhaps a matter of psychology as much as anything else? – assert that this is the movement in which a great release of energy will bring the symphony to an end. He is telling the whole orchestra, no fewer than four times, that we are just about to embark on the finale, and that *allegro*, emphatically, is to be the characterizing tempo for the entire movement.

RC That is close to what my feelings are about the finale. The fourth '*allegro*' on this first page is '*giocoso*', which means: 'in a happy mood'. The movement starts with freshness, ingenuity and purity. This '*giocoso*' is so important because it is the extreme opposite of the last bars of the *Adagietto*. To me, it feels like an escape, as if Mahler wants to get rid of the unsettling intensity of mood – *Drängend* – at the end of that movement. At the beginning of the finale he seems to be saying 'this is the happiest moment of my life', and he wants to shout it out from the rooftops. Maybe my interpretation is a little bit like a *romanza* . . .

DM  Not so; we have indeed finally arrived in a completely different world. But without the intervening *Adagietto*, Mahler could never have achieved this crucial moment of breakthrough. Can one imagine the finale following the scherzo without a break? Impossible! The fourfold assertion of '*allegro*' at the beginning of the movement is a kind of verbal fanfare, part of the message Mahler wants to get across that a dramatic change has occurred.

RC  That is true, though even in the finale there are some shadows in his music. But of course, the general mood of the movement is positive. Mahler was happy in the years 1901–1902, when he was working on the symphony. In his monograph on Mahler – *A Musical Physiognomy*, as its subtitle has it – Adorno writes that he could almost do without the finale,[12] perhaps because of the amount of unnecessary quavers running through the movement. Of course I do not agree with him! Without this movement, Mahler could not have ended the symphony. He probably needed the time and the space – and the abundance and continuity of notes – to describe this happy and, for him, almost unknown mood.

DM  There is that famous phrase from Adorno: 'Mahler was a poor yea-sayer.'[13] He could not see – or hear – Mahler as an artist capable of affirming life, and that is why he was so critical of this movement. It was not really a musical judgement, but a pessimistic, politico-ideological judgement with its origins in Adorno's own socio-politico-cultural philosophy. Adorno *had* to say that he did not like the last movement of the Fifth,

12  TWA *Mahler*, p. 137.
13  Ibid.

because Mahler, in other respects – especially the 'pessimistic' Mahler – seemed to support his ideological, socio-political approach. He was obliged to condemn the last movement of the Fifth because it didn't fit his politico-historical mindset.

The really interesting thing – and you put your finger on it – is the *continuity*. Whereas Part I of the symphony is born out of the idea of *dis*continuity, particularly in its second movement, when you get to the finale, everything is continuous. As Paul Banks has pointed out, Haydn might have been an influence on this finale. And Bach too, who without doubt plays a major role in the flowing figuration.

RC  It is all continuity!

DM  Continuity as against discontinuity! The *fugatos,* for example, are all part of that continuity, which counters the discontinuous materials of Part I with its very obverse. Counterpoint remains the basis of this movement, as it has been the basis of the allegro of Part I and the scherzo, but it is an entirely different kind of counterpoint, a continuous counterpoint, instead of the discontinuous web of polyphonic motives we have had in the preceding movements.

RC  I would like to add something about the positive mood of this finale, which is also about the non-stop continuity of the movement. A word, again, not typical in Mahler's music: it is the word '*grazioso*' – it is a 'Haydn' word, a 'Rossinian' word, almost. It is used at bar 100, at bar 191 . . .

DM  These passages you are quoting here are in fact the variations of the *Adagietto* theme, aren't they? These are episodes, incidentally, that for me throw further grave doubt on the theory that the *Adagietto* shares the same world as 'Ich bin der Welt abhanden gekommen'. Can you imagine that if Mahler had had 'Ich bin der Welt abhanden gekommen' in mind as a 'model' for the *Adagietto*, that he would then have transformed it into a '*grazioso*' – exuberant – mood in the course of the finale. That would not have been *spiritually* possible. With the *Adagietto* he was able to do it, because it was, I believe, a kind of love letter.

He could treat it in a gentle and sometimes very witty and elegant way. But it would have been difficult for him to be witty and elegant at the expense of 'Ich bin der Welt abhanden gekommen'.

RC  That is very true; it is the quotation of the *Adagietto* in accelerated motion that we are talking about. The third '*grazioso*' can be found at bar 373, the fourth at bar 606! Astonishing! In none of his other symphonies does he use the word so often.

DM  And what about the chorale?

RC  We arrive at the famous chorale at fig. 32. Alma believed that Mahler should leave chorales to Bruckner. But for me, the appearance of this noble chorale is perfectly timed – emotionally, that is.

DM  I would like to add one point to that. In Part I of the symphony, in the allegro, the second movement, the chorale has mysteriously collapsed. It could not be left hanging in the air, so the chorale *had* to come back in the finale – it would otherwise have been a piece of totally unfinished business. I mean, it would have been like somebody making a speech and then omitting the final paragraph that sums up and brings to a conclusion what the speech has been all about!

RC  In your analysis of the Fifth, you always mention the *raison d'être* in Mahler's music. Without the collapsed chorale in the second movement, there would be no *raison d'être* for it in the finale.

DM  Exactly. If you did not have the chorale at the end of the finale, it would not only deprive the end of the allegro in Part I of its meaning, but also deprive the trios in the *Trauermarsch* of their significance. Each of them aspires to a denouement, of which one gets a hint – a truncated vision – in the allegro. In the finale, the vision is not cut short – it blooms! The logic of it is inescapable. Also, it is a humane chorale, it is not, to my ears, a great celebration of the Godhead; it is not mystical in feeling. It is, as it were, an expression of human joy. And what, *pace* Adorno, is wrong with that, for goodness' sake?

There is one last point I should like to make about the end of the finale. For me, the *ultimate* affirmation of D major even precedes the materialization of the chorale. The passage I have in mind begins at fig. 21, when quite suddenly there is a switch away from counterpoint with 'classical' affiliations and instead we find ourselves in the midst of a luminous web of polyphony, ecstatic in character, with triplets prominent as part of the transfiguration – thus we are reminded of the rhythmic unit that is the very *first* thing we hear in the symphony – which to my ears directly anticipates Mahler's *Spätstil* [late style] that he was to develop in *Das Lied von der Erde* and the Ninth and Tenth Symphonies. For me, as I say, this is the finale's clinching *Höhepunkt* [climax], though I still have to hear a performance that rises to its challenge. And this, Riccardo, seems to me to be a good spot for ourselves to *dis*continue! A good moment to stop because, even while recognizing the formidable array of innovations the symphony introduces, Mahler seems to anticipate here, at fig. 21, the future of his own music as the world came to know it in those late masterpieces I have just mentioned, works that themselves were profoundly to influence the music of the future, the new music of the new century, the end of which we are just about to reach and the beginning of which, as I hope we may have shown, was initiated in Mahler's Fifth.

New Sounds, New Century!

# 'The only Sixth'

*To Claudio Abbado*

~: 1985 :~

'The only Sixth, despite the Pastoral.'
(Alban Berg)

It was during the summer of 1904 that Mahler worked on his Sixth
Symphony, a summer when, Alma Mahler tells us, he was visited by
Alexander von Zemlinsky: 'He revered Mahler as a god and Mahler
got to like him more and more.' (It was Zemlinsky who was to prepare for publication a piano-duet arrangement of the symphony.)

What Alma writes about Mahler's composing in those summer
months suggests that he was much preoccupied with death; and it
is a point to which she gives some emphasis:

> He finished the Sixth Symphony and added three more to the two
> *Kindertotenlieder* . . . [It is probable in fact that Nos. 1, 2 and 5 belong
> to 1901 and Nos. 3 and 4 to 1904.]
> 
> I found this incomprehensible. I can understand setting such
> frightful words to music if one had no children, or had lost those
> one had. Moreover, Friedrich Rückert did not write these harrow-
> ing elegies solely out of his imagination: they were dictated by the
> cruellest loss of his whole life. What I cannot understand is bewail-
> ing the deaths of children, who were in the best of health and
> spirits, hardly an hour after having kissed and fondled them. I
> exclaimed at the time: 'For heaven's sake, don't tempt Providence!'
> 
> The summer was beautiful, serene and happy. Before the holi-
> days came to an end he played me the completed Sixth Symphony.
> I had first to get everything done in the house, so as to have all my

First published as the programme note for Claudio Abbado's performance of Mahler's
Sixth Symphony with the London Symphony Orchestra at the Barbican on 24 October
1985, at the final concert of his LSO series, *Mahler, Vienna and the Twentieth Century*.

Claudio Abbado

time free. Once more we walked arm in arm up to his hut in the wood, where nothing could disturb us. These occasions were always very solemn ones.

After he had drafted the first movement he came down from the wood to tell me he had tried to express me in a theme. 'Whether I've succeeded, I don't know; but you'll have to put up with it.'

This is the great soaring theme [the second subject] of the first movement of the Sixth Symphony. In the third movement he represented the arhythmic games of the two little children, tottering in zigzags over the sand. Ominously, the childish voices became more and more tragic and at the end died out in a whimper. In the last movement he described himself and his downfall or, as he later said, that of his hero: 'It is the hero, on whom fall three blows of fate, the last of which fells him as a tree is felled.' Those were his words.

Not one of his works came so directly from his inmost heart as this. We both wept that day. The music and what it foretold touched us so deeply. The Sixth is the most completely personal of his works, and a prophetic one also. In the *Kindertotenlieder*, as also in the Sixth, he anticipated his own life in music. On him too fell three blows of fate, and the last felled him. But at the time he was serene; he was conscious of the greatness of his work. He was a tree in full leaf and flower.

Mahler's widow writes, as always, vividly and indeed, as often, illuminatingly. But one has to remember that the tone of her recollection was influenced retrospectively by how things turned out in Mahler's life and of course by the impact of the music itself. What if Mahler had been spared the heart disease that killed him? What if Marie, the elder daughter, had not succumbed to scarlet fever and diphtheria in the summer of 1907?

It is tempting but dangerous to draw precise parallels between art and events in an artist's life. Sometimes, naturally, there *are* parallels that it would be grotesque to overlook. Sometimes – perhaps often – coincidence, malign or benign, is at the root of the parallel. However that may be, there is one sentence in Alma's account of the Sixth that exemplifies the curious, often mystifying *non*-synchronization of art and life. 'The summer [of 1904]', she

writes, 'was beautiful, serene and happy', and Mahler himself 'was
serene . . . a tree in full leaf and flower'. The paradox could not be
*more* clearly exposed.

The fact remains, none the less, that death was a recurring image
in Mahler's works; and in the case of the works of his last period –
above all *Das Lied von der Erde* and the Ninth Symphony – we find
art and autobiography inextricably entangled. It would be absurd
here not to perceive a direct relationship between Mahler's consciousness of his own fate – a prediction that the time left to him
was brief – and the character of the music written in the light of
that prediction.

And yet what should concern us is not the fact of an established
interrelationship between a composer's life and his art, but, rather,
what it was the composer succeeded in making of his experience.

So far as *Das Lied* is concerned, we can answer with perfect confidence: a marvellous, self-sufficient and innovatory work of art that
clearly takes account of a profound personal experience and yet at
the same time wholly transforms it. Indeed it is precisely the
inspired reconciliation that Mahler achieves at the end of *Das Lied*
that is of particular interest to us in the context of the Sixth. For
whereas in *Das Lied*, in the context of his *actual* death, diagnosed
and shortly to come, Mahler writes a work that luminously transcends the idea of mortality, in the Sixth, when he was 'serene . . .
conscious of the greatness of his work . . . a tree in full leaf and
flower', he allowed himself, by an *imagined* death, to be felled, to be
defeated. To put it another way, it is the Sixth *alone* among Mahler's
symphonies or song-cycles – in which death triumphs.

In the last period, *Das Lied* transcends death (in C major), the
Ninth is resigned to it (in D flat major), the Tenth achieves some
kind of renewed if fragile reconciliation (in F sharp major); and in
the earlier and middle periods, in Symphony 2, for example,
'Resurrection' (in E flat) triumphs over the C minor of the opening Funeral March, while Symphonies 1, 3 and 4, and 5, 7 and 8, all
end variously but affirmatively in *major* keys, in D, D and E, and in
D, C and E flat. I spell out these details to emphasize the *singularity*
of the Sixth: the fact that the drama, the narrative, unlike all the
other symphonies of Mahler, ends in catastrophe, that the finale,

unlike all the other finales of Mahler, affirms (confirms!) the tonic *minor*.

This is enough, in truth, to single out the Sixth. In many other respects, naturally, it runs true to Mahler's concept of symphonic form, though we may note in passing that it was in the Sixth for the first time that Mahler most nearly approached the format of the 'classical', four-movement symphony.

In one dimension, certainly, the Sixth powerfully adheres to the principles of Mahler's own formal symphonic thinking. I refer to the idea of the 'frame' – two huge outer movements, the first movement and finale enclosing a diverse or contrasted middle; and a feature of the Mahlerian framing method is that the finale resolves the drama, the conflict, that is outlined in the first movement. We find frames almost throughout Mahler's symphonies, not excluding the song-cycles *Kindertotenlieder* and *Das Lied*; and always the musical consequences of the framing method are that the finale develops and elaborates and at length reconciles ideas adumbrated in the first movement. Or to put it another way round, Mahler's first movements are very carefully organized to leave in question the outcome of the inner drama; and it is precisely the business of the finale, both musically and dramatically, to reveal the denouement. The middle movements can bypass the rigour of the narrative argument, providing relaxation, consolation and contrast.

The Sixth offers just such a massive frame. The drama – virtually a life-and-death struggle – is set up in the first movement, *Allegro energico, ma non troppo*, which brilliantly crosses the character and momentum of a march, the remorseless rhythm of which carries all before it, with sonata form. This opening movement (one is almost inclined to write opening act of the drama), with its formal precedents in the Second and Fourth Symphonies, is one of the most 'classical' of Mahler's sonata formulations (he asks for the traditional repeat of the exposition). The duality that the sharp contrast between its first and second subjects reveals – the relentless march (conceived under the shadow of the great *Wunderhorn* marching song, 'Der Tamboursg'sell', composed in August 1901) and ensuing passionately lyrical melody predominantly for strings (the 'portrait' of Alma) – embodies the central conflict as tellingly as does the

work's famous motto, which combines the basic march rhythm
(drums) with a triad (three trumpets) which has hardly affirmed the
tonic major (A major) before it switches to the minor. It is a motto
that is both symbolic and highly functional in its ambivalence.
Which mode is eventually to gain the upper hand? Will the
supposed 'hero' of the symphony – the protagonist – live or die?

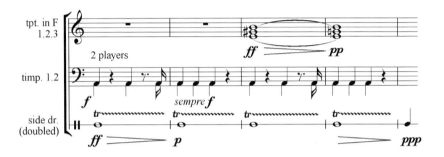

The first movement, as I have suggested, has to leave the drama
open-ended, for which reason in the epilogue or coda it is the lyrical, tumultuously life-affirming second subject (in the context of
the Eighth Symphony Mahler was to refer to Alma as his 'spiritus
creator') which rounds the movement off in a burst of A major.

For the same reason, Mahler also scrupulously avoids quite the
unambiguous concentration on A minor that one might have confidently expected at the crucial moment of recapitulation. Indeed,
there is first a brief revealing of the tonic *major*; and then, when the
pounding first introductory bars of the movement reassert themselves, it is not with pounding As but with pounding Es (a dominant pedal), which creates a certain ambiguity while of course not
really departing from the movement's tonal centre. When the second subject comes, it is in a bright D, the subdominant. It is not
until the end of the coda that the 'Alma' theme achieves and
apotheosizes the tonic major. (The visionary significance of the
cowbells* which have been heard from time to time in this first

---

\* See also 'Dearest Ted', pp. 625–32.

movement I touch on in the context of the andante and finale where they re-emerge.)

The struggle, then, is left in suspense at the end of the first movement, to be resumed in the finale, arguably the greatest of Mahler's finales and built on an epic scale even he did not rival elsewhere. But of course, before the finale picks up the unfinished business of the first movement, we have experienced the middle part of the symphony, which comprises the scherzo and the slow movement.

Mahler was often uncertain about how, precisely, to order the middle movements of his symphonies, and the sixth brings its own tale of indecision and resultant confusion. It is a complex issue, but the main events can be simply outlined. The first published edition of the symphony was ordered allegro – scherzo – andante – finale. But Mahler countermanded this sequence even before the premiere of the work given under his direction at Essen in May 1906, and in fact the premiere reflected the revision, i.e. the *Andante moderato* was placed second and the scherzo third. The second published edition of the full score followed this revised order. Later still, however, Mahler opted for revising the revision, i.e. to revert to the original order where the scherzo was placed second and the andante preceded the finale. We know that for the last performance of the work conducted by Mahler himself in 1907 he returned to this first option; and the *Critical Edition* of the symphony has chosen to establish this as the 'authentic' version.

In fact, as Paul Banks has suggested, and bearing in mind all we know of Mahler's changing attitudes to the middles of his frames, what we are confronted by here is perhaps the unique case of *two* authentic versions of the same symphony, a symphony that can be read (performed) in two ways (as it was indeed by the composer himself). There was, I think, absolutely no *last* word on the subject spoken by Mahler, and conductors in my view should adopt the sequence they themselves find the more convincing.*

When the order allegro – scherzo – andante – finale is adopted,

---

* A view I continue to hold in 2007, when revising this text for its publication here. See also Appendix 1, pp. 633–47, where Gastón Fournier-Facio comprehensively details the history of this debate, including correct details of the 1907 performance (p. 634). [DM]

**WIENER KONZERT-VEREIN.**

FREITAG, DEN 4. JÄNNER 1907

PÜNKTLICH

# AUSSERORDENTLICHES KONZERT

## (NOVITÄTEN-KONZERT)
im
### GROSSEN MUSIKVEREINS-SAALE.

---

### PROGRAMM:

## GUSTAV MAHLER:
Sechste Sinfonie (Tragische).

Allegro energico, ma non troppo.
Andante moderato.
Scherzo.
Finale (Allegro moderato).

Unter Leitung des Komponisten.

---

Viertes Sinfonie-Konzert im Mittwoch-Zyklus
am 16. Jänner 1907, pünktlich 1/2 Uhr abends.
PROGRAMM:

C. W. Gluck . . . . . . . . . . . . . Ouverture zur «Alceste» (mit dem Schluss von Felix Weingartner).
L. van Beethoven . . . . . . . . . . . . Violin-Solo.
Reger . . . . . . . . . . . . . Streichquartett.
(1. Aufführung in Wien.)
P. Tschaikowsky . . . . . . . . . . . . «Romeo und Julia», Phantasie.

Das vierte Sinfonie-Konzert im Dienstag-Zyklus findet am 22. Jänner 1907, pünktlich 1/2 Uhr abends, statt.

=== Dieses Programm unentgeltlich. ===

The concert programme for the Vienna premiere of the Sixth Symphony
on 4 January 1907

we are left in little doubt that the blaze of A major at the end of the first movement is only a temporary remission. The scherzo not only dauntingly reasserts A minor but is also built very conspicuously out of the march materials of the first movement: indeed from the outset the scherzo is projected over the pounding repeated As which generated the march rhythm in the opening movement and also form the drum part of the motto. One of the more extraordinary features of this scherzo is the way in which Mahler maintains the momentum of the march: we can almost imagine that what we are hearing is a march in triple time. Set against this energetic symmetry are two trios which as energetically introduce a constantly changing metre, e.g. 4/8, 3/8, 4/8, 3/8, 4/8 (two bars), 3/8, 4/8, 3/8, and often virtually bar by bar as my list of time signatures suggests. (These trios, Alma has written, 'represented the arhythmic games of our two little children, tottering in zigzags over the sand'.*)

While the scherzo is a kind of pendant to the first movement – the death march as it were redone *in dance form* – the ensuing *Andante moderato* provides the first real stretch of repose and relief. This sublime rondo (in E flat) starts by unfolding the principal melody to which Schoenberg pays special attention in *Style and Idea* (in his essay on Mahler). He points out the extraordinary consequences for the melody of the asymmetrical prolongation of the fourth bar; and indeed if one describes the melody as 'haunting', which it certainly is, the oddity of its construction is partly responsible for that impression. To my ears, though the melody is undeniably reposeful, its asymmetries embody a certain unease, as does its alternating major/minor mode. Perhaps a more genuine and stable point of repose is vouchsafed us in the first episode, when the tonality is uplifted a semitone to E (NB Mahler's 'heavenly' key: cf. Symphony 4!) and the cowbells are heard again. One is naturally, and no doubt intentionally, reminded of the visionary episode with cowbells in the first movement, which provided one of the few

---

\* Alma's memory is at fault. In the summer of 1903, when the scherzo was written, the Mahlers' elder daughter was only eight months old and the younger was not yet born. If there is some truth to the image of children zigzagging across the sand at Maiernigg, then it would have been children other than his own that Mahler had observed.

intimations in that movement of a remote peace beyond earthly and human strife. (The cowbells are three times to play a similar role amid the storms of the finale.)

After the temporary mitigation of the andante, the finale reopens the life-and-death conflict and once again in the shape of an all-engulfing march (*Allegro energico*) drives towards the inescapable denouement. But first a singular feature: the E flat of the andante becomes the C minor of an extensive introduction to the finale which almost constitutes a movement in its own right. Its formal function is to re-establish the link with the first movement, which it does by almost immediately reintroducing the motto and the tonic minor (and again a little later in G major/minor), and to lay out the materials which are to be developed in the gigantic movement that follows. (We note that Mahler does not overlook the visionary deep bells which, with the cowbells, recur throughout the finale and form a symbolic sonorous association with comparable passages in the first movement and andante.) It is precisely the lay-out and character of this introduction which are so fascinating. In atmosphere, if the preceding andante was relatively serene and visionary, and sometimes radiant, the introduction is agitated and nocturnal, but more nightmarish than dreamlike. It is made up of a mosaic of widely contrasting motives, themes and textures, precipitous slides and enormous leaps, shimmering tremolos and fiercely juxtaposed extremes of dynamics, all very freely treated, in the manner of a fantasia. Indeed, this introduction sometimes very closely approaches the quasi-improvisatory Expressionist manner of Schoenberg and Berg. One might think of it almost as an unnumbered *Orchesterstück* by Mahler, interpolated into his symphony. But free though the character may be, it remains the case that one dimension of it is strictly organized, i.e. the events in the first fifteen bars where first we hear the aspiring, ascending theme (over a pedal C, with celesta) which is to play a principal role in the finale and which, in bar 9 *et seq.*, is brilliantly combined with the first return of the motto (over a pedal A). Thus in the first fifteen bars Mahler unambiguously states in primal form the conflict which was left unresolved in the first movement and is now to be resolved.

The finale is virtually a one-movement symphony in itself. (Perhaps one might think of it even as a kind of symphonic poem – Mahler's answer to Strauss's *Death and Transfiguration*, though in the context of the Sixth the title would have had to be *Death and Extinction*.) Once again we encounter a basic sonata scheme, with exposition, development and recapitulation, and once again, as in the first movement, traditional sonata duality is used to embody the central struggle, i.e. contrasting first and second subject groups represent on the one hand the A minor, march- and death-oriented elements and on the other, the aspiring 'life' elements (which in the exposition emerge in D, the subdominant, which performed the same symbolic function in the recapitulation of the first movement).

The recapitulation of the finale is of special interest in this context, since, in order to avoid premature disclosure or confirmation of the inevitable victory of A minor (which in fact is only finally consummated in the last three bars of the symphony), the order of the first (negative) and second (positive) subject groups is *reversed*. This naturally means that the dramatic outcome of the finale is yet further held in suspense, and the re-establishment of the tonic minor postponed. It is another example of how Mahler modified his sonata schemes to serve the overriding *narrative* scheme and is on all fours with the comparable exercise in the recapitulation of the first movement.

Observation of the sonata outline of the finale is certainly important and significant. But perhaps a better perception of the real form of the movement is obtained by forgetting all about sonata form and concentrating on the movement's principal feature, which is a methodically planned series of monumental climaxes, each of which rises to a peak only to be terminated – *contradicted* – by the motto, or comparable, annihilating gesture, whereupon, until we come to the last climax, the process begins all over again. There is a parallel here with the Ninth, the first movement of which is built as surely about its recurring climaxes, disintegrations and re-assemblies as is the finale of the Sixth.

This question of the recurrent aspiring climaxes – often generated by page after page of some of the most extraordinary counterpoint Mahler ever wrote – is tied up with the notorious hammer blows, each of them punctuating a massive climactic point in the development, the first initiating its central section, the second both closing it and marking the beginning of the lead-back to the recapitulation. (The moment of recapitulation cannot be missed because it incorporates the return of the fantasia-like introduction.)

More words, in my view, have been spilled over the hammer blows than their importance justifies. Mahler found difficulty in alighting on the means to produce the muffled (yet reverberating!) *non*-metallic thud he wanted – cannot our electronic technology be pressed into service here? – and was then, we must believe, pursued by doubts about the third hammer blow (which originally initiated the coda) to which he came to attach superstitious significance and at length deleted.

It seems to me to be a moot point whether we should continue to feel obliged to conform to the composer's superstitious fear of the third blow, if indeed it was solely that. But was it? Can we be sure that there were not also purely musical reasons for the omission? For example, there is a telling symmetry about the siting of the two hammer blows at two crucial junctures in the development; and perhaps it could be argued that the absence of a comparable theatrical gesture in the recapitulation makes the denouement all the more powerful, just because of the restraint Mahler exercises. By that I am not suggesting that we are supposed to recognize and admire the *absence* of the pre-existing third blow at the precise spot where one would have previously expected to hear it, which is the somewhat idealistic point of view of some two-hammer-blows enthusiasts, but rather that by the time we experience the recapitulation the musical necessity for a third blow no longer exists.

Indeed, it is my guess that, all question of superstition apart, Mahler took it out because it added nothing to, and perhaps even detracted from, the most chilling, inexorable and obliterating blows of all – the two statements in the coda of the motto, the first a symmetrical reminder of the movement's opening bars and thus of the symphony's basic conflict, the second presenting the absolute end of the affair: a sustained, unrelenting, unyielding A minor triad, the blow which finally extinguishes the drama and the hero's life. We may continue to ponder, long after a performance of the work is over, on the paradox that for Mahler the *imagined* death enacted in the Sixth was the cause of more anxiety and foreboding than the *actuality* of death by which he was later faced and unforgettably transcended in *Das Lied*.

# Mahler on the Move:
# his Seventh Symphony

*To Colin Matthews*

⌐ 2001 ⌐

Is it the case that all great composers turn out to have given birth to a 'problem child' among their works? If so, then there can be little doubt that for Mahler it is the Seventh Symphony that fits the bill. In terms of public reception and affection – and, indeed comprehension – it has to be conceded that the Seventh has remained something of an enigma, though in fact the critical reception it was given at its premiere in Prague, in 1908, was generally positive, even enthusiastic. It was later performances elsewhere that seemed to arouse patent bewilderment, scepticism and hostility. However, although the Vienna premiere was not conducted by Mahler himself, it prompted a letter to him from Arnold Schoenberg who, up to this point, had been notably reserved in his response to Mahler's music. This, oddly, was contrary to the almost unbounded respect and admiration Schoenberg's own pupils – among them Berg, Webern and Erwin Stein – had for Mahler, the man and his works.

I have often wondered how it was that the conservative composer who was Schoenberg co-existed with the radical composer of the same name. Was it the *radical* Mahler who, for an appreciable period, Schoenberg found problematic? Whatever the reason for the paradox, the moment came when, by way of a much earlier positive impression (in 1904) of the Third Symphony, the younger composer's doubts, for the first time, were altogether stilled. The work that finally precipitated a dramatic change in attitude was the

First published as a liner note for the recording of Mahler's Symphony No. 7 by the Berlin Philharmonic Orchestra conducted by Claudio Abbado and issued in a special edition by the Salzburg Easter Festival, 2002.

Seventh. This is how the letter of 29 December 1909 – it has since become famous – ended:

> As for which movement I liked best: All of them! I cannot prefer any one to the others. Perhaps I was rather indifferent at the beginning of the first movement. But anyway only for a short time. And from then on steadily warming to it. From minute to minute I felt happier and warmer. And it did not let go of me for a single moment. In the mood right to the end. And everything struck me as pellucid. Finally, at the first hearing I perceived so many formal subtleties, while always able to follow a main line. It was an extraordinarily great treat. I simply cannot understand how I was not won over to this before.

Schoenberg's 'conversion', and that it was the Seventh that specifically activated it, has proved to be of historic significance. For here, surely, we have the 'radical' Schoenberg – and by 1909, the date of his letter, Schoenberg had already embarked on his revolutionary Expressionist period (*Erwartung*, for example, was composed in the same year) – reacting to a symphony that, as time has shown, has to be counted among Mahler's most radical and still provocative works.

What Schoenberg would have heard in Mahler's Seventh at its Vienna premiere in 1909, after which he wrote his letter to Mahler – and while Mahler succeeded in completing his work in the summer of 1905, its premiere was not given in Prague until September 1908 – was a preoccupation with the potentialities of the fourth, an interval deployed both vertically (superimposed fourths) and horizontally (in linear sequence). Schoenberg must have reflected on his own parallel preoccupation with the same interval in his first Chamber Symphony, Op. 9, composed in 1906: the ascending sequence of fourths proclaimed by the horn in its opening bars has endured as a famous manifestation of the new language for music that both Mahler and Schoenberg were in the process of creating. It is the fourth that unmistakably colours the sound of the Seventh's first movement, lending it a new, spare sonority that was to become one of the new century's most distinctive features. All the more appropriate then that at the stormy reception that greeted the premiere of Schoenberg's Chamber Symphony in Vienna in 1906 Mahler himself was highly visible and audible, defending his younger colleague's right to be heard. Who knows, perhaps he even reflected ironically on the fact that his own marshalling of fourths as yet remained unheard? Perhaps both composers shared more common ground at this specific moment in time than they had supposed.

Today, at the beginning of the twenty-first century, it has become virtually received opinion that the Seventh represents Mahler at his most 'modern', as one of the prime makers of the 'new' music that was to startle the world post-1900; and I have no doubt that it was the then novel presence of the fourth that suggested to listeners that the old euphony was on the brink of abandonment; add to that the peculiarly shrill and piercing character of Mahler's instrumentation of the first movement, for the woodwind especially, and it is scarcely surprising that the symphony's problematic reputation has persisted.

I would not wish for a moment to underrate the challenge but euphony had by no means been abolished, nor had tonality: the *Allegro risoluto* of the first movement powerfully establishes E minor as its tonic. As for euphony, one need seek no further than the eruption of the passionate second subject – think too of the second subject in the first movement of the Sixth! – in which Mahler instructs his players to release the surging melody with maximum momentum, 'Mit grossem Schwung'. An exceptional moment, not only the melody but also its tonality, a swamping C major; this departure from the 'classical' convention Mahler makes good in the development by reintroducing the second subject in the 'conventional' dominant, B major. While one of its functions is to restore the displaced 'classical' symmetry – we now have the second subject in the dominant – another is to mitigate the impact of the daunting B *minor* which opens the symphony.

This is another moment, the sheer beauty of which – its euphony! – must have raised the spirits of those who thought Mahler was advancing too swiftly into hitherto uncharted territories. He himself made sure no one could overlook the sublime modulation to B major by having its onset accompanied by *fortissimo arpeggios* on the harps; rather amusingly, perhaps, there was scarcely a critic at the premiere who did not praise this one bar's effulgence (bar 317). Here at least critical opinion was unanimous and positive.

One of the most remarkable aspects of this episode dedicated to transformation is the metamorphosis undergone by the materials of an intruding miniature slow march – march motive plus march rhythm in E minor! – we have already heard in the movement's spectacular B minor introduction, where, in typical Mahler fashion, it marches *across* the grand, sombre march that constitutes the first movement. The materials of that intrusive march now appear in the guise of a hushed quasi-chorale, distributed among different sections of the orchestra and, no less importantly, *combined* with the insistent repeated rhythm of the introduction which the intruder originally disrupted.

To be sure, fourths too remain a presence, but they are, so to say, pacified, subjected to the same radiant transforming process as all the other constituents that go to make up this part of the movement's development. (The whole passage is to be found between bars 298 and 337 in the orchestral score.)

Mahler, as we know, was a great traveller, musically speaking, and the idea of narrative was absolutely basic to his formal thinking: we depart at the beginning of one of the symphonies and arrive at our destination only at the end of its finale. Even in his early works there is an identifiable kind of 'travelling' music. Think, for example, of the timpani ostinato, heard at the start of *Das klagende Lied* (Part I of the original three-part version), or the animated, 'walking' melody to which the protagonist of the *Lieder eines fahrenden Gesellen* sets out on his journeying in the cycle's second song, an ostinato that resurfaces in the First Symphony and eventually leads us to the symphony's conclusion, somewhere very different from its point of departure. In between there has been a wealth of experience. Can we make an approach to the Seventh that takes these 'travelling' precedents into account?

I believe we can. Indeed, I believe that one of the reasons why Mahler had so much difficulty in completing the work's composition had something to do with the absence of what for him was indispensable: the idea (or ideas) that would initiate an ensuing journey. It is worth remembering that Mahler was in person a keen 'traveller', in particular a tireless walker. More specific to our purpose, when he came to compose his Seventh he was living in a villa on the Wörthersee, to reach which he sometimes had to be rowed across the lake. It was precisely this homeward-bound journey that proved to have such momentous consequences for the composition of the Seventh; indeed, it facilitated its completion. Two of the three middle movements, the two nocturnes, each to be entitled *Nachtmusik* by Mahler, had in fact been composed at Maiernigg during the summer of 1904; it was in that same summer that he also completed the *Kindertotenlieder* cycle and the Sixth Symphony. It was not, however, until the summer of the next year, 1905, that in an extraordinary eruption of creativity he finished work on the Seventh. Fascinatingly, it was the trip across the lake, and specifically the rhythm of the oars, that – in Mahler's own words in a letter to Alma – enabled him to overcome the block that had prevented him from finishing the symphony:

> I got into the boat to be rowed across. At the first stroke of the oars the theme (or rather the rhythm and character) of the introduction to the first movement came into my head – and in four weeks the first, third and fifth movements were done!

Thus it was that the new symphony came – almost literally – to be launched by a cross-lake trip. What I want to suggest is that the pronounced rhythm that opens the movement was also the beginning of a typical Mahlerian journey through a nocturnal landscape, punctuated by the shrieks and screams of nightbirds, the lowing and baying of cattle (the solo for tenor horn), and here and there watery noises: Mahler in his manuscript refers at one stage to a *pizzicato* passage (lower strings) generated, it seems, by the sound of stones as they 'plop in the water' ('*Steine* pumpeln ins Wasser').

For a long time it seemed to me that this extraordinary first movement depicted a nocturnal landscape – is it not in itself a *Nachtmusik* built on a gigantic scale? – inhabited by birds and beasts

The jetty at Krumpendorf looking across the Wörthersee. Mahler's villa is the large house on the far side of the lake in the centre.

and the forces of Nature but with humankind not much in evidence ('Die Welt schläft ein' ('The world falls asleep'), as Mahler has it in *Das Lied*). Now, however, with what we know of the inception of the introduction – Mahler himself *on the move* across the lake – I hear the movement afresh, first as the onset of a journey, and secondly as a graphic document of a nocturnal though not exclusively natural world. There *is* a human being at the centre of all of this, Mahler himself embarking and disembarking and then *continuing* his journey through the medium of his unique imagination. But it was a journey, we must remember, that got the symphony under way, and even more importantly the sombre, throbbing, drenched-in-darkness rhythm that we hear in the first movement's first bars, persists throughout the movement. It is a continuous, pervading presence, a later form of 'travelling music', reminding us that along with the composer we are in progress towards an unknown, undeclared destination. With hindsight we may well consider that the C major in which the sweeping second subject is first revealed is an anticipation of a distant goal yet to be achieved; furthermore, it is a melody that, albeit only temporarily, seems to run counter to the prevailing sombreness of spirit and landscape, and to have its roots in human passion. But while that surge of feeling, and its later sublime transformation in the new B major context that I have already mentioned, can be related meaningfully to the symphony's journeying protagonist, we have to note also how the melody itself, or motives drawn from it, are subjected to frequent distortion, if not indeed contortion. Nothing it seems is plain sailing.

For a moment I want to stick with the travelling idea, in fact with the concept of music that is itself constantly *on the move*; and there is no genre of music that is more self-evidently an image of motion, of mobility, than that of the march. It is true that the opening rhythm – the steady propulsion of the oars – runs like a thread throughout the first movement. But what that basic rhythmic idea leads into, though it is never lost sight of, never suppressed, is a monumental march-like allegro, a kind of complement to the first movement of the Sixth. In the Seventh the principal march theme and its associated materials likewise generate immense thrust and tension but of a quite distinctive character: those superimposed fourths create a gaunt, austere, unyielding soundworld of their own. And while, again like the Sixth, the Seventh's first movement ends (briefly) in the tonic *major*, E major, and without departing from the motives of the main march, the major mode is not charged with the intensity of the exuberant A major that rounds off the first movement of the Sixth. There the switch from minor to major, plus the fact that it is with a recall of the second subject that the tonic major is affirmed, makes an impact that, at least in retrospect, is seen to be intimately bound up with the work's overall narrative, its interior drama: which mode is it that will win out and bring with it the resolution of the symphony, victory or defeat? In the case of the Seventh, and on the basis of the first movement alone, it would be hard to predict what the work's eventual goal might be; and it is precisely at this point that we have to remind ourselves that when Mahler, in 1905, was completing movements 1, 3 and 5, the two

nocturnes, movements 2 and 4, were already composed and therefore inevitably influencing how, now the great journey had been
embarked upon, it was to continue. There is not of course a strict
parallel here between the process by which Mahler composed the
first three movements of his Fourth to culminate in an already
existing finale, 'Das himmlische Leben'. But he could hardly have
been unaware that at least some of the strategies involved were
similar.

I have mentioned earlier that the C major that inaugurates the
first appearance of the second subject of the first movement might
well, in retrospect, be regarded as a possible goal towards which the
symphony is moving. Was it this that Mahler had in mind when
composing his first movement? Because the first *Nachtmusik*, in its
own inimitable way, significantly spotlights the importance of C
(both major and minor: neither is given precedence) and sustains
the momentum of the first movement through its deployment of
new varieties and genres of march music. In short, the journey is
*resumed*.

In this first *Nachtmusik*, however, he has forsaken boat and oars
and the epic gestures of the first movement's march, where Mahler
was traversing the universe at night, and taken to the streets. What
confronts us now is a kind of domesticated military march music,
humble in scale, that an evening stroll through a town or city might
provide, not only march music but (in the trios) genial, serenade-
like tunes more appropriate to a Stadtpark than a regimental parade
ground. What is quite peculiar, however, and peculiar to the
Seventh, is the startling incorporation into the movement of the
shrill sounds of Nature that we thought we had left behind in the
first movement. On the contrary, after a few bars' articulation of
march motives and rhythms (horn solos) we are deluged by a torrential cadenza of birdsong for the woodwind, heralding the
appearance of the first march section proper; we note too that the
cadenza is cut short by a loud C major triad (horns and trumpets)
switching without a pause to the minor, the very motif that encapsulates the drama of the Sixth Symphony. (The issue of 'quotation',
yet another feature of the Seventh, turns up in relation to the finale.
I shall come back to it.)

There are other unforeseen events still to come. The birdsong cadenzas are singular enough; odder, surreal even, are the weird interpolations of cowbells, first heard at a far distance, the second time as part of a quite dense orchestral texture. At their first appearance, remote and mysterious, the chimes fall on the ear like sounds almost from another planet. The effect is startling, the summoning up of a *location* unimaginably distant from the materials that make up the rest of the movement. How does one relate to it, make sense of it? (One has had cowbells before in Mahler when, however, the context has been defined and provided a bridge to their reception.) The contrast between the cadenzas of bird cries and the sometimes humdrum character of the marches could not be sharper; and as this symphony progresses one may well come to conclude that contrast, contradiction, discontinuity, paradox and a manifest illogic are among its prime compositional tactics. In any event the march finds it difficult to sustain its own ideal of a comfortable stroll through everyday life: it never succeeds in making up its mind whether to commit itself to the major or minor mode of C. The consequent ambiguity is maintained virtually for the entire movement.

We have already heard in the first movement how often Mahler subjects his materials to subversive distortion. So it should not surprise us too much that Mahler himself undermines any disposition on the part of the march to become too cosy, too comfortable, too bourgeois. There is the extraordinary passage mid-movement where a continuation of the march tune finds itself contrapuntally combined with the busy triplets of the birdsong. How has this happened, one wonders? Have the birds joined the band? Yet more significant and unsettling are those unforgettable if brief moments when the principal march section loses its narrative drive, textural coherence and tonal direction and collapses – fragments – into short motives distributed among a handful of instruments, each one of which is allotted its own dynamic. A mosaic of dynamics is the result, along with a collage of dissected motives. One wonders, inevitably, where exactly we are being led.

As it turns out, to the lowest point of morale and optimism in the whole symphony, the scherzo, though it is certainly not a low point in terms of energy and mobility. Another instance this, of the paradoxes in which this work is so rich. The mobility that has characterized the first movement and first *Nachtmusik* is still an overt presence, but for the duration of the scherzo it is as if journeying has been suspended while we witness – or do we participate in it? – what is perhaps the most enigmatic of Mahler's scherzos, a wild dance, in a relentless D minor, for which he ordains 'Schattenhaft' ('Shadowy') as the principal feature of its characterization. This is a dance indeed from which the warmth of life has been almost entirely drained. Not even the trio offers significant relief, though it does vouchsafe almost the only – and brief – instance of extended melody. For the rest, the scherzo is compounded of a multitude of short themes and motives projected by an orchestra quite differently constituted from that which serves the first movement or the first *Nachtmusik*. Textures are gaunt and spare – it is rare that we encounter a tutti – and the instrumentation consistently shriller. 'Kreischend' ('screechingly') is what Mahler calls for in one spot from his oboes,[*] and it might well serve as a description of the spectral dance which this scherzo enacts.

There is not much to make a retrospective bridge to what we have experienced in the previous movements. However, the scherzo's ceaseless triplet motion, on which Mahler depends for the creation of his 'shadows', inevitably re-invokes the triplets of the preceding *Nachtmusik*, despite a different metre and dramatic context. My last point is this: the exceptional diversity of the dynamics in the scherzo is of a sophistication rarely equalled elsewhere in Mahler's symphonies.

That final stroke on the timpani (hard stick, quickly smothered) at the end of the scherzo could well be read – heard – as an indication of an end to travelling. The cessation of mobility has left us in a landscape peopled by ghosts. If the narrative is to resume, the only option is to pursue another direction.

In this sense I believe the second *Nachtmusik* (F major), marked, most unusually for Mahler, *Andante amoroso*, embarks on what should be understood as an ascent, an ascent *out* of the desolation to which the scherzo has reduced us. As Mahler himself seems to

---

[*] Bar 54ff.

suggest in his marking, human love and desire could now form part of the imagery that this symphony intends to explore. Not just the idea of love but possibly even an image of lovers and their discourse. This could be not only an amorous episode but one that makes love manifest; and Mahler seems to have been at pains to emphasize this dimension by incorporating instruments traditionally associated with serenading, not only the guitar but also a mandolin (an afterthought of Mahler's), while it is a solo violin that has an important role to play in the very first bar.

The scene, then, seems to be set for a nocturnal, romantic episode for which Mahler outwardly at least had prepared familiar ground. But like everything else in this symphony, though the trappings and furnishings of romanticism are in place, and expectations raised, what in the event we actually come to experience is not only far removed from convention but more often than not contradicts it or hangs a question mark over it, as if Mahler were asking of himself, and thence of ourselves, his audience, whether serenading, as it has been conducted in the past, is any longer meaningful. It is just another example of the serious questions about music itself – its past history, its present and its future – which Mahler continually raises as his symphony evolves. In the first movement, for instance, can the sweeping passion of the second subject still convince at the beginning of the twentieth century? Mahler subjects it to all kinds of sceptical tests, and finally – in B major – yes, he suggests, it can. And the curious march that comprises the first *Nachtmusik*? Where is it located? Town, countryside, outer space? Why does the march keep on collapsing, disintegrating? Where is it going? And then the sheer nihilism of the scherzo. Where does that leave us?

In the second *Nachtmusik*, interestingly, the concept of movement, of mobility, fundamental to the entire symphony, still remains potent. In fact after the miniature three-bar introduction which Mahler marks 'Mit Aufschwung' ('With impetus'), so he clearly wants to get the movement on the move, the 'serenade' begins, delivered over a characteristic harp ostinato, characteristic, that is, of Mahler's 'travelling' mode. We are, it seems, clearly at the beginning of yet another journey. Moreover, this is an andante that has been imagined in 2/4, not 4/4, which in turn suggests a tempo that should move along, on the slow side, undeniably, but certainly never lapse into lethargy. A serenade this may be, but if there is a protagonist then he or she or both are out for a stroll, leisurely perhaps, but with a defined sense of propulsion. This is clear above all in the syncopated figuration that we hear at once from the clarinets and oboes, in addition to which the horn's contribution clearly articulates a quasi-*march* motive and rhythm. In short, this is highly *active* music, asserting mobility not dawdling or dreams. And where, one almost immediately asks oneself, is the musical feature that is most directly associated with the strumming of guitar and mandolin? Where is the serenade itself, the irresistible tune, the immediately memorable, singable melody? The answer is, it isn't. In fact, the first time anything like an extended melody surfaces is midway through the movement in what functions as the movement's trio, and which, as it develops begins to speak with what we may care to identify as the accents of human passion: 'love' has made a late entry on the scene, but in a guise still pretty far removed from the familiar world of the serenade.

The recapitulation of the movement, if it is meaningful to think in such terms, is preceded by a restatement of the movement's initiating three bars, to which I now return. These proffer one of the most arresting and provocative ideas in the whole symphony. Who had ever before thought of opening a movement with a cadence that would normally close it? The cadence recurs throughout the movement, like a miniature ritornello, sometimes repeated, sometimes compressed with a degree of the descending scale omitted to strange foreshortening effect, sometimes tripping over itself, as if the ensemble were momentarily in disarray. Most important of all, while often signifying closure, it opens out at the end of the first section into a new rhythmic and chromaticized version of itself which, with ever expanding chromatic infiltration and increasing dynamics – piled up crescendi – comes to dominate the recapitulation.

This is some of the most powerful music in the movement, instinct with an agitated passion, constantly punctuated, the short phrases of which (rooted in the initiating cadence but now transformed) convey the breathlessness of a passion that is never to be fulfilled. On the contrary at the height of the climax the 'travelling' march tune is proclaimed and resumed and leads us into the coda, through which float fragments of many of the principal motives and rhythms we have heard on this strange journey, including vestiges of the cadence that set the whole thing in motion. One wonders if, from one point of view, part of Mahler's strategy was to see how much meaning and material could still be got out of a traditionally conceived cadence, hence the role allotted it in those unforgettable first bars. Calm is certainly restored and the journey ends in a bout of magical scoring which is exceeded only by the orchestral coda to 'Von der Schönheit' in *Das Lied von der Erde*. But the 'serenade' – if it was ever Mahler's intention to write one – has never materialized. Perhaps the opening cadence is, in fact, how the 'serenade' that we have never heard, *ended*? Or is this too paradoxical and ironic a gesture even for Mahler?

It was widely reported at the rehearsals in Prague in 1908 that when Mahler came to the finale he would remark 'And now for daylight [Der Tag]', or words to that effect. A pity that we have no information about his tone of voice or how he looked when he spoke – smiling, sceptical, stern? But there can be little doubt that on reaching the end of the epic journey through the night we find ourselves somewhere quite other from where we set out: darkness has given way to light.

In general, at the premiere, the finale was received with enthusiasm; it was thought to round off in an appropriately affirmative style what had been a sometimes puzzling and sometimes impenetrable narrative. The two nocturnes had offered some relief but there was need now for a resolution!

C major, of course, has long been hinted at *en route* as a possible goal – some have argued strongly for recognition of its status as an alternative tonic – and Mahler takes care to spell out that it is indeed C major that is to engulf us by making at the very beginning of his finale an undisguised reference to Wagner – a quote, almost – and specifically the music in Act III of his *Meistersinger* where darkness gives way to light: it is a transformation celebrated in the opera in a tumultuous C major. It is this music that forms the basis of Wagner's prelude and that Mahler was perfectly conscious of what he was doing is revealed by his including the *Meistersinger* Prelude in all the performances of the Seventh he conducted himself, in Munich, in The Hague and Amsterdam (twice). There would have been few among the work's audiences on those occasions who did not recognize the 'quote' and its association with – its glorification of – C major.

Throughout the Seventh we hear an astonishing number of contrasting musical genres, forms and styles which cumulatively, I want to suggest, represents a compositional journey through music – past, present, and (as we now come to realize) future – with Mahler, from his vantage point in the first decade of the twentieth century, acting as guide, commentator, and above all contributor to the history of which he himself had already formed a vital part (think of the 'modernity' of the Seventh's first movement). It is in this perspective that I believe we should approach the finale, the movement that has long remained an insoluble problem for many Mahlerians.

The idea of the march, as we know, has been a predominant influence throughout the work from its first bar and so it is scarcely surprising that the march, and its generating mobility, should be deployed yet again in the finale; and it is with a very grand march gesture that it opens. But as the movement proceeds, each stage of which is marked by a repeat of the initiating flourish, it becomes clear that what Mahler is doing is exactly what he has done in every other preceding movement: setting up an image, a convention, a context, and then testing it, to discover if it still has something to say to us, can still generate meaningful music.

In this sense, the finale not only sustains the probing spirit that is basic to the Seventh's aesthetic but also the protagonist's journeying. Unexpectedly often, at least for those who keep an ear focused on Mahler's bass lines, those ostinatos which I have identified as Mahler's 'travelling' music, can be found in the finale as elsewhere in the symphony. Their symbolic significance should not be underestimated. The journey is still in train.

Where in fact are we being led? The pomp and circumstance of the initiating ritornello over – it is as if Mahler needed Wagner's precedent to sanction so triumphalist a revival of C – we find ourselves exploring entirely different musical territories. The contrasting sections which alternate with the repeats of the ritornello are often as intimate and refined in texture as the ritornello is public and noisy. We hear reminiscences of past history – minuet-like passages marked *Grazioso* – quotes from eminent predecessors, not just from Wagner but Mozart too. How else can we respond to the 'Turkish' music that suddenly erupts, except by reference to Mozart's *Entführung*? Or are we to suppose that this is something our traveller hears on the street, much, one supposes, as Mozart may have heard it himself? There is self-quotation, too, for example those almost comically exaggerated glissandi for the strings: was Mahler remembering looking back (Eastwards again?) to his early years in Hungary where string glissandi were part of the soundscape?*

Large stretches of the musics Mahler compiles – my plural is deliberate – are conspicuously diatonic, a startling switch after the complex harmonic textures of the first four movements. A further contrast resides in their chamber-like texture and generally subdued dynamics. On the other hand what fascinatingly and unpredictably emerges in these episodes by way of contrast are ceaseless rhythmic dislocations and abrupt changes in tempo. To be sure, the idea of the march, so vigorously launched by the ritornello, continues to be a presence but it is a march far removed from the monumental character of the first movement or the subtle ironies of the first *Nachtmusik*. We are led, it seems to me, on a journey in which we encounter or overhear much music that strikes a new note, exploits a new vein, in Mahler.

The only words that I can find to describe the new musical territory through which we pass are 'a condition of innocence', and often very beautiful, benign and even gently humorous this state proves to be; it also perhaps counters – even subverts – the pretensions of the ritornello which keeps on interrupting the peculiar idyll that pursues its arhythmic, asymmetrical trail between one ritornello and the next.

Mahler has given us a clue to what is to be the eventual outcome in the very first two bars of the drum solo that opens the

---

\*   See also 'Mahler's Hungarian Glissando', pp. 125–30.

finale, pitches that outline the E minor triad before C major engulfs us. Thus Mahler juxtaposes the two 'alternative' tonics, leaving open at this stage the question of which is to triumph. However, at the climax of the movement, when intense pressure has accumulated, pressure, that is, to resolve the narrative, to terminate the journey, Mahler returns to the cyclic procedure that he had so often deployed in his past finales. The great march from the first move-ment is rediscovered, thereby transporting us back across acres of music and diverse experiences to one of the principal inspirations involved in getting the whole operation off the ground: the initi-ating march, itself a prime symbol of the mobility that underpins the Seventh from beginning to end. But we are not returned to E minor. It is in fact in *C minor* that the great march re-enters the scene, a moment of high drama and a tonal move that assaults the reality of the C major of the ritornello or at least hangs a huge question mark over it. There is something particularly arresting about Mahler's sketch for this precise moment of cyclic recapitula-tion, where he inscribes 'C-moll' ('C minor') above the passage in question. The inscription amounts almost to living proof of how acutely aware he was himself of the significance of the transposition.

Although it is true that the work is finally brought to an end in C, it is a C, in the light of that momentous C minor intervention, that we now hear differently, a response that inevitably incorporates elements of doubt and uncertainty. Mahler himself so to speak keeps sitting on the fence to the very last: even in the penultimate bar of the finale he introduces a vertiginous pause on an augmented triad that keeps us in suspense until the ultimate chord resounds.

What for me sounds a note of genuine triumph is less the final assertion of a C major that has had to bear a heavy load of scrutiny but Mahler's marvellous exploitation of bells, not only conventional orchestral bells but cowbells too, which forms part of the finale's rounding off. If I were asked to identify the point in the symphony when Mahler's journeying has taken him to an isolation and remote-ness beyond which it is not possible to proceed, it would have to be that extraordinary passage in the first *Nachtmusik* where the cowbells are heard at a vast distance. One seems to stand on the brink of an experience for which one has available no means of interpretation. It is inevitable that one should recall that moment when, in the finale, cowbells join with the orchestral bells to create a marvellous torrent of festive joy, reminding us that there may still be something to celebrate about mankind's capacity to survive, and make sense of, one of the most audacious of its travels through music, history, nature, space and time.

Questions naturally remain. How could it be otherwise with a symphony in which it was the composer's intention to question past certainties and to emphasize contrast, contradiction, dislocation and discontinuity, characteristics prominent in virtually whichever parameter of the work one cares to examine? The truth is, I believe, that if 'resolution' still stays with us as a problem, it was a problem brilliantly created by Mahler but not solved by him; it proved incapable of solution. If a 'defeat' of some sort in this symphony has to be conceded, it was a case of Mahler defeating himself. His journeying eventually took him beyond reach of resolution or conciliation. However, we can only begin to comprehend the Seventh if we first understand that the 'problem' was a conscious product of the unprecedented aesthetic that produced the symphony.

A last word: Mahler's Seventh would for a long time have remained a closed book to me if it had not been for all I have learned from Claudio Abbado's inspired and groundbreaking performances of the work in the concert hall and on disc. I salute him.

# Mahler's Seventh: A Dialogue with Bernard Haitink

## ⌐ 1994 ⌐

DONALD MITCHELL   Do you think that it is indeed important to publish the facsimile of the Mahler Seventh? There is something very magical about the history of the manuscript, and the way it has survived all these years, including the wartime years, is really astonishing. What do you think it might tell us that we don't already know, say, from the published version?

BERNARD HAITINK   The fact that Mahler's own handwriting will now be accessible to many people I find a wonderful idea. For me there is the emotional or sentimental fact that the manuscript which was in a safe in Amsterdam all those years, the only manuscript left in Amsterdam, will now be generally accessible. Mahler did so much for Amsterdam and the Netherlands, while later, in New York, Mengelberg was to do so much for Mahler. For me it is a very emotional thing, for many reasons. I was in the Netherlands during the Occupation, growing up in the midst of it, and then, after the Occupation, the Mahler revival started, cautiously. I remember Bruno Walter doing the Fourth Symphony and Van Beinum doing *Das Lied von der Erde* and the Sixth and Seventh Symphonies. Personally, I have a penchant for the Seventh. I know that it is often said to be one of the least successful, but I love and admire the Seventh, including the last movement. I think the finale is a fantastic piece, a kind of Mahlerian 'Symphonie fantastique'. And it is wonderful that now, for the 1995 Mahler Festival, the manuscript is to be published.

A conversation between Donald Mitchell and Bernard Haitink, recorded in London on 20 December 1994, and first published in the 1995 facsimile edition of Mahler's Seventh Symphony with a commentary by Donald Mitchell and Edward R. Reilly.

DM  It seems absolutely incontrovertible that the Seventh, for whatever reasons, has been the Cinderella among the Mahler symphonies. It really is almost the last symphony to have won any
kind of public esteem or popularity. Why do you think that was?

BH  First of all I think that shortly after the Second World War the
Sixth and the Seventh were more or less the stepchildren
among Mahler's symphonies, very rarely performed, not only
in Amsterdam, but also here in Britain. Mahler came late to
performances in Britain. Even in the 1970s, when I started
with the London Philharmonic, one had half-empty halls for a
Mahler symphony. And I think that, for me, the Sixth and the
Seventh Symphonies with the Ninth, are the most 'naked'
Mahler, the essential Mahler, lacking though they are the
immediate beauty of the songs. I love the songs above everything Mahler wrote; the *Wunderhorn* songs and the Rückert
songs are so wonderful. But they are very easily accessible, and
the Sixth, the Seventh and the Ninth, apart from that symphony's last movement, are very difficult to understand for the
general public. I think that conductors and performers were
always a bit worried, and it certainly took me a very long time
to get my teeth into these pieces. I admire the Sixth enormously; I value the Sixth more than the Second, to be honest.
I love the Second, of course, because it is such a fantastic piece,
with all those moving and theatrical effects at the end. But the
Sixth is such an honest symphonic structure and so typical of
Mahler in all his bitterness and aggressiveness, and not less in
the strange cool-warmth – if the contradiction may be forgiven – of the slow movement. The Seventh is much more of
a kaleidoscope, I think. It has so many different aspects and is
a piece which will always haunt me. I love the *Nachtmusiken* –
the second and the fourth movements – but it is the only work
of all Mahler's oeuvre that you could not do in a classic way.
No, you have to go through the whole shooting match of the
introduction to the first movement with the wonderful tenor
horn solo, and then through all the tribulations of the ensuing
allegro. The last movement also reveals this festive – again
kaleidoscopic – idea. It makes a wonderful conclusion.

Bernard Haitink in rehearsal with the Royal Concertgebouw Orchestra in 1975

DM  I would like to ask you about the early reception of it, the early performances in Prague and Munich, the performances Mahler conducted in the Netherlands, and then of course the performance in Vienna too, which Mahler didn't conduct himself, but which Ferdinand Löwe conducted. One curious consequence of that first Vienna performance, which, needless to add, got pretty awful reviews from the Viennese critics, was Schoenberg's conversion to Mahler. All his previous doubts about Mahler were finally removed by his experience of the Seventh.

BH  I am not surprised! You already feel Schoenberg hanging in the air. Listen to the first movement of the Ninth Symphony, especially at the pinnacle in the midst of those terrifying trombones. Apocalypse: that is typical Schoenberg already. And I think the Ninth is a work which – in that respect – indicates Schoenberg's future development. The Sixth starts to remind me of Alban Berg, especially the finale. I think the whole of the so-called Second Viennese School is already anticipated there.

DM  I have collected and we are going to publish in this edition of the facsimile some of the early reviews of the Seventh. They are fascinating because they also give one some idea of the difficulties that Mahler must have faced with the orchestras, particularly when conducting the Czech Philharmonic, which was not of the same calibre as, say, the Vienna Philharmonic in those days. There are some very vivid accounts of Mahler rehearsing the work in Prague.

BH  Let's also talk about the critics. How could they understand such a symphony? It was totally new for them. It is very easy, when you hear a thing for the first time, to say that you don't like it, that it is no good. It takes such a long time to know a piece really well. I don't want to be unnecessarily modest, but I am realistic. It took me years and years and years to work on these symphonies, to understand them and to perform them well. And I still find it very difficult. Perhaps even Mahler himself struggled with these works. We know from hearsay that he was a wonderful conductor. Still, how did a man with a very unpredictable temperament, confronted with his own work, perform with an orchestra when there was this terrible anti-pathy to his music – this anti-Semitism, even – in Vienna? I think all these things have to be taken into account. Every period has its reviewers, its critics. But I wonder what the performances were like at that time; I wonder how orchestras played these very complex works for the first time. I argued this question with a good friend of mine after a performance of a Mahler symphony where something inadvertent happened in the brass. I said, 'Listen, I have been conducting Mahler symphonies for thirty years and never, never have had one performance without a slip or two in the brass'. It is so testing for the players . . .

DM  You made a special point a little way back about the marvellous *Nachtmusiken* in the Seventh. The scherzo might just as well have been called *Nachtmusik*, of a rather spooky character. But surely it's that epic frame, the first movement and the finale, which contains this nocturnal trinity, that makes the symphony what it is. Everybody, even Mahler's opponents, grudgingly admired the *Nachtmusiken* when the work was first done. But it was the outer frame that really created a problem. Do you think that there is some kind of poetic or inner narrative? You know, Mahler used to say at rehearsals when he got to the finale, 'And now "Der Tag" [Daylight].' Do you find any merit in perceiving a logical progression from the very beginning of the symphony, passing through darkness and nighttime sounds and feelings and images, and arriving finally at the light? I myself believe there was in Mahler's mind a sense of night skies gradually dispersing and culminating in this great burst of light at the end of the work.

BH  Yes, I think there is. It is the dark beginning, from the tenor horn onwards. I don't think that it is necessary to put a sticker on the movement, because its character is explicit. I am not surprised by what Mahler said. I think that it is a kind of ascent into the light. Nevertheless, he wrote the symphony – not a rhapsody but a symphony and one has to treat it as a symphony unfolding a huge symphonic structure.

DM  Reading all these thousands of words of reviews, we find so
    many of the critics express themselves as bewildered by the
    absence of a programme. This is the only symphony to date,
    they often say, without an explicit, or at least an implicit, pro-
    gramme. This actually did create a problem for its later public
    reception. Mahler's hostility to the idea of a programme started
    quite early on, and particularly in relation to the Second. At an
    early stage there was an 'explanatory' programme; later it was
    vigorously suppressed. At the time of the Seventh he absolutely
    insisted that not a word of description or analysis was to be
    printed in the early programmes. If you look at the Prague
    programme it just has the tempo indications of the movements
    and nothing else. Did Mahler want to distance himself from
    'programme music', and from Strauss in particular?

BH  Why did Mahler withdraw his programme? That is what
    interests me. For example, there is always much discussion about
    Mahler's withdrawal of the programme for the Third Sym-
    phony, in which, as a conductor, you always try to find images
    to explain to musicians what is wanted. Mahler must have had
    a reason to say, 'No, I don't want any programme.' That's the
    interesting thing. Why did he not want them? Why did he not
    want to help? Well, he had a better understanding of his own
    work. It could be that he was annoyed with himself for
    making all those surtitles for the Third Symphony: 'What the
    flowers tell me', 'What love tells me', 'God', 'Nature'. Perhaps
    he found it a bit silly at the end. And he was such a fanatical
    man; maybe he said, 'Well, my time will come.' Maybe he said,
    'I will not be understood now but I will be understood later.
    Leave it for now', and so on. It is something that we, as lower
    inhabitants of this planet, see as the arrogance of a creative
    spirit who knows what he is doing and thinks, 'Well, my time
    will come anyway and for now I don't want to be bothered.'

DM  In any event, it seems to me that a work of art, whether a
    Mahler symphony or something else altogether, is perfectly
    explicit once one has really studied it and tried to understand
    it in and on its own terms.

BH   Yes, but there you use an interesting word: 'study'. But audi-
     ences, and also critics, I believe, very often go to a concert
     without really being prepared. One can still feel bewilderment
     with the Seventh Symphony and with the Sixth Symphony, at
     the end of those long finales. One can feel that the audience
     has been shattered by the experience, in the sense that demands
     have been made on them for which they are not fully pre-
     pared. I don't think that people are really prepared unless you
     have a very dedicated community. There may be people who
     go to Bayreuth for Wagner or to a Mahler Festival in Amster-
     dam, where you find a really dedicated nucleus of an audience.
     But I suspect that even many critics don't prepare themselves
     as thoroughly as one might wish. Maybe that's not very diplo-
     matic of me to say so, but I know how much time it has cost
     me really to understand the piece. To judge a performance of
     Mahler's Seventh when one may not have looked at the score
     for six months or so – one just has to look at it again. That,
     after all, is my experience.

DM   Could I just ask you about your experience of the Seventh and
     conducting it? The one movement that has really always in the
     past been a problem, certainly among the critics and audiences,
     was the last. I wondered whether there were any features of the
     finale that you found difficult to manage when you first started
     studying the work and preparing it for performance?

BH   I was and maybe still am slightly suspicious about Mahler in a
     festive mood. He is never purely festive like Wagner – one
     always uses this comparison – in the *Meistersinger* Overture.
     That, as it happens, is not the origin of the finale of the
     Seventh Symphony. At the very beginning it has the feeling of
     Wagner's overture, but then pursues a totally different direc-
     tion. Mahler tries to be optimistic at all costs, that's what I
     always feel about the finale. He wants to be affirmative, but in
     fact his last movement is not as affirmative as the finale of
     Beethoven's Ninth or the finale of a Bruckner symphony,
     where you have a feeling that you are really elevated, as one is,
     come to that, by the finale of Mahler's own Second Symphony.

The finale of the Seventh offers a more puzzling festive mood and I think that is what puts people off. Personally, I like it immensely. I find it an enormous talent of the composer to know how to put the kaleidoscope together. But I am suspicious of Mahler in a festive mood; after the last chord, after that strange diminuendo in the brass section, what remains is something that is not unclouded happiness. That's the feeling I am left with, and I think maybe that's what other people feel too.

DM  Mahler very rarely ever said much about new works in his letters, but he did make two remarks about the Seventh. To Emil Gutmann (the impresario who was to organize the premiere of the Eighth in Berlin) Mahler wrote, 'I've finished my Seventh.' He said – and these are his own words – 'It is my best work [this was in 1908, three years after he had finished it] and preponderantly cheerful in character.' In the same year he wrote to somebody else, 'It has a clear and engaging character.' Well, of course the finale certainly is 'cheerful' in its own odd way, but 'preponderantly cheerful' would hardly apply to either the wonderful first movement or those marvellous dark, shadowy serenades and the scherzo. But then composers have funny ideas about their own music. He had probably finished a few of the latest revisions of the work and had read through and heard the finale again, as it were, in his imagination, and he might have felt that it was a pretty cheerful piece. But it's a puzzling statement, particularly when you consider that the first movement is so tense.

BH  I think it is typical of the nature of an artist to think that the last thing he has done is his best work. You will see that at every level of the artistic community. Whether one is a composer or a performer or an orchestral member, one always thinks that the last thing one did was the best. That is the nature of the artist, so one should not take Mahler's remark too seriously.

DM  What has always interested me is the terrible difficulty Mahler had in starting the piece. There is a famous letter he wrote to Alma in which he said in effect, 'You will remember how I

wrote the two *Nachtmusiken* first and there they were lying
ready on my table'; a year later he came back to get on with
the symphony in the summer, and he described to her in the
same letter his despair at not knowing how to begin the symphony, how it should start. On being rowed home across the
lake to Maiernigg, the rhythmic stroke of the oars gave him the
idea of how the first movement of his symphony should open.
At once, the creative block was removed, he was able to return
to his studio, and within a few weeks the entire work was
brought to completion. Whenever I hear those first couple of
bars before the tenor horn enters, I cannot but think of that
extraordinary story of Mahler sitting in a boat with his hyper-
sensitive ears; the experience set him in motion, as if the starter
button on the motor of his creativity had been pressed. It is a
very odd case; I have never come across anything quite like it.

BH That is wonderful. In a way primitive and in another way
wonderful. So that's where he got that idea. He really had this
receptive musical imagination, this fertile soil waiting for
impressions. He was very vulnerable to impressions from
Nature apparently, and was very sensitive to what Nature told
him. I think that Beethoven was the same. He too was inspired
by Nature. Think of Debussy. He wrote *La Mer* at Eastbourne,
on the English Channel.

DM There is one interesting thing to say, I think, about the relationship between the finale and the *Meistersinger* Overture.
Mahler himself, it seems, did quite deliberately juxtapose the
overture and the finale of the Seventh. There was an occasion –
perhaps more than one – when he conducted the Seventh and
then played the *Meistersinger* Overture after the finale of his
own symphony; the overture was programmed to end the concert. It seems a very strange thing to have done because there
seems to be such an obvious relationship between the *Meistersinger* Overture and his finale. I agree with you absolutely that,
having made the point, Mahler then pursues his own independent path. None the less, most composers would have disguised or at least soft-pedalled the association, not gone out of

their way to draw our attention to it by juxtaposing the two works in the same programme!

BH Well, Mahler's finale is in the same festive mood. He was a great admirer of Wagner, and maybe it was a sort of secret homage to him. Far from disguising the relationship, so to speak, on the contrary it seems a very bold and even very witty thing to have done, to play the Wagner after the Seventh ... So he must have done it consciously; he must have included the *Meistersinger* because, to a very keen Wagnerian like Mahler, the *Meistersinger* represented the pinnacle of festivity, and, after all, he wanted to write a festive finale to end his symphony.

DM An extraordinary work and an extraordinary composer! Thank you very much for talking to me.

# On the Road to the Eighth Symphony: Mahler's New Worlds

*To Gastón Fournier-Facio – who has heard it all before*

### ～2003～

I remember very clearly the first time I heard Mahler's Eighth Symphony – it must have been in the 1950s, when I was not long out of my teens though already a committed Mahlerian, determined to explore, to enthuse, to espouse – above all to study – Mahler's works and learn everything I possibly could about this composer who had seized my imagination and has continued to do so ever since. On that first occasion, however, I found the Eighth something of a puzzle, in this particular sense: I found it difficult to relate what I had just heard to the works of Mahler with which I was already familiar.

I was born in 1925, and it was when I was a schoolboy, about fourteen years old, that I encountered the two works that were in fact to initiate and shape the history of my engagement with Mahler. Those works were *Das Lied von der Erde* and the Ninth Symphony, both of them in performances of historic importance by the Vienna Philharmonic Orchestra conducted by Bruno Walter, recorded respectively in 1936 and 1938. Two recordings, I must add, that played an absolutely vital role, at least in the UK, in bringing Mahler's genius to the attention of a wider public, not only to schoolboys like myself but to young composers like Benjamin Britten, who was similarly overwhelmed by his experiencing Walter's performance on record of *Das Lied*. This is what he wrote in a letter in 1937 when there was hardly a note of Mahler to be heard in England in public performance. He had been listening to 'Der Abschied', it seems over and over again. He writes of

Lecture given for the Associazione Amici di Santa Cecilia, Rome, on 9 February 2003.

Mahler achieving 'a serenity literally supernatural. I cannot understand it – it passes over me like a tidal wave – and that matters not
a jot either, because it goes on for ever, even if it is never performed
again – that final chord is printed on the atmosphere . . . At the
moment I can do no more than bask in its heavenly light – and it
is worth having lived to do that.'*

The voice of a young Mahler enthusiast from the 1930s.

Alas, the onset of the Second World War in 1939 put a brake on
the dissemination and comprehension of Mahler's music, though
there was one further recording – a performance of the Second
Symphony by Eugene Ormandy with the Philadelphia Orchestra
recorded as early as 1935 on shellac 78 rpm discs, a far cry from the
recording technologies of today. But here again in the case of the
Second, impressed of course I was, but puzzled too. To put it very
crudely, I found it hard at this stage to match up the composer of
the Second with the composer of *Das Lied* and the Ninth. I could
not discern the creative narrative – and that word *narrative* is of the
greatest significance whenever we talk about Mahler – that led us
from a relatively early work like the Second to late-style, other-
style works of the order of *Das Lied* and the Ninth.

My incomprehension was of course rooted in a past, in the 1920s
and 1930s, the period of my boyhood and youth, when, not only
for me, but virtually for all other musically inquisitive listeners,
there were simply very few performances of Mahler to be heard.
There were naturally memorable exceptions but in general there
was no place for Mahler in the landscape of musical culture in the
UK, or for the most part elsewhere in Europe – the big exception
was the Netherlands – in the period between the two world wars.
All the more reason to acknowledge the impact and influence of
those early recordings I have mentioned.

Now it is not my business you will be glad to hear to embark
on the history and significance of early Mahler recordings, fascinating though it is. Though having raised the subject I cannot leave it
without mentioning one still little-known fact that continues to

---

* Letter 103 in Donald Mitchell and Philip Reed (eds.), *Letters from a Life: Selected Letters
  and Diaries of Benjamin Britten*, vol. 1, p. 492.

surprise everyone every time I mention it, that one of the first commercial recordings* of Mahler was not made in Vienna or Philadelphia but in Tokyo, in 1930 – in 1930, I repeat that – when a recording of the Fourth, on the Parlophone label, was made by the Tokyo New Symphony Orchestra conducted by Hidemaro Konoye.

These days record stores in Tokyo and elsewhere in Japan are as packed with multiple copies of multiple performances of the Mahler symphonies as is every record store the world over. This in itself constitutes a remarkable cultural phenomenon, as indeed does the multiplicity of live performances of Mahler's music which it is in no way an exaggeration to describe as global in its scope. Before I conclude this talk, I hope I shall be able to identify some of the reasons why it is that Mahler's music today enjoys such huge popularity, why it is that in a very special way his music seems to speak to, to communicate with, the very large audiences who turn out to hear it.

All very different from the days of my youth. And I don't doubt if I had had available to me as a schoolboy a complete cycle of the Mahler symphonies, along with the songs and song-cycles, conducted, say, by Abbado or Chailly, Bernstein or Kubelik, Rattle or Haitink – I choose those names at random – I would not have been as puzzled as I was when I first heard the Eighth. The gap in creative continuity would have been filled.

But to leave it at that would be entirely inadequate. Because the truth is that while inevitably there is a continuity when we come to regard Mahler's work as a whole, it is a continuity of a kind quite *un*like the continuity – perhaps *evolution* would be the better word – that we are often familiar with in Mahler's predecessors, whether from the classical or romantic periods, where one work may be self-sufficient in itself but at the same time can be heard to be clearly related in retrospect to both what preceded it and what followed it.

With Mahler, however, it is by no means such plain sailing. I'm not for a moment suggesting that, now we have instant access to

---

* The first commercial recording (c. 1923) was of Mahler's Second Symphony conducted by Oskar Fried with the Berlin Cathedral Choir and the Berlin State Opera Orchestra.

the totality of Mahler's oeuvre, we could ever be unaware of the fact that each and every work has its roots in the one unique manifestation of creativity that we name and recognize to be Gustav Mahler's. But what still perhaps remains under-appreciated is the singularity and individuality of each specific work. If there is a consistency to be discerned in Mahler's oeuvre then it is the quite extraordinary compulsion that led him – no, *compelled* him – to explore and occupy a new concept of musical time and space in each succeeding symphony, and yet more importantly, especially in the context of this talk, a new philosophy that also on occasion might involve an altogether new aesthetic.

This may sound complicated, for which I apologize. But there is little point in pretending that Mahler was anything other than an extremely complex composer. The consoling thought is, that however complex words may prove to be when trying to describe music – something I'm very conscious of at this very moment – with luck they can prove to serve the music, not obscure it.

With this in mind I want, briefly, to say a word or two about the symphonies that preceded the composition of the Eighth because it is my belief that if we can understand the *dis*continuity that I have suggested is so marked a feature of Mahler's oeuvre as a whole, we stand a good chance of approaching the Eighth by means of the best guide available to us, the unique chronicle Mahler's own works narrate. I repeat, today we occupy in historical terms a privileged position, something denied our predecessors: our knowledge of the oeuvre is complete. But let me invite you to undertake a miniature historical exercise. Imagine, if you can, attending the first complete performance of the Third Symphony in Krefeld in 1902 – hitherto only fragments of the vast work had been heard in public – having heard the premiere of the Fourth in Munich a few months earlier in 1901. Just think for a moment of the scarcely to be believed contrasts between the two works, in the sizes of their orchestras alone. Might not our hypothetical listener at the turn of the century be forgiven his or her difficulty in concluding that it was the same composer who was responsible for both? Or to choose another example; if that same listener had been among the jubilant audience at the premiere of the Eighth in 1910 and by some magic means had had access to Mahler's desk, surely he or she would have been astonished, perhaps bewildered, to find there complete the autograph manuscript of *Das Lied von der Erde*, already composed in 1908, and to go unheard before Mahler himself died in 1911. Here again, as with the Third and Fourth, what confronts us are two distinct and independent works, each one of which, whether the Eighth or *Das Lied*, pursues its own narrative and its own philosophy and aesthetic in music – or music*s* (my plural is deliberate) – specific to the world that each work inhabits.

I am sure that some of you may be thinking that I am rolling out yet again that famous remark of Mahler's to Sibelius in 1907, when he said, 'The symphony must be like the world. It must be all embracing.' So far as Mahler himself was concerned this was indeed a major statement about his own innovative creative thinking which introduced into the specific world of the traditional symphony a variety of musics: birdsong, café music, fanfares, folksong, street music, the roar of Nature, marches, dances, military bands, an array of musics that one can only describe as vernacular in origin and character, comparable perhaps to what we mean when we refer to vernacular speech. Very few of the popular idioms I have mentioned had hitherto been allowed to play a role in the musical language thought proper to the concept of the symphony. At one stroke Mahler not only massively increased the vocabulary of that language but opened up whole areas of new feeling.

However, it is a rather different point that I want to make: that while Mahler indubitably proved that his idea of symphony was 'all embracing' as he put it, what I think was yet more extraordinary and still little comprehended was that each symphony he himself wrote was *a world in itself*, quite consciously so, I believe, as he developed throughout what proved to be a very short creative life. Perhaps we should remember more often that between the composition of the First Symphony and the unfinished Tenth there elapsed only twenty-five years – only twenty-five years! And while that sequence of symphonies can now be seen from our vantage point in history as a meaningful totality, what to my mind has been strangely neglected is Mahler's systematic exploration of a fresh philosophy for each new symphony that he created, which in sum one might claim to represent many of the leading new philosophies, psychologies and radical new aesthetics that characterized the end of the nineteenth and the first decades of the twentieth centuries. Let me hasten to add, I am in no way underplaying the unceasing *musical* innovations that of course were part and parcel of the fierce intellectual inquisitiveness that was a prominent feature of Mahler's personality and were to make such a huge impact on the twentieth century.

Let me try to explain what I mean. Take the first four symphonies, for instance. It may have taken Mahler significant time and effort to get his First Symphony into its final shape. (It had started life as a Symphonic Poem in Two Parts.) The work undoubtedly reveals a pretty clear narrative, touching on many aspects of the protagonist's journey through his life. We experience events and sometimes highly idiosyncratic commentaries on those events, events which we recognize without too much difficulty as part of the common experience of humanity. We note too that the symphony ends in a triumphant D major. Here, fascinatingly, the composer himself raised a question mark or left a question behind him rather, which has never been satisfactorily answered, claiming that his hero, the protagonist, had *not* succeeded in achieving ascendancy over his main adversary, death. We don't know precisely where Mahler thought that point was made in a seemingly triumphant finale. But we do know, again from the composer himself, that his hero's *funeral* is ceremonially evoked in the opening first movement of the Second Symphony, a movement Mahler embarked on almost before the ink was dry on the symphonic poem that was to become his First Symphony. Even more amazingly, Mahler pursues his hero *beyond* death. After the intervening middle movements, with their memories of a departed life, we embark on the incredible finale in which Mahler audaciously imagines life *after* death, the awakening call, the march to resurrection – a brilliant display of street music put to new effect – and a concluding chorale, for which by the way Mahler does not use an established Christian text but an Ode by the poet Klopstock, amended here and there by Mahler himself. This must surely be the first time in the history of music in which a composer had seriously explored the *after*life as new musical territory (for which by the way he had continually to invent new, albeit appropriate, musical and acoustic imagery).

But scarcely credible though it may seem, no sooner was Mahler's hero resurrected, whose narrative we now realize spanned *two* symphonies and *two* lives – first his life in the real world and then his life after death – than Mahler began work on a new symphony, his Third, which opens with a depiction of the world even *before* life as we know it had begun, generating some of the most remarkable music for orchestra Mahler was ever to write. The classical balance between the various sections of the orchestra was radically and dramatically reversed, with wind and brass and percussion predominant, the strings no longer in the lead. Something approaching traditional homogeneity is restored, and restored overwhelmingly, only in the last movement, Mahler thereby using an evolutionary approach to orchestral sound to mirror what is indeed the narrative that is the symphony's *raison d'être*, the very process – the philosophy, the science, the idea – of evolution. And it is in the magnificent concluding slow movement of the Third, the first of Mahler's great symphonic adagios, that the image of Love as perhaps the highest of mankind's spiritual objectives is clearly spelled out, something of importance for us here today because it foresees what I shall try to define as one of the much later Eighth Symphony's leading characteristics, the union of Eros – the god of love – and Creativity, in which the work eventually culminates.

Entirely typical of Mahler, I want to suggest, that having scrutinized the afterlife, he should turn to a leading theory of how life itself developed, the concept of evolution, much discussed, much debated, as the nineteenth century progressed, though it is not at all improbable that Mahler must have informed himself about the so-called 'chain of being' that had its origins in pre-Christian eras. His version of the 'chain' as we know it in the programme of the Third has quite remarkable parallels with accounts of mankind's evolution that date back to the fifth century. An intriguing thought this, that calls for research and future study.*

And then what next? The Fourth Symphony, at the very turn of

---

\* See also 'The Twentieth Century's Debt to Mahler', pp. 560–62.

SCRUTINY

the nineteenth into the twentieth century, and as distant from any theory of evolution as can possibly be imagined. Or rather, it puts evolution into reverse. Instead of the ascent of the Third to the highest plane of adult life, exalted Love, the Fourth, by means of a narrative articulated in music of the greatest sophistication, subtlety and brilliance, has returned us, by the time we reach the finale, to a condition of spiritual Innocence we identify with the child and childhood. Nothing child*ish* about it, I emphasize: *childlike* is the only word that fits. It is thus that bliss is finally established in the blissful E major that brings 'Das himmlische Leben' to its end, the pre-existing *Wunderhorn* song in which the Fourth culminates. And who but Mahler would ever have thought of ending a highly elaborate symphony with a solo song of this character? It is easy to forget the boldness of the idea and the disbelief amid audiences at early performances when the singer walked on stage. Furthermore, it was in the Fourth that we meet Mahler in the role of an historian of music, commenting in purely musical terms on the practices and procedures of his predecessors and thereby anticipating the neo-classical movement which was so marked a feature of later decades. And finally we have to note that the first three movements of the Fourth significantly anticipate the exclusive concentration on the orchestra in the ensuing three symphonies. Enough material for the world of one symphony, without doubt. That Mahler was able to co-ordinate and reconcile and make narrative sense of so complex an aesthetic is still cause for wonder, all of it by the way foreshadowed in the first handful of bars that introduce the first movement.

From even this brief survey it is apparent that the first four symphonies already reveal a pretty diverse sequence of imaginative territories, none of them I think ideological or doctrinal, all of them, however, related to common forms of human experience and universal preoccupations. Hence, surely, one of the reasons for Mahler's now exceptional command of wide audiences. His music, I believe, does address in spectacularly original shapes and sounds matters of life, love and death which, for most of us at any rate, are fundamental to our understanding of what being human entails.

In the past it has often been suggested that Mahler was committed to tragedy, was a composer haunted by death and mortality. There can certainly be no doubt that he was aware of the irrevocable challenge of death as a constant presence, as inescapably part of life. But in fact as we approach the symphonies that preceded the Eighth, I think it worth emphasizing that to my mind there is only one work of his, the Sixth Symphony, in which death, so to say, has the last word; and the power of that final utterance, the *finality* of it, given a performance that matches the intensity of those closing bars of the Sixth's finale, can, on occasion, come close to a virtual experience of death itself.

However, the Sixth, like all the Mahler symphonies, is a world in itself. One must never forget the sheer persistence with which Mahler explored new modes of thinking, even about death. For example, if it is in the Sixth that death emerges as victor, it is a very different narrative that he had already pursued in the immediately preceding Fifth. That symphony opens with a very large-scale funeral march, which inevitably stirs memories of the first movement of the Second. But in the Fifth, Mahler, with that inexhaustible energy with which he devised new means of occupying musical space, uses that funeral march constantly to *interrupt*, even to dislocate, the second movement. A reminder, to be sure, that death cannot be got rid of or wished away. Much more important, however, is to comprehend that the idea of Interruption has been raised to a new and highly original formal principle. Eventually, as we all know, in the finale of the Fifth life and love win through and the work ends in a blaze of D major and triumph. But the work's first two conjoined movements constitute one of the most daring and innovative forms in all of Mahler's oeuvre.

And it was in the Fifth – do I need to remark? – that he interposed the famous *Adagietto*, for strings and harp alone, which has been the subject of endless comment, most of it misconceived. What really matters today is to establish, by means of coherent and rational performance practice, the true musical character of the *Adagietto*. It is *not* a dirge, *not* a farewell to life, but a song of Love, for orchestra. Tempo here is a critical, determining factor; and it is the choice of the right, song-like tempo that will rescue the *Adagietto* from the false interpretation imposed on it by so many conductors – not to speak of film directors* — as music appropriate to funereal occasions. An ironic fate this, if it were to go unchallenged. The *Adagietto* is not an *Abschied*, but a song of Love, in which the soloist is an orchestra, one that, it should not go unnoticed, is compiled in a special way: it consists only of strings and harp, a texture that is often prominent in Mahler's late songs, not least in the *Kindertotenlieder* and his other settings of Rückert. Nor should Mahler's boldness in introducing into a symphony for very large orchestra a movement that represents so radical a reduction in forces go unnoticed. He once referred to his orchestral songs as *his* 'chamber music', true enough of the songs for voice, but true too of the song for orchestra that is the *Adagietto*. And mention of that characterizing texture reminds me of something else that is relevant, that it is often a predominant association of strings and harps that identifies those unmistakable affirmations of Love that I would claim to be the prime objective of the passionate second subjects in the first movements of both the Sixth and Seventh Symphonies to assert. I am thinking here in particular of the overwhelmingly ecstatic melody we hear in the Sixth. It sometimes goes unnoticed that it is this second subject which brings the first movement to an end in a radiant A major, in triumph, as if Mahler were telling us at this stage in the unfolding of his symphony that there remains the possibility of an alternative to tragedy, that the salvation of Love — which is the image I believe the strings and harp articulate — may yet spare us the annihilation of death. But as we know it is an incontrovertible extinction in an unalleviated A minor that awaits us in the finale.

As for the Seventh, the melody of the first movement's second subject is unmistakably of the same character as that of the Sixth, but, oddly, on its very first appearance, is harp-less. However, as the movement progresses and Mahler, so to say, elaborates on the significance of the melody, so too do harps play an increasingly prominent role. But, fascinatingly, while the movement ends positively (in E major), unlike the Sixth, it is not its second subject that is recapitulated in triumph.

You must forgive me if I seem to be concentrating on too much

---

* A reference to Visconti's use of the *Adagietto* in his film adaptation of *Death in Venice*.

detail, but in fact I believe this surfacing of the idea of Love, of human passion – Alma, Mahler's wife, I believe was central to the symbolism of the narratives we are discussing here – was much in Mahler's creative mind and imagination as he approached the composition of the Eighth, a preoccupation for which, as I have tried to suggest, he found a specific musical language.

Without doubt, if there is any opposition or source of opposition to the finality of death in the Sixth Symphony, we find it momentarily in the symbolic function of the first movement's second subject that I have just spelled out. In the Seventh, in the first movement that is a huge nocturnal landscape – a *night*scape – it is again only the second subject that puts us in direct touch with humankind; its apotheosis in B major, at the height of this extraordinary movement's development section, re-unites strings and harps. There is no denying the magic of this moment, and yet how, I wonder, does one interpret Mahler's direction to his first violins (in bar 320, to be precise) to play '*ohne Ausdruck*', '*without* expression'? There are always surprises to be found if we can take the trouble to look at Mahler's score and acquaint ourselves with what he himself asks for, and after that ask ourselves, Why? But, I must confess, not as yet to have come up with an answer in this particular instance.

But the truth is, ladies and gentlemen, that the Seventh is the joker in the pack – is there a comparable idiom in Italian? It is in many ways the most paradoxical of the symphonies, the most challenging because the most resistant to fitting into any of the patterns that I have been trying to discern in Mahler's symphonies, as he moves on from one symphony to the next. One has to conclude that the Seventh is indeed authentically Mahlerian in the sense that there is unquestionably a narrative that runs from beginning to end. The truth is, however, that one has to work hard to define where the narrative is leading us. Throughout a performance one often has to stop and ask: where are we now; where are we going? Not continuity but *dis*continuity seems to be the guiding principle. Undoubtedly too the Seventh has an aesthetic, one as odd as its narrative, though I am sure quite consciously contrived to raise our expectations and then deliberately contradict or dismiss them, or allow them to evaporate, to disintegrate into inaudibility.

Let me give you an example. Who, other than Mahler, would ever have thought of launching an amorous serenade, an *Andante amoroso* as the composer indicates, on a *cadence*, the device normally associated with closure? After that downright contradictory beginning it is perhaps less surprising to find that the most conspicuous feature of the movement as it continues is the omission, the *absence*, of anything that one might recognize as an extended, serenade-like melody? Or there is the famously capricious finale with its strange but unconcealed references to Wagner and his *Meistersinger* Overture and likewise to Mozart's *Entführung* Overture. What is Mahler trying to tell us? There are some who assess the Seventh as Mahler's most 'forward-looking' symphony, not so much 'modern' perhaps as a manifestation of a much later 'modernism', post First World War, that he did not live to see, one marked feature of which was a fashion for the 'irrational'.

Was Mahler here again ahead of his time, demonstrating, with typical rigour, that irrationality ultimately did not work, was self-defeating? In short, was his Seventh Symphony ultimately a victim of its own aesthetic? Mahler, a supreme ironist if there ever was one, would have appreciated the irony. Can we be certain indeed that the very self-defeat we experience in action in the Seventh, as the narrative progresses, was not in fact Mahler's ironic intention?

One certainly can't think of significant precedents in the established tradition of the symphony for such a systematic strategy of subversion, disruption and displacement (in the first *Nachtmusik* for instance how do we make sense of the juxtaposition of the torrent of birdsong and the street-band march music that immediately ensues?). And what about the triumphal C major that rounds off the finale? Is it an unambiguously conclusive conclusion, or is it Mahler in 1905, halfway through the first decade of the new century, asking himself – and us – whether it is possible still to make meaningful a gesture of this kind, bearing in mind, as we must, all the subversion that has preceded it?

There can be no denying, whatever we ourselves may conclude, that the aesthetic of the Seventh is quite unlike any other in Mahler's or for that matter any other composer's. Perhaps the only parallel in our own day would be with Shostakovich, who was indebted to Mahler in so many dimensions of his own thinking. What we can all agree on without question is that the Seventh represents a unique world of its own: who would have predicted that it would have been the symphony next in line after the Sixth? Who could have predicted that following the Seventh, the symphony the very aesthetic of which was seemingly dedicated to exposing how problematic the idea of 'symphony' had become, Mahler would embark on the Eighth and yet another audacious exploration of philosophy, musical time and space hard to relate at all to the aesthetic of the preceding Seventh? Which returns me to my opening thoughts and initiates what I hope may be a bit of fresh thinking about the Eighth. While the C major of the Seventh evokes as much doubt as conviction, it is not doubt I think that is aroused by the massive affirmation of E flat major with which the Eighth begins and ends. What it is affirming is precisely what I want to try to explain.

Let me start first by drawing attention to a feature of the symphony that has long been a source of confusion and puzzlement, the use in the symphony's two parts of two texts in different languages, one a Latin hymn, 'Veni creator spiritus', the other German – and a very famous German text at that – the final scene of Goethe's *Faust*, Part II. Many heads, including my own, have occasionally shaken in some bewilderment at the conjuction of two seemingly so dissimilar textual sources. How, in fact, did that come about? It is here that relatively recent research brings, I believe, important enlightenment. First of all that in April 1820 Goethe himself made a translation of the hymn into German, a hymn he proclaimed to be 'a call to the universal genius of the world'. Furthermore, we also know that Mahler's first acquaintance with the Latin hymn was not in its original Latin guise but in Goethe's German translation. Thus there was, I think we may safely assume, for Mahler a profound poetic and linguistic link between Parts I and II of his symphony; and the bond was Goethe. It must have been that Mahler was conscious that, in a very serious sense, both these texts belonged together. As Dieter Borchmeyer has remarked, the hymn in Mahler's Part I and the 'hymn' – Goethe's 'Chorus mysticus' – that

brings Part II of the symphony to an end, 'merge together in the
secularizing spirit of Goethe'. This togetherness of Parts I and II
I shall return to, but I think it will be useful to make a few further
comments first.

I think that so far today the name of Bach has not passed my lips.
His significance for Mahler cannot be exaggerated. It was the collected edition of Bach's works that Mahler kept close to hand in
whichever composing hut he found himself working in, volumes
that he frequently read and consulted and undoubtedly marvelled
at. The Bach–Mahler relationship is a long story, too long to
embark on here in much detail, but without question Bach was
central to Mahler's compositional thinking and as Mahler's creative
life progressed his influence grew.* A memorable event had
occurred in the year preceding the composition of the Eighth. In
the concert in Vienna in 1905 in which he conducted the Viennese
premiere of his Fifth Symphony, he arranged for a performance of
one of Bach's grandest motets, *Singet dem Herrn ein neues Lied*,
conducted by Franz Schalk, to precede the symphony, in the first
half of the programme. An imaginative bit of programme planning,
I assure you, because in those days it was by no means a familiar
concert-going experience to hear a Bach motet in the context of
a new Mahler symphony. This was a motet that especially aroused
Mahler's admiration, and in some very real sense he paid tribute to
its influence and inspiration in his setting of the Latin hymn that
forms the first part of the Eighth. But in truth the movement must
be heard in a much wider perspective than that of a salute to Bach.
It is fundamentally an audacious, comprehensive demonstration of
skills and compositional practices which have their roots specifically
in the art of counterpoint.

Part of Mahler's intention here I have no doubt was to remind
us of counterpoint's long history – one should never forget how
fascinated Mahler was by the *history* of music – furthermore, to
demonstrate how contrapuntal texture remained a brilliant, living
presence as the nineteenth century gave way to the twentieth. There
is scarcely a symphony of Mahler's that does not reveal a fresh aspect

---

* See also 'The Twentieth Century's Debt to Mahler', pp. 562–6.

of what contrapuntal thought meant to him – the first movement of the Fourth Symphony, for example – something that writers on Mahler frequently overlook.

But the Eighth, I suggest, is something of a special case. In the opening hymn, his own invocation of creativity, he was – if one may express it thus – putting on display with tireless energy the array of techniques he had at his command, that the art of music had at its command, at the turn of the nineteenth century into the twentieth.

It is no accident that it was precisely at this time that so many composers were renewing their contacts with the polyphonic past as a means of advance, not back to Bach, indeed, but *forward* from Bach, a movement in which now, rather belatedly, we recognize Mahler to have been a key figure. If Mahler were celebrating in his Part I exceptional contrapuntal ingenuity as a prime symbol of creativity, it would be at a climactic moment during this torrent of polyphony, in the movement's famous central developmental section, conceived as a double fugue and deploying an exhaustive compilation of contrapuntal devices, that we hear the words 'Accende lumen sensibus, Infunde amorem cordibus' – 'Illuminate our senses, Pour love into our hearts' – the theme of fervent aspiration which, in a diversity of derivations, pervades Part II and finally leads to the chorale, the hymn – Goethe's hymn – that brings the work to a close.

If this moment has a special radiance, and it is important to note that it is precisely at this moment that the images of Creativity and Love are so clearly spelled out, it is because the 'Accende' theme is projected with 'sudden upswing', as Mahler has it, in a powerful release of E major, a key that he often reserved for areas of feeling and expression distinctly not earthbound. Think, for instance, of the switch to E major with which the Fourth Symphony concludes and transports us to heaven ('Das himmlische Leben', the *Wunderhorn* song that is the work's finale). And once again in Part II, for a passage about which I shall have something to say a little later, Mahler re-introduces E major when Goethe's Mater gloriosa swims into view from on high. What other key, indeed, could possibly have served this event in the heavens?

I must confess to having wondered if Mahler might not have rounded off the Eighth with one of those characteristic semitonal shifts that is often a feature of his evolving tonal schemes across the span of a symphony, in which case we might have heard 'Alles Vergängliche ist nur ein Gleichnis' ('All that is past of us was but reflected') in a glorious E major. But Mahler of course, and quite rightly, stuck to his own rigorous logic. A heavenly goal is not at all what the symphony is seeking. Its musical and philosophical strength resides in its stubborn, unremitting celebration of Creativity, that 'universal genius of the world', for which reason the Eighth both at its beginning and at its end affirms E *flat* major, the tonal bedrock of the symphony. For once there is no narrative in Mahler's customary manner to land us at a destination elsewhere. I have talked a great deal today about the function of narrative in Mahler's symphonies and, true to form, in his Eighth he surprises us by omitting what hitherto has been a virtually established principle. And why, you may ask. Because in this instance the philosophy of the work cannot permit it. As we shall come to see I hope, Creativity and Love are inseparable and the whole point of the symphony is to affirm their unity, their interdependence.

What is so intriguing about the E major surfacings in both Parts I and II is the fact that the shift to a fresh tonal region was clearly prompted by the association, already firmly established in Mahler's inner ear, between E and some form of upwardness or upwards activity. 'Accende' speaks for itself (the very concept of aspiration must surely always imply uplift), while it is E, inevitably, that lends Mater gloriosa her wings. For Mahler, in both these instances, there could have been no other choice of key. But E flat had to remain the symphony's destination. As the poet T. S. Eliot famously observed, 'In my end is my beginning.'

In any event, it is the union of Creativity and Love that is spelled out musically in Part I, shown to be the *raison d'être* of the entire work, and unequivocally defined by the famous closing 'Chorus mysticus', 'Alles Vergängliche ist nur ein Gleichnis . . .':

> Alles Vergängliche
> Ist nur ein Gleichnis;
> Das Unzulängliche,
> Hier wird's Ereignis;

Das Unbeschreibliche,
Hier ist's getan;
Das Ewig-Weibliche
Zieht uns hinan.

*All that is past of us*
*Was but reflected;*
*All that was lost in us*
*Here is corrected;*
*All indescribables*
*Here we descry;*
*Eternal Womanhood*
*Leads us on high.*

We certainly experience the heights in Part II, but before I come to that, may I return for a moment to an aspect of the Eighth that has already surfaced in the shape of Bach and the precedent of his motet that inspired Part I? He often consciously made reference to the past in his own music while at the very same time he was busy creating music's future. A wholly typical Mahler paradox.

Part I of the Eighth, however, is single-minded in many respects: a sustained explosion of polyphony with roots in a single past form. However, when we come to Part II what greets us is no less than a comprehensive gathering together of almost every known vocal form and genre from the past, conscripted by Mahler to service his setting of *Faust*, Part II, in which it is fascinating to find that he incorporated into his published score all Goethe's 'stage directions', though this we have to believe for Goethe was a 'theatre of the mind' rather than a drama destined for the conventional stage.

None the less, one cannot but be conscious of Part II of the Eighth as in some sense representing the opera that Mahler himself never composed. Opera is certainly an important influence but is only one of the formal and stylistic influences that we encounter in Part II. In truth, Mahler gathers together here an almost comprehensive assembly of the vocal forms and genres of the past. In addition to opera, that is, we are confronted by oratorio; cantata; orchestral song, and aria; a chorus of boys' voices – an innovation

Mahler had himself anticipated in his Third Symphony – and choral writing of every description, from the full mixed choruses (two of them, though sparingly used *en masse*) to a constantly changing 'mix' of voices and registers in response to the changing levels and locations on which the drama is enacted; and the 'mix' of genders, of the natural and supernatural, the human and the mythical, the sacred and the secular. And finally we have to extend the list of genres to include 'symphony' itself, an unmistakable presence in the big orchestral prelude to Part II which, while marvellously raising the curtain musically – thematically, that is – on what is to follow, reminds us of those timeless stretches of slow music, those slow symphonic movements of which Mahler was such a master.

I'm not for a moment suggesting that the Eighth is all retrospection. Absolutely not. Who for example other than Mahler would ever have thought of setting 'Neige, neige' ('Turn, turn'), Gretchen's song – now one of the penitents – to an extraordinarily transparent and *pianissimo* accompaniment that includes solo mandolin, harps, celesta, harmonium, reduced wind, muted strings? Unquestionably authentic Mahler this, serenading away in a vein on which he had already embarked in the Seventh, though there the mandolin had a guitar as companion. (You may remember my comment about the second *Nachtmusik* in the Seventh: Mahler installed the appropriate instruments of accompaniment but forgot the tune!) It makes nonsense anyway, doesn't it, of all those tedious opinions of the Eighth in the past where the work from beginning to end was described as incontrovertible proof of Mahler's gigantism and megalomania. Nobody, it seems, had ever bothered to look at the score.

If they had, they would have discovered that it is only very occasionally that he uses anything like the total resources at his command simultaneously. The big tuttis are indeed very big, but relatively rare; and for much of the time, especially in Part II, we have vocal and orchestral textures of almost chamber-like refinement and sophistication, textures continuously re-imagined in ever fresh and ever new orchestral – and choral! – compilations. I want you to listen for a moment to one of those extraordinary, unique orchestras that Mahler compiles from the vast resources available to him. It functions in fact as the prelude to the chorale that brings the work to a close, 'Alles Vergängliche . . .'. It is an amazing passage in which dynamics are reduced to a hushed *pianissimo* and a handful of instruments (strings only minimally represented) constitute an 'orchestra' the like of which had never before been put together. This is the passage in question, and what we hear are, in order of their first appearance, piccolo, harmonium, celesta, piano, harps, flute, two oboes, two clarinets, four horns (with mutes), and a quartet of strings (playing harmonics). *In toto*, by the way, strings are heard in only three bars.

RECORDED MUSIC EXCERPT
Symphony No. 8, Part II, figs. 199–203

So it is not one huge orchestra we hear in the Eighth but a multiplicity of orchestras extrapolated from the main body, each one matching the different levels on which Goethe's imaginary drama – impossible to stage – takes place: only music could in fact 'realize' it. There's time for only one generalization: you'll notice in performance how relatively thin and bright the sound is, often in the high registers of the woodwind, when we hear what is going on upstairs among all those angels and heavenly boys etc., etc., whom Goethe depicts aloft in the upper regions. When we first encounter the angels in Part II there is no mistaking that we have been transported to a higher plane of sound. And while on the subject of Mahler's orchestras, the big preludial slow movement that opens Part II is a perfect example of how, for each unit of what in fact is the biggest stretch of orchestral music in the whole symphony, Mahler selects an individual assembly of instrumental colours as he explores Goethe's landscape of mountain gorges, forest, cliff and wilderness amid which the holy anchorites live. (It is exactly that same principle of deconstructing and then reconstructing his orchestras that Mahler then proceeds to apply to his choral resources.) Wonderful changing sounds and colours all of this, whether orchestral or choral, but still as it were earthbound. We're not yet upstairs.

Here again, simply to be able to accomplish all of this, Mahler needed to have available very large forces. But at the same time I

Mahler in rehearsal for the premiere of the Eighth Symphony in Munich
on 12 September 1910

believe there was another interesting ambition. He remarked to a
friend on one occasion that the Eighth was his 'gift to the nation'.
I don't think for one moment that what Mahler had in mind was
anything nationalistic or chauvinistic. He himself said famously that
he was at home *nowhere* in the world, something to which the viru-
lent anti-Semitism of his time would have contributed. I believe on
the contrary that his 'gift' to us and to the collective, communal
musical culture of his day was none other than this unparalleled
attempt in the Eighth to put on display every conceivable performing resource that was currently available at the turn of the century
and, through his own creative genius, his own creativity, to show
what riches in forms and compositional techniques were there to
exploit those resources.

That ambition I believe should be central to our understanding
of the work. But I repeat, of no less importance was the 'communal'
character of the Eighth, involving as it did the highest calibre of

professionals, vocal and orchestral, as well as amateurs among the many choruses. Above all there was the presence of children's voices, a unique culminating use of them (they had already been deployed in the Third) which was to have a profound influence on composers in the twentieth century. Think of Benjamin Britten alone and then think again of Britten and others in the context of evolving new means and methods of musical *education*. Fundamental to all of this was Mahler's initiating use of boys' voices in the Third and Eighth. It was in all of these ways, I suggest, that he thought of his symphony as a 'gift to the nation', and they add up to a 'communal' aesthetic that was entirely exclusive to the Eighth.

However, it was not only physical resources that Mahler so comprehensively assembled but also his remarkable historical retrospects. I've mentioned Bach, but there are many others – Wagner, of course, and, perhaps surprisingly, Verdi. Does everyone remember what Mahler once said of him, that it was from Verdi that he had learned 'a great deal' about orchestration? I've certainly found as I've grown older that I hear Verdi more and more as a profound influence on Mahler, especially in the later symphonies.

Indeed, the 'Italian' Mahler is almost a subject in itself,* and there is one supreme moment in Part II of the Eighth where we hear Mahler in what I think of as his unmistakably 'Italian' mode. The passage in question begins as a song for orchestra alone, as Goethe's Mater gloriosa swims into view. What we hear essentially is all strings, harps, and glissandi, the violins articulating – 'singing', that is – a breath-taking, heart-stopping *Liebeslied* – hence, without doubt, the ravishing presence of strings and harps. It is this ecstatic melody, a totally characteristic Mahlerian inspiration, searingly transparent in sound, that has aroused the disbelief and suspicion of critics since the work's premiere in 1910.§

I am conscious today of speaking to an audience more familiar than I with the origins of what I like to think of as Mahler's 'Italian' connection, a unique dimension of his music I believe in urgent

---

* So it is: see 'Chailly, Mahler and the Italian Connection', pp. 550–65.
§ See pp. 429–30 above, where the significance of the Fifth Symphony's *Adagietto* and its unique strings and harp orchestration is discussed.

The poster for the world premiere of the Eighth Symphony

need of serious study. Where else should the investigation be conducted other than here, in Italy? I have just mentioned Mahler's own salute to Verdi. But the composer I have in mind, especially in relation to the passage from the Eighth I've just described, and which we shall hear in my second and final music example in just one minute, is Bellini. Now, you may want to tell me that I've got it all wrong, that it was not Bellini who was Mahler's 'model'. But if not, and I shall be interested to hear your views, then surely it was Mahler *imagining* himself to be an Italian composer, deliberately deploying technical features that audiences in general, not only Italian audiences, would immediately identify as 'Italian', even 'operatic', in character. And, as if to make certain that his performers understand the link that is made in this passage with its cultural origins and context, Mahler goes out of his way to employ Italian language, when first instructing his first violins to play '*vibrando*' and then '*sempre molto cantando*'. It is thus that he wittily decodes his intention, which was, momentarily but significantly, to beguile us with music in specifically Italian guise – or perhaps to put it more accurately, *dis-guise*. Here then is Mater gloriosa as she swims into view in the Eighth Symphony:

RECORDED MUSIC EXCERPT
Symphony No. 8, Part II, figs. 106–9

I must not forget to mention an important preliminary sketch plan for the Eighth which shows that at one stage what Mahler had in mind was a four-movement version of the work. This was to end with a finale entitled 'Schöpfung durch Eros' ('Creation through Eros'), a movement perhaps envisaged to balance the opening hymn – already in place – of 'Veni creator'. As yet, however, there was no mention of Goethe and *Faust*.

It cannot be without significance that Mahler, in a letter written in 1910 to Alma, to whom the Eighth was to be dedicated, gives prominence to Eros, the god of Love. 'So long as Eros is the ruler of men and gods,' Mahler writes, 'so surely will I make a fresh conquest of all of the heart which once was mine and can only in unison with mine find its way to God and blessedness.'

This was clearly a reference to a period of pain and stress in his marriage. But no less clearly, 'Eros' had been much in his mind when composing the Eighth, which in turn must remind us of the new paths of psychology and psychoanalysis prominent at the beginning of the then new century. Among many other things these pioneering movements focused on the relationship of creativity to the fundamental act of human creation, the role sexuality has to play in the drive to create exalted and enduring works of art. Here too I believe Mahler was remarkably part of his time. As I have already suggested, it is Love and Creativity that eventually unite across Parts I and II to empower his symphony.

With the Eighth behind him, at least in terms of its composition, Mahler in 1908 embarked on another journey, this time eastwards. In *Das Lied von der Erde* he turned to classical Chinese poets, which led yet again to a new world, to the exploration of a new culture, a new aesthetic and above all to the acquisition of new compositional techniques which were undoubtedly indebted to his study of non-Western music, a topic much discussed in Vienna and Berlin during his last years. This time it was not Bach and his counterpoint, but heterophony, the contrapuntal method that services to this day so much music from the East and South-East Asia; while we are conscious, throughout *Das Lied*, of the high profile allotted pentatonicism. Perhaps it might be useful if I tried to explain what heterophony is, in the simplest possible terms. Imagine if you will a basic melody which is then combined simultaneously with different *rhythmic* versions of itself in all the parts, at different octaves or different transpositions as the case may be. But the fundamental idea is that of a non-synchronized unison, giving rise to a contrapuntal texture we identify as heterophony. So it was, ladies and gentlemen, that *Das Lied* explored yet another new world, one this time that ends in the most powerful invocation of a possible transcendence of death that has ever been heard, made meaningful, in music: 'Die liebe Erde allüberall, Blüht auf im Lenz und grünt aufs neu! Allüberall und ewig blauen licht die Fernen, Ewig . . . ewig!' ('The dear earth everywhere blossoms in Spring and grows green again! Everywhere and for ever the distance shines bright and blue, For ever . . . for ever!') Not a farewell to life, by the way, but an acceptance of mortality in the context of the earth's eternal renewal, something very different, which bestows on us our own immortality.

If nothing else, ladies and gentlemen, I hope I have left you with some idea of at least one of the leading characteristics of Mahler's legacy: that his symphonies comprise a chain of new worlds, one after the other, each one making a fresh start. Let's make sure that the 'liebe Erde', which was Mahler's and is ours still, remains intact for future generations the world over, who will want to explore his music, music that teaches us how to love, to live, to die. Mahler never wrote a last word or a last note. He was always creating new worlds. Why don't we give hate, war and destruction a rest and by following his example give creativity, love and peace a chance?

The first known photograph of Mahler and Alma together, Basel, 1903,
a year after their marriage.

# Mahler's Eighth Symphony:
# The Triumph of Eros

## ∻ 2001 ∻

Not one of Mahler's ten symphonies duplicates its predecessor in the manner or character of its opening gestures; each is unique in this respect. The Eighth, however, in its initiating release of an epic volume of sound from a huge and diverse assembly of choral and orchestral forces, offers an experience that is almost *extra*-musical. It not only comprises a statement of fundamental musical materials vigorously asserted but also marks the beginning of a philosophical narrative that underpins the symphony from beginning to end and is clarified and consummated only at the very end of Part II, Mahler's setting of the last scene of the second part of Goethe's *Faust*.

It is perhaps not surprising that special circumstances seemed to attend the birth of the work, which Mahler himself recalled in a letter to his wife Alma in 1910. He had left in 1906 for his customary summer vacation at Maiernigg 'with the firm resolution of idling the holiday away . . . and recruiting my strength. On the threshold of my old workshop . . . the *Spiritus creator* took hold of me and shook me and drove me on for the next eight weeks until my greatest work was done.'

The overwhelming momentum and impetuosity of that first fit of creativity was later confirmed by Alma herself in her reminiscences of her husband, when writing of the events of that summer:

> After we arrived at Maiernigg, there was the usual fortnight during which, nearly every year, he was haunted by the spectre of failing inspiration. Then one morning just as he crossed the threshold of

First published as liner note for the recording of Mahler's Eighth Symphony by the Royal Concertgebouw Orchestra conducted by Riccardo Chailly, Decca 467-314-2.

his studio up in the wood, it came to him – *Veni creator spiritus* ['Come, Creator Spirit']. He composed and wrote down the whole opening chorus to the half-forgotten words. But music and words did not fit – the music had overlapped the text. In a fever of excitement he telegraphed to Vienna and had the whole of the ancient Latin hymn telegraphed back. The complete text fitted the music exactly. Intuitively he had composed the music for all the strophes.

Alma Mahler writes of 'half-forgotten' words. But what is still not generally appreciated is the probability that Mahler's first acquaintance with the famous Latin hymn was in the shape of a German translation made by none other than Goethe himself in April 1820, the opening line of which reads, 'Komm heiliger Geist, du Schaffender' ('Come, Holy Spirit, You Creator'). Furthermore, Goethe considered the hymn 'to be a call to the universal genius of the world'. As Dieter Borchmeyer has observed – to whose research I am indebted – '*Veni, creator spiritus* and the Chorus mysticus [from *Faust*] merge together in the secularizing spirit of Goethe.' Seen in this context, what at first sight might seem to be two unrelated texts in two languages prove to unfold a remarkable inner logic and unity, the 'philosophical narrative' to which I have earlier referred, and to which I shall return.

The Munich premiere of the Eighth, of the 'Symphony of a Thousand' as it came to be known – eight soloists, a chorus of 850 (including a children's chorus of 350), organ and the augmented orchestra (170) of the Munich Konzertverein, conducted by the composer – was given on 12 September 1910 in the new concert hall in the city's exhibition park. It was an occasion like no other in the history of Mahler first performances. Bruno Walter was present and recalled in particular how, when the performance was over, and amid the enthusiastic applause of the audience, Mahler hurried up the steps of the platform to the children's chorus. He passed down their lines and pressed ecstatically every one of the little hands extended to him. It was a symbolic greeting to youth. Also present, along with innumerable friends and distinguished guests (Thomas Mann among them), was Alma, to whom the work was finally to be dedicated, only weeks before the premiere:

The Mahler family at Maiernigg in 1905: Alma and Gustav
with their daughters, Maria and Anna

The whole of Munich as well as all who had come there for the occasion were wrought up to the highest pitch of suspense. The final rehearsal provoked rapturous enthusiasm, but it was nothing to the performance itself. The whole audience rose to their feet as soon as Mahler took his place on the podium; and the breathless silence which followed was the most impressive homage an artist could be paid. I sat in a box almost insensible from excitement.

And then Mahler, god or demon, turned those tremendous volumes of sound into fountains of light. The experience was indescribable. Indescribable, too, the demonstration which followed. The whole audience surged towards the platform.

There followed, she concludes, a happy, relaxed evening when Mahler was 'acclaimed and honoured by all . . . We ended it up by talking until morning, with Gucki [Anna, the Mahlers' surviving daughter], our dear child, sleeping beside us.'

The title page of the piano score of the Eighth Symphony,
bearing the dedication 'To my dear wife, Alma Maria'

A certain irony resides in the fact that it was at this very time that Mahler's marriage was itself in a state of crisis (a brief, informal consultation of Sigmund Freud was only one of the signs of the engulfing turmoil); and yet Alma, however much one might deprecate the baffling insensitivity of her infidelity, undoubtedly played a major role in the conception and inspiration of the Eighth. Mahler's highly intelligent and probing letters to her about the 'meaning' of the Eighth are testimony to this, as was his undoubted passion for his remarkable, if unpredictable, companion. It would be a vulgar error to suggest that the Eighth was all 'about' Alma. But to recognize that Mahler's relationship to her was a fundamental part of the symphony's narrative – remember, the symphony ends unforgettably with Goethe's Chorus mysticus, the famous last words of which are 'Das Ewig-Weibliche/Zieht uns hinan' ('Eternal Womanhood/leads us on high') – is essential to our understanding of the complex coupling of private passion with high philosophy that was the Eighth's defining preoccupation. Seen in this light, and despite its use of a medieval Latin hymn and perhaps the most celebrated of classical German texts, the Eighth emerges, astonishingly, as very much a document of its critical and increasingly secularized time, when there was so much audacious new thinking about human psychology and prominent attention paid to sexuality as the fount of creativity.

As was habitual with Mahler, much thought was given to what form the work ultimately should take. An especially fascinating and revealing bit of evidence is provided by a *four*-movement scheme for the Eighth which was to open with *Veni, creator spiritus* and end with a 'Hymn', *Schöpfung durch Eros* ('Creation through Eros'). The second movement was to be entitled *Caritas,* a title that turns up among the innumerable schemes for the Fourth Symphony, while the third, a scherzo, was described as *Weihnachtsspiele mit dem Kindlein* ('Christmas games with the [Christ] child').

It is true that the *Caritas* idea was not pursued – did Mahler have in mind a slow movement dedicated to the concept of 'Love'? – but the imaginative thinking behind the scherzo most certainly was. In a letter to Alma, written not long before the premiere of the Eighth was given, Mahler spells out his concept of children 'as vessels for the most wonderful practical wisdom', and it is important for our comprehension of the sonorous world that the Eighth represents to recognize the novel role that children have to play; they represent not 'little adults', but emerge in their own right, with their own music, as vocal images of their own 'wise' innocence. We hear this not only in Part I, the Latin hymn, where the boys' voices introduce a unique thread of colour into the movement's ceaseless polyphony, but also in Part II, where the boys impersonate Goethe's 'Selige Knaben' ('Blessed boys').

I have no doubt that all of this explains Mahler's fervent public acknowledgement of his gratitude to the children's chorus at the end of the premiere.

The four-movement scheme shows us that the final 'Hymn' was envisaged as a celebration of Eros; and it is precisely from this point of view that Mahler, again writing to Alma, attempts to clarify his interpretation of the last scene of *Faust* Part II. 'The essence of it is really Goethe's idea that all love is generative, creative, and that there is a physical and spiritual generation which is the emanation of this "Eros".' He goes on to make a challenging comparison between Socrates and Christ, each, he concludes, an embodiment of 'Eros as Creator of the World'! Thus it is that Parts I and II share a common philosophy, the first a summons to the creative spirit, the second, in its climactic final chorus, demonstrating the link between creativity and the magnetism of the Eternal Feminine: Eros triumphant! Freud himself, if he had been more musical than he was, would have known what Mahler was saying.

In the light of this narrative that the work tells, it is scarcely surprising that Mahler thought of the Eighth as his 'grandest' in conception. Its philosophical ambitions are matched by the plurality of its resources and the wholly extraordinary scope and breadth of its music which presents a multiplicity of genres and forms, in themselves constituting a kind of overview of the history of music as Mahler saw it from his turn-of-the-century vantage point.

Across the span of Part II, for example, we encounter a profusion of vocal styles and genres, necessarily so since it was the human voice that was to be chief bearer of the philosophical or poetic ideas: cantata or oratorio, solo song or operatic aria, childlike

chorus or exalted chorale, each is plundered by Mahler and conscripted to serve its own innovative purposes. Nor should we overlook the overtly theatrical gestures that surface in Part II, especially at
that moment of (almost literally!) high drama when Mater gloriosa
floats into view – 'schwebt einher' as Mahler has it in his score,
taking over Goethe's own 'stage direction' for the 'theatre of the
mind', of the spirit, which was surely how the great poet must have
imagined the second part of *Faust*.

It is precisely here in the Eighth that the so often repeated question – why did Mahler never write an opera? – is gloriously
answered in music of riveting inspiration, with its roots, in fact, in
a clearly articulated Italian tradition. Mahler's Italianate style very
often goes unrecognized or underestimated. But as the Eighth
often teaches us, he knew not only his Verdi – as he once
remarked himself, the evolving of his own instrumental thinking
owed much to Verdi – but also works by other Italian composers
famous for their pronounced Italianate style and specifically for
their contributions to the history of opera.

A case in point is Bellini. Can there be much doubt that he was
the model for the ravishing music associated with the materializing of
Mater gloriosa? It is just as if Mahler were imagining the music –
the contour of the ecstatic melody above all – that he might have
written had he been, not Gustav Mahler from Vienna, but Vincenzo
Bellini from Sicily. Mahler of course makes the 'style' his own and
typically we hear Mahler-as-Bellini most pointedly and uncannily
in the 'aria' for orchestra *alone* that accompanies Mater gloriosa's
floating into view (Part II, fig. 106), conceived predominantly for
strings and harp, a texture Mahler had made his own in the years
preceding the composition of the Eighth (shades of the *Adagietto*
from the Fifth and the settings of Rückert). It cannot have been
altogether accidental that the tempo indication here is none other
than *Adagissimo*(!), nor that, as the aria's melody unfolds, Mahler
turns again to *Italian* to make his expressive intention clear: 'sempre
molto cantando' is what he asks for from the violins.

All of this discussion of forms, genres and styles goes to show
that it was not only the history of music past that Mahler exhaustively explored in the Eighth but also the history of his own music,

hence for instance the clear references to the Fourth Symphony and, not surprisingly, its 'heavenly' key of E major; moreover, when we are midstream in Part II, there surface no less audible (but always functional) uses of the style and character we closely associate with Mahler's *Wunderhorn* songs, the majority of which belong to a yet earlier compositional period.

However, of even greater significance, I venture to suggest, was Mahler's 'discovery' of Bach – his total immersion in Bach one is tempted to call it – which manifests itself so unmistakably in Part I, the setting of *Veni, creator spiritus* where what we hear to my mind is Mahler's tribute to Bach and to a particular motet by Bach, *Singet dem Herrn ein neues Lied*, which Mahler much admired and perhaps provided him with his point of departure for Part I of his new symphony.

It is Bach who stands behind the flow of teeming polyphonic textures and contrapuntal forms that characterize the movement. An exuberant example of the latter is the famous double fugue (Part I, fig. 46) which declares, as it gathers density and momentum, 'Per te sciamus da Patrem' ('Grant us knowledge of the Father, and of the Son'); and how better to have that prayer granted than by a virtuoso display of 'learned' counterpoint. But Mahler's pioneering passion for Bach before and beyond the turn of the nineteenth century into the twentieth was by no means part of the 'Back to Bach' aesthetic, which was a later phenomenon, but rather '*Forward* with Bach'. What Part I of the Eighth foretold was the future development in Mahler's own works of a mode of contrapuntal thinking that may have been generated by Bach in the first instance but in a movement like the wild *Rondo-Burleske* of the Ninth Symphony was to establish a virtually modernist type of dissonant counterpoint that had momentous consequences for the new music of the twentieth century.

Mahler not only described his Eighth to Willem Mengelberg, the great Dutch advocate of his music, as his 'grandest' work but also, on another occasion and to another friend, as a 'gift to the nation'. This has been misunderstood by some as an indication of a latent spirit of nationalism or cultural imperialism, which scarcely accords with what we know of Mahler's personality and politico-social sympathies. On the contrary, the 'gift' surely resided in the creation of a work that demanded for its delivery the participation of, virtually, a whole community of performers: children, choral societies, virtuoso soloists and a virtuoso orchestra. Furthermore, it seems only logical, having assembled under one roof the totality of performing resources available to a composer as the new century got under way, that Mahler should provide a matching summation of how the past history of music looked to him in 1906, when the Eighth itself was composed.

Mahler's summation of the past did not exclude prediction of how the future was going to look, partly as a consequence of his own tirelessly innovating creativity. But what will always remain a musico-philosophical landmark, even as the twenty-first century advances, was his bold union of the creative spirit and Eros, a frank avowal, albeit asserted at an exalted level, of the fundamental conjunction of creativity and sexuality, in which sexuality is finally acknowledged to be the fountainhead of creativity. The Eighth, gloriously, abundantly and radically, proclaims Eros – in Mahler's own words – to be the 'Creator of the World'.

# Das *Trink*lied von der Erde?

*To Oliver Knussen, 12.vi.2002 (op. 50)*

⌁ 2002 ⌁

'Every parting gives a foretaste of death.'
Schopenhauer

Before moving on to what might be termed the 'Chinese connection', in an effort to define how, and in what ways, it is meaningful to attribute to an authentic Chinese influence certain features of *Das Lied von der Erde* – Mahler's symphony for tenor, alto and orchestra, composed in 1908 – I should like to spend a few minutes on his choice of poems from Hans Bethge's *Chinesische Flöte* (*The Chinese Flute*). I believe that serious consideration of what prompted Mahler's choice can lead to a fuller understanding of the overall form of *Das Lied* and above all, perhaps, to bring final clarification to a narrative that we find Mahler to have pursued with exemplary rigour, virtually from first note to last.

For heaven knows how many years, discussion of the work's form was clouded by endless attempts to describe the work in terms associated with the 'classical' symphony: i.e., first movement, slow movement, scherzo, finale. This was clearly an absurdity from the start, and especially when trying to give a meaningful account of 'Der Abschied', of both its form and its formal function. None the less even today one still comes across approaches to the work that regard 'Der Einsame' as a kind of slow movement and the succeeding movements ('Von der Jugend', 'Von der Schönheit', 'Der Trunkene im Frühling') collectively representing a 'scherzo'. As for

Lecture given at a conference on *Das Lied von der Erde* at The Hague, May 2002, and published originally in Robert Becqué and Eveline Nikkels (eds.), *Die liebe Erde allüberall, Proceedings of* Das Lied von der Erde *Symposium, Den Haag, 2002.*

# HANS BETHGE∼DIE CHINEſIſCHE FLÖTE

## LEIPZIG∼ IM INſELVERLAG
### MDCCCCXIX

The title page of Hans Bethge's *Die chinesische Flöte*

'Der Abschied', well, that came last – which was about all that could be said about it from a perspective rooted in fallacy.

It was when thinking about what to say about *Das Lied* in a pre-concert talk I gave at the great Mahler Feest in Amsterdam in 1995 that for me a glimmer of light began to dawn. One aspect of it was the speculation that, had Mahler lived to perform the work himself and see it through the press for publication, it was more than possible – a belief I still hold – that he would have followed his own symphonic precedents in dividing the work into Part I and Part II, the first comprising the first five movements, the second, 'Der Abschied'. To spell this out to myself I put together this simple diagram:

| PART I | | | | | PART II | | |
|---|---|---|---|---|---|---|---|
| I | 2 | 3 | 4 | 5 | 6 | | CODA |
| a | | | | ➔ A | c ➔ | C | a/C |
| a | | | | | | ➔ | a/C |

If nothing else this crude little 'map' confirmed my guess that it made sense to think that the first five movements comprised one self-contained part which, having run its course, could the more easily embark on another, no less self-contained unit. (To the specific 'otherness' of Part II I shall certainly return.)

But let me first finish off my comments on Part I. My diagram indicates that for me the middle three movements of Part I are contained within a 'frame', a frame that is then itself framed by the overarching frame of the whole work, a trajectory that is initiated by the first movement, the first 'Trinklied', 'Das Trinklied vom Jammer der Erde', the title of which Mahler at one time considered using as a title for the entire work, and concludes only when the final, long sustained chord of 'Der Abschied' has been reached.

The work's similarly overarching tonal scheme precisely reflects the dichotomy of its form. The five movements of Part I are built around A: the first, in A minor, the key often associated with Mahler's darkest and bleakest thoughts and feelings, while the fifth – seemingly – affirms A major. But as I shall try to make clear, this is a desperate A major that if anything is even more dismaying, more undoing, than the tonic minor.

However, if A is unequivocally the tonic of Part I, it is C, with the minor very much in the lead until the final culmination of 'Der Abschied' in the major, that is the tonic around which Part II, in all its complexity, is constructed. Thus it is that in terms of its tonal organization *Das Lied* is bitonal, though not quite in the sense that we customarily use that term. On the other hand, it is one of the many miracles in which this symphony abounds that the famous last chord with which 'Der Abschied' concludes combines both tonal centres. What we hear is what the young Benjamin Britten unforgettably described in a letter written in June 1937. He had been listening to the Bruno Walter recording, and was over-whelmed by the work's coda ('Ewig . . . ewig!' ('Eternally . . . eternally')). 'I cannot understand it,' he writes, 'it passes over me like a tidal wave – and that matters not a jot either, because *it goes on for ever, even if it is never performed again – that final chord is printed on the atmosphere*.' [My italics.]

What of course haunted Britten was that final chord of 'Der Abschied' in which the work's double tonics are vertically conflated to form an added sixth, a chord incidentally that was always to remain for Britten one of exceptional significance; and it is on that chord that 'Der Abschied' blissfully and wellnigh inaudibly expires ('Ewig . . . ewig!'), with the very inspiration, so to say, on its lips that gave energetic birth to the work in its first bars (see Ex. 1). For me there is no more brilliant and arresting instance of Mahler's long-term powers of organization of his materials than the horizontal articulation of the work's basic motive which opens the first move-ment and the vertical conflation of those very same pitches which was to provide him at its end with the perfect sonorous equivalent of eternity. I hope my two music examples clarify what I've been saying:

Ex. 1 'Der Trinklied vom Jammer der Erde'

Ex. 2 'Der Abschied'

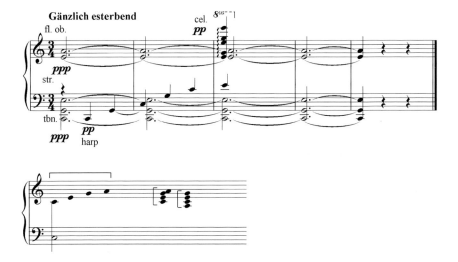

On this occasion, I am particularly anxious to draw your attention to a fact, perhaps still little appreciated, of the extraordinarily close scrutiny to which Mahler subjected his texts. The rigour and intensity of imagination he brought to bear are immediately apparent the moment we begin to understand how fundamental to the work is the complex organization of its poetic and symbolic imagery. It is my belief that it is precisely in this sphere that we come to comprehend the most subtle and most profound thinking that informs and shapes *Das Lied* and, above all, guides its narrative.

Recognition of Mahler's introduction of images of spring in both the first and fifth movements as clear and calculated anticipa-

tions of the renewal of the earth that 'Der Abschied' finally cele-
brates, has now become part of even the most modest of commentaries on the work. All I would wish to add here, and I address not
so much passive audiences or students as *performers* – those who
bear the responsibility of re-creating in the concert hall what we
must assume Mahler wanted to be heard – is the crucial importance of ensuring that those images are given the emphasis and
articulation, from the singers, from the orchestra, that guarantee
their resonating on in our memory, so that when they confront us
again in their final guise, 'Die liebe Erde allüberall blüht auf im
Lenz . . .' ('The dear Earth everywhere blossoms in spring'), we
come to realize that the symphony has at last reached its goal, the
goal that was targeted way back in the two drinking songs that
frame Part 1 (see my diagram above). How fervently I long from
time to time for singers in *Das Lied* to take as much trouble with
their words as Mahler did in choosing – and sometimes writing! –
them.

It must be of quite special significance that the image of spring
is crucially released in both of the drinking songs, the first and fifth
in the cycle of movements. Spring, in fact, has no place in the intervening songs: we have autumn in 'Der Einsame . . .' (No. 2) and
what must surely be regarded as high summer in 'Von der
Schönheit' (No. 4). However, what is no less important to recognize is the differences that characterize Mahler's use of his symbolic
springtime imagery. While in the first drinking song spring is
installed – and remains – as a symbol of possible hope amid the
song's pessimism, in the fifth, which concludes Part 1, a comparable
imagery is released only to be violently rejected, wholesale. The
protagonist finds his only means of warding off reality – intimations
of mortality? – is to resort to the bottle. 'Was geht mich denn der
Frühling an!?' ('For what does spring matter to me?'), he howls.
'Lasst mich betrunken sein!' ('Let me be drunk!') In short, we're
back to drinking again; and that this fifth movement culminates in
a seemingly exuberant A *major* makes the pain of it the more
intense. We are witnessing a moment of disconcerting self-delusion
and self-destruction.

Thus ends Part 1, and if we are allowed a real pause here before embarking on Part II – something I believe Mahler himself would have welcomed (introduced, even) – then it becomes impossible to avoid acknowledging the unique importance that the act of drinking has accumulated in Part I; as we shall see, 'Der Abschied' will identify an act of 'intoxication' to which, guilt-free, we may all aspire. (Drinking, I know, is a feature also of 'Von der Jugend', but there it is doubtless Chinese tea that the poet and composer had in mind.)

When 'Der Abschied' – Part II – opens, we find ourselves some place else. (Hence the importance of my suggested pause.) The stroke of the tam-tam alone, together with the onset of the new tonal centre on C, establishes that we are no longer where we were. The gong may also assert what we may finally come to recognize as the genuine 'Chinese' dimension of *Das Lied*, a sense, that is, of an 'otherness' that was essential to Mahler's purpose, and nowhere more so than in 'Der Abschied', a point to which I shall return. But what is certain is that we are no longer in a familiar world of love, Nature, human beauty, rage, despair, of recourse in sorrow to intoxication: the gong stroke cleanses the slate and propels us on a new journey.

Mahler, as I have so often remarked, was an inveterate, ceaseless traveller through numberless varieties of landscapes and human experience, through time, through musical history itself. So it came as no great surprise to me, years ago, when I realized that it was his knowledge of Bach's Passions and cantatas that helps us to comprehend the peculiar form of 'Der Abschied', the sixth and final movement of Mahler's symphony. With that knowledge in mind we can, I suggest, begin to understand that it is in fact an innovatory solo cantata that brings the work to its conclusion, a cantata, if you like, which we might justifiably regard as Mahler's own Passion, his solitary exercise (if that colourless word may be forgiven) in this form.

In this context, the recitatives, three of them, so astonishing in their impact, so totally unheralded, speak for themselves. Each, be it noted, defines a different stage in the protagonist's – the soloist's – journey. I use that word advisedly because it is now, with the onset of 'Der Abschied', that we realize that, as distinct from Part I, sealed off as that is by its tonal scheme and the framing function of the two *Trinklieder*, a journey is what we ourselves are to undertake, along with the protagonist. And the vehicle for that journey will be the great funeral march in C minor, which begins to assemble itself in fragmentary form in the brief orchestral prelude to 'Der Abschied' which precedes the first recitative.

There is much that might be said about the recitatives alone. However, I must content myself with remarking briefly on how Mahler chooses to compose them, for example that in the first two the singer–narrator is accompanied by an elaborate obbligato for the flute, improvisatory in character (though not in notation) and thereby reflecting in its deliberate irregularity the irregular sound, rhythms and patterns of Nature. This first recitative, indeed, marvellously depicts the world at sunset and prepares us for the sight of the rising moon and a world asleep. By the time we reach the second recitative the narrator, still accompanied by the flute, has been transformed into the protagonist whose journey we are about to share. Responses to and descriptions of Nature give way to exclamations of an altogether profounder identity with the Earth. In the 'aria' that succeeds this recitative its vocal climax is reached to words that summon up an image of spiritual intoxication generated by the earth's capacity ever to renew itself: 'O Schönheit! o ewigen Liebens, Lebens trunk'ne Welt!' ('O beauty! O eternal-love-and-life-intoxicated world!') Now it is the world that is the source of intoxication.

It is no accident that the liberating ecstasy of this passage clearly anticipates the character of the coda which brings the movement to a close. (Or, rather, it doesn't, because as the youthful Britten perceived in 1937 the final moment, that final chord of the added sixth, is 'printed on the atmosphere', 'goes on for ever'.) But, as we shall see, the calculated recall at this critical point of imagery central to the concept of *Das Lied* takes on additional significance, especially in the light of the path that the narrative is just about to pursue. (To the ultimate act of drinking I shall return below.)

I have already touched on the narrative concept that underpins *Das Lied* and suggested that with the onset of 'Der Abschied' we find ourselves not only somewhere else (both sonically and in location) but going somewhere else. It is for that last reason, I believe,

that after the second recitative (and ensuing 'aria') Mahler inter-
polates a funeral march in C minor for the orchestra alone, in which
all the fragmentary 'march' elements we have been aware of from
the start of the movement are developed, cohere, into an impassioned, extended lament. This is not, however, a stationary moment
of ritual but on the contrary an unequivocal *rite of passage*. When
we arrive – accompanied by climactic *sforzando* strokes on the tam-
tam, the very sonority that has initiated the movement *pianissimo* in
its first bars – we have indubitably passed over, passed to the other
side. (Mahler himself in his short score designates the strokes on the
tam-tam that mark the beginning of the funeral march, 'Grab-
gelaüte' (funeral bells).)

I am reminded here inevitably of the narrative sequence we
encounter in Mahler's Second Symphony, which opens with a
huge funeral march, again in C minor, the *Todtenfeier*. For me, as I
have argued elsewhere, this represents not so much a concluding
ceremony of death as a continuation of the narrative of the protagonist whom we have already got to know in the First
Symphony. According to the composer himself, the finale of the
First should not be 'read' as evidence of his protagonist's triumph
over adversity but in fact also embodies his defeat and eventual
death. 'The victory is won only with the death of my struggling
Titan,' Mahler remarked to Natalie Bauer-Lechner in Berlin in
1890. It is my view that the funeral march in the Second does not
represent so much a finite burial as the initiating stage in the self-
same protagonist's journey through the rest of the symphony until
Resurrection is attained. In short, there is a continuously evolving
narrative from the start of the First Symphony, on through death
and into the afterlife, until the culminating end of the Second. The
latter symphony's *Todtenfeier*, I believe, different though it is in style
and character, can be regarded as anticipating the comparable journeying function played by the funeral march of 'Der Abschied',
which transports us from life to death's door: we have died, and
when we get there it is Death who receives us.

But what in fact is the clear evidence for believing that in *Das
Lied* too, in its finale, at its most critical point, we have made the
crossing to the other side? I believe this rests with a feature of the

third and *last* recitative, which, again to my mind, has received insufficient scrutiny and assessment from scholars and performers. I refer first to the conspicuous absence of the flute obbligato that has previously characterized the first and second recitatives. I commented, it is true, on this absence in my earlier work on *Das Lied*,* noting that now, in recitative three, it is none other than a distantly tolling obbligato, this time for the *tam-tam* – the very sonority symbolic of death! – that accompanies the voice. But what I failed to do was to draw the obligatory conclusion that the abandonment of the flute had to be so. There was no longer any possibility for the protagonist to overhear the sounds of Nature or discern their irregularities; he is now somewhere quite else, in that silent no-man's-land, awaiting – or awaiting to confront – his final destiny. He is *beyond life*. The silencing of the flute, and the strokes of the tam-tam, tell us that. Furthermore, the momentum of the orchestral lament carries over into the contour and rhythm of the recitative's opening phrase, 'Er stieg vom Pferd . . .' ('He alighted from his horse . . .'). (After all, it is only logical that he should dismount to the music by which he has arrived.) There is also a purely practical consideration that I am certain Mahler would have had in mind at this critical moment in the narrative, to be as little distracted as was musically possible from the voice and – above all – the words.

It is not my purpose on this occasion to traverse ground that has been pretty thoroughly explored and commented on. I am thinking here of the seeming confusion of identity that Mahler, no doubt inadvertently – it would surely have been cleared up if he had lived to conduct a performance – brought on himself by necessarily substituting the third person ('Er'/'He') for Bethge's personal pronoun 'Ich'/'I'. In so doing, however, he created an ambiguity that persists to this day. I wrote about this at not inconsiderable length in *Songs and Symphonies of Life and Death* (pp. 424–32), and since then Stephen Hefling has returned to the topic in his monograph on *Das Lied*, suggesting that the 'musical persona [my "protagonist"] and the archetypal figure of Death have become one, inseparably fused, no longer adversaries'. Hefling puts this

---

* DMSSLD, p. 401.

very convincingly, though I think it was the late Christopher Palmer who was the first to suggest that it is 'symbolically, [Mahler's] old enemy, death, who arrives on horseback' and hands the waiting friend the drink, the draught, the elixir – call it what you will – that will enable him to experience, to become part of, the bliss that attends man's recognition of the life that death in fact bestows: our 'immortality' is embodied in the process by which the earth perpetually renews itself, and thereby its inhabitants. Small wonder that it was precisely here, for the coda, the work's denouement, no less, Mahler had to ditch Bethge and find his own words to match the culminating freedom of the music, for which we have been prepared by earlier stages in the movement's evolution:

> Die liebe Erde allüberall
> Blüht auf im Lenz und grünt aufs neu!
> Allüberall und ewig blauen licht die Fernen,
> Ewig . . . ewig!

> *The dear Earth everywhere*
> *Blossoms in spring and grows green again!*
> *Everywhere and eternally the distance shines bright and blue!*
> *Eternally . . . eternally . . .*

But intriguing though the question is of the identity of the participants in the final dialogue, it is not really the issue that for me is of prime importance. It is, rather, that in the special context of the third recitative, the moment we have reached in the narrative, Mahler turns yet again – and for the last time – to the image of an act of drinking:

> Er stieg vom Pferd und *reichte im den Trunk des Abschieds dar* [my italics].

> He alighted from his horse and *handed him the drink of farewell*.

Thus it is, though the significance of it has long gone unappreciated, that the image of drinking that has been central to the symphony's first part resurfaces in 'Der Abschied': we witness the consumption of the elixir that leads directly to the final intoxication and ecstasy – 'Die liebe Erde . . .' – by which we must now suppose the protagonist is himself consumed. All sense of a unique personal identity is gone but like the last chord, to quote Britten's words for the last time, we must imagine him continuing to exist for ever, 'printed on the atmosphere'. Here for the first time the image of spring is released in the guise of the Earth's capacity for perpetual renewal, wherein is incorporated mankind's immortality. It is that final enlightenment that constitutes the last image of 'intoxication', one this time that erases any distinction between death and an eternity of liberation from life. Ewig . . . ewig!

Should we not retitle the symphony? It is my belief that 'Das *Trink*lied von der Erde' would remind us of the image about which the whole work is built and, in Mahler's final articulation of it, finds its consummation.

How very strange it seems now that one of the work's critics after hearing its premiere under Bruno Walter in 1911 complained that the chief disappointment lay in the symphony's coda: what was missing, it seems, was any sense of 'redemption'! If nothing else this crass response is suggestive of how far removed in *Das Lied* was Mahler's philosophy from the conventional beliefs of his day about the afterlife.

There can be little doubt that the philosophy that generated *Das Lied* was significantly influenced by an interest in the philosophies of the East that had long been established in Europe by thinkers with whose work Mahler was known to have been familiar: Schopenhauer, for instance, and Nietzsche, and Gustav Theodor Fechner, who was perhaps not of a like stature, but undoubtedly one whose ideas clearly had a role in shaping Mahler's own. And there was Wagner, of course, himself a further channel of communication and influence, with his own undoubted interest in the East.

It is always a complex matter to try to pin down and assess the specific relationships between ideas, whether philosophical or aesthetic, and their realization in terms and images of music. In so far as this can be done it seems to me that Stephen Hefling in his monograph on *Das Lied* has admirably documented the relevant sources.

# TONHALLE

Montag, den 20. November, abends 8 Uhr

(Öffentliche Hauptprobe: Sonntag, den 19. November, vormittags 11 Uhr)

# ORCHESTER·KONZERT

Ausführende:

Dirigent: Hofkapellmeister BRUNO WALTER

Soli: M<sup>ME</sup> CHARLES CAHIER (Alt)

MARIE MÖHL-KNABL (Sopran)

WILLIAM MILLER k. k. Hofopernsänger (Tenor)

Chor: ORATORIEN-VEREIN AUGSBURG

unter dem hohen Protektorate
S. K. Hoheit des Prinzen Ludwig Ferdinand von Bayern

Orchester: KONZERTVEREINS-ORCHESTER

(auf 100 Künstler verstärkt)

Orgel: Hoforganist Prof. LUDWIG MAIER

———

I. ABTEILUNG:                    URAUFFÜHRUNG

## „DAS LIED VON DER ERDE"

Eine Symphonie für eine Tenor- und eine Altstimme und großes Orchester
(Dichtung aus Hans Bethge's „Chinesische Flöte") —

1. Das Trinklied vom Jammer der Erde
2. Der Einsame im Herbst
3. Von der Jugend
4. Von der Schönheit
5. Der Trunkene im Frühling
6. Der Abschied

II. ABTEILUNG:

## ZWEITE SYMPHONIE C-moll

für großes Orchester, Soli, Chor und Orgel

1. Allegro moderato
2. Andante moderato
3. In sehr ruhig fließender Bewegung
4. „Urlicht" (Sehr feierlich und schlicht)
5. Im Tempo des Scherzos (Sehr zurückhaltend) —
   „Der Rufer in der Wüste", — „Der große Appell".

The programme for the first performance of *Das Lied von der Erde*
on 20 November 1911

[FIRST PUBLICATION]

But the question that I find the most fascinating, though no less teasing and certainly no less complicated, is this: how do we discern what is undeniably 'Chinese' about *Das Lied*, purely in terms of music, and how, if we think we have found it, do we go about defining it? And, no less urgent and specific, what precisely was it that triggered off Mahler's voyage eastwards?

There is no overlooking Bethge, naturally, and I for one continue to be grateful to him for releasing in Mahler the inspiration that gave us *Das Lied*. I put some emphasis on 'releasing' because I believe it to be the case that the inspiration was already there, pre-Bethge, in the person and poetry of Friedrich Rückert, himself an orientalist and philologist of high repute (the language in question was Chinese).

Mahler himself let it be known how much Rückert's poetry meant to him during his last years, and it has often struck me as extremely odd that relatively little attention has been paid to Mahler's late Rückert settings, in particular the *Rückert-Lieder* of 1901–2. The unique beauty of these songs has long been recognized, and in the case of at least one of them, 'Ich bin der Welt abhanden gekommen', endless parallels have been drawn between the song and 'Der Abschied' of *Das Lied*, though often the significance of the most striking parallels in compositional technique has gone unremarked.

In short, the time has surely come when Bethge is no longer thought of as the 'onlie begetter', practically speaking, of *Das Lied* and for more serious work to be done on the Mahler–Rückert relationship, with especial attention being paid to what in fact were the first stirrings in Mahler of compositional techniques that can now be readily identified as themselves articulating his 'Chinese' dimension. And of course it is the existence of *Das Lied* that enables us retrospectively to make the identification and perhaps thereby document an *evolving* process in which Rückert played a crucial initiating role. I have no doubt now that this was the case and that when Mahler had Bethge brought to his notice by a friend, the techniques were already basically *in situ*. I do not one bit underestimate the importance of Bethge's contribution, but it was not by him that Mahler was prompted to acquire the new technical means that we encounter in his later masterpiece, *Das Lied*.

For all these reasons, I continue to harbour substantial doubts about any direct influence on Mahler supposedly exerted by a number of wax-cylinder recordings, issued, as I have now come to believe, in early shellac disc form, and which, as Henry-Louis de La Grange recounts in the third volume of the French edition of his biography of Mahler, p. 341, were discovered by a friend, the banker Paul Hammerschlag, in a shop near the Stefansdom in Vienna and passed on to the composer, at a time when an interest in perhaps what one might term the 'Chinese' dimension was still musically active in his mind. You will remember what I have just said about Mahler and the late Rückert songs, composed already in 1901.

I shall be returning to all these matters and in the context in particular of highly significant information conveyed to me by Peter Revers. But first I thought it might be helpful to be briefly reminded that it was Berlin that was one of the most important turn-of-the-century centres to pioneer the recording of authentic musics – my plural is deliberate – from the East, an activity that in itself was part of the growing exploration of, and fascination with, the arts of the East. Bethge was part of this powerful cultural trend which also included a widespread general taste for the consumption of the exotic. By the way, it is not only a scholarly or cultural appetite we encounter in these diverse fields but also the appetite of *commerce*.

Although we may never be able to be wholly confident which items of Chinese music Mahler himself might have heard, what we can inform ourselves about very precisely is the kind of sound Mahler would have encountered if he did indeed listen to recordings that first originated on wax cylinders at the turn of the century. It is for this reason that I have brought with me today a typical wax-cylinder recording (transferred to tape) made in Beijing in 1912–14 (a year or two after Mahler's death) by a field researcher from the Berlin Ethnomusicological Museum, a brief excerpt of background music to a theatre play, performed on the *sheng*, a kind of elaborate Chinese mouth organ. And please do understand my chief reason for playing this is to acquaint you with the extreme primitiveness of the sound and the inevitable brevity of the excerpt. The point I am making is principally to acquaint you with what recording techniques could at best achieve at the early stage of their evolution (electrical recording did not begin until 1925 or thereabouts):

RECORDED MUSIC EXCERPT
The recording referred to above

I in no way underestimate the importance of that illustration, nor that of the very many other similar recordings that date from the same period and earlier. I merely wonder seriously how realistic and meaningful in fact it is to suggest or believe that, if Mahler did find himself listening to the music represented on wax cylinders at the technical level we have just ourselves experienced, we could properly speak of a subsequent 'influence'. Judged purely from the perspective of information, one surely has to rate the possibility as pretty remote.

None the less, Mahler's, as I now think, probable contact with 'live' Chinese music remains of real importance, and it is exactly here that Peter Revers, himself a distinguished contributor to this conference, has come up with some highly significant evidence. In a ground-breaking text,* he draws our attention in its third and final section, 'Überlegungen zu Mahlers Rezeption fernöstlicher Musik' ('Considerations on Mahler's Reception of Far East Music'), to a series of recordings issued by Beka, a Berlin record company that made a special feature in 1906 (NB!) of a release on ten-inch shellac discs of a variety of 'exotic' musics, from China, Japan and Malaya (as it was at the time), along with many others.

The discs of particular relevance to our purpose are numbered 2086, 2130, 2175 and 2176, and represent a transfer of wax-cylinder recordings to shellac discs. We also learn from Revers that these discs formed part of the 'Phonogrammarchiv der Österreichischen Akademie der Wissenschaft' ('Phonographic Archive of the Austrian Academy of Science'), founded in 1899. These few facts lend weight to a point I was making earlier, the spread of investigative scholarship into new areas of technical documentation, from

---

* 'Aspekte der Ostasienrezeption Gustav Mahlers *Das Lied von der Erde*'.

wax cylinder to shellac disc, which in turn represents a shift from exclusive academic circles to a much broader public interest. We should also take note that from 1899 Vienna, like Berlin, was in the business of both meticulously exploring and, more broadly, disseminating the 'exotic' – selling it, in fact, to an eager public.

Once again through Professor Revers's kindness I have been able to hear a transcript on tape of the 'Beka-Grand-Record' (so the label reads) items numbered above; but once again, and despite some justifiable efforts to have improved the clarity of the sound, I find myself still in doubt about the *ultimate* – that is, creative – relevance of Mahler's supposed confrontation with 'authentic' Chinese music in recorded form. However, in the light of Revers's research, it seems to me now that the fact of that confrontation has now been virtually established, and that in itself is of no small importance. Furthermore, I also believe that it is more than likely that it was the Beka discs that Mahler would have heard, that were brought to him – bought *for* him – by Hammerschlag.

Revers remarks in his text on a feature of the music on the Beka discs that Adorno so memorably characterized in his Mahler study as 'unscharfes unisono' – 'blurred unison' is perhaps the best and most Adorno-like equivalent in English. In other words the unequivocal presence of 'heterophony'; and it is with that topic in mind, and with one last musical excerpt, that I wish to conclude.

What I want you to hear is a shellac disc issued by the famous German label Odeon. My guess, in which I have been valuably assisted by Joanna C. Lee, is that the recording belongs to the (early) 1930s, some years, that is, after the introduction of electrical recording in 1925, a date that puts it well beyond the reach of Mahler! But that is not the point I really want to make. It is, rather, to present you with an illustration that will show you first how rapid was the evolution of recording in the first decades of the twentieth century with remarkable advances being made in the quality and clarity of sound and secondly how these advances in technical achievement also made their impact in the sphere of exotic or, as I prefer, non-Western musics, above all on their accessibility and distribution. For here we find Odeon following in the footsteps of Beka in 1906, perhaps with less stress on 'authenticity', but undoubtedly with an eye on a growing market with customers in both East and West. As I have remarked before, commerce was soon playing an active role in the cultural trend – the 'mystery of the East' – that was so pronounced a feature at the turn of the century and inevitably, for good and ill, exploited by the new technologies.

The intertwining of culture and commerce is by no means an insignificant phenomenon, but my principal reason for playing this Odeon disc is that it enables us to hear very clearly Adorno's 'blurred unison' in audible action. It is a number for voice and flute, accompanied by percussion, with both the singer and flautist seemingly delivering an identical melody, though it will soon strike you that what we are actually hearing is a less than perfect unison, Adorno's 'unscharfes unisono', in fact, which in the West we identify as the practice of heterophony, a form of polyphony which, in many manifestations in the Orient and South East Asia, services the unique contrapuntal textures characteristic of the regions' musics:

RECORDED MUSIC EXCERPT
Odeon A 26012

I am bold enough to suggest that if Mahler had lived long enough to hear the example I have just played you, he might well have enjoyed it, admired it even, as I do. But none of this is really relevant to the main issue that I am trying to address. If it was not from wax cylinders or shellac discs, from what source was it precisely that Mahler derived the heterophony he practises so brilliantly in *Das Lied*?

You won't be surprised to hear that I believe the historical truth to be that the source that fundamentally inspired him was the pioneering investigative work prominent among scholars in Vienna at the turn of the century, activities that in many respects were in parallel with those in Berlin, though it was that city that led in the field of recording. If nothing else, the first of my two music examples testifies to that, as do the Beka records brought to our notice by Revers.

We know that Mahler was an insatiably inquisitive personality and no less intellectually curious and explorative. A close friend of his was the remarkable scholar Guido Adler, whom Edward Reilly has so valuably studied; and I have little doubt that during the years that were to culminate in the composition of *Das Lied*, Mahler and Adler must have conversed about the topic of 'other' musics from the East. I am pretty certain, moreover, that Mahler would have found himself an absorbed and stimulated reader of Adler's text of 1908 entitled 'Über Heterophonie' ('On Heterophony')* – might not Adler have shown it to him even before its appearance in print?

What we should never forget is that these topics and the issues they raised were vividly alive and the subject of vigorous discussion and debate in the culture of the time. Indeed, the work of pioneering investigative musicologists like Adler was, if you like, a comparable response to that being shown in almost all fields of creative and decorative activity in Mahler's day: the 'exotic' was a concept in full flower at all levels. It so happened that Mahler was more serious than most about finding out what the 'exotic' might, compositionally, have to offer him.

I want to read you a text that I believe to be crucial. Adler quotes it in his own 1908 article, a description of heterophony by a fellow musicologist, Carl Stumpf, to my mind a model of its kind. The music he writes about was Siamese in origin:

> It is not a question here of various themes being played simultaneously but rather of all the instruments compiling a texture out of basically identical materials whilst allowing themselves significant individual liberties: one instrument proceeds in simple crotchets, another plays around it with all kinds of ornamentation, a third resolves this completely into semiquaver passages, triplets and so on, at the same time as the semiquaver passages of the individual instruments are in utmost cohesion. In some principal motives, they all come together again in perfect unison.

The first 'Trinklied' in *Das Lied* tells us with dramatic energy that, master of counterpoint though Mahler was, what we are hearing is something arrestingly new in his polyphony. In fact, if we

* *Peters Jahrbuch* 1908, pp. 17–27.

listen to the first 'Trinklied', and after it read Stumpf, then we find ourselves reading a precise description of what, contrapuntally speaking, we have just heard. The *locus classicus*, I believe, is the fourth strophe, the critical point of recapitulation in the first song, 'Im Mondschein auf den Gräbern . . .' ('In the moonlight, on the graves . . .') (the first time incidentally that Ex. 1 is allotted to the voice!), where, between figs. 39 and 45, we hear Mahler in top-gear heterophonic action, a living example of a 'style' the promotion of which Adler was to call for in his concluding sentence: 'We are bound to have to acknowledge heterophony . . . theoretically to be the third category of style besides homophony and polyphony.' What Mahler gives us, of course, is not theory but practice, the first major breakthrough of heterophony in his music, which, after long-postponed recognition, can now be assessed as a moment of exceptional significance and eventual influence in the history of twentieth-century music.

(In this connection I should like briefly to mention my theory that it is composers who, in the course of their compositional histories, have shown a predilection for *canon*, and a conspicuous facility in the use of it, that are the more likely to succumb to the appeal and challenge of heterophony. Both Mahler and Britten, I would like to suggest, support my contention.)

Heterophony, ironically enough, for all its authenticity, would not necessarily have been heard by audiences (past, present or future) as an immediately audible sign or evidence of the informing presence of the East. Nor, for that matter, I suggest, transparently pentatonic though the conception of the symphony's basic motive is from the start (see Ex. 1), I do not think we can assume that the obligatory sense of 'otherness', of a different location, of embarking on a journey to another world, could have been achieved alone by the pentatonic and heterophonic features revealed in the first song. It was for this reason, I believe – and it was essential, surely, for Mahler to get the process going before 'Der Abschied' is reached – that he took such care to demonstrate the Chinese connection in a form that would have been readily recognizable. Hence the overt pentatonicism of, say, 'Von der Jugend' or 'Von der Schönheit', the Chinese-ness of which was part of the popular culture of Mahler's day, and has continued to be, to our own day.

We might well think that Mahler here was pursuing the merely decorative, but we would be wrong on two counts. First and foremost, perhaps, because of the wealth of imagination, the sophistication, subtlety of nuances, and refinement he brought to these numbers; and second, because, while the decorative was not his objective – though it seems to me that even here he achieves much more than any of his contemporaries – communication was; and it is in fact as a means of communication, of virtually instant accessibility to the idea of relocation, to awareness that we are now somewhere else than the world with which we are familiar, that Mahler puts overt pentatonicism to use. It is a means of preparing us for the eventual 'otherness' of 'Der Abschied', its music and its narrative, in which the 'Chinese' dimension of *Das Lied* finds its ultimate and most profound musical and philosophical expression.

There is much to be thought about, discussed, contended, debated, decoded; and there are surely fresh approaches still to be made. But of one thing I think we can be certain: that in the history of the creative relationship between East and West in the twentieth century, 'Das *Trink*lied von der Erde' must stand as an achievement of genius that has not been equalled or surpassed. It represents music's own contribution to the philosophy of life, death and – by way of that final draught – transcendence, no less.

# Mahler and Nature:
## Landscape into Music

### ∻ 1986 ∽

I am going to speculate about a possible relationship between landscape and music; and about one particular landscape – Toblach, now
Dobbiaco, in the Italian Dolomites – and Gustav Mahler. Before
the First World War the area was part of the Austro-Hungarian
Empire and accessible by train from Vienna. It was there, amid this
landscape of forests, lakes and mountains, that Mahler in the last
summers of his life, from 1908 until his death in May 1911, wrote
his last works, *Das Lied von der Erde,* the Ninth Symphony and the
incomplete Tenth.

Why Toblach? To answer that one has to look back to 1907,
when Mahler spent his summers composing in the only house he
ever owned, at Maiernigg on the Wörthersee. Here, three heavy
blows fell on him: it was in this year at Maiernigg that one of his
two daughters, Maria, caught diphtheria and cruelly died; at almost
the same time, Mahler's doctors diagnosed a heart condition that
certainly caused him anxiety, restricted his physical activities,
though not his creativity, and contributed to the weakening of his
hitherto powerful constitution, which finally succumbed to a viral
infection in 1911. In addition, in the same year, 1907, he found himself at loggerheads with the bureaucrats in Vienna; and, frustrated
and taxed beyond the tolerable, he resigned as Director of the
Hofoper – the Vienna Court Opera – and signed a contract to conduct at the Metropolitan Opera, New York.

Maiernigg could no longer offer him the serenity of spirit he
needed for composition. He had to find a new place to make a new
start. What was found was a farmhouse near Toblach, at Alt-

---

Lecture, 'Musikwoche *in memoriam* Gustav Mahler', Toblach, 22 July 1986; originally
given with recorded musical illustrations.

Mahler walking in the mountains near Toblach

Schluderbach, on the second floor of which Mahler in those last summers lived with his wife and surviving daughter. (It stands today virtually untouched.)

From that farmhouse Mahler continued to explore and absorb the sights and sounds of Nature, something he had done all his life, the impact of which we encounter in his earlier symphonies as much as in his later. But Mahler's enthusiasm for Nature was perhaps of a rather different order from the conventional kind. He was no passive observer of landscape but an active explorer of it, especially on foot. We know of his fondness for walking amid the lakes and mountains, and can guess with some certainty of being right that what attracted him to mountains at least was their *silence* – that unique silence which in fact constitutes an aural experience in itself, a silence that is itself a sound. It is a silence moreover that magically articulates any natural sound that may impinge upon it – the cry of a bird, cowbells from the valleys below, the murmuring of a mountain stream. All these sounds, the individuality of which might be lost when they form part of the larger chorus of noise that surrounds our day-to-day life on earth, are heard sharp and clear, each with its own sonorous physiognomy, in the context of silence.

Now all this may begin to sound like poetic 'rhapsody'; but in fact my purpose is not to rhapsodize but to remind us of something very essential about Mahler, namely that he walked not only on his feet but also *with his ears*: that a walk for this wholly extraordinary man was as much a *sonorous* experience as a matter of physical locomotion. We have to remember that for a walking composer his ears are at least as important as his eyes; while Mahler's eyes performed a much more complex role than drinking in, in a general way, the grand beauty of lake and mountain. His eyes, I think, could be almost as specific as his ears. (This is a point to which I shall return.)

To one form of Nature's music, birdsong, Mahler's ears had always been open. We don't have to wait until his late works, for example, to encounter the incorporation into his music of the song or cry of a bird. (I have often thought that in this respect alone Mahler and Messiaen might have had much to say to each other.)

I could quote many examples from the earlier works. But perhaps one is of particular interest and importance, the great cadenza in the finale of the Second Symphony, *Der grosse Appel* ('The Great Call'), the summons that leads to the final elevation of the dead to paradise. At this critical juncture in the symphony, which is both a *coup de théâtre* and a radical exploration of acoustic space, Mahler, after a great release of orchestral hubbub and activity, creates a moment of silence and then fills it with a huge instrumental cadenza compiled from horn calls and trumpet fanfares, and, no less significantly, birdsong. It is indeed the liquid aria of the bird, the flute and piccolo combined, that surely represents after the travail and tension of life on earth, the promise of hope, light and eternal life. The distant rumble of thunder on the drums also has a role to play in this remarkable passage, the innovatory techniques employed in which continue to surprise one. But what grips the attention especially is the free, quasi-improvisatory character of the cadenza and in particular the free, unmeasured nature of the birdsong, not bound by the tyranny of the barline, any more than the birds themselves in the real world are subject to the rules of composition. I have no doubt, moreover, that while that great cadenza in the finale of the Second is pre-eminently *symbolic* not *naturalistic* in its intention and effect, it none the less had its roots in Mahler's acoustic experience of the universe. The free mix of the sounds, the unmeasured birdsong, all these speak for the response of Mahler's ears to what they heard about them and to his capacity – wherein of course lies his genius – to assimilate them and transform them into music.

The free profile of the flute song in that cadenza reflects, one might think, the *freedom* of Nature, unconstrained by considerations of art, of classical proportion, of a need to discriminate between sounds and events which are proper to art while others are improper and to be excluded. Mahler, as he grew older and as his work developed, moved away more and more from a figurative, decorative or symbolic representation of Nature, and of birdsong in particular, towards a (for him) new kind of naturalism, of realism, in which the barriers between art music (*Kunstmusik*) and the sounds and events of Nature were further and radically lowered. There is a remarkable example of this development in the 'Abschied' of *Das Lied von der Erde* – the passage where Mahler graphically describes the nocturnal stirrings and twitterings of the birds and other noises and creatures of the night at the moment when night and silence descend. 'Description' indeed is entirely the wrong word. Mahler does not so much describe as faithfully *document* the sounds of Nature just before the world surrenders to sleep:

> Die Vogel hocken still in ihren Zweigen.
> Die Welt schläft ein!
>
> *The birds crouch in silence on their branches;*
> *the world goes to sleep!*

Here, the music that surrounds the voice is a music taken from Nature, received by Mahler's ears and then transformed by his imagination, but certainly not out of recognition. I have written about that passage elsewhere[1] and suggested that its extraordinary motivic organization and audacious instrumentation amount to a kind of Mahlerian Impressionism, but an Impressionism that does not aspire to a blend, a blur, but comprises a brilliant and incisive articulation of birdsong. Once again Mahler has created a moment of silence, as he did in the finale of the Second Symphony, but this time filled it not with symbolic but as it were with *actual* birdsong and other nocturnal noises. There is a big difference between the two aesthetic approaches.

Mahler of course did not altogether abandon in his last period the figurative, decorative or symbolic use of birdsong. When he needed it as a resource he made use of it. Indeed, in *Das Lied von der Erde* itself, the two modes of incorporating Nature, the two strategies, are juxtaposed in the same work. Take the fifth movement of *Das Lied,* 'Der Trunkene im Frühling'. In the third strophe of the song, it is a bird that brings the pessimistic singer a message of hope and reconciliation, a confirmation of the presence of spring – 'Der Lenz ist da, sei kommen über Nacht!' ('Spring is here,

---

1   See DMSSLD, pp. 373–6 and 380–81.

it's arrived overnight!'). And Mahler permits us to hear the tenor
overhearing the bird singing in the tree. But this is a very well-
trained and musically educated bird which impersonates the solo
flute, with a highly developed sense of melody, of symmetrical
phrasing and above all with a striking capacity to build its song out
of the motifs with which the composer has obligingly provided it
(see figs. $6^{+3}$–$6^{+10}$ and $9^{-2}$–$10^{-2}$). In short, this is principally a symbolic bird, whose song has been conditioned by long-established
tradition, a very different concept of sound from the nocturnal
passage from the 'Abschied' to which I referred above, or from the
free untrammelled birdsong in the cadenza from the Second
Symphony.

One might argue that there is nothing exceptional about a composer with an emphatic love of Nature building birdsong into his
music. Birds are Nature's musicians, Nature's own singers, and composers have long been in the habit of conscripting birdsong to serve
their own purposes. In 'Der Trunkene im Frühling' Mahler had one
foot in tradition; in the 'Abschied' he established a *new* tradition, a
kind of authenticity of reproduction that formed no part at all of
that earlier decorative or symbolic tradition. But Mahler, we may
be sure, was not in the business of achieving a faithful, literal replication of birdsong. What was it, then, that we should try to identify
as Mahler's particular interest in birdsong, in the sounds of the
natural universe? Or, to put it another way, are we able to identify
in any meaningful way other than the decorative the influence of
Nature on Mahler's musical thinking?

The aspect of the relationship between Mahler's own music and
the music of Nature that interests me most is the unmeasured freedom that characterizes the latter and the ever increasing freedom
of Mahler's late compositional techniques, especially in the fields of
rhythm and melody. I have perhaps talked about birdsong to excess.
But I should like to bring forward one final example from this
sphere, though in fact it is not a literal representation of birdsong at
all. You remember the cadenza from the finale of the Second
Symphony, and the marvellously free, quasi-improvised duet for
piccolo and flute which unfolds a continuous flow of unmeasured
melody. In a famous passage from the 'Abschied' – the first of the

recitatives – the flute obbligato that accompanies the voice has an innovatory, improvisatory unmeasuredness (see figs. 3–4). Now I am not suggesting that what we hear there is undiluted birdsong – if that were the case, it would be a virtuoso bird indeed! Moreover, it is clear to me that the concept of that recitative has its roots in Bach, in Bach's recitatives from the Passions in particular (Mahler was a great admirer of the *St Matthew Passion*) and in the style of Bach's instrumental obbligatos in his Passions and cantatas. One might think one could not get further away from Nature than the music of Bach. But as so often in Mahler's music, one thing does not exclude another; or, to put it another way, he integrates in and through his music elements and influences that normally would have been thought irreconcilable. In short, while recognizing the predominant Bach influence, at the same time the free shape of that extraordinary flute obbligato has been conditioned, I suggest, if only unconsciously, by the asymmetries, the irregularities, of the music of Nature. And when we take into account the poetic context and content of that first recitative from the 'Abschied', in which the protagonist responds to a nocturnal mountain landscape, it is not altogether far-fetched to hear in it an audacious mix of Bach and the last song of the bird before nightfall.

Let us leave birds for a moment and move on to other features of Nature which might have caught not only Mahler's ears but also his eyes. No doubt you will be asking whether it is really possible for a composer's music to be influenced by what he perceives with and through his eyes. I am reminded of something Mahler himself once said to a friend who was visiting him at Steinbach and admiring the mountain landscape. 'There's no need to look at that,' Mahler said, 'for it's all in my music' – he was working on his Third Symphony at the time.[2] Mahler of course was expressing the thought of the relationship between landscape and music in the form of a joke. But it is my conviction that there is more than an element of truth in it, a truth that became more pronounced as Mahler moved into his late phase. Let me illustrate this point with another example from the 'Abschied' of *Das Lied,* the extraordinary

2  Bruno Walter, *Gustav Mahler,* p. 33.

oboe melody that introduces the text describing both the sight and sound of a murmuring stream creating its own melody in the darkness amid flowers fading in the twilight (see figs. $7^{+2}$–$8^{+4}$). It is technically one of the most radical and challenging inspirations in *Das Lied*, and what is particularly striking about it is its rhythmic asymmetry. There is no bar in the melody that repeats a previously established rhythmic pattern: each bar is rhythmically unique. The melody extends itself systematically through bar-by-bar rhythmic variation. Moreover, this melody, which is built out of an additive chain of asymmetries, is itself accompanied by figuration with its own built-in rhythmic asymmetry: at the outset the clarinets' and harp's articulations of the rocking minor third make their irregular effect by alternating within the bar groups of 2s and 3s. There is scant harmonization of the melody in any conventional sense. After the ambiguous tonality of the first two bars of introduction, F is established, but an F – for the ensuing three bars – with a persistently sharpened fourth degree of the scale, B natural instead of B flat. This Lydian inflexion introduces a diatonic 'irregularity' into the melody that complements the associated irregularities of rhythm and asymmetries of phrase. Small wonder that the melody seems to wander irregularly on, without punctuation or traditional cadencing, until it is abruptly cut off, just before the voice enters with 'Der Bach singt . . .' ('The stream sings . . .') and with three words accounts for the characteristic of the musical process in one simple poetic image drawn from Nature.

This passage is not only a remarkable manifestation of Mahler's late style, of the development of new and surprising features, it is also something else: it is a graphic tone-picture of a mountain stream pursuing its irregular course, singing its song as it flows. It was not only the *sound* of it that worked on Mahler's imagination, but also the *sight* of it. It is a passage in which one might claim sight has been transformed into sound. This takes me back to the point I made earlier: that Mahler was as much a pair of walking eyes as a pair of walking ears.

I do not want to exaggerate the influence of Nature on Mahler to the degree that it loses all sense: I am far from suggesting that Mahler in his music was a kind of gazetteer or Baedeker. I *am* suggesting, however, that when we analyse some of the characteristics of the late style of Mahler and his growing preoccupation with the potentialities of asymmetry and irregularity, we should bear in mind that what was perhaps a development in his music that would have happened anyway, for purely musical reasons, was backed up, intensified, reinforced, by his *absorption* of the irregularities and asymmetries of the sounds and sights of the world of Nature by which he was so often surrounded. And where, as in *Das Lied,* the poetic content of the work is much bound up with observation of and reflections on Nature, then the influence surfaces in a highly original and immediately identifiable manner.

I have been expounding relatively marginal detail in order to support my general proposal that we may perceive a connection between Mahler's response to Nature and the manifestation of asymmetry and irregularity in his music. But while it is true that some of the asymmetries I have commented on and illustrated from *Das Lied* very clearly have their origins in Nature, there are other aspects of his systematic employment of asymmetry which altogether escape the graphic or depictive and assume a profound formal and symbolic significance. Perhaps not altogether surprisingly we find an elaborate example of a symbolic/formal use of asymmetry – the employment of asymmetry as a major musical and poetic resource – in the finale, the 'Abschied' of *Das Lied*. If I am to explain, even in the barest outline, how Mahler's method works, then I must say something very brief about what, I suggest, *Das Lied* is about, the poetic meaning of Mahler's song-cycle, and in particular the content of the 'Abschied'. I think there are various points on which we might reach ready agreement: for a start, that *Das Lied*'s principal preoccupation is with the idea of man's mortality, his struggle against the idea of death, the possibility of his being reconciled to the inescapable fact of his extinction. All this, we may think, was bound up with Mahler's own personal history, the events from 1907, and in particular the diagnosis of the heart condition that was to contribute to his untimely death in 1911.

*Das Lied*, I suggest, concerns itself both with the fight against oblivion and the transcending of it, an altogether typical Mahlerian conflict and dichotomy. It is a conflict that is played out and finally resolved in and by the 'Abschied' and in terms of the contrast, the opposition – I am now speaking purely musically – between the symmetrical and the asymmetrical, the regular and the irregular, the strict and the free.

We all know how important for Mahler was the concept of the march – marches of all shapes and sizes abound in his symphonies. But has it struck us that the finale of the 'Abschied' is also conceived as a gigantic march? Though with this difference: that it is a march that from the very outset of the movement never succeeds in establishing itself until a very late stage in the movement has been reached. The very opening prelude to the 'Abschied' unfolds the dichotomy: we hear the march, and above all its symmetrical march rhythm, trying to assert itself. But within the space of a few bars, the march breaks up or, rather, breaks down, disintegrating into a fragmenting music that leads us naturally into the first recitative and introduces us for the first time to the remarkable freedom and asymmetries of the flute obbligato. And Mahler, having thus concisely juxtaposed at the beginning of his finale the symmetrical and the asymmetrical, the regular and the irregular, then proceeds with extraordinary logic and consistency, to play off one kind of music against the other. Furthermore, as the movement extends itself, we come to realize that the two types of music, the strict and the free, the symmetrical and asymmetrical, are brilliantly identified with the two poles of experience which the song-cycle as a whole encompasses: the fact of mortality on the one hand, and the possibility of its transcendence – mitigation, reconciliation – on the other. Mortality and death are represented by the constraints of symmetry. The *escape* from mortality and its metrical bonds is represented by asymmetry, a freely conceived music, the irregularity of which is the very opposite of the metrical and the predictable. The contrast is as sharp as that between the fear of annihilation and a positive embracing of it. It is precisely the reconciliation of those seeming irreconcilables that it is the main formal business of the finale of *Das Lied* to achieve.

The march idea, naturally enough, represents the most intensive concentration of symmetry and rhythmic regularity; and when finally the march succeeds in establishing itself unequivocally in that extraordinary interpolation for orchestra alone that precedes the closing stages of the 'Abschied', Mahler leaves us in no possible doubt of the symbolic relationship between the concept of death and its embodiment in music which, of its very nature, is born out of symmetry and metricality. Moreover, it is a grand *funeral* march, a ritual celebration of death, that Mahler releases, has in truth reserved for this moment; could he have spelled out for us more clearly in the context of the finale of *Das Lied* the identification of mortality with metricality? This is the moment when what has been anticipated in – announced by – the prelude is at last fulfilled, at last materializes: a march.

But mortality and the metrical are not to triumph in *Das Lied* and do not, distinctly not, provide the work with its ultimate denouement. Throughout the 'Abschied', as I have already suggested, Mahler, with consummate skill, has played off the free against the strict, the asymmetrical against the symmetrical. Some of those intimations of the escape from mortality through a conspicuously free, unmeasured music I have already mentioned: not only the nocturnal passage, 'Die Welt schläft ein' ('The world is falling asleep') – and it must have been just such music that Adorno had in mind when referring in his monograph on Mahler to the 'unregimented voices of living things'[3] – but also that amazing passage, the oboe melody, which I have spoken about in connection with Mahler's observation, through his ears and eyes, of a mountain stream. It seems hardly credible that one movement should contain two such radically contrasted musics, one so improvisatory and irregular, and rhythmically amorphous, the other so definedly symmetrical in melody and regular in rhythm. But it is precisely the task of these two contrasted compositional techniques to represent the two poles of experience that I have suggested the 'Abschied' is built around.

It is revealing, I think, that one could argue that the innovating oboe melody – the liberated song of the stream – has its roots, its origins, in Nature. But by no means all the music that I should allot to the 'free' category in the 'Abschied' is bound up quite so

---

3 Theodor W. Adorno, *Mahler: Eine musikalische Physiognomik*, pp. 25–7.

unequivocally with Nature, with Mahler's depiction or observation of it. Take the long, seamless string and horn melody, for example, which, in its own way, is quite as free as the oboe melody, 'Der Bach singt' – transferred to the flute on the entry of the voice, which it succeeds and complements. The freely evolving, spontaneous character of that melody, which uncoils itself unpredictably *across* the barlines and is rarely punctuated by them, is typical of the asymmetrical, irregular and often very long string melodies that emerge with increasing frequency in Mahler's late works, though perhaps nowhere is there such a concentration of them as in the finale of *Das Lied*. In the example I have just cited, we may note that the melody is not directly linked with observation of Nature. On the other hand, it without doubt articulates the response of the protagonist in the 'Abschied' to the overwhelming beauties of Nature, of the physical world. I find it altogether fascinating that the protagonist in the finale, who was surely Mahler himself, chose to exploit the resources of asymmetry in expressing his felt response to Nature, just as asymmetry and irregularity were the means by which elsewhere he incorporates into his music the actual sounds (and some of the sights!) of the natural universe. Whatever Mahler's predisposition was towards the asymmetrical in shaping his melodies, we may conclude, I believe, that the influence of Nature was a heightening factor, especially in those works in which Nature is a central preoccupation, of which *Das Lied* is a prime example. Is there not something very magical, as well as logical, about Mahler's unleashing his tumultuous feelings *about* Nature in a melody whose contours are as unregimented as those of Nature herself?

And so amidst the very landscape amidst which *Das Lied* was conceived and created and which, I suggest, exercised a profound influence on the profile the musical materials assumed, we come to the apotheosis with which *Das Lied* ends. As I said earlier, it is not the metrical that finally triumphs in the 'Abschied' but its very opposite. In the ecstatic coda that rounds off the finale, indeed, Mahler achieves an unprecedented beatlessness, a suspension of pulse and beat which virtually erases rhythmic measurement. This, combined with the proliferation and heterophonic combinations of long spans of asymmetrical melodies, provides Mahler with that consummation of the free style – that other pole – in the 'Abschied', which at the same time signifies the *transcendence* of death, the reconciliation and identification with the perpetual renewal of earth's beauties which has been the goal of *Das Lied* from the outset. Through the manipulation of two contrasted compositional techniques, the strict and the free, Mahler plays out the poetic drama which is at the heart of *Das Lied* and brings it to its radiant denouement. I do not doubt myself that landscape and Nature – not pictorially, but at far deeper levels of the creative imagination – were profoundly influential in, as it were, drawing the contours of some of the music we find most remarkable in *Das Lied*. Landscape into music. A unique act of transformation, and like most things about Mahler, without precedent, and unsurpassed.

# Mahler's 'Abschied':
# A Wrong Note Righted

## ∼ 1985 ∼

Some recent work[1] on which I have been engaged has involved a detailed scrutiny of Mahler's *Das Lied* and some of its principal manuscript sources. One general impression I have been left with is the exceptional care and subtlety of Mahler's approach to word-setting, something I suppose I had been aware of but to which I had never before paid much attention.

I could quote many examples but shall introduce only one into this short essay because it proved to have rich consequences and resonances. The passage in question comes toward the end of 'Der Abschied' at fig. 57:

Ex. 1

Still ist mein Herz

There is nothing world-shaking, I concede, about that phrase. On the other hand, it is an admirable example of Mahler's scrupulous setting of his text. In particular, the repeated Cs clearly embody the level, steady, and serene beat of a heart at peace with itself.

I could quite easily quote a considerable number of like examples, some of them a good deal more complex. But it was this one

1   I acknowledge gratefully the kind co-operation and assistance of the Pierpont Morgan Library, New York (the Robert Owen Lehman deposit), the Willem Mengelberg Stichting and the Gemeente Museum of The Hague, and Dr Edward R. Reilly.

First published in *Musical Quarterly* 71/2 (1985), pp. 200–204; reprinted in DMCN, pp. 181–6.

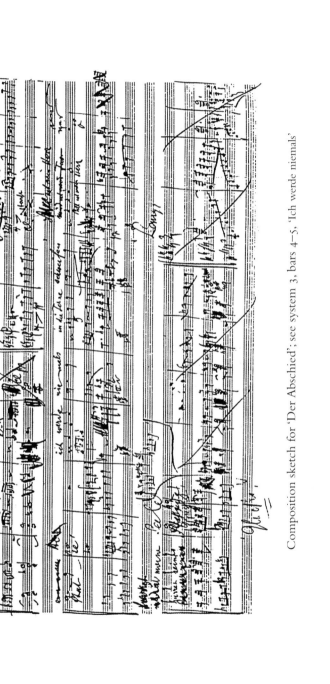

Composition sketch for 'Der Abschied'; see system 3, bars 4–5, 'Ich werde niemals'

that caught my ear and eye at a time when I was also busy with looking through the source materials of the movement; or, to be more precise, it was these bars and their immediate predecessors, five bars after fig. 56, that led me to investigate Mahler's composition sketch. For what we find in the published score is this:

Ex. 2

I confess that I had never in any sense questioned this phrase; on the contrary I had always thought of it as a neat example of the kind of integration of which Mahler was a master, that is, the complementary vocal phrase 'Still ist mein Herz' ('My heart is still') taking over the rhythmic pattern of 'Ich werde niemals' ('I shall never again') and the identical interval and pitches, but reversing their order and their direction. On this occasion, however, I wondered why, if Mahler were intent on making a point with the repeated notes in his setting of '*Still* ist mein Herz' (my emphasis), he used the same device only a few bars earlier in an entirely different context, where an image of stillness, of calm, was not involved.

It was this consideration I had casually in mind when turning over the pages of Mahler's short score of 'Der Abschied', his original composition sketch, which is owned by the Gemeente Museum of The Hague. What immediately leapt to my eye was, of course, 'Ich werde niemals . . .' which in the composer's hand quite clearly does *not* follow the repeated-note pattern of Ex. 2 but is laid out thus:

Ex. 3

There is no doubt about the composition sketch: the A (which appears in all published versions) is undeniably a G. How, then, did the repeated As arise?

This can be answered simply: because they appear thus in Mahler's fair manuscript full score of *Das Lied,* now part of the Robert Owen Lehman deposit at the Pierpont Morgan Library in New York City. There is no room for doubt either about what Mahler wrote in this autograph. It is what we are all thoroughly familiar with and reproduced in Ex. 2. One might well conclude, if this were all the evidence that might be assembled, that Mahler had had a change of mind at a very late stage or made a slip of the pen, but that it was impossible to determine which was the more likely explanation of an A replacing the G. For reasons I shall come to now, I think there can be hardly any doubt that it *was* a slip of the pen and that we should without more ado correct the errant A to G. I can outline my arguments as follows:

1   If we adopt G in bar 442, then the repeated-note response to the image of 'Still ist mein Herz' is no longer paradoxically anti-cipated and its impact thus diminished in bars 446–7.

2   The motif *with* the G appears not only in the composition sketch but also in the draft and probably earliest extant orchestral score in Mahler's hand (currently held by the Gemeente Museum) and in the autograph fair copy of the vocal score (owned by John Kallir, Scarsdale, New York).[2] So there are at least *three* manuscripts in Mahler's own hand in which the motif in its A–G–A form appears; and it is indisputable that it was with the G that Mahler first conceived the phrase.

3   There is one further piece of evidence which I personally find the most convincing of all and which derives from the special character of the counterpoint in *Das Lied* and in 'Der Abschied' in particular. Adorno was among the first to spot this: in his monograph on Mahler he refers to it as the manifestation of an

---

2   Mahler's piano reduction of *Das Lied* was published in 1989: see note 5 below. [Editorial note added by Mervyn Cooke for DMCN.]

*unscharfe Unisono* ('unfocused unison') in which 'identical voices differ slightly from one another in rhythm'.[3] This was a brilliant insight of Adorno's, and it is indeed the case that intensive study of 'Der Abschied' will reveal numerous examples of contrapuntal textures, which, in principle, are heterophonic, that is, it is a rhythmically dis-synchronized unison, shared between the parts, which is at the heart of the counterpoint.

It is precisely this relationship we encounter in bars 442–7, where the voice part and the counter-melody of the violins are built out of an identical melody and simultaneously combined, an octave apart, in two different rhythmic versions.[4] At least, that is how the passage was originally conceived by Mahler and how, in my estimation, we should hear it in the future, if my correction is accepted and becomes established performing practice:

Ex. 4

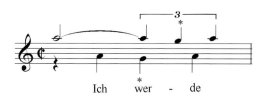

If we leave the repeated As as they appear, alas, in the so-called critical edition of the score (which makes no mention whatsoever of all this),[5] then of course this tiny but significant feature of Mahler's marvellous finale not only goes unheard but allows its

3    Theodor W. Adorno, *Mahler: Eine musikalische Physiognomik*, p. 194.
4    *Three,* actually. For, as David Matthews has pointed out to me, in the composition sketch the third part (system 3, stave 2, bar 4) yet again gives us the A–G–A pattern. (In the fair-copied full score this became a second violin part and is delivered at a different pitch.)
5    In the second volume of the *Supplement to the Mahler Critical Edition* (Universal Edition, Vienna, 1989), which published Mahler's own vocal score of *Das Lied von der Erde,* Stephen E. Hefling, in his table of errata (p. xxiv), lists and corrects the error that was originally Mahler's in his autograph fair copy of the full score (blindly followed in the *Critical Edition*'s published full score), without, however, acknowledging DM's thoroughly documented discovery of the mistake four years earlier. See, however, Hefling's contribution 'Perspectives on Sketch Studies' to M. T. Vogt (ed.), *Das Gustav-Mahler-Fest Hamburg 1989*, pp. 445–57. [Editorial note added by Mervyn Cooke for DMCN.]

erroneous substitution to blunt the effect of the stillness that is created by the (legitimately) repeated notes a few bars later.

A last point, though one not directly related to the manuscript sources. If there is one thing that I have learned from working closely alongside composers during the last twenty years or so, it is to be sceptical about claims of infallibility made for their autographs, even when those autographs are impressively tidy fair copies, wearing all the signs of finality and authority. It is in making his fair copy, into which, very often, a substantial element of the mechanical enters, that the composer can sometimes nod and commit – and thereby unwittingly perpetuate – an error. Of course, if Mahler had ever heard *Das Lied* in performance, he would doubtless have made the necessary correction. That was not to be. It is my guess that when he started to pen the voice part for 'Ich werde niemals', his mind had already raced ahead to the next vocal entry, 'Still ist mein Herz', and under the influence of those repeated Cs, A–G–A became repeated As.

We have become so familiar with 'Ich werde niemals' in its erroneous form that it may take a little while before we hear how natural, convincing, and expressive the correct version is: for instance it brings to life a crucial word, 'werde', which is otherwise locked into an accentless monotone.

The expressive gain was recently noticed by one of the London critics who attended the first performance of the revision. Simon Rattle adopted it for his performance of *Das Lied* at the Royal Festival Hall, London, on 19 April 1984, when he conducted the Philharmonia Orchestra, with the contralto Florence Quivar as soloist in 'Der Abschied'. Meirion Bowen, writing in the *Guardian* on 21 April, made it clear that in prospect the whole thing seemed slightly ridiculous, this recovery of *one* note, and I would be the first to concede that the whole affair might appear, in the abstract, to be grotesquely over-inflated (the same thought occurred to me, especially when, at the morning rehearsal, Mme Quivar quite overlooked the emendation and stuck to what she had always been used to singing). And yet, after Mr Bowen heard the wrong note righted, he declared that for him the phrase would never sound right again if sung in its old form. I would go along with that.

# Dualities, Contrasts, Conflicts:
# New Formal Thinking
# in Mahler's Last Symphonies

## ∝ 1988 ∾

It must have been said in print hundreds of times that after Mahler had composed his Fourth Symphony (1899–1900) the character and, as a consequence, the contents of most of his succeeding symphonies showed a fundamental modification. There were no more interpolations of orchestral songs into Symphonies Nos. 5, 6, 7, 9, or the incomplete No. 10. In the main, the middle and last symphonies are instrumental works (the exceptions are, of course, the Eighth and *Das Lied von der Erde*). But if we notice only the outward manifestation of change, we miss an essential and still more significant point: the very subtle way in which Mahler's songs *continued* to influence his symphonies.

I am not thinking of the occasional and sometimes meaningful relationship that can be heard between a song and one of the instrumental symphonies, for example the 'quotations' from the *Kindertotenlieder* in the Fifth and Sixth Symphonies; nor of even more substantial parallels, for example the first *Nachtmusik* from the Seventh, which might be considered as a kind of *Wunderhorn* song for orchestra alone. What I have in mind is the *formal* influence of Mahler's songs on his later symphonies. The key work here is the song-cycle already mentioned, the five *Kindertotenlieder,* whose composition was spread over an unusually extensive period – 1901–4, the years between which the Fifth (1901–2) and the Sixth (1903–4) were composed, and the Seventh begun (1904). In the *Kindertotenlieder* – much admired but little studied – we find in

First published as a liner note for the 1988 recording of Mahler's Ninth Symphony by the Vienna Philharmonic Orchestra, conducted by Claudio Abbado, DG 423–564–2. The final section of this note subsequently formed the basis of the extra (1995) material on the Tenth Symphony to be found on pp. 511–13.

embryo the formal innovations that Mahler introduced into his late symphonies, especially his first movements. It is, indeed, the cycle's first song, 'Nun will die Sonn' so hell aufgeh'n', that bears a critical relationship to the first movement of the Ninth Symphony, composed in 1908–9. Both the song and the symphonic movement are built round the juxtaposition of tonic major and minor. It is in the song that we first find the methodical alternation of D minor and D major, which (in reverse order) is so striking a feature of the opening movement of the symphony.

The alternation of mode in the song is brilliantly tied in with the imagery of the poem: the move from minor to major in each musical strophe parallels the move from the ritual of mourning and grief to the promise of renewed light (the sun rising) in the text. In the symphony's first movement, the tonal contrast or conflict is approached from a different angle: a warm, life-embracing D major is methodically assaulted by regular eruptions (in the first instance, in D minor) ever increasing in intensity, which lead to the movement's catastrophic climax (bar 314). There are occasional and unsuccessful attempts to establish D major as the 'victor' in the tonal conflict, but it is not until the very end of the movement that some sort of 'pacification' is achieved: while the original D major/minor juxtaposition is restated, it is on the tonic major – albeit of a somewhat fragile character – that the music fades into silence.

In its adherence to regular strophic form, 'Nun will die Sonn'' was following the pattern of the majority of Mahler's songs. But this was strophic form with radically new dimensions: a unique hybrid, the result of cross-fertilization between strophic and sonata forms. In the song, for example, the third strophe functions as a quasi-development section, the first and fourth as exposition and recapitulation respectively. In the first strophe the *duality* of contrasting tonalities, D minor and major, emerges as a remodelling of the traditional concept of *sonata-form* duality (with its contrasting first- and second-subject groups). It is precisely this refashioned and basically strophic idea that Mahler introduces into his Ninth Symphony. In a vastly extended and elaborated format it underpins the structure of the first movement and perhaps best represents the form of what has long been regarded as one of his supreme orchestral achievements. Furthermore, throughout the movement, as if to drive home the dominance of the principle of duality, Mahler offers not only contrasting tonalities, in which contrasting musical materials are embodied, but also contrasting tempi. It is true that when we first encounter the D major/minor juxtaposition, Mahler indicates no change in tempo. But thereafter the episodes derived from the contrasting D minor interpolation, each of them intended systematically to subvert the D major andante, are all designated as some kind of allegro. As a result, the andante indissolubly belongs to the major, the allegro to the destabilizing alternating episodes which have their origin in the D minor complex.

This bold notion of duality by no means exhausts Mahler's innovations in this first movement. Another highly original formal principle is also involved. The latter half of each dual statement (i.e. the contrasting section that follows each affirmation of the D major 'song') is shaped as a crescendo, and each of these exceeds its predecessor in momentum and dynamic power until the onset of what, in a conventional sonata movement, would be the recapitulation. Mahler himself marks the last and most violent climax *Hochste Kraft* ('Utmost force'), and it is at this point that the movement almost literally explodes before hurling itself into an abyss. Then, gradually, it reassembles itself and embarks on the concluding section which brings about a temporary reconciliation of the conflicting materials.

The dynamic principle was an aspect of the Ninth that caught the ear of Alban Berg, who wrote about it in the autumn of 1912 in a memorable letter to his wife Helene:

> The whole movement is based on a premonition of death which constantly recurs. All earthly dreams lead to it; that is why the tenderest passages are followed by tremendous climaxes, like new eruptions of a volcano. This, of course, is most obvious of all in the place where the premonition of death becomes certain knowledge, where, in the most profound and anguished love of life, death announces itself with utmost power [*mit hochster Gewalt*] ... Against that, there is no more resistance to be offered, and I see what follows as a sort of resignation.*

---

* Alban Berg, *Letters to his Wife*, p. 147.

# Wiener Musikfestwoche 1912

## Mittwoch den 26. Juni, abends 8 Uhr
## im Großen Musikvereins-Saale

# III. KONZERT

Ausführende:
## Das Wiener philharmonische Orchester

Dirigent: Hofopernkapellmeister
## BRUNO WALTER

## Programm

1. Josef Haydn ···················· Symphonie C-moll (Nr. 9)
   Geb. am 1. April 1732 in Rohrau an der Leitha, gestorben am
   31. Mai 1809 in Wien.
       Allegro
       Andante cantabile
       Menuetto
       Vivace

2. Gustav Mahler ··············· IX. Symphonie
   Geb. am 7. Juli 1860 in Kalisch (Böhmen), gestorben am
   18. Mai 1911 in Wien.
       Uraufführung aus dem Manuskript
       Andante comodo
       Im Tempo eines gemütlichen Ländlers
       Rondo, Burleske. Allegro assai
       Adagio

Während der Musikfestwoche Ausstellung musikalischer Zimelien im Prunksaale der k. k.
Hofbibliothek (I. Josefsplatz), täglich von 9 bis
4 Uhr, an Sonn- und Feiertagen von 10 bis 1 Uhr.

Preis mit Analysenheft 50 Heller, ohne Analysenheft 20 Heller.

Druck der „Kilbeműhl", Wien IX.

The programme for the first performance of Mahler's Ninth Symphony
in Vienna on 26 June 1912

Small wonder that Berg admired the Ninth so much! One only needs to hear his own Three Orchestral Pieces, Op. 6, to recognize how fundamental for the development of his orchestral style Mahler's Ninth (especially the first movement) was. It would scarcely have been possible for Berg – or, for that matter, Webern in his earlier works – to have arrived at so refined a plasticity of orchestral writing if it had not been for Mahler's pioneering example.

    With a composer's perspicuity, Berg early on isolated one of the first movement's generative principles, the sequence of volcanic climaxes. Besides this, and the principle of duality discussed above, there is a final dimension to which we should attend: the means by which, after each explosion, the music picks itself up and slowly finds its way back to the D major *Andante comodo* (where the whole process begins again). These extraordinary transitions between strophes, in which is heard some of the most spectral, defeated music of the whole symphony, form an essential part of the work's fabric, restoring what is continually rent apart. Typically, their musical source lies in the symphony's first six bars, a miniature introduction with a nest of motives, out of which grow not only the transitions but also much else that will attain emphatic, and symbolic, status during the course of the movement.

    In 1912, the year of the symphony's posthumous first performance by the Vienna Philharmonic Orchestra under Bruno Walter, Berg, as we have seen, was writing unequivocally of the 'premonition of death'. In *Das Lied von der Erde,* immediately preceding (1907–9), there had likewise been a preoccupation with issues of life and death, with the contrast of the transient and the eternal. *Das Lied,* too, went unheard by Mahler and was brought to posthumous performance only in 1911, a few months before the Ninth was first played. A strange feature, this, of Mahler's last years: it is as if the compulsion to get as much committed to paper as was possible in the years remaining to him far outweighed considerations of performance.

    In these late works Mahler was undeniably haunted by thoughts of his own mortality. In 1907 a doctor had diagnosed the serious heart ailment which in 1911 contributed to the condition leading to his death. But there was already a work, the *Kindertotenlieder*, written when Mahler's health was not in question and before he suffered the tragic loss of one of his daughters, in which the idea of death and its possible mitigation had already been profoundly touched on; there, as I have suggested, the age-old duality of life and death found perfect expression in the formal concept of the dual strophe. *Kindertotenlieder*, as we would expect, left its mark on *Das Lied*, whose forms reflect those of the earlier work. Likewise, I suggest, the first movement of the Ninth; and, after all, what could be more natural than this? There is a perfect, if tragic, logic in Mahler's return to the song-cycle where, a few years earlier, he had explored the contrast of mourning and reconciliation in a juxta-position of D minor/major. *Kindertotenlieder* provided him in his last completed symphony not only with specific tonalities but also with the formal idea to match the dual reality of his personal his-tory from 1907 onwards. Life-versus-death was no longer to be lived only in the imagination (as in the song-cycle) but as an immutable part of his own daily life.

While there is much that is new in the Ninth, Mahler remains faithful to the concept of the 'frame', long established in his music, in which the two outer movements bear the weight of the sym-phony, and its middle comprises movements of diverse character, one of them always a scherzo. After the exalted debate of the first movement, conducted in D major/minor, Mahler turns to more mundane, everyday topics – to a chain of dances, in fact; and he steps down a tone to C major, in this context a mundane, everyday key. The movement is exceptional not so much for its dazzling combination of the exuberant, the ironic, the poignant and the grotesque – all to be expected in a late Mahler scherzo – but for its comprehensive anthologizing of all the dances and dance forms which had been incorporated into his previous symphonies. The ländler, the waltz, the minuet – the familiar dances, or recollections (or distortions!) of them are unfolded in a continuous, cumulative sound-panorama which offers us a unique review of the history, indeed the prehistory, of the scherzo form. It is a movement in which Mahler emerges in the role of composer–historian, another aspect of his fascinating personality.

There is a historical dimension to the third movement too, the oddly titled *Rondo-Burleske,* because the contrapuntal textures with their unremitting energy undoubtedly have their origins in Mahler's passionate interest in the music of J. S. Bach. The Bach-Gesellschaft edition, one of Mahler's prized possessions, can have had no keener student. Not that there is anything retrospective about Mahler's dissonant counterpoint. On the contrary, the rondo pitches us headlong into the twentieth century. This is not so much back to Bach as forward with Bach, to the decades immediately after the First World War and neo-classicism though there is nothing Classical about Mahler's rondo if one equates 'Classical' with repose. He never wrote a more hectic movement than this, and although the influence of Bach had already shown up in the Eighth Symphony and *Das Lied,* the rondo of the Ninth remains the most concentrated manifestation of counterpoint in all Mahler's music. Its only moment of comparative relaxation emerges as a kind of still point at the centre of the polyphonic turmoil: a set of miniature variations which discloses a vision of the adagio finale and anticipates an essential feature – the turn – of its main theme.

The rondo pursues for the most part a ferocious A minor (the relative minor of the second movement's C major); the variations offer a glimpse of that warm D major essential to the conception of the first movement. Is the finale then to establish the tonality of D as the symphony's ultimate goal and, in fulfilling that goal, round off the work with an affirmation of 'life', the positive half of the original duality? Mahler was ever a truthful creator: an easy option was not for him. In the context of this symphony, and in the light of the duality expounded so forcefully in the first movement, to opt for D would have been to choose a facile solution. Hence D flat, a semitone lower than the symphony's first tonic, not a compromise solution but unblinkered recognition of the reality – true to Mahler's art *and* life – that D major was no longer possible. It would not, could not, ring 'true'.

To the last, though, Mahler maintains the dualities, contrasts and conflicts that have been the very *raison d'être* of this symphony, in ways already encountered (the juxtaposition of major and minor) and in fresh ones, among the most remarkable of which is the extreme contrast of textures. The rich, dense harmonization of the main melody, and its seemingly inexhaustible reharmonizations, are one thing. Quite another are the contrasting passages of spectral counterpoint, which follow immediately, for which there has been no preparation. On the contrary, their logic and justification rest in the starkness of the contrast they offer (they offer, too, another and even more audacious manifestation of Mahler's immersion in the music of Bach). What follows the final statement of the adagio's elegiac melody is a radical fragmentation and thinning out of its previously full-bodied texture and harmonization. In the coda, there is almost as much silence as sound; Mahler's last marking in the final bar is *ersterbend* (dying away). Words are clumsy, imprecise instruments here. Each listener must make his or her own decision about how to interpret – how to 'read' – this infinitely moving coda which brings the symphony to rest.

The Ninth was, in the main, composed in 1909. In 1910, the last full year of Mahler's life, he launched out, unabated, on a fresh symphony, his Tenth, which he was never to complete. Two movements, the *Adagio* (first movement) and the *Purgatorio* (third in a five-movement scheme), were both left at a compositional stage allowing them to be brought to first performance in Vienna on 14 October 1924, when the Vienna Philharmonic was conducted by Franz Schalk. Of the two movements, however, it was undoubtedly the *Adagio* that had attained something close to its final shape.

One senses that Mahler had hardly drawn breath before plunging into work on his new symphony; and that impression is surely confirmed by the Tenth's opening *Adagio* which, uniquely, picks up from the point where the preceding symphony left off. The formal type that rounded off the Ninth, a slow last movement, now opens the Tenth. We come face to face with a remarkable continuity; and, indeed, much of what has been said above about the Ninth (the first and last movements in particular) provides the context for a clear perception of the layout of the Tenth's *Adagio*. The movement's self-evident dualities impose themselves within the first twenty bars: a duality of tempi (*Andante* and *Adagio*), and one of contrasting tonalities (F sharp major/minor). While the movement is by no means a re-run of the procedures already encountered in the Ninth, we find Mahler using a formal method that, as I have suggested, reaches back to the seminal *Kindertotenlieder* of 1901–4, by way of the Ninth and *Das Lied*.

There are two aspects of the Tenth's *Adagio*, however, that seem to introduce fresh developments. The first is a concept of one single vertical event – one chord, in fact – replacing what in the past might have been a musical idea that occupied an extensive stretch of horizontal space. This is the famous – and frightening – dissonance which erupts between figs. 27 and 29 of the score. Here, one chord represents a concentrated, massive accumulation and expression of tension which in earlier symphonies Mahler achieved only by means of whole contrasting sections leading to a powerful climax (as in the first movement of the Ninth). In this instance, we have, as it were, the extreme climax without the crescendo. It is a new economy, a new intensity, a radical compression of musical time.

It would also – perhaps most remarkably of all – have provided the Tenth with its 'frame'. This is not to deprive the outer movements of their habitual weight. But what Deryck Cooke's brilliant deciphering and transcription of Mahler's original sketches showed us (an achievement quite distinct from the issues raised by the performing edition he based on those sketches) was the return of the explosive dissonance in the projected finale, where it was to be spelled out uncompromisingly yet again, before its ultimate resolution. Indeed, if the internal logic of the symphony was to be carried through, it could not be left unresolved.

And there, I think, we uncover the second innovation, and what would possibly have been the most striking feature of the Tenth, had Mahler lived to complete it. There was to be no acknowledgement of the reality of Mahler's circumstances along the lines of the finales of the Ninth and *Das Lied*. On the contrary, the Tenth, in its own terms, was to propose its own new reality: after the restatement of the great dissonant disruption – a premonition of death, to use Berg's term, as chilling as anything in the Ninth the music was to move to a serene, quiet but confident affirmation of the tonic major. Mahler had enjoyed no remission, he was granted no extra time. But if the Ninth had shown one way of creating meaning-fully out of the duality of life and death, the Tenth was planned to show another way: the work of art itself would prove that death, after all, would not have the last word. How ironic that death should have taken Mahler before he had brought the Tenth to completion and thus prevented him from making known to the world this last victory. His unfulfilled ambition was surely that which John Donne expressed in the last line of his Third Holy Sonnet: 'Death, thou shalt die.'

# Some Notes on Mahler's
# Tenth Symphony

## ⌐ 1955 / 1995 ⌐

The history of Mahler's unfinished Tenth Symphony is a curious one. The work was sketched in the summer of 1910, the last summer of Mahler's life. He was, very literally, under sentence of death and also deeply disturbed in his relationship to his wife, Alma (he consulted Freud in August, who seemed able to help him). The sketches for the last symphony, which vary greatly in their degree of completeness, were published in facsimile in 1924 by Mahler's widow. For long it was believed that Mahler had expressed the wish that, upon his death, the sketches should be destroyed, but this was not the case. It seems that he was, in fact, optimistic about the progress of the work during the last weeks of his life and told his wife that, should he not complete the work, she had his permission to do with the sketches what she thought best.

It is more than likely, however, that Mahler's attitude to his sketches was ambivalent. Altogether, he treated his last works in a very odd fashion. To put it crudely but concisely, he sat on them. He did nothing to promote a performance (or publication) of *Das Lied von der Erde* (completed in 1909), and took no steps to give the Ninth Symphony (completed in 1910) a hearing; it was three years before the Eighth Symphony (completed in 1907) received its premiere under the ailing composer's direction. It is very much open to doubt, in these circumstances, whether Mahler would have welcomed the publication of his Tenth Symphony's sketches in facsimile and *in toto* — as distinct from reconstructions where possible of nearly completed movements.

Main text first published in *Musical Times*, December 1955, with additional material from GMWL, pp. 2.104–5.

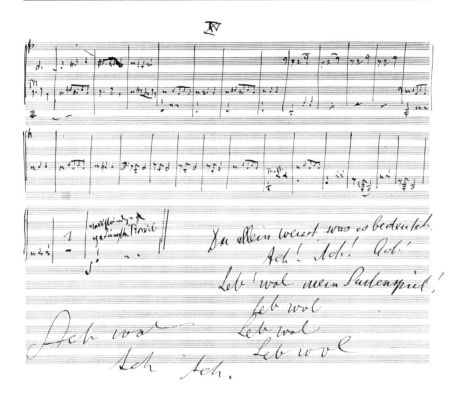

The manuscript of the Tenth Symphony, end of the fourth movement

In the event, the Tenth symphony has come down to us in both versions – as sketches and as edited scores of two of the symphony's
projectected five movements. The first score of the [*Andante*–]
*Adagio* and *Purgatorio* was edited by Ernst Krenek, with additions by
Franz Schalk and/or Alexander von Zemlinsky, and performed on
14 October 1924. The occasion was a Mahler concert given at the
Vienna State Opera during the Vienna Festival, when Schalk conducted the Vienna Philharmonic Orchestra. This 'performing' edition has not, I believe, been published. (Krenek, incidentally, has
implied that the contribution of Schalk and Berg to the editing was
slight.) In 1951, Associated Music Publishers, New York, issued a
pocket score of the two movements edited by Otto Jokl, a pupil of
Berg's, who bases his edition on Krenek's reconstructions but

incorporates the results of his own researches into the facsimiles. A defect of this otherwise valuable first publication is that editorial emendations are not distinguished from Mahler's own text.

The first English performance of the *Adagio* was a broadcast given on 20 November 1948 (and repeated on the 21st) by the BBC Orchestra under Scherchen. The first English public performance had to wait until 30 November 1955, when the *Adagio* was played by the Royal Philharmonic Orchestra under Richard Austin at the Festival Hall. To conclude these bibliographical data, it should be said that it was hoped originally that more than two of the five movements might be salvaged, but this scheme was abandoned by the sketches' first investigators. Attempts, however, have been made to reconstruct the remaining three movements, by Frederick Block in America, and by Joe Wheeler in England.

There can be no doubt whatever that publication of the Tenth Symphony's sketches – whether justified or not – revealed with terrible clarity the mental stress and strain under which Mahler was working. The manuscripts are littered with wounded cries and incoherent exclamations. It is from this kind of exposure that I think a fastidious mind must recoil. Some private agonies should be left private and the sketches, I feel, while they should not have been hidden or suppressed, might well have been left on deposit at a library where those with an interest deeper than mere curiosity might have freely consulted them. The third movement of the work is titled *Purgatorio or Inferno*; and though Mahler afterwards crossed through '*Inferno*', and would doubtless have eliminated '*Purgatorio*' had the work reached a final stage, the title is indeed appropriate. The state of mind in which the Tenth Symphony was composed must have approximated very closely to a private hell.

Strangely enough the *Purgatorio* movement itself is less infernal than some of its colleagues. The clue to its rather ironically reserved character lies in its prominent revival of a weary accompanimental figure from 'Das irdische Leben', a song, from the *Knaben Wunderhorn* collection, which Mahler composed in the 1890s. It is the purgatory of dull drudgery on earth that Mahler seemed to have in mind, not an apocalyptic vision of inferno. Hence the movement is quite undramatic. *Purgatorio*, moreover, is the shortest symphonic movement Mahler wrote. The indecisive impression it leaves would seem to suggest that it is incomplete or that Mahler would have radically recomposed it. The possibility cannot, of course, be ruled out. But the short score, from which the performing edition was constructed, gives a very clear indication of Mahler's intentions, and he rarely – if ever – changed the basic shape of the structures of his movements once they had reached even this preliminary stage of definitiveness. That Mahler had started off on the instrumentation of this movement is further proof that the outline of the movement was fixed. (It is a curious twist that while Mahler never meddled with the forms of his works, he could never stop tinkering with their instrumentation, with which he was rarely satisfied; yet it is Mahler's unique instrumentation that is universally admired.)

If *Purgatorio* sounds inconclusive, as I think it does, then we must seek for reasons outside the movement itself. The solution to the problem is to be found, in my view, in the disposition of the five movements. We cannot be certain that Mahler would have stuck to the order disclosed by the sketches – the order had been subjected to many variations – but what seems to have been his last arrangement is convincing:

|     |                       |
|-----|-----------------------|
| I   | [*Andante–*]*Adagio*  |
| II  | *Scherzo*             |
| III | *Purgatorio*          |
| IV  | *Scherzo*             |
| V   | *Finale*              |

The tri-partite outline of the work is reminiscent of the Fifth Symphony[1] but more especially of the Seventh, where two vast outer movements frame two nocturnes which themselves enclose a

---

1  More generally, the Tenth Symphony obviously adheres to the type of Mahler's middle-period instrumental symphonies. There is nothing in the sketches to suggest the use of vocal resources at any point. After the early symphonies, with their mixture of vocal and instrumental movements, Mahler composed either exclusively instrumental works or works exclusively vocal, e.g. in their different ways, the Eighth Symphony and *Das Lied*. The Tenth maintains the strict division.

brief, but vivid, scherzo. In the Tenth the two outer movements frame two large-scale scherzos which enclose the *Purgatorio*. It is obvious, I think, that this third movement will depend, for its effect, very much on its context, that it will not sound 'right' when torn out of it. In addition, certain movements of the Tenth show extensive inter-movement relationships – there are precedents in earlier symphonies – and it happens that the *Purgatorio* is further developed in the finale. Thus heard as part of the whole symphony, the movement would gain in immediate and retrospective significance; its integration is, as it were, actively demonstrated by its context and the role it plays elsewhere in the symphony.

That the great *Adagio* is placed first is evidence again of Mahler's continual experiments in the sphere of symphonic form. The two adagios with which this slow movement shares something in common may be found in Mahler's Third and Ninth Symphonies; in both works the slow movements function as finales. The Tenth exactly reverses that position, and the *Adagio* is placed first. But the movement is more than just a slow movement appearing, so to speak, 'out of order'. It bears, it is true, an intimate relationship to the adagio of the Ninth Symphony, but it is also partly based on the highly original model of the *first* movement, the *Andante comodo*, of the Ninth Symphony. We meet the same subtle combination of sonata and rondo and the same subtle combination of tempi, though the principal, 'walking-pace', tempo of the Ninth's first movement (the andante) is the subsidiary tempo of the Tenth's *Adagio*; nevertheless, the dualism is there and the andante contrasts with, and relieves, an otherwise strictly adagio character, just as the allegro tempi of the Ninth help to preserve the first-movement atmosphere of the andante. In other words, this striking *Adagio* in the Tenth Symphony, though predominantly a slow movement, offers something of what we customarily expect of a first movement. The symphony's finale attempts a complex synthesis to round off the whole work; its conclusion recalls the *Adagio*.

There is not space here to comment in detail upon the *Adagio*'s style and content, though since it is the movement that Mahler left most nearly complete there is most to discuss and the least need to reserve judgement. The *Adagio* never falls below Mahler's best level of inspiration, often transcends it, and most clearly and poignantly exposes both his love for a past tradition of romantic beauty and his quite extraordinary willingness to shoulder the responsibilities of newer concepts. This dual loyalty often emerges in his music as a fascinating conflict; but in the *Adagio* of the Tenth, Mahler seems to achieve a balance – albeit a precarious one – between two opposing worlds. Throughout the movement we find even the most traditional gestures fertilized by new ideas. We find it in his treatment of the big adagio tune, which appears straight, inverted and in both versions simultaneously combined; in the exceptional freedom of the part-writing, and in the movement's high degree of harmonic emancipation, especially in the disillusioned A flat minor passage which piles up immense harmonic tension and disrupts, indeed shatters, the recapitulation, a blow that, significantly, falls again in the finale.

Created under intolerable pressure, this slow movement represents one of Mahler's profoundest excursions into the territory of the twentieth century. He was, after all, something of a paradoxical composer, and it is only fitting, perhaps, that he should have succeeded in writing an almost painfully nostalgic movement in an idiom very much in touch with a musical future which he did not live to see.

★ ★ ★

One senses that Mahler had hardly drawn breath before immersing himself in his new symphony; and that impression is surely confirmed by the Tenth's opening *Adagio* which, uniquely, picks up from the point where the preceding symphony came to an end. The formal type that rounded off the Ninth, a slow last movement, now *opens* the Tenth – a slow first movement.

We come face to face with a remarkable continuity; and indeed very much of what I have already written about the Ninth, and its first and last movements in particular, provides the context for a clear perception of the layout of the Tenth's initiating *Adagio*. I shall not dwell on the movement's self-evident dualities, which impose themselves within the first twenty bars – a duality of tempi

(andante *and* adagio) and, later, a duality of contrasting tonalities,
F sharp major and minor. I am not suggesting for a moment that
the *Adagio* of the Tenth is a rerun of what we have already had in
the Ninth. Of course it isn't. But we find Mahler's mind, from a
formal point of view, working along the same lines, a formal
method that, as I have suggested, reaches back to the seminal
*Kindertotenlieder* of 1901–4, by way of the Ninth and *Das Lied*.

There are two aspects of the *Adagio*, however, that seem to me to
introduce fresh developments. The first is a concept of one single
vertical event – one chord, in fact – replacing what in the past
might have been a musical idea occupying an extensive stretch of
horizontal space. I am referring to the famous – and frightening –
dissonance that erupts in the *Adagio*, between figs. 27 and 29 in the
score (see the music example below). One chord here represents a
concentrated and massive accumulation and expression of tension
which in earlier symphonies Mahler achieved only by means of
whole contrasting sections leading to a powerful climax (compare
the first movement of the Ninth). Here, so to say, we have the
extreme climax without the crescendo. It is a new economy, a new
intensity, a radical compression of musical time.

It would also, perhaps most remarkable of all, have provided the
Tenth with its 'frame'. This is not to deprive the outer movements
of their habitual weight. But what Deryck Cooke's brilliant deciphering and transcription of Mahler's original sketches showed us
(a massive achievement quite distinct from the preparation of the
performing edition itself) was the return of the explosive dissonance in the projected finale, to be spelled out uncompromisingly
yet again before its ultimate resolution: indeed, if the internal logic
of the symphony were to be carried through, *it could not have been
left unresolved.*

And there, I think, we uncover the most striking feature of the Tenth. There was to be no compromise solution, no acknowledgement of the reality of Mahler's personal circumstances along the lines of the finales of the Ninth and *Das Lied*. On the contrary, the Tenth in its own terms proposes its own new reality: after the restatement of the great dissonant disruption – a premonition of death, to use Berg's term, as chilling as anything in the Ninth – the music moves to a serene, quiet but confident affirmation of the tonic major. Mahler had enjoyed no remission, was granted no extra time. But if the Ninth had showed one way of creating meaningfully out of the duality of life and death, the Tenth was planned to show another way: the work of art itself would prove that death after all need not have the last word.

How ironic that death should have taken Mahler before he had brought the Tenth to its final stage; and how grateful we should be to Cooke who laboured to make known to the world not Mahler's last defeat but his last victory. If I may amend a famous line of poetry by John Donne, at the end of the Tenth it is Death who dies.*

---

\* In Appendix II, pp. 646–7, Gastón Fournier-Facio lists the completions of Mahler's Tenth Symphony from the 1930s to the present day.

Arnold Schoenberg: *The Burial of Gustav Mahler (22 May 1911 in Vienna)*

REFLECTIONS

# Mahler: A Modern in Two Centuries

## ~: 1960 :~

'I could endure anything,' Mahler said in 1896, 'if only the future of my works seemed assured.'

In the same year he remarked, 'I shall not live to see my cause triumph! . . . People have not yet accepted my language, they have no idea what I am saying or what I mean; it all seems senseless and unintelligible to them. The very musicians who play my works hardly know what I am driving at.'

Could Mahler witness the widespread celebrations of his birth that are to take place this year, he might feel that his music had at last 'arrived', that his 'cause' had triumphed; and no doubt he would notice with amusement that many qualities for which he is cherished today were just those for which he was chastised by his contemporaries.

The Fourth Symphony, for example – now the most popular of his symphonies – had a very rough reception when it was first performed, and later.* Its reception caused Mahler no little distress. Many among these early audiences considered the whole thing a kind of hoax. Others were taken aback by the 'simplicity' of the tunes and then bewildered by the complexity of their development.

It is, of course, Mahler's brilliant manipulation of his seemingly innocent tunes that we find so fascinating. What we recognize as his 'originality', his own way of going about the business of composing, rests in his breaking-down of the tunes into their constituent motives and his magical re-assembly of them in new melodic and contrapuntal patterns, new combinations which he often views from a fresh harmonic angle or presents in startling instrumental colours – startling because the lines in the orchestral

---

First published in the *Daily Telegraph*, 23 January 1960.
\*   See '"Swallowing the Programme": Mahler's Fourth Symphony', pp. 173–4.

texture are so keenly drawn. It is a hundred other procedures of a like kind which make up the authentic Mahlerian 'voice'.

Not many of Mahler's comments on musical technique have survived (what a tragedy it is that the tape-recorder was not invented in time to document his famous conversations and disputes with the young Schoenberg), but one remark which has been handed down is certainly relevant in this context, that music is witness to the law of 'perpetual evolution, perpetual development'.

Mahler returned to this thought in more than one guise, making it clear that variation, the forsaking of repetition, was a constructive principle which actively occupied his mind. We hear the principle at work in his symphonies, in the first movement of the Fourth Symphony which, for that very reason, confused the audience at its premiere, and more complexly in later compositions. The 'diffuse' form with which Mahler is sometimes charged may well result from the listener losing his grasp on a method of musical argument which almost never restates its premises in their original shape.

Mahler's 'perpetual development' is plainly on the road which led to Schoenberg's later concept of 'perpetual variation'. (Who knows, this may have been one of the matters the two men discussed?) Schoenberg was a doughty champion of Mahler, all the more so for having started out in the opposite camp. He came to recognize the forward-looking nature of much of Mahler's music, a feature which is now more widely appreciated (Mahler's early opponents, who found his language unintelligible, were really more discerning in their misunderstanding than a later generation, who regarded his music as feebly 'Wagnerian'). For many years, indeed, the few faithful apart, Mahler was more of a composer's composer than anything else (a little like Schoenberg himself). But it was a sign of which way the wind might eventually blow that he enjoyed the respect not only of 'new' Vienna – Schoenberg, Berg and Webern – but of younger composers outside the Viennese tradition like Britten, Copland and Shostakovich. In fact, Mahler's singularly modern mind exerted a far-reaching influence through the music of these younger men, long before his own works attracted a wider public.

★

Today, I think, he is firmly established as a twentieth-century figure in his own right; and few will deny the aptness of the classification. But though he may be a founding father in the annals of modern music, part of Mahler's attraction lies in the valid claims two centuries can make upon him.

Out of the strain and friction of that conflict some of Mahler's finest and most personal music was born, and some of his most 'progressive' (a hateful word, but a serviceable one). His heroic gestures in the old style were as convincing and inspired as were his audacious ventures in the new, and often one finds both styles within a single movement, as in the adagio of the Ninth Symphony.

One cannot speak of division when faced with music so unified, music which can fall away into silence, and yet not crumble. The same is true of the man, a mass of contradictions, and yet the total impression left by his personality is a curiously consistent one, consistent in its inconsistencies.

He hated conducting, but was quite unable to give it up. He loathed the 'business' of the opera house, its administrative burdens, and yet supervised the detail of a new operatic production with boundless energy, not only the acting of the singers but in some cases the costumes, the sets and even the lighting.

The Mozart renaissance in this century owes much to his legendary performances of Mozart's operas, and he was one of the first conductors to reduce the size of the orchestra in the pit, for a production of *The Magic Flute*. Yet he could shamelessly talk about the 'progress' of music and play off Beethoven's Ninth against Mozart's G minor Symphony as if it were a legitimate comparison. Mozart, indeed, was not listed among the geniuses of 'universal significance' whom Mahler most admired (the musicians were Beethoven and Wagner).

No less surprising, the conductor who insisted upon chamber-orchestral textures for Mozart was convinced that Beethoven's late quartets were beyond the 'puny' talents of four players and must be transcribed for string orchestra. He was very much of his time and place in his patronizing attitude to Verdi, and yet, unfashionably, he could confess that he had learned a great deal from Verdi's orchestration. The contradictions continue, even down to his own beautiful-ugly face ('half genius, half monkey' was Freud's description of him).

The year 1960 will give us an opportunity to hear how all the contrasting fragments fit together to make an integral musical personality. For though Mahler was a much tormented man in his inner life, and born into a period of intense musical convulsion, it was the achievement of his creative genius that in his art, unimaginably and against all the odds, he succeeded in bringing the widest contrasts into close and meaningful relation, not by papering over the cracks — he was much too honest an artist for that — but by demonstrating the hidden unity and logic which can underpin seemingly irreconcilable elements.

The passion and skill he expended upon this task, the fruits of which form part of our musical landscape, cannot but command our respect and affection in this centenary year. Unlike his distinguished contemporary, Richard Strauss, Mahler remained a radical to the end of his life. He struggled on, neither corrupted by success nor wholly shattered by failure: anti-Semitic attacks did not deter him, despite their violence.

He was always extending his boundaries, feeling his way towards new horizons. 'Perpetual evolution, perpetual development' might well serve as this great composer's epitaph.

# Gustav Mahler: Prospect and Retrospect

## ~ 1961 ~

On 18 May, Mahler will have been dead for exactly fifty years. It is a convenient moment, perhaps, to survey, very briefly, the present state of Mahler studies and research.

It is a surprising fact, I think, that there is a need at all for the kind of research on documents and autographs that we associate with composers from the more distant past. Mahler, after all, was a public figure and lived in a glare of publicity. He was, undoubtedly, what the newspapers call 'news', and that means that a great deal of information about him of interest for later generations was recorded in the daily press or journals of the time.

So far, so good, one may think. But how accurate are those press reports, the advertisements, publishers' announcements, and so on, which are the very life blood of the industrious modern researcher, who pounces on a date here, a title there?

We are all of us indebted to the indefatigable Nicolas Slonimsky, that sleuth of the newspaper files, who has corrected many wrong dates and brought many forgotten dates to light. Newspapers, for him, at least for the most part, have the last word. But do they? And here I must add, that those of us associated with newspapers maintain a certain scepticism, even in the face of the daily black-and-white facts. It is, I sometimes think, the anonymous sub-editor who writes, or rather rewrites, the history that the unsuspecting reader has pushed through his door in the morning. This is not at all a flippant point. It can have all kinds of distressing consequences for the future.

Let us take one small example that concerns Mahler. The ordinary reader may well wish to know the date, place and circumstance of

Lecture given on 11 May 1961 and first published in *Proceedings of the Royal Musical Association*, no. 87 (11 May 1961), pp. 83–97.

the premiere of the most popular of Mahler's symphonies, the Fourth. If he looks for the information in the 5th edition of *Grove*, he will find none of it. But Mr Slonimsky's invaluable *Music Since 1900*[1] tells us that the work was first performed in Munich on 23 November 1901, conducted by Felix Weingartner. He has the date from a review in the Munich *Allgemeine Zeitung* of 26 November and from an advertisement in the paper on the day of performance.

Now Weingartner certainly was the conductor of the Kaim Orchestra in Munich, but it struck me as odd indeed that Mahler, who otherwise always conducted the premieres of his works, should have made an exception of the Fourth Symphony. On the face of it, there seemed no reason to doubt Mr Slonimsky's patient and convincing documentation. But a glance at Weingartner's autobiography solved the problem. There he makes it clear that while he conducted his part of the programme, it was Mahler who took over for the premiere of the Fourth Symphony. I haven't, naturally, wasted my time trying to find out why Mr Slonimsky was misled, but it would not surprise me at all to discover that it was the newspaper that got the facts wrong. Weingartner, needless to add, goes on conducting the premiere of Mahler's Fourth Symphony to this day. He is on the rostrum in Deryck Cooke's excellent Mahler handbook.[2] Once unleashed, these errors are extraordinarily difficult to kill.*

Well, that is a simple example of the kind of muddle still surrounding the bare facts of Mahler's life and music. Gradually, bit by bit, the pieces of the jigsaw puzzle are being fitted together. Gaps are being filled, misfits removed, the picture becomes a little clearer. It was only very recently, for instance, that I was able to attach a date and place to Mahler's baptism. An event of some biographical importance, one would have thought, but you will search the reference books in vain for a precise date. It seems strange that it was not until last year that someone was inquisitive enough to go along to the Kleine Michaelskirche in Hamburg and examine the baptismal

[1]   3rd edition, New York, 1949, p. 20.
[2]   Published by the BBC in 1960, p. 29.

---

*   Cooke's error was subsequently corrected on p. 66 of the 1980 (Faber Music) edition of this book.

register. And there, in his thirty-seventh year, Mahler was baptized on 23 February 1897. Another tiny detail has been completed.

All the work that needs to be done, in this sphere alone of Mahler research, really requires the support of a generous pair of wings from, shall we say, Gulbenkian or Fulbright.

It is a biographical handicap, a crippling one indeed, that so many of Mahler's contemporaries are no longer alive to be cross-examined, to be emptied of their memories. The great upsurge of interest in Mahler and his music, postponed by the war and before that by the censorship of the Nazis, has come just too late. We have lost the possibility of sifting the reminiscences of friends and colleagues who might have helped sketch in the blank pages of Mahler's life, especially those evasive early years. (The great figures of the Mahler era, his widow, for example, and Bruno Walter, have long told us all they know.)

But even about the early years, the odd fragment of information comes in which helps one to pencil in a shadow – it's rarely anything more substantial. I have this particular period of Mahler's life very much at heart, having written, as some reviewers were not slow to point out, a whole book about Mahler's early compositions, many of which no longer exist.[3] I freely confess to succumbing at times to something near panic as I added yet another lost work to an already very long list. I began to wonder, not if the work was lost, but if it had ever existed.

Just such a work was an early opera, *Herzog Ernst von Schwaben,* which I supposed Mahler to have worked on in 1877 or 1878,[*] when he was a youth of seventeen or eighteen. I notice that my own description of the opera begins, 'Very little is known about this work', the libretto of which was written by a boyhood friend, Josef Steiner. Imagine my surprise, when, only a few months ago, I found that a close relative of the librettist was living in London. She was able to tell me that the projected opera was a topic of discussion in the Steiner household. More than that, she remembered the

---

3   *Gustav Mahler: The Early Years,* London, 1958.

---

*   Now known to be written in the summer of 1875 while Mahler and Josef Steiner were on holiday at Ronow (see DMEY, p. 303 n. 129).

librettist picking out on the piano some of the tunes that his composer friend had imagined for the work. Steiner himself, of course,
is long dead. But some eighty-two years after the opera was abandoned, left incomplete and probably destroyed, confirmation did
come to me of the work's bodily existence. I had not, after all, been
pursuing a total fantasy. It is odd how these footnotes to history
come to be written.

There are some works from the early years, still extant, which
have not been placed at our disposal. For familiar reasons, certain
members of the composer's family sit on unpublished manuscripts*
which might add something to our knowledge of the young
Mahler's development. (I must add here that the composer's widow
is not among the squatters, though she has her compensating
foibles.)

The International Gustav Mahler Society, which has its head-
quarters in Vienna, and correspondents in most of the countries of
Europe, has been busy for some years collating and scrutinizing
Mahler's sketches and autographs. This is a particularly important
undertaking since it is by no means certain that the printed editions of the scores, though most of them appeared in the composer's lifetime, represent his final intentions. Hence the urgent
need for yet another *Kritische Gesamtausgabe.*§ The first volume of
the edition, a revised score of the Seventh Symphony, appeared last
year. It was scrupulously prepared for publication by the President
of the Mahler Society, Erwin Ratz, the distinguished Viennese
musicologist.

It is true to say, I think, that Mahler was never satisfied with the
instrumentation of his symphonies (he rarely altered the shape of a
work). The most celebrated example of wholesale revision we find
in the Fifth Symphony, of which two scores, both published by

---

*  A reference, above all, to the first version in three parts of the cantata *Das klagende Lied*,
    a manuscript that for many years was in the possession of Alfred Rosé, Mahler's nephew,
    who would not allow anyone to see it. The manuscript is now in the collection at Yale
    University.

§  For a list of current *Critical Editions*, see pp. 657–61.

Peters, were printed. The later version greatly clarifies the sound of the earlier, and very often by the cutting of superfluous duplication; but one can also clarify, of course, by making additions, by strengthening a part through doubling, by meticulous dynamic articulation. It is amazing what Mahler can accomplish in the way of clarity by the addition of a few rests. His amendments remind us that transparent scoring is not just a process of knocking things out but as much a process of knocking things in. A comparison of the two scores of the Fifth will provide any enquiring student with ample evidence of the principles upon which Mahler worked. His unceasing anxiety to improve his scores is well illustrated by a reminiscence of Otto Klemperer, who attended the rehearsals of the Seventh Symphony in Prague, in 1908. 'Every day', he tells us, 'after the rehearsal Mahler took the complete orchestral material home, to improve it, polish it up and retouch it. We attendant young musicians, Bruno Walter, Bodanzky, von Keussler and I, would gladly have helped him. He would not tolerate assistance and did everything alone.'[4] Typical of the man, and typical of his relentless drive after an ideal orchestral sound.

If we remember that this Klemperer experience may be applied to all the symphonies, that the retouching went on long after the premiere of a work and its publication, the importance of a critical edition of the works becomes self-evident. In a very real sense every performance of a Mahler symphony under Mahler was a premiere. What the Mahler Society has to do is to catch up on the final premiere in each case and fix it in music-type. One cannot but wonder what changes Mahler would have effected in the Ninth Symphony and *Das Lied van der Erde*, works that he never himself heard.

Obviously the *Gesamtausgabe* is of the first significance. But even when that is accomplished, a wide field of musical, as distinct from biographical, research remains. We are familiar with Mahler's editions of Schumann's symphonies; but what do we know in detail of his retouchings of Beethoven's symphonies and overtures; of

4   *Erinnerungen an Gustav Mahler,* Zurich, 1960, p. 10.

Schubert's Ninth Symphony; his edition of *Oberon*; his reconstruction of Weber's opera *Die drei Pintos;* his edition of *Figaro*, which adds a scene in the interests of dramatic clarification; his suite of movements from Bach's orchestral works, for which he realized the continuo part? One never knows what sudden illumination, of Mahler or his time, one may gain from exploration of these side-paths, and others like them.

The most incidental fact, indeed, can sometimes challenge the assumptions one has held for years. I had always imagined, for example, that Mahler, one of the most celebrated European conductors of his day, must have been kept busy conducting Beethoven's symphonies. It was quite extraordinary to find from Klemperer's little book of reminiscences, which appeared only last year, that one of the reasons why Mahler enjoyed his time in America, which came at the very end of his life, was that there he had a further opportunity to conduct the 'Pastoral' Symphony.* It makes an odd, if enlightening comment on the musical society of which, we know, Mahler was not always a very happy member.

One path that death decisively blocks, if the musician was born before the gramophone era, is that of performance. We can never know now what a Mahler performance was really like. None the less, rather in the same way that we can deduce the principles of Mahler's methods of revision from the comparison of different versions of the same work, we can at least estimate something of the impact and character of his performances by inspection of the scores from which he conducted. These provide, as minutely as possible within the limits of musical notation, a kind of map of Mahler's intentions. He applied phrase marks and dynamics to the scores of other composers with the same liberality with which he showered his own. If one knows Mahler's music well, which tells us how his mind worked, and can use one's imagination, one could, I think, arrive at a clear picture of how he approached the music he conducted – though nothing, of course, can restore to us Mahler's conception of tempo. But his scores are documents of considerable interest, and some day should receive the attention they merit. My own perusal of them (the scores were very carelessly preserved in

---

* Mahler had conducted Beethoven's Sixth Symphony in Hamburg in 1894 and 1895, and in Vienna in 1899.

Vienna, when I saw them) did not get very far. But I saw enough to convince me that the kind of ideal articulation of sound after which Mahler laboured in his own music must have been no less prominent a feature of his performances. And much of what he wanted to achieve, though not the achievement, could be demonstrated in music-type, so meticulous and plentiful are the signs and symbols with which he adorns his scores.

There I must leave the story of Mahler studies. Much, as you have heard, remains to be done. More, indeed, than I suggest, for I have only scratched the surface of the problems. (I have not mentioned, for example, the gaps there are in his correspondence.)

You may well wonder whether we are likely to be surprised by the discovery of unknown musical autographs. Not, I am sure, from Mahler's maturity. But there is one lost early work which might still turn up. Mahler composed it when he was twenty-three and a conductor at the Cassel Hoftheater: the incidental music for Scheffel's *Trompeter von Säkkingen,* which was performed in the Cassel theatre as a sequence of 'living pictures'.

The music was also successfully used in productions at Mannheim, Wiesbaden and Karlsruhe. Mahler quickly lost interest in what was undoubtedly an occasional piece and the work vanished. But I'm certain that there must be a set of parts buried somewhere in the archives of one of the opera houses that made use of the material.

A more tantalizing prospect – some might think it menacing – was opened up by an article which appeared in *Musical America* in 1938.[5] It was written by Paul Stefan, an intimate of the original Mahler circle in Vienna, but in 1938 he was an exile, and living in America, where he died in 1943. In this short article, which has received very little attention, he tells of a conversation with the late Willem Mengelberg, one of the most celebrated of Mahler's interpreters between the wars. Mengelberg claimed not only to have inspected, but to have played through at the piano, the manuscripts of four symphonies from Mahler's youth.* The autographs were in the possession of the then aged Baroness Weber who was living in Dresden and had promised the composer never to permit a performance of works which he would sooner have seen destroyed.

5  Issue of 10 April, p. 20. I am grateful to Jack Diether, New York, who sent me this article.

*  But see DMEY, p. 309 n. 133.

Fact or fancy? Here, of course, we're down among the dead men. Stefan is dead and Mengelberg is dead; Dresden was destroyed in the war and is now not the most accessible of cities.* It is improbable that the Baroness survives. Where does one start?

The information contained in the article matches up at many points with what we know of Mahler's early life and works. He was certainly very friendly with the Weber household in Leipzig and there is no doubt that symphonies, or at least attempts at symphonies, must be counted among his early exercises in composition. Whether these Dresden manuscripts, if they are, or were, authentic, may be identified with the lost symphonies of which we have a record, or whether they represent fresh attempts, remains a wholly open question which may now never be answered. Perhaps an echo of this address may stimulate inquiry in Dresden itself. Meanwhile we may remark upon the irony of Stefan's article appearing in a year – 1938 – that could not have been less auspicious for research of this kind; both the time itself and the very nature of the subject excluded the possibility of acting on Stefan's information. Just over a year later the Holocaust that many admirers have thought Mahler's music presaged, consumed the Europe of which he had been part.

His music, however – his published music – remains with us; and the centenary year has provided evidence of a most remarkable swing in Mahler's favour. The celebrations have been widespread, exhaustive and exhausting. England, which for many years was reluctant to take the plunge, has not been backward in paying generous tribute to this Austrian master. Who would have thought, ten or fifteen years ago, that a series of Mahler concerts in London would draw capacity audiences? That in the Festival Hall, an overflow audience would listen by relay to the programme that was being given in the main hall?§

---

* At the time of writing Germany was still divided, with Dresden in the Eastern sector.
§ A reference to the 'Mahler Centenary Year Programmes' given at the Royal Festival Hall in 1960, including performances of Symphony No. 4 (16 March), Symphony No. 9 (13 May), Symphony No. 6 (19 May), *Das Lied von der Erde* (24 June), the *Adagio* from Symphony No. 10, the *Rückert-Lieder* and Symphony No. 1 (26 October), *Kindertotenlieder* and Symphony No. 5 (30 October), and Symphony No. 2 (30 November). In the same period, in Leeds, on 20 October, the Hallé Orchestra gave a performance of Symphony No. 7.

The historian must take note of these movements in taste. After all, the ultimate status of a composer is determined neither by critics nor by historians but by his capacity to attract and hold an audience, which feeds the need to experience and re-experience his music. Historians may be the judges, critics the counsel for the defence or the prosecution; but the public is the jury.

One already hears voices, some of them influential voices, raising cries of 'fashion'. Composers, fortunately, are hardy perennials, at least the good ones are, and though fashion may freeze them one season and scorch them the next, they manage to survive these extremes of climate. Sibelius, I have no doubt, though now so senselessly, indeed sickeningly, downtrodden, will sprout again; perhaps a little less luxuriantly than before but still of a commanding size.

It may well be that Mahler will suffer the swings of fashion. But fashion is a two-way affair. For years, let us remember, in this country, Mahler – like some other composers – was subjected to the fashion of confident neglect. If one is obliged to choose between fashions, I prefer to rate as the more important a fashion that has its origins in aural experience of the music.

If there were historical reasons – those I concede – for the slow headway Mahler's music made in this country between the First and Second World Wars, there are good musical reasons, I think, for his present, relative, ascendancy. A substantial factor, undoubtedly, has been the discovery, in our own day, of Mahler's importance for some of the leading figures of twentieth-century music, not only composers of the intervening generation, like Berg and Schoenberg, but some of the most prominent composers of a later generation, often composers from a musical culture quite the opposite of Mahler's – Shostakovich, for example, or Britten. The influence of Mahler upon Shostakovich requires, I think, no detailed substantiation. It is self-evident. And if one looks at a work of Britten's as recent as his last orchestral song-cycle, the *Nocturne,* one finds there, above all in the concluding song, a clear extension of Mahler's style.

The chronology of musical understanding is often capricious in actual sequence. It does not surprise me at all that a keener interest in Mahler has been stimulated by the more general awareness of contemporary music we encounter today. A growing recognition of a new musical climate he helped to create, however distantly achieved, encourages one to come to terms with his own music. The understanding of what Mahler was about, as shown by later composers, can usefully guide our own appreciation of his music. In catching up on their music, we can catch up on his, too. There is a great deal to be learned, in fact, from listening to the history of music in reverse.

If nothing else, the centenary year has taught us, I think, that Mahler was, and is, of significance for the twentieth century. But it is one of the perils of centenaries that they unavoidably exaggerate and distort. (They also, let me add, tire a composer's friends and confirm the antagonism of his opponents. How one longs for the good old days when everyone was left in peace.)

I am particularly anxious on this occasion to avoid undue emphasis on the 'prophetic' Mahler. It is all too easy to decline into a curious kind of obsessive state in which one can't hear the music for the prophecies. Linear counterpoint in the finale of the Ninth Symphony, the systematic use of fourths in the first movement of the Seventh, intimations of a conscious neo-classicism in the first movement of the Fourth Symphony and the last movement of the Seventh – all very important, true and prophetic. But there is a real danger here that in following the signposts one assumes a condition of perpetual mobility that prevents one from resting for a moment and regarding the symphonies as things in themselves, not pointers to the future.

None the less, I should feel that I was failing in my duty if I did not mention a signpost that was brought to my mind only the other night when I heard Stockhausen's *Gruppen,* for three orchestras, for the first time. We live at this latest moment in a flood of news and views about musical space, stereophony, directional sound and multiple orchestras. During an idle moment in *Gruppen* – when the work, so to say, had moved away from me somewhere down the hall – it did strike me that Mahler too must be given his due as an early bird in the multiple-orchestra business. The Second Symphony, in particular, which makes use of an offstage brass band plus percussion, is rich in 'stereo' effects. It was doubtless the dramatic, 'resurrectional' character of the symphony that promoted the use of this device. But there is one passage in the finale in which the combination of the two orchestras gives us just those contrasts in texture and perspectives of sound which allow one to claim the passage as a clear and important historical precedent. Most significant of all, the orchestras enjoy a fair degree of rhythmic independence. My only excuse for adding yet another prophecy to the list is the fact that here we have Mahler foreshadowing the musical preoccupations of a generation of composers later than any I have previously mentioned. So far as his prophecies are concerned, Mahler seems to show a capacity to remain perpetually in fashion.

But how do the symphonies stand if we look at them as we might regard any of the other groups of symphonies by late romantic composers? By Tchaikovsky, for example, Brahms, Bruckner or Dvořák? (And by the way, if I do not talk about the songs or song-cycles of Mahler's maturity it is because they have been received in a way that the symphonies have not. In general, moreover, they share the characteristics of style which belong to the symphonies in any given period.)

We shall find, I think, that Mahler's symphonies show a width of contrasts, both between works and within individual symphonies, that we do not find in any of the other composers I have mentioned. This may strike you as an elementary observation, but some elementary things are also very unusual. For example, if one places the first movements of the Second and Fourth Symphonies side by side, one finds oneself poised between two virtually opposed worlds and textures, monumental symphony on the one hand and something that one might think approaches a divertimento on the other. Mahler often referred to his Fourth Symphony as his 'Humoreske'. If one compares the two finales, the contrast is even more striking – an epic, choral finale on the one hand, a solo song on the other. Within the symphonies, too, as I have said, there is this same, sometimes disconcerting, shock of violent contrast. There is the well-known pastoral andante from the Second Symphony, for example, which so surprisingly succeeds the solemnities of the huge first movement. Despite Mahler's call for a pause of five minutes – rarely observed in performance – the attempt to relax tension by way of extreme contrast does not, I think, come off. I was not surprised to discover that Mahler himself came to think that this juxtaposition of skyscraper and grass hut was a mistake, though not soon enough to prevent him from doing much the same thing in his Third Symphony, the first and second movements of which present a similar contrast in style and dimension. In later symphonies he was much more successful in holding a judicious balance between the relative weights of his sequence of movements.

But though, to return to my original point, the first movements of the Second and Fourth Symphonies exhibit such strikingly opposed features, they share, in form, an important unity. It is these two movements that represent, among the first group of Mahler's symphonies, his most successful handling of sonata structure. Yet paradox and contrast creep in even here. It is the first movement of the 'simple' Fourth Symphony which shows the greater degree of formal sophistication. The point of recapitulation alone is a master-piece of subtle compression. It simultaneously combines formal procedures which are normally exposed in sequence – the lead-back from the development and the recapitulation of the first group. The recapitulation proper, which at length finds its 'right' key, starts, so to speak, in midstream.

Let me add at once that the sonata principle haunted Mahler from the beginning to the end of his cycle of symphonies. We find in his works a number of extremely original approaches to a form which, by the end of the nineteenth century, had become highly problematic. In any history of the sonata idea, Mahler's symphonies must receive the most serious consideration. He kept the form on its feet with extraordinary resourcefulness even when, by all the rules of the game, it should long since have been carried out of the ring.

Of course, you may argue, quite properly, that the sonata prin-ciple is, above all, a scheme of ordered tonal relationships, the force of which was dissipated by romantic harmony. But we have to face the curious fact that 'sonata form' has gone on, I think quite mean-ingfully, even when tonal references have been completely aban-doned, as we find in Schoenberg, for example. I think we must view Mahler's sonata movements as part and parcel of a general development in the history of music, which resulted at length in a valid form independent of its original tonal basis. In this respect, Mahler was surely very much Schubert's successor.

In some important aspects, the Second Symphony is the odd man out among the first group of Mahler's symphonies. It anticipates the creative ambitions of the Eighth Symphony – his choral symphony – and the classical character of its first movement looks forward to the middle-period symphonies in which Mahler came closest, though perhaps not very close, to the house-style of the later Viennese symphonists.

It is in the First, Third and Fourth Symphonies that one finds Mahler's most comprehensive use of national musical materials, or perhaps it would be better to say 'local' rather than 'national'. In these three works, and of course in parts of the Second, one hears, as one does not hear to the same degree in the later works, the music that Mahler heard about him in his youth, folksong, military signals, brass bands, and birdsong (shades of Messiaen!). One has to remember that Mahler was born in Bohemia and lived the impressionable years of his youth in Moravia. He was not a self-conscious musical patriot but one cannot overlook the audible impact made on him by the world of sound which assailed his young ears. The most radical example of this influence occurs in the first movement of the Third Symphony, a movement of vast proportions which is largely built up out of military fanfares, folksong and popular march tunes, and throughout which the unmistakable sonority of the wind band predominates.

RECORDED MUSIC EXCERPT

Symphony No. 3, first movement, figs. 43–51

Many people find that music from the Third Symphony among the worst Mahler ever wrote. It certainly arouses in its acutest form the problem of his banality, about which so much has been written, on one side or the other, that I shall hold my peace on this occasion. I have said all I have to say elsewhere. But though one may dismiss the music, one is obliged to dismiss it for what it is – quintessential Mahler. One cannot account for it in terms of Strauss or Wagner, poles of reference, if you like, for much else in Mahler. Nor

can one explain it in terms of the Viennese symphony. It is something quite singular; and in so far as it expresses a sense of place, I
think we might approach the work as an offshoot, though a highly
idiosyncratic one, of the nationalism in music we readily accept
elsewhere. This is not, of course, the whole truth about Mahler's
early symphonies, but it is certainly one aspect of their style which
has not been very thoroughly explored.

There is something undeniably different about Mahler's concept
of nationalism – I would call it his 'factuality'. Mahler uses his
materials, as it were, straight, not touched up. It is this feature of
Mahler's early symphonies which has caught the very intelligent
ear of the German musicologist and sociologist, Theodor
Wiesengrund Adorno. In a new book,[6] devoted to the composer, a
perceptive study indeed but alarmingly unreadable, he writes, 'The
term socialist realism suits Mahler alone, were it not depraved by
current use; the Russian composers of 1960 frequently sound like
a disfigured Mahler.' I have already mentioned the influence of
Mahler on Shostakovich. Is not socialist realism, indeed, yet another
subdivision of a protracted nationalism?

I seem only to have scratched at the surface of Mahler's music.
The middle-period symphonies, Nos. 5, 6 and 7 – for that matter,
all Mahler's later symphonies – show a turning away from so radical a use of popular materials. But he still retains very clear links
with the style that gave us the first movement of the Third and
unique 'character' movements like the scherzos of the Second and
Third Symphonies, or the famous parody funeral march, the slow
movement, of the First Symphony. Character movements of the
new type are the second and fourth movements of the Seventh
Symphony, a pair of nocturnal serenades in which the popular
materials, the march tunes and birdcalls and military fanfares, have
undergone a remarkable refinement. One finds music like this
nowhere else in the symphonic literature.

But there is, in the later works, a distinct change of emphasis in
style. From the Fifth Symphony onwards – excluding the Eighth
because it is such a solitary achievement – it is possible to view

6   TWA *Mahler*, p. 67.

Mahler with more consistency as one of the last in the line in the tradition of the Austro-German romantic symphonists.

Neither leading the troops nor bringing up the rear is an enviable situation. But though Mahler was often obliged to compose, as it were, with his back to the wall, his prodigal inventiveness did not fail him; nor was he slow to make tactical use of the legacy left him by his predecessors in the field. He required, for instance, a new type of strong, long, lyrical melody, for these abstract symphonies, one free of the association with nature that we find in the big, singing themes of the First Symphony. His invention was equal to the task, and we find the new type of melody serving as second subjects in the first movements of both the Sixth and Seventh Symphonies. It characterizes, indeed, one of the best known of Mahler's movements, the *Adagietto* of the Fifth Symphony; melody, moreover, which wears a very personal face.

He was a tireless ransacker of musical resources which were certainly not conventional means of symphonic expression – the march, for example. I have never counted up the number of marches in Mahler's symphonies but they must amount to a formidable quantity. They certainly cover an extraordinarily wide range of mood. We march, it seems, not only into the grave but also out of it. But Mahler's successful promotion of the march, not just to symphonic status, but to first-movement status – above all in the first movement of the Sixth Symphony – deserves particular notice. There were distinguished precedents, Beethoven, Wagner, but no other composer has explored the possibilities of the march with such persistence.

The waltz, the ländler and the minuet – here, too, Mahler pursued these simple dance forms from the past and proved them capable of bearing new, if sometimes prickly, fruit. The scherzo of the Ninth Symphony juxtaposes all three dances, a synthesis which is perhaps characteristic of the artist who stands at the end of a tradition. There is much that is synthetic, in the exact sense of the word, about Mahler's symphonies.

In the middle-period symphonies, his adherence to the sonata principle in his first movements is, if anything, strengthened. But, characteristically, he seeks out fresh approaches. The two movements which go to make up the first part of the Fifth Symphony, for example, represent a novel attempt to divide between two movements the functions of exposition and development we normally find in one.

But it was not really until the Ninth Symphony that Mahler broke through with what might be claimed as a new form: the slow first movement, which is not a slow movement placed first, but a first movement in a slow tempo which retains, none the less, its time-honoured dramatic character and dynamic, developmental impetus, by a skilful handling of dual tempi. With some qualification, this same scheme and formal intention may be said to apply to the first movement of the unfinished Tenth Symphony.

And there, I fear, I must leave Mahler, with much left unsaid. It is clear from Mr Deryck Cooke's magnificent reconstruction, from the sketches, of the finale of the Tenth Symphony, that the work was by no means Mahler's last word. Far from giving, or cracking, up, we have every reason to suppose that he would have launched out on yet another project. Mr Cooke's great achievement, and the many Mahler performances we have heard this last year, in our concert halls and on the BBC, allow us, I think, to take a modest pride in the contribution this country has made to a just appreciation of Mahler's genius.

# Mahler and Smetana: significant influences or accidental parallels?

## ⌁ 1997 ⌁

Only comparatively recently – in 1991 during a visit to Prague – did I resume thinking about Mahler's musical relationships to those celebrated Bohemian composers, particularly Dvořák and Smetana, by whose works (especially operas) he was very likely influenced from time to time. Albeit in a rather random way, I touched on this topic in the second volume of my Mahler studies,[1] drawing attention to the similarity between a passage from Smetana's overture to *The Bartered Bride* and the transition to the recapitulation in the finale of the First Symphony (fig. 41), a connection that still seems to me very telling. What I write now remains narrow in focus, but suggests that in assessing the Bohemian influences on Mahler, we should be particularly mindful of Smetana.

To be sure, Mahler's preserved opinions of Smetana are not consistently enthusiastic. Nevertheless, his new production of *Dalibor* at the Vienna Opera, which opened on 4 October 1897, struck his friend and confidante Natalie Bauer-Lechner as something quite exceptional:

> He has been personally responsible for everything in it, having chosen and suggested the sets, costumes and lighting – not to mention his attention to the dramatic and musical aspects. In fact, he has even reworked the final section of the opera . . .
>
> Even apart from all this, I have perhaps never seen anything more perfect on the stage in every detail of performance and conception . . .

---

1  DMWY, pp. 209 and 291–2.

First published in Stephen E. Hefling (ed.), *Mahler Studies*, pp. 110–21.

Thus, although *Dalibor* had never been able to get a footing elsewhere, Mahler not only gave it a brilliant first night, but also assured it a genuine success.[2]

There can be no doubt about Bauer-Lechner's response to what was clearly a remarkable occasion; and to stage such an extraordinary event would have required, even of the hypercritical Mahler, a commitment and conviction based on the merits of Smetana's score (notwithstanding the fact that Mahler characteristically retouched and recomposed several passages of it).

Mahler conducted *Dalibor* a dozen times during 1897–98, but then only once or twice a season for the next six years.[3] Before the book was closed, so to say, he made one more comment to Bauer-Lechner, following the performance of 5 November 1901:

> You can't imagine how annoyed I was again today by the imperfection of this work, the work of so highly gifted an artist [*eines so hochbegabten Künstlers*]. He was defeated by his lack of technique and his Czech nationality (which hampered him even more effectively, and deprived him of the culture of the rest of Europe) . . . And when I'm conducting it I'm practically beside myself; there is a lot more I should like to cut and re-orchestrate, even recompose – so unskilfully is it written, in spite of its many beautiful passages.[4]

This makes odd reading as our twentieth century comes to an end, when it is difficult for us to imagine that being Czech could be regarded as a cultural deprivation. But composers' views on other composers are frequently unreliable, and more often than not tell us more about the composer uttering the criticism than the composer who is criticized. As I hope to show, despite Mahler's highly qualified admiration, Smetana's music influenced him beyond the previously noted instance of *The Bartered Bride*, and in ways by no

2   NB-L *Recollections*, pp. 101–2 and 209, n. 6.
3   Franz Willnauer, *Gustav Mahler und die Wiener Oper*, p. 232.
4   NB-L *Recollections*, pp. 180 and 227, n. 9.

means negligible. Composers have always behaved thus, and Mahler was no exception.

Smetana's *The Bartered Bride* entered the repertoire in 1866, and was swiftly recognized as a masterpiece of comedy and lyricism: according to Loewenthal, there had been one hundred performances by 1882 and five hundred by 1909.[5] Thus, there is nothing surprising about the 'quote' from the opera's overture in Mahler's First Symphony: this was music with which he would have been thoroughly familiar.[6] A few years later (January 1894) Mahler introduced a highly successful production of the work at the Hamburg Opera, and in Vienna he conducted ten performances of it between 1899 and 1907.[7] Nor did he neglect the *The Bartered Bride* at the Metropolitan Opera: the New York premiere took place under his baton on 19 February 1909. By all accounts this was a brilliant production, splendidly performed, but one that also aroused adverse commentary owing to Mahler's characteristic (although creative!) textual infidelities – among them, it seems, playing the overture before the second act. Although the production was highly praised, it did not capture the enthusiasm of New York audiences.

Clearly it was the 1894 triumph of *The Bartered Bride* in Hamburg that led Mahler later the same year to revive Smetana's *Two Widows* – said to be Richard Strauss's favourite opera. (Did Strauss also find Smetana's technique wanting, I wonder?) This work had been previously performed at Hamburg in 1881 – which was the first time, indeed, that any opera of Smetana's had been staged in a German theatre. Mahler continued to bring Smetana to his listeners with the Hamburg premiere of *The Kiss* in February 1895; among the cast were two stars whose names loom large in any chronicle of Mahler's theatrical activity, Bertha Förster-Lauterer and Ernestine Schumann-Heink. Indeed, during the 1894–95 season Hamburg witnessed virtually a miniature festival of

5   Alfred Loewenthal, *Annals of Opera*, p. 1866. Reviews of Mahler's 1909 New York performance appear in Zoltan Roman's invaluable *Gustav Mahler's American Years 1907–1911: A Documentary History*, pp. 220–23 and 238.

6   See also Henry-Louis de La Grange, 'Music about music in Mahler: reminiscences, allusions, or quotations?', pp. 122–68.

7   Willnauer, *Mahler und die Wiener Oper*, pp. 222 and 231.

Smetana operas conducted by Mahler – a self-contained event that is surely worth attention in its own right, particularly as regards the reception of these operas by both public and critics.

*The Kiss* – *Hubička* in Czech – is probably one of the least familiar of Smetana's operas outside the Czech Republic. Although today not nearly so popular as either the *Bartered Bride* or *Two Widows*,[8] at its Prague premiere on 7 November 1876, *Hubička* 'was the happiest and most successful of all of Smetana's operas and the work soon established itself as his most popular opera after *The Bartered Bride*.'[9] Mahler would not have been long unaware of such a successful work. When the premiere of *Hubička* took place, he was a sixteen-year-old student at the Vienna Conservatoire, and he was twenty when the vocal score of the opera was first published in 1880 (to coincide, perhaps, with the production of *Hubička* presented at the Provisional Theatre in Prague in honour of Smetana's fiftieth year as a performing pianist).[10] Mahler conducted his first performance of *Hubička* in Hamburg on 20 February 1895. The foregoing assembly of dates and data provides a necessary context for what follows; and what follows derives, quite simply, from my chance encounter with *Hubička* in September 1991 at the Smetana Theatre in Prague.

In Act I scene 7 of the opera, at the side of a cradle, Vendulka sings a lullaby – or rather, two lullabies. The first is a traditional one that begins (in F) as shown in Ex. 1. The second (in A), separated from the first by six bars of recitative, is Smetana's original composition. Two introductory bars establish the gently rocking motion of the slumber song as shown in Ex. 2. Both these lullabies seemed to me sublime inspirations (if I may be forgiven that tired old adjective). But what gripped my attention – so much so that I

8  Perhaps now one ought to add *Dalibor* to the short list, staged successfully as it was for the first time in England by English National Opera in 1976 and 1977.
9  John Tyrrell, 'The Kiss', *The New Grove Dictionary of Opera*, vol. ii, pp. 1000–2. Tyrrell's magisterial study *Czech Opera* provides detailed statistical information about the number of performances of Smetana's operas given at the National Theatre, Prague, between 1883 and 1886, years that include the period Mahler spent there as second conductor at the German theatre. See also Brian Large, *Smetana*, pp. 289–316 and 348.
10  Two further operas succeeded *Hubička*: *The Secret* (1878) and *The Devil's Wall* (1879–82). Smetana left a fragment of an opera entitled *Viola* (based on Shakespeare's *Twelfth Night*) that he was working on up to his death in 1884.

Ex. 1    Smetana, *Hubička*, Act 1 scene 7, first lullaby

Ex. 2    Smetana, *Hubička*, Act 1 scene 7, second lullaby

Ex. 3    Smetana, *Hubička*, Act 1 scene 7, ending of second lullaby

almost exclaimed out loud – was how the second lullaby *ended* (see
Ex. 3). Or, more precisely, how the lullaby did *not* end, but faded
out, dissolved into the sleep that overtakes Vendulka. In short, she
sings the child to sleep, and herself as well; Smetana graphically,
almost magically, captures this lyric–dramatic vignette and sustains it
for us.

That unresolved dominant with its lingering pedal,[11] which
leaves us suspended, like Vendulka, from the waking world of
action, immediately brought back to my mind in an almost Proustian
burst of memory the last bars of one of Mahler's orchestral *Wunderhorn* settings, 'Der Schildwache Nachtlied': this is another *Nachtstück* that, if not exactly a lullaby, none the less brings us to the edge

11  Nor does Smetana resolve it in any orthodox sense. However, the immediately ensuing
    opening of scene 8, a lively polka, is in F, the key of the first lullaby.

Ex. 4    Mahler, 'Der Schildwache Nachtlied', ending

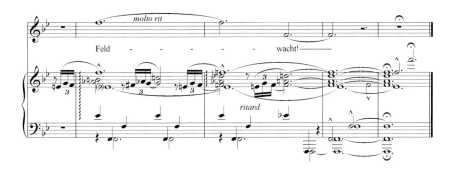

of dreams, whether through sleep or death (traditionally two closely associated states of being). And Mahler achieves the suspension of time and motion in the lyric–dramatic situation through virtually the same musical means as his Czech predecessor (see Ex. 4). We are left suspended on and over the dominant, another 'still', frozen, cinematic like, in its frame, fading, along with the sentry, into some other world on the threshold of which we are left standing.[12]

12  As I suggest above, whether the sentry drifts into dreams, sleep, or death remains to my mind an entirely open question: hence the unresolved dominant. The poem that Mahler set is surely enigmatic; although Deryck Cooke suggests without qualification that it tells of a sentry killed on duty while dreaming of his sweetheart, I am not sure that the text is not more ambiguous than this. (See DCGM, p. 42.)

It is curious, moreover, that there has been very little comment on Mahler's audacious 'dissolve' at the end of 'Der Schildwache Nachtlied'. To my knowledge, the first writer to draw attention to it was the perspicacious Ernst Decsey, who actually took the matter up with Mahler himself – only to be rebuffed for reading more into the treatment of the dominant than the composer was then prepared to concede. (Again, an altogether typical composer's response.) See Ernst Decsey, 'Stunden mit Mahler', *Die Musik* 10/21 (1910/11), pp. 144–5, translated in Norman Lebrecht (ed.), *Mahler Remembered*, p. 261.

An incomplete sketch for the song was once in the possession of Natalie Bauer-Lechner (now at the Library of Congress, Washington, DC; a photofacsimile of the first page is found in Emanuel Winternitz, *Musical Autographs from Monteverdi to Hindemith*, vol. II, plate 163). In her memoirs (*Recollections of Gustav Mahler*, p. 190) Bauer-Lechner associates it with an operatic project of 1888, as follows:

Mahler told me [in the summer of 1901] that in Leipzig, after finishing the *Pintos* with [Karl von] Weber [the composer's grandson], and at the request and urging of the latter's wife, he had wanted to write an opera of his own. He suggested the following subject to Weber for a libretto, outlining it in detail:

A soldier on his way to the gallows is – according to medieval custom – spared the

Had 'Der Schildwache Nachtlied' been composed after the
Hamburg premiere of *Hubička*, there could be little question of
Smetana's influence on Mahler's *Wunderhorn* song. But we know
with certainty that the voice-and-piano version of 'Der
Schildwache Nachtlied' was complete by 28 January 1892 (and the
orchestral score followed by 26 April the same year), whereas
*Hubička* was not staged in Hamburg until 20 February 1895. Yet it
seems very probable indeed that Mahler knew *Hubička* before he
came to conduct it himself in 1895. As noted above, the vocal score
appeared in 1880 and the opera had become fairly popular. In

death penalty when a girl, whose deepest sympathy he inspires, claims him in marriage
before the people and the judges. The mourning procession turns into one of jubilation,
and everyone goes home rejoicing. But the stubborn young fellow cannot bear the
shame of owing his life to the pity of a girl whom he, in turn, is beginning to love. His
inner conflict becomes so intolerable that he rejects her gift of freedom and marriage,
declaring that he would rather die. The last act was supposed to bring about the resolution of the matter with the girl's ardent pleading and confession of love.

Weber, however, had immediately altered this simple story. He introduced an earlier
love and sweetheart of the young man, running quite counter to Mahler's intentions, and
leading him very soon to abandon the whole idea. 'Der Schildwache Nachtlied' was
salvaged from this attempt. To it, Mahler owed his renewed acquaintance with *Des
Knaben Wunderhorn*, which was to become so significant for him.

This has never seemed probable to me, and the description of the sketch sent me by
Professor Edward R. Reilly, to whom I am much indebted, offers no evidence to support Bauer-Lechner's attribution. However, what prompted my query to Professor
Reilly was my interest in the song's concluding bars: were they, I wondered, present in
the sketch in the form that they appeared in the final version? Professor Reilly told me
(private communications, April and June 1994) that they were not:

The Library of Congress sketch does not show the end of the song. It is clear from the
manuscript that Mahler hit a snag at the equivalent of bar 97 [six bars after the beginning of the song's closing 6/4]. The vocal line for [the words] 'Verlorne Feldwacht' differs from the final form, and four further bars of unharmonized vocal line are cancelled.
So we don't know how he would have ended it at this stage. Most interesting, however,
is the fact that although the sketch begins in B flat, as in the final form of the song, the
passage beginning at bar 92 is in G, and in fact at bar 94 is marked 'G dur'.

The last three bars look as if they move in the direction of E minor. It would have been
fascinating, of course, for us to have had an early sketch from Mahler of a conclusion for
the song. It is almost more fascinating to know that at the stage of this sketch he clearly
didn't know himself how to end it.

As for the 'opera', it is difficult indeed to envisage a whole evening in the theatre
emerging from the outline Bauer-Lechner gives. Perhaps Weber and Mahler talked over
the kernel of an idea, but did not pursue it. Is it then not likely that Mahler's memory
of the 'project' of 1888 came back to mind when he was selecting *Wunderhorn* texts for
setting in the 1890s and helped determine his choice of 'Der Schildwache Nachtlied' –
i.e., that Mahler found the 'opera' had already been written for him in the shape of a
poem?

addition, it seems likely that the famous lullaby (or lullabies) may have been performed independently in concert halls here and there, a point to which I shall return below. More compelling, however, is the fact that Mahler spent the 1885–86 season in Prague, as temporary conductor at the Royal German Theatre (Deutsches Landestheater). At Prague's newer Czech National Theatre (Narodní divadlo), native works were presented in their original language, and it was here that Mahler came to know a number of Slavic operas, including those of Smetana, whose *Hubička* was performed at least four times during the first half of 1886.[13] Prior to his Prague engagement, however, Mahler had already signed a contract to become assistant conductor under Arthur Nikisch at the Leipzig Stadttheater for the 1886–87 season. In late June or early July he writes from Prague to the Director of the Leipzig house, Max Staegemann, as follows:

> Incidentally, I have several times been to the Bohemian National Theatre here and have heard a number of works by *Smetana* [Mahler's emphasis], Glinka, Dvořák, etc., and I must confess that Smetana in particular strikes me as very remarkable.
>
> Even if his operas will certainly never form part of the repertory in German, it would be worth while presenting such an entirely original and individual composer to audiences as cultivated as those in Leipzig.[14]

'An entirely original and individual composer': rather different words and tone from the judgement Mahler would later pronounce upon *Dalibor* when he was Director of the Vienna Court Opera! But that apart, it seems reasonable to assume that what Mahler had in mind in writing so persuasively to Staegemann was

---

13  See František Bartoš (ed.), *Mahler: Dopisy*, p. 185 – a valuably annotated edition of Mahler's letters, especially with regard to the years up to his appointment to the Opera at Vienna. See also HLG *Mahler*, vol. 1, pp. 203–4 and 226, n. 81, as well as Kurt Blaukopf (ed.), *Mahler: A Documentary Study*, pp. 174–5 and plates 61–9. According to Josef Bohuslav Foerster, *Der Pilger: Erinnerungen eines Musikers*, p. 374, *Hubička* (*Der Kuss* in German) was indeed among the operas Mahler heard during the 1885–86 season in Prague.

14  GM *Selected Letters*, no. 44.

precisely the sort of Smetana mini-festival that he finally brought to the boards in Hamburg during the 1894–95 season, comprising *The Bartered Bride, Two Widows*, and *Hubička*. Thus, although the evidence is not completely conclusive, it seems legitimate to me to suggest that the impact *Hubička* (or at any rate its lullabies) made on Mahler during his year in Prague became a significant influence on 'Der Schildwache Nachtlied' in 1892. It was not, I believe, a conscious influence, but a subconscious recollection that served him as a poetic and technical model for the concluding, or rather *inconcluding, bars of the sentry's *Nachtlied*. I find it not at all surprising that Mahler's preternaturally sensitive and all-consuming ear would have stored away a memory of Smetana's masterly little inspiration for future use.

The apparent connection between Smetana's lullabies and Mahler's song strikes me as a most telling and fascinating example of a creative legacy, inherited by Mahler from his great Bohemian predecessor, that transcended the bounds and boundaries of nationalism. But at least one further passage of *Hubička* made an uncanny impression on me when I heard it in Prague in 1991. It was, as it happens, yet another *Nachtstück,* but of a quite different character: not a lullaby, but a night patrol through a deep forest. The music in question is a chorus of smugglers, which John Tyrrell aptly characterizes as 'an atmospheric piece with a baroque crotchet tread and hushed voices above'.[15] I don't quarrel with any of that. Yet it was not an association with the baroque that floated into my mind, but rather a distinct evocation of a passage from the development in the first movement of Mahler's Second Symphony – the first version of which, entitled 'Todtenfeier', was completed in September 1888, in Prague. (Thus Mahler would already have heard the Smetana operas he mentioned to Staegemann in the letter of 1886 cited above.) Ex. 5 illustrates the nature of Smetana's nocturnal scene; undoubtedly it was the combination of the ostinato plus a tapestry of winds (bassoons, horns, clarinets, flutes and oboes) projected above the insistent bass tread that once again brought me, so to say, face to face with Mahler – and very much the Mahler of the 1880s.

---

15  Tyrrell, '*The Kiss*', p. 1001.

Ex. 5    Smetana, *Hubička*, Act II scene 1, chorus of smugglers (vocal parts omitted)

To make the point as clear as possible I have omitted from Ex. 5
all the vocal parts, which in themselves are of only secondary
musical significance. The parallel passage in Mahler, which is easily
accessible, is from fig. 16 to bar 270 in the score of the Second
Symphony.[16] It is, I repeat, the character of the Smetana example
that seems so embryonically yet authentically Mahlerian, together

16  In the 'Todtenfeier' full score published as Supplement Band 1 of *Gustav Mahler: Sämtliche*
    *Werke, Kritische Gesamtausgabe*, this passage runs from fig. 18 to fig. 19.

with its texture, its lay-out, and the colour of it. Was this once again music that Mahler had absorbed which resurfaced just below the threshold of consciousness when he found himself working on his own dark processional in the 'Todtenfeier' movement of the Second?

Although I cannot pretend to know all the answers to the questions that my own first faltering steps in this field have generated, it is clear to me that there is between Mahler and Smetana a creative relationship of potential significance which has not yet been thoroughly explored. Brian Large, in his voluminous work on Smetana,[17] makes only two very brief mentions of Mahler, in one of which he states that 'Mahler knew and loved *Má Vlast*, and *Tábor* and *Blanik* may well have inspired parts of the Sixth Symphony.' True or false? It seems to me that there is work to be done as regards *Má Vlast*. And what about *Dalibor*? Has anyone seriously examined the opera to discern what ignited Mahler's enthusiasm, qualified though it was? (His editing and retouching might tell us something as well.) As I write, moreover, additional correspondences occur to me. Of course all lullabies tend to have features in common, but in the sublime slumber song that closes the *Kindertotenlieder*, particularly in its gently ululating figuration, might there be a distant trace of Vendulka's second lullaby?

That possibility returns us to *Hubička,* and therewith to the last piece in this jigsaw puzzle, which comes from the very last year of Mahler's life. On 20 November 1910 at the Brooklyn Academy of Music Mahler conducted the New York Philharmonic in a programme (twice repeated at Carnegie Hall) that included Dvořák's *Carnival* overture and two pieces by Smetana – one of which (with soloist Alma Gluck) was none other than the 'Böhmisches Wiegenlied [Bohemian Lullaby] aus *Hubička*'.[18]

17  Large, *Smetana*, p. 185.
18  See Knud Martner, *Gustav Mahler im Konzertsaal, 1870–1911*, p. 139. A review of Mahler's
    1910 performance is to be found in Roman, *Gustav Mahler's American Years,* p. 408. The
    'arrangement' was made by Kurt Schindler; and it was no doubt in this shape that the
    excerpts from the opera had enjoyed some sort of independent life on the concert cir-
    cuit. I have not been able to locate this particular arrangement, but it must have found
    a way round the second lullaby's expiring on the dominant (which would not make
    much sense outside the theatre), while even the first lullaby is not rounded off but leads

into the brief recitative that acts as bridge between the two. Or perhaps Mahler came up with a solution of his own? A possibly relevant piece of evidence is a 1937 78rpm shellac disc of the lullaby made by Elisabeth Schumann with an anonymous conductor and orchestra. The very existence of the recording indicates that the lullaby was performed independently from the opera. As for the concluding bars, the arranger replaces Smetana's poetic open end with a conventional resolution. In all other respects, however, the performance is faithful to the text, and Schumann sings (in German, of course) with incomparable charm. The recording has been re-issued on CD on the Beulah label, 2PDH ('78 classics, Volume Two').

# Chailly, Mahler, and the Italian Connection

## ∾ 2005 ∾

I can still remember my surprise, many years ago now, when I was in the early stages of my discovery and understanding of Mahler, and read in one of those famous conversations that he had in the 1890s with Natalie Bauer-Lechner of how much he claimed to have learned about orchestration from none other than Verdi. This was in October 1901, not long after he had completed his Fourth Symphony. He went on to add that Verdi 'had blazed quite new trails in it'; and it struck me at the time, even if I did not fully take on board in those days the significance of what Mahler was saying or implying, that this was an observation that had to be taken seriously, coming from someone who was himself an innovatory trail-blazer in that very same field.

I soon came to realize how deep the Verdian link with Mahler was when I came to identify in the slow movement of the Fourth Symphony an unmistakable reference to the final duet* of the lovers in Verdi's *Aida*, an opera that Mahler frequently conducted when pursuing his 'other life' as a conductor of opera. Clearly, Verdi was very much in his mind when composing his Fourth, of which a quite exceptional performance forms part of this tribute to the legacy that Chailly's years in Amsterdam, as Chief Conductor of the Royal Concertgebouw Orchestra, represents. He remains Conductor Emeritus of the orchestra.

These Verdian reflections, I believe, are by no means irrelevant when considering the character and importance of Chailly's

---

Liner note for the recording *Mahler: The Symphonies*, Riccardo Chailly conducting the Royal Concertgebouw Orchestra and the Radio-Symphonie-Orchester Berlin, Decca 475–6686.
* 'O terra, addio', Act IV scene 2.

Amsterdam years, from 1988 to 2004. For one thing, he is a conductor of Verdi's operas of arresting brilliance and penetration. It is Mahler, for sure, who was a major figure in Chailly's programming throughout this period, but one should not forget other notable preoccupations, for example his commitment to radical contemporary music, which is also a feature of his recordings and of his principal musical enthusiasms. (I have in mind, for example, his striking attention to Varèse.) But let me for a moment continue with a further word or two about Verdi, because it was often after one of Chailly's performances in Amsterdam of one of the operas – I recall an unforgettable *Don Carlos* – that we would talk for a while, and it was rare if we did not find ourselves mentioning passages for which quite clear and fascinating parallels could be found in Mahler, evidence of how far-reaching was the influence of Verdi and how it came to be absorbed into Mahler's music. How fascinating too to remember that what certainly was regarded to be one of the greatest of productions in Vienna conducted by Mahler in his last years at the Vienna Opera was that of Verdi's last opera, *Falstaff*, for which Mahler's admiration was unbounded.

I am far from trying to make the simplistic point that from time to time we hear in Mahler a Verdian echo. The relationship goes far deeper than that. I am prepared to argue indeed that in a very real sense the closer we study Mahler's symphonies and song-cycles, the more aware we become that a whole culture, Italian culture no less, can sometimes be a fertilizing presence, perhaps lying just below the surface but there none the less; and if it has not been adequately recognized before, the reason for that is surely that for years it has been widely assumed that to think of Italy in any kind of specific musical relationship with Mahler was simply impossible.

For years we have been culturally conditioned to think of Mahler and Italy, culturally speaking, as diametric opposites, hard to speak of in the same breath. But it has long seemed to me that there are parallels that go beyond those I have already mentioned, for example the fact that each of Mahler's symphonies is itself a self-contained drama, an independent narrative each offering a theatrical experience in its own right. It is here surely that Chailly's own national musical tradition, out of which and into which he was born, proves to be so illuminating. He brings to each symphony indeed a riveting overall sense of drama which I cannot but believe has its roots in his own musical culture. We still today often hear the question still being asked, why did Mahler never write an opera? And my answer always has been that if we want to seek the answer, visit the symphonies and the huge range of dramas they traverse. It is precisely here that Chailly often and most valuably reminds us that Mahler's symphonies though they may have been born out of the concert hall, also belong to, and often were inspired by, the opera house. Think, for instance, of the finale of the Second Symphony, and the extraordinary theatricality of it. It is as if we are participating in the tumult and commotion of the Resurrection itself, a torrent of music of every kind engulfing us on all sides and from all directions, until, finally, the moment of climax is reached, the chorale which rounds off the movement. Mahler was never to write anything quite like it again, but it certainly goes a long way to providing the answer to the question about Mahler and opera. His operas *were* written. They are there, in the symphonies; and not surprisingly Chailly realizes them musically with outstanding brilliance. It is a world to which he himself belongs.

There is yet another fascinating example of Mahler in Italian mode. It occurs at a much later period in his Eighth Symphony, the second Part of which, the setting of Goethe's *Faust*, Part II, naturally enough called into play his theatrical resources; a case in point is the climactic moment when Goethe's Mater gloriosa glides into view, heralded by a *fortissimo* flourish of arpeggios (piano and multiple harps). This is then followed by a passage that could have been written only by Mahler but remains unique: there is nothing quite like it, in terms of intensity and ecstasy, elsewhere in his work. Ravishing it undoubtedly is in its articulation of love and passion (glissandi are prominent), music which seems to belong to a cultural world quite other than that of Goethe's *Faust*. To the never fully materialized world of Mahler's 'opera', I would suggest; and how appropriate it is that it is specifically *Italian* expression marks he turns to here. 'Sempre molto cantando' is what he calls for from his strings as they unfold their wordless aria; and as it proceeds we find ourselves encountering Mahler in undisguisedly Italian guise, briefly but unforgettably.* As one might expect, this extraordinary moment is meticulously spelled out in Chailly's performance. This is just one example of the many ways in which he brilliantly highlights an aspect, feature or dimension of one of the symphony's interior dramas. The diversity of his approaches is itself engrossing.

Take the Fourth Symphony, the denouement of which is Mahler's setting of a *Wunderhorn* text, 'Das himmlische Leben'. Surprising enough to find a song as a symphony's finale especially, as it so happens, that the work's first three movements very clearly anticipate the complex forms and above all hyperactive counterpoint of the immediately ensuing symphonies, the Fifth and Sixth. Mahler, of course, both rhythmically and thematically, has prepared us for the song when it arrives; but the real moment of revelation is postponed until the last stanza, with the advent of E major (and E major by the way is prominent in the Mater gloriosa scene of the Eighth I have already discussed) and, most conspicuous of all, the suppressed dynamics which Mahler calls for and which so few conductors observe. It is quite otherwise with Chailly, who reduces the volume of sound to an ultra-*pianissimo*, the effect of which, on the edge of inaudibility, offers a denouement as riveting – as dramatic – as it is magical.

To my mind, it has still not been sufficiently recognized how different one Mahler symphony is from another. For example, who could have predicted or imagined that the Ninth was to have a successor in the shape of the Tenth? That there was even the possibility of a Tenth? And it is precisely here that Chailly once again demonstrates his independence. He was among the earliest to recognize the importance of Deryck Cooke's performing version of Mahler's draft for the Tenth and his recording of the work is not only testimony to his conviction of its significance but also a revelation of the new world which Mahler was about to explore before death claimed him. Chailly has helped establish the Tenth as part of our experience of Mahler the symphonist. Like all of its predecessors it creates its own world of sound and is fired throughout by its own drama.

---

* A further Italian connection – with Bellini – is explored in 'On the Road to the Eighth Symphony', pp. 441–3, and in 'Mahler's Eighth Symphony: The Triumph of Eros', p. 453.

It is, I believe, Chailly's mastery of the individual narratives that will long lend his recordings of the works a special value and distinction. Or, to put it another way, each symphony, from the First onwards, embarks on a journey of exploration, each with a unique destination in mind, whether it is the remorseless momentum of the Sixth, ultimately proclaiming death as its goal, or the gradual unfolding in the Fifth of the eventual joy and triumph of its finale. Chailly leads us through the sequences of complex and contrasting movements which succeed the first movements of both symphonies. Among them, in the Fifth, is the famous and exquisite *Adagietto*, exquisitely performed here, with his customary attention to fine detail. It is fascinating to compare the agonized contrapuntal textures of the Sixth with the vigorous geniality of the fuguing in the last movement of the Fifth. Whether it is Mahler's pessimism or his optimism that is to the fore, however, Chailly's pronounced transparency of textures enables us to hear the totality of Mahler's polyphony.

Let me finish with a final comment on Chailly and Mahler's dramas. As one would expect of this remarkable conductor, noted for the independence of his thinking, it is the one symphony of Mahler's that superficially at least does not have a narrative or a programme, his Seventh, that he has very much made his own. Listeners will find that he has succeeded in finding a narrative, a drama – his own performance of the work, that is – which makes perfect sense of this most enigmatic of all Mahler's symphonies. (If the absence of a narrative can be one kind of problem, so too can be the presence of one, especially one as complicated as that of the Third Symphony. Yet Chailly rises to the challenge by focusing on what the music has to tell us about the 'programme' (not the other way round) and the problem disappears.)

When it came to the moment of Chailly's retirement from Amsterdam, for his last concert there was only one possible choice: Mahler's Ninth. It was an altogether memorable occasion and a performance charged with feeling by the orchestra and the conductor, feeling profoundly matched by the capacity audience that filled the hall, the Concertgebouw, in which Mahler himself had long ago conducted. I was there myself and shall never forget it.

The first movement, perhaps the composer's greatest single movement, was projected with unconstrained power, one climax following another in an ever increasing, overall crescendo. To be sure, the
movement ends in calm, if not exactly in peace; one knows in fact
the drama is by no means played out. It is Chailly's skill that, while
bringing off the two middle movements with passionate conviction, we continue to wonder, quite properly, how the symphony
will end. Probably 90 per cent of the audience present of course
knew precisely how the work would finish. But Chailly like
Mahler is a master of creating the art of expectation and sustaining
it over long stretches of musical time. Thus it was that it was not
until we reached the finale and actually heard the beginning of the
great slow movement, with its initiating, breathtaking semitonal
drop to D flat, that rounds off the symphony, that we knew we had
arrived. The drama was over. It was time to depart. How lucky we
are to have a recording of Chailly's concept of this amazing work.

I hope I may be allowed to conclude by expressing to Maestro
Chailly, as I must surely name him in the context of these thoughts
about the Italian connection, my now long-established esteem,
affection and admiration.

# The Twentieth Century's Debt to Mahler: Our Debt to Him in the Twenty-first

## ✑ 2001 ✑

I am rather often asked how it was that Mahler became one of the three leading musical passions of my life. (Britten and Mozart complete the trinity.) It is certainly not my intention to embark on autobiography; on the other hand what I am about to tell you says something of significance about the history of the reception of Mahler's music in the century we have just quitted.

I was born in 1925, which makes me just thirteen years old when I encountered Mahler's music for the first time through the medium of gramophone records. Those legendary performances, for so they have become, of *Das Lied von der Erde* and the Ninth Symphony, both conducted by Bruno Walter, with the Vienna Philharmonic Orchestra, were recorded on 78 rpm shellac discs respectively in 1936 and 1938. Already, then, there is a point I want to make, that at this specific moment in historical time, at the end of the period – those rather few years – between the end of the First World War, 1918, and the beginning of the second, in 1939, it was the gramophone record that had a highly significant role to play in the dissemination of Mahler's music and in the evolution of how it has become to be assimilated and comprehended, now on a virtually global scale. I shall have a bit more to say about this later on. These days, of course, we are all aware of the worldwide wonders of the Internet, and the extent of its communicative powers. We should not fail, however, to give a retrospective salute to a technology that was also innovative in its time, and, in Mahler's case, came to exercise a profound cultural influence.

Lecture given at the IVth MahlerFest, Colorado, 13 January 2001, and edited for publication on the MahlerFest website.

So what was it, some of you may ask, that prompted me to pester my very kind parents to buy me these recordings, which they did? Was it something of Mahler's that I had heard and was excited by? Of course not! And it is precisely that negative answer that says everything – well, almost everything – about the reception of Mahler's music, certainly in Britain, but I believe in most other parts of the world as well: in the 1920s and mid- and late 1930s there wasn't much to be received. Of course, there were remarkable exceptions, even – occasionally – in Britain, especially through the then new medium of broadcasting and an enlightened musical policy practised by the BBC. But for an inquisitive schoolboy of fourteen or fifteen in London there was simply no opportunity to have one's interest aroused by a live performance.

How then, you may ask, was that interest aroused? I was fortunate in having a mother who was herself a highly gifted musician who had been a student pre-First World War in Leipzig at the famous music Conservatoire there, which had enjoyed for many years the reputation of being Europe's leading music school for aspiring performers. When she returned to Britain, the war over, she brought home among her books, a famous two-volume encyclopaedia, Hugo Riemann's *Musik-Lexikon*, and as a boy I used to spend hours poring over the entries. Among them was a brief entry on Mahler in which of course there was a list of works which included *Das Lied von der Erde*. My mother patiently translated the entry for me, or those bits of it I couldn't make out, and for some inexplicable reason I was haunted by the title of Mahler's last song-cycle – *The Song of the Earth*, what could that be? – by his name, Gustav Mahler, and the very basic details of his life and work. It was that entry that set me off in search of Mahler, and from that moment what was a silence imposed by ignorance and by accidents of history and politics and cultural prejudices, from that moment the silence was broken, and I was, to put it with maximum economy, hooked. So it was that once that mysterious title, *Das Lied von der Erde*, was translated into sound, I set forth on a long journey that continues still and indeed has brought me to be with you now, in Colorado.

Just the other day I was reading a thoughtful review of the new volume in the series that constitutes my great friend's – Henry-Louis de La Grange's – unique biography of Mahler, which ended with a paragraph devoted to the generation of composers succeeding Mahler who had not only received Mahler's support and encouragement but eventually themselves won recognition as representing the New Music that was to engulf the twentieth century, among them Schoenberg, Berg, and Webern, not to speak of Zemlinsky whose music has had to wait longer for the serious attention it deserves and is now beginning to get. The review was written by a British composer and teacher, Hugh Wood, and it ends with this sentence in which he states that the 'aesthetic position' which made the whole work of Schoenberg, Berg and Webern possible 'had already been fought out' – and I applaud the choice of words – 'in the composition of Mahler's own symphonies'.

That is very much the territory at which I shall be taking a fresh look today and it seems to me to be of some significance that it was a composer, writing as the twenty-first century has just begun – the authentic start of the new millennium, is it not? – who made that comment. Because in fact it was in the first instance composers who realized the significance of Mahler's creativity, the unique worlds his symphonies represent, with the paradoxical consequence that even at a time when his music was in no way generally accessible, was not to be heard, it was composers – and I am not just thinking of Schoenberg, Berg, and Webern – who raised their voices on his behalf in the music they themselves were creating; in short, his influence on ensuing generations was to be heard, but only rarely recognized as such, long before his own music had become part of a living musical experience.

Two composers of remarkable genius, each – interestingly – from very different cultural traditions, have to be mentioned in this context: Dmitri Shostakovich, from Russia, and Benjamin Britten, from Britain. It is always inevitable that on occasions like this one cannot avoid making sweeping generalizations but it remains true none the less to claim that Shostakovich's prodigious symphonic legacy simply could not have happened if it had not been for Mahler's example: it was Mahler who served as Shostakovich's model, specifically, I suggest, in one area, the concept of narrative, when a formal process that is initiated by the first note – perhaps better, the first idea – of the work that we are hearing, is sustained over the length of it, and completed only when the last note has sounded. The constant, insistent presence throughout of an anticipated and thus awaited resolution, is a vital, indeed, obligatory part of the narrative process, and we experience it, time and time again, in Mahler. However much the individual forms of Mahler's movements may widely differ – the number of movements, their diverse characters – the over-arching idea of narrative is integral to all of them. The 'frame' – a beginning and end – is an indispensable part of the process of narrative.

Incidentally, it was not only in their music that Mahler's advocates and disciples proclaimed their enthusiasm. They were also vocal on his behalf in the sense of making propaganda to counter the absence of Mahler's music from the concert halls. I thought it might interest you to hear just one example of what I mean: propaganda in musical action in the early 1940s when Britten was resident in the USA and was thinking of ways in which the living sound of Mahler might persuade reluctant ears to open. Hence his version for an orchestra smaller than the composer's own – and remember that Mahler's mis-called 'gargantuan' forces were often used as a stick with which to beat him – of the minuet, the second movement, from the Third Symphony. Although the reduced version was made in 1941, it was not until 1969, at the Aldeburgh Festival, that Britten himself had the chance to conduct the English Chamber Orchestra in a performance of his reduction. A historical curiosity you may think, but one that still bears witness to the seriousness of his intention to bring Mahler's work to public attention in a climate very different from today's. I thought you might be interested to hear a fragment of Britten's arrangement, in an off-the-air recording of the 1969 performance, making its first appearance on CD. It is not of course an 'arrangement' in any real sense but, rather, a magical, almost chamber-orchestral realization of Mahler's original; and a chamber orchestra was very often at the heart of what today we acclaim as typical of Mahler's approach to orchestration:

RECORDED MUSIC EXCERPT
Symphony No. 3, minuet, from fig. 4 (double bar), bar 70,
fade from bar 107 onwards, out on flute triplets, bars 108–9

I am glad to have brought the question of Mahler's concept of
the orchestra into close focus at this early stage because it directly
relates to the fundamental theme of this talk – the massive debt that
the music of the twentieth century owes to him. Of course, one has
heard now for years past of his exceptional powers as an orchestra-
tor, his emphasis on instrumental solos, unusual combinations of
instruments, etc., etc., ad infinitum, but no one, or so it seems to
me, has isolated what I believe to be the two principal features of
what I think of as Mahler's revolutionary practice which over the
span of his creative lifetime changed the history of the modern
symphony orchestra as Mahler found it towards the end of the
nineteenth century. The first is the radical change in the traditional
balance between wind instruments – woodwind and brass, that is –
and the string body.

To be sure, as I have argued before, the liberation of the wind
had already begun with Mozart – it is no wonder that Mahler was
so passionate a Mozartian – but Mahler, true to his innovative self,
did not just modify the balance but reversed it. If I had to choose
one crucial turning point, then it would be the Third Symphony,
the long opening slow introduction of which is scored for wind,
percussion and strings – though mainly the lower strings – and
which must have astonished its first audiences because it released a
sound and instrumental style that had never before been heard in
the context of 'symphony', though it may have been anticipated here
and there in the musical theatre. As I play a bit, please try to think
back historically to the mid-1890s, when the work was conceived:

RECORDED MUSIC EXCERPT
Symphony No. 3, first movement, from fig. 13 (double bar)
to fig. 17, on trumpet motive, bars 208–12

The reversal of the conventional balance and abandonment of
any attempt at the homogeneity of the orchestra which had

hitherto been one of its chief glories are self-evident, are they not? But there is also another matter arising which I believe to be of no less significance. I have already mentioned Mahler's emphasis on solo writing for the instruments. Who, after all, had conceived quite such extraordinary, virtuoso writing for the trombone before Mahler? Berlioz, perhaps, was the artist who paved the way for him; Mahler himself acknowledged his influential predecessor in word and deed, that is to say, sound. But even Berlioz's boldness is exceeded by Mahler's. One might even describe this introduction of the Third without too much exaggeration as a kind of concertante number for solo trombones, tuba, wind and percussion.

But there is a rather subtler point I would like to make, one that still receives very little attention. I was asking that we imagine the first audiences' reaction to the new sound-world Mahler was unfolding in the Third Symphony. But what about the players? The shock, scepticism and sometimes downright resistance that Mahler not infrequently encountered from members of the orchestras he conducted has been amply documented. The exchanges between players and conductor could be tense, to put it mildly. But in the end Mahler had his way: the player having said his part was impossible, unplayable, found he could play it. Mahler had envisaged a possibility, a potentiality, for the instrument hitherto undreamed of. Thus it was that Mahler not only wrote undreamed of music for this instrument or that but at the same time extended the performing techniques and capacities of the players, a legacy that reverberated throughout the twentieth century and I am sure will continue to be a presence in the twenty-first. The modern symphony orchestra of today in terms of collective technical capacity owes a very real debt to Mahler, even when one has made allowances for the later generations of great orchestral innovators, among them Stravinsky and Bartók or Schoenberg and Webern, to name only four of the most important.

Stravinsky and Bartók? What on earth, I have sometimes been asked, have composers of that generation to do with Mahler? I will mention only one feature, what I name as the liberation of the percussion and its gradual evolution as the old century – the nineteenth – was quitted and the then new century – the twentieth –

began, into virtually an independent ensemble in its own right. One thinks of Bartók's *Music for Strings, Percussion and Celesta* (1936), or his Sonata for two pianos and percussion (1937), while the major role the percussion ensemble plays in works by Stravinsky is self-evident; one can hardly miss it. It was Stravinsky's stroke of revolutionary genius to turn the totality of a large symphony orchestra into a gigantic percussion orchestra; that was part of the unique breakthrough the *Rite of Spring* represents. But please don't misunderstand me. I am not suggesting a direct influence of Mahler on Stravinsky, say, or Bartók, though we know that Stravinsky heard Mahler conduct his Fifth in St Petersburg and was impressed by it – strange to think of the young Igor sitting in the audience. No, I am not talking about influence on style but about a whole process that was eventually to change the soundscape of twentieth-century music. And as even the hastiest scrutiny of almost any Mahler symphony will show, he was among the earliest to embark on changing the status of the percussion department and promoting its remarkable independence.

Mahler and the orchestra: a big subject of immense importance. After all, it was not just the percussion band that started on its journey towards independence under Mahler's guidance, but virtually every section of the orchestra. In short, the typical Mahler 'orchestra' consists of a collective or constellation of sectional orchestras – note the plural – which either achieve independence of their colleagues or, by means of cross-overs and cross-fertilization between sections, assemble themselves into unique combinations of instruments for the realization of a particular passage, a transition maybe, or a cadenza, or simply the affirmation of a marked contrast; and I stop there for a moment. How incredible it now seems that one of the sticks with which Mahler was so often beaten in the past, in the 1920s, 1930s and 1940s, was his dependence on 'gargantuan' orchestral forces, a sure sign of his 'megalomania'. These were the kinds of words and images that constantly recur in the adverse criticism of Mahler current in those decades. How incredible that the continuous process of de-construction and re-construction within the totality of the resources deployed, went virtually unnoticed and unheard by those who were too busy denouncing Mahler to open a score and examine what was really going on, on any typical page. How was it possible, I wonder, to go on and on about the 'grandiloquence', the 'gigantism', of the Eighth, and simply not notice a crucial transitional passage from that very symphony, for which Mahler compiles an idiosyncratic independent orchestra – piccolo, harmonium, celesta, piano, harps, flute, two clarinets, two solo violins, solo viola, and solo cello, the strings all playing harmonics pitched very high – to achieve the special colour and character that he was after; and all of it accomplished at a level of dynamics – triple piano – not normally associated with the 'grandiose'.

RECORDED MUSIC EXCERPT
Symphony No. 8, Part II, fig. 199, bar 1421 to fig. 202$^{+4}$,
fade on entry of chorus, 'Alles Vergängliche'

And, by the way, that passage enables me to remark on an additional aspect of Mahler's approach to the orchestra and its instruments: his exploring, that is, of new expressive possibilities in an instrument conventionally associated with the shrill or piercing. Mahler in fact raises the piccolo – that incredibly thin thread of sound we have just heard – to new, indeed unsuspected heights of poetry, a kind of piercing ecstatic serenity so pure and calm is it. And to bring that off, large resources had to be around from which the miraculous new sound could be assembled. Only Mahler could have thought of using the piccolo both to articulate and introduce the oncoming and exalted chorale, 'Alles vergängliche ist nur ein Gleichnis'.

How I wish I could stay a bit longer with the Eighth, but let me make at least two points. First, that one of the reasons for a large assembly of resources was nothing to do with affirming a vibrant nationalism as is sometimes claimed today – not very likely from Mahler in any event – but a lot to do with creating a work in which as many categories of performers as possible might participate, including children and both amateurs (the chorus) and professionals (soloists and orchestra). Certainly one of the least recognized aspects of the Eighth is its communal character, an apparatus designed for communal participation, to exalt and ennoble, inspire and enjoy. Secondly, and perhaps again little acknowledged, its narrative, to my mind, is one of Mahler's boldest. The conjunction of the Latin hymn, 'Veni Creator Spiritus', and the closing scene of Goethe's *Faust* may seem a problematic juxtaposition at first consideration, but I believe now that there is a perfect logic to it, one that I think Freud would have recognized if he had been musical, which alas he wasn't – the logic, that is, of the relationship between the creativity of an artist and man- and womankind's sexuality, sexuality, that is, as the *fons et origo* of humankind's creative instinct. It is in that light, I believe, we should perceive the invocation of the Latin hymn which is then fulfilled and spelled out in Goethe's closing scene. (Mahler in fact first got to know the hymn in a translation by Goethe – a fact of some significance.)

Let me return now for a moment or two to the Third Symphony, a work which for me incorporates so many of the features that I have been trying to describe. Certainly, the work is a powerful demonstration of that process of deconstruction and reconstruction, the concept not of an orchestra, but a collective of orchestras, that I have been at pains to emphasize. True enough, almost any single movement of the Third can be discussed in those terms. But there is a further truth; that while each movement of the symphony deploys an individual orchestra, the constitution of each is intimately related to its specific musical and, I would add, narrative ideas and images, the unfolding of which gives us the total, overall experience that is Mahler's objective. I think I have said enough about the symphony's opening act of deconstruction to have made the point. What the symphony's ensuing movements, the minuet, the scherzo, the solo vocal setting of Nietzsche's 'Um Mitternacht', the choral setting of the *Wunderhorn* poem, the 'Morgenglocken' (the 'Morning Bells') movement, what that sequence of movements vouchsafes is a series of orchestras, each orchestra appropriate to the strategy of the narrative. But the masterstroke, perhaps, is the culminating finale, the great adagio that concludes the symphony, where Mahler puts together again what he has so remarkably dismembered – in the last movement, we hear what we have scarcely once heard across the preceding one and a half hours, the 'homogeneity' of the traditional symphony orchestra with, moreover, the balance within the orchestra restored, that is, with the strings prominent and sometimes predominant. Thus it is that the sonorous architecture of the work is directly related to Mahler's evolving overall form which itself has its roots in the narrative that he wishes to tell – nothing less, and perhaps this is typical of our composer, than the creation of the world, of human-kind and Man's aspiring ascent to higher things.

I think Mahler leaves it to each of us to imagine what will offer us ultimate fulfilment. So, after the 'Resurrection' symphony, No. 2, we have what we might call Mahler's 'Creation' symphony, No. 3; and after that, another unique narrative embodied in the Fourth Symphony, that finally terminates in a childlike vision of 'heavenly life'; and it is the Fourth, perhaps, that represents the importance of narrative to Mahler at its most complex, most subtle and most orig-inal. Because, as a critic remarked after one of the very early per-formances of the work, to understand it, it has to be read backwards 'like the Hebrew Bible' if we are properly to understand and above all enjoy the phenomenal intricacy of the musical organization that gets us from start to finish. There can be no doubt that while overt narrative – which, even so, is very different from a 'programme', an important qualification, this, I believe – although overt narrative may, after the Fourth, take, so to say, a back seat, the narrative prin-ciple was never abandoned by Mahler and comprehension of that basic drive, that basic thrust, is obligatory if we are to help ourselves to follow Mahler's thinking in the later and indeed last symphonies. Need I add that it is no less essential that performers too, and per-haps conductors above all, understand how fundamental to Mahler's architecture was the narrative idea; it is their responsibili-ty to clarify for audiences the anticipations, interruptions, contra-dictions and evasions, even, all of which have a role to play in Mahler's narrative process – disruption, I sometimes think, was as basic to his creative thinking as continuity – and which eventually culminate in resolution and revelation.

Two last thoughts about the Third. Mahler, I believe, was not just a musician who had his head in his scores and was not aware of, or curious about, what was going on in the world about him. We know too how he kept abreast with, or was at least profoundly sympathetic to, the new music of his time; but he was inquisitive, and also well informed about psychology and philosophy, had many friends among leading painters, designers and architects of his day, and took more than a passing interest in the sciences. We should remember that he was married to Alma, the daughter of Emil Jakob Schindler, a famous artist of an earlier generation, that he knew the leading architect and designer Josef Hoffmann, one of whose remarkable houses he occupied when returning to Vienna from New York, during his American years, and we should recall what Freud wrote of him, expressing his admiration for 'the capability for psychological understanding of this man of genius'.★

It had always seemed probable to me, and I think to many others, that in conceiving the Third, Mahler was influenced by the current evolutionary theories of his time. We often find the name of the French evolutionary philosopher Henri Bergson mentioned in this context – I have often done so myself – though in fact his most famous theory, that of the 'Life Force' ('Élan vital') was not launched until well after the Third was completed. None the less, it had always seemed to me safe to assume that, given Mahler's inquiring mind, he had been intrigued by the then current post-Darwinian thinking. I was particularly interested therefore to be made acquainted by a friend (also of an enquiring mind) with an evolutionary scheme that long preceded Bergson or Mahler but most remarkably anticipates the sequence that Mahler finally came to adopt.

What I outline for you now derives from *The Elizabethan World Picture* (1943) by the famous historian E. M. W. Tillyard. In a chapter entitled 'The Chain of Being', he points out that the idea of the 'chain' 'began with Plato's *Timaeus*, was developed by Aristotle, was adopted by the Alexandrian Jews, was spread by the Neo-Platonists, and from the Middle Ages till the eighteenth century was one of those accepted commonplaces, more often hinted at or taken for granted than set forth'.

To attempt a complete history of this potent evolutionary idea would not be possible in the time available today but what is of

---

★ Ernest Jones, *Sigmund Freud: Life and Work*, vol. 11, p. 89.

specific relevance to the Third is to understand that the 'chain' was also a ladder, in Tillyard's words 'educative both in the marvels of its static self and in *its implications of ascent*' (my emphasis), in which, as the idea progressed – itself evolved across the centuries – Angels came to form 'the medium between the whole angelic hierarchy and man', functioning as 'God's messengers'. Thus it is that the chain or ladder describes a clear evolutionary progress, from the inanimate (think of the prelude to Mahler's first movement) to the vegetative (Nature), to creatures, birds and animals, and finally, by way of Angelic intervention, to man and his relation to God, the last rung on the ladder.

This, I am sure, is a very clumsy and inadequate summary of Tillyard's commentary, but I think I have given some indication of the need here for more research into the sources of Mahler's own evolutionary scheme which I believe Tillyard to show has its roots way back in pre-Christian beliefs which then developed to incorporate elements drawn from post-Christian imagery (the Angels, for example, and Man's own suffering). It is remarkable that so little attention has been paid to these parallels in Mahler's symphony, and we certainly need to find out more about how the medieval concept of the chain and ladder came to play such a fundamental role in the scheme – the programme – Mahler adopted in the 1890s. (I must express here my thanks to my friend David Meyer who drew my attention to Tillyard's classic text.)

It is my belief that Mahler's Third represents the first attempt to use music to enact the evolutionary history of mankind. But I believe too that there is another kind of history that surfaces in the Third, this time not a philosophical, religious or scientific past, but a musical past, and returns me to my very first music example which was, you will remember, the minuet. At first sight, or sound, one might well conclude that this movement is there simply because of the need for relaxation after the tumultuous sonic experience offered by the first movement. And up to a point that's right. A contrast is obligatory. But the more one thinks about it, the more fascinating the choice of minuet becomes. For one thing the minuet is immediately followed by a scherzo, and as Hans Keller was, I think, the first to point out, the result of this sequencing means we have the minuet juxtaposed with its historical successor, the scherzo; and given the context of this symphony, it can hardly have been accidental that Mahler introduced a bit of evolutionary musical history; it shows too that Mahler could be elegantly witty, a characteristic not often remarked upon. But of course there is more to it than that. The very concept of the minuet is deliberately classical in character, perhaps not exactly neo-classical, as we understand the term, but certainly a quite conscious reflection of, and reference to, the past, to music's past. And just for a moment or two I would like to talk about this singular feature of Mahler as a composer: his awareness of the past as a creative influence in his own work.

This shows up in diverse ways, among them for instance his constant references in his symphonies to past formal practice, to so-called sonata, first movement, form; a powerful component always in the thinking of his symphonic predecessors, it is very rarely absent from Mahler's own first movements. It may be vestigial, it may often almost disappear altogether, it certainly becomes an evermore distant preoccupation as the years passed. No matter; that awareness was always there, something to remember when considering his own revolutionary formal innovations. Mahler certainly never abandoned the past. On the contrary, he rigorously explored it, parts of it on occasion that were strikingly unfamiliar to performers and audiences in his own day. This again is a huge topic in its own right and I shall confine myself to a couple of observations.

How fascinating it is, for example, to scrutinize the programmes that Mahler embarked on, when he had done with the Met in New York and taken on the New York Philharmonic Orchestra. Mahler was never passive in his relationship to the past. The concerts that he planned as a 'historical series' were in their time, I suggest, remarkably and creatively inquisitive. Far from simply saluting or celebrating an established repertory, he was intent, it seems, on bringing to the attention of his audiences a whole range of musical experiences of a relatively unknown past. Unknown, or unfamiliar, even when the composer was J. S. Bach. Hence the historic importance of Mahler's Bach Suite first heard at a Philharmonic concert in New York. Of course New York audiences knew about Bach as had audiences in Vienna, say, or Berlin;

but what they did not know were Bach's glorious Orchestral Suites; and here was Mahler opening up a window on Bach, expanding his audiences' horizons. In Vienna, he wasn't given the chance.

Here in fact we find Mahler making history again, though in a rather different sense from which the term is normally associated with him. In this context we meet Mahler the educator, and it is perhaps in this area too that we should locate his arrangements for string orchestra of quartets by Beethoven and Schubert. At the same time however he was making history with and through Bach precisely in the sense that was most important for Mahler and for the evolution of music, of composition, in the twentieth century. His passion for Bach is now a familiar bit of Mahlerian history but we should not let our familiarity with it blind us to the sheer novelty of it when considered in historical context. I still recall my surprise when Mahler's surviving daughter Anna handed over to me in London a whole collection of scores of Mahler's, materials it must have been that he had had for study or performance, to find among them a number of Bach's cantatas, marked up in Mahler's characteristic blue pencil: dynamics, crescendos and diminuendos, and so forth; and these were publications in Mahler's hands well before his last years, his final period, when his exploration of Bach showed up so powerfully in his own music. In so doing he undoubtedly anticipated what was indeed to become another of the new century's – the twentieth's, that is – leading features, the so-called 'Back to Bach' movement and its bedfellow neoclassicism, 'Music about Music' – 'Musik über Musik' – as Adorno somewhere and somewhat sceptically remarked. But neither of those terms has much relevance to what Mahler was up to. In his amazing last years, his absorption of Bach released a creative storm, principally expressed, naturally, in polyphony and counterpoint, of a singular ferocity and ground-breaking originality. There was no element of 'Back' to anywhere in late Mahler; if anything, the message was 'Forward with Bach', a long way forward, as even the briefest of reminders from the *Rondo-Burleske* of the Ninth Symphony spells out:

RECORDED MUSIC EXCERPT
Symphony No. 9, *Rondo-Burleske*, from double bar, bar 180 to fig. 34

Even by Mahler's own exacting standards of voyaging out into new worlds of expression and finding the techniques to embody them – had seething counterpoint ever been put to quite such violent ends as this? – that movement from the Ninth remains a unique creative moment. To be sure, it would not have happened without Bach. But what did happen is testament to Mahler's extraordinary capacity to fuel the future from a past – chronologically distinct pasts have a role to play in Mahler's music – and then ignite it in an overpowering act of creative imagination. And how fascinating it is to hear that leap into the future and at the same time keep in mind Mahler the advocate, the pioneering educationalist, seriously trying to bring to his audiences' attention areas of Bach's own music that were by no means standard fare. Hence his Bach Suite that I mentioned a minute or two ago. It was given its premiere in New York in 1909.

It would be easy to spend all my remaining time on thinking about Mahler and Bach and the whole topic of counterpoint which, especially from the Fourth Symphony onwards, was to become one of his most prominent compositional techniques. It was indeed in the Fourth, precisely at the turn of the century, that Mahler's preoccupation with counterpoint first manifested itself in a passage like the one that I will play you in a moment, from the development of the first movement of the symphony, in which Mahler's motivic polyphony is revealed at its most intense and its most brilliant, brilliant in sound that is. One cannot, in fact, make any distinction between the sound and the counterpoint. The success of the latter is entirely dependent on the clarity secured by the former; which allows me to return to a feature that I mentioned way back, the revolution Mahler effected in the relationships between the constituent sections that in former times made up the homogeneity of the symphony orchestra. Here's the passage I have in mind, in which once again the wind deliver a high proportion of the developmental – that is to say, contrapuntal – argument:

RECORDED MUSIC EXCERPT
Symphony No. 4, first movement, fig. 14 (double bar) bar 177
to fig. 16, fade out by bar 211 or thereabouts

The complexity and intensity of the counterpointing there makes it all the less surprising that a few years on Bach should be more overtly acknowledged by Mahler in his late works as well as in his performance repertory; and this reminds me not to depart from this topic without reference to what remains for me one of the most original and far-reaching materializations of Bach in Mahler, in the great 'Abschied' of *Das Lied von der Erde*, where I have suggested, and passionately repeat now, that behind that movement stands Bach and his Passions and his cantatas, music well known to Mahler. This I believe explains how it is that he so astonishingly confronts us, almost at the very opening of the movement, with a recitative with minimal orchestral accompaniment plus flute obbligato; while thereafter, as the 'Abschied' proceeds, it proves itself to be what to my mind is virtually a self-contained cantata for solo voice and orchestra:

RECORDED MUSIC EXCERPT

*Das Lied von der Erde*, 'Der Abschied', figs. 22–23, bars 158–65

I don't need to be told that that's a million miles from Bach. The great gong stroke alone makes that clear, that we are in another world; but rooted in Bach, and generated by Mahler's absorption of Bach, which took no account of intervening centuries, the 'Abschied' most certainly is, in my considered view. What makes it all the more extraordinary in thinking about Bach in the context of *Das Lied*, is the fact that in this very same work Mahler opens up yet another path which I believe may find fulfilment in the new, the twenty-first, century, an encounter this time not with a past, and in some respects as I have said an unfamiliar past, but with a future, in which two world cultures, East and West, if one may be permitted such a preposterous generalization, may find a mode of mutual creative collaboration. We talk a great deal these days about globalization, for the most part its commercial evils; but what I am thinking about is the new resources in terms of compositional techniques that the West has learned from the East, while there has been no little traffic in the reverse direction in more recent decades. In this field too it seems to me that Mahler was undeniably a major pioneer. I am aware of the fact that as the nineteenth century turned into the twentieth, there was immense interest in the West in all the arts and crafts of the East, in painting, above all, but also in design, music and literature: Chinoiserie and Japonaiserie were key cultural buzz words in this period. But it was by no means all buzz and the acquisition of exotic knick-knacks. In music there was specifically Debussy and the impact made on him and his compositional processes by his encounter with a Javanese gamelan at the World Exhibition in Paris in 1899, and there was a decorative spin-off from a pursuit of Orientalism that we often find in Ravel and Stravinsky. Mahler himself, I think quite knowingly, introduced the decorative into *Das Lied*; an example is the charming pentatonicism of 'Von der Jugend':

RECORDED MUSIC EXCERPT<br>
Das Lied, 'Von der Jugend', from start to fig. 4, bar 29

That's the kind of pentatonic tune that we all knew as children and hammered out on the black notes of the piano. Part of Mahler's intention, I believe, was to use this relatively familiar musical idea, with its ready-made association with the 'Orient', as an indication, easily heard, that we are to be encouraged to enter, to experience, quite literally, another world. The overt pentatonicism spells that out immediately and audibly for audiences; it – so to say – sets the scene. However, when we begin to delve more deeply into the work, and into the techniques that are ultimately responsible for the unique experience it vouchsafes, we begin to discover features of the techniques Mahler deploys much more thoroughgoing in their 'Orientalism' and more innovative in their essential character than the decorative profiles of 'Von der Jugend' or 'Von der Schönheit', though the latter movement soon reaches out and way beyond the merely decorative.

One of the ways in which it does so is to embark on an exuberant canon, to describe the young men on their horses who crave the attention of the girls picking lotus alongside the river. Interesting – is it not? – that counterpoint once again emerges as a prominent characteristic. Canon, of course, is a specific contrapuntal device in the West, with a long tradition behind it; moreover, it occurs with increasing frequency in Mahler's late phase of composition, in the last – the two late – *Wunderhorn* songs, for example, and in *Kindertotenlieder*. It is also prominent in one of the four late Rückert settings, 'Ich bin der Welt abhanden gekommen', a magnificent song which so often seems to anticipate the style – no, 'style' is not adequate – the very language of the 'Abschied' in *Das Lied*. It brings to mind the movement's coda in particular, in which the ecstatic polyphony of 'Die liebe Erde allüberall/Blüht auf in Lenz . . . und ewig blauen licht die Fernen!' is finally released. (Mahler's own words colouring the pitches, by the way, not Hans Bethge's.)

I think we can summon up for ourselves the peculiar radiance with which the 'Abschied' concludes, without resort to a recording. What I should prefer to concentrate on for a moment is 'Ich bin der Welt . . .'. It is important to remember in the context of the Rückert settings that the poet himself was also a distinguished Oriental philologist. It must have been the case, though not often remarked upon, that Mahler's absorption of Rückert would have prepared him for his immediate creative response to the volume, shown him by a friend, of Hans Bethge's German-language versions of Chinese poems, poems that Mahler was later to use for the composition of *Das Lied*.

There is not only this significant literary link with the Orient by way of Rückert , pre-dating *Das Lied*, but – and more importantly – there are pronounced technical features of the Rückert settings, an overt pentatonicism, for example, that already prefigures the pentatonicism we meet again in *Das Lied*. But more important than this, I believe, is the character of the relationship between voice and orchestra in 'Ich bin der Welt . . .', a relationship Mahler was systematically to develop in *Das Lied* and, as you will now hear, one which is generated by an extended canonic interplay between the singer and his accompaniment:

RECORDED MUSIC EXCERPT
'Ich bin der Welt abhanden gekommen', figs. 3–6;
fade on cor anglais

It is impossible with the benefit of retrospective hindsight not to hear there that *Das Lied* was, so to say, just round the corner; but it is not, I want to suggest, just a matter of a shared spirit of resignation – call it what you will – that unites the 'Abschied' and 'Ich bin der Welt . . .', but the deployment of canon as the principal vehicle, the means, to achieve that expressive end; and it is precisely in this area, I believe, that Mahler and the Orient join hands.

To be sure, canon had been a long-standing preoccupation of Mahler's – one only needs to think back to the 'Bruder Martin' movement of the First Symphony, the funeral march, which opens with a round, a canon. Some might argue, then, that there is nothing very surprising about canon as a device surfacing, though in a much more elaborate form, in the late songs and in *Das Lied*. The surprise rests, I believe, in the fact that we also find in *Das Lied* a type of counterpoint, a form of contrapuntal activity, with a long tradition behind it in the East, in the Orient: heterophony; and I want to leave you with the thought that it is canon that provides a communicating bridge between the two musical cultures. Heterophony is in effect a unison melody simultaneously combined with different rhythmic versions of that same basic melody, often delivered at the octave, above or below. That is a very simplistic explanation of a technique that in South East Asia produces a polyphony of extraordinary rhythmic and textural complexity. It is, if you like, a challenge to musicians to see how much can be got out of a unison. It is by no means without parallels in Western tradition, for which very reason there is no doubt to my mind that heterophony in its Eastern guise has proved to be a technique that beckons to the growing number of Western composers interested in exploring the resources of the East; and it does not surprise me at all that composers with a pre-disposition to think canonically – that is, to exploit the possibilities of a melody that can, at a given distance and appropriately transposed, be combined with itself – should find heterophony particularly appealing. Such, I want to suggest, was certainly the case with both Mahler and Britten, to name only one later composer of genius who in his later years voyaged Eastwards on the wings of heterophony.

So it is, that *Das Lied*, in its course, juxtaposes both canon and heterophony, the latter notably servicing the impassioned first movement, 'Das Trinklied vom Jammer der Erde', with counterpoint that it can have been no accident has its roots unequivocally in classical Oriental practice. Mahler will take a motive and then, even though sticking to the same pitches, will create a voice and orchestra polyphony out of the combined statements of it in different rhythms and, not infrequently, octaves. One would never guess that so few pitches –

MUSIC EXCERPT: PIANO
'Das Trinklied vom Jammer der Erde', bars 1–16 (horns, strings)

– could produce music of such velocity, drama and passion. What you are going to hear is the end of the development section of the movement and the transition into the recapitulation; and I promise you that on close inspection you will find the texture is crammed with heterophonic practice:

RECORDED MUSIC EXCERPT
*Das Lied*, 'Das Trinklied vom Jammer der Erde',
from fig. 39 (double bar), upbeat to bar 325 to Fig. 44$^{+6}$;
fade on voice, out by bar 369

You will have noticed that at the exact moment of the recapitulation in the song the pentatonic idea that we have heard at the very onset returns. Nothing decorative about it or the uses to which it is put. I can't help, since I'm near a keyboard, but remind you that *Das Lied* ends unforgettably as it began, with the same pitches, now conflated into a chord that combines the A minor of the first movement with the C major and added sixth, the chord that concludes – or rather, doesn't conclude – the 'Abschied', the chord that for Benjamin Britten was a sonic image of eternity, though not eternal life perhaps so much as the perpetual renewal of the earth.

MUSIC EXCERPT: PIANO
'Der Abschied', bars 568–72

So it is then, for all the reasons that I have tried to touch on, I regard Mahler's last song-cycle as one of the first and most substantial, because creative, encounters between East and West in the twentieth century. It is simply not enough to think of Debussy alone as playing the principal historical role at this moment in time. Mahler has to join Debussy; Vienna has to join Paris. A profound cultural trend was located not in one European culture, but in two, cultures which, quite wrongly to my way of thinking, have so often been considered culturally opposed, a misjudgment that has led in turn to much cultural confusion.

In this specific context, it is ironic indeed that Berlioz, from whom Mahler learned so much, has never been wholly accepted by the culture of his own country as an integral, 'authentic', part of it; while Mahler, for so long dismissed in France post-First World War as an all too authentic manifestation of 'Germanic' tradition, has won, post-Second World War the acclaim and acceptance in France that he commands elsewhere. I shall have more to say about this cultural question a bit later.

I have focused so far on only one major dimension of *Das Lied*, but of course there are many others which like the Oriental dimension were to cast a long shadow on and into the twentieth century. Mahler raised the narrative power and scope of the song-cycle to new heights in *Das Lied*, not to speak of the remarkable formal innovation of the first movement, 'Das Trinklied', which unfolds an Exposition and its (varied) repeat, a Development section, and then, via a lead-back, a Recapitulation, a basic scheme we would not normally associate with the concept of a song-cycle but rather with the classical and romantic symphony. *Das Lied*, following the formal paths opened up in *Kindertotenlieder*, conjoins symphony and song-cycle, at least until the 'Abschied' when the narrative drama – no less than a transition from anticipations of mortality to death itself and its transformation in turn into renewal – required new forms to embody the new thought and feeling which characterize the 'Abschied'. Let me leave you with the reflection that the story of Mahler's three orchestral song-cycles is not one whit less innovative than the much more often told story of the symphonies and the suggestion that much more serious consideration should be given to the subtitle Mahler bestowed on his last song-cycle: 'Eine Symphonie'. *Das Lied*, in my view, cannot be separated out from the history of Mahler's symphonies and their ever newly evolving forms.

I sometimes think of Mahler's works – the totality of them – as constituting a kind of mythic, epic Praeludium to the twentieth century in the sense that wherever one turns, to whichever work one turns, it is virtually impossible not to hear outlined, somewhere along the way, an unmistakable anticipation of a significant technique, the opening up of new formal paths, of significant areas of expression to fresh exploration and fresh inspiration, by which the new century was to be motivated. I fear I may already have tried your patience, and if I were to attempt anything like comprehensiveness then you would find me taking up more or less permanent residence here in Boulder. Festivals would come and go but not I: I should become not a Phantom of the Opera but a Phantom of the Festival whose distinguishing feature was that he never stopped talking.

More seriously, I am conscious that time passes, and while there are still a number of topics and issues that I want to bring in train as further evidence of Mahler's unique unveiling of routes that were to lead directly to the new music of the new century, I have tried to choose items that, from my point of view, are relevant to the other part of my brief: what, in the twenty-first century we should be doing for Mahler, not in any sentimental sense, but to ensure that succeeding generations have a reasonable expectation of hearing his works in performances that realize, to put it not too ambitiously, what can be convincingly suggested were the composer's intentions when he wrote them.

I have said a fair amount already about Mahler's concept of the orchestra but perhaps have not given sufficient emphasis to one of his most striking contributions to the history of the orchestra, his creation of the idea – the concept – of the chamber orchestra. I believe that historically we have to attribute that quite specifically to the concert, a 'Lieder-Abend with Orchestra',* given in Vienna

---

★ See p. 107.

on 29 January 1905, in the small hall of the Musikverein, when the programme included not only the first performance of a group of *Wunderhorn* songs but also the premiere of *Kindertotenlieder*, the second of the orchestral song-cycles, along with the first public hearing of the four independent Rückert settings for voice and orchestra (one should write, in truth, for four differently compiled or constituted orchestras!). The programme was repeated, with minor variations a few days later, and then taken to Graz, some months later, where it formed part of the 'Tonkünstlerfest', whose director was Richard Strauss. It was in an exchange of letters with Strauss that Mahler momentously announced that his songs should be performed, 'in the manner of chamber music [*Kammermusik-ton*]';* and as is now well known, for the concerts I've just mentioned, he insisted on small halls with a correspondingly intimate acoustic. To be sure, this development, with hindsight, had already been anticipated in what I have earlier described as Mahler's deconstruction of the orchestra into a collective of orchestras or ensembles; to take that process one step further and, moreover, to write of it so unequivocally, was doubtless a consequence of practices that had been part of his orchestral thinking across the years which gave birth to his symphonies.

Once again the influence of Mahler's 'Kammermusik' precedents exercised a direct influence on succeeding generations of composers who embraced and absorbed the Mahler legacy and his specific aesthetic of the orchestra, composers, some of whom might be thought even to have been the very antithesis of Mahler in personality and aesthetic intention and ambition: Stravinsky, for example, or Bartók, or Hindemith. But once again it is not 'influence' as it is generally understood that I am talking about, but practice and principles embodied in compositional techniques which later proved to serve composers entirely distinct in style and belonging to contrasting cultural traditions. I return here to a point I made earlier, the inhibiting assumption that cultures with a specific national identity have about them a built-in, hands-off exclusiveness; if it is a French tradition you have in sight, then look else-

---

*   See p. 218.

where if it is an Austro-German tradition that you want to zoom in on. But the truth is, as I've tried to show in the case of the Orientalism of *Das Lied*, this was an event that traversed cultures, unthinkingly supposed to be mutually exclusive: Paris or Vienna, Mahler or Debussy. The concept of the chamber orchestra encountered no culturally imposed or imaginary borders.

And while on the topic of the convention of supposedly opposed cultures, when the artificial image of one culture has excluded comprehension and identification with the other, it is relevant perhaps to introduce into our discussion the composer I describe as the Italianate Mahler.* At first sight or sound this may seem to be a conjunction that makes little sense; but only to those, I suggest, whose closed minds and ears preclude their hearing, say, during a performance of Verdi's *Otello* or *Aida* a whole range of inspirations and influences that in the course of Mahler's lifetime were to leave their mark on his music. It is certainly not without significance that, in a conversation with Bauer-Lechner, he acknowledged his own debt to Verdi in the field of orchestration. But it was not by any means Verdi alone, whose operas he knew so well from conducting them, who was the source of Mahler's Italian connection. Among many others there was also Bellini; and it is Mahler in Bellini mode who surfaces unforgettably in the Eighth Symphony in the *Adagissimo*, when Mater gloriosa swims into view – strings and harp – and Mahler wittily and consciously lapses into Italian for his summons to the strings to play their ecstatic melody *sempre molto cantando*!

By far the clearest exposition I've ever read of the culturally impeding mindset I mentioned earlier – Paris vs Vienna (or Berlin) – is to be found in an early, sardonic essay by Marcel Proust, published in *Les Plaisirs et les jours*, long before he embarked on his monumental novel, *A la recherche du temps perdu*. Here is just part of an exchange between two imaginary friends, Bouvard and Pécuchet, whose names Proust pinched from Flaubert, one of his great predecessors. One of them – Bouvard – is a resolute Wagnerian. In fact he has never heard a score by that 'Brawler of

---

* See 'Chailly, Mahler and the Italian Connection', pp. 550–55.

Berlin' as Wagner is described by Bouvard's anti-Wagnerian friend, Pécuchet, himself 'always patriotic and always misinformed' (as Proust caustically remarks). And why was this? Because the Conservatoire – and remember Proust was writing in the 1890s – the Conservatoire, the equivalent in Paris of the Vienna Conservatoire which Mahler attended, was 'dying of routine between the stutterings of Colonne and the lispings of Lamoureux' (these last were two of the principal concert-giving orchestral societies of the time in Paris). Proust's 'dying of routine' inevitably brings to mind Mahler's 'Tradition ist Schlamperei' ('Tradition is sloppiness').

The absurdity of the exchange of cultural insults is exposed when Pécuchet wades in: 'In spite of the efforts of all your fine gentlemen' – the Wagner camp, that is – 'our beautiful country of France is still the country of clarity and French music will be clear, or there will be no French music'. Pécuchet, Proust continues, 'would strike the table with all his might to emphasize his words' and release yet further volleys of abuse: 'I doubt if the Valkyrie is even liked in Germany . . . but to French ears it will always be the most infernal torture, and the most cacophonic! and, let me add, the most humiliating to our national pride'. And so on, and so on.

This, let me hasten to remind you, is Proust in sardonic mode. He was himself a passionate Wagnerian; *The Ring* indeed was to have a demonstrable influence on the organization of his own epic masterpiece. But he is making in the 1890s a highly serious and combative point about the collisions between images of national cultures which bear little resemblance to reality, and – of particular relevance to what I'm saying today – were often used as instruments of aggressive criticism. For example, I can remember reading as a schoolboy in a compendium for music lovers, first published in 1934, and running through countless reprints, sentences prompted by an assessment of Mahler's Eighth, the last sentence of which reads – I'll spare you what precedes it – 'In this work and in Schönberg's *Gurrelieder* . . . the megalomania of Central Europe reached its apex.'* Wow! Not just a megalomaniac composer but

* A. L. Bacharach, *The Musical Companion*. See also 'A Mahlerian Odyssey: 1936–2003', pp. 598–9.

the whole of Central Europe. It makes odd reading now, does it not?, but it also shows how obsessive and inimical to rational thought the reaction against German *Kultur* had become.

To be sure, in the wake of the First World War, we have to recognize the force of the reaction against the arts, and music especially, of Austro-Germany. History and Politics and Nationalism all combined here to form a kind of united front against a tradition which in many fields had indeed reigned supreme for centuries. No doubt this was an insurrection that had to happen and was in fact to have some remarkably fruitful creative consequences. It could be argued that it was, historically speaking, a necessary liberation. But the supreme oddity of it, the irony of it, was the tarring of Mahler with a brush that was simply wide of the mark – 'grandiose', 'monumental', 'megalomaniac', 'megalithic', 'monomaniac', 'grandiloquent', 'mammoth', etc., etc. This was a vocabulary that once was commonly used to describe the character of Mahler's musical personality; and although those days, thank God, have passed, it is still possible to run across it here and there. The irony to which I have just referred was compounded by the general ignorance of the music which was dismissed so boldly, and above all by the woeful failure to realize that almost everywhere in Mahler were to be found signs and seeds and indeed deeds of the very counter-revolution that was then being espoused. It is a remarkable fact that, a few enlightened heroes apart, there was no general understanding that Mahler in his lifetime was in truth already part of that future which we now ourselves inhabit.

Pierre Boulez, without doubt, is symbolic of the change in cultural attitudes that has evolved during the last half of the twentieth century. He is one of the most radical creative figures post-Second World War, French and in the best sense an apostle of 'French' culture; but in addition, he is not only an admirer of Mahler but a fascinating interpreter of the symphonies. False cultural distinctions have at last been erased, it seems, and there is a kind of superb logic about the fact that at the end of the century in which Mahler died we were able to hear his works conducted by a one-time leading advocate of twentieth-century modernism. I think Mahler might have relished the logic of it; it might even have reminded him of his own cross-cultural espousal of Debussy during his last years in the United States. (I wonder however what Proust's Pécuchet might have made of Boulez conducting *The Ring* at Bayreuth! Just think of it – a Frenchman!)

This may have proved too lengthy a digression, but I think the relevance of it will strike you when I return to the topic that started it all off: the birth of the chamber orchestra that was an integral part of Mahler's later vocal music, which he came to regard as representing his *Kammermusikton*. And bearing that in mind, and all that I've said earlier about his deconstruction of the orchestra – just remember that each *Wunderhorn* song, each Rückert setting, in fact has its own orchestra, independent of its companions – and if one checks the reality of his orchestral imagination, of his sound, against the fictitious dismissal of him as a post-Wagnerian burdened with the mammoth baggage of an exhausting and exhausted past, one is then brought face to face with one of the most grotesque misconceptions that not so long ago plagued the reception of Mahler's music. And if I have chosen to concentrate on the idea of the chamber orchestra, it is, I repeat, because that concept often represents for composers of today and doubtless tomorrow the orchestral ideal, the ideal sonority, that in the past it was the function of the symphony orchestra to provide.

Now, we live in a period when all the Mahlerian battles may seem to have been won. Performances abound across the globe, there is a world audience for Mahler, an unceasing torrent of recordings: so why don't we just sit back and feel good? But it is precisely here, in the performance field, that I think there are battles still to be won. For example, to stick for a moment to the chamber music issue, it is of vital importance that now we have clear evidence of how Mahler wanted his songs performed, we should act upon it. I pay tribute here to the dedicated work done in this sphere by Renata Stark-Voit and Thomas Hampson in Vienna which has made accessible archival information about the string forces involved in Mahler's 1905 premieres of his songs. In my estimation, this results in a revelation of the songs themselves, of their unique, chamber-like sound, above all. I have been active myself in this area in very recent times and have had the luck to work with two conductors in Europe, Riccardo Chailly and Kent Nagano, in trying to secure performances that respected what we must believe to have been Mahler's radical reduction of the string body; and I can assure you that the contrast with what has been standard performance practice is extraordinary.

There are a couple of recordings on the way that I hope will claim your attention when they are released; in addition, they are recordings which have taken into account the voices that Mahler seems to have had in mind when composing the songs. I am not for a moment suggesting that we should close our ears to a Janet Baker performing *Kindertotenlieder* because Mahler composed the cycle for a baritone: that would be idiotic. None the less, it can never be other than helpful to performers to know what was the 'ideal' voice Mahler heard in his imagination when composing his songs. Of one thing one can be absolutely certain; he would have preferred an inspired contralto to an indifferent baritone. I must add finally that although progress is being made, for a performance I heard not so long ago in the Royal Albert Hall in London, the young and indisputably talented conductor on the podium, and himself a great Mahler enthusiast, had not done his homework. The platform to my prejudiced eyes, seemed to be awash with strings and the result, to my equally prejudiced ears, was horrible.

So it is, then, that I believe all of us who have something to offer in this field should take a New Year resolution at the beginning of the new century to do what we can to secure performances that are authentic in this sense, that they try to recover the freshness, boldness, unpredictability, surprise and sheer shock that we know formed part of the impact the symphonies made on their first hearing.

It is precisely these sometimes intendedly disturbing qualities, shock in particular, that I fear the now worldwide consumption of Mahler, the flood of recordings, the iconic status among aspiring conductors that the symphonies have attained, combine to put at risk. (No conductor it seems can be taken seriously these days if he does not have, along with his baton in his knapsack, the ambition to record a complete cycle of the symphonies.) I exaggerate; but there is to my mind a real danger of a cosmetic blandness, a soften-ing, disguising, smoothing over, in short a blunting of the sharp edges and thereby making acceptable a corpus of music that the composer more often than not wanted to arouse discomfort, anxiety, disbelief, pain, ambiguity. Here again I want to suggest that Mahler was far ahead of his time: the intent, the capacity to shock, was to become one more of those leading features of the twentieth century that he had substantially anticipated. Alas, in later decades, the 'shocking' in the arts, often deteriorated into triviality. Mahler in fact was no stranger to triviality; but he used it, characteristically and creatively, time and time again, as a means of caustic commentary on slovenly expectations and the threadbare feelings that accompany them.

Everyone here I am sure is familiar with one of the most famous examples in all Mahler of his capacity, his intent, to shock by a highly original manipulation of the seemingly trivial in a context in which audience expectations would have led them to expect something quite other. I believe it was part of his strategy not to produce an unprecedented shock of his own but also – though this may have been an over-optimistic ambition – to remind his public that they had got into the habit of receiving a 'funeral march' whether by Beethoven, say, or Wagner, as just another piece of lovely music, just the thing for a comfortable Sunday afternoon in the concert hall. (Mahler was an enemy of habit.) We all know the saying that familiarity can breed contempt. I'm not sure it was contempt exactly that Mahler had as a target, but rather a whole culture whereby audiences ceased to respond to, to be aware of, even, the challenge that many masterpieces from the past had originally presented. It was to correct this corruption induced by familiarity that I think was at least part of his intention in his First Symphony, in the slow movement, which he permitted to be described as an 'Andante grottesco' in an early performance that he conducted himself. But I guess no one at all could have been prepared for what they actually heard themselves listening to. These opening bars of the movement remain one of the most discussed passages in all of Mahler:

MUSIC
Symphony No. 1, slow movement, from start to 4 bars after fig. 4; fade on continuation of lower strings' entry

It is my conviction that that performance, from which my excerpt comes, marvellously realizes what Mahler wanted his audience to hear, yes, to be, shocked by; and I expect many of you will have recognized the recording itself, where Dimitri Mitropoulos conducts the Minneapolis Symphony Orchestra – a recording that belongs to 1940 and, as far as I can determine, the first recording to be made of the symphony. A historic recording from more than one point of view. That wiry, truly grotesque, out of tune sound, has nothing 'beautiful' about it, certainly nothing solemn about it; and if we can think back to 1889, it realizes, I believe, what was Mahler's intent, to challenge his audiences' assumptions about what a funeral march ought to be. But that much about the First Symphony's slow movement has been said often enough, and I don't want to try your patience by repeating it. Instead, I pose a question: how often in fact do we in a performance of the First in our own day hear from the solo double-bass anything that remotely resembles what we've just heard from that rightly celebrated Mitropoulos recording?

It might amuse you to know that when working with one of the major European orchestras on the First, an orchestra renowned for its Mahler performances, I spent a long time trying to persuade the principal double-bass, an outstanding young player, to persuade him – no, to stop him beautifying that opening solo and thus stripping it of its intended character and above all of its power to shock. Here was a living example of that unconscious process of cosmetic beautification that I believe to be a creeping threat to the genuine authenticity of Mahler performances today. There was no ill-will on the player's part, simply an inability – and this in itself is an interesting point – to shed, even temporarily, all that he had ever been taught about playing the double-bass. You will recall that I mentioned way back the extraordinary advances made in instrumental techniques by the sheer difficulty and novelty of what Mahler habitually demanded of his players. Eventually they rose to the occasion, met the challenges, and in so doing, they not only advanced their techniques but also generated the tension that was, I'm sure, characteristic of performances that Mahler conducted himself. It was of course a tension that in the very first place was an in-built component of the musical ideas themselves. Nowadays, all these challenges have been overcome. Orchestral virtuosity flourishes, and there is no denying that Mahler's own works played a fundamental role in creating it. But it brings its own perils, and I hope in this century, as it progresses, we can campaign against the smoothness and blandness which can often contradict the very contradictions with which Mahler wants to confront us.

The funeral march from the First is, as a whole, a *locus classicus* in Mahler's oeuvre, replete as it is with so many examples of innovations that were to form the basis of his unique world of experience, and most of which were to have a role to play in the music of the generations of younger composers who succeeded him, irrespective of their national origin. In my doubtless untidy way I've mentioned quite a few of these influential anticipations of how the twentieth century was to sound; but one could scarcely move on from the andante of the First without noting that it was here that Mahler seriously launched the concept of the vernacular – after all, the movement opens with music from a vernacular repertory, the 'Bruder Martin' round or catch, relocated however in a disorienting minor key – a bold strategy that led to an extraordinary expansion of the language and resources of romantic music that was indeed Mahler's inheritance. His feat in incorporating into the symphony so many kinds of vernacular musics – my plural is deliberate – that had hitherto been kept out in the cold, obliged to keep their distance, cannot be over-estimated. It is surely the case that he broke down more cultural barriers, in purely musical terms, than almost any other composer one can think of, certainly of his generation. His music, to put it perhaps rather oddly, is class-less in the materials it deploys, and traverses the spectrum of the diverse musics – from the streets, concert halls, theatres, parade grounds, dance halls and ballrooms – that serviced the society of which he was part. It is surely that comprehensiveness, that huge inclusiveness, that must be one of the reasons for the breadth of appeal his works have proved to make to a global audience itself of incalculable diversity. (I think, by the way, this was a point very well made by Robert Olson in his introductory note to the Festival Programme Book this year.)

Mahler and the vernacular is another huge subject in itself. Those of my generation will remember that one of the earliest criticisms of him was aimed at his unconscionable 'vulgarity', because, I assure you, that was how his innovative deployment of the vernacular was almost always heard in the past. This alone goes to show the kind of cultural barriers that had to be brought down before much progress could be made in comprehending the kind of realities with which his music confronts us.

And of course there were many different kinds of vernacular realities that Mahler dealt in; 'Bruder Martin' is only one of them in the movement from the First we're thinking about. For instance there's the street band, complete with obligatory bass drum and cymbal, that erupts mid-stream, a vernacular intrusion that is one of the earliest examples again of a process that was to become ever more important throughout Mahler's life, what I identify as his preoccupation with the mobility of music, of music approaching, intruding and receding; music as it were overheard by a stationary, captive audience at every conceivable distance, near or far; music that approaches, passes us by, fades; one music that picks up the thread of the discourse while another music altogether, in its own rhythm, marches off.

Mention of this mobility reaffirms for me the absolute necessity, often lost sight of in present-day concert performances, of striving to realize Mahler's array of dynamics, which so often are directly related to this concept of mobility both within the orchestra and without. And here I am bold enough to suggest that a work like Karlheinz Stockhausen's *Gruppen*, in which three diversely constituted orchestras are strategically located around a concert hall and the sound each group generates either passed round, so that the music is in continuous motion – continuously mobile – or heard simultaneously in different combinations of the groups. *Gruppen*, I suggest, could never have happened without the precedents for mobility, interplay and simultaneous combination first explored, consciously, as an aesthetic strategy, by Mahler. The exploitation of acoustic space has to have a high place in any accounting of his excursions into a future that has become very much our present.

It may also strike some of you as far-fetched to introduce the name of Webern into the context of this talk, though we should always remember that he was an ardent advocate of Mahler during the composer's lifetime; and after his death was, from all reports, a remarkable Mahler interpreter, of the Second Symphony in particular. He was, too, in the audience in 1905 at that memorable 'Lieder-Abend' in Vienna which I have mentioned so often for one reason or another. In any event, my approach to the Webern/Mahler compositional relationship is one that I believe has not often been remarked upon: their joint deployment of a positive deluge of dynamic markings. If one scrutinizes almost any typical page from one of Mahler's symphonies, especially a highly active page, with a lot going on, one has to conclude that the proliferation of teeming dynamics in fact represents – almost – an independent compositional dimension. I am not just thinking of the distinctions of *fortes* and *pianos*, but subtle gradations of sound that articulate distance, not just in an onstage/offstage dichotomy but within the orchestra, e.g. the layering of dynamics between simultaneously combined parts. This process initiated and developed by Mahler across decades, undoubtedly left its mark on Webern, whose dynamics – often at the extreme end of the *pianissimo*, for which Mahler again provided him with ample precedents – took the process several stages further forward; and the result of that was the systematic ordering of dynamics to form an independent compositional parameter along with all the other components of composition – pitch, rhythm, motive, etc., etc. – an ultimate evolution which came to characterize the music of the European avant-garde post-1945.

Having raised this issue of dynamics – but it was Mahler who raised it first! – it seems only logical to pursue it for a moment in the context of the performances I still hope to hear as the twenty-first century progresses. It has only been during the last few years, when I have had the good fortune to be involved in performances with orchestras, conductors, soloists – the whole performing apparatus – that I first became aware of the difficulties that Mahler's multiple dynamics pose. Trying to persuade an orchestra to play really softly, achieving the triple or quadruple *pianissimo* that Mahler sometimes calls for, is very hard work. The players may have the best of intentions and for a handful of bars they may produce the ideal sound; but sustaining an intense *pianissimo* for any length of time is one of the most challenging technical feats that they have to face: the rigour, the concentration, slackens, and all too soon they revert to a blank, featureless *mezzo piano* or *mezzo forte*.

Mahler especially in his last years was a master of sighs and whispers, especially for the strings. Just because these passages – the closing bars of the slow movement of the Ninth, for instance – are dramatic, albeit the manifestation of a fragmenting interior or spiritual drama, and because Mahler himself helps the players by his disposition of his fragments among divided strings, the composer's dynamics are often scrupulously realized in performance. But to turn to a much earlier work and to a relatively simple – in principle – example, how often have any of us heard the final stanza of 'Das himmlische Leben' in which the orchestra – and the soloist too – deliver the triple *pianissimo* that Mahler calls for? I'm sure that the performance of the Fourth we're going to hear as part of this MahlerFest will not disappoint us; but I stress, this example I've chosen is not a matter of pedantry or poetic sentiment but, rather, a crucial illustration of the overall narrative role that Mahler's dynamics can play as an integral part of his symphonic thinking, spelling out the relationship between dynamics and overall form. This is, for sure, the transcendent movement in the symphony, both a moment of revelation (so this is what heaven is going to be like) and the end of a long and complex narrative initiated by the symphony's opening bars; the goal has been reached, but it is not only the end that has been achieved but a final clarification and justification of the otherwise ambiguous beginning, the point (B minor) we started from, embodied in the hushed affirmation of E major which it is the business of the last stanza of the concluding song to render. In all of this the role of the given but so often disregarded dynamics has a vital role to play. The more we have to strain our ears to hear what that last stanza is telling us – and away with any notions of a false naivety or the importation of a child's treble – the closer we get I am convinced to what Mahler wanted. I recognize that this demands a lot of time and hard slog from conductor, singer and players, but the rewards of a barely audible *pianissimo* are transforming: it comes as a shock of a totally unique kind. And it's because shock is almost always associated with loudness, an explosion, a crescendo, that I deliberately focused in on the transfiguring *pianissimo* that should bring 'Das himmlische Leben', and with it the symphony, to a close.

Mahler, I need hardly tell you, also knew how to summon up music of an exceptional intensity that is also exceptionally loud, though here again there are multiple distinctions to be made between the degrees of loudness that he calls for and which, no less than his *pianos* and *pianissimos*, demand not just the closest scrutiny but precise realization if we are to hear his orchestration in depth; and dynamics are intimately related to textural depth.

I emphasize once again the relationship in Mahler between organization of dynamics and form. The first movement of the Ninth, one of the basic documents of twentieth-century music, is built I believe round a dynamic concept, the idea of a recurring crescendo that leads to a climax, each repetition of which grows in dynamic intensity until, almost literally, the music – the movement – explodes, detonates, and falls to pieces; the process of re-forming – picking up the pieces – constitutes the movement's unforgettable transitions. In the case, then, of one of the formally most innovative of all Mahler's first movements, its form is dictated by its dynamic. I might be accused of over-simplification, but it is my conviction that in this movement, my early schoolboy experience of which left me physically shaken, shocked, such was the impact of it, Mahler, as no one else before him – perhaps it is only in Wagner that we might uncover a precedent or two – systematically exploits the hyper-expressive potentialities of just one dynamic marking – the hairpin – the crescendo. That, ultimately, tells us all we need to know about the principle that generates the movement's unique form.

You will have noticed that shock has been one of many sub-themes of this talk today; and it is not surprising that I find I have returned to that topic in the context of Mahler's dynamics. That the wheel seems to be turning full circle suggests that it is time to begin to draw this already long enough session to a close. But before I do so, please bear with me while, with my last few examples, I try to complete the circle. For a start, it seems to me that the capacity to shock was already part of Mahler's burgeoning creative personality, already a weapon in his strategic armoury, at a very early stage, in fact in his first major work, the cantata, *Das klagende Lied*.* In recent years we've been able to familiarize ourselves with the first version of the work, in performance and a recording, along with the hitherto unpublished score of the *Urfassung*. The passage I'm going to play you from the original second part of the cantata is interesting judged by any standards, the more so if one bears in mind that it is an eighteen-year-old composer we are listening to. Here already is Mahler exploring the mobility of sound that figures high on my list of his contributions to twentieth-century music. But in this particular instance, taken from the first version of *Klagende Lied*, he introduces something in addition to mobility, in fact an engagement between two tonalities a semitone apart, C major, for the off-stage ensemble of trumpets, timpani and cymbals, and C flat major, for the main orchestra. To be sure, these are relatively brief confrontations and fall short of a fully fledged polytonal collision. John Williamson has wisely remarked that the passage resists conventional analysis if only because of Mahler's obvious intention that 'the two musical streams should not coalesce into a single harmonic field'; and to add to the dis-synchronization, Mahler has the off-stage ensemble in 3/4 and the main-stage orchestra in 4/4. Let's hear the early precedent for so much of what was to come later in Mahler's music, the exploration by diverse means of acoustic space:

RECORDED MUSIC EXCERPT
*Das klagende Lied, Urfassung*, orchestral score, Part ii,
*Der Spielmann*, fade in from bar 219; fade out bar 230
(interventions of offstage ensemble)

These days we may not find that so much of a shock; but remember, that music belongs to 1878–80. What I wonder, or who, was Mahler's specific model? And if there was one group of people

---

* See pp. 73–90.

(Brahms and Goldmark among them) it did shock, it was almost certainly the members of the Beethoven Prize Committee to whom he submitted his score and by whom it was adjudicated and rejected in 1881. It could well have been a passage like the one we have just heard that proved the final straw. But we also know, fascinatingly, that when Mahler returned to the cantata to revise it, he was astonished to find, in his own words, 'the Mahler whom you all know was already fully and instantly developed at that time'; and promptly christened it his Opus 1. To be sure, that C major/C flat bit he came to omit; it is my guess that when he came to look at it years later, he decided that if it were going to be done at all, then it would have to be done substantially, not fleetingly; and revision on that scale would have raised all kinds of other issues, proportion, duration, and above all the coherence of the overall language, which, we must never forget, he had only finally arrived at while he was still in the process of composing the cantata. But the passage remains evidence of Mahler's bold, experimental spirit, even at so early an age, and I should not have been happy to ignore it. Moreover, the offstage/onstage dichotomy he was to retain, reserving it for the finale of the cantata, where the intrusion of the offstage music – festive noises off – on the chilling moment of revenge, of catastrophe, represents the first manifestation in Mahler of his ironic juxtaposition of two seemingly mutually exclusive genres of music to comment on the tragic denouement of the drama, to intensify it indeed.

To follow that excerpt from Mahler's first major work, I want to end, yes, really end, with music from Mahler's last symphony, his Tenth, so at least I can pretend to have traversed the full chronological span of his life's work. When talking about the first movement of the Ninth I made the point that Mahler raised the idea of the crescendo to new expressive and formal heights. In this last paragraph and example, before I attempt to sum up, I want to concentrate on just one chord which to my ears in itself represents in Mahler's oeuvre a unique attempt to concentrate within the scope of a single vertical conflation of nine different pitches an expressivity that one might be forgiven for thinking in earlier times would have demanded a whole movement to match the explosive discharge of feeling that Mahler accomplishes in one massive vertical gesture, which – just in case we don't get it first time round – he sustains. Dissonance abounds in Mahler; but this I think is the most radical moment of dissonance we encounter in all of his music, and it fiercely articulates what was to become, indeed was already becoming, the most revolutionary of the leading features of the music of the new century: the Emancipation of the Dissonance, to use a famous phrase of Arnold Schoenberg's, which heralded, for some at least, the eventual abandonment of tonality. Here in the Tenth Mahler reveals himself in the throes of that process of Emancipation, which as it developed was fundamentally to change the face, the sound, of music:

RECORDED MUSIC EXCERPT
Symphony No. 10, first movement (Cooke edition),
bars 203–13; quick fade

The means by which Mahler achieves the intensity of that vertical explosion are themselves of particular interest, given the preoccupations of the period in which the Tenth was written. For a start, the chord conflates nine out of the available twelve pitches of the chromatic scale; I was amused only the other day to read a respected music critic in London writing about Mahler's '12-note chord'* in the Tenth as evidence of his anticipatory genius. I think he can be forgiven his error, for there is no doubt that the sonority the pitches produce remind one powerfully of similar gestures in the non-tonal Expressionist period of Schoenberg's music, before the 12-tone system was born out of that historic emancipation, a system itself born out of the need to impose order on the freedom that had been unleashed.

It has interested me too that in this same movement Mahler's treatment of his melody, especially in counterpoint with versions of itself, irresistibly bring to mind the treatment of the row – the potentialities of the row – as spelled out in the 12-tone system. I am far from suggesting that had Mahler lived longer, he would have found himself pursuing, consciously or unconsciously, strictly Schoenbergian paths. But it remains remarkable, I think, that here

---

* See p. 510.

and there in the Tenth one cannot but be aware of these anticipations of a future that, for a time at least – a time I believe that has now passed – seemed to offer the possibility of a new language for music.

But that was a future Mahler was not to experience. Let me return to the chord for a moment, the extreme, violent expressiveness of which brings Mahler into the style we identify as Expressionism, one of the best definitions of which was made by Webern in 1912 when defining the role of the theme in Expressionist composition. There can be no development, he claimed, no repetition: 'Once stated, the theme expresses all it has to say'. Substitute 'chord' for 'theme' – 'once stated, [the chord] expresses all it has to say' – and one understands precisely why Mahler's nine-note chord makes the overwhelming impact it does. It is Mahler exploring the expressive possibilities of radically heightened dissonance, embodying it in one overwhelming gesture, and undeniably thereby making a bit of musical history at the same time. Perhaps we might hear it one last time?

MUSIC

Symphony No. 10 (repeat of last example)

Music of that order of surprise and power, demands silence rather than words. On the other hand, what could be more appropriate to a Mahlerian occasion like this than a coda? So let me attempt a summing up with as few repetitions as possible.

I'm conscious that there are many avenues I've left unexplored. But to try to cover a lifetime's work and omit nothing would require a talk of a lifetime's duration. Mahler however has not only been a generous enricher of generations of successor composers in terms of techniques, forms, and the manipulation of sound, from near inaudibility to towering walls or waves of sound. He has in addition – and I know that I speak for many here today – immeasurably enriched the lives of those of us, who may not be composers or performers, but in whose lives his music has played a leading role. For me, and I suspect many others, he has been one of the great interpreters of experience, that is, the experience of being human and being alive, with all that implies in terms of triumph, tragedy, sorrow, happiness, anger, despair, desolation, reconciliation, innocence, humour, love. Is there indeed an aspect of the human condition that Mahler has not, as it were, translated for us into sound, into music? That is a criterion by which we recognize genius and esteem it. None the less, I cannot call to mind another composer quite so all-embracing in the sheer range of experience that Mahler so astonishingly demonstrated from the *Klagende Lied* to the Tenth; and I am sure that it is that comprehensiveness, along with the arsenal of techniques he invented to service it, that is responsible for the phenomenal global reception his music now enjoys.

But for that to continue, at the level of comprehension and reception that I would fervently wish to see it continue, we should, all of us, I believe, pay attention to some of the issues of performance that I have raised as a subtext throughout this talk. It is one important thing to recognize how profoundly creative and innovatory and fruitful was Mahler's influence on the preceding century; it has proved to be a truly staggering legacy. The best way of trying to repay the consequent debt that we owe his genius is now, I suggest, to give much more thought to how his works are performed, above all to their interpretation.

I have long been convinced of the importance of the relationship between analysis and interpretation and I believe there is a growing desire among conductors, among them some with a special feel, a special talent, for Mahler, to bring off an 'authentic' interpretation. A much used and abused word but I use it to mean the re-igniting, or perhaps better, re-discovery, so far as is humanly possible, of the inspiration that originally gave birth to the work, and thereby established its unique character. A lofty ambition I agree, but analysis must I believe be the first crucial step in the journey towards achieving that end.

It has always seemed to me a great flaw in the training of musicians – at least, it is so in Britain – that analysis, in the sense that I ascribe to it, plays a very minor role in the syllabus. The unbridgeable gulf that supposedly separates performers from 'academics' is still very much an inhibiting presence. In my ideal educational world, young conductors, and above all aspiring conductors of Mahler, would have the chance to approach analysis conceived of, not as an 'academic' exercise, but as a means of practical enlightenment, the sole aim of which is to provide the performer with the information which, will enable him or her first to comprehend and then to realize the composer's intentions. That of course requires extensive study of the works, perhaps in particular from angles and approaches some of which I have touched on in this talk, but also the assimilation of information gleaned from reception history, from consideration of the culture in which Mahler lived and worked, and from what knowledge we have of his practice as an interpreter of his own works. A tall order you might say, but I promise you every detail of any syllabus in which I had a hand would be oriented to the specific practicalities and problems with which in truth each individual work of Mahler's confronts the performer, the conductor above all. Too much analysis today, to my mind, is insufficiently music-directed to be of much help to the performer. And would it be too bold of me to suggest that those who engage in the problematic business of music criticism, of assessing the validity of a given performance, might benefit from such an initiative?

You will know that I have not attempted to disguise my resistance to the false beautification of Mahler, to smoothness, the application of cosmetics, to routine, to blandness, to the reduction of the shock that is so often integral to his aesthetic. I most earnestly hope that younger generations of Mahler students, scholars, analysts and critics, indeed all who have direct contact with Mahler's genius, will unite and campaign to find a way, perhaps through the collaboration of a sympathetically inclined institution, to build this vital bridge of communication between analysis and interpretation. It could form a brilliant future area of Mahler studies which would also attract much public attention. Unless that happens, I am fearful of a future when Mahler may be performed not one whit less than he is now, but when, in the wake of a thousand performances of this symphony or that, members of the audiences might be heard asking themselves, homeward bound, 'I wonder what all the fuss was about?'

# A Mahlerian Odyssey: 1936–2003

*To Eveline Nikkels and Robert Becqué*

⌐⁓2003 ⁓

Ladies and gentlemen, I hope I may be forgiven if I start this memorable occasion by talking for a few minutes about myself. I promise you that I shall not spend too long on this autobiographical prelude, but as is the case with all convincing preludes in the field of musical composition, it is what follows a prelude that finally justifies its existence. I very much hope that the relevance of what I am about to embark on now will become apparent before I have finished.

To make a start on all of this then, let me tell you that I was born in 1925. I first encountered Mahler in 1936 or 1937, when I was a schoolboy, eleven or twelve years old, not in the first instance as a composer – that was to come a little later – but in the shape of a text, in fact a biographical entry in Hugo Riemann's famous *Musik-Lexikon*. The presence of this dictionary – perhaps not everyday reading in a typical middle-class home in London in the 1930s – was due to the fact that my mother, a gifted soprano, had been sent by her father, who was Swiss, to the Conservatoire in Leipzig, where she studied and indeed resided throughout the whole of the First World War. Perhaps at least some of my inquisitiveness about Europe and its music can be attributed to this unusual domestic history. When my mother returned to England, to marry an Englishman and have a family, she brought with her a piano, a lot of music, books – German classics mostly – and, for me most importantly, an edition of Riemann, in the company of which I

Lecture given at the Concertgebouw, Amsterdam, 2 May 2003, as part of the celebration of a hundred years of Mahler tradition in the Netherlands, before a performance of Symphony No. 3, given by the Royal Concertgebouw Orchestra conducted by Riccardo Chailly.

pursued many hours of investigation, assimilating as best I could as much information as possible.

What caught my attention in the entry on Mahler, a name altogether strange to me, was the mention in the list of works of something called *Das Lied von der Erde*; and I very clearly remember going to my mother to ask her what this puzzling title meant. Remember, please, because it is of striking relevance when I move on a little later to talk about the reception of Mahler's music in England, that at this period in my life I had not *heard* a note of Mahler's music, for the very good reason that there was not a note to hear. I exaggerate of course, but only slightly: the chances of a schoolboy, even an enquiring one as I was, coming across Mahler in terms of a live performance were very, very remote.

One possibility might have been picking up a live broadcast from a radio station like Hilversum (and probably long after my bedtime), but that, alas, was not my luck to experience. To be sure, the BBC, as distinct from the established concert-giving organizations, was in contrast relatively adventurous. But it remains true that in the general musical culture in England in the 1930s, and in many other cultures elsewhere – the Netherlands always excepted – there was simply no place for Mahler, no opportunity that is to hear for oneself *why* precisely it was that his music went unheard. I hope that sentence survives its somewhat tortuous logic, for it makes an important point to which I shall return. Indeed I want to pursue it now by illustrating briefly the climate of opinion that in England was prevalent at the time.

Naturally enough, I looked elsewhere for some enlightenment in the shape of basic information about Mahler. I was given as a present for my birthday or Christmas, I don't remember which, a highly popular and many times reprinted compendium entitled *The Musical Companion*, edited by A. L. Bacharach and published by Victor Gollancz; its team of contributors included names such as Eric Blom (who was later to edit the first post-war edition of *Grove's Dictionary*); Edward J. Dent, the celebrated Mozart scholar; Edwin Evans (who was to succeed Dent as President of the International Society for Contemporary Music in 1938); and Julius Harrison, a by no means untalented conductor it would seem, who helped both Nikisch and Weingartner prepare their performances of Wagner in Paris in 1914; and there were other names too, all of them writers on music of significant reputation.

You can imagine then with what eagerness I leafed through the pages, locating the references to Mahler, hoping for illumination. This must have been in 1938 or thereabouts, when I was thirteen. Naturally enough, I turned first to *Das Lied von der Erde*, the title for which I had sought an explanation. But this is what Dyneley Hussey, a well-known critic, who was still writing in the 1950s and 1960s, had to say in his chapter on Mahler's vocal music in 1934 in *The Musical Companion*:

> The most important of his later [vocal] works on a large scale is *Das Lied von der Erde*. One says 'on a large scale' because, although these are only six songs from Hans Bethge's *Chinese Flute*, Mahler has transformed them from miniatures into a work of symphonic proportions. Indeed, there is something rather ridiculous in his solemn and literal-minded treatment of the word 'ewig' ('eternal') at the end. But these songs are far preferable to the imposing finale of the ninth [*sic*] symphony, where the Latin hymn 'Veni, Creator Spiritus' and some of the more metaphysical passages from the second part of Goethe's *Faust* are allotted to eight solo voices, a double chorus and a boys' choir, the performers numbering, together with the vast orchestra, about a thousand. In this work and in Schoenberg's *Gurrelieder*, written about the same time under Mahler's influence, the megalomania of Central Europe reached its apex.

As for the symphonies, Julius Harrison proved no more insightful to his eager young reader, who was told that Mahler's symphonies were works of 'enormous size, interesting at times but laboriously put together and lacking that vital spark of inspiration that made Beethoven's nine . . .', etc., etc. Need I continue? The sheer dumbness, deafness and downright ignorance of Mahler in England in the 1930s can still arouse my indignation, even today in 2003. You can imagine how I felt when I later made the acquaintance of Eric Blom himself, who at our first meeting in the 1950s promptly remarked, 'You know, Donald, we just don't want Mahler here', as if the composer were an unwelcome immigrant seeking admission to the United Kingdom.

There had been of course exceptions: Samuel Langford, who wrote for what was then entitled the *Manchester Guardian* and attended the great Mahler Festival in Amsterdam in 1920, organized by Mengelberg, and important occasional pieces by the biographer of Wagner, Ernest Newman. Most important of all, however, in these years was the role of *composers*, and one in particular, Benjamin Britten, whom of course I did not know as a schoolboy but with whom I was to work very closely from the 1960s until his death, and with whom from time to time I would talk about Mahler. Why composers, and composers of an altogether later generation, you may well ask? Because for my generation, it was often through the works of those composers, who themselves owed a substantial creative debt to Mahler, that wider audiences first made their acquaintance with his genius, even though, paradoxically, they may never have heard his music. I have mentioned Britten. Already in 1937 – just three years or so after the first publication of that wretched compendium I have just referred to – he was writing to a friend – and remember Britten was a young man of twenty-three, not the famous composer we are familiar with today – after listening over and over again to Bruno Walter's historic first recording of *Das Lied*, which, as you will hear, was also to play a vital role in initiating my own first encounter with the composer. This is Britten's letter to his friend Henry Boys, himself a notable musician and pioneering writer:

> It is now well past midnight & society dictates that I should stop playing the Abschied. Otherwise I might possibly have gone on repeating the last record indefinitely – for 'ewig' keit of course.
>
> It is cruel, you know, that music should be so beautiful. It has the beauty of loneliness & of pain: of strength & freedom. The beauty of disappointment & never-satisfied love. The cruel beauty of nature, and everlasting beauty of monotony.
>
> And the essentially 'pretty' colours of the normal orchestral palette are used to paint this extraordinary picture of loneliness. And there is nothing morbid about it. The same harmonic progressions that Wagner used to colour his essentially morbid love-scenes

(his 'Liebes' is naturally followed by 'Tod') are used here to paint a serenity literally supernatural. I cannot understand it – it passes over me like a tidal wave – and that matters not a jot either, because it goes on for ever, even if it is never performed again – that final chord is printed on the atmosphere.

   . . . At the moment I can do no more than bask in its Heavenly light – & it is worth having lived to do that.*

I hope I may be forgiven for returning for a moment to my own odyssey, which in some ways ran parallel with Britten's, by trying to resurrect for you the excitement I felt on learning that for the first time I was going to have the opportunity actually to *hear* a work by the composer who had hitherto been locked away in the pages of Riemann's dictionary. Moreover, it was the recording of *Das Lied* itself, that historic recording of a live performance in Vienna on 24 May 1936, when Bruno Walter conducted the Vienna Philharmonic with Kerstin Thorborg and Charles Kullmann as soloists, at a concert in the Musikvereinsaal, that Britten was describing in his letter of 1937.

The album of 78 rpm shellac discs – a massive pile by today's standards – was given to me by my generous parents, and from the moment I played it through, not knowing what to expect, hardly comprehending what it was I was hearing, I was seized by the music as I had never been seized before and only very rarely since. I cannot describe or explain the experience. I was simply possessed by a music which up to now I had known only as a title in a dictionary in a foreign tongue. My life was changed and has remained changed as a result of that first encounter, which was followed, a year or so later, by my acquiring the similarly historic Walter recording of the Ninth Symphony, made in Vienna in 1938, when the impact was no less. Indeed, I was shaken *physically* by the huge, menacing, explosive climaxes of the work's first movement. I had never experienced anything like it before: I was simply overwhelmed, possessed, transformed by a new world of sound, swamped by a new world of feeling.

My experience, along with Britten's, testifies to the quite special

---

* Letter 103 in Donald Mitchell and Philip Reed (eds.), *Letters from a Life: Selected Letters and Diaries of Benjamin Britten*, vol. 1, p. 492.

and significant role played by Walter's recordings of *Das Lied* and the Ninth in contributing to changed attitudes to Mahler in the late 1930s, and not only in England. But for a moment I want to continue to think a bit more about this question of Mahler's influence even while his music was still largely unheard. One of the most telling examples I know is the interaction between the second movement of Mahler's Fifth Symphony and one of Britten's own most famous orchestral pieces, the so-called 'Storm' Interlude from his opera *Peter Grimes*. Here, to begin with, is a reminder of the relevant movement from the Mahler:

RECORDED MUSIC EXCERPT
Mahler: Fifth Symphony, second movement, from start

The performers there were the Royal Concertgebouw Orchestra under Riccardo Chailly, a recording made in 1997. And now the 'Storm' Interlude from *Grimes* (Act I), where the composer conducts the Orchestra of the Royal Opera House, Covent Garden, in a recording made in 1958:

RECORDED MUSIC EXCERPT
Britten: *Peter Grimes*, 'Storm' Interlude, from start

I believe the juxtaposition of those two excerpts makes the relationship – in fact the *source* of Britten's inspiration – very clear indeed, while a word about dates helps me to make the point I'm trying to get across.

The young Britten in fact had been given a score of the Fifth by his teacher, the composer Frank Bridge, in 1930. Prodigious score-reader that he was, a live performance was less essential for him than for the rest of us and we may be sure that the process of assimilation was extremely rapid. But what lends the chronology of this very clear instance of influence a quite special and ironic significance is this: that in fact the world premiere of *Peter Grimes* and its famous 'Storm' Interlude took place some five months *before* the first ever public live performance in London of Mahler's Fifth, in October 1945. This enables me mischievously but truthfully to suggest that some members of the audience attending the premiere of the opera were probably hearing Mahler's Fifth for the first time too, albeit unknowingly. (It was not until 1947 indeed that the first commercial recording of the symphony was made, as it happens by Bruno Walter.)

If one is trying to assess – to measure – the extent of Mahler's influence on the twentieth century, in terms of the creativity he generated – released – in succeeding generations of composers out-side the territories of middle Europe with which by birth and culture he is most closely associated – Schoenberg, Berg, Webern, Zemlinsky and so on – there can be no question that we should accord the Russian Shostakovich no less recognition than the British Britten.

I would put it quite bluntly like this: without Mahler, would we have had Britten's song-cycles? I think not. Without Mahler, would we have had Shostakovich's symphonies? Again, I think not. Furthermore, it is Shostakovich who provides an additional layer of inter-relationships and inter-action. Consider his Fourteenth Sym-phony, for soprano, bass, and string orchestra, an eleven-movement work dedicated to Britten. (The two men were great friends and admirers.) Shostakovich's vocal symphony would hardly have existed without the precedent of Mahler's own 'Symphony for tenor and contralto (or baritone) voices and orchestra' that is *Das Lied*. Nor, on the other hand, can the influence of Britten's own orchestral song-cycles be discounted, which again patently owe their origins to Mahler and *Das Lied*. I find the mutual relationship of Shostakovich and Britten and their joint relationship to Mahler of quite exceptional interest, and illustrative of Mahler's influence in the twentieth century across generations, cultures and national boundaries. These unique crossovers and cross-fertilizations form a highly important part of the history of Mahler reception in the twentieth century.

But why, you may well ask, perhaps impatiently, this focusing on two composers, one Russian, one English, both of them securely established as composers who command world audiences, along of course with Mahler himself? To be sure, at the same time as they won recognition for themselves, they were preparing the ground for the eventual triumph of the composer, whom they tirelessly advocated (except – in Shostakovich's case – when politics intervened) and passionately admired. Yes, Mahler's triumph; and it is precisely that new culture in which we find ourselves that I want to talk about, identify some of its consequences, and perhaps come up with a few ideas that may encourage us to step back and remind ourselves of the composer that Mahler actually *was* rather than the composer who for many decades either went unheard or was ignorantly dismissed, even by those who should have known better, such as the famous radical philosopher Ludwig Wittgenstein who, I quote, was to write like this, dismayingly, in 1948 [his italics]:

> If it is true that Mahler's music is worthless, as I believe to be the case, then the question is what I think he ought to have done with his talent. For quite obviously it took a *set of very rare talents* to produce this bad music. Should he, say, have written his symphonies and then burnt them? Or should he have done violence to himself and not written them? Should he have written them and realized that they were worthless? But how could he have realized that? I can see it, because I can compare his music with what the great composers wrote. But *he* could not, because though perhaps someone to whom such a comparison has occurred may have *misgivings* about the value of his work through seeing, as it were, that his nature is not that of the other great composers, – that still does not mean that he will recognize its worthlessness; because he can always tell himself that though he is certainly *different* from the rest (whom he nevertheless admires), his work has a different kind of value.

Mahler's works 'worthless'? Having written his symphonies, he should have 'burnt them'? I confess to wondering why it was that Wittgenstein did not address to himself all those questions he asks about Mahler. Indeed are we not left with the impression that it must have taken 'a set of very rare talents' to produce an example of such very bad criticism? Perhaps he should have burnt it! The fact however that this quotation of Wittgenstein is given prominence at the very start of a new volume of Mahler studies published by an academic press in the United States in 2002 to accompany an important Mahler event makes me nervous. Are we to experience now a period of 'revisionist' criticism which seeks to imply that maybe Wittgenstein, and the contributors to the *Musical Companion* I mentioned way back, got it more right than we have hitherto supposed? If so, then I think it makes all the more important what my ambition is today – what I am hoping to communicate to you today – living as we do in an entirely different critical and cultural climate.

Now, Mahler's music is pretty much everywhere, both in terms of live performance and, above all, accessibility, by means of all the new recording technologies. The schoolboy of today would find it hard to imagine even, what another world it was in the 1930s. Furthermore today there is an ample quantity of Mahler literature, the best of which, and I am thinking in particular of the masterly biography by my friend and colleague, Henry-Louis de La Grange; the tireless study of Mahler's manuscripts and sketches by the doyen of American Mahler scholars, Edward Reilly, and those specific essays, memories and tributes which have punctuated the decades since Mahler's death; and here perhaps I can dare to drop a few names – Schoenberg, Adorno, Boulez, in particular – without risking unwelcome comparisons.

Great names, indeed. But if there were one feature common to what all these highly individual and independent advocates had to say, it was this, that whatever their differences in age, nationality, historic period and approach, they were all intent on *making a case for Mahler*; and given the largely negative reception that prevailed until, in effect, the second half of the century, that was obligatory. I am in no way underrating the importance of what was achieved. You will not think me intolerably immodest, I hope, if I claim to have helped a little at least to bring about changed attitudes in England. But looking back as I do today at the work I myself did in past decades I begin to realize that there were consequences, in some respects because of the narrowness of the focus, necessary and significant though that may have been at the time. Now, I believe, this may have to be questioned and perhaps rethought.

For example, I am second to none in my admiration of Theodor Adorno. There is scarcely a current Mahler scholar who does not

owe him a profound debt of gratitude, in particular for his monograph of 1960: *Gustav Mahler: Eine musikalische Physiognomik*, a small
volume but undoubtedly one of the monuments of Mahler literature. Perhaps his only fault was when he occasionally permitted his
Marxist dialectic convictions to dictate an *adverse* musical judgement. It was vital to Adorno's case that Mahler's music could be
interpreted as critical of the 'bourgeois' society in which he lived,
which was probably one of the reasons why he found, say, the finale
of the Fifth lacking characteristic weight and substance. But just the
other day I was reading a much earlier essay of his on Mahler –
thirty years earlier than his 1960 monograph – in which a couple
of sentences gripped my attention. They come right at the end of
the essay, after he has spent several pages *defending* Mahler from
those who would hear in him nothing more than an inflated, exaggerated late romanticism. He wrote: '*All contemporary compositional
technique* lies ready in Mahler's work under the thin cover of the
late romantic language of expression. It needs only authentic interpretation to bring it out.' (That last observation is in itself of great
importance. How lucky I have been in this very hall to have heard
so many remarkable performances of Mahler, which, to my ears,
have been distinguished by the ambition and ability to achieve
*authenticity* of interpretation, by fearlessly penetrating, puncturing
even, the 'romantic' surface to which Adorno refers.) But the more
important for me, at least in the context of this talk, is that remarkable opening claim, '*All contemporary compositional technique* lies ready
in Mahler's work . . .' As I repeat that, think back, if you can bear it,
to those breathtakingly ignorant English views of Mahler I quoted
way back, and remember that they too, astonishingly, belonged to
the very same decade as Adorno's 1930 essay.

   And it was precisely under that Adorno flag, that I and many
others pursued our ambition to reveal the truth about Mahler: that
far from being representative of an exhausted past, he was, on the
contrary, herald of a compositional *future* that was already very
much the *present* that was ours in the 1950s and 1960s. I would not
wish for a moment to retract a single one of those claims, for
example his innovatory approach to the orchestra, the homogeneity
of which he systematically deconstructed, so that the orchestra that

was 'traditional' for Mahler was in fact a collective, a multiplicity, of orchestras, each assembled to realize, in perfectly imagined sound, the needs and demands of each event in the specific narrative – a word I shall be returning to – the *narrative* in which to my mind each symphony of Mahler is grounded. To talk in such general terms may not – cannot – spell out the extraordinary anticipations of contemporary practice that Mahler continuously introduced into his orchestration, for example the astounding sophistication of his dynamics. This last, I believe, amounts in quantity and complexity to what is almost an independent layer of his compositional method, along with melody, harmony and rhythm. It is a feature that to date has received relatively little analytic attention from Mahler students, and I hope one day someone might be sufficiently interested to examine form and texture in a movement or extended passage by Mahler and come up with some observations on the organization of their dynamics, for here the influence on Webern was for sure a profoundly creative one. Organized dynamics had suddenly become absolutely integral to the compositional concept.

In this area of orchestration alone – and how inadequate the very word 'orchestration' seems when it is a Mahler symphony, song or song-cycle one has in one's ears or before one's eyes – it would take hours, literally, to reach the end of what might be said about it. And likewise almost any other dimension of his music. I choose this one example, one dimension, to emphasize again how it was that the case *for* Mahler was presented, perfectly properly but sometimes exclusively and therefore excludingly, as a composer *par excellence* whose music opened up a never-ending series of windows on the future.

Let me say at once that this was an approach – both a vigorous defence and a sharp attack on entrenched opinion – that I wholeheartedly pursued myself and for which I make no apology. It contains a huge element of truth in it. But in more recent years, as the battle in that area has surely been *won*, I have begun to ask myself whether we might not have been rather seriously neglecting and therefore underappraising other and equally highly original aspects of Mahler that, when we have come to identify them, perhaps go a long way to explaining the phenomenon of exceptional popularity his music now enjoys worldwide. It is with that ambition in mind that I shall, if I may, devote the rest of my text today.

You may think I am altogether losing my wits when I suggest that we urgently need to remind ourselves of just how extreme the contrasts are between one Mahler symphony and another. Be patient with me while I briefly return to my boyhood and my total immersion in *Das Lied* and the Ninth. Rather oddly, this unforgettable confrontation, totally inspiring though it was, led to my having quite serious difficulties when, on an enforced random basis – we're back for a moment in the 1930s – I succeeded in getting to know some of his other music. For example, I was excited inevitably by my first acquaintance with the Second Symphony (in that famous old 78 rpm shellac recording made in the USA by Ormandy and the Minneapolis Symphony Orchestra in 1935), but also puzzled by it. I found it hard to relate it to those two late-period, late-style (genuinely *Spätstil*) works, *Das Lied* and the Ninth, which had so totally hijacked my receptivity and defined my comprehension of who and what compositionally speaking Mahler was. This, naturally, was but a temporary impediment, one that study, knowledge and information eventually helped overcome. But it was a real problem. Something analogous might have been trying to get to know Beethoven when the only work accessible to one was, say, the C sharp minor String Quartet.

But what my earlier experiences of Mahler went to prove – and this I believe is something that we have lost sight of a bit today – was his sheer *unpredictability*, which as he set off on his unique creative journey became ever more evident: indeed, unpredictability has to be recognized to be a leading if unconscious principle of his symphonic art. Whereas in the music of past masters of the, let us say, symphony a discernible pattern of an evolving continuity can be discerned, it is almost impossible in fact to use the term *evolution* meaningfully in relation to Mahler.

Let me try out a couple of examples on you. Mahler completed his Eighth Symphony, that 'gesture of megalomania' as we learned from Julius Harrison in 1934, in for him an unusually brief period of intense creativity in the summer of 1906. In 1908 he completed *Das Lied*. The Eighth, for reasons of organization and the multiple forces involved – I'll have something to say about those before I finish – did not attain its first performance in Munich until quite late in 1910, while *Das Lied* and the Ninth were to go unheard and unperformed until *after* Mahler's death in 1911.

Imagine if you will that you were a member of the tumultuously enthusiastic audience attending the premiere of the Eighth in 1910 who left the hall and by some magical means were transported back to his desk where he had left the draft manuscript full score of *Das Lied*, and taken a look at it; and not only at *Das Lied* but the Ninth too! Could you have made sense of what you read in the scores of *Das Lied* and the Ninth in the light of the symphony, the Eighth, you had just heard in Munich? I doubt it. Perhaps you had *already* been surprised when encountering the Eighth for the first time after attending the premiere of the Seventh in Prague, which had been composed in 1904 and 1905. You – and by 'you' of course I mean my hypothetical traveller from one Mahler premiere to another – you might yourself have wondered then how possible it would have been on the evidence of the Seventh to have predicted the creation of the Eighth in 1906? As for *Das Lied*, the impact must have been even more challenging. For here you were in another world altogether, of sound, of philosophy, of narrative, of belief; and likewise the Ninth.

The crucial word here, I believe, is 'world', not in the sense that Mahler famously used it when remarking to Sibelius in Helsinki in 1907, 'Symphony is like the world, it must include everything' – that was an exclusively musical injunction. I use the word in a different though I hope no less musical sense, at least with regard to Mahler's own symphonies. Each of them to my mind constitutes an independent world of sound, form and thought, which is precisely why, the more I think about this raising of the issue of unpredictability, of non-evolution, not, I emphasize, within the scope of a single symphony but between a symphony's predecessor and its successor, the more significant for me it becomes to bring fresh attention to a now little remarked upon feature of Mahler's originality. We may indeed be helped freshly to define what we mean by 'originality', that over-familiar descriptive term.

I have not the space or time, nor you I am sure the patience, to plod through all the symphonies in turn. But even at the most elementary level the spelling out in chronological order of the symphonies and the ever-changing number, sequence and character of the movements that make up each one can be illuminating and challenging. How was it possible for a composer across the span of a relatively brief creative life – of what? thirty years odd? – never to repeat himself, to eschew repetition and evolution, to go on building and exploring new worlds, new worlds of forms, one by one? All this, remember, on top of, or, perhaps better, part of a compositional methodology in which, as Adorno remarks, 'all contemporary compositional technique' was to be found.

But there is much more to be said about the process that led to the creation of this succession of independent worlds. What fascinates me here is the remarkable plethora of diverse philosophies, aesthetics, and above all *narratives* that in combination service each symphony. I've been giving recent thought to Mahler's narratives and have been astonished by their wealth of imagination and, I believe, yet more importantly the unique range of human experience, belief, philosophy and diverse aesthetics they represent. We all know, for sure, that our point of departure in a Mahler symphony is going to lead us into and onwards through a journey that will land us eventually somewhere else. Hence, of course, the fundamental role played by his tonal schemes in the devising and interpretation of his narratives. And even when, as is rarely the case, a symphony ends in the same key that it begins, it is a memorable narrative point that is still being made. The Sixth and Eighth Symphonies, in their very different ways, make that point: the *absence* of a tonal shift, narrative-wise, can be as telling as its presence. But has it been sufficiently comprehended, I wonder, just how elaborate and investigative these narratives are? For me it is almost without doubt that Mahler quite consciously, in one symphony after another, one world after another, explores basic human concerns and issues from many different perspectives which on occasion themselves reflect the prime intellectual debates of his day.

I shall not be able to traverse, you will be glad to hear, the whole of Mahler's œuvre from this angle of approach but I start with the First Symphony, first because of its absolutely explicit and familiar journeying narrative, and secondly because of its extraordinary relationship to the Second Symphony, something unique in fact in Mahler's output if we are looking for what lessons might be drawn from the line of succession. Undeniably the Second is something of a special case because, although Mahler set about composing the great funeral march that was intended to be the first movement of his new symphony, hardly had the ink dried on the paper of its predecessor, he found acute difficulty in bringing the work to an end – he suffered no less than a composing block for a significant number of years.

Here one has to recall the narrative of the First – a symphony that it took Mahler no inconsiderable time to establish in its four-movement form and with a traditional title, 'Symphony No. 1' – where Mahler himself claimed that his protagonist, whom we have to assume was himself, did *not* in fact achieve the victory over death that the finale of the symphony would seem to imply, hence the massive funeral march which opens the Second and commemorates that defeat.

While I don't doubt Mahler's own words, I have not myself been able to find a convincing location in the finale of the First to which that moment of defeat might be attributed. It is my guess that one or other of Mahler's extensive revisions excised it and thereby the evidence for its existence was lost. But what in the symphony grips my imagination, and self-evidently Mahler's imagination too, was the extraordinary extension of the journeying narrative initiated in the First but not concluded by its finale.

The huge funeral march of the Second speaks for itself. But who could ever have predicted that the symphony was to continue and eventually to end with a unique venture into the *afterlife*? The protagonist – there is no room for doubt – is dead and buried. There follow the three movements that make up the middle part of the symphony, the first two of which to my mind clearly function as memories of former life, memories, both pleasurable and painful, until the vocal third movement 'Urlicht' intervenes – and remember, if Mahler wasn't able to finish his symphony, he *was* able to compose at this time of frustration some of the most marvellous of his *Wunderhorn* songs, 'Urlicht' in fact among them –

by means of which we embark on the final journey to resurrection.

An incredible narrative! Had anyone ever thought of so extensive, unnerving a realization of life *beyond* death and tried to give it shape and substance in terms of music? And what music! The extraordinary acoustic experiments alone, on and off the platform, along with many others, for which I have not space to describe, confirm Adorno's observation of the preparation we find in Mahler of so many features of a language of contemporary music to be achieved in later decades, and this in a symphony the narrative of which was *out of real time* altogether, a characteristic Mahlerian paradox. For us today, more than forty years after Adorno wrote his essay, those techniques form part of a familiar language that generations of composers post-Mahler speak with ease. Yet they prove to have lost none of their novelty, provided – always – that an authentic performance of the Second resurrects the inspiration that gave birth to them in the first place.

And now once more to return to the principle of unpredictability. Who could have foreseen that the Third Symphony should take the shape it did? Sufficient one would have thought for Mahler to have explored the afterlife so forcefully in the Second. But not a bit. What he turned to next – and philosophically it could hardly have been a more powerful contrast – was the articulation of the so-called 'chain of being', 'chain of becoming', which begins pre-life and then, by a process of evolution, conducted by means of its narrative as well as within the symphony itself, ascends to images of Angels (boys' voices!) and Love, the last representing for Man- and Womankind an exalted spiritual destiny which all should strive to attain.

What do I mean by evolution as we hear it within the symphony itself? The huge introduction to the huge first movement graphically describes the world *before* life as we understand it evolved. To achieve this, Mahler deploys a highly idiosyncratic orchestra in which homogeneity is eschewed and the traditional relationship between strings and wind reversed. It is now wind and percussion that predominate, and the introduction carries to what at the time must have been an extreme – even allowing for Berlioz, Wagner, and Strauss – the virtuoso solo roles allotted the brass. By any standards, what Mahler demanded of his trombones in the 1890s was exceptional. Let me give you a brief example, which I think illustrates the point I'm trying to get across. There cannot have been at the time of the complete première of the symphony in 1902 a more startling point of departure in terms of orchestral sound than this:

RECORDED MUSIC EXCERPT
Mahler: Third Symphony, introduction to first movement,
figs. 15–17$^{+9}$
Berlin Phiharmonic Orchestra, Abbado

Mahler was ever a great deconstructor of the orchestra; but after starting from the complete reversal of the 'traditional' relationship between strings and wind, he proceeds to *re*construct the orchestra across the span of the entire symphony so that by the time we reach the sixth and last movement, the great slow movement, the string body is restored to a more traditional equality with the wind, indeed for the first forty bars of the movement it is only a string orchestra that we hear. Mahler could hardly have made the evolutionary point more clearly: we have 'evolved' in orchestral terms from one orchestral concept to another, and as the sixth and last movement continues, the totality of the orchestra presents an image of the triumphant completion of the 'chain of being': human life has been established and human love revealed as one of the principal objectives of humankind.

I have little doubt that in his choice of narrative Mahler was influenced by current debates in his day about evolution. It is tempting to think he may have been influenced by Henri Bergson and his theory of the *élan vital*. But in fact Bergson's monograph on this topic (*Creative Evolution*) was not published until 1907. All the more fascinating perhaps that Mahler's 'programme' for the Third so meticulously follows the scheme I have already spelled out, the 'chain of being', a concept of evolution that goes back to pre-Christian eras, as was meticulously documented by the distinguished English historian, E. M. W. Tillyard, in 1943. (I must say thank you here to my friend David Meyer who brought Tillyard's work to my attention.) It is interesting, is it not, that as profound as the contrasts are between the Second and the Third, both narratives are, as I like to put it, *out of real time*, which is not to suggest they are irrelevant to our immediate present or were to that of Mahler himself. After all, both narratives, time-less though they may be, have matters of life and death as their very *raisons d'être*.

And what next? Another unpredictable successor, in the shape of the Fourth, even though – and how splendidly ironical it is to remember it – even though the Fourth in fact would never have happened at all without the Third; it was, so to say, stored away in the womb of the Third until finally released publicly in 1901. But who, I wonder, could have guessed its parentage? A radically fresh world of sound; a hugely reduced orchestra; a remarkable preoccupation with and proliferation of elaborate contrapuntal textures which in retrospect anticipate the often polyphonic profiles of the coming exclusively orchestral symphonies, Five, Six and Seven. There is too a conscious 'classical' awareness, manifesting itself in the dialogue that Mahler conducts with himself at crucial formal junctures – transitions and formal recapitulations in particular – in his chosen forms (sonata form and variations, prominent among them).

At times indeed Mahler's role as practising historian of the symphony can result in the Fourth in a typically idiosyncratic kind of neo-classicism. But what no one at all could have been prepared for was that surplus *Wunderhorn* song, 'Das himmlische Leben', discarded from the Third, and now functioning, to most critics' and audiences' disbelief at the time, as the Fourth's finale. There was only one critic, I believe, who got the point, Max Graf, I think it was, who wittily suggested that the symphony, if it were to be understood, had to be 'read' from back to front, like the Hebrew Bible. In short, one cannot fully comprehend the work until one turns the pages back and comes to realize that from the very outset, the first bars of the first movement, we have been systematically prepared to receive the finale when we reach it. In no other work of Mahler's is the function of memory more important both for listener and performers. The finale we might think is the musical equivalent of Proust's famous *madeleine*, in *A la recherche du temps perdu*.

All of this is wonderfully managed by the composer decreasing the work's complexities and increasing its transparency across its total span, thereby conditioning us to receive the finale as a perfectly logical denouement. But what, needless to add, has intrigued me is something different. Perhaps no less surprising as the song finale – and who other than Mahler would ever have come up with such an outlandish idea? – is the nature of the narrative, which to my mind is a theory of evolution alternative to that of the Third and describes not an ascent to a vision of what humankind might, should, achieve through exalted Love, but a reverse process, a *return* to the innocent condition of childhood – to the child*like* – if we are fully to comprehend the sublime E major which 'Das himmlische Leben' finally comes to affirm. This is not a Darwinian survival of the fittest but the survival of Innocence, and I think it can be demonstrated that every dimension of the symphony's composition is geared to achieve that sublime end.

A line has to be drawn somewhere, and I think this is the moment at least to begin to draw it. Could one in fact have a more convincing illustration of the accumulation of new worlds than the juxtaposition of Five, Six and Seven, not one of which shared its overall form with its predecessor and each of which pursued an independent narrative and an independent philosophy and, in one case, at least, an independent aesthetic? The Fifth progresses from death to triumph across the span of a five-movement sequence that constitutes one of the most formally innovative symphonies that Mahler ever wrote. In its two-movement first part, he raises both 'interruption' and 'quotation' to the status of formal principles and prime components of the symphony's compositional process. I can think of no precedents for this. Mahler was not commenting on history, but making it.

The Sixth, by way of contrast, is in four movements plus, and by 'plus' I have in mind its finale of epic proportions, almost constituting a one-movement symphony in itself. I often wonder, had Mahler lived longer, if he might not have brought to birth the concept of a one-movement symphony. The finale of the Sixth is an indication, while the first movement of the Ninth, to my mind, is almost a realization of that ideal. The Sixth of course reverses the narrative of the Fifth in the sense that its huge finale asserts without qualification or mitigation the victory of death, not life. On the other hand, love – human passion – which I believe became an increasingly prominent source of Mahler's inspiration and for which he invented an unmistakable sonorous image of passion (strings and harps always to the fore), makes, I believe, its first and unforgettable appearance as the second subject of the Sixth's first movement which is then recapitulated in an overwhelming A *major* to bring the movement to a close. It is the finale, however, that brings the narrative to an end with an annihilating A minor.

It was, I believe, a very specific kind of music that during Mahler's final years came to represent for him the idea of passion, sexual passion even, as distinct from the exalted concept of Love we have encountered in earlier works. As for the Seventh, who would have predicted it after the experience of the Sixth? And who after the Seventh could have expected the Eighth? The Seventh to be sure has long been considered the most 'modernist' of Mahler's symphonies. I have never been quite sure what that means though it certainly suggests the difficulty some have in making total – that is to say, narrative – sense of it. I myself find it not so much 'modernist' as *surreal*, the manifestation of an extraordinary *dis*continuity and *dis*location that becomes the more apparent as the work unfolds. The finale indeed exudes a kind of challenging *ir*rationality unlike anything elsewhere in Mahler. The trouble is, or so it seems to me, that ultimately the aesthetic he chose to explore subverts the work itself, prevents the composer from bringing it to a successful, that is, convincingly rational conclusion.* Perhaps that was Mahler's ironic intention?

Room, you see, for another lecture; but before I leave the Seventh let me give you just one example of the subversion I have mentioned in compositional action. One might well think that the second *Nachtmusik*, so intriguingly marked *Andante amoroso*, would prove to be a revival of the serenade, a favourite genre of romanticism both in music and literature. Our expectations are certainly aroused but only to be, not so much disappointed as contradicted.

---

* For a somewhat different perspective, however, see 'Mahler on the Move: His Seventh Symphony', pp. 406–10. [DM]

For a start – if that's the right word – Mahler begins his *Nacht-musik* with a cadence, a progression that normally would close a movement, not open it. What then follows, if one is an enquiring listener, is a vain search for anything that might resemble an extended, serenade-like melody (the trio perhaps is the only exception). In short, this is a serenade from which the serenade has gone absent. Or was that cadence we heard at the beginning the closure of a serenade – *Con amoroso* – that has somehow got lost? I speculate, of course, and perhaps exaggerate. But there can be no denying that the capacity of the Seventh to *dis*concert was part of its aesthetic intention.

I've already mentioned that a juxtaposition of the Seventh and Eighth presents a striking discontinuity of its own. But I'm not going to say much about that now, only to make a few remarks about the Eighth. First, I don't believe there was anything at all 'nationalistic' about Mahler's reported remark that the symphony was to be regarded as 'a gift to the nation'. I hear the Eighth quite otherwise, as an attempt first to salute one aspect of the creative spirit by demonstrating with maximum inspiration, energy and skill as many of the techniques of composition that were around, and live and well, as the nineteenth century ended and the twentieth began, the art of counterpoint especially.

Hence the exhaustive contrapuntal textures that characterize the opening hymn, 'Veni creator spiritus'. In the second part of the symphony, and in a very real sense both parts are united by *Goethe*, whose German translation of the Latin hymn was how Mahler first got to know it, the spirit of creativity is identified in quite another way, through the medium of the closing scene of Goethe's *Faust*. Here, I am convinced, the unifying bond is not only Goethe but also the images of love and passion. In the opening invocation to the creative spirit, love is prominently identified in both words and music – 'Accende lumen sensibus, Infunde amorem cordibus' ('Illuminate our sense, Pour love into our hearts') – while it can be no accident that when Mater gloriosa floats into view, in Goethe's and Mahler's 'theatre of the mind', we not only hear strings and harps but she flies transcendentally in E major, the key which for Mahler often represented bliss. The ultimate chorale that concludes Part II tells us that it is 'Eternal Womanhood' that leads us on high.

In that context we should bear in mind a remarkable conjunction that Mahler made in a letter to Alma in 1910: 'So long as *Eros* is the ruler of men and gods,' he wrote, 'so surely will I make a fresh conquest of all of the heart which once was mine and can only in unison with mine find its way to God and blessedness.' Here again, in the Eighth the central thrust of the narrative – 'Eros . . . the ruler of men and gods' – forcefully reminds me that the decade in which the Eighth was composed was a period when the relationship between creativity and the fundamental act of human creation was a prominent feature of the new paths in psychology and psychoanalysis: the role our sexual drive plays in creating not only new life but exalted and enduring works of art. In that historical context, Mahler's summoning up of the creative spirit – 'Veni creator spiritus' – must be given fresh significance. It is the union of love and creativity that empowers the Eighth.

Secondly and finally there is what I would call the *communal* dimension of the Eighth. In parallel to Mahler's extraordinary compilation of compositional techniques and, let it be added, genres – motet, cantata, opera, aria, choruses of every description, stretches of orchestral music that are patently 'symphonic' – he assembled in the Eighth virtually every performing resource that was available to him at the time, both professional and amateur (the choruses, for instance), and strikingly incorporated the special timbre of boys' voices into his vocal textures. All of this, I am sure, was part of Mahler's collective intention, a gift not so much to the 'nation' as to the culture and community of which he himself was part.

The wheel has turned full circle and I am back now with *Das Lied von der Erde*, the work that ignited, inspired, transported me when a schoolboy all those years ago in 1938. Needless to add, and this is almost always the case with Mahler in my experience, I continually find new things to think about even in those works with which I am most familiar, among them *Das Lied*. I want in fact to end today with a comment or two on the marvellous narrative of this masterpiece which in so many ways explores new territory, both musical and philosophical, though in one way it returns us to a form of narrative that Mahler had first made his own in the Second Symphony. Let me explain what I mean.

In 'Der Abschied', I guess most of us will know that Mahler introduces into his finale, three recitatives for the solo voice and the Mahlerian equivalent of the continuo. Here is the first recitative, and naturally I'm using the Bruno Walter performance of 1936, the recording of which not only overwhelmed me but, as we've heard way back, the youthful Benjamin Britten too:

RECORDED MUSIC EXCERPT
*Das Lied von der Erde*, 'Der Abschied', figs. 2–4
Vienna Philharmonic Orchestra, Bruno Walter, Kerstin Thorborg

That marvellous flute obbligato recurs in the second recitative, but not in the third and last, which follows the big C minor interlude for orchestra alone. Here it is:

RECORDED MUSIC EXCERPT
'Der Abschied', figs. 48–49

Of course you'll have noticed there the omission of the flute obbligato; and it was in trying to answer that question (*why* no flute?) that I came to realize two things, first that the protagonist (the soloist) is now somewhere else – the big preceding orchestral interlude is in fact one of those Mahlerian journeys, *a crossing to the other side* – and secondly that there is in fact still an obbligato, an inverted obbligato as it were; and this time for the tam-tam, the instrument in *Das Lied* that is undoubtedly the sonorous symbol of death. Hence the absence of the flute. We are beyond life and the sounds of Nature; in fact we are in the immediate afterlife, having made the crossing from life to death. Mahler has returned again to that extraordinary territory which had preoccupied him when composing the Second in the 1890s, though in very, very different music.

If I may, I shall play in a moment that third and last recitative once more, and ask you to think not so much about the absent flute but about the presence of its successor, the tam-tam. And not only

the tam-tam but the text, the words, that it accompanies: 'He
alighted from his horse', the protagonist sings, 'and handed him the
*drink* of farewell.' ('Er stieg vom Pferd und reichte ihm den *Trunk*
des Abschieds dar.') It is to the word 'Drink' ('Trunk') that we,
whether audiences, or performers and interpreters, must pay
crucial attention, for it is vital at this moment that we recall how
fundamental the act of *drinking* has been to the total concept of *Das
Lied von der Erde*. After all, it is *two* songs, both dedicated to drinking, that *frame* the first five movements of the work, and it is no
accident, but part of Mahler's brilliant organization of his poetic
symbols and images, that the third recitative, after the protagonist
has dismounted, re-introduces, no less, an act of drinking. The text
continues, '. . . and handed him the drink of farewell' ('. . . und
reichte ihm den *Trunk* des Abschieds dar'). Here, again, is the third
recitative:

RECORDED MUSIC EXCERPT
Repeat of previous music example

That last drink, of course, is not of alcohol but of the *elixir* that
Death hands the protagonist, that does not so much intoxicate us
as liberate us from life while at the same time affirming that in the
renewal of the earth – and remember, the image of spring is carefully preserved throughout *Das Lied*, even in the contexts of
protest, anger, despair and rejection – and our eventual dissolution
within it, we may find the guarantee of our immortality. Let me
remind you of how the movement ends, where we encounter a
world of sound – celesta, mandolin, harps prominent – from which
the tam-tam has at last been banished:

RECORDED MUSIC EXCERPT
*Das Lied von der Erde*, 'Der Abschied', figs 58-9–65

Die liebe Erde allüberall
Blüht auf im Lenz und grünt aufs neu!
Allüberall und ewig blauen Licht die Fernen!

> *The beloved earth everywhere*
> *Blossoms in Spring and grows green anew!*
> *Everywhere and for ever the horizon shines blue!*

Mahler's own words, not Bethge's.

In the past, Mahler has often been thought of, type-cast, as a 'tragic' composer *par excellence*, that his art as a whole was haunted by images of death. I would not contest for a moment that an awareness of the presence of mortality was part of his fantastically rich awareness of life. But it is in fact only in the Sixth that death, after a heroic resistance, is allowed to triumph. As for *Das Lied*, in which a fresh philosophy is expounded, accompanied by all kinds of extensions of his musical language, many of them rooted in what he had learned from friends and scholars about non-Western music, I find it hard to interpret 'Der Abschied' as a *farewell* to life. Is it not in fact the attainment of a selfless bliss that the music we have just heard represents? How odd to recall that one of the early critics of an early performance of *Das Lied* complained that what was missing from 'Der Abschied' was any concluding sense of *redemption*! He had surely got his theologies and philosophies hopelessly confused.

I must leave it there, I think appropriately, with a work that perhaps more than any other has shaped my own life and no doubt helped prepare me for that last journey that awaits us all. It seems to me that great art, of the scale of Mahler's works, teaches us now to live, to love, to die. So many of the values for which he stood, and his works stand, are under threat today in a world in which violence and hate and collateral damage, the new and shameful idealogy of 'shock and awe', too often seem to triumph. Mahler's agenda was something altogether different; and it is with a profound sense of gratitude and esteem that I have attempted today to honour his memory and the legacy of his genius.

RESONANCE

# 'Dearest Ted'

*To Edward R. Reilly (1929–2002)*
*doyen of Mahler scholars in America*

~ 2005 ~

From one point of view I know perfectly well that it would be use-less to post this to you by conventional means: it would not reach you. But in the context of the specific volume of letters in which this, my very last letter to you, will be published, all anyone needs to know is that it is my heart that not only dictates the text but serves as a unique postage stamp. I have no doubt that this tribute to our very long friendship will circulate among those many Mahlerians, and many others besides, for whom you and your work were so fundamental a source of information and insight, and, no less, objects of admiration.

But let me begin to explain why it is that I am, so to say retro-spectively, bothering you with this letter. Our own Mahlerian dia-logues, maintained over many years – we first met in the States in 1967 – would take place whenever and wherever we found our-selves together. When not, then letters or telephone calls filled the gap. That vital thread of continuity was never broken; and though it may sound strange to say so, it remains to this day. I still speak with you whenever I have some bit of fresh Mahlerian news to impart and discuss or puzzle to solve. For me this is an indispens-able habit of communication that testifies to your living presence in my life. For me you have never died and never will.

Thus it was that the terrible terrorist events in London on 7 July 2005 – as I write, only two or three weeks ago – while they cer-tainly renewed my awareness of your physical absence, prompted me almost at once to commit to paper what we would have talked

---

Contribution to *Letters to Posterity* (Amsterdam: Nexus Institute, 2005).

about and, more importantly, why during the hours immediately
following the bomb attacks, Mahler too was much in my thoughts.

I need hardly spell out to you, dearest Ted, that nothing I write
here implies any underestimation on my part of the loss of life that
Kathleen and I realized all too swiftly was the result of the bombs.
But after the initial shock was over — you will already have understood how close the events were to where we live — Bloomsbury —
a part of central London with which you are wholly familiar: how
often in fact have we strolled together, and with Van,* past Tavistock
Square and across Russell Square — it dawned on me that there
were features associated with the date itself, which I am absolutely
sure we would have discussed with a kind of horrified surprise.

First of all, of course, that it was on 7 July 1860 that Mahler was
born, 145 years ago. Furthermore, and I know you will not think
of me as in some way obsessed with myself, that very evening, by
which time London had been brought to a virtual standstill, I had
been invited to attend the annual dinner of the Gustav Mahler
Society in the UK and give a short address. This, it very soon
emerged, had to be cancelled; and it was then that I thought of
your probable response to all of this, and to remember above all our
many past discussions of Mahler's preoccupation with irony, which
so many of his early audiences found hard to accept.

There were, I fully realize, other vastly more weighty and challenging issues that we found ourselves debating on 7 July than the
forced abandonment of my talk. But I was certainly reflecting on
Mahler and his fascination with irony when I recall what it was that
I had intended to talk about, however briefly, and indeed illustrate.
Specifically, my topic was to be Mahler's addition of cowbells to the
substantial array of percussion in his Sixth and Seventh Symphonies, and his use of them, undeniably new to the resources of
percussion hitherto deployed in the symphony, to represent a vision
of an altogether 'other world' where peace reigned and which in
some distant future might even be attained.

I could not, could not, dear Ted, but reflect on the gross irony
that it was on this very day when, in celebration of Mahler, I
intended to invoke cowbells as an image of peace, a catastrophic

---

*    Edward Reilly's wife, Evangeline.

manifestation of terrorism should have occurred here. All of this, I might remind you – we certainly talked about it at the time – had been anticipated in 1999 when I was attending performances of Britten's *War Requiem* in Oslo. Irony again, in fact, since on the occasion of the second performance (on 25 March, I think it was) I switched on the TV when I got back to my hotel and, with horror and shame, learned of the hail of bombs dropped on Belgrade, a climactic event in the long history of the Kosovo crisis. God knows how I managed to reconcile what I was doing, introducing Britten's unique pacifist masterpiece to undoubtedly dismayed Norwegian audiences at a moment when violence, death and war were to be witnessed daily on our screens, images that have seemingly been with us ever since. It was a final irony when I learned that our ambassador in Oslo was to be among those who were to attend my final pre-concert talk. I felt inclined to ask him not to attend, but in the event it was quite evident from the exchanges we had time for, that his sympathies were closer to the composer's convictions, and to mine, than I had thought possible.

What I want to do now, Ted, if I may rely on your patience for a while longer, is to return to Mahler's cowbells and set out, briefly, what I had hoped to say on the evening of 7 July, the day of the terrorist attacks in London. By that time the shock had diminished a little, to be replaced by a sense of frustration that while the bombers had had their say, Mahler had not had *his*, the more so since it was in the spirit of evoking an affirmation of peace from another world that had led him to use cowbells in the first place.

Mahler in fact had quite a bit of importance to say about the significance of the bells and, no less importantly, about how they should be performed; perhaps better, how they should be *heard*. What follows is the unusually elaborate note that he added, at fig. $21^{+3}$, in the first movement of the score published in 1906:

> The cowbells must be played very discreetly, in a realistic imitation of the bells, sometimes together [*vereinigt*], sometimes at random [*vereinzelnt*] (higher and lower) like those of a herd grazing in the distance. It is explicitly stated that these indications do not imply a programmatic interpretation.

It was not Mahler's custom to write extensive notes with regard to how his music should be performed and this rare instance, highly significant though it is, leaves us with as many issues unresolved as resolved. To many of those I shall return later. But by now, dear Ted, you must be asking yourself why it is that I am pursuing this matter of Mahler's cowbells? To which my answer is that I now believe – am finally convinced! – that we very rarely, whether in live performance in the concert hall or on disc, hear the cowbells as Mahler wanted us to hear them.

This sudden realization came to me as the result of a curious and recent incident in my own life two or three years ago. Because of my Swiss connections – my mother was half-Swiss, my Swiss grandfather, Carl Brenner, a prominent international merchant, much travelled and travelling – because of these connections, I was visiting some of my Swiss relatives who now live in Scharnachtal, in the Bernese Oberland. I sat late one sunny afternoon amid the foothills of the mountains, a landscape Mahler would surely have much loved, and as I thought of him on one of his famous walks, a small herd of cows moved across the field and closely approached where I was sitting and thinking. Next moment, what was ringing in my ears was the sound of cowbells as I had never heard them before.

What astounded me was the fascinating polyphony that resulted from the cows' movements: munching the grass, occasionally mooing or lowing, raising their heads and necks in observation of their surroundings and their companions, and shaking their heads and their bodies to discourage or rid themselves of unwelcome insects. It was the sheer unpredictability of this collective demonstration of a contrapuntal texture of total freedom that was so brilliant and arresting, a texture that incorporated silence, *tutti*, occasional solos and ever-varied grouping and re-grouping among the members of the ensemble; and what beautiful creatures they were, seen at close hand.

No doubt I fantasize just a little about this event, but what I describe I believe to be pretty close to the truth, a truth moreover that I am sure Mahler himself had recognized. It was, I suggest, the randomness of the polyphony that must have made a particular

Scharnachtal – where Mahlerian cowbells may still be heard

appeal to him. For which reason I believe, even more importantly, that we now have to find a way of introducing into those passages in the Sixth and Seventh Symphonies creative thinking among performers – not only percussionists but conductors too – creative thinking about the means by which Mahler's ambitions might be achieved.

I can see that at any moment, Ted, you are going to intervene and ask, 'Is all of this really necessary?' 'Yes, it is,' is my reply, and the need for action was brought home to me when, to prepare for the informal address that I was going to give on 7 July (and I am aware even as I complete this letter that further terrorist threats have been made in London), I listened to a number of established recordings of the Sixth, one of the most recent of which was conducted by a renowned Mahler conductor of the highest standing and much admired by me. And what did I find? A *barely audible anonymous tinkling and jingling* that no one I think could argue was even remotely

what Mahler had in mind. There can be no disputing that he did
not want cowbells swamping the sonorous scene nor the crucial
element of 'distance' to be lost. However, the problem, as I see it, is
clearly exposed if we take a look at an example of what the per-
cussionist will have in front of him or her when attempting to fulfil Mahler's imaginative ambition. What follows, to be precise, are
characteristic bars from the orchestral part for the *Herdenglocken*
in the first movement of the Sixth Symphony. To be sure, Mahler
indicates 'placed at a distance' at the beginning of the passage in
question and 'closer' towards the end of it, indisputable evidence of
course that 'distance', far and near, was a prime component of the
sound he was aiming to achieve. But that said, how else is Mahler's
wavy line to be 'read', interpreted, *realized* in actual performance?

Pretty much a *blank*, isn't it? In particular, Mahler's wavy line may
indicate start, stop, and continuity in between, but gives not the
slightest idea of the riveting, intricate polyphony of rhythms, pitches,
and what we might hear as 'motives', all of it accidentally and
unconsciously released by an ensemble of cows going about their
daily business.

   No one should think I am making a joke of all this. On the contrary I have thought about it a lot and am convinced that what I
have had a shot at describing above was precisely what Mahler
heard but for which he failed to find an adequate means of transcription. The wavy line simply leads all too often to feeble, colourless, noises off.

   Something should surely be done about this? The suggestions I
make might strike some with horror and disbelief, though I very
much doubt, Ted, that your response would be wholly negative. I
wonder, for example, if it might not be possible to use some form
of pre-recorded cowbells which could be played with discreet
amplification, all the appropriate durations, dynamics and differen-
tiations of distance having been secured, during those bars the

extent of which is determined by Mahler's wavy lines. Do we have the technology that could fulfil this ambition? Could it work?

Yet more rewarding and practical perhaps, might not two or three composers with particular Mahlerian expertise and enthusiasm – how about Colin and David Matthews for instance, who together did so much to bring the performing version of the Tenth to its final shape? – get together and devise a fully written out, fully realized, percussion part which at long last would enable the relevant players in the Sixth and Seventh Symphonies to realize in sound the extraordinarily important symbolic role that Mahler's cowbells ought to be heard fulfilling?

What we should seek is not a 'realistic' representation, as he himself spells out clearly in his note, but an adequate realization of the cowbells' symbolic significance, the existence, that is, of another world in which among other things peace prevails. Kurt Blaukopf for one, assesses Mahler's experience which gave birth to the cowbells' imagery in these terms: 'high mountain pastures . . . the loneliness of freedom, the peace, the relaxed breathing under a blissful sky'. These run-of-the-mill observations, it seems to me, do not go very far in communicating what Mahler was really after. It is, in short, only music itself, not words, that can reveal to us the reality, the crucial 'otherness' that Mahler found in the unique, random polyphony that comprises – must comprise in performance – the cowbells' counterpoint. This very point Mahler surely makes himself by his use of the word 'vereinzeln' in his note which I quote above?

How extraordinary it is that in these passages which (but for the exemplary Norman Del Mar) have received so little critical attention, Mahler was already heralding a mode of composition that was to become one of the leading compositional practices in the latter half of the twentieth century! For here was Mahler, in 1903–4, undoubtedly fascinated by the musical potentialities of randomness.

There can be no question that work needs to be done to find the ways and means to bring to fruition a bold dimension of Mahler's late imagination that I believe has yet to be adequately heard in our concert halls and recording studios. Perhaps later generations of Mahler performers, percussionists especially, will follow this up. What better legacy could I hope for than that?

Moreover, if in the future we can hear Mahler's cowbells as a symbol of peace still to be attained, who knows – perhaps, perhaps, perhaps – the world in which all of us live, racked by violence, will eventually listen and strive to make his distant vision a reality; in which case his bells will have cause for ceaseless, though no doubt random, celebration.

As always, dearest Ted, in living and loving memory,

DONALD

Brigueuil, France, 24 July 2005

# The 'Correct' Order of the Middle Movements in Mahler's Sixth Symphony –

*Scherzo: Wuchtig–Andante moderato* or
*Andante moderato–Scherzo: Wuchtig*

### Gastón Fournier-Facio

Mahler was often uncertain about how, precisely, to order the middle movements of his symphonies. This uncertainty was particularly important regarding the Sixth. To choose between the two possible alternatives is no light issue, around which a fierce controversy has developed during the years. In order to map the relevant elements, I will start with the chronology of all the changes in the middle movements' order. Later I will argue that the only way to clarify the controversy is to study both the historical and musical facts involved.

*Chronology of the middle movements' order*

1904   Mahler finishes the symphony. The order of the middle movements is: scherzo–andante (S–A).

1905   The autograph of the full score (dated 1 May) also presents the middle movements in the S–A order. During the autumn the 'fair copy' is sent to his new publisher, C. F. Kahnt in Leipzig, who prepares, again in the S–A order:
(a) a full-size conducting score;
(b) a smaller 'study score';

(c) a four-hand piano reduction prepared by the composer Alexander Zemlinsky;

(d) a 'Thematic Analysis' prepared by the musicologist Richard Specht.

1906    On 1 May, in Vienna, Mahler reads through the symphony with the Vienna Philharmonic, keeping the s–a order.

The symphony is programmed for its first public performance at the Allgemeiner Deutscher Musikverein held in Essen in May. At the dress rehearsal the order is still s–a. On 27 May, at the premiere, Mahler suddenly decides to reverse the order of the middle movements to a–s; he requests that slips of paper be inserted into the printed programmes to advise concertgoers that the order shown there (and in the three scores published thus far) had been changed. He also requests that an erratum slip be inserted in each of the unsold copies of all three scores to advise buyers that order of the middle movements had now been reversed.

Furthermore, in November, at Mahler's request, Kahnt publishes new editions of all the already printed scores as well as Specht's 'Thematic Analysis' booklet with the new order of the middle movements.

No other editions appear until 1963.

On 8 November, in Munich, Mahler conducts the Sixth with the a–s order.

1907    On 4 January, in Vienna, Mahler conducts the Sixth for the last time, keeping the a–s order.

1909    In a letter postmarked 6 July, Mahler asks Mengelberg to send him his score of the Sixth, presumably so that the former can enter some further changes. Mengelberg's conducting score shows Mahler's last known changes to the Sixth, neatly entered in red ink. These changes do not include reverting to the s–a order of movements.

On 10 October Mahler conducts his Seventh Symphony in Amsterdam. This was probably the occasion for further discussion of the Sixth with Mengelberg. The composer might once again have expressed doubts as to the order of the middle movements. According to La Grange, this most likely explains why Mengelberg contacted Alma in 1919, and requested her advice for his forthcoming performance (cf. La Grange, p. 815*).

NB It can be argued that, if Mahler in 1909 in Amsterdam expressed doubts to Mengelberg about the middle movements' order, it is not easy to understand why the latter did not raise the question with Alma when he conducted the symphony in 1916 in Amsterdam (cf. Gantz, p. 4; see also the year 1919 below).

1910    Universal Edition takes over the Kahnt edition of the Sixth, retaining the A–S order.

1916    Willem Mengelberg conducts the Dutch premiere of the Sixth in the A–S order.

1919    Willem Mengelberg now becomes uncertain about the order of the inner movements and decides to question Mahler's widow about it.

On 1 October Alma responded with a succinct telegram: 'First scherzo, then andante, affectionately Alma', without specifying any basis for her categorical statement.

Upon receipt of Alma's telegram, Mengelberg writes on the title page of his own conducting score: 'According to Mahler's instruction II first scherzo then III andante.'

This inscription from the hand of Willem Mengelberg has since been quoted as evidence of Mahler's final intention (or 'third thoughts', as D. Matthews, p. 372, puts it) to revert to his original ordering of movements. That Mengelberg subsequently trusted the accuracy of Alma's memory, rather than consulting Mahler's close friends, musical associates or his publisher, Bruck considers surprisingly naive. Nevertheless, it has since been responsible for fostering a 'tragic legacy', 'igniting a controversy that has spanned the decades since' (Bruck, pp. 26, 13).

On 5 October, Mengelberg performs the symphony in its

original s–a order, printing in the programme note for this concert the above-quoted statement that he had written into his own score.

1920   On 14 October, at the great Amsterdam Mahler Festival, Mengelberg performs the Sixth in the original s–a order; printing once again in the programme note for the concert his above-quoted statement.

Paul Stefan, an early devoted supporter of Mahler, publishes a revised version of his 1910 study on the composer, changing the order of the middle movements, stating that 'the definite order of the middle movements determined by Mahler is: scherzo before the andante' (Stefan, p. 132).

1921   Nevertheless, many Mahler biographers and analysts following his death spoke of the andante as the second movement of the symphony, including Ernst Decsey and Richard Specht. In this year Paul Bekker's major work on Mahler's symphonies is published, in which the a–s order appears.

1940   In her *Memories and Letters* Alma refers to the scherzo as the third movement (A. Mahler, p. 70).

1963   Erwin Ratz, founder of the Internationale Gustav Mahler Gesellschaft (IGMG), edits the first *Critical Edition* of the Sixth using the original s–a order of the middle movements. In his *Revisionsbericht* (cf. Ratz, p. 1968) he claims that such an order is justified by what he describes as the 'unfortunate practice hitherto over the matter of the movement order', stating that Mahler reversed the order in the first place only 'to some extent under pressure' and that 'he had . . . soon recognized the destructive effect of the change and put back the original order'. Though he offers no evidence to support his position (cf. Del Mar, p. 91; C. Matthews, p. x, Bruck, pp. 29–30), it is certain that his claim has altered 'performance practice of the Sixth up to the present day' (Bruck, p. 14). According to Kaplan, this was the result not only of a mistake but of a 'wilful act' from the part of Ratz (Kaplan, p. 7).

2000   Karl Heinz Füssl publishes his revised IGMG *Critical Edition* of the Sixth (dated 1998) keeping Ratz's s–A ordering of the middle movements, and basing the IGMG decision primarily on the inscription in the Mengelberg score (cf. Füssl, 1998).

2004   As the current Chief Editor of the *Complete Critical Edition*, Kubik publishes 'the official position of the institution I represent': 'The correct order of the middle movements of Mahler's Sixth Symphony is andante–scherzo'; 'I have now informed C. F. Peters, the current publisher, that the score and parts should be corrected at the next available opportunity.' (Kubik, p. 43)

*Historical Facts*

In his 2004 text, Jerry Bruck draws a most precise and passionate picture of the relevant historical facts of the controversy. He collects all the currently available evidence which clearly supports the A–s order of middle movements which he summarizes as follows:

> All of Mahler's own performances of his Sixth Symphony [Essen, 27 May 1906; Munich, 8 November 1906; Vienna, 4 January 1907], without exception, had its andante precede the scherzo.
>
> All other performances of the Sixth during Mahler's lifetime, and for almost a decade thereafter, observed his final A–s order.
>
> No record exists of any written or verbal instruction by Mahler himself to his friends, associates, other conductors or his publishers to indicate that he ever intended to revert to his earlier ordering of these movements. (Bruck, p. 15)

On this basis, the three authors taking part in the 2004 Kaplan Foundation publication on our subject challenge the s–A ordering of the middle movements of the Sixth from several perspectives.

Regarding Alma's 1919 telegram which finally convinced Mengelberg to change his view on the subject and go back to Mahler's original s–A order, Kaplan quotes La Grange's statement that 'Alma was never a scrupulous observer of her husband's creative life' (Kaplan, p.10); and goes on to say that 'Alma's general unreliability is compounded here, as Bruck points out, by her contradicting herself on this very point in her memoirs (where she refers to the scherzo as the third movement)' (Kaplan: 10; cf. also the year 1940 above).

Furthermore, Kubik points out Alma's 1957 mistake (she had written to Ratz talking about a non-existent Mahler performance of the Sixth in Amsterdam with the s–a order of the middle movements) in order to criticize 'the already well-known unreliability of Alma's information', as she 'can no longer remember those things exactly'(Kubik, pp. 38–40).

Ratz is presented as 'an analyst, not a historian or a philologist' (Kubik, p. 37). And he is said to have 'both misrepresented the facts and failed to disclose evidence that undermined his personal position' (Kaplan, p. 10)

It is pointed out that many international conductors as significant as Barbirolli, Rattle, Slatkin, Jansons, Mackerras, Mehta, Tilson Thomas have already adopted the a–s order in their recordings (Bruck, pp. 33–4). A list to which one could also add the recent 2005 Abbado recording.

Even though the historical arguments in the Kaplan Foundation publication are very convincing, there are none the less some queries still open to discussion.

Herta Blaukopf, for example, drastically contests the Kaplan Foundation's negative view on Ratz; someone she knew personally rather well (cf. Blaukopf, p. 76).

Similarly, she presents a contrasting perspective with regard to Alma. Blaukopf is convinced that Alma, before replying to Mengelberg's 1919 request, herself consulted with Schoenberg and Webern who, incidentally, were responsible for performances of the Sixth Symphony using the s–a order of the middle movements (cf. Blaukopf, pp. 71–5).

Kubik is right, though, in stating that it remains an open question whether Alma's message 'was a genuine mistake or an expression of her own preference' (Kubik, p. 42). On the other hand, one should note that Kubik's harsh criticism of Alma's 'unreliability' and 'memory lapses' is much based on her scant correspondence with

Ratz in the years 1955 and 1957, just a few years before her death, when she was elderly, infirm and approaching her eightieth birthday. This I find somewhat unfair, since at the time Alma sent her famous 1919 telegram to Mengelberg she was half that age!

In any case Alma's telegram could imply that, 'near the end of his life (when he worked on new versions of the Fourth and Fifth Symphonies), Mahler had expressed to her a wish to revert to the original order; unless (which is unlikely but not inconceivable) Alma had made her own independent decision based on her preference for Mahler's original conception of the symphony' (D. Matthews, p. 372).

What is certain, La Grange writes, is that 'Mengelberg's Mahler Festival was for Alma an all-important event. Much as I have sometimes felt compelled to cast doubt on her testimony, either because of her memory lapses or because at times she intentionally distorted the truth, I see every reason here to believe she was passing on Mahler's final decision to a conductor who had, more than any other, performed and defended Mahler's music' (La Grange, p. 815).

## Musical Facts

As important as the *historical* facts are, I strongly believe that the only way to have a full and clear picture of the problem is to look, also, at the *musical* ones. In the Introduction to the 2004 Kaplan Foundation publication, we are invited to 'examine what is at issue here *musically*' (Kaplan, p. 8; my italics). But, alas, this publication systematically avoids talking about music!

Some of those who, beyond the sole historical facts, have looked at the score itself, have a different opinion: 'I think that from a musical point of view there can be no doubt that the original version is far superior' (D. Matthews, p. 374).

POSSIBLE REASONS FOR CHANGING THE ORIGINAL ORDER
AT THE 1906 ESSEN PREMIERE

'When she arrived at Essen on Friday, 25 May, Alma found Mahler "sad and worried", almost ill with anxiety' (La Grange, p. 410).

Klaus Pringsheim, Thomas Mann's brother-in-law and Mahler's assistant in Essen, describes with great eloquence the composer's state at the Essen rehearsals:

> Those close to him were well aware of Mahler's 'uncertainty'. Even after the final rehearsal he was still not sure whether or not he had found the right tempo for the scherzo, and he wondered whether he should invert the order of the second and third movements (which he subsequently did) . . . After each rehearsal he asked everyone around him, musicians and friends, for their impressions, trying to determine down to the smallest technical detail, to what extent, in their impact on the listener, he had achieved what he intended. (Pringsheim, 1920 and 1923; cf. also La Grange, p. 408).

It is difficult to know exactly why the composer changed his mind about the order of the middle movements. In his intense, uncertain state, it is plausible that some of his colleagues and friends (Pringsheim himself?!), called to Mahler's attention, as a possible weakness, the resemblance between the openings of the original first and second movements: a repeated ostinato on A in the low strings. Also the fact 'that the scherzo was too similar in style and dynamism to follow directly upon the enormously strenuous twenty-two-minute [actually twenty-three minutes in Mahler's own Essen timing] opening movement. Equally, for the andante to precede the long slow introduction that opens the monumental finale was not really satisfactory, whereas by reversing the order the necessary contrast and relief on both counts was solved at a single stroke' (Del Mar, p. 90; cf. also Zander, p. 6).

Bekker believes that perhaps 'it was the significant emergence of the motto [from the first movement] in the scherzo that caused Mahler to move this movement to the third position from its original second place, and thus to give an immediate preparation for the finale. After the scherzo, which dies away in eerily tense gloom, the outbreak of the finale's beginning has the effect of a release' (Bekker, p. 225).

One could also speculate 'that the chief, perhaps even the only reason why Mahler reversed the order of the two movements was the same as that which led him to remove the third hammer blow in the finale: fear of the symphony's prophetic power ["the tragic argument"], and an instinctive wish to diminish it' (D. Matthews, p. 373; cf. also C. Matthews, p. x). We know that Mahler was terrified by what he had written. As Alma writes:

> None of his works moved him so deeply at its first hearing as this ...When [the dress rehearsal] was over Mahler walked up and down in the artists' room, sobbing, wringing his hands, unable to control himself . . . On the day of the concert Mahler was so afraid that his agitation might get the better of him that out of shame and anxiety he did not conduct the symphony well. He hesitated to bring out the dark omen behind this terrible last movement (A. Mahler, p. 100; cf. also D. Matthews, pp. 372–3, and La Grange, p. 816).

'DEVELOPING VARIATION' BETWEEN THE ORIGINAL FIRST
AND SECOND MOVEMENTS

But are the musical similarities between the allegro (first movement) and the scherzo (second movement) of the Sixth really a problem?

In this sense, one should remember the deep parallels between movements in Mahler's own Fifth Symphony. In movements two and five of this symphony he develops at length the actual material used in the previous movements (first and fourth, respectively: the allegro (second) takes up and develops the material of the preceding funeral march (first); the *Rondo-Finale* (fifth), again, developing materials already heard in the *Adagietto* (fourth). What is curious is that this has always been pointed out as one of the great achievements of the Fifth Symphony. If nobody has ever questioned the Fifth's inter-movement connections, why should one use the parallels between the allegro (first) and the scherzo (second) in the Sixth as a criticism of its original movement order ?!

As Karl Heinz Füssl has convincingly stated, the scherzo belongs after – and with – the opening allegro because it varies and carries forward some of its thematic material and could be considered an example of '*entwickelnde Variation*' ('developing variation'), the device defined and used by Schoenberg. The A–S order would destroy the intended thematic and harmonic unity of the work (Füssl, p. 6).

The strength of such 'developing variation' between the two original first and second movements is eloquently described by Donald Mitchell:

> To one's utter astonishment, it seems for a moment as if one has returned to the march of the first movement and to A minor. But there is something distinctly odd about it: the great death march has been re-done in dance form, in triple time – in short, it has become a dance of death. This is one of the most daring of Mahler's many feats of imagination . . . (Mitchell 2005, p. 5).

'TRAGIC' SIGNIFICANCE OF THE HARMONIC RELATIONS
BETWEEN THE ORIGINAL MOVEMENTS

Karl Heinz Füssl (to whom Bruck devotes only a short paragraph without going into any of its important musical evidence – cf. Bruck, p. 31). has convincingly analysed and enumerated the 'hermeneutic and musical' reasons (Füssl, p. 7) which make the Ratz edition a convincing one. According to Füssl: (a) the scherzo uses the same keys as the first movement, A minor in the beginning and F major for the trio; (b) the key of the andante, E flat, is the furthest removed [a tritone apart] from that of the end of the allegro, A major, whereas the C minor beginning of the introduction to the finale serves as transition from E flat major to A minor which is the main key of the last movement; (c) a slow movement precedes the finale in five other of Mahler's Symphonies: 1, 2, 4, 5, and 7 (Füssl, p. 6; cf. also La Grange, p. 816).

TIMING AND SIGNIFICANCE OF THE USE OF A MINOR BETWEEN
THE FIRST AND SECOND (SCHERZO) MOVEMENTS

David Matthews illustrates in great harmonic detail, how carefully Mahler has avoided A minor in the second half of the first movement (which starts in that gloomy key). There

> is no more A minor in the remaining 137 bars of the movement. Indeed, the final thirty-eight bars are in A major, with the 'Alma' theme triumphant, so that the plunge back into A minor at the

beginning of the scherzo comes as a shock. We had temporarily forgotten that A major must turn irrevocably to the minor [cf. the symbolic, 'tragic' modulation, in the symphony's recurrent motto, between A major and A minor], as it does here with sudden and dreadful impact' (D. Matthews, p. 373).

HARMONIC RELATIONS BETWEEN E FLAT MAJOR (ANDANTE)
AND C MINOR (INTRODUCTION TO THE FINALE)

D. Matthews draws an even more clinching point:

The andante's E flat major, and the whole idyllic character of the movement, 'lost to the world', like Mahler's Rückert song, has once again caused us to forget the fundamental tonal conflict between A major and A minor. E flat was the key to which the 'visionary interlude' of the first movement (bars 196–250) aspired (see bars 225–50), and the andante is full of reminiscences of this interlude, particularly in its scoring (compare the horn solos in bars 225–33 of the first movement and bars 28–32 of the andante, and the use of cowbells and celesta). The ultimate haven of tranquillity in the andante is reached in A *major* (bars 124–45), before the music returns, via a passionate climax in E major, to E flat. The finale opens in C minor, the relative minor of E flat major, but at bar 9 there is a sudden and quite unexpected return to A major/minor for the reappearance of the motto, like the spectre at the feast . . . Note especially the chilling clash between C natural in the melody line and C sharp in the motto (bar 10). The devastating power of this reappearance depends almost entirely on our not having heard A minor since the scherzo, but it makes very little impact if we have just heard the scherzo. The C minor of the introduction again makes little sense as a bridge from A minor back again to A minor in a few bars. (D. Matthews, p. 373–4)

According to Henry-Louis de La Grange, the

sequence of keys (E flat–C minor), and the need for the moment of repose provided by the meditative andante before the hurricanes of the finale, seem to be all-powerful arguments in favour of placing the andante next to the finale. Moreover, the ironic and distorted scherzo, which denies the exultant coda of the first movement of which it is a parody or caricature, loses its meaning altogether when it is not heard immediately after it. (La Grange, p. 816)

David Matthews tells us that Paul Banks, a distinguished Mahlerian scholar, 'has argued [personal communication] that Mahler's indecision over the order of the movements leaves us with no alternative but to think of two separate versions of the symphony' (D. Matthews, p. 374; a similar position is presented in Zander, p. 7, as well as in the Colorado MahlerFest XVI CD set, compiled from performances given on 11–12 January 2003).

Donald Mitchell writes that 'conductors in my view should adopt the sequence they themselves find most convincing' (Mitchell 1995, p. 2.75). 'I myself believe that any serious musical discussion of the symphony must take into account both Mahler's first and second thoughts about the placing of the scherzo . . .' (Mitchell 2005, p. 4).

The 'two versions' position is violently rejected by Jerry Bruck: 'Those who reluctantly acknowledge the facts cited here but are still determined to have their Sixth s–a argue that there are really two Mahler Sixths, the one that he composed and the one he performed.' This, he suggests, would open

> a musical Pandora's Box in which we can find at least two First Symphonies (with and without 'Blumine'), two Second Symphonies (Mahler once performed it with the andante and scherzo movements reversed!), a two- or three-movement *Das klagende Lied* (with and without *Waldmärchen*), and so on. As musicological curiosities, such performances may occasionally be of interest, but in fairness to Mahler (as to any other composer) a concert audience should at least be advised in advance that what they are about to hear is not the form in which its composer left the work and meant it to be heard. (Bruck, pp. 32–3)

But can one really reject that bluntly the historical value of listening to Mahler's original version of his First Symphony, which he himself conducted in Budapest in 1889, in Hamburg in 1893 and in Weimar in 1894? (By the way, one wonders if Bruck knows that one of the significant conductors he reports as having accepted the reversed A–S order of the middle movements of the Sixth, Zubin Mehta, has made an important EMI recording of the first version of the First Symphony, including the subsequently rejected 'Blumine' movement?)

And, though respecting Mahler's revised version in two parts which he himself premiered in Vienna on 17 February 1901, could one really reject today the historical and musical importance of the original 1880 version in three parts of *Das klagende Lied*, which was premiered by Kent Nagano and the Hallé Orchestra and Choir in 1997 and which is now often performed around the world?

There's no way one could reject the historical value of the A–S order. But I would like to remind the reader that, trying to bring the best out of his most-loved composers, Mahler did make changes in the original scores of symphonies by untouchable icons as important as Beethoven and Schumann, convinced that by his interventions he was 'helping' them to bring out their unrealized intentions. Without going as far as that, with all the above-listed musical reasons considered, should not one at least allow today's listener to have the possibility of hearing as well the original version composed by Mahler, in which the 'tragic' narrative of his Sixth Symphony is most powerfully articulated?!

TEXTS CITED

Bekker, Paul, *Gustav Mahlers Sinfonien* (Berlin: Schuster & Loeffler, 1921)

Blaukopf, Herta, 'Aus drei mach zwei, aus zwei mach drei!', *Nachrichten zur Mahler-Forschung* 51 (Vienna: Internationalen Gustav Mahler Gesellschaft, spring 2004)

Bruck, Jerry, 'Undoing a "tragic" mistake', in Kaplan, 2004, pp. 13–35

Del Mar, Norman, *Mahler's Sixth Symphony: A Study* (London: Eulenburg Books, 1980)

Füssl, Karl Heinz, 'Zur Stellung der Mittelsätze in Mahlers Sechster', *Nachrichten zur Mahler-Forschung* 27 (Vienna: Internationalen Gustav Mahler Gesellschaft, March 1991)

– *Gustav Mahler. Symphonie Nr. 6. Revisionsbericht*, Sämtliche Weke. Kritische Gesamtausgabe (Herausgegeben von der Internationalen Gustav Mahler Gesellschaft,Vienna; Frankfurt/M: C. F. Kahnt, 1998)

Gantz, Jeffrey, 'Myth and Reality in Mahler's Sixth Symphony' (Colorado: Mahlerfest, 2003)

Kaplan, Gilbert (ed.), *The Correct Movement Order in Mahler's Sixth Symphony* (New York: Kaplan Foundation, 2004)

– 'Rescuing Mahler from the "Rescuer"'', in Kaplan, 2004, pp. 7–11

Kubik, Reinhold, 'Analysis versus History: Erwin Ratz and the Sixth Symphony' in Kaplan, 2004, pp. 37–43

La Grange, Henry-Louis de, *Gustav Mahler*, vol. 3: *Vienna: Triumph and Disillusion (1904–1907)* (Oxford and New York: Oxford University Press, 1999); in particular: 'Première of the Sixth', pp. 401–25, and 'Mahler's Sixth Symphony in A minor (1903–1904)', pp. 808–41

Mahler, Alma, *Gustav Mahler: Memories and Letters*, translated by Basil Creighton, edited by Donald Mitchell and Knud Martner, 4th edn (London: Sphere Books, 1990); in particular: pp. 70–71 and 99-101

Matthews, Colin, Introduction to Del Mar, 1980, pp. ix–xi

Matthews, David, 'The Sixth Symphony', in Donald Mitchell and Andrew Nicholson (eds.), *The Mahler Companion* (Oxford and New York: Oxford University Press, 1999), pp. 366–75

Mitchell, Donald, 'Mahler: Symphony No. 6', in *Gustav Mahler. The World Listens*, editor-in-chief: Donald Mitchell, published to commemorate the Mahler Festival 1995 in Amsterdam (Harlem: TEMA Uitgevers, 1995), pp. 2.71–7

– 'Mahler's Sixth Symphony: Triumph in Tragedy', liner note for the DGG recording of Mahler's Sixth Symphony by the Berlin Philharmonic Orchestra conducted by Claudio Abbado, 2005

Pringsheim, Klaus, 'Zur Uraufführung von Gustav Mahlers Sechster Symphonie', *Musikblätter des Anbruch*, vol. 2, no. 14 (1920), pp. 496ff.

– 'Erinnerungen an die Uraufführung von Gustav Mahlers Sechster Symphonie', *Neues Wiener Journal*, 15 September 1923

Ratz, Erwin, *Gustav Mahler. Symphonie Nr. 6. Revisionsbericht*, Sämtliche Weke. Kritische Gesamtausgabe. Herausgegeben von der Internationalen Gustav Mahler Gesellschaft (Vienna; Frankfurt/M: C. F. Kahnt, 1968)

Stefan, Paul, *Gustav Mahler. Eine Studie über Persönlichkeit und Werk. Neue, vermehrte und veränderte Ausgabe* (Munich: R. Piper & Co. Verlag, 1920)

Zander, Benjamin, 'A Note from the Conductor', liner note for the Telarc recording of Mahler's Sixth Symphony by the Phlharmonia Orchestra conducted by Benjamin Zander, 2002

# Completions of Mahler's Tenth

*Gastón Fournier-Facio*

Friedrich Block (1899–1945)
Piano four-hands version from the 1930s of movements 2, 4 and 5.

Krenek – Schalk – Zemlinsky – Jokl
Movements 1–3; with autograph notes by Alban Berg which are not included by the publisher (New York: Associated Music Publishers, 1951)

Zsolnay (publisher)
Facsimile print (1924)

In 1942, Jack Diether contacts Shostakovich, who responds, saying he does not have enough time to do a complete version.

In 1950, Schoenberg is approached, but judges it an impossible task.

Clinton Carpenter (1921–)
Piano four-hands version (1946)

Between 1949 and 1964 Carpenter makes six different orchestral versions and is the first to attempt a full version of the symphony for full orchestra.

Joe Wheeler (1927–1977) makes four different orchestral versions between 1953 and 1965. The fourth version is performed in 1966.

Hans Vieugels (1899–1978) attempts a full version in 1952.

Vieugels's pupil, Hans Kreutz, establishes contact with Bruno Walter and Alma Mahler. Nothing comes of it.

In 1972 the publisher Hans Wollschlaeger retires his version which, according to Erwin Ratz, was too rich.

Deryck Cooke (1917–1976)
1960: realization of a performing version (incomplete). First broadcast, conducted by Berthold Goldschmidt
1964: first complete version. Performed in London under Goldschmidt.
1972: second version.
1976: full score published (incorporating a complete transcription of the sketches): *Gustav Mahler: A Performing Version of the Draft for the Tenth Symphony*, prepared by Deryck Cooke in collaboration with Berthold Goldschmidt, Colin Matthews and David Matthews (Faber Music–Associated Music Publishers).

Remo Mazzetti (1957–); American
Completed version in 1985.

Rudolf Barshai
*Rekonstruktion und Orchestrierung nach Mahlers Entwurf* (Universal Edition, 2001)

Nicola Samale (1941–) and Giuseppe Mazzuca (1939–)
Full orchestral version completed in 2001; performed the same year in Perugia at the Sagra Musicale Umbra, by the Vienna Symphony Orchestra conducted by Martin Sieghart. This version will be recorded in December 2007 by the Arnhem Het Gelders Orkest, conducted by Martin Sieghart.

# Bibliography

Adorno, Theodor W., *Mahler: Eine musikalische Physiognomik* (Frankfurt am Main: Suhrkamp, 1960)
- *Philosophy of Modern Music,* translated by Anne G. Mitchell and Wesley V. Blooffister (London: Sheed & Ward, 1973)
- *Mahler: A Musical Physiognomy,* translated by Edmund Jephcott (Chicago and London: University of Chicago Press, 1992)
- *Quasi una Fantasia: Essays on Modern Music,* translated by Rodney Livingstone (London: Verso, 1992)

Bacharach, A. L. (ed.), *The Musical Companion* (London: Gollancz, 1934)

Banks, Paul (ed.), 'Aspects of Mahler's Fifth Symphony: Performance Practice and Interpretation', *Musical Times*, 130 (May 1989), pp. 258–65
- *The Making of 'Peter Grimes',* vol. 2, *Notes and Commentaries* (Woodbridge: The Britten Estate/The Boydell Press, 1996)

Bartoš, František (ed.), *Mahler: Dopisy,* translated by František and Marie Bartoš (Prague: Státí Hudebnī Vydavatelstvī, 1962)

Bauer-Lechner, Natalie, *Recollections of Gustav Mahler*, translated by Dika Newlin, edited by Peter Franklin (London: Faber and Faber, 1980)

Becqué, Robert, and Eveline Nikkels, *Die Liebe Erde Allüberall: Proceedings of* Das Lied von der Erde *Symposium, Den Haag, 2002* (Amsterdam: Stichting Rondom Mahler, 2005)

Bekker, Paul, *Gustav Mahlers Sinfonien* (Berlin: Schuster und Loeffler, 1921; reprinted 1969)

Berg, Alban, *Letters to his Wife* (London: Faber and Faber, 1971)

Blaukopf, Herta (ed.), *Gustav Mahler–Richard Strauss: Correspondence 1888–1911,* translated by Edmund Jephcott (London: Faber and Faber, 1984)

Blaukopf, Kurt (ed. and comp.), *Mahler: A Documentary Study,* with annotations by Zoltan Roman, translated by Paul Baker et al. (London: Thames and Hudson, 1976)

Block, Geoffrey, and J. Peter Burkholder (eds.), *Charles Ives and the Classical Tradition* (New Haven and London: Yale University Press, 1996)

Botstein, Leon, 'Innovation and Nostalgia: Ives, Mahler and the Origins of Modernism', in Burkholder (ed.), *Charles Ives and his World*, pp. 35–74

Burkholder, J. Peter (ed.), *Charles Ives and his World* (Princeton: Princeton University Press, 1996)

Burton, Humphrey, *Leonard Bernstein* (London: Faber and Faber, 1994)

Cooke, Deryck, *Gustav Mahler: An Introduction to his Music* (London: Faber and Faber, 1980)

Craig, Gordon A., *Theodor Fontane, Literature and History in the Bismarck Reich* (New York and Oxford: Oxford University Press, 1999)

Decsey, Ernst, 'Stunden mit Mahler', *Die Musik* 10/21 (1910/11), translated in Lebrecht (ed.), *Mahler Remembered*

Del Mar, Norman, *Mahler's Sixth Symphony* (London: Eulenberg, 1980)

Downes, Graeme Alexander, 'An Axial System of Tonality Applied to Progressive Tonality in the Works of Gustav Mahler and Nineteenth-Century Antecedents', Ph.D. thesis, University of Otago, Dunedin, 1991

Eliot, T. S., *Poems 1920* (New York: A. A. Knopf, 1920)

Floros, Constantin, *Gustav Mahler: The Symphonies*, translated by Vernon Wicker (Aldershot: Scolar, 1994)

Foerster, Josef Bohuslav, *Der Pilger: Erinnerungen eines Musikers*, translated by Pavel Eisner (Prague, 1955)

Gülke, Peter, 'The Orchestra as Medium of Realization: Thoughts on the Finale of Brahms's First Symphony, on the Different Versions of Bruckner's Sixth Symphony, and on "Part One" of Mahler's Fifth', *Musical Quarterly*, 80 (1996), pp. 269–75

Harrison, Julius, '"Absolute" Music and the Symphonists', in A. L. Bacharach (ed.), *The Musical Companion*, p. 237

Hefling, Stephen E. (ed.), *Mahler Studies* (Cambridge: Cambridge University Press, 1997)

– *Mahler: Das Lied von der Erde* (Cambridge: Cambridge University Press, 2000)

Hilmar-Voit, Renate, 'Symphonic Sound or in the Style of Chamber Music? The Current Performing Forces of the *Wunderhorn* Lieder and the Sources', *News about Mahler Research*, 28 (October 1992), pp. 8–12

Hussey, Dyneley, 'Vocal Music in the Twentieth Century', in A. L. Bacharach (ed.), *The Musical Companion*, pp. 454–6

Jones, Ernest, *Sigmund Freud: Life and Work* (London, Hogarth Press, 1955)

Kaplan, Gilbert E. (ed.), *Gustav Mahler: Adagietto: Facsimile, Documentation, Recording* (New York: The Kaplan Foundation, 1992)

Kennedy, Michael, *Mahler* (London: J. M. Dent, 1974; 2nd edn, 1990)

Klemm, Eberhardt, 'Zur Geschichte der Fünften Sinfonie van Gustav Mahler: Der Briefwechsel zwischen Mahler und dem Verlag C. F. Peters und andere Dokumente', in *Jahrbuch Peters*, 1979

Klemperer, Otto, *Erinnerungen an Gustav Mahler* (Zurich: Atlantis, 1960)

Kravitt, Edward F., 'Mahler's Dirges for his Death', *Musical Quarterly*, 64 (1978), pp. 329–53.

La Grange, Henry-Louis de, *Mahler*, 2 vols.: I (London: Gollancz, 1974); II *Vienna: The Years of Challenge (1897–1904)* (Oxford: Oxford University Press, 1995)

— *Gustav Mahler: Chronique d'une vie*, 3 vols.: I *Les Chemins de la gloire (1860–1900)* (Paris: Fayard, 1973); II *L'Âge d'or de Vienne (1900–1907)* (1983); III *Le Génie foudroyé (1907–1911)* (1984)

— 'Music about Music in Mahler: Reminiscences, Allusions, or Quotations?', in Hefling (ed.), *Mahler Studies*, pp. 122–68

La Grange, Henry-Louis and Günther Weiss (eds.), *Ein Glück ohne Ruh'. Die Briefe Gustav Mahlers an Alma*. Erste Gesamtausgabe. Redaktion: Knud Martner (Berlin: Siedler, 1995)

Large, Brian, *Smetana* (London: Duckworth, 1970)

Lawford-Hinrichsen, Irene, *Music Publishing and Patronage: C. F. Peters, 1800 to the Holocaust* (Kenton, Middlesex: Edition Press, 2000)

Lebrecht, Norman, *Mahler Remembered* (London: Faber and Faber, 1987)

Leur, Truus de, 'Gustav Mahler in the Netherlands', in Mitchell (ed.), *Gustav Mahler: The World Listens* (Haarlem: TEMA Uitgevers, 1995), pp. 1:15–40

— 'Mahler's Fifth Symphony and the Royal Concertgebouw Orchestra', in Mitchell and Straub (eds.), *New Sounds, New Century: Mahler's Fifth Symphony and the Royal Concertgebouw Orchestra*, pp. 76–101

Lewis, Christopher O., 'On the Chronology of the *Kindertotenlieder*', *Revue Mahler*, 1 (Paris: Bibliothèque Gustav Mahler, 1987)

Loewenberg, Alfred, *Annals of Opera* (Cambridge: W. Heffer, 1943)

Mahler, Alma, *Gustav Mahler: Memories and Letters*, translated by Basil Creighton, edited by Donald Mitchell and Knud Martner, 4th edn (London: Sphere Books, 1990)

Mahler, Gustav, *Selected Letters of Gustav Mahler*, translated by Eithne Wilkins, Ernst Kaiser and Bill Hopkins, edited by Knud Martner (London: Faber and Faber, 1979)

*Mahler a Romo* (Rome: Accademia Nazionale di Santa Cecilia, 2000)

Mahler Werfel, Alma, *And the Bridge is Love* (London: Hutchinson, 1959)

Martner, Knud, *Gustav Mahler im Konzertsaal, 1870–1911* (Copenhagen: private publication, 1985)

Matter, Jean, *Connaissance de Mahler. Documents, analyses et synthèses* (Lausanne: Editions L'Age de l'homme, 1974)

Matthews, Colin, *Mahler at Work: Aspects of the Creative Process* (New York and London: Garland Publishing Inc., 1989)

Matthews, Colin, 'Mahler and Self-Renewal', in Reed (ed.), *Britten and Mahler: Essays in Honour of Donald Mitchell*, pp. 85–8

Mitchell, Donald, *Gustav Mahler: The Wunderhorn Years* (London: Faber and Faber, 1975; new paperback edition, Woodbridge: The Boydell Press, 2005)

— *Gustav Mahler: Songs and Symphonies of Life and Death* (London: Faber and Faber, 1985; new paperback edition, Woodbridge: The Boydell Press, 2002)

— 'Mahler's "Orchestral" Orchestral Songs', Rondom Mahler II Congress and Workshop, Rotterdam, May 1990

— 'Mahler's Longest Journey', liner note for DGG 439 953–2 (1994), Claudio Abbado's recording of Mahler's Second Symphony with the Vienna Philharmonic Orchestra

— 'Contexts of Violence: The Sources of *Peter Grimes*', *Aldeburgh Festival Programme Book*, 1995, pp. 91–6

— *Cradles of the New: Writings on Music, 1951–1991*, edited by Christopher Palmer and Mervyn Cooke (London: Faber and Faber, 1995)

— '*Peter Grimes:* Fifty Years On', in Paul Banks (ed.), *The Making of*

'Peter Grimes', vol. 2, *Notes and Commentaries* (Woodbridge, The Britten Estate/The Boydell Press, 1996), pp. 125–51

- 'Mahler and Smetana: Significant Influences or Accidental Parallels?', in Hefling (ed.), *Mahler Studies*, pp. 110–21

- 'The Modernity of Gustav Mahler', in Weiss (ed.), *Neue Mahleriana: Essays in Honour of Henry-Louis de La Grange on his Seventieth Birthday*, pp. 125–51

- 'Mahler's "Lieder-Abend": Many Songs, Many Orchestras', liner note for Teldec CD 8573–865730–2 (2001)

Mitchell, Donald (ed.), *Benjamin Britten: Death in Venice* (Cambridge: Cambridge University Press, 1987)

- *Gustav Mahler: The World Listens* (Haarlem: TEMA Uitgevers, 1995)

Mitchell, Donald, and Hans Keller (eds.), *Benjamin Britten: A Commentary on his Works* (London: Rockliff, 1952; Westport, Conn.: Greenwood Press, 1971)

Mitchell, Donald, and Andrew Nicholson (eds.), *The Mahler Companion* (Oxford: Oxford University Press, 1999)

Mitchell, Donald, and Philip Reed (eds.), *Letters from a Life: Selected Letters and Diaries of Benjamin Britten*, vol. 1: *1923–39* (London: Faber and Faber, 1991)

Mitchell, Donald, and Henriette Straub (eds.), *New Sounds, New Century: Mahler's Fifth Symphony and the Royal Concertgebouw Orchestra* (Bussum: THOTH/Amsterdam, Royal Concertgebouw Orchestra, 1997)

Morgan, Robert P., 'Ives and Mahler: Mutual Responses at the End of an Era', in Block and Burkholder (eds.), *Charles Ives and the Classical Tradition*, pp. 75–86

Natter, G. Tobias, and Gerbert Frodl, *Carl Moll* (Vienna: Osterreichische Galerie, 1998), catalogue to accompany the exhibition, 'Carl Moll: Maler und Organisator', at the Belvedere, September–November 1998

Newlin, Dika, 'Secret Tonality in Schoenberg's Piano Concerto', *Perspectives of New Music*, 13 (1974), pp. 137–9

- *Bruckner, Mahler, Schoenberg* (London: Marion Boyars, 1979)

Oltmanns, Michael Johannes, '"Ich bin der Welt abhanden gekommen" und "Der Tamboursg'sell" – Zwei Liedkonzeptionen Gustav

Mahlers', *Archiv für Musikwissenschaft*, 43 (1986), pp. 69–88

Pamer, Fritz Egon, 'Gustav Mahlers Lieder', *Studien zur Musikwissenschaft* (Vienna, 1929 and 1930), vol. XVI, pp. 116–38, and vol. XVIII, pp. 105–27

Reed, John, *The Schubert Song Companion* (Manchester: Manchester University Press, 1985)

Reed, Philip, 'Aschenbach becomes Mahler: Thomas Mann as Film', in Mitchell (ed.), *Benjamin Britten: Death in Venice*, pp. 178–83

Reed, Philip (ed.), *On Mahler and Britten: Essays in Honour of Donald Mitchell on his Seventieth Birthday* (Woodbridge: The Boydell Press/ The Britten–Pears Library, 1995)

Reeser, Eduard (ed.), *Alphons Diepenbrock. Brieven en documenten*, vol. 5 (Amsterdam: Vereniging voor Nederlandse Muziekgeschiedenis, 1981)

Reik, Theodor, *The Haunting Melody: Psychoanalytic Experiences in Life and Music* (New York: Farrar, Straus and Young, 1953)

Reilly, Edward R., *Gustav Mahler and Guido Adler: Records of a Friendship* (Cambridge: Cambridge University Press, 1982)

– 'The Manuscripts of Mahler's Fifth Symphony', in Mitchell and Straub (eds.), *New Sounds, New Century: Mahler's Fifth Symphony and the Royal Concertgebouw Orchestra*, pp. 58–63

– '*Todtenfeier* and the Second Symphony', in Mitchell and Nicholson (eds.), *The Mahler Companion*, pp. 84–125

Revers, Peter, 'Aspekte der Ostasienrezeption Gustav Mahlers *Das Lied von der Erde*', in *Musik als Text: Bericht über den Internationalen Kongress der Gesellschaft für Musikforschung* (Freiburg im Breslau, 1993)

Roman, Zoltan, *Gustav Mahler's American Years: 1907–1911. A Documentary History* (Stuyvesant, NY: Pendragon Press, 1989)

Sadie, Stanley (ed.), *The New Grove Dictionary of Music and Musicians* (London: Macmillan, 1980)

Schmierer, Elisabeth, *Die Orchesterlieder Gustav Mahlers* (Kassel: Bärenreiter, 1991)

– 'Between Lied and Symphony: On Mahler's "Tamboursg'sell"', *News about Mahler Research*, 33 (March 1995), pp. 15–22

Schoenberg, Arnold, *Style and Idea* (London: Faber and Faber, 1975)

Slonimsky, Nicolas, *Music Since 1900*, 3rd edn (New York: W. W. Norton, 1937)

Specht, Richard, *Gustav Mahler* (Berlin: Gose und Tetsslaff, 1905)

– *Gustav Mahler* (Berlin: Schuster und Loeffler, 1913)

Sponheuer, Bernd, *Logik des Zerfalls: Untersuchungen zum Finalproblem in den Symphonien Gustav Mahlers* (Tutzing: Hans Schneider, 1978)

Tyrrell, John, *Czech Opera* (Cambridge, Cambridge University Press, 1988)

– '*The Kiss*', *The New Grove Dictionary of Opera* (London: Macmillan, 1992), vol. II, pp. 1000–1002

Vill, Susanne, *Vermittlungsformen verbalisierter und musikalischer Inhalte in der Musik Gustav Mahlers* (Tutzing: Hans Schneider, 1979)

Vogt, M. T. (ed.), *Das Gustav-Mahler-Fest Hamburg 1989* (Kassell: Bären-reiter, 1991)

Walter, Bruno, *Gustav Mahler* (London: Hamish Hamilton, 1958); US edition, translated by J. Galston, with a biographical essay by Ernst Krenek (New York: Greystone Press, 1941)

Weiss, Günther (ed.), *Neue Mahleriana: Essays in Honour of Henry-Louis de La Grange on his Seventieth Birthday* (Bern: Peter Lang AG, 1997)

Wilkens, Sander, *Gustav Mahlers Fünfte Symphonie: Quellen und Instrumentationsprozess* (Frankfurt: C. F. Peters, 1989)

Williams, Ralph Vaughan, *National Music and Other Essays*, 2nd edn (Oxford: Oxford University Press, 1987)

Willnauer, Franz, *Gustav Mahler und die Wiener Oper*, new edn (Vienna: Löcker Verlag, 1993)

Winternitz, Emanuel, *Musical Autographs from Monteverdi to Hindemith* (New York: Dover, 1965)

# Critical Editions of Mahler's Scores

Klavierquartett. 1. Satz
*Editor* Manfred Wagner-Artzt
*Publisher* Universal Edition, Vienna, 1997

Das klagende Lied
(original (1880) version in three movements)
*Editor* Reinhold Kubik
*Publisher* Universal Edition, Mainz, 1999

(1898 version in two movements)
*Editor* Rudolf Stephan
*Publisher* Universal Edition, Vienna, 1978

Verschiedene Lieder
'Im Lenz', 'Winterlied', 'Maitanz im Grünen', 'Frühlingsmorgen',
'Erinnerung', 'Hans und Grete', 'Serenade', 'Phantasie'
*Editor* Zoltan Roman
*Publisher* Schott, Mainz, 1990

Lieder eines fahrenden Gesellen
(for solo voice and piano)
*Editor* Zoltan Roman
*Publisher* Josef Weinberger, Vienna–Frankfurt/M.–London, 1982

(for solo voice and orchestra)
*Editor* Zoltan Roman
*Publisher* Josef Weinberger, Vienna–Frankfurt/M.–London, 1982

Symphony No. 1
*Editor* Erwin Ratz
*Publisher* Universal Edition, Vienna, 1967

*Editors* Erwin Ratz and Karl Heinz Füssl
*Publisher* Universal Edition, Vienna, 1973

*Editor* Sander Wilkens
*Publisher* Universal Edition, Vienna, 1992; revised edition, 1995

## Neun Lieder und Gesänge aus 'Des Knaben Wunderhorn'
(for voice and piano)
*Editor* Peter Revers
*Publisher* Schott, Mainz, 1991

## Todtenfeier
(original (1888) version of the first movement of the Second Symphony)
*Editor* Rudolf Stephan
*Publisher* Universal Edition, Vienna, 1988

## Symphony No. 2
*Editor* Erwin Ratz
*Publisher* Universal Edition, Vienna, 1970

*Editors* Mark Kaplan and Renate Stark-Voit
*Publisher* Universal Edition, Vienna, 2007

## Fünfzehn Lieder, Humoresken und Balladen aus 'Des Knaben Wunderhorn'
(for voice and piano)
*Editor* Renate Hilmar-Voit
*Publisher* Universal Edition, Mainz, 1993

## 'Des Knaben Wunderhorn'
(for solo voice with orchestral accompaniment)
*Editor* Renate Hilmar-Voit
*Publisher* Universal Edition, Mainz, 1998

## Symphony No. 3
*Editors* Erwin Ratz and Karl Heinz Füssl
*Publisher* Universal Edition, Vienna, 1974

## Symphony No. 4
*Editor* Erwin Ratz
*Publisher* Universal Edition, London, 1963; revised edition, 1995

## Lieder nach Texten von Friedrich Rückert
'Blicke mir nicht in die Lieder', Ich atmet' einen linden Duft',
'Um Mitternacht', 'Ich bin der Welt abhanden gekommen',
'Liebst du um Schönheit'
(for solo voice and piano)
*Editor* Zoltan Roman
*Publisher* C. F. Kahnt, Frankfurt/M/, 1984; C. F. Peters, Frankfurt/M., 1989

## Lieder nach Texten von Friedrich Rückert
'Blicke mir nicht in die Lieder', Ich atmet' einen linden Duft',
'Um Mitternacht', 'Ich bin der Welt abhanden gekommen'
(for solo voice and orchestra)
*Editor* Zoltan Roman
*Publisher* C. F. Kahnt, Frankfurt/M/, 1984; C. F. Peters, Frankfurt/M., 1989

## Symphony No. 5
*Editor* Erwin Ratz
*Publisher* C. F. Peters, Frankfurt/M., 1964

*Editor* Karl Heinz Füssl
*Publisher* C. F. Peters, Frankfurt/M., 1989

*Editor* Reinhold Kubik
*Publisher* C. F. Peters, Frankfurt/M., 2001

## Kindertotenlieder
(for solo voice and piano)
*Editor* Zoltan Roman
*Publisher* C. F. Kahnt, Frankfurt/M., 1979; C. F. Peters, Frankfurt/M.,
   1989

(for solo voice and orchestra)
*Editor* Zoltan Roman
*Publisher* C. F. Kahnt, Frankfurt/M., 1979; C. F. Peters, Frankfurt/M.,
   1989

## Symphony No. 6
*Editor* Erwin Ratz
*Publisher* C. F. Kahnt, Wasserburg, 1963

*Editors* Karl Heinz Füssl and Reinhold Kubik
*Publisher* C. F. Kahnt, Frankfurt/M., 1998

## Symphony No. 7
*Editor* Erwin Ratz
*Publisher* Bote & Bock, Berlin, 1960

## Symphony No. 8
*Editor* Karl Heinz Füssl
*Publisher* Universal Edition, Vienna, 1977

## Das Lied von der Erde
*Editor* Erwin Ratz
*Publisher* Universal Edition, Vienna, 1964

*Editor* Karl Heinz Füssl
*Publisher* Universal Edition, Vienna, 1990

## Symphony No. 9
*Editor* Erwin Ratz
*Publisher* Universal Edition, Vienna, 1969; revised edition, 1998

## *Adagio*, Symphony No. 10
*Editor* Erwin Ratz
*Publisher* Universal Edition, Vienna, 1964

## Symphony No. 10
*Performing edition prepared by* Deryck Cooke
*in collaboration with* Berthold Goldschmidt, Colin Matthews
*and* David Matthews
*Publisher* Faber Music/Associated Music Publishers, London/New York, 1976

Carl Maria von Weber–Gustav Mahler: *Die drei Pintos*
*Editor* J. Zychowicz
*Publisher* A-R Editions, Inc., Madison, 2000

Suite aus den Orchesterwerken von Johann Sebastian Bach
*Ouverture, Rondeau und Badinerie, Air, Gavotte 1 und 2*
(with continuo realized for concert performance by GM)
*Publisher* G. Schirmer, New York, 1910

Ludwig van Beethoven, Symphony Nr. 9
(revised orchestration by GM)
*Publisher* Internationale Gustav Mahler Gesellschaft, Vienna,
  in preparation

Franz Schubert, String Quartet in D minor (D. 810)
'Der Tod und das Mädchen'
(orchestral arrangement by GM)
*Editors* Donald Mitchell and Colin Matthews
*Publisher* Josef Weinberger, Vienna–Frankfurt/M.–London, 1984

# General Index

Major references are <u>underlined</u>; references to illustrations are shown in *italics*.

*Die Meistersinger* Prelude, 406–8, 417,
419–20, 432; *The Ring*, 580, 582; *Tristan
und Isolde*, 187, 338n; compositional practices, 26; influence on GM, 4, 7, 28, 86, 441
Wagner-Artzt, Manfred, 657
Walter, Bruno, XXIII, 175n, 317, 326n, 333,
411, 421, 448, 459, 467, 500, 523, 525, 556,
600–603, 619, 648; *Gustav Mahler. Ein
Porträt*, XXIII
Wang-Sei, XLV
Wasserburg: place of publication, 660
Weber, Baroness, 527–8
Weber, Carl Maria von, 104n; *Die drei Pintos*
(orchestration by GM), XLVI, 19, 526, 543n,
661; *Der Freischütz* overture, 329; *Oberon*
(performing edition by GM and Gustav
Brecher), 236, 526; influence on GM, 4, 28
Weber, Captain Karl von, XLVI, 104n,
543–4n
Webern, Anton, XXIII, 66, 108, 323, 360, 394,
500, 518, 558, 561, 588, 594, 603, 638;
Symphony (1928) Op. 21, 366; on GM, 47
Webster, John, 46
Wedekind, Frank: *Spring Awakening*, XX
Weidemann, Friedrich, 213
Weimar: performances, 645
Weinberger, Josef (publisher), XXXVI, XXXVII,

XXXVIII, XXXIX, XLI, 334n, 657, 661
Weingartner, Felix, 175, 522, 599
Wheeler, Joe, 508, 648
Wicker, Vernon, 315
Wiesbaden: performances, 527
Wigglesworth, Mark, 217
Wilkens, Sander, 658
Willem Mengelberg Stichting, 490
Williamson, John, 591
Wittgenstein, Ludwig, 604–5
Wolf, Hugo: 'Hochbeglückt in deiner
Liebe', 214
Wollschlaeger, Hans, 649
Wood, Hugh, 558
Woolf, Virginia, XX, 69; *To the Lighthouse*, 69
Wörthersee, XXV, 226, 398, 399, 477

Yale University, 524n
*Youth's Magic Horn, The, see Knaben
Wunderhorn, Des*

Zemlinsky, Alexander von, 381, 507, 558,
603, 634, 648
Zsolnay (publisher), 648
Zychowicz, James J., 661; *The Seventh
Symphony of Gustav Mahler: A Symposium*,
XXIII

# Index of Mahler's Works

Major references are <u>underlined</u>; references to illustrations are shown in *italics*.

scheme, 7, 114–16; manuscript, 8; narrative element, 6, 8, 112–13, 120–21; orchestration, 9, 118; performance, xxxvii, 116, 117, 118–20; publication, xxxvii, 657; voice-and-piano version, 118
*Lieder und Gesänge*: volume i, *see also 5 Lieder*; volume ii, 104n, *see also 9 Wunderhorn Lieder*; volume iii, 98, *see also 9 Wunderhorn Lieder*; publication, 92
'Little Rhine Legend', *see Knaben Wunderhorn, Des*: 'Rheinlegendchen'
'Lob des hohen Verstandes', *see Knaben Wunderhorn, Des*
'Lonely One in Autumn, The', *see Lied von der Erde, Das*: 'Der Einsame im Herbst'

'Maitanz im Grünen', xxxv, 91; *see also Lieder und Gesänge*, vol. i: 'Hans und Grethe', *and Verschiedene Lieder*
'Minstrel, The', *see klagende Lied, Das: Der Spielmann*

'Never to Meet Again', *see 9 Wunderhorn Lieder*: 'Nicht wiedersehen!'
'Nicht wiedersehen!', *see 9 Wunderhorn Lieder*
'Now I see clearly why such ardent flames', *see Kindertotenlieder*: 'Nun seh' ich wohl, warum so dunkle Flammen'
'Now will the sun as brightly rise', *see Kindertotenlieder*: 'Nun will die Sonn' so hell aufgeh'n'
'Nun seh' ich wohl, warum so dunkle Flammen', *see Kindertotenlieder*
'Nun will die Sonn' so hell aufgeh'n', *see Kindertotenlieder*

'Oft denk' ich, sie sind nur ausgegangen', *see Kindertotenlieder*
'On the Ramparts of Strassburg', *see 9 Wunderhorn Lieder*: 'Zu Strassburg auf der Schanz'

'Phantasie aus Don Juan', *see 5 Lieder and Verschiedene Lieder*
Piano Quartet in A minor, xxxv; composition, xxxv; *Critical Edition*, 657; performance, xxxv; publication, xxxv, 657

'Primeval Light', *see Knaben Wunderhorn, Des*: 'Urlicht'

'Remembering', *see 5 Lieder*: 'Erinnerung'
'Reveille', *see 7 Lieder*: 'Revelge'
'Revelge', *see 7 Lieder*
'Rheinlegendchen', *see Knaben Wunderhorn, Des*
*Rübezahl*, xxxv; composition, xxxv
*Rückert-Lieder*: analysis/commentary, xv, 33, 105, 187, 206, 215–16, 222, 259, 285, 288, 331, 333–5, 339, 343–4, 412, 430, 453, 469–70, 573, 582; composition, 108, 220; *Critical Edition*, 659; performance, 528n, 578; *and see individual songs*

'Scheiden und Meiden', *see 9 Wunderhorn Lieder*
'Schildwache Nachtlied', *see Des Knaben Wunderhorn*
'Selbstgefühl', *see 9 Wunderhorn Lieder*
'Self-Assurance', *see 9 Wunderhorn Lieder*: 'Selbstgefühl'
'Sentry's Night Song, The', *see Knaben Wunderhorn, Des*: 'Der Schildwache Nachtlied'
'Serenade aus Don Juan', *see 5 Lieder and Verschiedene Lieder*
'Serenade from Don Juan', *see 5 Lieder*: 'Serenade aus Don Juan'
'Song of Lament, The', *see klagende Lied, Das*
'Song of the Prisoner in the Tower', *see Knaben Wunderhorn, Des*: 'Lied des Verfolgten im Turm'
*Songs on the Death of Children*, *see Kindertotenlieder*
*Songs of a Wayfaring Lad*, *see Lieder eines fahrenden Gesellen*
'Spring Morning', *see 5 Lieder*: 'Frühlingsmorgen'
'Springtime Dance in the Countryside', *see* 'Maitanz im Grünen'
'Ständchen am Rhein, Der', *see Trompeter von Säkkingen, Der*
'Starke Einbildungskraft', *see 9 Wunderhorn Lieder*
'Strong Imagination', *see 9 Wunderhorn Lieder*: 'Stark Einbildungskraft'